IN THEIR OWN WORDS

Criminals on Crime: An Anthology

Fifth Edition

Paul Cromwell
Wichita State University

New York   Oxford
OXFORD UNIVERSITY PRESS
2010

Oxford University Press

Oxford University Press, Inc., publishes works that further
Oxford University's objective of excellence
in research, scholarship, and education.

Oxford New York
Auckland Cape Town Dar es Salaam Hong Kong Karachi
Kuala Lumpur Madrid Melbourne Mexico City Nairobi
New Delhi Shanghai Taipei Toronto

With offices in
Argentina Austria Brazil Chile Czech Republic France Greece
Guatemala Hungary Italy Japan Poland Portugal Singapore
South Korea Switzerland Thailand Turkey Ukraine Vietnam

Published by Oxford University Press, Inc.
198 Madison Avenue, New York, New York 10016
http://www.oup.com

Oxford is a registered trademark of Oxford University Press

Library of Congress Cataloging-in-Publication Data

In their own words : criminals on crime, an anthology / [edited by] Paul
Cromwell.—5th ed.
    p. cm.
  Includes bibliographical references and index.
  ISBN 978-0-19-538319-5 (alk. paper)
 1. Criminology—Fieldwork. 2. Crime—Research. 3. Criminals—Research.
I. Cromwell, Paul F.
  HV6030.I488 2010
  364—dc22

                                                          2009002070

Printing number: 9 8 7 6 5 4
Printed in the United States of America
on acid-free paper

This book is dedicated to the memory of my friend and former colleague, John Byrd, who passed away in April 2008. In a distinguished career that included service as a United States Probation Officer, Chief Clerk of the United States District Court for New Mexico, Executive Director of the Texas Board of Pardons and Paroles, Chief United States Pre-trial Services Officer for the Western District of Texas, and finally as Instructor in Criminal Justice at the University of Texas at San Antonio, John was one of the most highly respected and most dedicated persons in the profession. He was a good man and he will be greatly missed.

PREFACE

This anthology provides the reader with an opportunity to view the world from the perspective of criminal offenders. *In Their Own Words*, 5th edition, is a collection of field studies of crime and criminals derived from a long tradition of field research in criminology. In this new 5th edition, which contains 11 new chapters, students will encounter a diverse array of criminals, including new studies of international terrorists, criminal computer hackers, perpetrators of domestic violence, and identity theft—all of whom discuss their motives, perceptions, strategies, and rationalizations of crime. Readers will note that the "methods" section of each chapter from the original has been redacted for brevity. Instead, a brief note in the introduction to the chapter describes the methods and the respondents in the study. Readers are encouraged to go to the original source of the material for a fuller and more complete methodology.

METHODS OF FIELD RESEARCH

Field research is not a single research methodology. Field research, also called *ethnography*, provides a way of looking at the complex contexts in which any research problem exists. Good field research results in what Glassner and Carpenter (1985) call *thick description*—access to the often conflicting and detailed views of the social world held by the subjects being studied.

According to Maxfield and Babbie (1995), field research "encompasses two different methods of obtaining data: direct observation and asking questions." *Asking questions* involves in-depth interviews (also called ethnographic interviews) with research subjects. Field study interviews are much less structured than survey research interviews. At one level, field interviews may be likened to a conversation (Maxfield and Babbie, 1995). At a more structured level, researchers ask open-ended questions in which a specific response is elicited, but the respondent is allowed and encouraged to explain more completely and to clarify responses. The question is simply a guide, structuring but not limiting the interviewee's responses.

Observation takes several forms in field research. These techniques may be categorized on a continuum according to the role played by the researcher (Gold, 1969; Maxfield and Babbie, 1995). At one degree of involvement, the researcher observes an activity or individuals without their knowledge. A researcher watching shoplifters through a one-way mirror in a department store is an example of this technique. Gold (1969) labels this method *the complete observer*.

At a more involved level of interaction, the researcher is identified as a researcher and interacts with the participants in the course of their activities but does not actually become a participant (Maxfield and Babbie, 1995). Gold (1969) identified this technique as *observer-as-participant*.

The *participant-as-observer* (Gold 1969) technique involves participating with the group under study while making clear the purpose of conducting research. Wilson Palacios and Melissa Fenwick used a version this technique in their study of the Ecstasy club scene in south Florida (Chapter 21 in this book).

The most complete involvement of researcher with subjects is the complete participant. Gold (1969, p. 33) describes this role: "*The true identity and purpose of the complete participant in field research are not known to those he observes. He interacts with them as naturally as possible in whatever areas of their living interest him and are acceptable to him in situations in which he can play or learn to play requisite day-to-day roles successfully.*"

A number of ethical, legal, and personal risk considerations are involved in the complete participant role, and the researcher must tread carefully to avoid pitfalls. Because of these problems, complete participation is seldom possible in criminological research.

USE OF FIELD RESEARCH IN CRIMINAL JUSTICE AND CRIMINOLOGY

Field studies are particularly well suited to investigating several important issues in criminology and criminal justice. Only through field research may we observe the everyday activities of offenders: how they interact with others, how they perceive the objects and events in their everyday lives, and how they perceive the sanction threat of the criminal justice system. By understanding the offenders' perspective, decision making, and motivation, field research may inform crime prevention and control strategies. Wright and Decker (1994) point out that criminal justice policymaking is predicated on assumptions about the perceptions of criminals:

> The traditional policy of deterrence rests squarely on the notion that offenders are utilitarian persons who carefully weigh the potential costs and rewards of their illegal actions...

However, the studies in this collection offer strong arguments for other, perhaps as compelling motivations for many crimes, including so-called economic crimes. Even robbery and burglary, crimes assumed to be driven almost entirely by instrumental (economic) motivations, may have expressive roots as well. Burglars report that excitement, thrills, and a "rush" often accompany the criminal act. Some burglars report having occasionally committed a burglary out of revenge or anger against the victim (see Shover and Honaker, "The Socially Bounded Decisions of Persistent Property Offenders," in this book). By contrast, gang membership, which traditionally has been thought to be turf oriented and centered on conflict, is shown to be increasingly about money—drugs and drug sales. Thus, effective crime control strategies must take into account the factors that drive crime. Field research that allows offenders to "speak for themselves" is ideally suited to these issues.

Field studies such as those in this book also have great value in educating students in criminal justice and criminology. The field has sometimes suffered from the "distance" between student and subject of the study. Would anyone argue that it is possible to train a physician without contact with sick people? The essence of medical training is of course the gaining of experience diagnosing and treating the sick. Yet, in 15 years as a criminal justice practitioner and administrator, and 25 years as a criminal justice and criminology educator, I have been troubled by the realization that most graduates never encounter an actual criminal during the course of their education. Some universities provide internships or practicums or arrange field trips to prisons or other correctional facilities. Despite these efforts, however, few students ever experience a "real criminal" during their education. By viewing the criminal event from the perspective of the participants, these studies can make the decision by an individual to engage in crime "up close and personal" and supplement the statistical data from other research.

In Their Own Words enriches the reader's understanding of criminal typologies, criminal decision making, criminological theories, and criminal subcultures and lifestyles. The studies contained in this book vary in terms of the settings, the crimes being studied, and the researcher's involvement and role in the environment. In every case, however, the story is told from the perspective of, and in the words of, the offender. In each case, the researcher places the offender's words in a theoretical context and provides analyses and conclusions.

References

Campbell, A. (1984). *Girls in the Gang.* Oxford, UK: Basil Blackwell.

Cressey, D. R. (1953). *Other People's Money.* Glencoe, IL: Free Press.

Glassner, B., and Carpenter, C. (1985). *The Feasibility of an Ethnographic Study of Property Offenders: A Report Prepared for the National Institute of Justice.* Washington, DC: NIJ Mimeo.

Gold, R. (1969). Roles in sociological field observation. In G. J. McCall and J. L. Simmons (Eds.), *Issues in Participant Observation.* Reading, MA: Addison-Wesley.

Inciardi, J. (1977). In search of class cannon: A field study of professional pickpockets. In R. S. Weppner (Ed.), *Street Ethnography: Selected Studies of Crime and Drug Use in Natural Settings.* Beverly Hills: Sage.

Irwin, J. (1970). *The Felon*. Englewood Cliffs, NJ: Prentice Hall.

Klockars, C. (1974). *The Professional Fence*. New York: Macmillan.

Letkemann, E. (1973). *Crime as Work*. Englewood Cliffs, NJ: Prentice Hall.

Maxfield, M. G., and Babbie, E. (1995). *Research Methods for Criminal Justice and Criminology*. Belmont, CA: Wadsworth.

Shover, N. (1971). Burglary as an occupation. Ph.D. diss., University of Illinois.

Sutherland, E. H. (1937). *The Professional Thief*. Chicago: University of Chicago Press.

Wright, R. T., and Decker, S. H. (1994). *Burglars on the Job: Streetlife and Residential Break-Ins*. Boston: Northeastern University Press.

ACKNOWLEDGMENTS

In this 5th edition of *In Their Own Words*, it is again important to express my deep appreciation for the researchers and authors of the studies that are presented here. The credit for an anthology such as this goes to those individuals. My task was simply to select the best exemplars of contemporary field research in crime and criminal behavior and to attempt to bring them together in an integrated and effective manner. I gratefully acknowledge the scholarly efforts of these researchers. It is truly their book.

Over the life span of this book, several colleague have contributed in important ways, not only by allowing me to use the fruits of their scholarly labors but also by serving as consultants and advisors as I attempted to organize the materials and to locate new qualitative studies. Among these individuals who have helped me in many ways since the first edition in 1996, and who rightly should share the editorship, are Neal Shover at the University of Tennessee at Knoxville, Scott Decker at Arizona State University, and Richard Wright at the University of Missouri-St. Louis. More recently, Bruce Jacobs at the University of Texas-Dallas, John Heith Copes at the University of Alabama-Birmingham, Dean Dabney at Georgia State University, and Andy Hochstetler at Iowa State University have become valuable contributors and helpful colleagues in developing and identifying new material for the book.

In the process of preparing this new edition, I have also benefited from the numerous reviewers who commented on the selections, organization and integration of materials, and on the general worth of the project. Special appreciation is extended to Sarah Becker, University of Massachusetts—Amherst, Rebecca Bordt, DePauw University, Elizabeth Q. DeValve, Fayetteville State University, Mary Ann Eastep, University of Central Florida, Richard Felson, Pennsylvania State University, James Lasley, California State-Fullerton and Peter J.Venturelli, Valparaiso University.

At the 2007 American Society of Criminology annual meeting in Atlanta, Richard Felson suggested that I include a test bank with the next edition. I did. Thanks, Richard.

Special thanks are owed to my editor, Sherith Pankratz, and Assistant Editor, Whitney Laemmli, at Oxford. They have been there when I need them and have supported this effort in every way imaginable.

I must also express my appreciation to my Graduate Research Assistant, Donisha Ross at Wichita State University. Not only did she do all the clerical work associated with a project like this, such as obtaining all the reprint permissions, but also prepared the test bank. It is often said, but in this case is really true, "I could not have done it without her."

Finally, as always, I owe Jimmie Cromwell, my wife of 32 years and my best friend, the greatest debt and my deepest appreciation. I suspect that living with me all these years cannot have been the easiest job. I am grateful for her patience.

Paul Cromwell
Wichita, Kansas

CONTENTS

About the Contributors   xix

Section I   Criminal Lifestyles and Decision Making

Introduction   /   01

1   The Socially Bounded Decision Making of Persistent
Property Offenders   /   03
Neal Shover and David Honaker

Shover and Honaker argue that improved understanding of
the decision-making processes of property offenders is gained
through exploring how their decisions are shaped by their
lifestyles.

2   The Reasoning Offender: Motives and Decision-Making
Strategies   /   22
Paul Cromwell and James N. Olson

Cromwell and Olson examine the decision-making processes of
residential burglars. They explore the factors that motivate the
burglar and those that deter or promote a burglary.

3   Opportunities and Decisions: Interactional Dynamics in
Robbery and Burglary Groups   /   46
Andy Hochstetler

The author analyzes the decision-making processes of offenders
working in groups.

Section II   Property Crime

Introduction   /   67

4   The Key to Auto Theft: Emerging Methods of Auto Theft
from the Offenders' Perspective   /   69
Heith Copes and Michael Cherbonneau

The authors interviewed auto thieves regarding the techniques
and strategies used to commit their crimes.

5 The Five-Finger Discount: An Analysis of Motivations for Shoplifting / 90

Paul Cromwell, Lee Parker, and Shawna Mobley

The authors examine the motivations for shoplifting and suggest prevention strategies.

6 Becoming a Computer Hacker: Examining the Enculturation and Development of Computer Deviants / 109

Thomas J. Holt

Holt explores the development of computer hackers and how they define and justify their actions through subcultural norms.

7 Identity Theft: Assessing Offenders' Motivations and Strategies / 124

Heith Copes and Lynne Vieraitis

Copes and Vieraitis shed light on the motives, perceptions of risk, and strategies involved in identity theft.

Section III Violent Crime

Introduction / 139

8 The New Face of Terrorism: Socio-Cultural Foundations of Contemporary Terrorism / 141

Jerrold M. Post

Drawing on interviews with 35 incarcerated radical Middle-eastern terrorists, Post contrasts the motivations of the social-revolutionary terrorists groups of the past with the emerging nationalist-separatist fundamentalist groups of the 21st century.

9 Creating the Illusion of Impending Death: Armed Robbers in Action / 158

Richard T. Wright and Scott H. Decker

In this study, Wright and Decker explore the dynamics of offender-victim confrontations in armed robbery.

10 Gendering Violence: Masculinity and Power in Men's Accounts of Domestic Violence / 168

Kristin L. Anderson and Debra Umberson

The authors reveal the strategies used by abusing males in an effort to portray themselves as rational and non-violent.

11 Retrospective Accounts of Violent Events
by Gun Offenders   /   187

Mark R. Pogrebin, Paul B. Stretesky, N. Prabha Unnithan, and Gerry Venor

The authors explain the narrative explanations gun offenders
provide for engaging in their violent acts.

Section IV   Occupational Crime

Introduction   /   203

12 Crime on the Line: Telemarketing and the Changing
Nature of Professional Crime   /   205

Neal Shover, Glenn S. Coffey, and Dick Hobbs

In this selection, Shover and his associates examine the lifestyles
and motivations of individuals engaged in illegal telemarketing.

13 Denying the Guilty Mind: Accounting for Involvement
in a White-Collar Crime   /   224

Michael L. Benson

Benson explains the process by which white-collar offenders
deny criminal intent are thus able to defeat the process of
criminalization.

14 Neutralization and Deviance in the Workplace: Theft
of Supplies and Medicines by Hospital Nurses   /   235

Dean Dabney

In this selection, Dabney examines thefts by hospital nurses and
the means by which they rationalize and neutralize guilt.

Section V   Illegal Occupations

Introduction   /   249

15 The "Myth of Organization" of International Drug
Smugglers   /   251

Scott H. Decker and Jana S. Benson

The authors examine drug smuggling from the perspective of
those most in the know, the individuals whose roles facilitate the
trade.

16 Fencing: Avenues for Redistribution of Stolen
Property   /   265

Paul Cromwell and James N. Olson

Cromwell and Olson discuss the various avenues utilized by burglars to dispose of stolen property and develop a typology of fences

17 The Second Step in Double Jeopardy: Appropriating the Labor of Female Street Hustlers / 283

Kim Romenesko and Eleanor M. Miller

In chapter, the authors studied 14 female street prostitutes and analyzed their relationships to the men who controlled their activities.

Section VI Gangs and Crime

Introduction / 299

18 Gang-Related Gun Violence: Socialization, Identity, and Self / 301

Paul B. Stretesky and Mark R. Pogrebin

The authors examine how gang socialization leads to gun-related violence.

19 Gender and Victimization Risk Among Young Women in Gangs / 324

Jody Miller

Miller explores the extent that female members of youth gangs shapes their risk for victimization

20 Homeboys, Dope Fiends, Legits, and New Jacks / 338

John M. Hagedorn

Hagedorn identifies four categories of gang members based on their commitment to gang life.

Section VII Drugs and Crime

Introduction / 351

21 "E" Is for Ecstasy: A Participant Observation Study of Ecstasy Use / 353

Wilson R. Palacios and Melissa E. Fenwick

Palacios and Fenwick examine the "rave" culture and associated drug use in south Florida.

22 The Drugs-Crime Connection among Stable Addicts / 363

Charles E. Faupel

In a field study of heroin addicts, Faupel explores the connection between drugs and crime.

23 Property Crime and Women Drug Dealers in Australia / 375

Barbara Denton and Pat O'Malley

Denton and O'Malley analyze involvement in property crime as a way to finance participation in the drug culture.

24 Researching Crack Dealers: Dilemmas and Contradictions / 392

Bruce A. Jacobs

Jacobs points out the inherent dangers associated with studying street criminals.

Section VIII   Quitting Crime

Introduction / 407

25 Aging Criminals: Changes in the Criminal Calculus / 409

Neal Shover

Shover analyzes the factors which contribute to desistence from criminal activity.

ABOUT THE CONTRIBUTORS

Kristin L. Anderson is Associate Professor of Sociology at Western Washington University.

Jana S. Benson is a doctoral student at Arizona State University.

Michael L. Benson is Professor of Criminal Justice at the University of Cincinnati.

Michael Cherbonneau is a doctoral candidate at the University of Missouri-St. Louis.

Glenn S. Coffey is Assistant Professor of Criminology and Criminal Justice at the University of North Florida.

Heith Copes is Assistant Professor of Criminology and Criminal Justice at the University of Alabama at Birmingham.

Paul Cromwell is Professor of Criminal Justice at Wichita State University.

Dean Dabney is Associate Professor of Criminal Justice at Georgia State University.

Scott H. Decker is Chairperson and Professor of Criminal Justice and Criminology at Arizona State University.

Barbara Denton is a lawyer and sociologist in Melbourne, Australia.

Charles E. Faupel is Professor of Sociology and Director of Graduate Studies at Auburn University.

Melissa E. Fenwick is an Instructor of Criminal Justice at Western Connecticut State Uiversity.

John M. Hagedorn is Associate Professor of Criminal Justice at the University of Illinois at Chicago.

Andy Hochstetler is Assistant Professor of Sociology at Iowa State University.

Dick Hobbs is Head and Professor of Sociology at the London School of Economics.

Thomas J. Holt is Assistant Professor of Criminal Justice at the University of North Carolina-Charlotte.

David Honaker is deceased. He was formerly employed by the University of Tennessee at Knoxville.

Bruce A. Jacobs is Professor of Crime and Justice Studies in the School of Economic, Political, and Policy Sciences at the University of Texas at Dallas.

Eleanor M. Miller is Dean of the College of Arts and Sciences at the University of Vermont.

Jody Miller is Professor of Criminal Justice and Criminology at the University of Missouri-St. Louis.

Shawna Mobley is Director of Correctional Counseling of Kansas in Wichita, Kansas.

Pat O'Malley is Professor at the University of Sydney Law School in Sydney, Australia.

James N. Olson is Professor of Psychology at the University of Texas–Permian Basin.

Wilson R. Palacios is Associate Professor of Criminology at the University of South Florida.

Lee Parker is an attorney and judge in Wichita, Kansas.

Mark R. Pogrebin is Professor of Criminal Justice at the University of Colorado at Denver.

Jerrold M. Post is Professor of Psychiatry, Political Psychology and International Affairs and Director of the Political Psychology at the George Washington University.

Kim Romenesko is a Senior Administrative Specialist at the University of Wisconsin-Milwaukee.

Neal Shover is Professor of Sociology at the University of Tennessee–Knoxville.

Paul B. Stretesky is Associate Professor of Sociology at Colorado State University.

Debra Umberson is Professor of Sociology at the University of Texas at Austin.

N. Prabha Unnithan is Professor of Sociology at Colorado State University.

Gerry Venor is an Instructor in the Department of Criminal Justice at Metropolitan State University in Denver, Colorado.

Lynne Vieraitis is Associate Professor of Crime and Justice Studies in the School of Economic, Political, and Policy Sciences at the University of Texas at Dallas.

Richard T. Wright is Curators Professor in the Department of Criminology and Criminal Justice at the University of Missouri–St. Louis.

IN THEIR OWN WORDS

CRIMINAL LIFESTYLES
AND DECISION MAKING

This section explores the lifestyles and the decision-making strategies of criminals. We are concerned here with offenders' views and attitudes about both criminal and conventional activities and their perceptions of the risks and benefits associated with a criminal lifestyle. How those perceptions are formed and how they change over time are also examined. Because the nature of the criminal lifestyle is hidden from public view and open only to the initiated, criminologists know little about these important issues. The research studies in this book are a step toward understanding the dynamics of criminal lifestyles and criminal decision making in that context.

In Chapter 1, Neal Shover and David Honaker ("The Socially Bounded Decision Making of Persistent Property Offenders") argue that an adequate understanding of the decision-making processes of property offenders can be gained only through exploring how these offenders' decisions are influenced by their lifestyles. They argue that offenders' risk assessments can best be understood by exploring the personal and social contexts in which decisions are made. They examine how the lifestyles of persistent property offenders affect their assessment of the risks and benefits of crime. The research focuses on the decision to commit a crime, emphasizing how closely that decision fits the rational choice model, in which decisions are based on an "assessment of potential returns from alternative courses of action and the risk of legal sanctions."

Chapter 2, "The Reasoning Burglar: Motives and Decision Strategies," by Cromwell and Olson, is based on a study of 30 active, "free-world" burglars. The authors interviewed and observed their behavior over an 18-month span. They examined the decision processes, target selection strategies, and methods involved in committing burglaries.

In Chapter 3, "Opportunities and Decisions: Interactional Dynamics in Robbery and Burglary Groups," Andy Hochstetler analyzes the decision-making processes of criminals working in groups. He argues that although the role of co-offenders has been recognized for decades, it has not been adequately studied. He found that interaction among groups of offenders can "reduce the appeal of law abidance" and make criminal opportunities appear to be more attractive. Although the role and influence of co-offenders varies widely, participants mutually influence each other both in terms of decisions to offend, target selection and evaluating the risk-gain calculus.

The Socially Bounded Decision Making of Persistent Property Offenders

Neal Shover and David Honaker

The last decade has witnessed a renewal of interest in understanding crime based on the degree of rationality attributed to criminals as they contemplate offending. The rational choice model recognizes that individuals choose crime from other possible alternative courses of action. The argument holds that prospective criminals weigh the possible consequences of their actions—potential risks and possible gains—and take advantage of a criminal opportunity only when it is in their self-interest to do so. This model stresses the offender's perceptions of the costs and benefits and the anticipated net utilities of crime, arguing that an objective appraisal of the costs and benefits of any course of action cannot be completely known or acted upon.

In the following selection, Neal Shover and David Honaker argue that the risk assessments of offenders are best understood by exploring the personal and social contexts in which decisions are made. They examine the lifestyles of persistent property offenders relative to the influence of these lifestyles on how criminals assess the risks and benefits of crime. The focus of the research is on the decision to commit a crime, with emphasis on how closely that decision fits the rational choice model.

The study population includes a sample of 60 recidivist property offenders incarcerated in Tennessee state prisons, but who were nearing their release date. Subjects ranged in age from 23 to 70 years of age, with an average age of 34.1 years. Each member of the sample was interviewed approximately one month before his release from prison. Seven to 10 months after release, the authors traced, contacted, and interviewed 46 of the original sample of 60 men. The data used in this study were collected in the postrelease interviews. Semistructured ethnographic interviews were the principal data collection technique.

The interviews produced detailed descriptions of the most recent, easiest recalled crime that each subject had committed before the interview. Some of these crimes were committed by these individuals before their incarceration and some after their release. The objective was to gain, through the eyes of the offender, an understanding of the decision to commit a specific criminal act. The subjects were asked to focus their recollection on how the decision was made and to provide a detailed account of the risks and rewards they assessed while doing so.

Source: Neal Shover and David Honaker, "The Socially Bounded Decision Making of Persistent Property Offender," in *Howard Journal of Criminal Justice*, v.31, pp. 276–293. Copyright © 1992 by Blackwell Publishers Ltd. Reprinted by permission.

INTRODUCTION

The 1970s were marked by the eclipse of labeling theory as the dominant individual-level criminological theory and by the reappearance of interest in approaches originally advanced by classical theorists. Economists and cognitive psychologists, along with many in the criminological mainstream, advanced an interpretation of crime as *choice*, offering models of criminal decision-making grounded in the assumption that the decision to commit a criminal act springs from the offender's assessment of its anticipated net utilities (e.g., Becker 1968; Heineke 1978; Carroll 1978; Reynolds 1985). This movement in favor of rational-choice approaches to crime spurred empirical investigation of problems that heretofore were limited primarily to studies of the death penalty and its impact on the homicide rate.

Early investigations of a rational-choice interpretation of crime reported a weak but persistent relationship between the certainty of punishment and the rates of serious property crimes (Blumstein, Cohen, and Nagin 1978). It was recognized, however, that an understanding of criminal decision-making also requires knowledge about individual perceptions and beliefs about legal threats and other constraints on decision-making (e.g., Manski 1978). Investigators moved on two main fronts to meet this need. Some used survey methods to explore differential involvement in minor forms of deviance in samples of restricted age ranges, typically high school and college students (e.g., Waldo and Chiricos 1972). Alternatively, they examined the link between risk assessments and criminal participation in samples more representative of the general population. Serious shortcomings of these studies are that most either ignore the potential rewards of crime entirely or fail to examine its emotional and interpersonal utilities. Still other investigators turned attention to serious criminal offenders and began expanding the narrow existing knowledge base (e.g., Claster 1967), chiefly through the use of cross-sectional research designs and survey methods.

For more than a decade now, investigators have studied offenders' attitudes toward legitimate and criminal pursuits, their perceptions of and beliefs about the risks of criminal behavior, and their estimates of the payoffs from conventional and criminal pursuits (e.g., Petersilia et al. 1978; Peterson and Braiker 1980). These studies raise serious questions about the fit between offenders' calculus and a priori assumptions about their utilities and criminal decision-making. One investigation of 589 incarcerated property offenders concluded, for example, that the subjects apparently do not utilize "a sensible cost-benefit analysis" when weighing the utilities of crime (Figgie International 1988, p. 25). They substantially underestimate the risk of arrest for most crimes, routinely overestimate the monetary benefit they expect, and seem to have "grossly inaccurate perceptions of the costs and benefits associated with property crime" (Figgie International 1988, p. 81). Unfortunately, both design and conceptual problems undermine confidence in the findings of this and similar studies. Cross-sectional survey methods, for example, are poorly suited for examining dynamic decision-making processes. Most such studies also fail to examine offenders' estimates of the likely payoffs from noncriminal alternatives or their nonmonetary utilities, such as emotional satisfaction (Katz 1998).

As newer, empirically based models of criminal decision-making have been developed (e.g., Clarke and Cornish 1985; Cornish and Clarke 1986), a growing number of investigators are using ethnographic methods to examine the offender's criminal calculus, often in real or simulated natural settings (e.g., Carroll 1982; Carroll and Weaver 1986). The research reported here continues this line of ethnographic inquiry by using retrospective interviews to examine criminal decision-making by serious and persistent property offenders. The focus of our attention is the decision to commit a crime rather than the target-selection decision that has received substantial attention elsewhere (e.g., Scarr 1973; Repetto 1974; Maguire 1982; Bennett and Wright 1984a; Rengert and Wasilchick 1985; Cromwell, Olson, and Avary 1991). The first objective is to examine how closely the decision to commit a crime conforms to a classical rational-choice model in which it is assumed that decisions are based largely on an assessment of potential returns from alternative courses of action and the risk of legal sanctions. A second objective is to examine the influence of the lifestyle pursued by many persistent property offenders on the salience of their utilities and the risks they assess in criminal decision making.

FINDINGS

Analysis reveals that the most striking aspect of the subjects' decision-making for the crimes they described is that a majority gave little or no thought to the possibility of arrest and confinement. Of 34 subjects who were asked specifically whether they considered the risk of arrest or who spontaneously indicated whether they did so, 21 (62%) said they did not. The comments of two subjects are typical:

Q: Did you think about ... getting caught?

A: No.

Q: [H]ow did you manage to put that out of your mind?

A: [It] never did come into it.

Q: Never did come into it?

A: Never did, you know. It didn't bother me.

Q: Were you thinking about bad things that might happen to you?

A: None whatsoever.

Q: No?

A: I wasn't worried about getting caught or anything, you know. I was a positive thinker through everything, you know. I didn't have no negative thoughts about it whatsoever.

The 13 remaining subjects (38%) acknowledged that they gave some thought to the possibility of arrest, but most said they managed to dismiss it easily and to carry through with their plans:

Q: Did you worry much about getting caught? On a scale of one to ten, how would you rank your degree of worry that day?

A: [T]he worry was probably a one. You know what I mean? The worry was probably one. I didn't think about the consequences, you know. I know it's stupidity, but it didn't that I might go to jail, I mean it crossed my mind but it didn't make much difference.

Q: As you thought about doing that [armed robbery], were there things that you were worried about?

A: Well, the only thing that I was worried about was ... getting arrested didn't even cross my mind, just worrying about getting killed is the only thing, you know, getting shot. That's the only thing ... but, you know, you'd have to be really be crazy not to think about that ... you could possibly get in trouble. It crossed my mind, but I didn't worry about it all that much.

Some members of our sample said they managed deliberately and consciously to put out of mind all thoughts of possible arrest:

When I went out to steal, I didn't think about the negative things. 'Cause if you think negative, negative things are going to happen. And that's the way I looked at it ... I done it just like it was a job or something. Go out and do it, don't think about getting caught, 'cause that would make you jumpy, edgy, nervous. If you looked like you were doing something wrong, then something wrong is gonna happen to you....You just, you just put [the thought of arrest] out of your mind, you know.

Q: Did you think about [the possibility of getting caught] very much that night?

A: I didn't think about it that much, you know.... [I]t comes but, you know, you can wipe it away.

Q: How do you wipe it away?

A: You just blank it out. You blank it out.

Another subject said simply that "I try to put that [thought of arrest] the farthest thing from my mind that I can."

Many subjects attribute their ability to ignore or to dismiss all thought of possible arrest to a state of intoxication or drug-altered consciousness:

Q: You didn't think about going to prison?

A: Never did. I guess it was all that alcohol and stuff, and drugs.... The day I pulled that robbery? No. I was so high I didn't think about nothing.

Another subject told us that he had been drinking the entire day that he committed the crime and, by the time it occurred, he was in "nightlight city."

Although it is clear that the formal risks of crime were not considered carefully by most members of the sample, equally striking is the finding that very few thought about or assessed legitimate alternatives before opting to commit a criminal act. Of 22 subjects who were asked specifically whether they had done so, 16 indicated they gave no thought whatsoever to legitimate alternatives. The six subjects who did either ignored or quickly dismissed them as inapplicable, given their immediate circumstances.

We recognize the methodological shortcomings of the descriptions of criminal decision-making and behavior used as data for this study. Because the subjects were questioned in detail only about specific offenses they could remember well, the sample of descriptions may not be representative of the range of crimes they committed. By definition, they are memorable ones. Moreover, the recall period for these crimes ranged from one to 15 years, raising the possibility of errors caused by selective recall. Whether or not this could have produced systematic bias in the data is unknown. We cannot rule out the possibility that past crimes are remembered as being less rational than they actually were at the time of commission. Such a tendency could account in part for our interpretation of the data and our description of their style of decision-making. The fact that we limited the sample to recidivists means also that we cannot determine how much their behavior may reflect either innate differences (Gottfredson and Hirschi 1990) or experiential effects, that is, the effects of past success in committing crime and avoiding arrest (Nagin and Paternoster 1991). It could be argued that the behavior of our subjects, precisely because they had demonstrated a willingness to commit property crimes and had done so in the past, limits the external validity of their reports. Given sample selection criteria and these potential data problems, generalizations beyond the study population must be made with caution.

This said, we believe that the remarkable similarity between our findings and the picture of criminal decision-making reported by others who have studied serious property offenders strengthens their credibility significantly. A study of 83 imprisoned burglars revealed that 49% did not think about the chances of getting caught for any particular offense during their last period of offending. Although 37% of them did think about it, most thought there was little or no chance it would happen (Bennett and Wright 1984a, Table a14). Interviews with 113 men convicted of robbery or an offense related to robbery revealed that "over 60 percent ... said they had not even thought about getting caught." Another 17% said that they had thought about the possibility but "did not believe it to be a problem" (Feeney 1986, pp. 59–60). Analysis of prison interviews with 77 robbers and 45 burglars likewise revealed their "general obliviousness toward the consequences [of their crimes] and no thought of being caught" (Walsh 1986, p. 157). In summation, our findings along with the findings from other studies suggest strongly that many serious property offenders seem to be remarkably casual in weighing the formal risks of criminal participation. As one of our subjects put it, "you think about going to prison about like you think about dying, you know." The impact of alcohol and drug use in diminishing concern with possible penalties also has been reported by many others (e.g., Bennett and Wright 1984b; Cromwell, Olson, and Avary 1991).

If the potential legal consequences of crime do not figure prominently in crime commission decision-making by persistent thieves, what do they think about when choosing to commit crime? Walsh (1980; 1986) shows that typically they focus their thoughts on the money that committing a crime may yield and the good times they expect to have with it when the crime is behind them. Carroll's data (1982) likewise indicate that the amount of gain offenders expect to receive is "the most important dimension" in their decision-making, whereas the certainty of punishment is the least important of the four dimensions on which his subjects assessed crime opportunities. Our findings are consistent with these reports; our subjects said that they focused on the expected gains from their crimes:

> I didn't think about nothing but what I was going to do when I got that money, how I was going to spend it, what I was going to do with it, you know.
>
> See, you're not thinking about those things [possibility of being arrested]. You're thinking about that big pay check at the end of thirty to forty-five minutes worth of work.
>
> [A]t the time [that you commit crime], you throw all your instincts out the window.... Because you're just thinking about money, and money only. That's all that's on your mind, because you want that money. And you throw, you block everything off until you get the money.

Although confidence in our findings is bolstered by the number of points on which they are similar to reports by others who have explored crime commission decision-making, they do paint a picture of decision-making that is different from what is known about the way at least some of them make target selection decisions. Investigators (e.g., Cromwell, Olson, and Avary 1991) have shown that target decisions approximate simple commonsense conceptions of rational behavior (Shover 1991). A resolution of the problem presented by these contradictory findings is suggested by others (Cromwell, Olson, and Avary 1991) and also apparent in our data: Criminal participation often results from a *sequence* of experientially and analytically discrete decisions, all of potentially varying degrees of intentional rationality. Therefore, once a *motivational* crime commission decision has been made, offenders may move quickly to selecting, or to exploiting an apparently suitable target. At this stage of the criminal participation process, offenders are preoccupied with the *technical* challenge of avoiding failure at what now is seen as a *practical* task. As one subject put it, "you don't think about getting caught, you think about how in hell you're going to do it *not* to get caught, you know." His comments were echoed by another man: "The only thing you're thinking about is looking and acting and trying *not* to get caught." Last, consider the comments of a third subject: "I wasn't afraid of getting caught, but I was cautious, you know. Like I said, I was thinking only in the way to prevent me from getting caught." Just as bricklayers do not visualize graphically or deliberate over the bodily carnage that could follow from a collapsed scaffold once there is a job to be done, many thieves apparently do not dwell at length on the likelihood of arrest or on the pains of imprisonment when proceeding to search out or exploit suitable criminal opportunities.

The accumulated evidence on crime commission decision-making by persistent offenders is substantial and persuasive: the rationality they employ is limited or bounded severely (e.g., Carroll 1982; Cromwell, Olson, and Avary 1991). Although unsuccessful persistent offenders may calculate potential benefits and costs before committing criminal acts, they apparently do so differently or weigh utilities differently than as sketched in a priori decision-making models. As Walsh (1980, p. 141) suggests, offenders' "definitions of costs and rewards seem to be at variance with society's estimates of them." This does not mean that their decision making is *irrational*, but it does point to the difficulties of understanding it and then refining theoretical models of the process. Our objective in the remainder of this chapter is an improved understanding of criminal decision-making based on analysis of the socially anchored purposes, utilities, and risks of the acts that offenders commit. Put differently, we explore the contextual origins of their bounded rationality.

Lifestyle, Utilities, and Risk

It is instructive to examine the decision-making of persistent property offenders in context of the lifestyle that is characteristic of many in their ranks: life as party. The hallmark of *life as party* is the enjoyment of "good times" with minimal concern for obligations and commitments that are external to the person's immediate social setting. It is a lifestyle distinguished in many cases by two repetitively cyclical phases and correspondingly distinctive approaches to crime. When offenders' efforts to maintain the lifestyle (i.e., their party pursuits) are largely successful, crimes are committed in order to sustain circumstances or a pattern of activities they experience as pleasurable. As Walsh (1986, p. 15) puts it, crimes committed under these circumstances are "part of a continuing satisfactory way of life." By contrast, when offenders are less successful at party pursuits, their crimes are committed in order to forestall or avoid circumstances experienced as threatening, unpleasant, or precarious. Corresponding to each of these two phases of party pursuits is a distinctive set of utilities and stance toward legal risk.

Life as Party

Survey and ethnographic studies alike show that persistent property offenders spend much of their criminal gains on alcohol and other drugs (Petersilia et al. 1978; Maguire 1982; Gibbs and Shelley 1982; Figgie International 1988; Cromwell, Olson, and Avary 1991). The proceeds of their crimes, as Walsh has noted (1986, p. 72), "typically [are] used for personal, nonessential consumption (e.g., 'nights out'), rather than, for example, to be given to family or used for basic needs." Thieves spend much of their leisure hours enjoying good times. Our subjects were no different in this regard. For example:

> I smoked an ounce of pot in a day, a day and a half. Every other day I had to go buy a bag of pot, at the least. And sometimes I've went two or three days in a row.... And there was never a day went by that I didn't [drink] a case, case and a half of beer. And [I] did a 'script of pills every two days.

Although much of their money is consumed by the high cost of drugs, a portion may be used for ostentatious enjoyment and display of luxury items and activities that probably would be unattainable on the returns from blue-collar employment:

> [I]t was all just, it was all just a big money thing to me at the time, you know. Really, what it was impressing everybody, you know. "Here Floyd is, and he's never had nothing in his life, and now look at him: he's driving new cars, and wearing jewelry," you know.

Life as party is enjoyed in the company of others. Typically it includes shared consumption of alcohol or other drugs in bars and lounges, on street corners, or while cruising in automobiles. In these venues, party pursuers celebrate and affirm values of spontaneity, autonomy, independence, and resourcefulness. Spontaneity means that rationality and long-range planning are eschewed in favor of enjoying the moment and permitting the day's activities and pleasures to develop in an unconstrained fashion. This may mean, for example, getting up late, usually after a night of partying, and then setting out to contact and enjoy the company of friends and associates who are known to be predisposed to partying:

> I got up around about eight-thirty that morning....
> Q: Eight-thirty? Was that the usual time that you got up?
> A: Yeah, if I didn't have a hangover from the night before....
> Q: What kind of drugs were you doing then?
> A: I was doing.... Percadans, Dilauds, taking Valiums, drinking. ... [A]nyway, I got up that morning about eight-thirty, took me a bath, put on some clothes and ... decided to walk [over to his mother's home]. [T]his particular day, ... my nephew was over [there].... He was just sitting in the yard and talking and drinking beer, you know.... It was me, him and my sister. We was sitting out there in the yard talking. And this guy that we know, he came up, he pulled up. So my nephew got in the car with him and they left. So, you know, I was sitting there talking to my sister.... And then, in the meantime, while we was talking, they come back, about thirty minutes later with a case of beer, some marijuana and everything, and there was another one of my nephews in the car with them. So me, two of my sisters, and two of

my nephews, we got in the car with this guy here and we just went riding. So we went to Hadley Park and ... we stayed out there. There were so many people out there, they were parked on the grass and things, and the vice squad come and run everybody away. So when they done that, we left.... So we went back out [toward his mother's home] but instead of going over to my mother's house we went to this little joint [tavern]. Now we're steady drinking and smoking weed all during this day. So when we get there, we park and get out and see a few friends. We [were] talking and getting high, you know, blowing each other a shotgun [sharing marijuana].

Enjoyment of party pursuits in group context is enhanced through the collective emphasis on personal autonomy. Because it is understood by all that participants are free to leave if they no longer enjoy or do not support group activities, the continuing presence of each participant affirms for the remainder the pleasures of the lifestyle. Uncoerced participation thus reinforces the shared assumption that group activities are appropriate and enjoyable. The behavioral result of the emphasis on autonomy is acceptance of or acquiescence in group decisions and activities.

Party pursuits also appeal to offenders because they permit conspicuous display of independence (Persson 1981). This generally means avoidance of the world of routine work and freedom from being "under someone's thumb." It also may include being free to avoid or to escape from restrictive routines:

I just wanted to be doing something. Instead of being at home, or something like that. I wanted to be running, I wanted to be going to clubs, and picking up women and shooting pool. And I liked to go to [a nearby resort community] and just drive around over there. A lot of things like that.... I was drinking two pints or more a day.... I was doing Valiums and I was doing Demerol.... I didn't want to work.

The proper pursuit and enjoyment of life as party is expensive, largely because of the costs of drugs. As one of our subjects remarked: "We was doing a lot of cocaine, so cash didn't last long, you know. If we made $3,000, two thousand of it almost instantly went for cocaine." Some party pursuers must meet other expenses as well if the lifestyle is to be maintained:

Believe it or not, I was spending [$700] a day.

Q: On what?

A: Pot, alcohol, women, gas, motel rooms, food.

Q: You were living in hotels, motels?

A: Yeah, a lot of times, I was. I'd take a woman to a motel. I bought a lot of clothes. I used to like to dress pretty nicely, I'd buy suits.

Party pursuits require continuous infusions of money and no single method of generating funds allows enjoyment of it for more than a few days. Consequently, the emphasis on spontaneity, autonomy, and independence is matched by the importance attached to financial resourcefulness. This is evidenced by the ability to sustain the lifestyle over a period of time. Doing so earns for offenders a measure of respect from peers for their demonstrated ability to "get over." It translates into "self-esteem ... as a folk hero beating the bureaucratic system of routinized dependence" (Walsh 1986, p. 16). The value of and respect for those who demonstrate resourcefulness means that criminal acts, as a means of sustaining life as party, generally are not condemned by the offender's peers.

The risks of employing criminal solutions to the need for funds are approached blithely but confidently in the same spontaneous and playful manner as are the rewards of life as party. In fact, avoidance of careful and detailed planning is a way of demonstrating possession of valued personal qualities and commitment to the lifestyle. Combined with the twin assumptions that peers have chosen freely and that one should not interfere with their autonomy, avoidance of rational planning finds expression in a reluctance to suggest that peers should weigh carefully the possible consequences of whatever they choose to do. Therefore, the interaction that precedes criminal incidents is distinguished by circumspection and the use of linguistic devices that relegate risk and fear to the background of attention. The act of stealing, for example, is referred to obliquely but knowingly as "doing something" or as "making money":

> [After a day of partying,] I [got] to talking about making some money, because I didn't have no money. This guy that we were riding with, he had all the money .... So me and him and my nephew, we get together, talking about making some money. This guy tells me, he said, "man, I know where there's a good place at."
>
> Q: Okay, so you suggested you all go somewhere and rob?
> A: Yeah, "make some" well, we called it "making money."
> Q: Okay. So, then you and this fellow met up in the bar .... Tell me about the conversation?
> A: Well, there wasn't much of a conversation to it, really .... I asked him if he was ready to go, if he wanted to go do something, you know. And he knew what I meant. He wanted to go make some money somehow, any way it took.

To the external observer, inattention to risk at the moment when it would seem most appropriate may seem to border on irrationality. For the offender engaged in party pursuits, however, it is but one aspect of behaviors that are rational in other respects. It opens up opportunities to enjoy life as party and to demonstrate commitment to values shared by peers. Resourcefulness and disdain for conventional rationality affirm individual character and style, both of which are important in the world of party pursuits (Goffman 1967).

Party Pursuits and Eroding Resources

Paradoxically, the pursuit of life as party can be appreciated and enjoyed to the fullest extent only if participants moderate their involvement in it while maintaining identities and routines in the straight world. Doing so maintains its "escape value" but it also requires an uncommon measure of discipline and forbearance. The fact is that extended and enthusiastic enjoyment of life as party threatens constantly to deplete irrevocably the resources needed to sustain enjoyment of its pleasures. Three aspects of the life-as-party lifestyle can contribute to this end.

First, some offenders become ensnared increasingly by the chemical substances and drug-using routines that are common there. In doing so, the meaning of drug consumption changes:

> See, I was doing drugs every day. It just wasn't every other day, it was to the point that, after the first few months doing drugs, I would have to do "X amount" of drugs, say, just for instance, just to feel like I do now. Which is normal.

Once the party pursuer's physical or psychological tolerance increases significantly, drugs are consumed not for the high they once produced but instead to maintain a sense of normality by avoiding sickness or withdrawal.

Second, party pursuits erode legitimate fiscal and social capital. They cannot be sustained by legitimate employment and they may in fact undermine both one's ability and inclination to hold a job. Even if offenders are willing to work at the kinds of employment available to them, and evidence suggests that many are not (Cromwell, Olson, and Avary 1991), the time schedules of work and party pursuits conflict. The best times of the day for committing many property crimes are also the times the offender would be at work and it is nearly impossible to do both consistently and well. For those who pursue life as a party, legitimate employment often is foregone or sacrificed (Rengert and Wasilchick 1985). The absence of income from noncriminal sources thus reinforces the need to find other sources of money.

Determined pursuit of life as party also may affect participants' relationships with legitimate significant others. Many offenders manage to enjoy the lifestyle successfully only by exploiting the concern and largesse of family and friends. This may take the form of repeated requests for and receipt of personal loans that go unreturned, occasional thefts, or other forms of exploitation:

> I lived well for awhile. I lived well ... until I started shooting cocaine real bad, intravenously.... [A]nd then everything, you know, went up in smoke, you know. Up my arm. The watches, the rings ... the car, you know. I used to have a girl, man, and her daddy had two horses. I put them in my arm. You know what I mean? I made her sell them horses. My clothes and all that stuff, a lot of it, they went up in smoke when I started messing with that cocaine.

Eventually, friends and even family members may come to believe that they have been exploited or that continued assistance will only prolong a process that must be terminated. As one subject told us, "Oh, I tried to borrow money, and borrow money and, you know, nobody would loan it to me.

Because they knew what I was doing." After first refusing further assistance, acquaintances, friends, and even family members may avoid social contacts with the party pursuer or sever ties altogether. This dialogue occurred between the interviewer and one of our subjects:

Q: [B]esides doing something wrong, did you think of anything else that you could do to get money? ... Borrow it?

A: No, I'd done run that in the ground. See, you burn that up. That's burned up, right there, borrowing, you know.... Once I borrow, you know, I might get $10 from you today and, see, I'll be expecting to be getting $10 tomorrow, if I could. And then, when I see you [and] you see me coming, you say, "no, I don't have none." [A]s the guys in the penitentiary say, "you absorb all of your remedies," you see. And that's what I did: I burned my remedies up, you know.

Last, when party pursuits are not going well, feelings of shame and self-disgust are not uncommon (Frazier and Meisenhelder 1985). Unsuccessful party pursuers as a result may take steps to reduce these feelings by distancing themselves voluntarily from conventional others:

Q: You were married to your wife at that time?

A: Yeah, I was married.

Q: Where was she living then?

A: I finally forced her to go home, you know.... I made her go home, you know. And it caused an argument, for her to go home to her mother's. I felt like that was the best thing I did for her, you know. She hated me ... for it at the time, didn't understand none of it. But, really, I intentionally made her go. I really spared her the misery that we were going to have. And it came. It came in bundles.

When party pursuers sustain severe losses of legitimate income and social resources, regardless of how it occurs, they grow increasingly isolated from conventional significant others. The obvious consequence is that this reduces interpersonal constraints on their behavior.

As their pursuit of life as party increasingly assumes qualities of difficulty and struggle, offenders' utilities and risk perceptions also change. Increasingly, crimes are committed not to enhance or sustain the lifestyle so much as to forestall unpleasant circumstances. Those addicted to alcohol or other drugs, for example, must devote increasing time and energy to the quest for monies to purchase their chemicals of choice. Both their drug consumption and the frequency of their criminal acts increase (Ball et al. 1983; Johnson et al. 1985). For them, as for others, inability to draw on legitimate or low risk resources eventually may precipitate a crisis. One of our respondents retold how, facing a court appearance on a burglary charge, he needed funds to hire an attorney:

I needed some money bad or if I didn't, if I went to court the following day, I was going to be locked up. The judge was going to lock me up. Because I didn't have no lawyer. And I had went and talked to several lawyers and they told me ... they wanted a thousand dollars, that if I couldn't come up with no thousand dollars, they couldn't come to court with me.... [S]o I went to my sister. I asked my sister, I said, "look here, what about letting me have seven or eight hundred dollars" which I knowed she had the money because she ... had been in a wreck and she had gotten some money out of a suit. And she said, "well, if I give you the money you won't do the right thing with it." And I was telling her, "no, no, I need a lawyer." But I couldn't convince her to let me have the money. So I left.... I said, shit, I'm fixin' to go back to jail.... [S]o as I left her house and was walking I was going to catch the bus the [convenience store] and bus stop was right there by each other. So, I said I'm going to buy me some gum.... [A]nd in the process of me buying the chewing gum, I seen two ladies, they was counting money. So I figured sooner or later one of them was going to come out with the money.... I waited on them until ... one came out with the money, and I got it.

Confronted by crisis and preoccupied increasingly with relieving immediate distress, the offender eventually may experience and define himself as propelled by forces beyond his control. Behavioral options become dichotomized into those that hold out some possibility of relief, however risky, and those that promise little but continued pain. Legitimate options are few and are seen as unlikely solutions. A criminal act may offer some hope of relief, however temporary. The offender may imbue the criminal option with almost magical prospects for ending or reversing the state of discomfort:

I said, "well, look at it like this"; if I don't do it, then tomorrow morning I've got the same [problems] that I've got right now. I could be hungry. I'm going to want food more. I'm going to want cigarettes more. I'm going to want everything more. But, if I do it, and if I make it, then I've got all I want.

Acts that once were the result of blithe unconcern with risk can over time come to be based on a personal determination to master or reverse what is experienced as desperately unpleasant circumstances. As a result, inattention to risk in the offender's decision making may give way to the perception that he has nothing to lose:

It ... gets to the point that you get into such a desperation. You're not working, you can't work. You're drunk as hell, been that way two or three weeks. You're no good to yourself, and you're no good to anybody else. Self-esteem is gone [and you are] spiritually, mentally, physically, financially bankrupt. You ain't got *nothing to lose*.

Desperate to maintain or reestablish a sense of normality, the offender pursues emotional relief with a decision to act decisively, albeit in the face of legal odds recognized as narrowing. By acting boldly and resolutely to make the best of a grim situation, one gains a measure of respect, if not from others, then at least from oneself.

> I think, when you're doing drugs like I was doing, I don't think you tend to rationalize much at all. I think it's just a decision you make. You don't weigh the consequences, the pros and the cons. You just do it.
> You know, all kinds of things started running through my mind. If I get caught, then there, there I am with another charge. Then I said, well if I don't do something, I'm going to be in jail. And I just said, "I'm going to do it."

The fact that sustained party pursuits often cause offenders to increase the number of offenses they commit and to exploit criminal opportunities that formerly were seen as risky should not be interpreted as meaning they believe they can continue committing crime with impunity. The opposite is true. Many offenders engaged in crimes intended to halt or reverse eroding fortunes are aware that eventually they will be arrested if they continue doing so:

Q: How did you manage not to think about, you know, that you could go to prison?

A: Well, you think about it afterwards. You think, "wow, boy, I got away with it again." But you know, sooner or later, the law of averages is "gonna catch up with you. You just can't do it [commit crime] forever and ever and ever. And don't think you're not gonna get caught," cause you will.

Bennett and Wright (1984a) likewise show that a majority of persistent offenders endorse the statement that they will be caught "eventually." The cyclical transformations of party pursuits from pleasant and enjoyable to desperate and tenuous is one reason they are able to commit crimes despite awareness of inevitable and potentially severe legal penalties.

The threat posed by possible arrest and imprisonment, however, may not seem severe to some desperate offenders. As compared to their marginal and precarious existence, it may be seen as offering a form of relief:

> [When he was straight], I'd think about [getting caught]: I could get this, and that [penalties].... [A]nd then I would think, well, I know this is going to end one day, you know. But, you know, you get so far out there, and get so far off into it that it really don't matter, you know. But you think about that.... I knew, eventually, I would get caught, you know.... I was off into drugs and I just didn't care if I got caught or not.
> When I [got] caught and they caught me right at the house it's kind of like, you feel good, because you're glad it's over, you know. I mean, a weight being lifted off your head. And you say, well, I don't have to worry about this shit no more, because they've caught me. And it's over, you know.

In sum, because of offenders' eroding access to legitimately secured funds, their diminishing contact with and support from conventional significant others, and their efforts to maintain drug consumption habits, crimes that once were committed for recreational purposes increasingly become desperate attempts to forestall or reverse uncomfortable or frustrating situations. Pursuing the short-term goal of maximizing enjoyment of life, legal threats can appear to the offender either as remote and improbable contingencies when party pursuits fulfill their recreational purposes or as an acceptable risk in the face of continued isolation, penury, and desperation.

We analyzed the descriptions of crime provided by our subjects, and their activities on the day the crime occurred. We focused specifically on: (1) the primary purpose of their crimes, that is, whether they planned to use the proceeds of crime for pleasure or to cope with unpleasant contingencies, and (2) the extent and subjective meaning of their drug use at the time they decided to commit the crime in question. On the basis of the analysis, we classified the crimes of 15 subjects as behaviors committed in the enjoyment of life as a party and 13 as behaviors committed to enhance or restore enjoyment of this lifestyle. The 12 remaining offenders could not be classified because of insufficient information in the crime descriptions or because they committed isolated criminal acts that do not represent a specific lifestyle. Two subjects, for example, described crimes that were acts of vengeance directed at the property of individuals who had treated them or their relatives improperly. One of the men related how he decided to burglarize a home for reasons of revenge:

> I was mad.... When I was in the penitentiary, my wife went to his house for a party and he give her a bunch of cocaine.... It happened, I think, about a week before I got out.... I just had it in my mind what I wanted to do: I wanted to hurt him like I was hurt.... I was pretty drunk, when I went by [his home], and I saw there wasn't no car there. So, I just pulled my car in.

The other subject told how an acquaintance had stolen drugs and other possessions from his automobile. In response the subject "staked out the places where he would be for several days before I caught him, at gun point, [and] made him take me to his home, [which] I ransacked, and found some of the narcotics that he had stolen from me." Although neither of these crimes was committed in pursuit of life as party, other crimes committed by both these subjects during their criminal careers did occur as part of that lifestyle. Other investigators have similarly reported that revenge is the dominant motive in a minority of property offenses (e.g., Cromwell, Olson, and Avary 1991, p. 22).

Implications

We have suggested that daily routines characteristic of the partying lifestyle of persistent and unsuccessful offenders may modify both the salience of their various decision utilities and their perceptions of legal risk in the process of their crime commission decisions. This is not to say that these decisions are irrational, only that they do not conform to decision-making as sketched by rational-choice theories. Our objective was not to falsify the rational-choice approach to criminal decision-making, for we know of no way this could be accomplished. Whatever it is, moreover, rationality is not a dichotomous variable. Indeed, offenders' target selection decision-making appears more rational in the conventional sense than do crime commission decisions.

The lesson here for theories of criminal decision-making is that although utilities and risk assessment may be properties of individuals, they also are shaped by the social and personal contexts in which decisions are made. Whether their pursuit of life as party is interpreted theoretically as the product of structural strain, choice, or even happenstance is of limited importance to an understanding of persistent offenders' discrete criminal forays. What is important is that their lifestyle places them in situations that may facilitate important transformations in the utilities of prospective actions. If nothing else, this means that some situations more than others make it possible to discount or ignore risk. We are not the first to call attention to this phenomenon:

> [The] situational nature of sanction properties has escaped the scales and indicators employed in official record and self-report survey research. In this body of research an arrest and a year in prison are generally assumed to have the same meaning for all persons and across all situations. The situational grounding of sanction properties suggests, [however,] that we look beyond official definitions of sanctions and the attitudinal structure of individuals to the properties of situations. (Ekland-Olson et al. 1984, p.174)

Along the same line, a longitudinal survey of adult offenders concludes that decision making "may be conditioned by elements within the immediate situation confronting the individual ... [such that] perceptions of the opportunity, returns, and support for crime within a given situation may influence ... perceptions of risks and the extent to which those risks are discounted" (Piliavin et al. 1986, p. 115). The same interpretation has been suggested by Shover and Thompson (1992) for their failure to find an expected positive relationship between risk estimates and crime desistance among former prison inmates.

In light of the sample and data limitations of this study we cannot and have not argued that the lifestyle we described generates or produces the characteristic decision-making behaviors of persistent property offenders. The evidence does not permit such interpretive liberties. It does seem reasonable to suggest, however, that the focal concerns and shared perspectives of those who pursue life as party may function to sustain offenders' freewheeling, but purposeful, decision-making style. Without question there is a close correspondence between the two. Our ability to explain and predict decision-making requires that we gain a better understanding of how utilities and risk perceptions are constrained by the properties of situations encountered typically by persons in their daily rounds. In other words, we must learn more about the daily worlds that comprise the immediate contexts of criminal decision-making behavior.

References

Ball, J. C., Shaffer, J. W. & Nurco, D. N. (1983). The day-to-day criminality of heroin addicts in Baltimore: A study in the continuity of offense rates, *Drug and Alcohol Dependence*, *12*, 119–142.

Becker, G. (1968). Crime and punishment: An economic approach. *Journal of Political Economy*, *76*, 169–217.

Bennett, T. & Wright, R. (1984a). *Burglars on Burglary*. Hampshire, U.K.: Gower.

———. (1984b). The relationship between alcohol use and burglary. *British Journal of Addiction*, *79*, 431–437.

Blumstein, A., Cohen, J. & Nagin, D., (Eds.). (1978). *Deterrence and Incapacitation: Estimating the Effects of Criminal Sanctions on Crime Rates*. Washington, D.C.: National Academy of Sciences.

Carroll, J. S. (1978). A psychological approach to deterrence: The evaluation of crime opportunities. *Journal of Personality and Social Psychology*, *36*, 1512–1520.

———. (1982). Committing a crime: The offender's decision. In J. Konecni & E. B.

Carroll, J. S. & Weaver, F. (1986). Shoplifters' perceptions of crime opportunities: A process-tracing study. In D. B. Cornish & R. V. Clarke (Eds.), *The Reasoning Criminal: Rational Choice Perspectives on Offending* (pp.19–38). New York: Springer-Verlag.

Clarke, R. V. & Cornish, D. B. (1985). Modeling offenders' decisions: A framework for research and policy. In M. Tonry & N. Morris (Eds.), *Crime and Justice: A Review of Research*, Vol. 4 (pp. 147–185). Chicago: University of Chicago Press.

Claster, D. S. (1967). Comparison of risk perception between delinquents and nondelinquents. *Journal of Criminal Law, Criminology, and Police Science*, *58*, 80–86.

Cornish, D. B. & Clarke, R. V., (Eds.). (1986). *The Reasoning Criminal: Rational Choice Perspectives on Offending*. New York: Springer-Verlag.

Cromwell, P. F., Olson, J. N. & Avary, D. W. (1991). *Breaking and Entering: An Ethnographic Analysis of Burglary*. Newbury Park, CA: Sage.

Ekland-Olson, S., Lieb, J. & Zurcher, L. (1984). The paradoxical impact of criminal sanctions: Some microstructural findings. *Law and Society Review*, *18*, 159–178.

Feeney, F. (1986). Robbers as decision-makers. In D. B. Cornish & R. V. Clarke (Eds.), *The Reasoning Criminal: Rational Choice Perspectives on Offending*. New York: Springer-Verlag.

Figgie International (1988). *The Figgie Report Part VI The Business of Crime: The Criminal Perspective*. Richmond, Va.: Figgie International Inc.

Frazier, C. E. & Meisenhelder, T. (1985). Criminality and emotional ambivalence: Exploratory notes on an overlooked dimension. *Qualitative Sociology*, *8*, 266–284.

Gibbs, J. J. & Shelley, P. L. (1982). Life in the fast lane: A retrospective view by commercial thieves. *Journal of Research in Crime and Delinquency, 19,* 299–330.

Goffman, E. (1967). *Interaction Ritual.* Garden City, N.Y.: Anchor.

Gottfredson, M. R. & Hirschi, T. (1990). *A General Theory of Crime.* Stanford, CA: Stanford University Press.

Heineke, J. M. (Ed.). (1978). *Economic Models of Criminal Behavior.* Amsterdam: North-Holland.

Johnson, B. D., Goldstein, P. J., Preble, E., Schmeidler, J., Lipton, D. D., Spunt, B., et al. (1985). *Taking Care of Business: The Economics of Crime by Heroin Addicts.* Lexington, Ma: D.C. Heath.

Katz, J. (1998). *Seductions of Crime.* New York: Basic Books.

Konecni, V. J. & Ebbesen, E. B. (Eds.). (1982). *The Criminal Justice System: A Social-Psychological Analysis.* San Francisco: W.H. Freeman.

Maguire, M. in collaboration with Bennett, T. (1982). *Burglary in a Dwelling.* London: Heinemann.

Manski, C. F. (1978). Prospects for inference on deterrence through empirical analysis of individual criminal behavior. In A. Blumstein, J. Cohen & D. Nagin (Eds.), *Deterrence and Incapacitation: Estimating the Effects of Criminal Sanctions on Crime Rates.* Washington, D.C.: National Academy of Sciences.

Nagin, D. S. & Paternoster, R. (1991). On the relationship of past to future participation in delinquency. *Criminology, 29,* 163–189.

Persson, M. (1981). Time-perspectives amongst criminals. *Acta Sociologica, 24,* 149–165.

Petersilia, J. (1980). Criminal career research: A review of recent evidence. In N. Morris & M. Tonry (Eds.), *Crime and Justice: An Annual Review of Research,* Vol. 2, (pp. 321–379). Chicago: University of Chicago Press.

Petersilia, J., Greenwood, P. W. & Lavin, M. (1978). *Criminal Careers of Habitual Felons.* Washington, D.C.: U.S. Department of Justice, National Institute of Law Enforcement and Criminal Justice.

Peterson, M. A. & Braiker, H. B. (1980). *Doing Crime: A Survey of California Prison Inmates.* Santa Monica, Calif.: Rand Corporation.

Piliavin, I., Gartner, R. & Matsueda, R. (1986). Crime, deterrence, and rational choice. *American Sociological Review, 51,* 101–119.

Rengert, G. F. & Wasilchick, J. (1985). *Suburban Burglary.* Springfield, Ill.: Charles C. Thomas.

Repetto, T. A. (1974). *Residential Crime.* Cambridge, Mass.: Ballinger.

Reynolds, M. O. (1985). *Crime by Choice: An Economic Analysis.* Dallas, Tex.: Fisher Institute.

Scarr, H. A. (1973). *Patterns of Burglary* (2nd ed.). Washington, D.C.: U.S. Department of Justice, National Institute of Law Enforcement and Criminal Justice.

Seidel, J. V., Kjolseth, R. & Seymour, E. (1988). *The Ethnograph: A User's Guide* (Version 3.0). Littleton, CO: Qualis Research Associates.

Shover, N. (1991). Burglary. In M. Tonry (Ed.), *Crime and Justice: An Annual Review of Research,* Vol. 14. Chicago: University of Chicago Press.

Shover, N. & Thompson, C. Y. (1992). Age, differential expectations, and crime desistance. *Criminology, 30,* 89–104.

Waldo, G. P. & Chiricos, T. G. (1972). Perceived penal sanction and self-reported criminality: A neglected approach to deterrence research. *Social Problems, 19,* 522–540.

Walsh, D. (1980). *Break-Ins: Burglary from Private Houses.* London: Constable.

——. (1986). *Heavy Business.* London: Routledge and Kegan Paul.

The Reasoning Offender: Motives and Decision-Making Strategies

Paul Cromwell and James N. Olson

*I*f you want to know something about burglary, what better way than to talk with burglars and to ask them to recreate their past crimes as you observe and ask questions. This is what the authors of this study did. Using a snowball sampling technique, they selected a group of 30 active burglars and spent many hours with each of them. First they conducted an extensive semi-structured interview with each subject, asking them questions about their decisions to commit burglaries, their drug use, their co-defendants, the techniques they used to select targets, methods of breaking into houses, how they searched once inside, and what they did with the stolen items once obtained. Following the interview, the burglar subjects were asked to ride along with the researchers and to recreate past burglaries (up to the point of actually committing the crime). They were asked to identify the factors that made up their decision to burglarize a particular residence and those factors which deterred them from a burglary. Findings from this study inform crime prevention policies at both he individual and the community level. Burglars are found to make decisions based on their perceptions of risk and gain at the site of the prospective target and on factors which have immediate consequences. Risk variables such as the possibility to future arrest and criminal justice sanctions play a very minor role in their decision making processes. Thus, criminal justice practices and legislation which establish severe penalties for burglary (and most other property crime) do not usually deter the burglar. On-site practices,, such as target hardening, increasing visibility and surveillance from the street and neighbors homes, do have a deterrent effect.*

Much of the recent research on property crime (Copes, 2003; Cromwell, Olson, & Avary, 1991, 2004; Hochstetler & Copes, 2003; Jacobs, 1999; Shachmurove et al., 1997; Shover, 1996; Wright & Decker, 1994) has focused on the rational processes by which an offender chooses a criminal career, selects targets, and carries out criminal acts. Rational choice theory is predicated on the assumption that individuals *choose* to commit crimes. The theory predicts that individuals evaluate alternative courses of action, weighing the possible

Source: Excerpted from Paul Cromwell and James N. Olson, *Breaking and Entering: Burglars on Burglary*. Belmont, CA: Wadsworth. 2004. Used with permission of the publisher.

rewards against the costs and risks, and choosing the action that maximizes their gain.

The notion of rational choice has its origins in both the classical theories of Cesare Beccaria and Jeremy Bentham in the late eighteenth century and in relatively recent economic theory, specifically in the work of Gary Becker (1968). According to classical theory, criminals are free, rational, and hedonistic. They choose among alternative courses of action according to their perceptions of the risks and gains associated, seeking to maximize gain (or pleasure) and minimize risk (or pain).

Modern classical explanations are derived from economic theory, which views the decision to commit crime as essentially like any other decision— that is, one made on the basis of a calculation of the costs and benefits of the action. The benefits of a criminal action are the net rewards of crime and include not only the gains but also intangible benefits such as emotional pleasure or satisfaction. The individual may receive immense satisfaction from the excitement of crime, from the independent lifestyle afforded by crime, or from outwitting the authorities. The risks or costs of crime are those associated with formal punishment should the individual be discovered, apprehended, and convicted, as well as psychological or social costs, such as pangs of conscience, social disapproval, marital and family discord, or loss of self-esteem (Void & Bernard, 1986).

The degree of rationality that can be attributed to offenders in planning and executing their crimes and how rationality is related to crime prevention measures have been central issues of debate (Clarke & Cornish, 1985; Cook, 1980; Cornish, 1993; Cornish & Clarke, 1986). Brezina (2002) characterizes the major positions as the "narrow" and the "wide" models of rational choice. The narrow model assumes that offenders consider all possible consequences of their actions and choose the course that maximizes their personal gain and utility. The wide model, in contrast, suggests that offenders do not operate under optimal conditions; that the complete range of possible consequences is always unknown to the actor, and that even if all possible consequences were known, most individuals are not capable of the intricate and complex calculations necessary to choose the course of action to maximize outcomes. In other words, the wide model assumes that information necessary to make good decisions is frequently unavailable and that even if were, most people are not particularly competent decision-makers.

The concept of limited rationality proposes that for behavior to be rational, it does not have to be carefully preconceived and planned or require hierarchical, sequential decision making. It is enough that decisions are perceived to be optimal. It does not require deliberate weighing of carefully considered alternatives and consequences. It is sufficient that decision makers choose between alternatives based upon their immediate perception of the risks and gains involved. The decision does not have to be the best possible under the circumstances, nor does it have to be based upon an accurate assessment of the situation. A burglar can never calculate with assurance the value of the property he or she expects to take away in a burglary or know

with confidence the extent of the punishment should he or she be apprehended. The concept of limited rationality recognizes the limited capacity
and willingness of most persons to acquire and process information from
more than one input or source simultaneously.

Cornish and Clarke (1986) concluded that people usually pay attention
to only some of the facts or sources at their disposal, employing shortcuts
or rules of thumb to speed the decision process. These rules of thumb are
analogous to Cook's (1980) concept of "standing decisions," which negate the
need to weigh carefully all the alternatives and consequences before making a decision in many cases. A standing decision may simply be a decision
made beforehand to take advantage of certain types of criminal opportunities or to avoid others. In effect, these are rational processes that do not
require conscious analysis each time they are employed.

In this chapter we consider the rational processes that motivate offenders to commit burglary and the decision strategy they use in committing
the crime. When considering the motives that underlie crime, we must
first differentiate between *criminality* and *crime*. Crime refers to the criminal event itself. Criminality refers to processes through which individuals originally become involved in crime and which create a "readiness"
to offend. Tonry and Morris (1985) identify factors such as temperament,
intelligence, broken homes, parental crime, self perception, criminal associates, and so on as being involved in the development of readiness to commit crimes. Cornish and Clarke (1986, p. 2) assert that the development of
criminality is a process that is usually multistaged and extends over an
extended period of time. For example, a person from a broken home might
not develop adequate social bonds allowing him or her to perceive of theft
as a reasonable means of dealing with an urgent need for cash. Having
associates who commit criminal acts might further cement the perception
that crime is an appropriate solution to the problem. For purposes of this
study, we assume a readiness to commit crimes and we do not delve into
the dynamics of the burglar's criminality. Of more immediate concern are
those variables which translate the readiness into a criminal event into the
criminal event itself.

MOTIVATION FOR BURGLARY

The motivation that drives the burglary event is a consistent factor in the
literature. Scarr (1973) found that burglars in his study cited four general
motives; in order of importance:

1. need for money to buy drugs and alcohol,
2. need for money to lead a "fast expensive life,"
3. social motives (gangs, delinquent subcultures, peer approval, status), and
4. idiosyncratic motives (kicks, thrills, pathological behavior, rebellion).

Reppetto's (1974) subjects reported satisfaction of their need for money as the primary motivation for their robberies and burglaries. Subsidiary satisfactions such as excitement, revenge, and curiosity were cited by a significant but smaller percentage of the subjects. Excitement as a motive was mentioned most often by the younger burglars and less often by the older. Only 10% of Reppetto's subjects stated that they would continue to commit burglary if their need for money, including money for drugs, was satisfied (p. 22).

Rengert and Wasilchick (1985) concluded, "The primary reason stated by burglars we interviewed for deciding to commit a burglary was simply to obtain money.... The need for money arose out of psychologically defined needs, not subsistence needs" (p. 54).

Wright and Decker (1994) reported that the decision to commit a burglary was driven primarily by a need for cash. Due to the "then and there" lifestyle of most thievesBliving entirely in the presentBgetting a job and working for the money was not a viable alternative. They explained that much of the offending by the burglars in their study was directed toward obtaining the funds necessary to sustain activities that constituted the essence of "streetlife" (pp. 194–195).

Shover (1996) argues that the lives of burglars and other thieves is one of an unending "party." Their crimes are committed to allow them to maintain a lifestyle that is essentially the pursuit of a pattern of activities that they experience as pleasurable (p. 93). They are seeking to "keep the party going." Shover states that those who live this lifestyle share a minimal concern for serious matters in favor of enjoying the moment (p. 93).

> Persistent thieves spend much of their criminal gains on alcohol and other drugs. The proceeds of their crimes "typically" are used for personal, non-essential consumption, rather than, for example, to be given to family or used for basic needs. ... Thieves and hustlers spend many of their leisure hours enjoying good times, albeit there is a decidedly frenetic and always precarious quality to the way these times are lived. (p. 94)

In an early study of theft and thieves, Jackson (1969) wrote:

> [Burglars] if the had any money...[they] wouldn't be out stealing, they'd be partying. Its as simple as that. If they have money they're partying and when they're broke, they start stealing again. (p. 136)

Our subjects lived similar lives and expressed similar motives for their crimes. They stressed the need for money to fulfill expressive needs as the primary motivation for their offending. Only one burglar in our study reported a primary need for money for something other than to purchase drugs or alcohol or for other "partying"activities--and he used the money to support his gambling habit. Although virtually every burglar used some of the money from criminal activity to buy food and clothing and to pay for shelter, transportation, and other licit needs, the greatest percentage of the proceeds from burglary went toward the purchase of drugs and alcohol and to the activity they loosely labeled as partying. Many of the burglars discussed the importance of maintaining a "fast, expensive life." Keeping up appearances was stressed by many as a primary concern. This was especially true for the African American burglars. One burglar summed up the attitude this way:

> You gotta understand about blacks. It's important to keep up a front, to have money and for people to know you have money. Looking good is important. You can't get women if you don't have some bread.

All 30 of our burglar subjects abused drugs and/or alcohol. Most were addicts. Some were so addicted that they took their stolen items directly to a local drug dealer who was known to trade drugs for quality stolen goods. They did not want to spend the extra time converting their goods to cash before buying drugs. Most, however, converted their loot to money and then went immediately to a drug dealer or to a bar where they ingested or self-administered their way into temporary oblivion. The length of their "party" determined the time span between burglaries, for when they ran out of drugs and alcohol and had "slept it off," they began again the search for a new burglary target.

We recognize that our sample was not an exact reflection of the nation's population of residential burglars in so far as drug and alcohol abusers may have been over-represented. However, Shover (1971, 1996) and Wright and Decker (1994) arrived at similar conclusions concerning the lifestyles of burglars and other thieves. Jerry, one of our more articulate burglar subjects, summed it up as follows:

> Once I got into the life, I liked itBa lot. I always liked to party and if you party you can't keep a job for any length of time. I like the ladies too. And the ladies like dudes with lots of folding money. You can't keep it up working for hourly wages. I've had some pretty good jobs before, but it was never enough. Not enough money. Not enough time. Not enough freedomBwhen you work. Now I work for myself. I'm a self-employed thief. I can party all I want to and when I run out of green, I go get some more.

Although drugs, alcohol and "party" were the dominant motives for the burglars in our study, other factors also played a role for some burglars. Excitement and thrills were mentioned by almost every informant; however, only a few would commit a burglary for that purpose only. Like Reppetto (1974), we concluded that the younger, less experienced burglars were more prone to commit crimes for thrills and excitement.

Gerald, a 22-year-old burglar, stated:

> I used to love that adrenaline rush you get when you first go in the window. It's as good as coke. Heart starts thumping and you get shaky and feel super alive. When I was 15-16 years old, I lived for that feeling. I still get scared and get the rush, but now I do it [burglarize] for money.

Another informant, Steve, a 36-year-old, said:

> There's no feeling like it. It's fear and sex and danger and every other exciting feeling you ever had all rolled into one. I'd do crime just for that rush. I do do crime just for that rush. Sometimes.

About 30% of the informants reported committing at least one burglary for revenge. They seldom obtained much material reward in revenge burglaries, reporting instead that they "trashed" the victim's house. This tendency was more pronounced among burglars under 25 years of age. One burglar reported:

> I was helping this friend move into a new house and the white lady next door saw that we were black. I heard her tell another neighbor that she was upset about a black man moving in next door. I decided to come back the next day and "do" her house for revenge.

Another said that he had burglarized the house of a former friend after that individual had "snitched" on him. He said:

> I didn't take nothin' except some food. Mainly I just trashed his place. I was really pissed off.

THE DECISION STRATEGY AND TARGET SELECTION

Being motivated to commit a crime is a necessary but not a sufficient condition for the actual commission of the act. Even a highly motivated burglar—one who has immediate need for moneyBmust still locate a vulnerable target and manage to effect entry without detection. These tasks are not as simple as they may appear to be. As Wright and Decker (1994) observe, "In theory, the supply of residential properties seems so vast that finding a target would seem to be a simple matter. In practice, however, potential targets are fairly limited" (p. 62). The potential burglary target must:

- be unoccupied (90% of the burglars we interviewed stated that they would not knowingly enter a residence where they knew someone was at home);
- not be easily observed from the street of neighboring homes;
- be in a neighborhood or area where the burglar would not "stand out" or be noticed as a suspicious stranger;
- be accessible—relatively easy to break in to; and
- contain items worth stealing.

Gerald, an experienced burglar, explained:

> First off, you gotta find a place that's empty, you know, no one's home. Sometimes it's hard to tell. Place look empty but you go check it out and there's

somebody there. One time I rang the doorbell to see if anybody was home at this one house and nobody answered, so I go in the back and break in through the sliding door. Next thing I know there's this old lady sleeping in front of the TV. I got the Hell out of there....Sometimes you can check out a whole bunch of places and none look good.

Jerry, an African American burglar, agreed:

It ain't easy ...looking for places to hit. Me, I gotta pretty much stay in neighborhoods where I fit in. Some of these rich white neighborhoods are too dangerous. I stand out...people watch me and if I hang around too long, somebody be calling the law.

Interestingly, during the initial interview, virtually every burglar in our study reported a rational decision-making strategy in selecting burglary targets. The following dialogue is typical of responses during the first interview:

Q: Before you decide to break into a house, what kinds of things do you think aboutBI mean what makes you decide whether a house is a good place to burglarize or too risky?
A: First, I gotta case the place. Sometimes I watch the place for two, three days before I go in.
Q: Really? You take that much time? What are you looking for?
A: Fuckin' A! Can't be too careful. I'm looking for, you know, when they come and go, and how many people live there, when the police come by, have they got good stuff. You know, is it going to be worth it to hit the place?

But, when we went with them to reconstruct their past crimes, we found important variations between what they initially told us (in the semistructured interview)about the process of selecting a target and committing a burglary, and what they actually did when presented with a field simulation. Most of our burglars could design a textbook burglary. However, when subsequently visiting sites of burglaries they had previously committed, the characteristics of the target sites and the techniques used to burglarize those targets were seldom congruent with the completely rational approach they had constructed during the initial interview. The sites, more often than not, were targets of opportunity rather than purposeful selections. There were three common patterns:

(a) the burglar happened by the potential burglary site at an opportune moment when the occupants were clearly absent and the target was perceived as vulnerable (open garage door, windows, etc.);
(b) the site was one that had been previously visited by the burglar for a legitimate purpose (as a guest, delivery person, maintenance worker, or other such activity); or

(c) the site was chosen after "cruising" neighborhoods searching for a criminal opportunity and detecting some overt or subtle cue as to vulnerability or potential for material gain.

One of the purposes of the study was to determine which environmental cue or complexes of cues caused a burglar to perceive of a potential burglary target as vulnerable to burglary. Some researchers (Bennett & Wright, 1984; Brantingham & Brantingham, 1978, 1981; Brown & Altman, 1981; Wright & Decker, 1994) have focused on the burglar's use of distinctive environmental stimuli that function as signals or cues to provide salient information about the environment's temporal, spatial, sociocultural, psychological, and legal characteristics. An individual who is motivated to commit a crime uses these discriminative cues to locate and identify target sites. With practice, the individual gains experience and learns which discriminative cues and which combination or sequence of cues are associated with "good" targets. These cues then serve as a "template" which is used in victim or target selection. Potential victims or targets are compared to the template and either rejected or accepted, depending on the congruence (Brantingham & Brantingham, 1978, 1991, 1993). In effect, these are standing decisions that do not require conscious analysis each time they are employed. Regardless of whether the individual is consciously aware of the construction and implementation of the template, each time it is successfully employed it is reinforced and becomes relatively automatic. The Brantinghams state:

> The templates are not a simple list of easily identifiable and measurable characteristics, but more a holistic image with a complex interaction of past and relationships seen from varying perspectives. (1993, p. 12)

As one of our burglary subjects said:

> I just know how I feel about it. I drive around and see a place and think, AThis is a good one." It's experienceBknow what I'm saying? I been doing this a long time and I just know.

Another burglar informant perhaps stated it better. He said:

> I got a criminal mind, you know. Something just tells me a place is hot or cold. It's like intuition.

Finding that most burglars have developed an intuitive mental template of what constitutes a good or a bad burglary target, we set out to determine which discriminative cues or sequence of cues composed the template. Knowing what cues cause a site to be more or less attractive to a burglar should allow development of effective burglary prevention strategies.

We also wished to understand the decision-making processes involved. How does the burglar use cues that represent risk and gain? What factors might cause a burglar to be deterred from burglary? What makes a site more attractive to the burglar? What are the cues that the burglar uses to makes the decision to commit the burglary? How does the burglar determine whether a target site is unoccupied? Is there a favored time of day, or day of the week? How does he or she effect entry into a locked residence?

Interviews with our 30 burglar subjects and the recreations of past burglaries by the subjects suggest that a burglar's decision to "hit" a specific target is based primarily on environmental cues that are perceived to have **immediate** consequences. Most burglars seem to attend only to the present; future events or consequences do not appear to weigh heavily in their risk-versus-gain calculation. Drug-using burglars and juveniles are particularly oriented to this immediate-gain and immediate-risk decision process. Non-drug-using experienced burglars are probably less likely to attend only to immediate risks and gains. Our informants, although experienced burglars, were all drug users, and tended to have a "here and now" orientation toward the rewards and costs associated with burglary. As one informant stated:

> I don't think about the future. Today is all that counts with me. You might be dead tomorrow, so live the best you can right now, today. I knew this dude that was always planning what he was gonna do someday, how he was gonna have a big car and a house and be rich and stuff—he got killed by some other dudes in a dope deal All that planning didn't do no good for him. Wasted all that time, you know. I don't think that way.

Another burglar assessed his life in the following manner:

> Ever day I live past 15–16 years old is just luck. I don't expect to get to 25 or 30. I just ain't goin' to worry about what might happen. I'm just goin' to have a good time while I'm here.

And another stated:

> I don't think about it. I might think about it later, but when I'm doing a crime, I worry about the here and now. The police and the joint aren't part of my thinking, you know what I mean. Can't let those things bother you.

These findings suggest that the rational choice process must be considered as it is perceived through the eyes of the offender. Long-term rewards and future punishment appears to have little effect on most burglars. They are concerned about danger at the crime site and the immediate rewards to be had there.

ASSESSING GAIN

There is considerable research supporting the position that reward or gain is the most important element in the decision to commit a burglary.

Shover (1996) found that instead of paying close attention to the potential consequences of their actions and planning carefully to avoid arrest, offenders tend to focus on the money that committing a crime will yield and how they will spend that money. Shover cited one subject, who stated:

> I didn't think about nothing but what I was going to do when I got that money and how I was going to spend it, you know. See, you're not thinking about those things [possibility of being arrested]. You're thinking about that big paycheck at the end of thirty or forty minutes of work. (1996, pp. 158–159)

The decision strategy employed by our informants began with an appraisal of the circumstances at the potential target site. Most burglars in the study expended minimal energy and time assessing gain cues. They estimated potential gain quickly and intuitively. They tended to make assessments of individual target sites based upon their evaluation of the general affluence of the neighborhood in which the target is located. The assumption is that most residences in a neighborhood contain essentially the same quality and quantity of "stealable" items. As one burglar stated:

> It don't take no Einstein to know [what's in a house]. I can look at a neighborhood and almost tell you what's in every house there. Poor neighborhoods got poor stuff. Rich neighborhoods got rich stuff.

Luis, a heroin addict/burglar, told the interviewer:

> Most houses in this neighborhood have got at least two color TVs, a VCR, some stereo equipment, and some good jewelry. A lot of 'em have got guns, too.

Wright and Decker (1994) found that almost all of the offenders in their study were attracted to residences "which, judging from the outside, appeared to them to contain 'good stuff'" The most obvious cue was the size of the house. "Other things being equal, a large house was regarded as promising the biggest payoff" (Wright & Decker, 1994, p. 82). Well-maintained property was considered by their burglar informants to contain the most desirable goods. The type of car parked in the driveway was also a gain cue to the subjects in Wright and Decker's study. One of their subjects stated:

> Here's this big old house sittin' up there and in the driveway is two BMWs and a Mercedes. This other house might have a van or something like that....So I visualize that [the intended target] must have more things than that house. (pp. 82–83)

Our burglar subjects expressed similar preferences. Donna stated:

> I'm always looking for signs that they got something worthwhile. Big expensive houses, rich cars, stuff like that.

Another subject expressed a preference for houses in a certain part of time where the lots were all over an acre in size and the houses large and expensive. He said:

> These people mostly have gardeners and other people doing their work for them. When I see somebody mowing that ain't the owners and a gardener's truck parked in the street and lots of expensive trees and flowers, I know these people got money. Top of that, if I go on the property, people next door and passing by probably goin' to think I work there.

Inside Information

In some cases, the assessment of gain does not require use of the mental template. The burglar actually knows what is inside the house through the use of informants who have been in the house and have given inside information to the burglar. Experienced burglars often work with "inside men" who have access to potential targets and advise the burglar about things to steal. They may also provide such critical information as times when the owner is away and of weaknesses in security. One female informant maintained close contact with several women who worked as maids in affluent sections of the community. She would gain the necessary information from these women and later come back and break into the house, often entering by a door or window left open for her by the accomplice. A more common scenario was for the burglar to learn of the habits and activities of homeowners from maids, gardeners, and others who had no intention of knowingly assisting a burglar. Friends who worked in these jobs would alert him to possible burglaries through casual talks about their job or their employer, mentioning, for instance, that the family they worked for was leaving for a two-week vacation, or that they had just purchased a new television or VCR. The burglar then used that otherwise innocent information to commit a burglary.

People involved in a variety of service jobs (repair, carpet cleaning, pizza delivery, lawn maintenance, plumbing, carpentry) enter many homes each day and have the opportunity to assess the amount and quality of potential stolen merchandise and security measures taken by the residents. Burglars will often establish contact with employees of these businesses for purposes of obtaining this inside information. One informant said:

> My homie, he works for [a carpet cleaning service] and he in 5–6 different houses every day. He always keeps an eye out for places where they have expensive stuff. I give him somethin' off every job if he clues me in to a place.

One of the burglars in our study worked closely with an employee of a maid service. The maid provided information to the burglar about security, times when the residents were away from home, and a list with specific locations of valuable goods inside the house.

Information about potential targets was frequently gained from fences—persons who purchase stolen property for later resale. Because many fences have legitimate occupations, they may have knowledge of the existence of valuable property from social or business relationships. They can often provide the burglar with information about the owners' schedules and the security arrangements at the target site (see Chapter 16 in this book, "Fencing: Avenues for Redistribution of Stolen Property," for a more detailed discussion). Pawnshop employees may also be able to provide burglars with information about potential targets. One professional burglar told the interviewer that an employee at a pawnshop provided him with copies of jewelry appraisals and the addresses of potential targets.

Inside knowledge is also obtained by persons who work regularly in a neighborhood but who never actually enter a potential target residence. Several of our informants worked sporadically as carpenters' helpers or roofers. During the course of residential construction jobs they became aware of the habits of the people living nearby. They used this knowledge later or provided inside information to other burglars for a fee or a split of the take. Larry, a burglar and heroin addict, told us:

> One time I was working on this roofing job in this real nice area. I got to know the schedules of almost everybody on the block. I knew when they left in the morning and came home at night, and who stayed home during the day. About two weeks after the job was done I came back and did [burglarized] almost every house on that block.

ASSESSING RISK

The risk side of the decision-making equation is one of the most difficult to study and one of the most controversial. Do burglars carefully plan their crimes? Do they act spontaneously, taking advantage of opportunity? Do they act without giving thought to short term or long-term risk? The answer to these questions is central to developing burglary prevention strategies. Although it may be difficult for a homeowner to hide or disguise indicators of gain, such as affluence of neighborhood, size of residence, or type of automobile driven, controlling risk cues may be more easily accomplished.

As stated earlier, consideration of long-term risk is almost nonexistent in the decision processes of most burglars. Burglars and many other criminals tend to live in the here and now. Not only do they not consider next month or next year, most do not even consider the next day. By contrast, immediate risks do play a significant role in target selection. Shover (1996) found that "burglars pay close attention to whether or not a residence is occupied and how easily potential entry points can be seen by neighbors and passers-by" (p. 161).

We learned that although most burglars stated a preference for the homes of the affluent as presenting the greatest opportunity for gain, they tended to avoid these houses and neighborhoods due to increased risk. Affluent homes are more likely to have alarm systems and private security patrols, as well as to be occupied during the day by residents and/or servants. Burglars also perceived themselves as more likely to "stand-out"—to be noticed and observed—in such neighborhoods. One of the burglars interviewed for a study by George Rengert (1989), commenting on the possibility of committing a burglary in a very affluent neighborhood near Philadelphia, remarked:

> These houses are too good. Probably have alarms, or servants. And they're rich and probably watch out for each other all the time. (p. 22)

Likewise, an African American burglar in our study, declared:

> Man, I'd stand out in that neighborhood. What's a black man doing over here? That's what they'd be saying. They might think I was working somewhere, but they'd still keep a eye on me all the time I was around. When I'm out doing my thing, I like to be invisible. Man gotta fit in a place, then he be invisible. Can't be invisible in this neighborhood.

The immediate risk cues considered by burglars in the target selection decision fell into three categories: visibility, occupancy, and accessibility.

Visibility

Visibility refers to the extent to which a house is overseen and observable by neighbors or passers-by. Visibility cues include the location of the house on the block; whether or not the windows and doors of the target site can be observed from neighbors' houses, and from the street. The visibility of a potential burglary target was considered by our informants as a primary factor in target selection. These cues provide answers to several questions of primary importance to the burglar. Are there neighbors present? Can the neighbors observe the target house from inside their homes? Can the proposed point of entry into the target site be observed by passers-by? Are there dogs that might bark and arouse neighbors? Are there shrubs, blind doorways, corners, or fences that will hide the burglar during entry? Is there traffic near the house that might see and report the burglar? Are there people in the neighborhood who "watch the street and know who is and who is not at home"?

The location and type of windows both at the target site and at neighbors' houses were considered critical by almost all informants. One burglar in our study stated:

> Notice how that picture window looks out onto the street. The curtains stay open all the time and both the houses across the street can see straight into the living room. I wouldn't do [burglarize] this place.

Another said:

> I'm looking at that upstairs window next door. You can see almost everything that goes on at this house from there. I'm worried about that window.

Wright and Decker (1994) also found that burglars considered visibility a major factor in their decision calculus. The burglars in their study preferred to enter from the rear of a house. They stated:

> I never [break in] through the front, unless I go through, like, a porch or some-thing that could hide me. Its too obvious on the front. See, on the back it's not that obvious. The other ... houses ain't facing the back. You don't find too many [potential onlookers] on the back, you mostly find them on the front

Although the average burglar fears being seen, many professional burglars do not. Rather, they fear being seen *and reported*. The more experienced bur-glars stated that it was important to fit into a neighborhood or situation. They attempted to make their presence in a neighborhood seem normal and natu-ral. The most professional of the burglars in our study, Robert, always drove a car that fit the neighborhood's socioeconomic level or a van disguised as a delivery vehicle. He dressed befitting the circumstances: as a plumber, deliv-eryman, or businessman. He would walk to the door of a potential target residence, open the screen door, and unobtrusively hold it open with his foot while he pretended to be having a conversation with a nonexistent person inside. He would then enter the house if the door was unlocked (he reported that many of his target houses were unlocked). If the door was locked, he pantomimed a conversation that appeared to instruct him to go around to the backyard. He would then walk around the house, sometimes stopping to gaze at some feature of the house or landscape, and take notes on a clip-board. When he got to the backyard, he entered the house from that point. To possible onlookers, he had knocked on the door, talked with the owner, and, following instructions, had gone to the rear of the house on some legitimate errand. Other times he would stop his car near a proposed target residence, open the hood, tinker around under the hood, appear to be angry, kick a tire, and angrily walk over to the potential target house. A neighbor or any-one else who might be watching saw only an angry man with a broken car, walking to a house to ask for assistance. Robert was not concerned about being seen. He expected to be seen, but because of his role-playing he did not expect to be reported (and he seldom was).

Visibility cues also include the extent of natural cover such as trees, shrub-bery, and other landscaping. Houses with dense shrubbery near windows and doors were considered very vulnerable by the informants. One of the most important forms of cover was the privacy fence, a 6- to 8-foot-high board or masonry fence enclosing a backyard. These fences were common in the area studied, and most informants considered them important in the target selection process. Some stated that they would not consider burglar-izing a house that did not have a privacy fence. Although burglars were at risk while climbing the fence or entering through an unlocked gate, once inside, they were effectively protected from prying eyes by the fence. As one burglar stated:

> Once I'm inside this fence, I can slow down and take my time. The place is mine.

Occupancy

The second category of risk cues are those that indicate *occupancy*. Occupancy cues include the presence of cars in the driveway or garage, visible residents, noise or voices emanating from the house, and other cues that indicate someone is at home. Research both before and after our study confirms the preference for unoccupied targets (Bennett & Wright, 1984; MacDonald 1980; Reppetto, 1974; Scarr, 1973; Wright & Decker, 1994). Twenty-eight of the thirty burglars in our study stated that they would never purposely enter an occupied residence. Many reported that their greatest fear was that they would encounter the resident upon entering or that the resident would return home while they were still there.

The typical burglar is much more aware of our use of time than we are. As Rengert and Wasilchick (1985, p. 52) conclude, "We are all waiting to become victims of a burglar whose intuition about time coincides with our routine." Robert, a professional burglar in our sample revealed that he was not only aware of his victim's use of time but also that of police and law enforcement:

> You know when is the best time to do a burglary? Three o'clock in the afternoon. Mothers are picking up their kids at school and the police are doing shift change. Even if someone called the cops on me, they'd be in the middle of shift change and it would take longer to get here.

Our research confirmed that burglars work during periods when residences are left unguarded. They concluded that if a home is guarded (occupied) during the day, it is likely to be guarded by women. Rengert and Wasilchick (1985) stated that women who do not work outside the home tend to develop predictable patterns regarding the use of discretionary time for the purpose of shopping, errands, or visiting friends and relatives. Women who work outside the home develop similar patterns of time use on Saturday and Sunday. In either case, the use of discretionary time for the purpose of shopping and running errands is observable and predictable by residential burglars. Whenever the house is left unguarded, it is susceptible to burglary. They wrote, "When we combine the daily activities of many women, we can identify times when the typical house is not likely to be guarded" (Rengert & Wasilchick, 1985, p. 26). They found burglars to be most active between 10:00 and 11:00 a.m. and from 1:00 to 3:00 p.m.

The burglars in our study stated they preferred to work between 9:00 and 11:00 a.m. and in mid-afternoon. Most organized their working hours around school hours, particularly during the times when parents (usually mothers) took children to school and picked them up after school. Several told us that they waited "until the wife left to take the kids to school or go shopping." Most stated that they did not do burglaries on Saturday because people were usually home then. However, Sunday morning during church hours was considered prime time for weekend burglary.

Only a small number (n = 3) of burglars in our study committed residential burglaries at night. Most preferred to commit their crimes during daylight hours when they expected people to be at work and out of the home. Those who did commit nighttime burglary usually knew the victims and their schedules or took advantage of people being away from home in the evening during special events, such as high school football games. Pep squads at the high schools in the area studied decorate the front yards of the football team members with signs that identify the player, position, and uniform number. Burglars told us that they knew these houses would most likely be empty on Friday nights because the families attended the game. One said: Man! Wait until football season. I clean up then. When they are at the game, I'm at their house.

Accessibility

Accessibility cues are those factors that indicate how easily the residence can be entered and how well the site is protected. These cues include location and type of doors and windows, as well as the extent of target hardening such as locks, burglar alarms, fences, walls, burglar bars, and dogs. Accessibility also includes neighborhood and street permeability. Houses on corners or on through streets are more accessible than those on dead-end streets, cul de sacs, and other streets with few intersections. Houses in gated communities are much less susceptible than those open to all. Burglars generally agree (Bennett & Wright, 1984; Taylor & Nee, 1988; Wright & Decker, 1994) that the critical elements in assessing vulnerability to break-in are:

- Larger, more expensive residences are more difficult to break in to.
- Houses on cul-de-sacs, streets with few intersections, barricaded streets and those in gated communities are among the least vulnerable to burglary.
- Alarm systems increase the risk.
- Dogs increase the risk.
- Burglar bars and good quality locks increase both the effort and the risk.

Large, Expensive Homes

Although many burglars express a preference for burglarizing homes in the "rich" part of town, all agree that expensive homes are much more risky targets. Not only is the burglar less likely to know the neighborhood and more likely to be noticed and identified as an outsider, they also recognize that homes in these areas have more security technology than smaller, less expensive homes. As one of our burglar subjects complained:

> These people got solid wood doors and locks and alarms ... maybe even laser guns protecting their house. It's just too hard. I don't mess with rich people's houses.

Complex Street Layouts, Barricaded Streets, and Gated Communities

Accessibility also applies to the location of houses and other potential burglary targets. The more difficult the route to the prospective crime site, the less likely it will be targeted by the burglar. There has been a moderate amount of research on the susceptibility of houses on cul de sacs, less permeable streets, and those in gated communities to burglary and other forms of predatory crime. In a study of a residential area of Hartford, Connecticut, R. A. Gardiner (1978) demonstrated that closing off some streets to cars resulted in an overall decrease in crime. A study by James Lasley (1996) found a reduction in drive-by shootings in Los Angeles when some streets were closed to cars (1996). Atlas and LeBlanc (1994) found a significant reduction in burglary in a south Florida community after implementation of street closures and barricades. Others (Beavon, 1984; Bevis & Nutter, 1977) have shown that the farther a residence is from main thoroughfares and arterial roads, the less likely it is to become a burglary target. The Brantinghams (1975) in a study of residential burglary in Tallahassee, Florida, found that burglary rates decreased sharply toward the core of residential areas.

A recent analysis of burglary in Greenwich, Connecticut, sought to determine the attributes of homes that attract burglars (Shachmurove, Fishman, & Hakin, 1997). The researchers obtained self-report data from 3,014 households, of which 339 had experienced burglary incidents. They found that homes closer to major arterial routes (providing escape opportunities for the burglars) corner homes, and those adjacent to wooded areas tended to have a greater probability of being burglarized.

Jesse, one of our experienced burglars, stated:

> I don't like to go too deep [inside a neighborhood]. You get kinda lost once you get in those winding streets and stuff. I like to stay close to the main road so I can find my way out and escape fast.

Roberto, a professional burglar in our sample, adamantly declared:

> [I] don't do cul-de-sacs. Or dead end streets. Always gotta have an escape route.

Burglar Alarms

Burglar alarms can serve as occupancy proxies. As such, burglars try to avoid them (Wright & Decker, 1994). As one burglar told Wright and Decker (p. 96):

> If I see an alarm out, like I say, they usually have them outside the house. I'll leave them alone automatically.

A major study of the effectiveness of burglar alarms was conducted by the Cedar Rapids, Iowa, Police Department. Matched pairs of 100 businesses and schools with previous burglaries were chosen for the experiment. One member of each pair was given a burglar alarm that sounded directly at the police station. The other half served as a control group. There was a reduction of 55% in attempted burglaries in sites with alarms compared to a reduction of only 8% for the control group (Rubenstein, Murray, Motoyama, & Rouse, 1980).

In their study of burglary in Greenwich, Connecticut, Shachmurove et al. (1997) concluded that "if the home is protected by an alarm the probability for a burglary is virtually nil" (p.11). Our findings confirm these studies. One burglary subject advised:

> Sometimes I pick a house to do and when I get up close I can see the wires taped to the window and I know they got an alarm. I just move on.

Another stated:

> Most houses got a sign, like "This house protected by Westinghouse Security" or one of those other security companies. I just pass them by. People stupid to hit a house with an alarm system. Just go to one without it. That's common sense, you know. ... Sometimes you see this blue sign that just says something like "This house protected by an electronic alarm system" without no company name on it. That's not real .... They just trying to scam you. You can get those signs at Radio Shack. Don't mean nothing.

Wright and Decker (1994) found that, "Most offenders...wanted to avoid alarms altogether and, upon encountering such devices, abandoned all thought of attacking the dwelling. Indeed, 56 of 86 subjects we questioned about this issue said that they were not prepared to burglarize an alarmed residence under *any* circumstances"(p. 125). One of their burglar subjects reported:

> When I check the house out and be ready to get in it and I see an alarm, I'm ready to bust a window and I see that, I just back off it. (p. 126)

Although several burglars in our study boasted about disarming alarms, when pressed for details, almost all admitted that they did not know how to accomplish that task. Two informants had disarmed alarm systems and were not particularly deterred by them. They stated that the presence of an alarm system gave them an additional cue as to the affluence of the residents, telling them that there was something worth protecting inside. One informant had purposely taken a job installing alarm systems in order to learn to disarm them. Another informant stated that alarm systems did not deter her because she still had time to complete the burglary and escape before police or private security arrived in response to the alarm. She stated that she never took more than 10 minutes to enter, search, and exit a house. She advised:

> Police take 15 to 20 minutes to respond to an alarm. Security [private security] sometimes gets there a little faster. I'm gone before any of them gets there.

Another professional burglar advised that he did not care whether a house had an alarm or not. He would go ahead and enter and begin to gather the goods he planned to steal. He said that after about 5 minutes the telephone would ring (the alarm company calling to verify the alarm). After the call, he stated that he had 5 to 15 minutes before someone arrived.

In general, however, burglars agreed that alarms were a definite deterrent to their activities. Other factors being equal, they preferred to locate a target that did not have an alarm rather than to take the additional risk involved in attempting to burglarize a house with an alarm system. Over 90% of the informants would not choose a target with an alarm system. Most (about 75%) were deterred by a sign or window sticker that stated that the house was protected by an alarm system. As Richard, an experienced burglar, stated:

> Why take a chance? There's lots of places without alarms. Maybe they're bluffing, maybe they ain't.

Locks, Burglar Bars, and Other Target-Hardening Devices

Past research has been inconsistent regarding the importance of locks on windows and doors. Scarr (1973) and Rengert and Wasilchick (1985) found that burglars consider the type of lock installed at a prospective target site. Others (Bennett & Wright, 1984; Reppetto, 1974; Walsh, 1980) did not find locks to be a significant factor in the target selection process.

Early research evaluating "target hardening" techniques in four public housing projects in Seattle (1975) and in Chicago's Cabrini-Green public housing (1979) found that installation of deadbolt locks and other such techniques significantly reduced the burglary rate in those areas. From their review of these programs, Rubenstein et al. (1980) concluded that locks are a factor considered by burglars in target selection. Rengert and Wasilchick (1985) wrote: "... most of the burglars we interviewed are easily discouraged by a tough lock. With so many opportunities, many burglars will move on rather than struggle with a deadbolt lock" (p. 90).

Wright and Decker (1994) found that locks and windows and doors were usually not considered during the initial phase of the target selections process because they were not able to be seen from a distance. They wrote, "If locks were considered at all, this usually occurred at a later stage" (p. 98). Once a target was selected, the burglar would deal with the problem of locked doors and windows when the problem was actually encountered:

> Locks play a part [in discouraging burglars], but...[if] you got the right tools, you could go up to the front door and open it as quickly and as easy as if you had your own key...(Wright and Decker, p. 120)

The majority of informants in our study initially stated that they were not deterred by locks, just as in the case of alarm systems. However, during burglary reconstructions, we discovered that given two potential target sites, all other factors being equal, burglars prefer not to deal with a deadbolt lock. After the burglar compared a few sites and discovered his or her own preference for doors without deadbolt locks, they were better able to evaluate their own preferences. A typical response to our questions about deadbolt locks was:

> I gotta be in and out in 2–3 minutes. I ain't got time to mess with no tough lock.

Another of our subjects said:

> I never really thought about it. I can bust open a deadbolt if I got time, but going back on it, I usually just find a house without one.

The variation in findings regarding security hardware appears to be related to the degree to which burglars are either rational or opportunistic. To the extent to which burglars are primarily opportunistic, locks appear to have some deterrent value. The opportunistic burglar chooses a target based upon its perceived vulnerability to burglary at a given time. Given a large number of potential targets, the burglar tends to select the most vulnerable of the target pool. A target with a good lock and fitted with other security hardware will usually not be perceived to be as vulnerable as one without those items. The rational, planning burglar chooses targets on the basis of factors other than situational vulnerability and conceives ways in which he or she can overcome impediments to the burglary (such as the target site being fitted with a high quality deadbolt lock). Thus, to the extent that burglars are rational planners, deadbolt locks have limited utility for crime prevention. Our findings, however, support the deterrent value of deadbolt locks; 75% of the burglaries reconstructed during our research were opportunistic offenses. Many of those burglaries would have been prevented (or displaced) by the presence of a quality deadbolt lock. It is important to note that nearly one half of the burglary sites in the present study were entered through open or unlocked windows and doors. The findings are very similar to those of Rengert and Wasilchick (1985), who found that burglary through unlocked doors was a "surprisingly frequent occurrence." They wrote:

> Many burglars build their careers on the mistaken belief held by residents that "it can't happen here," or "I'll only be next door for a minute." More than one of the burglars we talked to burglarized open houses while the residents were in the backyard doing yard work.

Dogs

Almost all studies agree that dogs are an effective deterrent to burglary. Wright and Decker (1994, p. 208) stated that few of the burglars in their study were prepared to tackle a house with a dog. Reppetto (1974) found that only about one-third of burglars under the age of 25 years reported that dogs would not be a deterrent. Although there is some individual variation among burglars, the general rule is to bypass a house with a dog—any dog. Large dogs represent a physical threat to the burglar and small ones are often noisy, attracting attention to the burglar's activities. We found that although many burglars have developed contingency plans to deal with dogs (petting them, feeding them, or even killing them), most burglars prefer to avoid them. When asked what were considered absolute "no go" factors, most burglars responded that dogs were second only to occupancy.

Approximately 30% of the informants, however, initially discounted the presence of dogs as a deterrent. Yet, during ride-alongs the sight or sound of a dog at a potential target site almost invariably resulted in a "no go" decision. As Richard said:

> I don't mess with no dogs. If they got dogs I go someplace else.

Debbie told us that she was concerned primarily with small dogs:

> Big dogs don't bark much. I talk to them through the fence or door and get them excited. Then I open the gate or the door and when they charge out, I go in and shut the door behind me. They are outside and I'm in. Little dogs yap too much. They [neighbors] look to see what they are so excited about. I don't like little yapping dogs.

Some of the more professional burglars were less concerned with dogs and had developed techniques for dealing with them. In general, however, the presence of a dog was considered an effective deterrent.

SUMMARY

Burglary appears to be a highly instrumental crime, being committed almost exclusively to obtain money. Although thrill, excitement, and revenge do play a minor role in the etiology of the offense, it is primarily young, inexperienced burglars who report such motives. Once the decision is made to commit a burglary, the burglars must select a likely target. We found that most of them employ a decision-making strategy that has three components. The burglar begins with an assumption that each proposed target site contains at least some minimal potential gain. He or she must then determine whether the target site can be entered without being seen and reported, whether the site might be occupied, and whether the site can be broken into readily. These determinations are made on the basis of evidence obtained from observing environmental cues at or near the target site and employing the mental template constructed through past experience and the recounted experiences of others.

Burglars use three categories of environmental cues to assess these risk factors: (a) cues that indicate the visibility of the proposed target site; (b) cues that indicate whether the target site is occupied; and (c) cues that indicate the degree of difficulty that might be expected in actually breaking into the site. The specific content of these cues has varied widely across prior studies.

We found that burglars are opportunistic and are easily deterred or displaced from one target site to another. Situational factors such as the presence of a dog, an alarm system, security hardware, and alert neighbors may be effective deterrents. However, criminal justice system sanctions appear to have little role in the risk-gain calculus employed by burglars. Their "here and now" orientation tends to negate the role of future consequences in their decision making and thus reduce the impact of most public policy regarding burglary in particular and property crime in general.

References

Atlas, R., & LeBlanc, W. C. (1994). The impact on crime of street closures and barricades: A Florida study. *Security Journal, 5,* 140–145.

Beavon, D. J. (1984). Crime and the Environmental Opportunity Structure: The Influence of Street Networks on the Patterning of Property Offenders. Unpublished Master's thesis. Simon Fraser University, Burnaby, BC.

Becker, G. (1968). Crime and punishment: An economic approach. *Journal of Political Economy, 76,* 169–217.

Bennett, T., & Wright, R. (1984). *Burglars on burglary: Prevention and the offender.* Aldershot, UK: Gower.

Bevis, C., & Nutter, J. B. (1977). Changing Street Layout to Reduce Residential Burglary. Paper presented at American Society of Criminology annual meeting. Atlanta, GA.

Brantingham, P. L., & Brantingham, P. J. (1975). Residential burglary and urban form. *Urban Studies, 12,* 273–286.

Brantingham, P. J., & Brantingham, P. L. (1978). A theoretical model of crime site selection. In M. D. Krohn & R. L. Akers (Eds.), *Crime, law and sanctions.* Beverly Hills, CA: Sage.

Brantingham, P. J., & Brantingham, P. L. (1981). *Environmental criminology.* Beverly Hills, CA: Sage.

Brantingham, P. J., & Brantingham, P. L. (1991). *Environmental criminology.* Prospect Heights, IL: Waveland Press.

Brantingham, P. L., & Brantingham P. J. (1993). Nodes, paths and edges: Considerations on the complexity of crime on the physical environment. *Journal of Environmental Psychology, 13,* 3–28.

Brezina, T. (2002). Assessing the rationality of criminal and delinquent behavior: A focus on actual utility. In R. P. Alex & T. G. Tibbetts (Eds.), *Rational choice and criminal behavior: Recent research and future challenges* (pp. 241–264). New York: Routledge.

Brown, B. B., & Altman, I. (1981).Territoriality and residential crime: A conceptual framework. In P. J. Brantingham & P. L. Brantingham (Eds.), *Environmental criminology.* Beverly Hills, CA: Sage.

Clarke, R. V., & Cornish, D. (1985). Modeling offenders' decisions: A framework for policy and research. In M. Tonry & N. Morris (Eds.), *Crime and justice: An annual review of research* (4th ed.). Chicago: University of Chicago Press.

Clarke, R. V., & Cornish, D. B. (1980). Rational choice. In R. Paternoster & R. Bachman (Eds.), Research in criminal deterrence: Laying the groundwork for the second decade. In M. Tonry & N. Morris (Eds.) *Crime and Justice: An Annual Review of Research* (Vol. 2). Chicago: University of Chicago Press.

Cook, P. J. (1980). Research in criminal deterrence: laying the ground work for the second decade. In Morris, N. and Tonry, M. (Eds.) *Crime and Justice: an annual review of research* (Vol. 2). Chicago: University of Chicago Press.

Cornish, D. B. (1993). Theories of action in criminology: Learning theory and rational choice approaches. In V. C. Ronald & F. Marcus (Eds.), *Advances in criminological theory, Vol. 5. Routine activity and rational choice* (351—382). New Brunswick, NJ: Transaction.

Cornish, D. B., & Clarke, R. V. (1986). Situational prevention, displacement of crime and rational choice theory. In K. Heal & G. Laycock (Eds.), *Situational crime prevention: From theory into practice.* London: HMSO.

Cromwell, P. F., Olson, J. N., & Avary, D. W. (1991). *Breaking and Entering: An Ethnographic Analysis of Burglary.* Newbury Park, CA: Sage Publications.

Cromwell, P. F., Olson, J. N., & Avary, D. W. (2004). *Breaking and Entering: Burglars on Burglary.* Belmont, CA: Wadsworth Publishing Co.

Gardiner R. A. (1978). *Design for safe neighborhoods.* Washington, DC: Law Enforcement Assistance Administration.

Jackson, A. (1969). *A thief's primer.* New York: Macmillan.

Jacobs, B. A. (1999). *Dealing crack: The social world of streetcorner selling.* Boston: Northeastern University Press.

Lasley, J. R. (1996). Using Traffic Barriers to "Design Out" Crime: A Program Evaluation of L.A.P.D.'s Operation Cul de Sac. Report to the National Institute of Design. Fullerton, CA: California State University Fullerton.

MacDonald, J. M. (1980). *Burglary and theft.* Springfield, IL: Charles C. Thomas.

Rengert, G. (1989). Burglary in Philadelphia: A critique of an opportunity structure model. In P. Brantingham & P. Brantingham (Eds.), *Environmental criminology.* Beverly Hills, CA: Sage.

Rengert, G., & Wasilchick, J. (1985). *Suburban burglary: A time and a place for everything.* Springfield, IL: Charles C. Thomas.

Rengert, G., & Wasilchick, J. (1989). Space, time and crime: Ethnographic insights into residential burglary. A report prepared for the National Institute of justice (mimeo).

Reppetto, T. G. (1974). *Residential crime.* Cambridge, MA: Ballinger.

Rubenstein, H., Murray, C., Motoyama, T. & Rouse, W. V. (1980). *The link between crime and the built environment: The current state of the knowledge* (Vol. 1). Washington, DC: National Institute of Justice.

Scarr, H. A. (1973). *Patterns of burglary.* Washington, DC: U.S. Government Printing Office.

Shachmurove, Y., Fishman, G., & Hakin, S. (1997). The burglar as a rational economic agent. CARESS Working Paper, 97-7. Mimeo.

Shover, N. (1971). Burglary. In M. Tonry (Ed.), *Crime and justice: A review of research* (Vol. 14, pp. 73–114). Chicago: University of Chicago Press.

Shover, N. (1996). *The great pretenders: Pursuits and careers of persistent thieves.* Boulder, CO: Westview Press.

Taylor, M., & Nee, C. (1988). The role of cues in residential burglary. *British Journal of Criminology, 238,* 396–401.

Void, G., & Bernard, T. (1986). *Theoretical criminology* (3rd ed.). New York: Oxford University Press.

Walsh, D. P. (1980). *Break-ins: Burglary from private houses.* London: Constable.

Wright, R. T., & Decker, S. H. (1994). *Burglars on the Job: Street life and residential burglary.* Boston: Northeastern University Press.

3

Opportunities and Decisions: Interactional Dynamics in Robbery and Burglary Groups

Andy Hochstetler

S *treet offenders more often than not are co-offenders. The theoretical impor-*
tance of understanding how co-offending shapes conduct has been recognized
for decades but is often ignored by investigators. Drawing from interviews
with 50 male robbers and burglars who committed their crimes with others, this
paper examines how interactional dynamics modify both the perception of crimi-
nal opportunities and criminal decision making. Offenders construct opportunity
by improvising situational interpretations, communicating expectations and nego-
tiating shared meanings. As opposed to many prevailing notions of criminal deci-
sion making, decisions in groups are incremental, contextually situated, and affected
significantly by variation in members' influence. The findings, therefore, highlight
shortcomings of decision-making investigations that obscure marked variation
in choice by focusing narrowly on individual assessments of risks and utilities.

Criminologists generally focus their research either on the correlates of crime in offenders' backgrounds or else on characteristics of situations and environments where crime is likely to occur. The immediate social context in which offenders construct criminal decisions is a rich and largely unexplored area. Only a few investigators focus on mental processes, action, and inter- actions that link offenders' backgrounds to immediate environments and discrete criminal choices (Short, 1998, p. 25). This empirical neglect results in understandings of crime that emphasize offender characteristics and situa- tional correlates of offending without considering the processes and events through which these correlates and characteristics result in criminal agency. It is well known, for example, that most street offenders in the United States choose crime in the presence of co-offenders (Bureau of Justice Statistics, 1999; Reiss, 1988; Zimring, 1981). However, little research into the potential influence of co-offenders on construction of criminal opportunity or on how criminal groups negotiate meaning and align action to offend exists.

The theoretical importance of understanding how co-offending sha- pes conduct is recognized in many of criminology's classics. However,

Source: Criminology, 39(3), pp. 737–763. 2001. Used with permission of the American Society of Criminology.

investigators generally assume that co-offending influences choice without analysis of the interpersonal interactions that create group effects (McCarthy, Hagan, & Cohen, 1998; Reiss, 1988; Reiss & Farrington, 1991; Tremblay, 1993; Warr, 1996). In this paper, I apply an interactionist approach to investigating the processes by which offenders subjectively interpret and define situations in choosing to commit crime (Athens, 1997; Groves & Lynch, 1990; Katz, 1988, 1991). I draw on interviews with 50 robbers and burglars who committed their crimes with others. Analysis of these interviews reveals some common patterns of interpersonal dynamics, rooted in street activities, which contribute to situational construction of criminal opportunity. By incrementally signaling to communicate their emerging preferences, by referring to target characteristics, and by referencing identities and expectations attributed to co-offenders, group thieves negotiate a shared sense of opportunity. Interaction can reduce the appeal of law abidance to group participants and make developing criminal opportunity difficult to refuse. In addition, co-offender interaction can act as a catalyst for crime by increasing access to illicit pathways and easing the pursuit of criminal objectives.

BACKGROUND

Revival of interest in deterrence and control interpretations of crime in the closing decades of the twentieth century gave new impetus to investigations of criminal decision making. The resulting corpus of research reveals two recurrent approaches to examining the decision-making process. One depicts criminal decisions as the outcome of a straightforward cognitive process in which offenders weigh rewards against costs. Investigators informed by this approach typically require subjects to imagine themselves in hypothetical settings and to evaluate the potential rewards and risks of choosing crime (Carrol & Weaver, 1986; Cornish & Clarke, 1986; Nagin & Paternoster, 1993; Piliavin, Gartner, Thorton, & Matsueda, 1986; Piquero & Rengert, 1999; Taylor & Nee, 1988; Wright, Logie, & Decker, 1996). The vignettes presented to subjects typically contain a small number of variables. Investigators consistently find that expected risks and rewards are significant considerations in offending decisions and target selection. However, research designs that utilize artificial criminal scenarios obscure motivational and contextual factors that potentially complicate offenders' opportunity assessments. Moreover, investigators usually proceed as if criminal decisions are made by lone offenders and fail to consider that interactional dynamics produce decision-making contexts that potential offenders cannot fully anticipate through advance calculation of risk and benefits.

The second approach to criminal choice situates offending decisions in the context of offenders' larger lives and lifestyles (Eckland-Olson, Lieb, & Zurcher, 1984; Gibbs & Shelley, 1982; Jacobs & Wright, 1999; McCarthy et al., 1998; Shover, 1996; Tunnell, 1992; Wright & Decker, 1994, 1997). Investigators informed by this approach typically draw from interviews conducted with active or inactive thieves. Their findings show that criminal decisions are embedded in offenders' chaotic lifestyles. The lifestyles and routines of street life place offenders in situations that impede careful choice and that evoke motivations and cultural outlooks that make crime attractive. One observer, for example, notes that "contexts populated almost exclusively by young, drug-using males simply are not the kind in which decision makers pay close attention to threat and virtue" (Shover, 1996, p. 170). However, investigators of criminal decision making and context typically slight the role of situations immediately antecedent to crime and favor analysis of offenders' more entrenched habits and routines (Fleisher, 1995; Jacobs & Wright, 1999; Tunnell, 1992; Wright & Decker, 1994, 1997). This led Hagan and McCarthy (1992, p. 556) to conclude that although the context of street life produces delinquency, "exactly what aspects of life on the street cause delinquency" remain unclear (Hagan & McCarthy, 1992, p. 556). Although many investigators note that offenders share a style of living and often socialize with other offenders, researchers rarely examine how co-offending affects the decision to commit a particular crime (Cordilia, 1986).

Decision making in criminal groups is seldom a focus of investigation, but acceptance of group effects on individual criminal motivation is widespread. Many investigators note that participation and interaction with co-offenders may moderate individuals' fear of punishment and increase chances of offending (Cloward & Ohlin, 1960; Eckland-Olson et al., 1984; Erikson & Jensen, 1977; Short & Strodtbeck, 1965; Shover & Henderson, 1995). There also is reason to suspect that some participants play a much greater part in encouraging criminal decisions in groups than do others. Results of self-report surveys of youthful offenders document reported variation in individual influence on group decisions to commit crime (McCarthy et al., 1998; Warr, 1996). Even experienced thieves often contend that they "got involved primarily because of partners" (Feeney, 1986, p. 58; see also Bennet & Wright, 1984). Despite widespread acceptance of group effects on choice, some observers find evidence for the effects of interpersonal dynamics on crime choice unconvincing. Gottfredson and Hirschi (1990, p. 158) acknowledge that criminal cooperation eases individual effort required to offend, but are skeptical of imprecise assertions that interpersonal dynamics heavily influence offending decisions. Nevertheless, denying the presence of significant group effects is premature given the substantial evidence that interaction significantly affects choice in other types of small groups.

In classic sociological experiments, investigators found that subjects provided with simple estimating tasks modified their estimates to comply with the estimates of copresent others (Asch, 1951; Sherif, 1936). These early experiments on group conformity inspired scores of scholars in diverse disciplines to investigate interaction and decisions in small groups. In studies ranging from experiments on shifts in individual preferences resulting from accommodation of other group members' preferences to *post hoc* interpretations of foreign policy, investigators find that dynamics of small group interaction affect choice (t'Hart, Stern, & Sundelius, 1997; Turner, Wetherall, &

Hogg, 1989). One explanation for individual conformity to group preferences is that some participants persuade others to conform, but individuals modify their preferences and behavior to suit expectations even in the absence of communication with other group participants (Kameda & Davis, 1990; Maas, West, & Cialdini, 1987; Shelley, 1998; Turner et al., 1989; Wright & Ayton, 1994). Group effects result not only from communication, but also from individual participants' expectations and attempts to gauge preferences of others in their group. Group participants predict the group's likely course and adjust their actions to suit their expectations.

Failure to examine choice processes in crime groups potentially is a significant oversight. This article contributes to our understanding of criminal choice in three ways. First, it bridges an empirical gap in the literature between offenders' abstract motivations and lifestyles and their choice of a target. Second, it examines how interaction between co-offenders influences assessments of criminal opportunity and subsequently offending decisions. Offenders construct their sense of opportunity incrementally and in accord with expectations derived from the situational context and the actions of others. The discussion emphasizes that offenders do not respond passively to situational opportunity; they create it by selecting and transforming the situations they confront. Third, and relatedly, findings reinforce the importance of continued investigation of the varied processes and interpersonal interactions that contribute to the construction of criminal opportunity and criminal decisions.

STREET ACTIVITIES AS CONTEXT

Street thieves' descriptions of decision making contrast with depictions of crime choice that cast it as calculating and purposeful. Many thieves report that they do not plan their crimes or spend only a few minutes planning (Cromwell, Olson, & Avary, 1991, p. 61; Feeney, 1986; Short, 1998, p. 10; Tracy, 1987). As other investigators have found, thieves often ignore and can put out of mind consequences of being caught while considering a crime (Cromwell et al., 1991; Shover & Honaker, 1992). In this study, several subjects exhibited an extreme lack of concern with consequences by choosing to commit crimes in which they were sure to be suspects. Some pawned goods using accurate identification, loitered or aimlessly drove their cars near the scene of recently completed robberies, robbed victims they knew, or indifferently allowed themselves to be photographed during an offense. To reconcile offenders' descriptions of criminal deliberation with assumptions of calculating actors, decision making is best understood as "socially bounded" (Shover & Honaker, 1992). Offenders construct decisions in accord with conduct norms and during the activities of street life (Feeney, 1986; Jacobs & Wright, 1999; Shover, 1996; Tunnell, 1992; Wright & Decker, 1994, 1997).

The hallmark of street life, as a style of living, is pursuit of pleasure and status through conspicuous leisure and consumption "with minimal concern for obligations and commitments that are external to the immediate social setting" (Shover & Honaker, 1992, p. 283). Street-offenders live for the moment (Fleisher, 1995, pp. 213–214). A burglar explains that his attitude prevented due attention to consequences:

> You just don't care, you know. You get the attitude that, hey, whatever happens happens. I'm not gonna worry about that [consequences] until it happens, and that's...the frame of mind you are in [when stealing].

Commitment to street life and crime coincides with periods of drug use and related family and economic crises. Many offenders explain that they had temporarily given up on conventional living and devoted themselves fully to partying. Investigators find that a host of problems accompany theft and that it is much more common during offenders' heaviest periods of overindulgence in drugs and drink (Deschenes, Anglin, & Speckhart, 1991; Faupel, 1987; Horney, Osgood, & Marshall, 1995). A burglar recalls that a lengthy period of intoxication and reckless living made stealing a sensible option:

> Things were crazy anyway. I was worried and paranoid all the time. We sat around the apartment and listened to a police scanner, for Christsakes. Our apartment was full of stolen stuff and crank, and we were living off of hot credit cards [purchased from other thieves and hotel bartenders]. If you're like that anyway, why not do a crime so you got something to really worry about.

Thieves share their chaotic lifestyles and parties with compatible friends and a loose network of associates who live similarly (Cordilia, 1986; Katz, 1988, p. 212; McCarthy et al., 1998). Expensive drug and alcohol habits, fighting, shoplifting, writing bad checks, and amassing debt to drug dealers, lawyers, and other creditors are normal in their circles of friends. Street-offenders often sleep in cheap motels or on associates' couches or move from party to party with little idea of where they will rest next (Wright & Decker, 1997, p. 38). Curtis, a heroin addict, explains that a continuous and mobile party allowed him to maintain his drug habit by reciprocal sharing with others. His lifestyle made locating criminal opportunities effortless and led him to his robbery co-offender, a man that he scarcely knew. When I asked Curtis, "were you partying with Willie?" He responded:

> To an extent, you know, because you go from one place to another place. I'd been like that for some time. You have a car, or he has a car and that's the situation. Then this turns into a better situation, and then you get high some more. It's kind of a balance, who's going to do something [crime] last. Who is doing things just kind of shift back and forth...I guess most people who have been doing it understand.

During the activities of street life, offenders encounter audiences who admire risk-taking, fearlessness, and the ability to provide money and drugs for the party (Katz, 1988; Miller, 1998; Shover, 1996). As one burglar notes, "you never know how many friends you've got until you got a pocket full of pills." Criminal events provide money and drugs for conspicuous consumption and are ideal venues for displaying courage and familiarity with dangerous situations (Katz, 1988, p. 148). Offenders often purport that one goal of their crimes is "showing off" courage or ability by exhibiting lack of hesitation, willingness to take risks, or exaggerated calm in the face of danger (Katz, 1988, p. 304; Matza, 1964; Shover, 1996, p. 110). Crime is a form of "edgework" or voluntary chance-taking that contains "a serious threat to one's physical or mental well-being or one's sense of an ordered existence" (Lyng, 1990, p. 857). Part of the enjoyment of edgework is that it sets capable risk-takers who can "maintain control over a situation that borders on chaos" apart from others (Lyng, 1990, p. 859; Shover, 1996). A middle-aged thief proudly recalls his group's management of challenging criminal events: "it's bad to say, but we was good at what we done."

All group participants define a range of appropriate action from a broad understanding of the situation and how they expect copresent others to act in it (Fine, 1979). Street crime originates in "permissive environs allowing the performance of various respectable and non-respectable activities" (Luckenbill, 1977, p. 178). Small groups of friends intent on "partying," a word unambiguously meaning drug consumption and action-seeking to offenders, comprise most theft groups (Giordano, Cernkovich, & Pugh, 1986; Katz, 1988, p. 198; Shover, 1996). In this sample, 44 subjects were drinking or under the influence of controlled substances during their crime. Levels of consumption on the day of the crime were extreme even by the standards of men who construct their lives around drug use and drinking. A robber reports: "I drank a lot. After my divorce, I drank a lot. But, on that day I drank more. We was drinking a *whole lot* on that day!" A robber currently serving his third sentence for the crime describes the occasion preceding his last offense:

> Well, it more or less started out like most of them do: getting high with my buddy there and riding around drinking. Stopped off to get a few Valiums, and we was just riding around here and there. You know, stopped at a buddy's here. It was an all day thing, drinking and driving, driving and drinking.... I was in and out [of consciousness]. I would get so drunk he would drive, and then he would get so drunk I would drive while he was sleeping. And just more or less the whole day went on like that.

Offenders encounter many people during their extended parties. As a result, the composition of a group often changes as it proceeds toward crime. Some participants excuse themselves from company suspected to be on a criminal course, whereas others are quick to volunteer. A persistent robber remembers the outcome of his group's plan to rob a gas station: "[t]he other guys backed out, didn't show...just me and the guy that worked at the station, we carried out the plan." Continued participation in a scene already construed by others as potentially criminal conveys approval of a criminal course. Restraining influences on a group diminish as those wary of crime and less committed to the party depart. A burglar recalls recognizing the apparent criminal potential in his companions:

> We were at a party and everyone else goes to bed. They go to sleep. We just sittin' around doing nothing. Now, when you have got a bunch of crank heads sitting around at four in the morning with nothing to do, they are scheming. There is nothing to do but scheme.

Experienced offenders are adept at sizing up trustworthiness and criminal willingness in associates (Gould, Walker, Crane, & Lidz, 1974, pp. 45–46; McCarthy et al., 1998, p. 174). Of course, many street offenders are so committed to street life that they can safely assume that those around them are open to criminal proposals. When I asked Greg, a burglar whose most recent conviction contained 32 counts, what happens when his associates refuse to accompany him for a burglary, he answered: "I never had that problem. If they have hit a lick before, they know you can make pretty good money...everybody needs more money."

INTERACTIONAL DYNAMICS

Antecedent events and copresent others open group participants' eyes to opportunity, but interaction begins enactment of a criminal course and the more intentional stages of decision making. All interactions are temporally embedded and contextual. Offenders' forward-looking opportunity appraisals are based on the sense they make of situations using contextually relevant precedent and experience (Vaughan, 1998), but actors do not simply apply lessons from experience to static situations. They "continuously engage patterns and repertoires from the past, project hypothetical pathways forward in time and adjust their actions to the exigencies of emerging situations" (Emirbayer & Mische, 1998, p. 1012). How do group offenders interact with each other and their environments to reach a criminal decision?

Subjects described three general styles of interaction that made illicit opportunity apparent and readily accessible. Most crime groups made criminal sense of a scene by referencing group identities, improvisational communicative signals, or conspicuously attractive targets. These styles of decision making are fluid and overlapping; all three considerations play a part in the decisions of many groups. However, qualitative differences in group decisions are apparent. The relative importance of the three recurring considerations in criminal choice is contingent on a group's shared criminal experience and on the experience and motivation of individual participants. Participants in groups with extensive experience frame their situations and opportunities using this experience; groups without shared experience improvise and rely on situational and interactional cues.

INCREMENTAL SIGNALING

In many cases, small decisions and incremental actions made more or less intentionally and by multiple participants alter situations and perceptions until criminal choice is attractive, what I term *incremental signaling.* Offenders without shared experience or on the periphery of street life are especially likely to approach crime gradually using incremental gestural or verbal moves. When offenders are unsure of others' objectives, they use signals to negotiate shared definitions. One offender makes a move toward crime, and then checks others' responses to find out if they see similar potential and are receptive to the directive (Cromwell et al., 1991, p. 67).

Shared contexts and immediate precipitating experiences turn actors' attention to similar reference signals and solutions to mutual problems; signaling articulates these anticipatory courses of action (Hilton & Slugowski, 1998; Wade, 1994). A burglar explains that his partners easily interpreted his otherwise oblique suggestion because their recently incurred obligations made criminal potential apparent:

> I guess I figured they owed me. I mean I wouldn't have cared a bit, the thought would have never crossed my mind if I had went out and bought $100 worth of pot and smoked every bit. I wouldn't have thought [that] they owed me anything. But, I bought $300 worth of rock, and it was gone in like two hours....He shared it (burglary profit] with me because he better have. Bubba was telling Tommy "we have to get some more money." I had spent my whole paycheck on them. So I told them, "Look, I got no more money! All my money was left back in Memphis, it's about time y'all come up with something."

Deliberation begins ambiguously, but escalates quickly. Typically, someone in the group mentions an apparent need for money. The context makes it clear that a suggestion is being made that the group has the potential for acquiring money illegally. Next, a participant mentions a specific type of crime or target. This statement of intent is similar conceptually to a *keynote,* a term familiar to collective behavior scholars. Keynotes are exploratory directives that resonate with those thinking along similar lines, but who are still turning over multiple interpretations of a situation (Turner & Killian, 1987, p. 59). In consequential and urgent situations, keynotes inspire action. Urgent situations are sufficiently ambivalent to encourage actors to turn to others for guidance but convey a finite set of appropriate preferences (Fine, 1979; Kohn & Williams, 1956, p. 173; McPhail, 1991; Turner & Killian, 1987, p. 53). Two robbers recall definitive progressions in verbal deliberation:

> Yeah, it went, "we need some damn money" and then here he sat and told us all. Well, we were all sittin' there, and he was telling us about robberies or whatever, and he told us how to do it.

We was riding around gettin' high, and I was telling them that I needed to make some money for Christmas. They kinda looked at each other and started laughin'. They pretty much said, "you need some easy money, you're with the right people." I said, "that's what I'm talking about." When they said fast and easy, I didn't know they meant armed robbery.

Decisions are based on the style of presentation provided for alternatives as well as on the objective situation (Kuehberger, 1996). Offenders often build confidence using optimistic conversation referred to as "talking it up" or "gassing each other up" (Cromwell et al., 1991, p. 69; Shover, 1996; Tunnell, 1992). Several subjects in this study noted that what is most significant about the optimistic talk preceding crime is what participants do not say. They contend that selective omission of information by some participants reduced fear for others. For example, two burglars reported that the homes they targeted belonged to a co-offender's family members. This information was withheld, however, and the subjects were surprised when their partners were suspected and arrested immediately.

Because conversations are short and criminal consent is often unspoken, many participants are not sure that a crime really will be committed until the last minute (Katz, 1988, p. 225; Matza, 1964, p. 54). A heroin addict engaged in a payroll dispute with his employer approached an older man in his neighborhood with a reputation as a competent thief. He explains how the incremental banter and actions before their robbery allowed the group to work toward a crime and postpone consideration of the risks:

> It is not like you approach him and say "hey, look here, I have this problem." It's more like you are getting high and everything like that. You talkin' about "this son of a bitch who did this to you" and "that son of a bitch that did that to you" and then I said, "I ought to go over there and take my money! Et cetera, et cetera, et cetera." One guy goes, "yeah, yeah, yeah, I ought to!" I ought to do this, and I ought to do that. And one thing leads to another, and basically I find myself in a situation where like I'm laying on the side of a hill saying, "what the hell am I doing this for?"

Criminal proposals are provisional but are often made by those participants who have established a relatively firm definition of a situation. One thief reported that his drug habit did not allow him to be selective about criminal opportunity. When conversations turn to crime, he immediately directs the group toward action with a challenge: "let's go then...if they are for real, if they really want to do something, then they will do it right then cuz there ain't no sense talking about it." Because criminal conversations often begin with ambiguous or exploratory statements, the influence of people who speak tersely and forcefully during decision making is substantial, particularly if other participants do not openly oppose their position (DeGrada, Kruglanski, Mannetti, & Pierro, 1999; Turner & Killian, 1987, p. 85). An offender remembers how an outspoken participant influenced his group's decision making:

> He wanted them how he wanted them, and he was the main one who hollered at people to get things done. He said, "let's go do this!" And I tell you, he had a way of talking you into it. He had this way, "oh come on pussy" and this and

that and the other. There was one that was real dominant. It was almost like, how do I want to word this? It was almost manipulation as far as getting us to do something that we didn't want to. Like, I'm not saying that any of us didn't want to do what we did; it's like we are skeptical and he would manipulate us into going on into it.

Unchecked assertive directives result in a situation in which "each thinks others are committed" to offending (Matza, 1964, p. 54). Therefore, conversations can rapidly evolve past the point where participants begin to see statements that discourage crime as evidence of cowardice or the speaker's inability to meet the demands of a situation.

TARGET CONVERGENCE

Some groups reach criminal decisions when participants mutually and instantaneously recognize an appealing target, what I term *target convergence*. These groups seemingly converge on a target with only the slightest communication between offenders. The eight subjects whose groups clearly reached their decisions in this manner had participants with extensive criminal experience and exposure to street life. However, none of these groups had committed a robbery or burglary together previously. The groups did not discuss crime because they did not set out to commit one, but when an opportunity appeared, talk was not necessary. Appealing targets trigger a group's partially formed and contingent criminal frame of a situation. Targets stand out against a recently constructed backdrop of illicit potential.

Many spontaneous robbers find conspicuous contrast between their situational understandings and ignorant victims who, without realizing the danger, "flash their money around" or "play [the robbers] for punks" or who simply are "somewhere they don't belong." In these situations, deliberative communication with robbery partners is limited to abrupt gestures, nods, or a few words. A robber recalls that his crime began when an older group of men challenged his friends to a fight. When the younger men did not balk, the groups made a frail peace by mentioning mutual associates and sharing a bottle. The newfound allies, apparently on edge from the averted fight, assaulted a stranger who entered the scene minutes later:

> We were just sitting there chillin,' and I asked one of the guys do he got a cigarette....About this time, he says "nah," and he says "but I bet you this dude got one coming down the street." So, I went over there and, you know, asked the dude for a cigarette. One of them dudes comes runnin' across the parking lot and hit him—just Boom! So, when he hit him, [he] hit the ground, and just immediately we started kicking him. While we was beating him, others was going in his pockets gettin' everything he got.

Target convergence typifies mugging and robbery during drug deals, but burglars also can become instantly aware of opportunity. A burglar explains how an encounter with an inviting target during an interstate drug run aligned action in his group:

> I was all high and stuff and seeing tracers and blown away. A big snow come up, and we pulled into this cul-de-sac to stop. There was this hunting lodge or a big house, like an A-frame, and I was sure there was nobody in there. I don't think nothing was even said. I don't know if he said something or I did. We were high and just talking gibberish, like in rhymes. We just ran up there and busted in a window.

ESTABLISHING IDENTITY

Criminality can be a group identity or a mental device shared by participants for organizing events and predicting group action (Cromwell et al., 1991; Short & Strodtbeck, 1965). Participants' knowledge of others in the group, whether gained in firsthand experience or by reputation, frames how a group sees its potential. The characters inhabiting street scenes often have reputations for criminal capability that precede them. These reputations play a significant part in turning group participants' heads toward illicit opportunity. James, a habitual burglar, reported that a young accomplice probably knew how their group would fund a spontaneous beach vacation: "[t]his is what I do. I am a burglar. He knows that and he knows that if he is with me, we are going to steal." Another experienced burglar reflects on why an accomplice who had never committed a burglary volunteered for their crime: "I am sure he looked at me as someone who could give him an alternative."

Most group offenders have firsthand knowledge of co-offenders' criminal potential. Interaction in these experienced groups retains some of its improvisational character. However, subjects from experienced groups report that their group interaction began and proceeded with the potential for crime in participants' minds. Shared criminal experiences are especially salient in ascribing criminal potential to a group (Wood, Gove, Wilson, & Cochran, 1997; Wright & Decker, 1994, p. 37). Several subjects knew others in their group for years before committing a felony together, but stole every time they were together after the first offense. Although individual criminal careers are usually diverse, crime groups often specialize in method and target selection. This shared specialization suggests that participants associate assembly of the practiced group with particular opportunity (Warr, 1996). An offender with several years experience installing burglar alarms and with some expertise in burglary reports that after he revealed his skills to younger relatives during a spontaneous theft: "They come to get me to get high about every night. I would have been stealing some, but not near as much."

A modicum of success enthuses some crime groups. A young man remembers the discussion that followed his first burglary: "We sat and joked about it, we was talking about how easy it was...hey, we can do this every day."

After many successful crimes, stealing with a group becomes a routine that provides offenders with a sense of security. Confidence in partners and in the group's criminal ability and good fortune reinforces the group's criminal identity. One addict recalls that he regularly met with co-offenders and that theft plans needed no discussion in his group: "we were beginning to use stealing as a job; we got up of a morning; we did us a pill and then we were out and in the process and looking for something to steal."

INFLUENCE AND SCENE SETTING

To this point, I have described how offenders cooperatively negotiate shared recognition of criminal opportunity. Indeed, most subjects took care to assert that crime participants mutually influence each other and that each offender exercises considerable agency in crime choice. Nevertheless, as the preceding discussion of interactional dynamics implies, some participants have more influence on a group's behavior than do others (Warr, 1996). Almost all subjects readily identified the most influential person(s) in their group's decision. Nine interviewees identified themselves as leaders and several more viewed themselves as instigators in their last offense. A self-proclaimed instigator describes a burglary in which he stole a van from a residential garage:

> I don't know him that well. I had the idea of gettin' the van, you know. Whenever I had the idea of getting the van, he went along with it. We were coming from a friend's house. He was just following me. He was ten years younger.

Directives made to a group have the greatest influence when participants attribute relevant expertise or experience to the speaker (Berger, Fisek, Norman, & Zelditch, 1977; Foddy & Smithson, 1996; Levine & Russo, 1987; Maas et al., 1987; Shelley, 1998; Warr, 1996). Offenders sometimes ascribe expertise to partners with a paucity of information, however. Subjects cite co-offenders' age, toughness, confident demeanor, and criminal reputations as sources of influence. Partners' presumed and proven criminal abilities not only lead others to look toward criminal opportunity, but also define power relations in the group. A novice burglar explains that a co-offender's past exploits increased his influence over the group:

> Whether we wanted to do it or not, we would, cuz we figured he was right. I mean, it was like we knew he had been around more than we had. I mean, just getting around into things; like just getting high or stealing or whatever. He wasn't scared of nothin'.

Groups ascribe influence to some participants. In turn, these participants enact their influence. Suspecting that present company and surroundings approximate opportunity, actors adjust the situation to fit their preferred perspective for understanding events (Best, 1982; Goffman, 1969; Heise, 1979).

With motives of helping friends, showing off, and benefitting from task cooperation, some offenders maneuver so that others make criminal sense of a scene. Actors accomplish scene setting by "moving about to confirm that all the parts of a scene are present,...or assembling required paraphernalia or mustering human participants,...or locomoting to a setting where a required situation exists intact" (Heise, 1979, p. 39).

In some groups, offenders provide drugs and alcohol to reduce fear of criminal participation (Cromwell et al., 1991, p. 64). A severe alcoholic reports that when he refused a criminal proposal, his partner bought more liquor in an attempt to "get me drunk...to where I didn't give a damn." Collecting and displaying weapons or other facilitating hardware also elicits criminal ideas and shapes the behavior of others (Carlson, Marcus-Newhall, & Miller, 1990; Lofland, 1969, pp. 69–72). A young man recalls his surprise when his partners suddenly presented tools needed to stage a robbery: "The guns was theirs; they had them and some ski masks already in the car." A habitual burglar explains why it may seem to some offenders that tools suddenly appear in a potentially criminal scene: "Burglary tools, always did have them with me. You never know when you are going to run up on something." A young burglar describes using a set of keys in his effort to recruit accomplices for a burglary:

> Sometimes it just happens to be luck—like one time a store. One day I was in front of the store, it was closed and I walked to the store and tried to open the doors. It was locked. It was closed, and when I was walking away from the store I happened to look at the ground and seen a set of keys. So...I pick up the keys, and I go to the lock and open the door. I lock it back up, go home and tell about two or three friends. We was just livin' across the street from the store. Four of us come back,...took all kind of stuff out that store.

Most subjects reported that at least one group participant contemplated or made some preparation for their crime before the group assembled. The consistent finding that many thieves keep a store of potential targets in mind until they need them or an opportune situation arises supports their claim (Maguire, 1982; Wright & Decker, 1994, p. 63, 1997). Six subjects said that before discussing specific criminal plans their group arrived at a target that was preselected by another participant. A home invasion robber contends that until he saw the target, he thought his group's plan was to intimidate a nonpaying drug customer as his partners had implied:

> I mean, as soon as we pulled up—and they had gone in and come out to get me—and when I got inside, that's when I first knew. I mean, they didn't tell me outside before I went in; that's the part I couldn't understand about it. All I knew is that the people in there [a wealthy attorney's home] wouldn't mess with these two guys.

Offenders who are the most hesitant or uninformed often become acutely aware of the influence of others on their actions in the instant before they offend. When confronting a target, they realize that their previous decisions and the actions of co-offenders constrain their options. The most motivated offenders in a group often turn from subtle to overt means of influence in an attempt to overcome this late hesitation. When confronting a target, a decisive move finally "brings into relief" criminal definitions and polarizes options (Katz, 1988, p. 305). A burglar reports that his presumed consent placed him in a situation that compelled him to respond:

> [By the] time he got the one [partner] and put him through the window, I mean, what am I gonna do, you know? I didn't want to look like a punk and leave. I wouldn't leave them standing there and me a punk. Then, if they got away from it, then I would be a punk for leaving. That's how I was. I mean, I thought I was in a little gang or whatever.

A robber remembers that he was disgusted with his partners' failure to follow through on the group's quickly formulated plan. He explains that frustration led to his decision to take the initiative:

> We pulled into a couple of places, and nobody would do it. It was driving me crazy. I can't take that. They were findin' every little thing that could go wrong. I finally said, "all right, by god, pull in the next place you see." I went in and said, "I have a gun" and robbed it.

DISCUSSION

Understanding why people who are not determined to commit a crime one minute become so the next requires attention to the immediate situations that link street life and criminal decisions (Jacobs & Wright, 1999, p. 150; Katz, 1988, p. 3; Short, 1998). This paper shows that interaction with other people in distinctive compositional settings and organizing activities conditions criminal choice. Findings support portrayals of criminal decision making as complex, bounded by the desperate circumstances of offenders' lives, and framed by the pursuit of an escapist party. Moreover, findings suggest that examining offenders' fallible perceptions of costs and benefits or their commitment to conduct norms of street life only begins to capture complexity in criminal decision making.

Inadequate attention to the many sources of extrasituational, situational, and interactional variation in individual offenders' considerations in choosing crime, particularly in studies of target selection, structures research findings and creates an overly rational and simplistic understanding of choice (Bennet & Wright, 1984; Rankin & Wells, 1982; Tunnell, 1992). Burglars obviously scan for signs of occupancy, witnesses, and escape routes in the instant before stealing (Bennet & Wright, 1984). This utilitarian rationality is commensurable with extended, less deliberate, and complex routes to offending. When given freedom to describe events, offenders depict improvisational, contextual, and variable processes leading to their choice. To varying degrees, incremental signaling, target convergence, constraining and enabling actions by others, and the situational dynamics of the criminal setting shape their decisions.

The abstract context of crime is a style of living that creates need for disposable cash and provides few feasible approaches for getting it (Jacobs & Wright, 1999; Wright & Decker, 1994, p. 39). In the immediate context of criminal events, motivation often results from collaboratively constructed perceptions of opportunity. The most insightful and self-reflective thieves refer to both lasting and situational contexts when they report that a learned approach to crime avoidance is "staying out of trouble" or "off the streets." For them, the law-abiding path seems narrow and crime results from inaction and failure to take precautions by avoiding street life, its activities, and potential crime partners.

Many investigators portray criminal motivation either as an enduring predisposition or else as an attraction to offending that remains dormant until an encounter with a target (Jacobs & Wright, 1999, p. 164). Criminological theories suggest models of overdetermined individuals who are driven to crime and waiting for a chance to satisfy their preferences. However, conceptual distinctions between opportunity and motivation blur when ethnographers and situational analysts examine decisions and interaction preceding crime (Athens, 1997; Short & Strodtbeck, 1965; Wolfgang, 1958). Burglars and robbers construct criminal opportunity by comparing recently formulated understandings with developing events and adjusting situations to make events and understanding correspond. Criminal choice "blends indiscriminately into the flow of practical activity" as offenders improvise action and expectations to suit ever-shifting circumstances in informal situations (Emirbayer & Mische, 1998). Some crime groups are more goal directed than are others, but only a few pursue determined and consistent ends known equally to all; more typically, the rational path mutates as options open and close and as participants interact to make sequential choices. Participants in this study contend that the immediate allure of crime is incomprehensible without considering preparation, cajoling, encouragement, and other enabling and constraining action by others.

Findings from investigations of the situational complexities of choice have significant implications for future research. On the one hand, offending results when offenders stumble into developing crime. Therefore, social and geographic proximity to crime groups and situations that precipitate thoughts of crime have causal significance (Fagan, Piper, & Cheng, 1987, p. 588). Those without experience in street life are unlikely to find themselves in the presence of men considering a burglary, but theft groups are difficult for many impoverished young men to avoid. On the other hand, this study reveals that purposive, but contingent, action by some actors often precedes even unplanned crime. Dangerous places, alcohol and drug use, appropriate victims, tools, and supportive co-offenders are correlates of criminal situations, but these elements do not converge in scenes spontaneously (see Sampson & Lauritsen, 1994, p. 39). Actors assemble the elements of criminal situations to direct action, play with danger, and create opportunity.

The complexity of situations and variability in offenders' situational skills and constructions of opportunity receives little empirical attention (Birkbeck & LaFree, 1993). Therefore, the intersections between offenders' lives and the effects of these encounters on variation in their decision making are largely unexplored. For example, many robbers are motivated sufficiently to wait in the car while partners rob a store, but contend that they would never serve as gunmen. Others may never attempt a burglary unless in the presence of people who they assume burglarize routinely. In an event, one offender can be an experienced thief who displays unusual forethought in scouting out a target, whereas his co-offenders are drunken young men who join the decision in its last stages.

Qualitative and interactionist studies of crime have great potential. This paper, however, is not a call for a particular methodology, but for empirical attention to "immediate background and context of offenders' action" (Katz, 1991). Examining event characteristics may support well-worn theories and improve specification of established models. For example, offenders without biographical characteristics correlated with street crime may offend when their lives take a short-term turn for the worse or when they are in the company of those who clearly are at risk of offending. Reducing the accessibility of targets may deter groups without experience. Groups that have committed many crimes may be willing to take on greater risks or only be displaced by a challenging target. In methodologies that examine crime as an outcome of individual offenders' characteristics, potential sources of variation escape notice. Group crimes are an intersection of participants' pathways in which characters and their characteristics meld and interact with environments to shape events.

References

Asch, S. E. (1951). Effects of group pressure upon the modification and distortion of judgment. In H. Guetzkow (Ed.), *Groups, leadership and men* (pp. 177–190). Pittsburgh: Carnegie Press.

Athens, L. H. (1997). *Violent criminal acts and actors revisited.* Chicago: University of Chicago Press.

Bennet, T., & Wright, R. T. (1984). *Burglars on burglary: Prevention and the offender.* Aldershot, UK: Bower.

Berger, J., Fisek, M. H., Norman, R. Z., & Zelditch, M. J. (1977). *Status characteristics and social interaction: An expectation-states theory.* New York: Elsevier.

Best, J. (1982). Crime as strategic interaction. *Urban Life, 11,* 107–128.

Birkbeck, C. B., & LaFree, G. (1993). The situational analysis of crime and deviance. *Annual Review of Sociology, 19,* 133–137.

Bureau of Justice Statistics. (1999). *Criminal victimization in the United States.* Washington, DC: Department of Justice.

Carlson, M., Marcus-Newhall, A., & Miller, N. (1990). Effects of situational aggression cues: A quantitative review. *Journal of Personality and Social Psychology, 58,* 622–633.

Carrol, F. M., & Weaver, J. S. (1986). Crime perceptions in a natural setting by expert and novice shoplifters. *Social Psychology Quarterly, 48,* 349–359.

Cloward, R. A., & Ohlin, L. E. (1960). *Delinquency and opportunity.* New York: Free Press.

Cordilia, A. T. (1986). Robbery arising out of a group drinking context. In A. Campbell & J. J. Gibbs (Eds.), *Violent transactions.* New York: Blackwell.

Cornish, D. B., & Clarke, R. V. (1986). *The reasoning criminal: Rational choice perspectives on offending.* New York: Springer-Verlag.

Cromwell, P. F., Olson, J. N., & Avary, D. W. (1991). *Breaking and entering: An ethnographic analysis of burglary.* Newbury Park, CA: Sage.

DeGrada, E., Kruglanski, A. W., Mannetti, L., & Pierro, A. (1999). Motivated cognition and group interaction: Need for closure affects the contents and processes of collective negotiations. *Journal of Experimental Social Psychology, 35,* 346–365.

Deschenes, E. P., Anglin, M. D., & Speckhart, G. (1991). Narcotics addiction: Related criminal careers, social and economic costs. *Journal of Drug Issues, 21,* 405–434.

Eckland-Olson, S., Lieb, J., & Zurcher, L. (1984). The paradoxical impact of criminal sanctions: Some microstructural findings. *Law and Society Review, 18,* 159–178.

Emirbayer, M., & Mische, A. (1998). What is agency? *American Journal of Sociology, 103,* 962–1023.

Erikson, M. L., & Jensen, G. F. (1977). Delinquency is still group behavior: Toward revitalizing the group premise in the sociology of deviance. *Journal of Criminal Law and Criminology, 70,* 102–116.

Fagan, J., Piper, E., & Cheng, Y. (1987). Contribution of victimization to delinquency in inner cities. *Journal of Criminal Law and Criminology, 78,* 586–613.

Faupel, C. E. (1987). Drugs-crime connections: Elaborations from the life of hard-core heroin addicts. *Social Problems, 34,* 54–68.

Feeney, F. (1986). Robbers as decision-makers. In D. B. Cornish & R. V. Clarke (Eds.), *The reasoning criminal: Rational choice perspective on offending.* New York: Springer-Verlag.

Fine, G. (1979). Rethinking subculture: An interactionist analysis. *American Journal of Sociology, 85,* 1–20.

Fleisher, M. S. (1995). *Beggars and thieves: Lives of urban street criminals.* Madison: University of Wisconsin Press.

Foddy, M., & Smithson, M. (1996). Relative ability, paths of relevance, and influence in task oriented groups. *Social Psychology Quarterly, 59,* 40–53.

Gibbs, J. J., & Shelley, P. L. (1982). Life in the fast lane: A retrospective view by commercial thieves. *Journal of Research in Crime and Delinquency, 19,* 299–330.

Giordano, P. C., Cernkovich, S. A., & Pugh, M. D. (1986). Friendship and delinquency. *American Journal of Sociology, 91,* 1170–1202.

Goffman, E. (1969). *Where the Action is.* London: Allen Lane.

Gottfredson, M. R., & Hirschi, T. (1990). *A general theory of crime.* Stanford, CA: Stanford University Press.

Gould, L., Walker, A. L., Crane, L. E., & Lidz, C. W. (1974). *Connections: Notes from the heroin world.* New Haven, CT: Yale University Press.

Groves, W. B., & Lynch, M. J. (1990). Reconciling structural and subjective approaches to the study of crime. *Journal of Research in Crime and Delinquency, 27,* 348–375.

Hagan, J., & McCarthy, B. (1992). Street life and delinquency. *British Journal of Sociology, 43,* 533–561.

Heise, D. (1979). *Understanding events: Affect and the construction of social action.* New York: Cambridge University Press.

Hilton, D. J., & Slugowski, B. R. (1998). Judgment and decisionmaking in social context: Discourse processes and rational inference. In T. Connoly & H. R. Arkes (Eds.), *Judgment and decisionmaking: An interdisciplinary reader* (2nd ed.). New York: Cambridge University Press.

Horney, J., Osgood, D. W., & Marshall, I. H. (1995). Criminal careers in the short term: Intra-individual variability in crime and relation to local life circumstances. *American Sociological Review, 60,* 655–673.

Jacobs, B. A., & Wright, R. T. (1999). Stick-up, street culture, and offender motivation. *Criminology, 37,* 149–174.

Kameda, T., & Davis, J. H. (1990). The function of reference point in individual and group risk decision making. *Organizational Behavior and Human Decision Processes, 46,* 55–76.

Katz, J. (1988). *The seductions of crime: Moral and sensual attractions in doing evil.* New York: Basic Books.

Katz, J. (1991). The motivation of persistent robbers. In M. Tonry (Ed.), *Crime and justice: An annual review of research* (Vol. 14, pp. 277–306). Chicago: University of Chicago Press.

Kohn, M. L., & Williams, R. M. (1956). Situational patterning in intergroup relations. *American Sociological Review, 21,* 164–174.

Kuehberger, A. (1996). The influence of framing on risky decisions: A meta-analysis. *Organizational Behavior and Human Decision Processes, 75,* 23–55.

Levine, J. M., & Russo, E. M. (1987). Majority and minority influence. In C. Hendrick (Ed.), *Group Processes.* Newbery Park, CA: Sage.

Lofland, J. (1969). *Deviance and identity.* Englewood Cliffs, NJ: Prentice-Hall.

Luckenbill, D. F. (1977). Criminal homicide as situated transaction. *Social Problems, 25,* 176–186.

Lyng, S. (1990). Edgework: A social-psychological analysis of voluntary risk-taking. *American Journal of Sociology, 95,* 851–886.

Maas, A., West, S. G., & Cialdini, R. B. (1987). Minority influence and conversion. In C. Hendrick (Ed.), *Group processes*. Newbery Park, CA: Sage.

Maguire, M. (1982). *Burglary in a dwelling*. London: Heinemann.

Matza, D. (1964). *Delinquency and drift*. New York: John Wiley.

McCarthy, B., Hagan, J., & Cohen, L. E. (1998). Uncertainty, cooperation and crime: Understanding the decision to co-offend. *Social Forces, 77*, 155–176.

McPhail, C. (1991). *The myth of the madding crowd*. New York: Aldine de Gruyter.

Miller, J. (1998). Up it up: Gender and accomplishment of street robbery. *Criminology, 36*, 37–66.

Nagin, D., & Paternoster, R. (1993). Enduring individual differences and rational choice theories of crime. *Law and Society Review, 27*, 467–496.

Piliavin, I. M., Gartner, R., Thorton, C., & Matsueda, R. L. (1986). Crime, deterrence and rational choice. *American Sociological Review, 51*, 101–119.

Piquero, A., & Rengert, G. F. (1999). Specifying deterrence with active residential burglars. *Justice Quarterly, 16*, 450–480.

Rankin, J. H., & Wells, L. E. (1982). The social context of deterrence. *Sociology and Social Research, 67*, 18–39.

Reiss, A. J., Jr. (1988). Co-offending and criminal careers. In M. Tonry & N. Morris (Eds.), *Crime and justice: A review of research* (Vol. 10). Chicago: University of Chicago Press.

Reiss, A. J., Jr., & Farrington, D. (1991). Advancing knowledge about co-offending: Results from a prospective longitudinal survey of London males. *Journal of Criminal Law and Criminology, 82*, 360–395.

Sampson, R., & Lauritsen, J. L. (1994). Violent victimization and offending: Individual-, situational-, and community-level risk factors. In A. J. Reiss & J. A. Roth (Eds.), *Understanding and preventing violence* (Vol. 3). Washington, DC: National Academy Press.

Shelley, R. K. (1998). Some developments in expectation states theory: Graduated expectations? In *Advances in Group Processes* (Vol. 15). Stamford, CT: JAI Press.

Sherif, M. (1936). *The psychology of social norms*. New York: Harper & Row.

Short, J. F. (1998). The level of explanation problem revisited. *Criminology, 36*, 1–36.

Short, J. F., & Strodtbeck, F. (1965). *Group process and gang delinquency*. Chicago: University of Chicago Press.

Shover, N. (1996). *Great pretenders: Pursuits and careers of persistent thieves*. Boulder, CO: Westview.

Shover, N., & Henderson, B. (1995). Repressive crime control and male persistent thieves. In H. D. Barlow (Ed.), *Crime and public policy: Putting theory to work*. Boulder, CO: Westview.

Shover, N., & Honaker, D. (1992). The socially bounded decision making of persistent property offenders. *Howard Journal of Criminal Justice, 31*, 276–290.

Taylor, M., & Nee, C. (1988). The role of cues in simulated residential burglary. *British Journal of Criminology, 28*, 396–401.

t'Hart, P. T., Stern, E. K., & Sundelius, B. (1997). *Beyond groupthink: Political group dynamics and policy-making.* Ann Arbor: University of Michigan Press.

Tracy, P. E., Jr. (1987). Race and class differences in self-reported delinquency. In M. E. Wolfgang & T. P. Thornberry (Eds.), *From boy to man, from delinquency to crime.* Chicago: University of Chicago Press.

Tremblay, P. (1993). Searching for suitable co-offenders. In R. V. Clarke & M. Felson (Eds.), *Advances in criminological theory: Routine activity and rational choice* (Vol. 5). New York: Transaction Publishing.

Tunnell, K. D. (1992). *Choosing crime: The criminal calculus of property offenders.* Chicago: Nelson Hall.

Turner, R. H., & Killian, L. (1987). *Collective behavior* (3rd ed.). Englewood Cliffs, NJ: Prentice Hall.

Turner, J. C., Wetherall, M. S., & Hogg, M. A. (1989). Referent informational influence and group polarization. *British Journal of Social Psychology, 28*, 135–147.

Vaughan, D. (1998). Rational choice, situated action, and the social control of organizations. *Law and Society Review, 32*, 501–538.

Wade, A. L. (1994). Social processes in the act of juvenile vandalism. In M. B. Clinard, R. Quinney, & J. Wildeman (Eds.), *Criminal behavior systems: A typology* (3rd ed.). New York: Anderson.

Warr, M. (1996). Organization and instigation in delinquent groups. *Criminology, 34*, 11–37.

Wolfgang, M. E. (1958). *Patterns in criminal homicide.* Philadelphia: University of Pennsylvania Press.

Wood, P. B., Gove, W. R., Wilson, J. A., & Cochran, J. K. (1997). Nonsocial reinforcement and habitual criminal conduct: An extension of learning theory. *Criminology, 35*, 335–366.

Wright, G., & Ayton, P. (1994). *Subjective probability.* Chichester, UK: John Wiley.

Wright, R. T., & Decker, S. (1994). *Burglars on the job: Streetlife and residential break-ins.* Boston: Northeastern University Press.

Wright, R. T., & Decker, S. (1997). *Armed robbers in action.* Boston: Northeastern University Press.

Wright, R. T., Logie, R. H., & Decker, S. (1996). Criminal expertise and offender decision making: An experimental study of the target selection process in residential burglary. *Journal of research in crime and delinquency, 29*, 148–161.

Zimring, F. E. (1981). Kids, groups and crime: Some implications of a well-known secret. *Journal of Criminal Law and Criminology, 72*, 867–885.

SECTION II

PROPERTY CRIME

Most crime is nonviolent, solely intended to bring financial benefit to the offender. Property crime is usually differentiated from violent crime in its lack of the use of force or serious injury to the victim. Property crimes make up more than 90% of all victimizations. In addition to being more frequent than violent crimes, property crimes usually occur without interaction between the victim and the criminal. In contrast, violent offenders and their victims interact with each other and are often known to each other, although stranger-to-stranger violence is becoming more common

This section includes three new studies of property offenders. In recent years, the issues of identity theft and computer hacking have become increasingly important. In this new edition, these critical issues are addressed, as well as topics on auto theft, burglary, and selling and receiving stolen property. The offenders in these chapters discuss their perspectives on crime as a way of life and the strategies and decisions involved in their criminal activities.

In Chapter 4, "The Key to Auto Theft: Emerging Methods of Auto Theft from the Offender's Perspective," Copes and Cherbonneau interviewed incarcerated auto thieves to determine how they adapted to increasingly sophisticated antitheft devices installed on newer automobiles. Although these new advances have made it harder to steal cars, auto thieves have adapted their techniques, suggesting thieves are not merely opportunistic but exhibit some degree of planning and skill. The authors also suggest strategies for prevention and control of auto theft.

In Chapter 5, Cromwell, Parker, and Mobley ("The Five-Finger Discount") analyze the motivations that underlie shoplifting. They found that although most shoplifters acted to obtain cash or desired merchandise, few individuals used a single, stable criminal calculus.

Chapter 6, a new topic for this edition, "Becoming a Computer Hacker: Examining the Enculturation and Development of Computer Deviants," by Tom Holt examines the development, motivations, subcultural norms, and justifications of criminal computer hacking.

Chapter 7, "Identity Theft: Assessing Offenders' Strategies and Perceptions of Risk," by Copes and Vieraitis, is an in-depth examination of variables associated identity theft. This emerging crime exists today at a near epidemic rate. The authors focus on the motivations underlying the offense and the skills and techniques used in the perpetration of the crime.

The studies included in this section and throughout the book illustrate that criminal decision making is neither purely opportunistic nor completely rational. It is frequently directed at solving immediate problems and satisfying immediate needs. Age, lifestyle, and previous criminal experience combine to create a "limited rationality" based on what seems reasonable to the offender.

4

The Key to Auto Theft: Emerging Methods of Auto Theft from the Offenders' Perspective

Heith Copes and Michael Cherbonneau

ecent improvements in vehicle security have reduced the opportunities for auto *theft for many would-be thieves. Auto thieves have adapted to these changes by illegally obtaining keys to accomplish their misdeeds. To combat this trend in auto theft, it is necessary to determine commonly preferred methods of key theft. The authors conducted interviews with two to determine their strategies for committing their crimes. One group consisted of 42 individuals on community supervision in a metropolitan area in Tennessee. The second group consisted of 12 incarcerated auto thieves in Louisiana. The subjects ranged in age from 18 to 50. The average age was 29. In terms of experience as auto thieves, they ranged from relatively inexperienced to those whop were very prolific, having stolen more than 50 cars in their "careers." They relied on the accounts of these auto thieves to shed light on the techniques and strategies that they employed to obtain keys. Offenders' accounts show that although some of them simply found keys left in cars, many took more active steps in locating and stealing keys. They relied on strategies such as burglary, robbery, or fraud to acquire keys. Our results suggest that key thieves are not solely opportunistic but instead exhibit some degree of reasoning when offending.*

Theft of motor vehicles constitutes a sizeable portion of the crime problem in North America and Great Britain. In 2003, auto thefts accounted for 12% of all property crimes reported to police in the United States (FBI, 2004) and 13% of all property crimes reported to police in England and Wales (Dodd, Nicholas, Povey, & Walker, 2004). These figures are even more troubling when one considers the financial losses emanating from such offences. Of the $17 billion lost by victims of property crime in the United States in 2003, over $8.6 billion (roughly 51%) was the result of auto theft (FBI, 2004; see also Hough & Mayhew, 1985). Canadian estimates suggest the annual cost of vehicle theft to be around $1 billion (Wallace, 2003). When these costs are

Source: Copes, J. H., & Cherbonneau, M. (2006). The key to auto theft: Emerging methods of auto theft from the offender's perspective. *British Journal of Criminology, 46*, 917–934.

69

coupled with increases in insurance premiums, monies spent protecting vehicles and the costs associated with the unavailability of vehicles, it is clear that auto theft exacts a heavy financial and psychological toll on victims and the larger society (Field, 1993).

These high costs were instrumental in prompting legislation that forced automobile manufacturers to make vehicles more secure. Manufacturers were deemed partly responsible for high auto theft rates because poor designs made it easy for thieves to break into and start vehicles (Brill, 1982; Clarke & Harris, 1992; Karmen, 1981; Southall & Ekblom, 1985). The weak ignition lock of certain Ford models manufactured between 1969 and 1974 was thought to be a major cause of their disproportionately high rate of theft in the United States. After Ford replaced the old locks with more secure ones in 1975, theft rates for Fords decreased by 25% (Karmen, 1981). In 1969, federal legislation in the United States required manufacturers to equip vehicles with steering column locks. Evidence shows that the introduction of locking steering columns dramatically lowered auto theft rates, at least temporarily (Webb, 1994). A more recent development in "target hardening" from manufacturers is the electronic immobilizer. In 1995, the European Union mandated that all cars manufactured after October 1998 be fitted with electronic immobilizers (Levesley, Braun, Wilkinson, & Powell, 2004). This antitheft device involves the use of a computer chip, fitted on the key, that restricts a would-be thief from bypassing the vehicle's ignition. Police reports from Great Britain show that there was a decline in the rate of auto thefts for cars manufactured after 1998. This decline is attributed to the implementation of the immobilizer (Levesley et al., 2004).

Offenders are quick to adjust to changing opportunity structures of crime (Inciardi, 1975; Shover, 1996) and auto thieves are no exception. The new advances in target hardening have certainly made auto theft more difficult, but auto thieves have adapted by employing new strategies and tactics to accomplish their misdeeds (Flood-Page & Taylor, 2003). One emerging strategy to bypass many of the new built-in security measures is to use keys to start the vehicles (Beekman, 1994; Levesley et al., 2004). Evidence shows that this strategy is becoming increasingly more common. For example, the proportion of vehicles stolen using keys in England and Wales rose from 7 to 12% from 1998 to 2001 (Flood-Page & Taylor, 2003).

Although the exact number of vehicles stolen using keys is not known, it is clear that these types of theft account for a nontrivial proportion of the vehicles stolen in Britain, Canada, and the United States. Levesley et al. (2004) obtained police data on 8,303 incidents of thefts and attempted thefts of newly registered cars (i.e., those equipped with electronic immobilizers) in the Northumbria and Greater Manchester areas. Overall, they found that keys were used in 85% of auto thefts. Other estimates based on police reports suggest that the percentage of offenders who used keys in vehicle thefts ranged from 10% (Kinshott, 2001) to 48.7% (Sandvik, 1996). Using data collected from recovered stolen vehicles, the Maryland Vehicle Theft Prevention Council (2003) estimates that between 25 and 32% of recovered stolen vehicles still had the keys in them. A survey of juvenile car thieves in Great Britain found that 16% of them said they were able to steal cars because the key had been left in the vehicle (Webb & Laycock, 1992). A victimization survey of known auto theft victims in British Columbia, Canada, revealed that "roughly 20% of the vehicles in this sample were stolen with the owner's keys, most often because they were left in the ignition or had been hidden in or on the vehicle" (Fleming, Brantingham, & Brantingham, 1994, p. 58). This finding is consistent with other studies of auto theft in Canada (Morrison, 1991; Ogrodnik & Paiement, 1992). Using a variety of data sources and geographic contexts, it is evident that theft of keys accounts for a relatively large proportion of auto thefts.

To combat this trend of illegally obtaining keys, it is necessary to determine commonly preferred methods of key theft. In line with this thinking, Levesley et al. (2004, p. 4) conclude their report on the theft of keys by suggesting that "something could be learnt from speaking with offenders who are involved in this type of offence. Interviews could be conducted to examine: commonly preferred methods of key theft, perceptions of associated risks, types and value of vehicle stolen." A better understanding of how auto thieves get keys can help direct crime prevention efforts, particularly those based on situational crime prevention principles.

Situational crime prevention involves the systematic manipulation of the immediate environment in order to reduce the opportunities and increase the risks associated with highly specific forms of crime (Clarke, 1997). All situational crime prevention measures are designed based on assumptions about the nature of the target crime and the typical characteristics of those who commit it. In the best of circumstances, these profiles are grounded in knowledge gained directly from offenders. Some have suggested, in fact, that "There can be no more critical element in understanding and ultimately preventing crime than understanding the criminal's perceptions of the opportunities and risks associated with [crime]" (Rengert & Wasilchick, 1989, p. 1). Development of situational crime prevention initiatives frequently begins with offender interviews as a way of learning the skill sets and techniques of the crime in question (Clarke, 1995; Decker, 2005; Hesseling, 1994). It is for this reason that we sought out auto thieves to gain their perspectives and insights. We rely on the accounts of auto thieves who used keys to steal vehicles to shed light on the techniques and strategies that they employed to obtain keys.

OBTAINING KEYS FOR AUTO THEFT

Alert Opportunism

Opportunities for auto theft can emerge at any time. One only needs the "larceny sense" to recognize them and the willingness to exploit these conditions (Sutherland, 1937). Alert opportunists claimed that they did not set out to steal a vehicle but during the course of their daily activities, an easy opportunity emerged and they seized it (see Bennett & Wright, 1984; Topalli & Wright, 2004). In the words of one opportunist:

> It is not that I set my mind before I seen the bike, "O.K., today I'm going to steal a motorcycle.' It was the fact that the dude was stupid enough to leave the key in the motorcycle. Right there all the way at the end of a driveway. Down an old road. It's an old abandoned highway. He wanted someone to steal it!

Here, the decision to steal was precipitated by the chance discovery of an easy, low-risk opportunity, which he simply could not pass up.

Those with larceny in their heart are often aware of potential criminal opportunities that go unnoticed by law-abiding citizens (Wright, Logie, & Decker, 1995). From the perspective of experienced thieves, these opportunities appear to materialize out of thin air, and the easier these opportunities seem, in terms of effort and risk, the more they engender an irresistible desire to take full advantage of them. When asked if he was looking for a vehicle to steal, one offender responded "Nope. When I seen it I knew it was for me. It was calling my name. It was calling my name." The temptation of ill-gotten gains makes lines of action to the contrary easy to ignore (Katz, 1988). When describing how the intent to steal emerged, one offender stated:

> I went off up in this neighborhood by General Hospital. They had this convertible Benz, it was parked up under the garage, you know. And I kind of found that funny. The top down in the garage with the door open. So I waited for a little while and I ain't seen nobody come out So I went in and the keys were just sitting right there. I was like damn. So I cranked it up and I pulled out.

Another offender had a taste for high-end car audio accessories. While driving around with friends, he stumbled upon a car that had an attractive radio and the keys in the ignition. Without hesitation, he seized this moment to upgrade his own car stereo system:

> We just driving by and I see a running car just parked [and] I'm looking out the passenger window and I see a "fire' radio one of them little flip in and flip down 3 disk CD players. But the car [was] just running.... So we parked the car we were in like two blocks away.... We go back and I get in the [running] car.

Clearly, the presentation of enticing opportunities (e.g., those with low effort, minimal risk and high reward) made thieves out of many individuals.

Participation in street life facilitates crime by instilling a general openness to offend, by creating situations in which offending is seen as a viable option, and by fostering offenders' abilities to recognize criminal opportunities (Topalli & Wright, 2004). In relation to auto theft, the spontaneity of street life and late-night partying often leaves offenders stranded in places far from home with no means of getting back (Copes, 2003a). To overcome such situations, offenders seize opportunities that are available: "On a few occasions I got stranded and I seen somebody's car parked at a gas station. You know how they just out and run in there and get cigarettes or something? I would just jump in their car and just pull out." Another offender recalled a similar situation: "I had went to a club [and] got dropped off at my girls house and I didn't have the key or she wasn't there.... I wasn't even planning on stealing a car. All I knew I was stuck." Thus, taking advantage of an easy opportunity was commonplace for thieves immersed in the street lifestyle (Shover, 1996; Wright & Decker, 1994).

Participation in street life also dictates that personal or symbolic affronts be confronted directly (Anderson, 1999). Thus, victims' public displays of bravado coupled with a bit of carelessness are the sparks needed to move an auto thief from an unmotivated state to a motivated one (Copes, 2003b). The following account exemplifies this mentality toward punishing affronts:

> I took a car one time, dude was just at Wal-Mart. He parked his car there, a black Z-28 IROC-SS. He parked his car out there and left his car running like he's the shit or something. Man I hopped in that. "I'm a holler at you partner.' I just took it, I had to get somewhere. He parking like he just, you know, a big bad bull. Like nobody won't jump up in there. Man, I was gone before he even much knew it. His mistake.... In a situation like this, he got caught slipping. He got caught slipping. Shouldn't be slacking off [or] it could happen. I know the thought came to him, "Should I park? Should I turn my car off? Let me hurry up and go run up in here ain't nobody going to take it' Oh yeah? You ain't never know who watching.... That's why I caught the boy slipping with his IROC.

Alert opportunities for auto theft also materialized while offenders engaged in a variety of other property crimes. One offender, in need of fast cash, burglarized a business. Since he had never stolen a car before, he had no intention of doing so until he came across a set of keys inside the establishment. Below, he describes the unique situation that led to his first auto theft:

> I broke into a like rent-a-car place and stole the keys to a Lexus.... I remember it was so easy. I went in there looking for money but I didn't find any. I found these keys, so I took the keys. I went and tried it out in the front that night to see which car it was for. It opened up a black Lexus.

Offenders also found keys in the course of committing a variety of car crimes, such as burglarizing cars. While rummaging through a car's interior to uncover valuables, they sometimes stumbled upon a set of keys. The first auto theft committed by the following offender emerged in this fashion:

> I had a group of friends that we actually used to go out and break into cars already. This particular night I happened to be by myself. I was looking for some CDs. Not to sell but just something I might enjoy personally. And I came

across an Acura. Brand new. It had about 200 miles on it. And I pulled the trunk release and they had the brand new package. The package they give you when you buy your car, I suppose. It had an extra set of keys, an ink pen, and all this other luxury stuff. I thought well I wonder how fast it will go. So I quietly rolled it out of the drive way, cranked it up, and took it out for a drive.

Not all who seize alert opportunities lack the ability to create their own opportunities for auto theft. But these thefts do result from the most primitive techniques and easily can be thwarted by more careful car owners. Again, such offences do not occur because an offender sets out to steal a car. Offenders merely seize opportunities that are created by car owners who let their "guard down" and, thus, these crimes can occur at any hour of the day and in a variety of locations (Felson & Clarke, 1998).

Active Search

Whereas alert opportunists simply seize opportunities as they emerge, active searchers set out with the desire and the intent to steal. They are motivated offenders who actively seek out opportunities to "capitalize on other people's carelessness." These thieves are optimistic about their ability to find keys in their searches. As one young searcher who stole approximately 30 cars in 2 months said:

> We always had a set of keys. We found it either in that car or in the car sitting right next to it where they had a spare set of keys....If we searched for two hours we would find a car with the keys in it and we would get that one.

With a little diligence and luck, anyone can eventually find a vehicle with keys.

Unlike more skillful thieves who can break into and start the cars they desire, active searchers are limited in their target selection and prey upon "Whatever is open and has a key in it." Thus, the hardest part of accomplishing this type of theft is finding a target fitting these criteria. This task, however, can be made less grueling. Through experience, offenders learn to identify those places and situations in which they are most likely to succeed and those in which they face the greatest risk (Brantingham & Brantingham, 1978; Topalli, 2005). Some offenders prefer to target "nice residential neighborhoods" because "a lot of people leave their shit open in [those] neighbourhoods." Others believe that they would have better luck elsewhere, such as "standard middle-class" areas, because residents in wealthy neighborhoods "would have something really nice and they would lock it up."

Rather than neighborhoods, some offenders preferred to target specific venues in which people are more likely to let their guard down or be caught "slipping." These offenders simply went to highly populated areas and "walked down the curb or down a line of cars in a parking lot looking for one with the keys in the ignition" (Rapp, 1989, p. 10). Two offenders living in

New Orleans, Louisiana, searched for unlocked cars at times and places at which they believed that tourists would be the most careless:

> During [holidays] is the best time you know because all the cars are lined up in the street.... That be the best days because New Orleans is a main attraction for tourists and stuff, and tourists they get drunk, they might leave the keys in the car. Hell, the door might be open! All we got to do is open it up [and] go up in there, you know.

Others preferred to stake out establishments where people are likely to be drinking because "that's where you will mostly find them, you know. People getting drunk, their vehicle will be there, the keys in there because they are not in their right mind." Although offenders had different beliefs about what constitutes a fruitful search area, in the end, this decision came down to the accessibility of an area in relation to the searcher, especially with regards to convenience and familiarity, and, of course, those areas with an abundance of cars to check. After all, most of these offenders did their searching on foot.

Active searchers are not limited to searching vehicles for keys. Many expand their searches to include private residences and businesses. They commit burglary with the intent to steal keys so that they can then drive off in the occupants' vehicles. Keys obtained through burglaries accounted for 37% of all cars stolen in the study conducted by Levesley and his colleagues (2004). Often, these "burglar car thieves" maraud used-car lots or car-rental businesses. One offender explained, "I done seen myself on a Saturday night break into [a used car lot] and take me a set of keys. I mainly targeted the cars that were parked on the corner [of the lot]. I could just drive clean off the lot." Another said:

> I went over to the dealership like I was going to check out one of these used cars on the lot. Right there they have a big old board up with all the keys of the cars in the showroom. I had already done peeped that out. I done seen that and I had spotted the keys to the car. I went back later on that night with two five gallon cans of gas and filled [the car] up.

A few respondents mentioned breaking into people's homes with the intention of getting car keys. These offenders claimed that while they did steal other valuables in the residence, their primary targets were car keys. In the words of one burglar car thief, "I went in the trailer and they had keys hanging up on the side of the wall right there. I took the keys, you know. I hurried up and peeled out. I shot out."

Some searchers capitalize on the mistakes of others by waiting for people to make mistakes. These "active waiters" position themselves in places where they believe opportunities will present themselves. The most common waiting spots were outside gas stations and corner shops because of the steady flow of traffic:

> I would hang around service stations [and wait for] somebody to go in the store and leave their keys in the car or leave the car running. I would jump in

and go about my business....Did I plan them? When I be waiting for someone to make a mistake that is planning. Sometimes it be all day and no one leave their keys in the car, you know. But sooner or later somebody will. Like they got this black dude, he got a Trans-Am and he has music playing. Some people like their music to be heard so he left his music on went in the store, and shit, when he came out I was burning rubber.

Because waiting can be time-consuming, a main concern of offenders is that their loitering will attract the attention of passers-by and employees who could later identify them. Some reduce this risk through displays of normalcy as evidenced by the following offender: "I keep on a work uniform. That's what I steal in, do my dirt in. You got on all work clothes [and] work boots, people don't give you much attention. You look like a working man."

Force

Most car thieves try to avoid direct contact with the owners of the vehicles they are stealing. This is common among those who use keys to steal and among those who use more traditional auto theft techniques. Most would agree that forcefully taking a vehicle from someone is more dangerous than stealing them through nonconfrontational means. In the words of one car thief, "I'll steal them any day. Carjacking? Naw, you got to be ignorant and have balls of steel." Thus, using threatened or actual violence to steal cars is not for all auto thieves. Many are simply unable to stomach the violence and/ or muster the courage to "draw down on somebody." Beyond this, the vast majority of car thieves avoid owners because they want to be neither seen or reported nor injured or killed by an unruly victim.

But despite having good reasons to avoid owners, a small group of car thieves opt to forcefully confront them. Many experts predicted that as vehicle security became more sophisticated, the number of armed auto thefts would rise correspondingly (Beekman, 1994; Clarke & Harris, 1992). Research on the theft of cars with electronic immobilizers lends some support to these claims. Levesley et al. (2004) found that armed key theft increased from 2 to 4% over the three years of their study. Although predictions of a rise in carjacking may have been smaller than predicted or simply a product of sensational media reports (Cherbonneau & Copes, 2003), there is little doubt that carjackings have become a facet of the urban landscape (Jacobs, Topalli, & Wright, 2003; Topalli & Wright, 2004).

The carjackings in our sample emerged from both alert and motivated opportunism (Topalli & Wright, 2004). For some thieves, it was not uncommon to seize an opportunity that manifested in the face of self-defined desperation. The following case of an auto thief turned carjacker exemplifies this pattern of carjacking. He resorted to carjacking after the vehicle he stole earlier stopped running. Believing that the police would be called to the scene, he became paranoid and agitated. Because he did not know how to steal a car without a key and he believed that there was little time to actively search or wait for someone to let their guard down, he carjacked the first person he saw:

> So the lady was coming out of the car. She had her keys and her purse in her hands. She was like getting ready to close the door, but before that I walked up on her and I said, "I'm not going to hurt you. I just want your keys." She turned around and she just kind of froze. I was like, "Give me the keys." She was trying to back up. I kept repeating, "Give me the keys." I guess she thought I was going to cause her bodily harm. But I didn't. So I just took-the keys and she didn't want to let go so I jerked them out of her hand.

Other carjackings came about when the offender purposely sought out a person to rob. Typically, these robberies occurred because the offender desired a vehicle but did not have the skills to steal it: "Certain luxury cars that the people had we couldn't pop them bitches up [start the vehicles without a key], like the BMW. Man, certain cars we couldn't pop up so that brings in the carjacking shit. Have to pull out the pistol and shit." His remarks were echoed by another respondent: "[I've done] about four or five [carjackings]. It wasn't really my big one. My big one was stealing them. But sometimes certain [cars] in order to steal you got to go get the keys."

Not all forceful taking of keys were as outwardly violent as carjacking. Some offenders drugged their victims and then stole the keys while the victims were immobilized. In one incident, a respondent, after striking up friendly conversation, put sleeping pills in the victim's drink while he went to the bathroom. In his words:

> I'm standing on the outside of the bar waiting to see someone get out of a nice car. I want to see the car so when I put something in their drink I know what car to go to when I get a key. I walk in with them like we're buddies, talking to them [and] making conversation as we are going through the door so I be noticed by the bartender or whoever. Look like we were friends, you know. So if I be noticed when I get the keys, you know, they think it's my boy.

This method was used at bars and nightclubs because these venues offer offenders innocuous and naturally occurring opportunities to drug unsuspecting victims.

Manipulation

Of all the offenders who used keys to steal cars, perhaps the most skilled were those who manipulated and/or conned keys away from victims. Although carjackers rely on brute force to take keys, fraudsters rely on their "wits, 'front,' and talking ability" (Sutherland, 1937, p. 197). Levesley et al. (2004) estimate that 5% of all key-related auto thefts in Greater Manchester and Northumbria were accomplished by using forgery or fraud.

The key to being successful at auto theft for these offenders is their ability to control the interaction between themselves and their victims. For a fraud to be successful, it is "necessary to be a good actor, a good salesman, and have good manners and a good appearance" (Sutherland, 1937, p. 56). The following fraudster exemplifies Sutherland's claim about the importance of being a good talker and a good salesman:

> Conversation rules the nation. Word of mouth is always good. If you got a good conversation and you can talk to people and manipulate them and stuff, you always going to conquer this person....Like I said, you know, I just manipulated the conversation and my appearance and just the way I presented myself to them.

Although controlling the conversation is a necessary element in most successful cons, as the previous offender pointed out, additional factors such as appearance increase the likelihood that a con will be successful. Some offenders went to great lengths to portray themselves as honest and legit:

> I wasn't sloppy with it. I mean I stayed well-dressed every time I went to the car lot. You know any kind of interview or any kind of scenery your first impression is your best impression. I always try to look legit, you know. I had a double breasted suit on, tie, shoes, briefcase everything, nice looking female on the side of me, you know.

Offenders who used conversation and appearance to manipulate the keys away from victims mainly targeted car dealerships. There were two ways they would do this. The first involves slight-of-hand techniques to swap the keys while test-driving a car:

> You can go to a dealership to test drive [the car]. And they get in a car with you. They are so bent on selling you the car that you can get permission and they let you drive. They sit in their car with you because people done got in their car and drove off, right. So you can't do that no more. But you get the key and the key ring is nothing but a little, old, thin piece of wire with a couple of keys on it. You know how easy it is to take that key off? When you finish your test drive you park the car back and when you are getting out of the car you switch the keys. Give him a new key. Then you got a key to that car, you know. I mean they so lame. Then you can go back [at night] and just drive off because you got the keys.

The second approach involves making a mould of the vehicle's key. This too is performed while test-driving a car but is more discrete than the slight-of-hand method just described. These offenders keep a small piece of clay in their pocket and while test-driving a car, they mould the key's groove signature into the clay (Rapp, 1989). This is often done while entering or exiting the vehicle—a moment when the salesman is the most likely to be distracted:

> I would sit and talk to them like they was an associate, you know. Like we fixing to do business. I would like more or less take advantage of the conversation....I would have a lot of play-dough in my pocket and as I was getting in the car to start it and test drive it I would make a copy of it in the

play-dough and I bring it to a locksmith friend of mine and he would make keys.

Like offenders who swap the keys, maintaining appearances is very important if they want to take advantage of the salesman's overwhelming desire to make a sale.

Less elaborate cons were played out upon unsuspecting car owners, especially those considered weak, such as drunks or drug addicts. Once again, conversation and trickery were used to lure the keys away from victims (see also Brickell & Cole, 1975). Patrons at bars are often ideal targets, as the following offender describes:

> I was at this bar with this dude [and] he was drinking.... He had a nice car and stuff. I'm a good conartist. I done talked him into letting me drive for him. I got the keys and he's in the bar drinking and stuff. I sneaked off with the car.

In another incident, one offender befriended a fellow drug user and then, at an opportune moment, drove off in this person's vehicle:

> I would get in the car with them and I smoke with them. I'd say, "Man, look pull over man. You go get a lighter." Give him a dollar or whatever and they would go get a lighter. When he come out the store I'm gone, you know.

Crack users are often considered ideal victims for auto theft because of their tendency to rent out their vehicles for a small amount of crack (a practice known as rock renting) and their reluctance to go to the police. Although rock rentals are used for recreation, transportation, anonymous crime commission or to simply keep up appearances, for many it was an ideal situation for auto theft. "I done like rented some cars like for drugs and never brought them back." The following thief would frequently sell cars he rented from unfamiliar crack users:

> Once I started selling dope I could rent dope fiend cars. They got dope fiends that drive Porsches and stuff or a Benz. You go to Houston up in they car.... All the [chop shop[1]] is going to do is buy the car from you for $4,000 or $5,000.

For the most part, rock rentals go as planned; that is, the crack user does not inform the police or try to get their car back too soon and the dealer/renter returns the dope fiend's car in the allotted time (Cherbonneau, Copes, & Forsyth, 2006). After all, users and dealers are often acquainted, thereby making identification possible. More important, a breech of contract by either party would disrupt future drug transactions, block future opportunities and cause a great deal of hassle. This is especially true from the perspective

---

[1] A chop shop is a place where stolen cars are disassembled for parts that are then sold (Harris and Clarke, 1991).

of the dealer/renter: "When you sell drugs you kind of build up a friendship with your clientele. You know, I might need to go back and use that car one day and I ain't going to have it [if I stole it]." Even with these natural safeguards in place, thefts do occur, especially when renting cars from strangers or from unfamiliar customers.

Master Keys and Close-Cousin Keys

Auto thieves do not have to obtain the personal keys of a vehicle's owner to steal a car. They can use "master keys" or "close-cousin keys" to open, start and abscond with other people's vehicles. For some time, many police departments were skeptical about the existence of master keys. In fact, some police departments have had reports of master keys for years, but discarded them as "street lore" until they actually arrested thieves in possession of master keys (McCoy, 2003).

Master keys are cut with a universal groove signature that allows them to fit a variety of models within a certain car manufacture. By using these keys, thieves can open and start cars in a matter of seconds. Master keys are vehicle-specific and typically work best on older models. Most offenders said they used them on Toyotas and Hondas manufactured in the early 1990s. The following offender, however, worked for a chop shop and claimed that the owner had master keys for more recent cars:

> The man I worked for gets pictures of certain cars that he wanted. The exact same car and make. So he'd give us keys to start the cars. So we'd drive around in a stolen car looking for this certain car. Once we find it, we steal it and head back to the dealership....Certain models of cars say, Ford Mustang, a master key will start any one. Once you have a master key it is easy to do.

One offender claimed that master keys could be acquired through car "dealerships, like when you lose your keys for a Toyota or when you lock your keys in the car. They are like 'Here take this, it will open it up.' And people make copies of it." Although media reports and police officials have found that they can obtain these keys from an Internet site for $25 dollars ("Master Keys," 2003; Randles, 2005), none of the offenders interviewed here went to such lengths. They mainly obtained master keys from friends or acquaintances:

> In the gang we was in everybody had [a master key]. There were so many of us and everybody had one. You put it on your key chain and as soon as you see a Toyota you can break into it. Like an '89 or '90. You can start them up right there.
>
> [My drug dealer] gave us a master key for the '88 to '89 model Camry, the boxy ones before they changed the body style. He had a master key that opened all Camrys, like the door, the trunk, and the ignition. Like it was our car.

Some vehicle manufacturers only create a limited number of key signatures for a given model and thus one key can open numerous vehicles. By keeping spare keys, offenders could eventually find the right car. The uncertainty inherent in this type of theft requires offenders to invest a great deal of time and effort to be successful. Nevertheless, this did not inhibit the following offender:

> You can just find lost keys. And one day [when you] see a car for that key, go up in there and keep turning it and one eventually going to work. You just hold it and one day you going to run across a car with that key.... Like not everything you run across going to be something you going to get in, but when you do get in something, oh, yeah man, you all in.

Auto thieves can also modify keys to serve as master keys. They do this by shaving down an existing set of keys to create "close-cousin" keys (Fleming et al., 1994; Plouffe & Sampson, 2004):

> The last car theft I did was easy. I had the keys and everything. Because for some cars you can just take a key and scratch it up, you can open the car door with it and you can turn over the ignition for it. We call them master keys.

Makeshift master keys work best on cars with worn discs in the ignition (Geason & Wilson, 1990). Again, shaved keys worked particularly well on Japanese models:

> You can take any kind of key [but] if you got a pair of Honda keys or Toyota keys you take them and file them down make them real thin. They will fit in the slot but loosely. You move it up and down. When you move it up and down what it does is push the prongs up. When you turn it they fit into the hub and they stay in there.... You had to have a good rhythm to make them pop. When you get used to it you can get real good at it. It's like a natural skill that becomes a bad habit.

For these thieves, master keys become crime facilitators (Clarke, 1995; Ekblom & Tilley, 2000). Like carrying a weapon, possession of a master key makes crime an easy, attractive and viable solution to overcome a desperate situation.

There is little evidence from our offenders or elsewhere that master keys can be used with newer cars, especially those with electronic immobilizers. The availability and use of master keys are nevertheless a problem (McCoy, 2003). Although the possession of or use of a master key falls under the burglary tool statutes of most U.S. states, in recent years, several states (e.g., Maryland, Michigan, and New Jersey) revised their vehicle antitheft codes to address the illegal use of master keys to open or operate motor vehicles.

CONCLUSION

The primary method of preventing auto thefts in North America and Great Britain has been the reduction of opportunities for theft through target hardening. Vehicles are now much harder to steal than ever before. But these opportunity-reducing strategies have not completely stopped auto theft. Offenders have adapted to the changing opportunity structure of auto theft by seeking out more effective ways to appropriate cars (e.g., key theft). In an age in which mechanical theft is available to fewer people, the techniques of the practiced key thief likely will receive a more receptive audience. In fact, recent research on auto theft indicates that there has been a growth in the prevalence of auto thefts involving keys (Flood-Page & Taylor, 2003; Levesley et al., 2004).

There are two reasons to believe that the trend toward auto theft involving keys will continue. First, auto theft using keys is an ideal method for auto thieves, especially with respect to the effort, financial gain, and formal risk associated with committing the offence. For the mechanically unskilled offender, keys provide the only tool they need to accomplish their tasks. For others, keys are sought because using them can minimize damage done to the vehicle, which will ultimately increase the vehicle's resale value. And regardless of their motivation or skill level, car thieves attempt to avoid detection by creating an illusion of normalcy; that is, they try to present themselves as normal drivers in normal vehicles. This allows them to not call attention to themselves while driving and thereby increases their likelihood of avoiding arrest (Cherbonneau & Copes, 2005). Having a key in the vehicle's ignition and/or using a key to minimize damage upon entry and start-up go a long way in fostering this illusion (see also Light, Nee, & Ingham, 1993).

Second, in an attempt to deter would-be auto thieves, car manufacturers and car owners have begun to better secure vehicles (Hazelbaker, 1997). Car manufactures have strengthened built-in security designs to include fuel cut-offs, kill switches, electronic immobilizers, and tracking devices. What is more, these features are not limited to high-end makes and models. Many now come standard in several lines of mid-range vehicles. Although target hardening measures may prevent traditional auto thefts (those involving more mechanical techniques such as jimmying door locks or breaking ignitions), it likely will have little impact on the methods of theft described here. If anything, target-hardening measures have encouraged the use of keys to steal cars. Now that vehicle security has put auto theft beyond the reach of many would-be auto thieves, they are forced to use keys if they wish to be successful at auto theft.

When thinking about who steals vehicles with keys, it would be a mistake to assume that these offenders are all low-skilled, opportunistic joyriders. The accounts given by those we interviewed reveal that stealing cars with keys involves more than simply stumbling across random opportunities. Indeed, some car thieves go to great lengths to steal, find or manipulate keys from owners. The diligence involved in locating keys may explain why many anti-car theft programs that focus on "lock-your-car" campaigns are unsuccessful (Burrows & Heal, 1979; Riley & Mayhew, 1980). They may prevent thefts resulting from alert opportunism, but it is unlikely that those motivated to find keys will be deterred. These offenders will likely only search longer and harder or devise new strategies for obtaining keys (La Vigne, 1994).

Our results are consistent with those who have found that offenders exhibit at least some degree of rationality when offending. The rationality, although limited, shown by key thieves is important for crime prevention and suggests two things: (1) that these offenders are keenly aware of the perceived difficulty in stealing cars with advanced target hardening; and (2) in response to increased security, offenders are likely to engage in some sort of behavioral change, either through discouragement or displacement. Offenders may be discouraged outright and ultimately desist from auto theft, but this will not be the case for all. Offenders are known to adapt to the changing opportunity structure of crime (Bennett & Wright, 1984; Hesseling, 1994). Those who do not possess the necessary skills to overcome advanced target hardening can still be successful at auto theft simply by turning to more violent, cunning or simplistic methods of theft (Levesley et al., 2004; Topalli & Wright, 2004). If the outcomes of past attempts to improve vehicle security are any indication of future trends, then both target and tactical displacements are likely to occur.

The problem with many antitheft programs, as Clarke (1983, p. 246) notes, is that "Within easy reach of every house with a burglar alarm, or car with an antitheft device, are many others without such protection." In accordance with government mandates, new passenger cars manufactured in or imported to Britain after 1971 had to be fitted with steering-column locks. Although there was an immediate and substantial decline in the number of cars stolen that had column locks, the risk of theft to older cars where these devices were not made compulsory nearly doubled by 1973 (Mayhew, Clarke, Sturman, & Hough, 1976; Webb, 1994). The overall benefits of the recent legislation mandating electronic immobilizers to newer cars manufactured after 1997 may only exist until a sufficiently large proportion of cars are protected by immobilizers; meanwhile, target displacement to unprotected vehicles is likely to occur. In order to have enduring effects on the auto theft problem, older cars, whose security typically can be readily defeated, must also be protected. Such an approach to guard both old and newer cars was taken with the introduction of steering-column locks in West Germany in 1963 and this program has had long-lasting effects (Webb, 1994).

Inevitably, as the pool of unprotected targets shrinks, offenders must alter their *modus operandi* if they are to persist at auto theft. It is unlikely that immobilizers will decrease the enthusiasm joyriders have for cars or the black-market demand for stolen car parts. Thus, once immobilizers become commonplace, so, too, may be key theft. On the surface, this adaptation may be counter-intuitive, as offenders are more likely to displace in other ways (i.e., spatially, temporally, target) rather than tactically.

But the likelihood that offenders will adapt tactically depends largely on how familiar these methods or types of offending are to the offender (Eck, 1993). Many of the methods and techniques involved in acquiring keys entail committing a crime separate from that of the actual auto theft, such as burglary, robbery, or fraud. These additional crimes are certainly not unfamiliar to most street offenders and thus support the likelihood of tactical displacement.

The predicted rise in key thefts suggests that it may be timely to rethink the effectiveness of "lock-your-car" campaigns. Previous campaigns have done little to reduce the overall scale of auto theft. This is likely a result of the large pool of suitable targets that are available, even if the proportion of locked cars does increase (Clarke & Harris, 1992). But if increasing vehicle security has compelled offenders to rely on keys, then these campaigns may be more viable now.

Publicity campaigns should remind individual owners to make concerted efforts to protect keys in and away from the home. There are few places those motivated to search for keys would not go. Consequently, there are few places owners can be careless with their keys. Given this, vehicle owners who park on streets or in open areas should always lock their cars and protect their keys. When possible, cars should be parked in garages or other secure locations. In addition, spare keys are better protected in the home, no matter how well they are hidden within the vehicle. Levesley et al. (2004) found that keys obtained during burglaries accounted for the largest proportion of cars equipped with immobilization technology being stolen. Even in their homes, people should take steps to guard their keys. Using insights gained from residential burglars, we know that it is safer to hide valuables, including spare car keys, in places away from common searching areas. These safer areas include basements, utility rooms, guest rooms and children's bedrooms (Wright & Decker, 1994).

Also, vehicle owners should never leave their keys in the ignition when away from the vehicle. People are apt to do so when running quick errands or when they will be leaving their cars untended for only a couple of minutes. The consensus among those we interviewed is that these are ideal situations for theft because it only takes a moment to get in the car and drive away. Vehicle owners should always remove keys from the ignition, no matter how quick the errand is or how safe the area appears because, in the words of one offender, "you never know who's watching."

Little attention has been paid to thefts from commercial dealerships. Those who work at dealerships should be aware of the frauds that auto thieves use to obtain keys. They could then better guard the keys and the vehicles on their lots. When obtaining keys from car lots, thieves used two primary approaches: burglary or fraud. One group burglarized dealerships for the sole purpose of acquiring keys and ransacked the building until a set was found. In other cases, offenders relied on inside information or prior knowledge to quickly locate keys. Some thieves looked for these "windows of vulnerability" (Walsh, 1986) during the day while acting like normal customers.

Safeguarding spare car keys is vital to thwarting these types of key theft. Keys should be stored away from the view of customers and secured in a safe or lock box at night.

The second strategy used at dealerships was endorsed by more shrewd offenders. Here, they approached salespeople during the day under the guise of being a buyer and purloined keys by swapping the real keys for fake ones or by making copies of the keys. These thieves returned after regular business hours to steal the car. Since such offenders may be hard to discern from legitimate buyers, dealerships should instruct employees to never let customers handle the keys. When allowing customers to test-drive cars, the salesman should insert and remove the key from the ignition. This would at least deter those who make a last-minute swap before handing the keys to the dealer. In cases in which this cannot be done, the following offenders' comments on prevention are instructive:

> The dealerships can do better than they do. As far as the salesmen getting keys switched on him, the salesmen should always be cautious to go back and check after each time somebody touches that key, regardless of how honest this person looks. Regardless.

In addition, records should be kept on customers who test-drive cars to assist police if a theft occurs. Records should include customers' general identification information (e.g., name, date of birth, driver's license number, address, and telephone number) and the vehicle identification numbers for the vehicles. Taking down this information should be made mandatory for all customers who test-drive cars.

Many believe that car crime can be stamped out if car manufactures made security and design their highest priority (Karmen, 1981). Car manufactures have made great strides in recent years toward this end. However, to place sole responsibility in the hands of manufacturers implies that offenders possess limited skills and predominately rely on found opportunities to be successful at crime. Our results do not fully support this implication. Owners must make efforts to protect their keys and not solely rely on built-in security measures. Just as police cannot be expected to prevent all crime, nor can car manufactures be expected to be the sole bearer of responsibility in this regard. Those who control access to keys are in the best positions to successfully reduce opportunities for key thefts and, thus, the overall scale of the auto theft problem.

Blocking opportunities for key theft may diffuse prevention benefits beyond the criminal event. Many scholars maintain that "opportunity makes the thief" (Felson & Clarke, 1998). This was true of the auto thieves we spoke with. Many of their first auto thefts were sparked by easy opportunities created by careless car owners. Even the criminal careers of the most prolific offenders began with such opportunities. Once an appetite is whetted, thieves can become remarkably innovative in their theft patterns and it may be more difficult to discourage them. It is certainly intriguing that if such opportunities never existed, these offenders' careers in auto theft may have been much different Thus, when car owners protect their keys, they may be preventing more than just the theft of their own vehicles.

References

Anderson, E. (1999). *Code of the street: Decency, violence, and the moral life of the inner city.* New York: W. W. Norton.

Beekman, M. E. (1994). Auto theft: Countering violent trends. In A. R. Roberts (Ed.), *Critical issues in crime and justice* (pp. 145–154). Thousand Oaks, CA: Sage.

Bennett, T., & Wright, R. (1984). *Burglars on burglary: Prevention and the offender.* Brookfield, VT: Gower.

Brantingham, P., & Brantingham, P. (1978). A theoretical model of crime site selection. In M. D. Krohn & R. L. Akers (Eds.), *Crime, law and sanctions* (pp. 105–118). Beverly Hills, CA: Sage.

Brickell, D., & Cole, L. (1975). *Vehicle theft investigation.* Santa Cruz, CA: Davis.

Brill, H. (1982, Winter). Auto theft and the role of big business. *Crime and Social Justice,* 62–68.

Burrows, J., & Heal, K. (1979). *Crime prevention and the police* (Home Office Research Study 55). London: Home Office.

Cherbonneau, M., & Copes, H. (2003). Media construction of carjacking: A content analysis of newspaper articles from 1993–2002. *Journal of Crime and Justice, 26,* 1–21.

Cherbonneau, M., & Copes, H. (2005). Drive it like you stole it: Auto theft and the illusion of normalcy. *British Journal of Criminology, 46,* 193–211.

Cherbonneau, M., Copes, H., & Forsyth, C. J. (2006, March). *Rock rentals: The social organization and interpersonal dynamics of crack for cars transactions.* Paper presented at the annual meeting of the Southern Sociological Society, New Orleans, LA.

Clarke, R. V. (1983). Situational crime prevention: Its theoretical basis and practical scope. In M. Tonry & N. Morris (Eds.), *Crime and justice: A review of research* (Vol. 4, pp. 225–256). Chicago: University of Chicago Press.

Clarke, R. V. (1995). Situational crime prevention. In M. Tonry & D. Farrington (Eds.), *Crime and justice: A review of research* (Vol. 19, pp. 91–150). Chicago: University of Chicago Press.

Clarke, R. V. (1997). Introduction. In R. V. Clarke (Ed.), *Situational crime prevention: Successful case studies* (2nd ed., pp. 2–43). Guilderland, NY: Harrow and Heston.

Clarke, R. V., & Harris, P. (1992). Auto theft and its prevention. In M. Tonry (Ed.), *Crime and justice: An annual review of research* (Vol. 16, pp. 1–54). Chicago: University of Chicago Press.

Copes, H. (2003a). Streetlife and the rewards of auto theft. *Deviant Behavior, 24,* 309–332.

Copes, H. (2003b). Societal attachments, offending frequency, and techniques of neutralization. *Deviant Behavior, 24,* 101–127.

Decker, S. (2005). *Using offender interviews to inform police problem solving: Problem-Solving Tools Series, Guide No. 3.* Washington, DC: U.S. Department of Justice.

Dodd, T., Nicholas, S., Povey, D., & Walker, A. (2004). *Crime in England and Wales 2003/2004: Supplementary volume* (Home Office Statistical Bulletin 10/04). London: Home Office.

Eck, J. E. (1993). The threat of crime displacement. *Criminal Justice Abstracts, 25,* 527–546.

Ekblom, P., & Tilley, N. (2000). Going equipped: Criminology, situational crime prevention and the resourceful offender. *British Journal of Criminology, 40,* 376–390.

Federal Bureau of Investigation, Department of Justice. (2004). *Uniform crime report: Crime in the United States.* Washington, DC: U.S. Government Printing Office.

Felson, M., & Clarke, R. V. (1998). *Opportunity makes the thief: Practical theory for crime prevention* (Police Research Series Paper 98). London: Home Office.

Field, S. (1993). Crime prevention and the costs of auto theft an economic analysis. In R. V. Clarke (Ed.), *Crime prevention studies* (Vol. 1, pp. 69–91). Monsey, NY: Criminal Justice Press.

Fleming, Z., Brantingham, P., & Brantingham, P. (1994). Exploring auto theft in British Columbia. In R. V. Clarke (Ed.), *Crime prevention studies* (Vol. 3, pp. 47–90). Monsey, NY: Criminal Justice Press.

Flood-Page, C., & Taylor, J. (2003). *Crime in England and Wales 2001/2002: Supplementary Volume* (Home Office Statistical Bulletin 1/03). London: Home Office.

Geason, S., & Wilson, P. R. (1990). *Preventing car theft and crime in car parks.* Canberra: Australian Institute of Criminology.

Hazelbaker, K. (1997). Insurance industry analyses and the prevention of motor vehicle theft. In M. Felson & R. Clarke (Eds.), *Business and crime prevention* (pp. 283–293). Monsey, NY: Criminal Justice Press.

Hesseling, R. (1994). Displacement: A review of the empirical literature. In R. V. Clarke (Ed.), *Crime prevention studies* (Vol. 3, pp. 197–230). Monsey, NY: Criminal Justice Press.

Hough, M., & Mayhew, P. (1985). *Taking account of crime: Key findings from the British Crime Survey* (Home Office Research Study 85). London: Home Office.

Inciardi, J. (1975). *Careers in crime.* Chicago: Rand McNally.

Jacobs, B. A., Topalli, V., & Wright, R. (2003). Carjacking, streetlife and offender motivation. *British Journal of Criminology, 43,* 673–688.

Karmen, A. A. (1981). Auto theft and corporate irresponsibility. *Contemporary Crisis, 5,* 83–91.

Katz, J. (1988). *Seductions of crime.* New York: Basic Books.

Kinshott, G. (2001). *Vehicle related thefts: Practice messages for the British Crime Survey* (Briefing Note 6/01). London: Home Office.

La Vigne, N. G. (1994). Rational choice and inmate disputes over phone use on Rikers Island. In R. V. Clarke (Ed.), *Crime prevention studies* (Vol. 3, pp. 109–125). Monsey, NY: Criminal Justice Press.

Levesley, T., Braun, G., Wilkinson, M., & Powell, C. (2004). *Emerging methods of car theft: Theft of keys* (Findings 239). London: Home Office.

Light, R., Nee, C., & Ingham, H. (1993). *Car theft: The offender's perspective* (Home Office Research Study 130). London: Home Office.

Maryland Vehicle Theft Prevention Council. (2003). *2002 annual report.* Cumberland, MD: Author.

Master keys. (2003). Retrieved May 16, 2005, from www.fox5dc.com/ezpost/data/1256.shtml

Mayhew, P., Clarke, R. V., Sturman, A., & Hough, J. M. (1976). *Crime as opportunity* (Home Office Research Study 34). London: Home Office.

McCoy, C. R. (2003, September 28). A potent new tool for auto thieves. *Philadelphia Inquirer,* pp. B1.

Morrison, P. (1991). Motor vehicle theft. *Juristat Service Bulletin, 11*(2).

Ogrodnik, L., & Paiement, R. (1992). Motor vehicle theft. *Jurists Service Bulletin, 12*(12).

Plouffe, N., & Sampson, R. (2004). Auto theft and theft from autos in parking lots in Chula Vista, CA: Crime analysis for local and regional action. In M. G. Maxfield & R. V. Clarke (Eds.), *Crime prevention studies* (Vol. 17, pp. 147–171). Monsey, NY: Criminal Justice Press.

Randles, T. (2005). *Can someone buy keys to steal your car?* Retrieved May 16, 2005, from www.wtkr.com/global/story.asp?s=3334264&clienttype=printable

Rapp, B. (1989). *Vehicle theft investigation: A complete handbook.* Port Townsend, WA: Loompanics Unlimited.

Rengert, G., & Wasilchick, J. (1989). *Space, time and crime: Ethnographic insights into residential burglary.* Final Report to the National Institute of Justice, U.S. Department of Justice, Washington, DC.

Riley, D., & Mayhew, P. (1980). *Crime prevention publicity: An assessment* (Home Office Research Study 63). London: Home Office.

Sandvik, E. (1996). *The role of technology in reducing auto theft.* Tallahassee: Florida Department of Law Enforcement.

Shover, N. (1996). *Great pretenders: Pursuits and careers of persistent thieves.* Boulder, CO: Westview.

Southall, D., & Ekblom, P. (1985). *Designing for car security: Towards a crime free car* (Crime Prevention Unit Series Paper 4). London: Home Office.

Sutherland, E. (1937). *The professional thief.* Chicago: University of Chicago Press.

Topalli, V. (2005). Criminal expertise and offender decision-making: An experimental analysis of how offenders and non-offenders differentially perceive social stimuli. *British Journal of Criminology, 45,* 269–295.

Topalli, V., & Wright, R. (2004). Dubs and dees, beats and rims: Carjackers and urban violence. In D. Dabney (Ed.), *Crime types: A text reader* (pp. 149–169). Belmont, CA: Wadsworth.

Wallace, M. (2003). Motor vehicle theft in Canada—2001. *Juristat Service Bulletin,* 23(1).

Walsh, D. (1986). Victim selection procedures among economic criminals: The rational choice perspective. In D. B. Cornish & R. V. Clarke (Eds.), *The reasoning criminal: Rational choice perspectives on offending* (pp. 39–52). New York: Springer-Verlag.

Webb, B. (1994). Steering column locks and motor vehicle theft: Evaluations from three countries. In R. V. Clarke (Ed.), *Crime prevention studies* (Vol. 2, pp. 71–89). Monsey, NY: Criminal Justice Press.

Webb, B., & Laycock, G. (1992). *Tackling car crime: The nature and extent of the problem* (Home Office Research Study 32). London: Home Office.

Welsh, E. (2002). Dealing with data: Using NVivo in the qualitative data analysis process. *Qualitative Social Research, 3*(2). Retrieved January 8, 2004, from www.qualitative-research.net/fqs/fqs-eng.htm

Wright, R., & Decker, S. (1994). *Burglars on the job: Street life and residential break-ins.* Boston: Northeastern University Press.

Wright, R., Logie, R., & Decker, S. (1995). Criminal expertise and offender decision-making: An experimental study of the target selection process in residential burglary. *Journal of Research in Crime and Delinquency, 32,* 39–53.

5

The Five-Finger Discount: An Analysis of Motivations for Shoplifting

Paul Cromwell, Lee Parker, and Shawna Mobley

S *o, why study shoplifting? It is perhaps the most commonly committed crime. It is widely distributed in the population and appears to cross racial, ethnic, gender, and class lines. Studies have shown that 1 in every 10–15 shoppers shoplifts (Lo, 1994; Russell, 1973; Turner & Cashdan, 1988). The Federal Bureau of Investigation estimates that shoplifting accounts for approximately 15% of all larcenies (Freeh, 1996). According to the Monitoring the Future data, shoplifting is the most prevalent and most frequent crime among high school seniors over time, with over 30% of respondents reporting having taken something from a store without paying on one or more occasions (Johnston, O'Malley, & O'Malley, 1984–1995). And a study by Ellen Nimick (1990) identified shoplifting as the most common offense for which youth under the age of 15 are referred to juvenile court. Estimates of losses attributable to shoplifting range from $12 to $30 billion annually (Griffin, 1988; Klemke, 1992; Nimick, 1990). Although shoplifting is considered by most to be a relatively minor offense, it is a violation of the law, and when the stolen items exceed a certain value, it is a felony. Petty offenses, although not as dramatic as more serious ones, raise the same questions of explanation and policy as do more serious offenses. The purpose of this study was to analyze the various motives that underlie shoplifting behavior and to suggest prevention strategies based on the types of shoplifters identified and the motives that drive their behavior. The study is based on data obtained over a 9-year period in three states. In summary, shoplifting data were gathered from 320 persons who admitted to one or more shoplifting incidents and more extensive interviews were conducted with 115 of those respondents. The respondents ranged from youthful first offenders to professionals who made the bulk of their living from shoplifting.*

The study found that shoplifting is not simple behavior with a simple causal dynamic. Although shoplifters appeared to make conscious decisions to shoplift and did usually attend to considerations of risk and gain in their decision calculus, many reported that they stole for different reasons at different times. There were few individuals who employed a single, stable criminal calculus. Although most stole for economic reasons, they also occasionally chose to steal to satisfy some emotional need, and an otherwise rational offender might on occasion steal some item for which he or she had no need or purpose. Although the findings support a rational choice model of offending, some noted cases of shoplifting with apparent nonrational motives.

Shoplifting may be the one crime that most people have committed at one time or another in their lives, and yet it is a relatively unstudied crime. There have been few large-scale studies yielding systematically collected data. Prior research on this subject tends to focus on small convenience or student populations (Katz, 1988; Moore, 1983; Turner & Cashdan, 1988), data gathered from criminal justice or store security records (Cameron, 1964; Moore, 1984; Robin, 1963), special populations, such as the elderly (Feinburg, 1984), juveniles (Hindelang, Hirschi, & Weis, 1981; Klemke, 1982; Osgood, O'Malley, Bachman, & Johnston, 1989), or psychiatric patients (Arboleda-Florez, Durie, & Costello, 1977), or involve a few questions about shoplifting as part of a larger more general survey (Johnston et al., 1984–1995). And, although there have been some large-scale studies (e.g. Fear, 1974; Griffin, 1970, 1971; Won & Yamamoto, 1968), most of these have been conducted with apprehended shoplifters and have concentrated primarily on collecting demographic data on the subjects.

There are several apparent reasons for the lack of interest on the part of scholars and the public. First, most shoplifting is a minor, nonviolent offense. It does not engender public outrage or fear. It is seldom the focus of legislative or media investigations. In fact, most studies place shoplifting near the bottom of the seriousness scale, along with such offenses as painting graffiti and trespassing (Warr, 1989). In her classic study, Mary Cameron (1964) wrote:

> Most people have been tempted to steal from stores, and many have been guilty (at least as children) of "snitching" an item or two from counter tops. With merchandise so attractively displayed in department stores and supermarkets, and much of it apparently there for the taking, one may ask why everyone isn't a thief. (p. xi)

Lloyd Klemke (1992) explains that shoplifting does not result in "eye-catching 'body counts' or astronomical dollar losses generated by individual shoplifters" (p. 5). He argues:

> Without sensational evidence of cataclysmic harm to foster and fuel public concern, most people consider shoplifting to be an interesting but not a very serious type of crime. (p. 6)

Second, shoplifters do not conform to most people's perception of what a criminal is like. Instead, shoplifters tend to be demographically similar to the "average person." In a large-scale study of nondelinquents, Klemke (1982) reported that as many as 63% had shoplifted at some point in their lives. Students, housewives, business and professional persons, as well as professional thieves constitute the population of shoplifters. Loss prevention experts routinely counsel retail merchants that there is no "profile" of a potential shoplifter. Klemke (1992) contends, "... adult middle-class female shoplifters continue to be a significant segment of the contemporary shoplifting population" (p. 24). Turner and Cashdan (1988) conclude, "While clearly a criminal activity, shoplifting borders on what might be considered a 'folk crime.'"

Another reason for the relative lack of interest in shoplifting is the public's attitude toward the "victim." Although most people understand that the costs of shoplifting are passed on to the consumer through higher prices, few people view a large, impersonal department store or other commercial establishment with much sympathy. Shoplifters themselves frequently characterize their crimes as "victimless," or, the victim as deserving it.

SO, WHY STUDY SHOPLIFTING?

It is for many of these same reasons that shoplifting should be more widely and systematically examined. It is perhaps the most commonly committed crime. It is widely distributed in the population and appears to cross racial, ethnic, gender, and class lines. Studies have shown that 1 in every 10–15 shoppers shoplifts (Lo, 1994; Russell, 1973; Turner & Cashdan, 1988). The Federal Bureau of Investigation estimates that shoplifting accounts for approximately 15% of all larcenies (Freeh, 1996). According to the *Monitoring the Future* data, shoplifting is the most prevalent and most frequent crime among high-school seniors over time, with over 30% of respondents reporting having taken something from a store without paying on one or more occasions (Johnston et al., 1984–1995). And a study by Ellen Nimick (1990) identified shoplifting as the most common offense for which youth under the age of 15 are referred to juvenile court. Estimates of losses attributable to shoplifting range from $12 to $30 billion annually (Griffin, 1988; Klemke, 1992; Nimick, 1990).

Although shoplifting is considered by most to be a relatively minor offense, it is a violation of the law, and when the stolen items exceed a certain value, it is a felony. Petty offenses, although not as dramatic as more serious ones, raise the same questions of explanation and policy as do more serious offenses.

The very fact that shoplifting is considered to be a "folk crime" enables us to see some things about the origin and motivation for crime that more serious offenses such as burglary and robbery may not. And explaining why people shoplift may help explain why most of us at some time or another engage in deviant behavior and why some persist and some do not.

If shoplifting is as prevalent as studies have shown and the losses attributed to shoplifting as great as estimates indicate, this criminal activity has major economic and social consequences and should be more widely and systematically studied.

PURPOSE OF THIS STUDY

The purpose of this study is to analyze the various motives that underlie shoplifting behavior and to suggest prevention policy strategies based on the types of shoplifters identified and the motives which drive their behavior.

CONCEPTUAL FRAMEWORK

Rational Choice Theory

This research focuses on the factors that motivate an offender to commit a crime—in this case, to shoplift. Although some studies have attributed shoplifting to psychological maladjustments, to compulsion, or to other forces beyond the conscious control of the offender (Arboleda-Florez et al., 1977; Beck & McEntyre, 1977; Solomon & Ray, 1984), most research has noted that shoplifters often employ decision strategies involving calculation of the risks and gains associated with committing the offense. This rational choice perspective is predicated on the assumption that individuals choose to commit crimes. It predicts that individuals will evaluate alternative courses of action, weigh the possible rewards against the costs and risks, and choose the action that maximizes their gain. The benefits of a criminal action are the net rewards of crime and include not only the material gains but also intangible benefits such as emotional satisfaction. The individual may receive immense satisfaction from the excitement of crime, from the independent lifestyle afforded by crime, or from outwitting the authorities. The risks or costs of crime are those associated with the formal punishment should the individual be discovered, apprehended, and convicted, as well as psychological or social costs, such as pangs of conscience, social disapproval, marital and family discord, or loss of self-esteem (Vold & Bernard, 1986).

Rational choice theory is a theory of crime, not a theory of criminality. It assumes a general "readiness" for crime, that is, someone who has sufficient criminal motivation to act on a criminal opportunity or to seek out an opportunity to commit a crime (Brantingham & Brantingham, 1991). Criminal "readiness" is not constant in any individual. It varies over time and space according to any individual's background, circumstances, and opportunity structure. On one occasion, shoplifting might be a product of the individual's mood and perceptions brought on by drugs or alcohol, and by the need for money on another (Brantingham & Brantingham, 1993).

The degree of rationality that can be attributed to offenders in planning and executing their crimes and how rationality is related to crime prevention measures has been a central issue of debate (Clarke & Cornish, 1986; Cook, 1989). In the classical version of rational choice, the individual gathers information relevant to risk and gain and combines this information in making a reasoned decision. There is little reason to believe that this "strict" form of rationality is correct. Offenders seldom have all the information regarding risk and gain and have little or no accurate knowledge of the probabilities of reward or punishment associated with the act. However, in order for an act to be rational, it is not necessary that it be carefully preconceived and planned. Behavioral decision making theorists (Kahneman, Slovic, & Tversky, 1982; March, 1994; Newell & Simon, 1972; Slovic et al., 1977) have shown that individuals do not behave consistently with normative rationality; rather, they take shortcuts or make simplifications that are reasonable but may not produce maximized outcomes (Carroll & Weaver, 1986). This view of rationality does not require deliberate weighing of carefully considered alternatives and consequences. It is sufficient that decision makers choose between alternatives based upon their immediate perception of the risks and gains involved. The decision does not have to be the best possible under the circumstances, nor does it have to be based on an accurate assessment of the situation. And, as Wilson and Herrnstein (1985) conclude, the value of any reward or punishment associated with a criminal action is always uncertain. It is enough that decisions are perceived to be optimal.

The concept of "limited rationality" recognizes the limited capacity and willingness of most persons to acquire and process information from more than one input or source simultaneously. Clarke and Cornish (1986) concluded that people usually pay attention to only some of the facts or sources at their disposal, employing short cuts or rules of thumb to speed the decision process. These rules of thumb are analogous to Cook's (1989) concept of "standing decisions" which negate the need to carefully weigh all the alternatives and consequences before making a decision in many cases. A standing decision may simply be a decision made beforehand to take advantage of certain types of criminal opportunities or to avoid others. None of this, however, implies irrationality. Rational choice theories need only presume that some minimal degree of planning and foresight occurs (Hirschi, 1986).

Many prior studies have noted a rational element in the motivations of shoplifters. Cameron (1964) classified shoplifters into two classes: *boosters*, who "steal merchandise as one way of making a living," and *snitches*, described as "deliberate thieves who manifest intent to steal by preparation beforehand and who carry out their crimes with system and method" (pp. 58–59). She noted that they are "not impulsive, erratic individuals who are suddenly 'taken' with an uncontrollable urge for a pretty bauble" (p. 59). She concluded that there may be individuals who act impulsively; however, their numbers are few and their impact on the justice system or on business institutions is minimal.

Moore (1983) also found little evidence that pathology or maladjustment were significant contributing factors in shoplifting. He found no meaningful differences in the MMPI between shoplifters and nonshoplifters. Instead, he found that college students experience psychological satisfaction from acquiring personally attractive goods and saving money for other purposes. Kraut (1976) also argued that the motive for most shoplifting was the acquisition of goods at minimum cost. He claimed that the decision to shoplift is "an inverse function of the perceived risks associated with stealing" (Kraut, 1976, p. 365).

Turner and Cashdan (1988) asked college students to provide information about the reasons their classmates and friends shoplifted. It was assumed that their responses would function as a projective self-report, in effect, revealing information about the respondents' real or potential motives for shoplifting. They found that poverty, "self-indulgence," and some variant of "thrill," "risk," "fun," or "challenge" were the most prevalent motives reported. Those who reported poverty (mentioned by 64% of the subjects) as a motive shoplifted to obtain items they needed but could not afford to buy. Self-indulgence (mentioned by 40% of the respondents) was defined as stealing items that were desired, but not necessarily needed. Sixty-six percent of the respondents listed "excitement," "thrill," "challenge," or "fun" as a primary motive for their illegal behavior.

Katz (1988), in research with a college student population, concluded that "various property crimes share an appeal to young people, independent of the material gain or esteem from peers" (p. 52). He found that such offenses as vandalism, joyriding, and shoplifting are "all sneaky crimes that frequently thrill their practioneers" (p. 53).

Each of these studies—whether attributing shoplifting to the desire to obtain material goods at minimal cost or to attain some psychosocial reward (thrill, excitement, fun, self-indulgence, etc.)—involves a choice by the offender based on (at least minimally) his or her perceptions of the risks and gains associated with the act.

RESULTS

The subjects were asked to explain the primary motivation for their shoplifting. They were asked, "Why do you shoplift?" They were allowed to list as many reasons as they believed applied to them, but were asked to be specific about the "main reason you shoplift." Many subjects reported more than one motive for their behavior. Table 5.1 illustrates the range of responses reported by the study subjects:

Table 5.1 Reported Motivations for Shoplifting

Primary Motivation	Percent	
1. Wanted item but did not want to pay for it	82	25.6
2. Peer pressure	49	15.3
3. Steal for a living	46	14.4
4. Wanted the item but could not afford it	41	12.8
5. I don't know why. It was an impulse thing	37	11.6
6. I was under the influence of drugs or alcohol	17	5.3
7. I enjoy the thrill/rush/danger involved	15	4.7
8. I was under a lot of stress	13	4.1
9. I can't help myself. It's compulsive	10	3.1
10. Other	10	3.1

It was difficult to determine the *primary* motivation driving the shoplifting activity for most of the informants, as they shoplifted for different reasons at different times. Many reported multiple reasons for single shoplifting events. For example, one Wichita subject stated, "I wanted it. It's kind of a rush to take things, and I was mad at my mother at the time." When a subject expressed difficulty listing a primary motivation, the first motivation mentioned was considered primary. In the example above, the primary motive was recorded as "I wanted it." The subject was then asked if he had the money to pay for the item. If he or she said "yes," the motive was classified as "I wanted the item but did not want to pay for it." If he or she said "no," the motive was classified as "I wanted the item but could not afford to pay for it."

A Miami student reported, "My girlfriend dared me to do it. It was real exciting—I was pumped." In this case, the motive was recorded as "peer pressure."

This finding of within-individual variation in motivation may be important, as most of the literature in criminal decision making suggests a single, stable criminal calculus. However, it appears that many of the subjects in this study shoplifted for economic gain on some occasions and to satisfy some psychosocial need on others. Occasionally, the two motives were intertwined in a single offense.

In the following section each of the identified motives for shoplifting and representative statements by study subjects are presented.

"I Wanted the Item(s) but Didn't Want to Pay for It"

Eighty-two subjects listed this motive as primary. These shoplifters admitted to having the money to pay for the items they stole, but preferred to steal them anyway. Over 60% (64.6%) of males and only 47.5% of females reported this motivation as their primary reason for shoplifting. Many of these subjects also reported stealing for the thrill or rush, by impulse, or for some other "noneconomic" reason on occasion. White respondents (42.6%) were more likely than African American respondents (24.4%) or Hispanics (32.9%) to report this motivation. Some examples of their responses include:

I did it because I didn't want to pay for anything. I've got better things to do with my money. (Wichita: 18-year-old white male)

I have a long shoplifting history. There are a lot of expensive things and I want them. (Miami student: 22-year-old white female)

I got two kids I gotta raise and I don't get no help from that shit of an ex-husband of mine. They like nice things and it makes me feel good seeing them dressed nice to go to school. It ain't hard to take stuff. I just take what I want, anytime I want it. I've got three televisions and three VCRs in my house. I took 'em all from Wal Mart....I once went a whole year without washing clothes. Just threw them in the basement when they was dirty and "went shopping" for some more. (Wichita: 29-year-old African American female)

I've got better things to spend my money on. Some things you can't lift—movie tickets, a Big Mac, gas, stuff like that—everything that I can lift, I do. (Miami student: 23-year-old African American male)

"It Was Peer Pressure"

Forty-nine (49) subjects reported peer pressure as the primary motivation for their shoplifting. Peer pressure—the second most cited motive in the present study—may be a highly rational motive for behavior as perceived by the offender. Approval from peers is one of the most powerful motivators of youthful behavior. Robert Agnew writes, "This pressure might be direct, with respondents reporting that their friends explicitly encouraged them to commit the delinquent act. This pressure might also be indirect, with respondents stating that they were trying to impress their friends or simply act in conformity with them" (Agnew, 1990, p. 279).

Two-thirds of all the subjects reported shoplifting because of peer influences at one time or another in their life. However, only those subjects who were in the early stages of a shoplifting career or those who had shoplifted only a few times reported peer influence as the primary motivation for their current behavior. White respondents were three to four times more likely to report peer pressure as their main motive. Males were somewhat more likely than females to report peer pressure as a motive for their behavior. Many of the professional thieves reported shoplifting as a result of peer influence, but they seemed to be referring to their early experiences. Twenty-two Miami students (15 male and 7 female) and 27 Wichita informants (20 male and 7 female) listed peer influence as the primary motivation of their behavior.

> My mom is a shoplifter. Both my sisters do it. I got it from them. My oldest sister said, "Don't be stupid. Take what you want." (Wichita: 20-year-old African American female)
>
> I started out learning from my cousins. They always stole candy from the [neighborhood store]. They let me go with them but at first I just was the lookout—watching if the manager was looking. If he looked at them, I dropped a can or a box on the floor and he looked at me and they knew he was watching. (Wichita: 38-year-old Hispanic male)
>
> My mother taught me. Ever since I was a baby she used me to hide stuff. She'd push me in my stroller and put things under my blanket. After I got older she would give me stuff to walk out of the store with. Nobody paid any attention to a little kid. (Wichita: 25-year-old white female)
>
> I never stole anything in my life until I changed schools in the seventh grade. These girls had a sorority and to get in you had to shoplift something. They would tell you what to take.... I had to get a pair of earrings from a Woolworth store. Red ones. It was too easy. I still do it sometimes. (Miami student: 22-year-old white female)

In some cases, need or greed supplied the primary motive, but peer pressure facilitated the actual offense. One Wichita subject stated:

> I had been wanting this CD and my friend started egging me on to steal it. I was afraid I'd get caught and stuff, but he just kept bugging me about it and finally I went in the store and put in down my pants and just walked out. It set

off the alarm by the door and I just ran out. Now I can't ever go back in there 'cause they know what I look like. (Wichita: 19-year-old female)

"I Steal for a Living"

These subjects shoplifted for resale and much of their income was derived from shoplifting. Most, but not all, were or had been drug addicts with daily habits which ranged from $50 to $500. They engaged in a range of legal and illegal activities to support their habits. Most preferred shoplifting to other criminal activity because of the ease of committing the crime and the minimal sanctions associated with apprehension and conviction. Twenty of the Texas subjects (18 males and 2 females), 22 of the Miami drug clinic informants (21 males and 1 female), and 4 of the Wichita subjects (1 male and 3 females) were so categorized. In every case, these subjects looked on their shoplifting as "work." One subject in Wichita told the interviewer, "I'm a self-employed thief." Typical responses included:

I changed from doing houses [burglary] to boosting cause it was getting too hot for me in Odessa. I couldn't go out of the house without being dragged down for some burglary I didn't commit. I've been down to TDC [Texas Department of Corrections] two times already and I could get the "bitch" next time [life imprisonment as a habitual criminal] so I went to boosting. It's a misdemeanor. Oughta have changed years ago. Boosting is easy and safer. [Y]ou steal a TV from a house and maybe you get $50 for it. I got a 19-inch Magnavox at Walmart last week and sold it for half the sticker price. (Texas: 47-year-old Hispanic male)

I make more than you do [referring to the writer] just stealing from stores. Yesterday I rolled up six silk dresses inside my shirt and walked out of Dillards [an upscale department store in Ft. Lauderdale]. They was worth over $1000 and I sold 'em for $300. That was 30 minutes' work. (Miami drug clinic: 39-year-old white female)

I'm the Prince of Thieves. Everybody in my family are crooks. My father is a shoplifter. My mother is a shoplifter. My sister is a shoplifter. I'm sure my son will probably be a shoplifter, too. I can't imagine making a living any other way. I'm proud of what I do and I'm proud that I've only been caught once—after over 20 years. (Wichita: 40-year-old white male)

I don't boost every day. Sometimes not even every week. My girlfriend and I go out whenever we need some money and spend the whole day. We fill up big garbage bags full of stuff—clothes mostly. We make enough to live good for a week, two weeks. (Wichita: 28-year-old African American female)

I gotta have $200 every day—day in and day out. I gotta boost a $1000, $1500 worth to get it. I just do what I gotta do....Do I feel bad about what I do? Not really. If I wasn't boosting, I'd be robbing people and maybe somebody would get hurt or killed. (Miami drug addict: 28-year-old white male)

Taking stuff from stores is a lot easier than robbing people or burglary. Nobody ever shoots boosters. Even if I get caught, nothing much gonna happen. Probation—a few days in county. It's like it's my job. (Texas drug addict: 35-year-old African American female)

"I Wanted the Item(s) and Could Not Afford It"

Another common response to the motivation question was "I wanted [the item] and didn't have enough money, so I lifted it." This motivation was reported much more often by women (80%) than by men. Some of the women who reported this motivation were single parents with few financial resources. However, the majority simply coveted some item they could not then afford to buy and took it. In many cases, this was one of the motivations for their first shoplifting experience. Five Miami student respondents (0 males and 5 females) and 36 Wichita subjects (8 males and 28 females) listed this as their primary motive for shoplifting. Typical responses included:

I want nice things for my family but I can't afford to buy them. My husband and kids have the best wardrobe in town. My husband doesn't know, but I don't know how he doesn't. Where does he think all this stuff comes from? He never asks. Course, he doesn't know how much anything costs. (Wichita: 39-year-old white female)

My mom wouldn't buy me a pair of $30 jeans…so I took 'em. (Wichita: 18-year-old African American female)

I stole a wallet from Sears for my boyfriend. I didn't have the money so I took it. After that I became quite the klepto. If I saw something I wanted, I took it…it's hard to raise three children without help and my ex hasn't paid a cent of child support.…I was willing to steal to give them things they needed. It's hard to see something you want and can't have it. (Wichita: 33-year-old white female)

The first time I ever lifted anything, there was this CD I wanted real bad. I didn't have any money and me and my friend decided to steal it. We were scared to death, but it was easy. I've probably stolen $10,000 worth of stuff since. (Miami student: 22-year-old white female)

"I Don't Know Why. It Was Just an Impulse"

A few subjects expressed the belief that their acts were impulsive and done without thought or planning. Nine Miami college students (four males and five females) and 28 Wichita subjects (10 males and 18 females) reported impulse as the primary motive for their shoplifting. Over one-half of all the subjects reported impulse as one of the motives for their first shoplifting experiences. Typical responses included:

I want to say "spur of the moment." It was a watch and I just wanted that watch then. The amazing thing was that I had the money in my pocket to pay for it. I wish I could say that I had been drinking, but I can't. (Wichita: 33-year-old African American male)

It was sort of an impulse. I didn't plan to do it. I'm really embarrassed by all this. (Wichita: 22-year-old white female)

I didn't really plan on it. It just kinda happened. I've never stolen anything before. (Wichita student: 19-year-old white male)

I've been doing it since I was in elementary school. [I] see something in a store and even if I don't need it, I just take it. I don't know why. I'm a klepto. (Miami student: 18-year-old Hispanic female)

I've done this since I was eight. To me it comes natural. I don't know why I do it. I've done it so many times that I don't think about it. (Wichita: 18-year-old white male)

I took a shirt at K-Mart. I don't understand why I did it. I have friends who take things, but I never did. I liked this shirt and on the spur of the moment I stuffed it in my purse. (Wichita: 19-year-old white female)

"I Was Under the Influence of Drugs or Alcohol"

Eleven of the subjects in the Wichita diversion sample (seven males and four females) and six in the Miami student sample (three males and three females) reported shoplifting only when intoxicated or under the influence of drugs. Many stated that they never stole when sober and blamed the disinhibition of alcohol or drug use for their crimes. In fact, in most cases, they reported taking minor items such as beer, cigarettes, or candy. Subjects reported:

I picked up a pack of cigarettes and put them into my pocket. I forgot I had them there. I'd been drinking most of the afternoon. (Wichita: 30-year-old white male)

Drinking causes it. I should stop altogether. Makes me impulsive. That's when I take things. Usually I'm too drunk to be a good thief. (Wichita: 40-year-old African American male)

Sometimes when everybody is drinking or smoking, we go down to the [shopping area] and pick up stuff. It doesn't seem bad then but sometimes I do feel guilty about it the next day. (Miami: 21-year-old white female)

When I'm drunk or stoned, it's like I'm invisible. No, it's like I'm Superman. I ain't scared of nothing. Nobody can touch me. It seems like that's what always gets me in trouble. I'll just walk in and take something and walk out. (Wichita: 37-year-old white male)

We were sitting around drinking. My roommate bet me I couldn't go across the street and steal a pack of cigarettes. (Miami: 20-year-old white male)

"I Enjoy the Thrill/Excitement/Rush/Danger"

Many informants viewed shoplifting as a challenge and a thrill. They enjoyed the risk taking and many discussed the "rush" they received from the act. Many of the subjects reported "excitement" or "rush" as one of the motivations for their illegal behavior, however, only 15 informants, six Miami students (six males and no females) and nine Wichita subjects (seven males and two females), considered this motivation as primary.

I do it for the rush. Adrenaline rush, you know. You get all excited and you feel kinda crazy inside. I can't explain it. It's adrenaline. (Wichita: 25-year-old white male)

It's like an addiction. I like the feeling I get when I might get caught. Once you get in the car and you got away with it, it's like, wow, I did it. It's a buzz. An adrenaline buzz. I love that feeling—while I'm still in the store, my heart is pumping real loud and fast. It's so loud I know people can hear it. I'm really scared, but once I get away, I'm exhilarated. (Miami student: 21-year-old white female)

It is really fun. It got to be quite a lark doing it. It was an art and I was good at it. (Wichita: 44-year-old white male)

It's not hard. Actually, it's fun. It's fun when you get away with it. It's scary in the store. Heart pumping—adrenaline pumping. It's exciting. Addicting. (Wichita: 30-year-old white female)

It's a thrill—the excitement, danger. Fear. Dude, my heart pounded like a drum. Like it was gonna come out of my chest. It made me feel alive. (Miami: 20-year-old white male)

"I Can't Help Myself. It's Compulsive"

A small number of informants reported that their behavior was beyond their control. This category is differentiated from the "Impulse" category by the subjects' assertions that they could not seem to stop. Many argued that they were addicted to shoplifting. There was significant crossover between those who reported compulsive behavior and those who reported shoplifting for thrill and excitement. Seven Miami students (no males and seven females) and six Wichita subjects (two males and four females) reported that they could not easily control their shoplifting behavior. Typical responses include:

I don't plan on stealing. I tell myself I'm not going to do it again and then I see something I want and I lift it. I already have it in my purse before I think about it. It's like, you know, automatic pilot. I'm addicted—that's all I know. (Miami student: 19-year-old white female)

I'm a kleptomanic. I steal anything I can get in my purse. The other day I stole a key chain—can you believe it? Took a chance on going to jail with a stupid key chain. (Wichita: 35-year-old white female)

Shoplifting is an addiction for me. It built up over time. I tried seeing a counselor but it didn't help. Didn't stop me. (Wichita: 44-year-old African American male)

"I Was Under a Lot of Stress"

A small number of subjects reported shoplifting as a response to stressful life situations. Five Wichita (two males and three females) and five Miami students (no males and five females) listed stress as the primary factor in their shoplifting behavior. Typical responses included:

I was worried about my ex-wife back in New York. She was being evicted from her apartment. I also didn't get a promotion I thought I was going to get. (Wichita: 46-year-old African American male)

I was working long hours and not getting along with my wife and we had a lot of bills and some sickness. I don't know what happened to me. Next thing I know I'm stealing things. Books from Barnes and Nobles, cigarettes, meat from [grocery store]. (Wichita: 40-year-old white male)

I used to shoplift before I got married. Then I stopped.... The divorce started me up again. It gave me something to think about, I guess. I think maybe

I wanted to get caught, but I didn't for a long time. (Wichita: 35-year-old white female)

I get depressed. Things start to pile up and I start shoplifting. Sometimes it's at finals [final exams] or when I have a fight with my boyfriend. One time when I thought I was pregnant. Who knows why. It's like I take out my feelings on them [the stores]. (Miami student: 24-year-old white female)

Other Responses

Other responses not mentioned often enough to rate a separate category included: "It was so easy" (n = 1), "I had a fight with my husband and I wanted to embarrass him" (n = 1), "I hate my boss. When he gives me shit about something, I give myself a little reward" (n = 1), "I needed some condoms and was too embarrassed to take them to the check-out" (n = 2), and "the check-out line was too long and I didn't want to wait" (n = 5). Six Wichita respondents (three males and three females) and four Miami students (two males and two females) listed these motives.

CONCLUSIONS AND DISCUSSION

It is obvious, now, that to speak of shoplifting as having a simple causal dynamic is to misunderstand the diversity and complexity of the behavior. When asked "Why do you shoplift?" the 320 shoplifters in this study revealed motivations that ranged from purely economic to apparent manifestations of emotional maladjustment. Most of the subjects reported that they shoplifted for some economic benefit. These subjects chose to steal as a means of satisfying their material needs and desires. Others satisfied some emotional need by their shoplifting activity. Still others sought to avoid some unpleasant or painful encounter or activity. These behaviors—satisfying economic or emotional needs—may be seen as highly utilitarian and rational. Motivations in these categories included (1) wanting the item but not being able to afford it, (2) wanting the item but not wanting to pay for it, (3) pressure from peers, (4) stealing for a living, and (5) feelings of thrill, rush, or danger. A small number of subjects reported that they stole to avoid embarrassment of paying for condoms, to avoid long lines at the check-out station, to embarrass a spouse or parent, or to exact revenge on an employer or store where they perceived they had been mistreated.

Of critical importance, however, was the finding that people who shoplift steal for different reasons at different times. In the 115 cases more extensively interviewed, there were few individuals who reported a single, stable criminal calculus. An otherwise "rational" shoplifter might occasionally act impulsively, stealing some item for which he or she had no need or purpose. The informants often expressed bewilderment over their motives in such cases. Of course, it is recognized that subjects may not have good insight into their own behavior or motives. Subjects may have reported their motive as "impulse" or "compulsive" because they could not articulate the dynamics of their behavior. Others may have reported stealing because of the disinhi-bition brought on by drugs or alcohol as a rationalization for behavior which they could not otherwise justify.

This points out the situational nature of offending. The motivation to shop-lift is closely tied to the offenders' current circumstances. In most instances offenders perceive the act as a means of satisfying some need. The "need" may be for cash, for some item(s) they wish to obtain for their personal use, or to satisfy some psychosocial need, such as revenge, self-esteem, peer approval, or for thrill and excitement. However, the same individuals might also commit offenses without a clear motive. Several informants reported that they simply went along with friends who decided to shoplift during an otherwise legitimate shopping excursion. They joined in for no reason other than, as one informant said, "It seemed like a good idea at the time." Crozier and Friedberg (1977) argued that people seldom have clear objectives. They do not know exactly where they are going or what they want. Maurice Cusson (1983) notes that to imagine that people carry out only projects that are conceived in advance and act in terms that are clearly foreseen is "sheer idealism" (p. 19). A shoplifter may drift into crime on one day, following the lead of a friend or acquaintance, whereas on another occasion he or she may utilize a more thoughtful planning strategy before committing a crime. Wright and Decker (1994) argued that this type of offending is not the result of a thoughtful decision strategy, but rather "emerges out of the natural flow of events, seemingly coming out of nowhere" (p. 40). They conclude:

> [i]t is not so much that these actors consciously choose to commit crime, as they elect to get involved in situations that drive them toward lawbreaking. (p. 40)

Some "otherwise rational" shoplifters reported that they occasionally took an item, not out of need or because they wanted it, but because they could do so without being observed. In these cases, the relative lack of risk appeared to be the major factor in the offenders' calculus. They were individuals with a "readiness" to commit offenses if the circumstances were favorable, and they did so even when they had no specific need for the items taken. Like the proverbial mountain that was climbed "because it was there," these shoplift-ers stole because they could.

Approximately 20% (n = 60) of the informants reported occasionally committing offenses for what appeared to be nonrational motives. These included shoplifting as a response to stress, as a result of compulsion, or an impulse. Women were more than twice as likely to report a nonrational motive than men. Of the 60 individuals who reported a nonrational motive for their shoplifting, 42 were women. Such shoplifters often asserted that they did not know why they committed their acts or that they did not under-stand their own behavior. The behavior was seldom obviously goal-oriented and it frequently did not have a significant acquisitive element. Many of these shoplifters took small, inexpensive items such as candy, cigarettes, and nonsensical items like keychains or small toys for which they had no use.

However, on closer examination, we found that all of these individuals recognized that they had a tendency to "compulsively" or "impulsively" shoplift, and yet they consciously entered places of business for that very purpose. Others appeared to attribute their shoplifting to forces over which they had no control as a means of maintaining their sense of self-worth or to impress the interviewer with their "basic goodness." One informant summed it up stating, "I'm basically a good person. Sometimes I lift things and when it's over, I can't even tell you why. It's not like me at all."

These findings are important because they call attention to a wider range of behaviors and motives associated with shoplifting than have previous studies, which depended on limited samples or on data developed through criminal justice sources. They also suggest the need for further systematic research with both apprehended and nonapprehended shoplifter populations.

IMPLICATIONS FOR PREVENTION STRATEGIES

The study suggests that shoplifting is not simple behavior with simple motives. Shoplifting is more complex than previously thought and the motives of shoplifters, although not stable, are more rational than those noted in some previous research. These findings, if borne out by further research, have policy implications both for law enforcement and for businesses.

If a substantial proportion of shoplifters are compulsive and nonrational, policies based on deterrence have little impact. They do not calculate the risks and gains, but rather steal without "reason." However, if shoplifting is perceived as rational behavior, then deterrence-based policies may be effective. The existence of a strong deterrent effect does not require that the individual be fully informed or fully rational in their decisions. The deterrence argument holds that an increase in the probability or severity of punishment for a particular crime will reduce the rate at which that crime is committed, other things being equal (Cook, 1989, p. 51). This suggests that arrest and prosecution for shoplifting might reduce its incidence. However, during the course of this study we discussed store policy regarding shoplifting with store mangers and loss-control personnel. A substantial number of these individuals reported that they prosecuted few shoplifters because of fear of lawsuits by those arrested or belief that penalties for the offense were so minor compared to the time and effort required for the store to carry out the prosecution as to render prosecution not worthwhile. Others reported that their loss-control technology or manpower was too limited to provide the evidence needed to prosecute suspected shoplifters. In many of these stores, suspected shoplifters were detained briefly, the stolen items recovered, and the thieves warned not to return to the store under threat of prosecution.

Interviews revealed that shoplifters are easily deterred if the threat of apprehension is obvious. Their perceptions of the risks involved at a particular store were gained from their own experiences and those of friends and acquaintances. They said that when a store had a reputation for arresting and prosecuting shoplifters, they tended to give it a wide berth. They also reported that once in a store, if they were being overtly watched by clerks or loss-prevention staff, they left the store immediately. These findings have several implications for loss control.

First, effective shoplifting control requires visible and obvious threat communication. Stores should post signs stating their policies regarding shoplifting. Clarke (1992) has shown that "rule setting" has a significant effect on behavior. Where the rules are clearly and openly established and stated, people tend to adhere to them. Where the rules are ambiguous or unclear, there is less adherence.

Second, shoplifting can be effectively reduced by strategic siting of store clerks' work stations, proper layout of display counters, check-out areas and dressing rooms. Stores which pile merchandise high, crowd aisles, and do not maintain adequate sight line between aisles and check-out stations may expect higher rates of shoplifting. Unattended dressing rooms and inattentive clerks also facilitate theft. Some small but expensive items, such as cigarettes, batteries, and razor blades should be placed in locked display cabinets or immediately under the watchful eyes of clerks. Clerks should be trained in shoplifting prevention and incentives should be established to encourage attentiveness. Closed-circuit television, strategically placed mirrors, and merchandise tagging, bar-coding, and "electronic point of sales" systems also play a major role in theft reduction.

Third, if store personnel openly and overtly observed suspected shoplifters, following them about the store, most of them would leave without committing an offense. However, there is little glory or credit given to employees who "scare off" potential thieves. Most store security personnel prefer to apprehend suspected shoplifters and will thus observe them covertly, waiting for a theft to occur before revealing themselves. This course of action results in lost time spent processing the shoplifter in the store, taking statements, calling the police, if warranted by the evidence and store policy, and subsequently testifying in court if necessary.

Fourth, if store policy demands that the shoplifter be apprehended, then the store should be committed to carrying out the prosecution to the end. If word gets out in the shoplifter population (and it will) that a store releases apprehended shoplifters with a warning, or does not follow up with charges and court appearances by its staff, shoplifters will not weigh risk too heavily in their risk-gain calculus. That store will become a favorite for shoplifters.

Finally, police, prosecutors, and courts must agree to aggressively prosecute shoplifting. If shoplifters find that they are rarely arrested, unlikely to be convicted if arrested, and unlikely to receive a substantial punishment if convicted, then they may justifiably begin to believe that they are free to commit their offenses at will.

Policies, once established and communicated to the public, should be carried out faithfully. If the policy is to prosecute "to the fullest extent of the law," as the anti-shoplifting signs often threaten, then stores should follow through on the promise. These actions reverberate throughout the shoplifter population and should quickly pay dividends in reduced levels of theft.

These conclusions suggest that most shoplifters can be deterred. Their behavior, while not rational in the Benthamite sense, has a rational component in most cases.

References

Agnew, R. (1990). The origins of delinquent events: An examination of offender accounts. *Journal of Research in Crime and Delinquency, 27,* 267–294.

Arboleda-Florez, J., Durie, H., & Costello, J. (1977). Shoplifting—An ordinary crime. *Journal of Offender Therapy and Comparative Criminology, 21,* 201–207.

Beck, E. A., & McEntyre, S. C. (1977). MMPI patterns of shoplifters within a college population. *Psychological Reports, 41,* 1035–1040.

Brantingham, P. J., & Brantingham, P. L. (1991). *Environmental criminology.* Prospect Heights, IL: Waveland.

Brantingham, P. L., & Brantingham, P. J. (1993). Environment, routine, and situation: Toward a pattern theory of crime. In R. V. Clarke and M. Felson (Eds.), *Routine Activity and Rational Choice* (pp. 259-294). New Brunswick, NJ: Transaction.

Cameron, M. (1964). *The booster and the snitch.* New York: The Free Press.

Carroll, J., & Weaver, F. (1986). Shoplifters' perceptions of crime opportunities: A process tracing study. In D. B. Cornish & R. V. Clarke (Eds.), *The reasoning criminal: Rational choice perspectives on offending* (pp. 19-38). New York: Springer-Verlag.

Clarke, R. V. (Ed.). (1992). *Situational crime prevention: Successful case studies.* New York: Harrow and Heston.

Clarke, R. V., & Cornish, D. (1986). *The reasoning criminal: Rational choice perspectives on offending.* New York: Springer-Verlag.

Cook, P. J. (1989). The economics of criminal sanctions. In M. L. Friedland (Ed.), *Sanctions and rewards in the legal system: A multidisciplinary approach* (pp. 50–78). Toronto, Ontario, Canada: University of Toronto Press.

Crozier, M., & Friedberg, E. (1977). *L'Acteur et le système.* Paris: Le Seuil. Cited in Cusson (1983).

Cusson, M. (1983). *Why delinquency?* Toronto, Ontario, Canada: University of Toronto Press.

Fear, R. W. G. (1974, July). An analysis of shoplifting. *Security Gazette,* 262–263.

Feinburg, G. (1984). Profile of the elderly shoplifter. In E. Newman, D. J. Newman, and M. Gerwitz (Eds.), *Elderly Criminals* (pp. 35-50). Cambridge, MA: Oelgeshlager, Gunn and Hain.

Freeh, L. (1996). *Crime in the United States—1995.* Washington, DC: U.S. Department of Justice.

Griffin, R. (1988). *Annual report: Shoplifting in supermarkets.* Van Nuys, CA: Commercial Service Systems.

Griffin, R. K. (1970). Shoplifting: A statistical survey. *Security World, 7,* Part 10, 21–25.

Griffin, R. K. (1971). Behavioral patterns in shoplifting. *Security World, 10*, Part 2, 21–25.

Hindelang, M., Hirschi, T., & Weis, J. (1981). *Measuring delinquency.* Beverly Hills, CA: Sage.

Hirschi, T. (1986). On the compatibility of rational choice and social control theories. In D. R. Cornish & R. V. Clarke (Eds.), *The reasoning criminal: Rational choice perspectives on offending* (pp. 105-118). New York: Springer-Verlag.

Johnston, L. D., O'Malley, P. M., & Bachman, J. G. (2002). *Monitoring the future survey.* Ann Arbor, MI: Institute for Social Research, University of Michigan.

Kahneman, D., Slovic, P., & Tversky, A. (Eds.). (1982). *Judgement under uncertainty: Heuristics and biases.* New York: Cambridge University Press.

Katz, J. (1988). *The seductions of crime.* New York: Basic Books.

Klemke, L. W. (1982). Exploring juvenile shoplifting. *Sociology and Social Research, 67,* 59–75.

Klemke, L. W. (1992). *The sociology of shoplifting: Boosters and snitches today.* Westport, CT: Praeger.

Kraut, R. (1976). Deterrent and definitional influences on shoplifting. *Social Problems, 25,* 358–368.

Lo, L. (1994). Exploring teenage shoplifting behavior. *Environment and Behavior, 26,* 613–639.

March, J. G. (1994). *A primer on decision making: How decisions happen.* New York: Free Press.

Moore, R. (1983). College shoplifters: Rebuttal of Beck and McIntyre. *Psychological Reports, 53,* 1111–1116.

Moore, R. (1984). Shoplifting in middle America: Patterns and motivational correlates. *International Journal of Offender Therapy and Comparative Criminology, 28*(1), 53–64.

Newell, A., & Simon, H. A. (1972). *Human problem solving.* Englewood Cliff, NJ: Prentice Hall.

Nimick, E. (1990). Juvenile court property cases. *OJJDP Update on Statistics.* Washington, DC: U.S. Department of Justice.

Osgood, W. D., O'Malley, P. M., Bachman, G. G., & Johnston, L. D. (1989). Time trends and age trends in arrests and self-reported behavior. *Criminology, 27,* 389–415.

Robin, G. D. (1963). Patterns of department store shoplifting. *Crime & Delinquency, 9,* 163–172.

Russell, D. H. (1973). Emotional aspects of shoplifting. *Psychiatric Annals, 3,* 77–79.

Schlueter, G. R., O'Neal, F. C., Hickey, J., & Seiler, G. (1989). Rational and nonrational shoplifter types. *International Journal of Offender Therapy and Comparative Criminology, 33,* 227–238.

Solomon, G. S., & Ray, J. B. (1984). Irrational beliefs of shoplifters. *Journal of Clinical Psychology, 40,*1075-1077.

Turner, C. T., & Cashdan, S. (1988). Perceptions of college students' motivations for shoplifting. *Psychological Reports, 62,* 855–862.

Vold, G., & Bernard, T. (1986). *Theoretical criminology.* New York: Oxford University Press.

Warr, M. (1989). What is the perceived seriousness of crimes? *Criminology, 27,* 801.

Wilson, J. Q., & Herrnstein, R. J. (1985). *Crime and human nature.* New York: Simon and Schuster.

Won, G., & Yamamoto, G. (1968). Social structure and deviant behavior: A study of shoplifting. *Sociology and Social Research, 53,* Part 1, 45–55.

Wright, R. T., & Decker, S. (1994). *Burglars on the Job: Street-life and Recidential Break-ins.* Boston: Northeastern University Press.

Becoming a Computer Hacker: Examining the Enculturation and Development of Computer Deviants

Thomas J. Holt

C omputer hackers represent an increasingly significant yet misunderstood problem for computer users across the globe. Hackers are one of the most immediately recognized threats to computer security, although there is relatively little knowledge of the process by which an individual becomes interested in these behaviors. This study will explore the development of computer hackers in their own words, as well as the ways that they define and justify their actions through subcultural norms. This qualitative study attempts to address this gap using three data sets, including a series of 365 strings from six hacker web forums, interviews with 13 active hackers, and observations from Defcon, a hacker convention held annually in Las Vegas, Nevada. These multiple data sources are triangulated and used to explore the behaviors hackers engage in, as well as the development and enculturation process of computer hackers. This is followed by an exploration of the ways that experiences in virtual and real social settings impact the socialization process and growth of computer hackers.

Computer technology and the Internet have dramatically affected the way people communicate and do business across the world (see Jewkes & Sharp, 2003). Businesses depend on the Internet to draw in commerce and make information available on demand. The banking and financial industries have implemented new technology enabling customers to gain access to their funds and accounts with relative ease. As the world comes to rely on computers and rapidly changing technologies, the threat posed by computer criminals has become increasingly significant (see Furnell, 2002; Jewkes & Sharp, 2003).

In particular, a great deal of concern stems from one of the most recognized computer criminals: hackers (see Furnell, 2002). Computer hackers are individuals with a profound interest in computers and technology that have used their knowledge to access computer systems, often with malicious illegal consequences (see Schell, Dodge, & Moutsatsos, 2002). For example, unauthorized access and theft from computer systems cost U.S. businesses

---

Source: Prepared especially for this volume. Used with permission of the author. 2008.

over $15 million dollars in 2007 alone (CSI & FBI, 2007). Hackers have also been linked with the creation of malicious viruses, such as the Melissa virus which infected computers worldwide causing at least $80 million in damages (Furnell, 2002).

Research suggests computer hackers operate within a subculture where its members place significant value on profound and deep connections to technology, and judge others based on their capacity to utilize computers in unique and innovative ways (Holt, 2007; Jordan & Taylor, 1998; Taylor, 1999; Thomas, 2002). Hackers also have shifting ethical beliefs about the consequences of their actions, and can justify and rationalize their actions in a number of ways (Holt, 2007; Jordan & Taylor, 1998; Taylor, 1999; Thomas, 2002). Furthermore, a relatively large community has formed around the act of hacking, particularly in online environments (Holt, 2007, 2008). Web forums, irc channels, blogs, and other online resources provide social links to electronically connect with other hackers, as well as resources to facilitate hacking activities (Furnell, 2002; Holt, 2008). Despite the communal nature of hacking, most hackers suggest that they operate within loose social networks with limited numbers of people on- and off-line (Holt, 2008). These collegial relationships enable the exchange of information, tools, and normative values and goals, though hackers largely offend alone (Holt, 2008).

The growing body of literature on hackers provides important insight into the nature of hacker subculture, though few have examined the process of becoming a hacker. Understanding the ways individuals develop their skills and become a part of hacker subculture is vital to improve our knowledge of computer crime, and its relationship to traditional forms of offending.

HACKS, CRACKS, AND DEVIANCE

To understand hacking, it is necessary to explore the various activities in which hackers engage on a day-to-day basis. Computer hackers are involved in behaviors that range from legitimate, lawful practices to blatantly illegal acts. For example, some hackers define a hack as any legitimate or useful alteration or adjustment to computer hardware or software that enable technology to be used in a new way. This definition recognizes behaviors such as increasing the processing speed of a computer through unusual means or testing their own computer's security programs. Such activity may not violate any legal statutes, although hackers do not always act within the letter of the law. In fact, hackers often apply the term "crack" to refer to any alteration of technology that has a negative or potentially criminal application. For instance, one of the hackers interviewed for this study named Mack Diesel suggested he performed a crack when he:

> downloaded what's called a password dictionary file which contains hundreds of words and used it to hack [a university's] password system and...get a number of passwords for accounts. I just let this program run and I got the information for access to a number of different accounts.

Mack occasionally used these accounts to steal Internet access, and considered this a crack because he used this service without authorization. Mack used hacking skills to gain access to these accounts, but he did not view it a hack because of his intentions and beliefs about the illegal use of services. Thus, the attribution of "hack value" has significant weight within hacker subculture as hackers differentiate between individuals based on their use of hacks and cracks (Schell et al., 2002). There is, however, no consensus on these terms, as the same act may be perceived as a hack or crack depending on individuals' ethics and beliefs (see also Holt, 2007).

This example is just one of the illegal acts a hacker may perform using computer technology. Some may create fraudulent credentials within a system in order to access other services, whereas others may delete or change data files. For example, one of the forum users described hacking his school's Web server and discovering information about the system administrator, stating: "We had made an admin account and looked through [the real administrator's] files. We found he had loads of very disturbing images...lets just say he like Star Trek way to much....So we emailed to all pupils in the school, everyone now knows." Hackers may also utilize malicious software, such as viruses and Trojan horse programs to gain access to and destroy computer systems.

Computer hackers are also actively involved in software and media piracy. Specifically, some hackers actively remove or "crack" the copyright protections on a piece of software or media. When someone "cracks" media, they can then distribute the material free of charge to others. Cracked media are also called warez, and are hosted on Websites that allow hackers to obtain software and media at no charge (Furnell, 2002, p. 44). A variety of materials can be found on warez sites, such as operating systems, software suites, antivirus programs, games, music, and tools that may help hackers to develop their skills.

Hackers also practice wardriving as a result of the increasing popularity of wireless technology. This term refers to the process of driving or traveling through an area using a laptop and various pieces of equipment to look for wireless Internet (or Wi-Fi) access points. If an access point is identified, hackers may attempt to access the Internet without authorization from the owner. This sort of theft of services is common, and some in the hacker community have made a hobby out of simply identifying Wi-Fi spots. For example, a multistage wardriving game was held at Defcon. In one game, competitors had to drive around Las Vegas seeking out and logging all open wireless Internet access points. The individual who found the largest number of points won, though the game required driving through Las Vegas for 48 hours strait in order to log the largest number of Wi-Fi points.

INITIAL INTEREST IN HACKING

Regardless of the legal or illegal behaviors a hacker engages in, it is vital that researchers explore how an individual becomes a hacker. The process of becoming a computer hacker started with an individuals' interest in technology. Hackers clearly possessed a deep connection to computers and technology, which played an important role in structuring their interests and activities (see also Holt, 2007; Jordan & Taylor, 1998; Taylor, 1999; Thomas, 2002). Three of the thirteen interviewees said their relationship with technology began by age five, such as Mack Diesel who said:

> I was, yeah, I was about four and [my mother] would take me up to school with her sometimes and they had a computer there. If I got bored, she would let me, uh, fool around with the computer, you know, to keep me occupied, and after a while I enjoyed playing around with it.

Two other interviewees suggested they became fascinated with technology by age seven. Spuds wrote, "my Grandparents saw my aptitude for all things technical at an early age. At the age of seven, my grandparents decided to nurture that interest and aptitude by purchasing me my first PC." The remaining interviewees took an interest in technology during adolescence. Mutha Canucker wrote, "I got a computer when I was 12, and my interest grew from there. The more I played with it, the more I realized what I could do."

Gaining access to computers deepened hackers' interest in technology. Most of the interviewed hackers received a system from either a parent or loved one, but they were not always the best machines available. Dark Oz explained, "I really started with computers when I graduated from eighth grade and was given an Amstat PC20 8086 PC. It was slow, even by the standards of those days." Once they had a computer, hackers spent their time becoming acquainted with its functions in a variety of ways. Video game technology commonly introduced hackers to the ins and outs of their system. Indiana Tones explained:

> It was a little tough, and uh, my mom basically worked with computers at work so she kind of helped me out with my games, getting games installed and told me like how to do things like that. And as I started playing more games I kept having to tweak the system settings to free up RAM and get the games to run because it was an old piece of junk computer, uh, because my parents couldn't really afford more. So then I started having to do research on how to tweak it out to get the best performance.

Adjusting their system in minor ways allowed budding hackers to improve their game play or compete against others. At the same time, it introduced them to a variety of skill sets. For example, some hackers learned to program their own games like Vile Syn:

> I was quickly introduced to the vast array of games that were made during that time, and how to execute them from the C64's [Commodore 64 computer] BASIC shell. By the time I was 7 the Computer Gazette was my newfound

interest, full of raw BASIC code for games and applications. I coded around a total of 50 of these programs taking up to 5 hours to type each one.

The interviewed hackers' interest in technology quickly moved beyond games into the basics of computers through discovery and exploration. R. Shack wrote that, "continuing to play with computers got me further involved" in hacking, and interested him in the "capabilities that can be done with computers." By understanding how individuals could be connected together through telephone lines or delving into how compression software functioned, budding hackers became interested in the many different facets of computer technology. This gave them an understanding and appreciation for a variety of technical skills such as programming, software, hardware, and computer security. For example, Spuds "learned how to program the machine to make my own programs to do things for which there were no programs readily available to do. I learned how to fix the machine, upgrade the machine, and so much more."

Understanding the interrelated elements of computer systems is critical as a hacker's knowledge level directly relates to their ability and skill (see Thomas, 2002, p. 44). Therefore, hackers must have an intense desire to understand computer technology. This was exemplified in the following comment from a forum poster named Binkels, who wrote:

> Hacking allows people to learn more about computers. I am really into computers and try to learn as much as I can. I want to be a hacker to exploit systems/programs and using them to learn from and go further into my limited knowledge of computers.

The urge to learn about computers and technology could be met through a variety of resources, especially Web forums. These online resources allow individuals to post questions and receive answers from a range of interested parties. Forums have tremendous utility, as noted by the forum user MorGnweB:

> You might want to remember that this forum is designed for people to ask questions, despite the fact that you can find almost anything on google. Soif [sic] we all should just searched [sic] for things ourselves thered [sic] be no forums.

Technical questions were frequently posted in the six forums analyzed. In fact, 387 questions were posted to start the strings, representing 72% of all strings analyzed. A range of questions were asked, including how to hack specific targets or assistance in identifying specific software or tools:

> I'm looking for a special keylogger. The keylogger must collect the windows 98 login passwords and usernames. Is this possible. Does anyone know such a good keylogger and the place where I can download it?

Some individuals had questions about software programming and included samples of their coding procedures. Others wanted general information on hacking. For instance, g00fu5 wrote:

> I'm planning on printing out a bunch of different texts to print out and take around with me so I can read them in my spare time. I was wondering if anyone could recommend any good texts that are actually worth printing out for me. I am printing out the SQL [programming language] white pages so far, but I need more. I am interested in just about anything hacking-related.

Thus, the forums engendered hackers' significant interest in and desire to comprehend technology.

Defcon was also an important resource for hackers to learn more about all facets of technology. Most all of the panels held during the course of the convention related to various computer software and hardware. A wide range of topics were discussed, including hardware hacking, phreaking, computer security, exploits, privacy protections, and the legal issues surrounding hacking and piracy. Presenters provided new information to attendees along with tools, security tactics, and creative applications of existing products. In fact, a data disk was given to all attendees that contained programs and data relating to the panel presentations. This provided hands-on access to 13 different pieces of software and over 30 different applications from data on exploits to programming information. Thus, hackers at Defcon placed great value on spreading innovative uses of technology to others.

LEARNING TO HACK

The various technologies and resources available to hackers make it difficult to identify a common starting point for new hackers. Individuals across the data sets, however, stressed that new hackers begin their learning process with the basic components of computer technology. Forum poster dBones suggested, "you will have to start learning the basic techniques and you will surely progress to be a better hacker." An understanding of the rudimentary functions of computers provided hackers with an appreciation for the interrelated nature of computer systems. The interviewee Dark Oz explained his own learning experience:

> I tried to learn assembler [software that translates an assembly language into machine language]. Too low level for me, I was board [sic] with it, but in just trying to learn it, I taught myself a lot about how a PC works, how the processor and memory relate to each other, and this low-level of information has been extremely valuable to have. It's helped me to understand why things work the way they do, and why they were designed the way they were.

Similar comments were pervasive across the interview and forum data. Developing a broad knowledge of systems, hardware, programming, and networking was extremely important to interviewed hackers because it influenced their ability to hack. For example, 10 of the 13 hackers indicated they had a variety of skills that allowed them to complete multiple tasks during a hack. Such a diffuse understanding of computers and technology was beneficial, as Indiana Tones explained:

> Everybody's got their own cup of tea, whether it be hardware, software, programming. Because the more you know about networking, the more that might help you program your program that's going to run over the network, you know.

Many interviewees reported developing their knowledge of computer technology on their own through "trial and error" and "playing with computers." Experimentation allowed hackers to determine the rules and parameters of software and hardware. Mack Diesel indicated, "I picked up most of my knowledge and skill through reading a lot, taking classes, but primarily from just sitting down and experimenting and seeing what works and what doesn't." J. Rose suggested he learned through "trial and error, which I believe is the only effective way to learn computing techniques." Hands-on experience provided a fundamental way to recognize the limits of systems and push beyond them (see Jordan & Taylor, 1998, p. 764). As Mutha Canucker explained, "the motto was: try it, if it works, write it down, if not, get out the DOS disks."

Forum users made similar comments on the importance of learning, especially on one's own. The forum poster dBones wrote, "What I'm trying to get at is that you will become more knowledgeable if you were to find out information by yourself and then teach yourself that information." This sentiment was also evident in the following exchange when a poster asked for information to learn to hack:

STFUser: ok im quite new to this and need some mega help i need to know the basics of this hacking [I am] on my quest to becoming elite so if someone can help and give me the info and tell me where i can get it [information on how to hack] form [sic] i would much appreciate it.

3nf0r3c3r: arrrrr how cute, seriously mate why would anyone want to go out of their way to help some random person hack computers?

H3H3: Nah man, you want a teacher, you can pay lol [laughing out loud]. Besides that, read whatever you can get your hands on and understand the shit that you read.

Thus, forum users both explicitly and implicitly demonstrated the importance of learning on one's own. To assist in this process, forum users provided Web links in almost every string in each forum. These links provided specific information about an issue or topic discussed in the string without repetition or wasted time for the reader. Tutorials were also posted, giving detailed explanations on topics from programming to the use of hack tools. In some instances, users made actual programs available for download to help individuals learn.

Learning was not, however, an entirely solitary enterprise for hackers. Social networks played an important role in educating hackers by introducing new concepts or providing tools and resources to hack (see Schell et al., 2002). For instance, Defcon attendees sat at communal tables between and during panels discussing issues. Individuals lined the halls and common areas of the hotel with laptops connected together to share files and information. The interviewees stressed the importance of peers in learning and facilitating hacks as well. This was exemplified by Kamron who wrote that he learned about computers and technology when he "asked friends and did a lot of trial and error." Vile Syn described a similar situation stating "we [a small group of hackers] would constantly spend time trading pirated software, and discussing the next find. Here my interest in electronic engineering, cryptography and the lack of respect for software copyrights developed."

Almost all (84%) of the hackers interviewed for this project went to friends or associates for guidance and assistance when hacking (see also Schell et al., 2002). For example, hackers sometimes did not have enough knowledge to complete a hack on their own. Kamron described such an incident, when he "collaborated with friends who acquired information on the mechanics" of an online game server, enabling them to evade a ban in place. Others simply exchanged information with friends to expand their knowledge of systems and technology. Indiana Tones explained this in some detail:

> I just liked listening to their [his phreak friends'] stories because they basically told me how the phone system works. See, I was more into computers and things...they always wanted me to make like good little boxes, [phreaking tool] you know. They were never really good at soldering or anything like that, so I mean I took that up and tried to help them out here and there.

Hacker social networks were not limited to physical connections. Bulletin Board Systems and forums allowed hackers to connect with one another and share information without actual face-to-face contact. One forum user elaborated on this concept stating: "we are always trying to provide an atmosphere where any user can feel comfortable asking any question." The interviewee Mutha Canucker discussed this issue in some detail:

> I made a lot of friends in much the same way as people make friends online now. Even though we all lived in the same city, we never saw each other. Where I live, public transit is bad and when your 14 you not just going to borrow the car for the evening. It was through these friends, one in particular, that I learned most of the techniques.

Nine of the thirteen interviewees also reported using Web forums or Bulletin Board System (BBS) to get information. Through these resources, hackers could procure data on the weaknesses of targets. Spuds suggested he "would consult a resource online to find out about vulnerabilities of particular OS [Operating System] or service that was being run on that OS." Hackers downloaded different tools and software from online sources as well. Vile Syn explained that he would "dial into the BBS and interact with the BBS for files, documents, pictures, and anything else that was shared." Bob Jones also used online resources to get cracked software, or warez, explaining, "if you go on-line and you take the time to search for cracks and serial numbers…you can find a source with a lot of cracks, a lot of times they'll have tools to create worms or to install worms. Actual programs so you don't have to do any programming yourself." The availability of malicious software was noted by Dark Oz who recounted his experiences with BBS:

> With the modem I was exposed to more things, and had access to more software and text files. Since I had more things to play with and read, I continued to learn more and more. One day I found an underground BBS that had a virus collection, and so I downloaded a few and started experimenting with them on my PC, and collecting them (similar to how one collects stamps).

The previous comments also indicate that there is value in visiting more than one forum. Membership in multiple forums was necessary because each had different specializations and purposes. This was exemplified in a post from Toastly describing what individuals should do to learn how to hack. He provided links to nine tutorials and forums, writing "Besides reading all these newbie tutorials, you should defintely [sic] join some forums that will help on your way. If you always keep to the n00b tutorials, then your knowledge will never increase and you'll give up quite quickly."

COMMITMENT TO HACKING

The previous statements also stress the important role of learning in hacker subculture. In order to become a hacker, individuals must be committed to continued study and practice of hacking techniques. This point was reinforced across the data set. For example, forum posters indicated it took a tremendous amount of time to learn to hack. Wiggum wrote, "For me…the most important thing to have if u wanna be a hacker is to 'love it' and [be] ready to give your time to learn and master it." Ashy Larrie also provided some insight:

> If you are just starting you might not have a clue what to learn, or what you should know. As for me, I just started reading texts for a long time…when I started I didn't understand most of what was said in the texts but just kept on reading, after awhile things become more clear and you get the idea of what hacking is all about.

Hackers had to spend a significant amount of time learning and understanding computers and technology. Without such an investment of their time, hackers would not discover what issues they truly find interesting. In addition, continuous changes and improvements in technology compounded the length of time required to learn. Thus, hackers must be committed to the continuous identification and acquisition of new information. Mack Diesel emphasized the importance of commitment, saying, "the minute you feel you've learned everything is the minute you're out. There's always something new to learn."

In fact, the tremendous value placed on constant learning over time influenced the structure and meaning of hacker identity. As one forum poster suggested, "if you want to be a hacker, then you should start to learn...hacking is all about learning new stuff and exploring." Forum users and interviewed hackers stressed the notion of curiosity and a desire to learn (see also Furnell, 2002; Jordan & Taylor, 1998). For example, a forum poster wrote, "a hacker is someone who loves to find alternative applications for any given technology, another word for this is inventor or innovator." The interviewee MG also defined a hacker as "any person with a sincere desire for knowledge about all things and is constantly trying to find it." Spuds also indicated in his interview that hackers have a "natural curiosity about how things work and how they can be improved."

The more time individuals spent learning the tradecraft of hacking, the more skilled a hacker they could become. Dark Oz reflected on this, writing, "You do this long enough, with many technical projects, and you begin to really learn a lot, and then it becomes quicker to pick up more things faster then you did before." Although this statement references the importance of learning, it clearly indicates the value of expending constant and consistent effort in the process of learning. In fact, a hacker's willingness and desire to learn affected how he or she was viewed and labeled by others within the subculture. Several different terms were used by interviewees, forum users, and even at Defcon, to differentiate between hackers based on their skill level. An individual who was new to hacking or had little knowledge was often labeled a noob (Furnell, 2002). Those with little skill who used tools and techniques without truly understanding their functionality were called script kiddies (Furnell, 2002). Both the script kiddie and the noob were also sometimes designated as a "lamer" as a sign of disrespect based on their lack of skill. Because noob, script kiddie, and lamer had negative associations, individuals often applied these terms to the unskilled or uninitiated. Those with a deep understanding of technology were referred to as hackers. The extremely skilled hacker was also called elite, spelled "1337," or 'leet (see also Thomas, 2002).

If an individual did not prove they put effort forth to learn on their own, they were disrespected. This was most evident in the forums when hackers tried to obtain information from others. For example, a user named Heshopolis asked for assistance to make an attack script work and stated that he did not want to spend his own time to do so. Several people replied, stating:

THE MONKEY: If you can't even fucking compile someone else's exploits, think about actually learning what you're doing before you try doing it....Get your head out of your ass, fuck off, and read a book.

T0mp3t3r5: Get off your dead ass and code your own exploits, you fucking script kiddie.

These comments plainly demonstrate the forum users' stance on the importance of understanding how hacks actually work, which can only be gleaned through hard work and dedication. As such, Heshopolis was flamed, disrespected, and derogatorily referred to as a script kiddie.

The intense commitment required to learn and apply knowledge is necessary as complex hacks may require hours or days to complete. For example, Indiana Tones said "it probably took me a year" to hack his Internet Service Provider's mail server. The process of a hack could be difficult and required creative thinking, as Bob Jones suggested:

You've got to take something that's broke and fix it and taking something that's fixed and break it and that takes a lot of perseverance. A lot of persistence. A lot of just, OK I've tried this, this, and this. You've got to think OK, how haven't I tried? Or what can I twist a little to try a different way.

The challenging nature of hacking and the constant effort required became a motive for some hackers. Completing challenging tasks fueled some hackers forward to persist in the face of failure. Mack Diesel explained:

It's [hacking] is challenging and that is what spurs most people forward, is that getting past a hard obstacle. You are going to see a lot of reading, and there are going to be a lot of hard points and times where you fail. But if you succeed and try a lot of different things by learning and doing, then there are going to be times when you get up from the computer and clap your hands together and say yeah, you know. Getting past something difficult is what will keep you going forward.

Thus, commitment to hacking has a significant impact on the activities and interests of hackers. The importance of commitment makes it clear why the forum poster WisdomCub3 wrote, "hacking is a lifestyle. Spend all your time on it and you will get better and better." Many forum users and interviewees echoed this sentiment, especially when defining the term hacker. For instance, MG wrote, "to be a hacker, you must live the life, not just play the part. You must be hacker in everything you do." In fact, Mack Diesel suggested a deep commitment to hacking is a "part of who they [hackers] are, it's their nature, so it be very difficult for that person to just turn it off like a switch."

JUSTIFYING HACKING

In addition to exchanging information to facilitate hacking, individuals also discussed the legality of hacking and information sharing in the real world and in cyberspace. Hackers in the forums often discussed whether some hacks or related activities were legal, and if they should be performed. There was a split between hackers who felt no illegal hacks were appropriate and those who viewed hacking in any form as acceptable. Such competing perspectives were addressed in the following exchange. An individual asked for information on a password cracking tool and how to use it. Pilferer answered the poster's question and gave an admonition that was quickly contradicted:

PILFERER: You do understand that using these password crackers on machines which you don't own or have no permission to access is ILLEGAL?

LEETER: Illegal...So is masturbation in a public place, but we don't get reminded of that every time anyone thinks about it do we? ;-)

Legal matters were also addressed off-line during multiple different presentations at Defcon. For example, a panel of attorneys from the Electronic Freedom Foundation, a legal foundation supporting digital free speech rights and hacker interests, spoke on the current state of law relative to computer hacking. A similar talk was given by an attorney addressing the ways that the Digital Millennium Copyright Act could be used to deal with civil and criminal hacking cases. There was also a panel titled "Meet The Fed," where attendees could ask a number of different law enforcement agents questions on the law and hacking.

However, concern over potential law violations appeared to have little effect on hacker behavior. Individuals across the data sets provided information that could be used to perform a hack regardless of their attitude toward the law. This led to a contradiction in the process of information sharing. If a hacker shared knowledge with possible illegal applications, they justified its necessity. Individuals on- and off-line stated they provided information in the hopes of educating others, as in this statement from a tutorial posted in one of the forums on macrovirus construction:

> This is an educational document, I take no responsibility for what use the information in this document is used for. I am unable to blamed for any troubles you get into with the police, FBI, or any other department....It is not illegal to write viruses, but it is illegal to spread them- something I do not condone and take responsibility for.

Similar justifications were used at Defcon, especially when a presenter's content had rather obvious or serious illegal applications. An excellent example of this was a presentation titled "Weakness in Satellite Television Protection Schemes or 'How I learned to Love The Dish.'" The presenter, *A*, indicated, "I will not be teaching you how to steal [satellite Internet connectivity] service, but I will give you the background and information to understand how it could be done." The second slide in his presentation, however, included the message "Many topics covered may be illegal!," as well as the potential laws they may break by stealing service.

This legal warning reduced the presenter's accountability for how individuals used the information he provided. He simply shared his knowledge on satellite systems and television service. If someone used the information to break the law, *A* had clearly described the laws that could be violated by engaging in these actions. Just as with the warning in the macrovirus tutorial, he justified sharing information that could be used to engage in illegal behavior, stealing satellite service, as part of the pursuit of knowledge.

Nevertheless, forum users and the Defcon staff did not condone the exchange or supply of overtly illegal information. In the forums, hackers eschewed posting blatantly illegal content and forcefully explained this idea. For example, an individual proclaimed himself, "the kind of hacker police really hate" and posted someone's credit card information. One of the senior users posted the following comments in reply:

> No only do the police hate you Regardless if this is a honey-card and regardless if its good or bad to card (btw its bad), someone should delete it because it IS illegal and this is an open forum Go away

Thus, overtly illegal information was not tolerated. Suggesting individuals engage in criminal activities or giving access to illegally obtained or questionable materials were not welcome in public settings on or off-line. At the same time, sharing information that could potentially be used to perform criminal activity was acceptable.

The dichotomy of information sharing present in hacker subculture on and off-line may stem from the potential for law enforcement attention. It is possible that law enforcement agents examine hacker web forums on a regular basis. Limiting the amount of illegal information traded in the forums reduced the risk of law enforcement intervention. The same can be said for Defcon because it is open to the public. The convention organizers used their own security staff, called "goons," to deter illegal behavior on the hotel grounds. Also, the convention organizers and some attendees noted that the presence of law enforcement agents was greater than in previous years. As a result, hackers limited the exchange of information in public settings on and off-line and distanced themselves from overtly illegal activity activities.

DISCUSSION AND CONCLUSIONS

This study sought to explore the process of becoming a hacker and the ways that individuals become a part of hacker subculture. The findings suggest that hackers develop their skills slowly through constant learning and experience over time. Hackers utilized on- and off-line social networks to improve their knowledge of all facets of computing. Web forums provided access to a range of materials and information, and peer connections enabled and reinforced their interest in hacking and technology. Thus, hacking mirrors the social learning process of other types of crime, such as burglary (Wright & Decker, 1994) and car theft (Copes & Cherbonneau, 2006).

At the same time, this study suggests that hacking is not a static process like some other forms of street crime. Hackers had to be committed to constant learning and new application of their knowledge. In fact, status and labels were conferred on individuals based on their skill and ability. Individuals with demonstrable knowledge were shown a great deal of respect and were referred to as hackers (see also Thomas, 2002). Poorly skilled hackers with no interest in developing their skills were called script kiddies and given very little respect, especially in web forums.

Hackers also demonstrated significant concern and awareness of the threat of law enforcement in cyberspace and the real world. As a result, they frequently discussed the legal nature of hacks and whether or not they should be performed. Hackers also actively structured their interactions to reduce exposure to law enforcement on and off-line (see also Jordan & Taylor, 1998; Taylor, 1999). For example, forum users noted the potential for law enforcement observation and limited the public exchange of overtly illegal information. The Defcon convention placed similar restrictions on the behavior of those in attendance. Yet individuals legitimized sharing information with potentially illegal applications on or off-line under the guise of educating others.

Thus, hackers placed significant value on concealing blatantly illegal behavior from law enforcement on- and off-line, but justified open involvement in certain activities. In addition, this research found hackers used similar methods to reduce legal attention in both virtual and real contexts. Few studies have considered any relationships between the methods used by deviants and criminals to limit their exposure to social control agents on- and off-line. Further research should examine this issue with other deviant groups to improve our knowledge of the ways that subcultures react to the consequences of socially unacceptable behavior on- and off-line.

Taken as a whole, this study has demonstrated that hacking is a complex and challenging behavior structured by experiences in cyberspace and the real world. Computer hacking is, however, just one of several crimes that stem directly from technological innovations (see also Furnell 2002). Research is needed exploring other technology-centered crimes to understand the ways they differ from traditional street crimes, such as robbery and assault. This will improve our understanding of the influence of technology on the nature of crime and deviance in the 21st century.

References

Computer Security Institute & Federal Bureau of Investigation. (2007). *Computer crime and security survey.* Retrieved August 15, 2007, from http://www.cybercrime.gov

Copes, H., & Cherbonneau, M. (2006). The key to auto theft: Emerging methods of auto theft from the offenders' perspective. *British Journal of Criminology, 46,* 917–934.

Furnell, S. (2002). *Cybercrime: Vandalizing the information society.* Boston: Addison-Wesley.

Holt, T. J. (2007). Subcultural evolution? Examining the influence of on- and off-line experiences on deviant subcultures. *Deviant Behavior, 28,* 171–198.

Holt, T. J. (2008). Lone hacks or group cracks: Examining the social organization of computer hackers. In F. Schmalleger & M. Pittaro (Eds.), *Crimes of the Internet* (pp. 336–355). Upper Saddle River, NJ: Pearson Prentice Hall.

Jewkes, Y., & Sharp, K. (2003). Crime, deviance and the disembodied self: transcending the dangers of corporeality. In Y. Jewkes (Ed.), *Dot.cons: Crime, deviance and identity on the Internet* (pp. 1–14). Portland, OR: Willan.

Jordan, T., & Taylor, P. (1998). A sociology of hackers. *The Sociological Review, 46,* 757–780.

Schell, B. H., Dodge, J. L., & Moutsatsos. S. S. (2002). *The hacking of America: Who's doing it, why, and how.* Westport, CT: Quorum Books.

Taylor, P. A. (1999). *Hackers: Crime in the digital sublime.* New York: Routledge.

Thomas, D. (2002). *Hacker culture.* Minneapolis: University of Minnesota Press.

Wright, R., & Decker, S. H. (1994). *Burglars on the job: Streetlife and residential break-ins.* Boston: Northeastern University Press.

Identity Theft: Assessing Offenders' Motivations and Strategies

Heith Copes and Lynne Vieraitis

*D*espite rates of identity theft, little is known about those who engage in this crime. The current study is exploratory in nature and is designed to shed light on the offenders' perspectives. To do this we interviewed 59 identity thieves incarcerated in federal prisons. Results show that identity thieves are a diverse group, hailing from both working-class and middle-class backgrounds. Nearly half of those we interviewed led lifestyles similar to those of persistent street offenders. The rest used the proceeds of their crimes to live "respectable" middle-class lives. Regardless of their chosen lifestyle, they were primarily motivated by the quick need for cash and see identity theft as an easy, relatively risk-free way to get it. They employed a variety of methods to both acquire information and convert it to cash. The most common methods of acquiring information were to buy it from others, steal it from mailboxes or trashcans, or to obtain it from people they knew. Identity thieves have developed a set of skills to enable them to be successful at their crimes. These skills included social skills, technical skills, intuitive skills, and system knowledge. By developing these skills they thought they could commit identity theft with impunity.*

Over the past several years, the United States has enjoyed a significant decline in rates of serious street crime. However, crimes of fraud continue to increase and with emerging opportunities for economic crime this trend is expected to continue (Shover & Hochstetler, 2006). In the last 10 years, one form of fraud, identity theft, has garnered America's attention as it became one of the most common economic crimes in the nation (Bernstein, 2004; Perl, 2003). According to recent data from the Federal Trade Commission, 685,000 complaints of fraud were reported in 2005. Thirty-seven percent of these complaints (255,565) were for identity theft, making it the most prevalent form of fraud in the United States (Federal Trade Commission, 2006).

Source: Excerpted and adapted from Heith Copes and Lynn Vieraitis, Identity Theft: Assessing Offender's Strategies and Perceptions of Risk" A project funded by the National Institute of Justice, Grant # 2005-IJ-CX-0012. For a complete version of the study, go to http://www.ncjrs.gov/App/Publications/Abstract.aspx?ID=240910. Used with permission of the authors.

To combat these rising rates, Congress passed the Identity Theft and Assumption Deterrence Act (ITADA) in 1998. According to ITADA, it is unlawful if a person:

> knowingly transfers or uses, without lawful authority, a means of identification of another person with the intent to commit, or to aid or abet, any unlawful activity that constitutes a violation of Federal law, or that constitutes a felony under any applicable State or local law.

This law made identity theft a separate crime against the person whose identity was stolen, broadened the scope of the offense to include the misuse of information and documents, and provided punishment of up to 15 years of imprisonment and a maximum fine of $250,000. Under U.S. Sentencing Commission guidelines a sentence of 10 to 16 months' incarceration can be imposed even if there is no monetary loss and the perpetrator has no prior criminal convictions (GAO, 2002).[1]

Identity theft occurs when a criminal appropriates an individual's personal information such as name, address, date of birth, or Social Security number to assume that person's identity to commit theft or multiple types of fraud. Identity thieves utilize a variety of methods to acquire victims' identities, most of which are "low-tech" (Newman & McNally, 2005). These methods include stealing wallets or purses, dumpster diving, stealing mail from residential and business mail boxes, and buying information on the street or from employees with access to personal information. More sophisticated methods or "high-tech" methods include hacking into corporate computers and stealing customer and/or employee databases, skimming, and using the Internet to purchase information from Websites or trick consumers into divulging account information (Newman & McNally, 2005).

By exploiting personal and financial information, an identity thief can obtain a person's credit history; access existing financial accounts; file false tax returns, open new credit accounts, bank accounts, charge accounts, and utility accounts; enter into a residential lease, and even obtain additional false identification documents such as a duplicate driver's license, birth certificate, or passport. Identity theft also occurs when an offender commits crimes in the victim's name and gives that person a criminal record. Identity

---

[1] In 2004, the Identity Theft Penalty Enhancement Act established a new federal crime, aggravated identity theft. Aggravated identity theft prohibits the knowing and unlawful transfer, possession, or use of a means of identification of another person during and in relation to any of more than 100 felony offenses, including mail, bank, and wire fraud, immigration and passport fraud, and any unlawful use of a Social Security number. The law mandates a minimum two years in prison consecutive to the sentence for the underlying felony. In addition, if the offense is committed during and in relation to one of the more than 40 federal terrorism-related felonies, the penalty is a minimum mandatory five years in prison consecutive to the sentence for the underlying felony.

thieves may use the victim's personal information "to evade legal sanctions and criminal records (thus leaving the victim with a wrongful criminal or other legal record)" (Perl, 2003).

Although estimates of the costs vary, identity theft is one of the most expensive financial crimes in America, costing consumers an estimated $5 billion and businesses $48 billion each year. The FTC Identity Theft Clearinghouse estimates that the total financial cost of identity theft to be over $50 billion a year, with the average loss to businesses being $4,800 per incident and an average of $500 to the victim whose identity is misused (FTC, 2006).

Despite the fact that identity theft is one of the fastest growing economic crimes in the United States, researchers have devoted little attention to understanding those who engage in this offense. To date, no one has conducted a systematic examination on a sample of offenders to ascertain a reliable or comprehensive picture of identity theft and how it can be controlled more effectively (for an exception, see Allison, Schuck, & Lersch, 2005). The goal of the current research is to explore the offenders' perspectives. Through semistructured interviews with 59 identity thieves incarcerated in federal prisons, we examine their life experiences, and criminal careers, the apparent rewards and risks of identity theft, and measures employed to carry out their crime. Because so little is known about those who commit identity theft the current study is exploratory and is designed to act as a springboard for future research on identity theft.

DESCRIPTIVE STATISTICS

The common perception of identity thieves is that they are more akin to white-collar fraudsters than they are to street level property offenders. That is, they hail disproportionately from the middle classes, they are college educated and they have stable family lives. To determine if identity thieves, at least the ones we interviewed, resemble other fraudsters we collected various demographic characteristics, including age, race, gender, employment status, and educational achievement. We also asked offenders about their socioeconomic status, family status, and criminal history including prior arrests, convictions, and drug use. Overall, we found identity theft to be quite democratic with participants from all walks of life. In fact, they were just as likely to resemble persistent street offenders as they were middle-class fraudsters.

Gender, Race/ethnicity, and Age

Our final sample of 59 inmates included 23 men and 36 women. This discrepancy in gender is likely as a result of our sampling strategy and the higher response rate from female inmates rather than the actual proportion of identity theft offenders. In addition, more males were unavailable for interviews because of disciplinary problems and/or prison lockdowns. Offenders in our sample ranged in age from 23 to 60 years with a mean age of 38 years.

They included 18 white females, 16 black females, 2 Asian females, 8 white males, and 15 black males.

MOTIVATIONS FOR IDENTITY THEFT

Numerous studies of street-level property offenders and of fraudsters find that the primary motivation for instigating these events is the need for money (Shover, 1996; Shover, Coffey, & Sanders, 2004; Wright & Decker, 1994). When asked what prompted their criminal involvement, the overwhelming response was money. Lawrence[2] probably best reflects this belief, "It's all about the money. That's all it's about. It's all about the money. If there ain't no money, it don't make sense." Indeed, identity theft is financially rewarding. Gladys estimated that she could make "two thousand dollars in three days." Lawrence made even larger claims, "I'll put it to you like this, forging checks, counterfeiting checks... in an hour, depending on the proximity of the banks—the banks that you're working—I have made seven thousand dollars in one hour." These estimates were consistent with those given by other offenders in the sample and with previous estimates (BJS, 2006).

Although estimates on how much they made from their crimes varied widely among respondents, most brought in incomes greater than they could have earned with the types of legitimate work they were qualified for or from other illegal enterprises. In fact, several of them described how they gave up other criminal endeavors for identity theft because they could make more money. When asked why she stopped selling drugs, Bridgette answered, "[Selling drugs is] not the answer. That's not where the money is." Dale switched from burglaries to identity theft arguing, "[Identity theft] is easier and you keep the money, you know. You keep a lot of money."

But how did they spend the money gained through their illegal enterprises? Ethnographic studies of street offenders indicate that few "mentioned needing money for subsistence" (Wright, Brookman, & Bennet, 2006, p. 6). This was also true for the majority of those with whom we spoke. Jacob said that he spent most of his money on "a lot of nice clothes." When asked what he did with the money Lawrence replied, "Partying. Females. I gave a lot of money away. I bought a lot of things." Finally Carlos said, "We're spending it pretty much as fast as we can get it, you know?" The majority of them spent the money on luxury items, drugs, and partying.

But not all identity thieves were so frivolous with their proceeds. In fact, many of them claimed that they spent money on everyday items. When asked what he did with the money Jake answered, "Nothing more than living off it, putting it away, saving it... Nothing flashy. Just living off it." Similarly, Bonnie responded, "Just having extra money to do things with... but nothing extravagant or anything like that." Oscar simply stated, "Just pay bills, you know."

---

[2] The offenders' names have been changed.

Identity thieves used the proceeds of their crimes to fund their chosen lifestyles. Much has been written describing the self-indulgent lifestyles of persistent street offenders. Of the 54 for which we had information about their lifestyle, 23 led lifestyles similar to persistent street-offenders. Like their street-offender counterparts, these individuals led a "life of party." Proceeds were more likely to be spent maintaining partying lifestyles filled with drug use and fast living than putting money aside for long-term plans. Bridgette explained succinctly why she committed identity theft, "getting money and getting high." This lifestyle was described by Lawrence:

> I made a lot of money and lost a lot of money. It comes in and you throw it out.... Partying, females. I gave a lot of money away. I bought a lot of things. A lot of people put things in their names.... Back and forth to Miami, to Atlanta. I mean it's a party.... Just to party, go to clubs, strip clubs and stuff. Just to party.

The ease at which money was made and spent is reflected in the words of Sheila:

> I was eating great food, buying clothes, going shopping, getting my hair done, you know, wasting it. I wish I would have bought a house or something like that, but it probably would have got taken away anyways.

However, not all indulged in such a lifestyle. In fact, some showed restraint in their spending. Nearly half of those we had lifestyle information on used the money they gained from identity theft to support what could be considered conventional lives (n = 24). In addition, seven others could be classified as drifting between a party lifestyle and a more conventional one. These offenders made efforts to conceal their misdeeds from their friends and family and to present a law-abiding front to outsiders. They used the proceeds of identity theft to finance comfortable middle-class lives, including paying rent or mortgages, buying expensive vehicles, and splurging on the latest technological gadgets. Bruce engaged in identity theft "to maintain an upper class lifestyle. To be able to ride in first class, the best hotels, the best everything." Their lifestyles were in line with the telemarketers interviewed by Shover, Coffey, and Sanders (2004). This is not to say that they did not indulge in the trappings of drugs and partying. Many did. As Denise explains, "I didn't do a lot of partying. I bought a lot of weed, paid out a lot, kept insurance going and the car note, put stereos in my car." Nevertheless, they put forth an image of middle-class respectability.

Offenders have a variety of options when seeking means to fund their chosen lifestyles. Regardless of their lifestyle offenders are often confronted with a perceived need for quick cash. This was certainly true for the identity thieves we spoke with, regardless of their lifestyle. These self-defined desperate situations included drug habits, gambling debts, family crises, and loss of jobs. Shover's (1996, p. 100) description is applicable here: "Confronted by crisis and preoccupied increasingly with relieving immediate distress, the offender may experience and define himself as propelled by forces beyond his control." Edgar succinctly described why he engaged in identity theft, "Poverty. Poverty makes you do things." When asked how she got involved in identity theft Sherry explained, "Well, let's see. I had been laid off at work, my son was in trouble, about to go to jail. I needed money for a lawyer." Sylvia described the situations that led her to start her crimes:

> I had a mortgage company that went under. My partner embezzled a bunch of money. Certain events happened and you find yourself out there almost to be homeless and I knew people that did this but they never went to jail. And back then they didn't go to jail, so it was a calculated risk I took.

In the face of mounting financial problems, she like other identity thieves, thought identity theft could offer hope of relief, even if only temporarily.

For those who were addicted to alcohol or other drugs (n = 22), their addictions led them to devote increasing time and energy to the quest for monies to fund their habits. For identity thieves, as for others offenders, the inability to draw on legitimate or low risk resources eventually may precipitate a crisis that they believe can only be relieved through crime. Penni explained, "I started smoking meth and then when I started smoking meth, I stopped working and then I started doing this for money." In explaining how her and her husband relapsed into drug use Sherry said, "My husband had lost his job at [an airline] and I was working at a doctor's office and then I lost my job. So we were both on unemployment." The loss of both sources of incomes set them onto a path of drug use and identity theft. Finally, Heidi claimed that her relapse precipitated her crimes. In her words, "I was clean for three and a half years before I relapsed on methamphetamines and that's what brought me back into this."

In addition to the financial rewards of identity theft there are also intrinsic ones. Criminologists should not forget that crime can be fun and exciting (Katz, 1988). Eleven interviewees mentioned that they found identity theft "fun" or "exciting." These offenders said that they enjoyed the "adrenaline rush" provided by entering banks and stores and by "getting over" on people. Bruce describes what it was like going into banks, "It was fairly exciting to…I mean, every time you went to a retail establishment and you gave them the credit card you don't know what's going to happen." Similarly, Cori described, "It's just, it was, it was like a rush.…At first it was kind of fun. The lifestyle is addicting you know." Bridgette describes what it was like, "It was like a high.…It's all about getting over." When asked to describe the rush he felt from engaging in identity theft Lawrence replied:

> It's money. It's knowing I'm getting over on them. Knowing I can manipulate the things and the person I got going in there. It's everything. It wasn't just…I guess you can say it is a little fear, but it's not fear for me, though. It's fear for the person I got going in there. I don't know. It's kind of weird. I don't know how to explain it…But it's the rush. Knowing that I created this thing to manipulate these banks, you know what I'm saying? They're going to pay

me for it and I'm going to manipulate this dude out of the money when they cashing those checks.

Dustin attributed his continuance with identity theft to the thrill:

I like to go out with money. But eventually it got to the point where I didn't need money. I was just doing it for the high. But that is basically what it was. The rush of standing there in her face and lying. [Laughter]. That's what it was. I'm being honest. I didn't need the money. I had plenty.

But even for these individuals, except Dustin, the thrill factor of identity theft was a secondary motivation to the money. Thrills alone did not instigate or propel identity theft. It is possible, however, that offenders persisted with identity theft because of the excitement of these crimes.

Previous reports on identity theft have pointed out that some of these crimes are precipitated by the desire to hide from the law or to get utilities or phone service activated (Newman, 2004). Only three people with whom we spoke mentioned such reasons. Jolyn told us that she had a warrant out so she used another's identity to get a telephone. Although her crimes started as a means to get telephone services, she eventually used this information to garner social security benefits. Additionally, Jamie said, "I needed my utilities on. [I did it] for that reason. I've never used it as far as applying for a credit card though because I knew that was a no."

METHODS AND TECHNIQUES OF IDENTITY THEFT

Acquiring Information

Offenders in our sample utilized a variety of methods to procure information and then convert this information into cash and/or goods. In fact, most did not specialize in a single method, instead, they preferred to use a variety of strategies. Although some offenders in our sample acquired identities from their place of employment (35%), mainly mortgage companies, the most common method of obtaining a victim's information was to buy it (n = 13). Offenders in our sample bought identities from employees of various businesses and state agencies who had access to personal information such as name, address, date of birth, and Social Security number (n = 5). Information was purchased from employees of banks, credit agencies, a state law enforcement agency, mortgage companies, state departments of motor vehicles, hospitals, doctor's offices, a university, car dealerships, and furniture stores. Those buying information said that it was easy to find someone willing to sell them what they wanted. According to Gladys, "It's so easy to get information and everybody has a price." Penni, said:

people that work at a lot of places, they give you a lot of stuff...hospitals, DMV, like Wal-Mart, a lot of places, like [local phone company]. People fill out applications. A lot of stuff like that and you get it from a lot of people. There's a lot of tweekers [drug addicts] out there and everybody's trying to make a dollar and always trading something for something.

When describing how she obtained information from a bank employee, Kristin said:

she was willing to make some money too, so she had the good information. She would have the information that would allow me to have a copy of the signature card, passwords, work address, everything, everything that's legit.

Eight offenders who purchased information did so from persons they knew or who they were acquainted with "on the streets." Lawrence explained, "...[people on the streets] knew what I was buying. I mean any city, there's always somebody buying some information." The identity thieves bought information from other offenders who obtained it from burglaries, thefts from motor vehicles, prostitution, and pick-pocketing. One offender purchased information from boyfriends or girlfriends of the victims. For the most part, those with whom we spoke did not know nor care where their sellers obtained their information. As long as the information was good they asked no questions.

Five individuals obtained information by using the mailbox method and another two got information by searching trash cans. Those offenders typically stole mail from small businesses such as insurance companies or from residential mailboxes in front of homes or apartments. Some offenders simply drove through residential areas and pulled mail out, often taking steps to appear to be legitimate, that is, they placed flyers advertising a business in mailboxes. Mailboxes and trashcans for businesses that send out mail with personal information (account numbers, Social Security numbers, and date of birth) such as insurance companies were also popular targets.

Although most of the offenders we interviewed did not know their victims, of those who did six said that the victim willingly gave them the information in exchange for a cut of the profits. In these cases, the "victim" gave the offender information to commit the identity theft and then reported that their identity had been stolen. According to Lawrence, "What I did was I had got this guy's personal information, he actually willingly gave it to me." Five offenders used family members' information without their knowledge and in one case the information was on family members who were deceased. Another five stole from friends or acquaintances without their knowledge.

Other methods of acquiring victims' information included various thefts (house and car burglary, purse-snatching) (n = 3) and socially engineering people to get their information (n = 2). One individual set up a fake employment site to get information from job applicants. Another used the birth announcements in newspapers to get the names of new parents and, posing as an insurance representative, called the parents to get information for "billing purposes." Interestingly, the offender made the phone calls from the waiting room of the hospitals where the infants were born so that the name of the hospital would appear on the victims' Caller ID if they had it. Another offender used rogue Internet sites to run background checks and order credit reports on potential victims. In addition, nine individuals claimed to work in a group where others obtained information. These thieves chose not to ask where the information came from.

Converting Information

After they obtain a victim's information the offender must convert that information to cash or goods. Most commonly, offenders used the information to acquire or produce additional identity related documents such as driver's licenses or state identification cards. Some offenders created the cards themselves with software and materials, for example, paper and ink, purchased at office supply stores or given to them by an employee of a state department of motor vehicles. Other offenders knew someone or had someone working for them who produced IDs. Identification cards were needed to withdraw cash from the victim's existing bank account or to open a new account.

Offenders used a variety of methods to profit from the stolen identities. The most common strategies were applying for credit cards in the victims' names (including major credit cards and department store credit cards), opening new bank accounts and depositing counterfeit checks, withdrawing money from existing bank accounts, applying for loans, and applying for public assistance programs. Identity thieves often used more than one technique when cashing in on their crimes.

The most common strategy for converting stolen identities into cash was by applying for credit cards. Twenty-three offenders used the information to order new credit cards. In a few cases, the information was used to get the credit card agency to issue a duplicate card on an existing account. They used credit cards to buy merchandise for their own personal use, to resell the merchandise to friends and/or acquaintances, or to return the merchandise for cash. Offenders also used the checks that are routinely sent to credit card holders to deposit in the victim's account and then withdraw cash or to open new accounts. Offenders also applied for store credit cards such as department stores and home improvement stores. According to Emma:

> [I would] go to different department stores or most often it was Lowes or Home Depot, go in, fill out an application with all the information, and then receive instant credit in the amount from say $1,500 to $7,500. Every store is different. Every individual is different. And then at that time, I would purchase as much as that balance that I could at one time. So if it was $2,500, I would buy $2,500 worth of merchandise.

Another common strategy is to produce counterfeit checks. Sixteen offenders either made fraudulent checks on their own or knew someone who would produce these checks for them. Although most offenders who counterfeited checks made personal checks, others made insurance checks or payroll checks. They cashed these checks at grocery stores, purchased merchandise, and paid bills such as utilities or cell phones.

Sometimes identity thieves would use the stolen identities to either open new bank accounts as a way to deposit fraudulent checks or to withdraw money from an existing account. Sixteen of the people we interviewed used this approach. Using this strategy required the offender to have information about the victims' bank account.

Another method of conversion included applying for and receiving loans. Fourteen individuals used this strategy. The majority of those who applied for loans engaged in some type of mortgage fraud. These types of scams often involved using victim's information to purchase homes for themselves. In one case, the offenders were buying houses and then renting them for a profit. Others applied for various auto loans, home equity loans, or personal loans.

SKILL SETS

As with any behavior, skills improve with experience. With practice, persistent burglars learn to assess the risks and value of homes almost instantaneously, crack dealers and prostitutes learn to discern undercover officers, and hustlers learn to recognize potential marks. Identity thieves have also developed a skill set to successfully accomplish their crimes. Four broad categories of skills emerged in our analysis of the interviews: (1) social skills, (2) intuitive skills, (3) technical skills, and (4) system knowledge.

Good social skills is perhaps the most important skill that identity thieves claim to possess. Social skills is the ability to manipulate the social situation through verbal and nonverbal communication. To be successful, an identity thief must possess the ability to "pass" as a regular customer in stores and banks and "be" the person they claim to be. This ability allows identity thieves to construct a larcenous situation as real and remove any doubts about the legitimacy of the situation. Identity thieves accomplish this through dress, mannerisms, and speech. When questioned as to what skills make a "good" identity thief, Gladys responded:

> I mean I can go into a place....Knowing how to look the part in certain situations...you go up to a place and you look in there and get the feeling about how a person would look and I'd take off a ring or something, put on a ring, take off some of your make-up, or go put on a hat or a scarf, put some glasses on.

Bridgette also made sure that whomever she sent into the bank was dressed to appear to be the person he/she claimed to be.

> I always made them dress accordingly, if you're going in to cash an insurance check, I want to dress nice and casual. If you were cashing a payroll check, you got to wear a uniform. I always try to find a uniform that match whatever company we were using. With the lab tech, we went right to the uniform shop and got it, the little nurse scrub sets and everything.

Tameka also "dressed" the part, "I might have on a nurse uniform, a lot of these they had me on I had on a nurse uniform." In describing what it was like interacting with bank and store employees Bruce, an experienced thief, said:

> You definitely have to be adaptable. It's not even being pleasant with people. It's just having authority. You have to have authority of whatever situation you are in. And if you have that authority, people will not go any further than to peripherally question you. That's about it.

Emma explained:

> I would just act as if I were that person and I would go in and I'd be talking to the person processing the application and, say if it were at Home Depot, I would be saying, "Oh, we're doing some remodeling of our home" or something like that and I'd engage the people.

The ability to socially engineer people and situations is especially important when things go wrong. When describing how she would conduct herself in a bank when questioned by employees, Tameka said:

> [i]f it was a tricky question you should be able to talk to the bank manager cause there were times when I asked to speak to the manager if I was withdrawing a large sum of money. In essence you had to become these people.

A second skill that identity thieves develop is intuitive skills, which can be defined as "an acute sensitization to and awareness of one's external surrounding" (Faupel, 1986). Some offenders superstitiously believed they have developed the ability to sense trouble, believing that if they do not "feel bad" about a crime then they are safe. April replied, "You kind of get, I don't know, almost like you dreaded walking into it." The ability to recognize criminal opportunity, sense danger and know when to call off a criminal plan has been referred to as "larceny sense," "grift sense," and "intuitive sense" (Faupel, 1986; Maurer, 1951; Sutherland, 1937). When asked how he got better at identity theft Bruce responded:

> Sensing…sensing what was going on within a situation, like at a bank, like I could sense what was going on with tellers. I could tell how they were looking at the screen, how long they were looking at it and I could sense whether something had been written or if I was cashing too many checks. Just a sense of how people react in situations and then also just the situations themselves. As many as they presented themselves, I would find a way around them. So I guess just honing the thinking on your feet…in the situations that came up.

Several offenders in this study believed they would not have been caught if they had paid attention to their premonitions. For instance, Kimi describes the moments before she was arrested:

> I knew the detectives were watching. I knew that and I had the feeling and I told [my co-defendant] but he was trying to kick heroin that day. And this

stupid fool was shooting and I'm all surrounded by heroin addicts. So one person, up all night, she was smoking meth and smoking weed, but everyone else was shooting heroin and I'm surrounded by them. And I told him I said, we got to leave. I have this freaking feeling something's going to go wrong.

Whether or not repeat offenders have a heightened ability to sense danger is less important than the fact that many believe they do.

A third type of skill identity thieves develop are technical skills. This refers to the technical knowledge needed to produce fraudulent documents such as identification, checks and credit applications. Making these documents look real is an increasingly difficult task. For example, determining the right types of paper to print checks on, how to replicate watermarks, and matching the colors on driver's licenses are necessary skills that must be learned. Lawrence describes:

I use a different type of paper. I use a regular document. The paper always came straight from the bank. A lot of people, they would get paper out of like Target or Office Max or places like that. That kind of paper right there, it's not always efficient. Nine times out of ten, the bank may stop it. They want to check the company payroll.

Although many identity thieves contract out for their documents, a sizable number learn these tricks through experimentation and practice. Kimi described her process:

We studied IDs then I went to the stamp shop, the paint shop, got the logos right and I know the [Bank] was one of the hardest banks for us to get money out, but when I found out about the logos, when I passed it through the black light, it became real easy.... I went to the stamp shop and bought a stamp and sat there for hours and hours with the colors and I made like seven different IDs before it come through under the black light.

The final skill discussed by identity thieves is system knowledge. This includes knowing how banks and credit agencies operate and knowing which stores require identification when cashing checks.

You have to have an idea of how banks work. At some point in your life, live a normal life and understand how credit is extended and things like that. (Sherry)

I was a bank teller. I knew how to approach a person. I knew the insights, you know, what they would look for, how much I could get, when to go out. (Sheila)

The development of these various skills plays an important role in crime persistence. By developing these skills identity thieves increase their chances of being successful at crime; that is, these skills allow them to avoid the formal sanctions associated with identity theft. Those who commit crime with impunity have overly optimistic views of their crimes (Cusson, 1993; Paternoster, Saltzman, Chiricos, & Waldo, 1982), which was the case for many of those we interviewed. Offenders come to believe that they could continue offending because they could rely on their skills to evade sanctions thereby nullifying the deterrent effects of criminal sanctions.

CONCLUSION

Our interviews with 59 offenders incarcerated in federal prisons revealed information about their motivations for identity theft and the methods they employ to acquire information and convert it into cash and/or goods. Results show that identity thieves are a diverse group. Offenders are primarily motivated by the quick need for cash and see identity theft as an easy, relatively risk-free way to get it. They employ a variety of methods to both acquire information and convert it to cash and have developed a set of skills to enable them to do so successfully.

References

Allison, S. F. H., Schuck, A. M., & Lersch, K. M. (2005). Exploring the crime of identity theft: Prevalence, clearance rates, and victim/offender characteristics. *Journal of Criminal Justice, 33*, 19–29.

Bernstein, S, E. (2004). New privacy concern for employee benefit plans: Combating identity theft. *Compensation and Benefits Review, 36*, 65–68.

Bureau of Justice Statistics. (2006, April). *Identity theft, 2004* (NCJ 212213). Washington, DC: U.S. Department of Justice.

Cusson, M. (1993). Situational deterrence: Fear during the criminal event. In R. Clarke (Ed.), *Crime prevention studies* (Vol. 1, pp. 55–68). Monsey, NY: Willow Tree Press.

Faupel, C. E. (1986). Heroin use, street crime, and the "main hustle": Implications for the validity of official crime data. *Deviant Behavior, 7,* 31–45.

Federal Trade Commission. (2006). *Consumer fraud and identity theft complaint data: January–December 2005.* Retrieved December 9, 2008, from http://www.consumer.gov/sentinel/pubs/Top10Fraud2005.pdf

Katz, J. (1988). *Seductions of crime.* New York: Basic Books.

Maurer, D. W. (1951). *Whiz mob: A correlation of the technical argot of pickpockets with their behavior patterns.* Gainesville, FL: American Dialect Society.

Newman, G. R. (2004). *Identity theft.* Washington, DC: U.S. Department of Justice.

Newman, G. R., & McNally, M. M. (2005). *Identity theft literature review.* Presented at the National Institute of Justice Focus Group Meeting. Retrieved December 9, 2008, from http://www.ncjrs.gov/pdffiles1/nij/grants/210459.pdf

Paternoster, R., Saltzman, L., Chiricos, T., & Waldo, G. (1982). Perceived risk and deterrence: Methodological artifacts in perceptual deterrence research. *Journal of Criminal Law and Criminology, 73*, 1238–1258.

Perl, M. W. (2003). It's not always about the money: Why the state identity theft laws fail to address criminal record identity theft. *Journal of Criminal Law and Criminology, 94,* 169–208.

Shover, N. (1996). *Great pretenders: Pursuits and careers of persistent thieves.* Boulder, CO: Westview.

Shover, N., Coffey, G., & Sanders, C. (2004). Dialing for dollars: Opportunities, justifications and telemarketing fraud. *Qualitative Sociology, 27,* 59–75.

Shover, N., & Hochstetler, A. (2006). *Choosing white-collar crime.* Cambridge, UK: Cambridge University Press.

Sutherland, E. (1937). *The professional thief.* Chicago: University of Chicago Press.

U.S. General Accounting Office (2002). *Identity theft Prevalence and cost appear to be growing.* GAO 02–363. U.S.

Wright, R. T., Brookman, F., & Bennet, T. (2006). The foreground dynamics of street robbery in Britain. *British Journal of Criminology, 46,* 1–15.

Wright, R., & Decker, S. (1994). *Burglars on the job.* Boston: Northeastern University Press.

VIOLENT CRIME

Violent crime refers to any criminal act committed through the threat of harm or actual physical harm to the victim. Violent crimes such as robbery, rape, and murder have profoundly affected the way we live and have clearly altered our lifestyles. Although the per capita crime rates for violent crime decreased slightly in the 1990s, because of increased population, the over-all incidence of violent crime has increased significantly in the past two decades.

Violent crime is often considered less rationally conceived than property crime. Violent behavior is often expressed in the "heat of passion"—during periods of great emotional turmoil. The violent act is thought to be more expressive than instrumental, having no real functional purpose or accept-able rationale. However, recent studies have shown that violence can be highly instrumental.

Chapter 8, "The New Faces of Terrorism: Socio-Cultural Foundations of Contemporary Terrorism," is new to this edition and is a rare study of actual Middle-Eastern terrorists," in their own words." Professor Jerrold Post inter-viewed 35 incarcerated terrorists, analyzing their motives and contrasting the religious fundamentalist terrorists of today with the leftist social-revolu-tionary terrorists of the last century.

In Chapter 9, "Creating the Illusion of Impending Death," Wright and Decker reported that violence can play an important role in the commission of armed robberies by overcoming the resistance of the victims. Violence is thus rationally employed to accomplish the goal of the robbery.

Chapter 10, "Gendering Violence: Masculinity and Power in Men's Accounts of Domestic Violence" by Kristin L. Anderson and Debra Umberson, reveals the strategies used by males in an effort to portray themselves as rational and non-violent. The authors found that offenders claim that women are responsible for their own victimization and that they (the men) are victims of a biased criminal justice system.

Chapter 11, "Retrospective Accounts of Violent Gun Offenders," exam-ines the excuses, explanations, and justifications provided by incarcerated offenders who have committed violent crimes using a firearm. The authors found that inmates frequently stated that their victims deserved their injury and did not offer further explanations. Others, however, offered justifications and excuses for their behavior.

In these selections we see violent crime as having both expressive and instrumental roots. The motives for their behavior, strategies used by the offenders to accomplish their crimes, and rationalizations used to avoid responsibility for their acts are graphically illustrated in this anthology.

8

The New Face of Terrorism: Socio-Cultural Foundations of Contemporary Terrorism

Jerrold M. Post

*A*fter the terrorist attacks of 9/11, President George W. Bush declared that this was "the first war of the 21st century," but in fact the modern era of terrorism is usually dated back to the early 1970s, as represented by the radical Palestinian terrorist group Black September seizure of the Israeli Olympic village at the 1972 Munich Olympics, an event which captured an immense international television audience and demonstrated powerfully the amplifying effect of the electronic media in the information age.

In the early years of the modern era of terrorism, two terrorist types dominated the landscape. They were the social-revolutionary terrorists, also known as terrorism of the left, groups seeking to overthrow the capitalist economic and social order, exemplified by the Red Army Faction in Germany and the Red Brigades in Italy, and nationalist-separatist terrorists, such as al-Fatah and other radical secular Palestinian terrorists, the Provisional Irish Republican Army of Northern Ireland (PIRA), and the Basque separatist group Euskadi ta Askatasuna (ETA) (Freedom for the Basque Homeland), seeking to establish a separate nation for their national minority. Both of these group types wished to call attention to their cause and would regularly claim responsibility for their acts. They were seeking to influence the West and the establishment. Often there were multiple claims of responsibility for the same act. Social-revolutionary terrorist groups have experienced a significant decline over the last two decades, paralleling the collapse of communism in Europe and the end of the cold war.

The author obtained semi-structured interviews with 35 incarcerated Middle Eastern terrorists, including 21 Muslim extremists from Hamas (and its armed wing, Iza a-Din al Qassan), Islamic Jihad, and Hizballah and 14 secular subjects from Fatah and its military wing (PFLP and DFLP), as well as interviews with an Abu Nidal and al-Qaeda terrorists in connection with federal trials. The incarcerated terrorists were convicted by Israeli courts and were serving their sentences in

Source: Post, J. M. (2005a). The New Face of Terrorism: Socio-Cultural Foundations of Contemporary Terrorism. *Behavioral Sciences and the Law*, 23, 451–465. This article is drawn in part from the Nevitt Sanford Award Lecture "When Hatred is Bred to the Bone" presented to the International Society of Political Psychology, July 2003 (Post, 2005b).

either Israeli or Palestinian prisons. The interviews were conducted with the under-standing that the subjects would remain anonymous. One subject, Hassan Salame, a suicide bomber commander, allowed his name to be used and signed a release.

NATIONALIST–SEPARATIST TERRORISM

In contrast to the social-revolutionary terrorist groups, nationalist-separatist terrorism continues as one of the two predominant terrorist types active today. Also known as ethnonationalist terrorism, these groups are fighting to establish a new political order or state based on ethnic dominance or homogeneity. They are carrying on the mission of their parents and grand-parents who have been damaged by, or are disloyal to, the regime. They are loyal to families that are disloyal to the regime. Their acts of terrorism are acts of vengeance against the regime that damaged their families. This is in vivid contrast to the social-revolutionary terrorists who are rebelling against the generation of their parents, who are loyal to the regime. They are disloyal to the generation of their families that is loyal to the regime. Their acts of ter-rorism are acts of revenge against the generation of their families that they hold responsible for their failures in this world (Post, 1984).

ISLAMIST FUNDAMENTALIST TERRORISM

However, in recent decades, no responsibility has been claimed for upward of 40% of terrorist acts. We believe this is because of the increasing frequency of terrorist acts by radical religious extremist terrorists, in particular radical Islamist fundamentalist terrorists. They are not trying to influence the West. Rather, the radical Islamist terrorists are trying to expel the secular modern-izing West. And they do not need recognition by having their name identi-fied in a *New York Times* headline or on a story on CNN. They are "killing in the name of God" and do not need official notice; after all, God knows.

Traditional groups include Islamic, Jewish, Christian, and Sikh radical fundamentalist extremists. In contrast to social revolutionary and nation-alist-separatist terrorists, for religious fundamentalist extremist groups, the decision-making role of the preeminent leader is of central importance. For these true believers, the radical cleric is seen as the authentic interpreter of God's word, not only eliminating any ambivalence about killing but also endowing the destruction of the defined enemy with sacred significance. These groups are accordingly particularly dangerous, for they are not seek-ing to influence the West but to expel the West with its secular moderniz-ing values and hence are not constrained by Western reactions. They have shown a willingness to perpetrate acts of mass casualty terrorism, as exem-plified by the bombings of Khobar Towers in Saudi Arabia, the World Trade Center in the United States, the U.S. embassies in Kenya and Tanzania, the U.S.S. *Cole,* and the mass casualty terrorism on a scale never seen before in the coordinated attacks on the World Trade Center in New York and the Pentagon in Washington, DC. Osama bin Laden, directly responsible for a number of these events, has actively discussed the use of weapons of mass destruction in public interviews.

Although he is not a religious authority, Osama bin Laden is known for his piety and has been granted the title emir. Like Khomeini, Osama bin Laden regularly cites verses from the Koran to justify his acts of terror and extreme violence, employing many of the same verses as earlier cited by Khomeini. Consider this extract from the February 1998 *Fatwa*, Jihad Against Jews and Crusaders, World Islamic Front Statement:

> In compliance with God's order, we issue the following *fatwa* to all Muslims:
>
> The ruling to kill the Americans and their allies—civilians and military—is an individual duty for every Muslim who can do it in any country in which it is possible to do it, in order to liberate the al-Aqsa Mosque and the holy mosque [Mecca] from their grip, and in order for their armies to move out of all the lands of Islam, defeated and unable to threaten any Muslim. This is in accordance with the words of Almighty God, "and fight the pagans all together as they fight you all together," and "fight them until there is no more tumult or oppression, and there prevail justice and faith in God."
>
> We—with God's help—call on every Muslim who believes in God and wishes to be rewarded to comply with God's order to kill the Americans and plunder their money wherever and whenever they find it.

Note that it is not Osama bin Laden who is ordering his followers to kill Americans. It is God! Osama bin Laden is the messenger, relaying the commands of God, which are justified with verses from the Koran. The author discussed this language with a moderate Muslim cleric, who indicated that this was blasphemous, that bin Laden was speaking as if he were the new prophet and was the authentic interpreter of the Koran. He emphasized that many of the actions for which bin Laden found justification in the Koran were in fact prohibited by the Koran.

Al-Qaeda, Hamas, Hezbollah, and the Islamic Jihad all have found an abundance of recruits, eager to join these Islamic fundamentalist terrorist organizations. Indeed, Ariel Merari (personal communication), a prominent Israeli expert on terrorism, noted wryly that for every terrorist killed or captured there were ten waiting to take his (or her) place, and that there were now more terrorist volunteers than there are suicide explosive belts. For them, like the youth drawn to the path of nationalist-separatist terrorism, hatred has been "bred in the bone."

These two groups—nationalist–separatist terrorists and Islamist religious fundamentalist terrorists—represent the major threats to contemporary society and will be the focus of the balance of this article. To bring the readers into their minds, we will draw upon the words of terrorists themselves, drawing on material from a research project (Post, Sprinzak, & Denny, 2002) funded by the Smith Richardson Foundation involving semistructured interviews with 35 incarcerated radical Middle Eastern terrorists, both radical Islamist terrorists from Hamas, Islamic Jihad, and Hezbollah, and secular terrorists from Fatah and the Palestinian Front for the Liberation of Palestine, as well as from interviews conducted by the author with an Abu Nidal terrorist and al-Qaeda terrorists in connection with federal trials.

NATIONALIST—SEPARATIST SECULAR PALESTINIAN TERRORISM

Secular Palestinian Terrorists in their Own Words

Although most Fatah members reported that their families had good social standing, their status and experience as refugees was paramount in their development of self-identity:

> I belong to the generation of occupation. My family are refugees from the 1967 war. The war and my refugee status were the seminal events that formed my political consciousness and provided the incentive for doing all. I could to help regain our legitimate rights in our occupied country.

For the secular terrorists, enlistment was a natural step. The identity of the members was well known in the community and joining led to enhanced social status:

> Enlistment was for me the natural and done thing...in a way, it can be com-pared to a young Israeli from a nationalist Zionist family who wants to fulfill himself through army service.
>
> My motivation in joining Fatah was both ideological and personal. It was a question of self-fulfillment, of honor and a feeling of independence...the goal of every young Palestinian was to be a fighter.
>
> After recruitment, my social status was greatly enhanced. I got a lot of respect from my acquaintances and from the young people in the village.

In addition to causing as many casualties as possible, armed action pro-vided a sense of control or power for Palestinians in a society that had stripped them of it. Inflicting pain on the enemy was paramount in the early days of the Fatah movement:

> I regarded armed actions to be essential; it is the very basis of my organiza-tion and I am sure that was the case in the other Palestinian organizations. An armed action proclaims that I am here, I exist, I am strong, I am in control, I am in the field, I am on the map. An armed action against soldiers was the most admired....the armed actions and their results were a major tool for penetrat-ing the public consciousness.
>
> The various armed actions (stabbing collaborators, martyrdom opera-tions, attacks on Israeli soldiers) all had different ratings. An armed action that caused casualties was rated highly and seen to be of great importance.

An armed action without casualties was not rated. No distinction was made between armed actions on soldiers or on civilians; the main thing was the amount of blood. The aim was to cause as much carnage as possible.

View of Armed Attacks

Armed attacks are viewed as essential to the operation of the organization. There is no question about the necessity of these types of attack to the success of the cause:

> You have to understand that armed attacks are an integral part of the organization's struggle against the Zionist occupier. There is no other way to redeem the land of Palestine and expel the occupier. Our goals can only be achieved through force, but force is the means, not the end. History shows that without force it will be impossible to achieve independence.

Socialization of Hatred

The hatred socialized toward the Israelis was remarkable, especially given that few reported any contact with Israelis:

> You Israelis are Nazis in your souls and in your conduct. In your occupation you never distinguish between men and women, or between old people and children. You adopted methods of collective punishment; you uprooted people from their homeland and from their homes and chased them into exile. You fired live ammunition at women and children. You smashed the skulls of defenseless civilians. You set up detention camps for thousands of people in sub-human conditions. You destroyed homes and turned children into orphans. You prevented people from making a living, you stole their property, you trampled on their honor. Given that kind of conduct, there is no choice but to strike at you without mercy in every possible way.

The Cauldron of Life Experiences of an Abu Nidal Terrorist

In 1996, the author had the opportunity and challenge of assisting the Department of Justice as an expert on terrorist psychology in the trial in Federal Court in Washington, DC, of Mohammad Rezaq, an Abu Nidal terrorist who played a leading role in the skyjacking of an Egypt Air passenger jet in which more than 50 lost their lives in the skyjacking and the subsequent SWAT team attack on the hijacked plane in Malta (Post, 2000).

The defendant epitomized the life and psychology of the nationalist-separatist terrorist. The defendant assuredly did not believe that what he was doing was wrong, for from boyhood on Rezaq had been socialized to be a heroic revolutionary fighting for the Palestinian nation. Demonstrating the generational transmission of hatred, his case can be considered emblematic of many from the ranks of ethnic/nationalist terrorist groups, from Northern Ireland to Palestine, from Armenia to the Basque region of Spain.

In 1948, when the subject's mother was 8, as a consequence of the 1948 Arab–Israeli war, her family was forced to flee their home in Jaffa in Israel.

They left for the West Bank, where Rezaq was raised. In 1967, when Rezaq was 8, the 1967 war occurred, and the family was forced to flee their pleasant West Bank existence, ending up in a crowded Palestinian refugee camp in Jordan. Rezaq's mother told him bitterly that this was the second time this had happened to her.

There he went to a school funded by the UN and was taught by a member of Fatah whom he came to idolize. At the time, Arafat's stature as a heroic freedom fighter was celebrated in the camps. He was taught that the only way to become a man was to join the revolution and take back the lands stolen from his parents and grandparents. Two years of obligatory service in the Jordanian army were required, and in 1977, at age 19, he was sent to a camp near Iraq for military training. There, the Palestinians were treated as second-class citizens, leading many to desert.

After only 3 months in the Jordanian army, Rezaq deserted and joined Fatah. When he first participated in a terrorist action, he felt at last he was doing what he should do. He left Fatah after becoming disillusioned with Arafat's leadership. He moved from terrorist group to terrorist group, initially enthused then disillusioned, with each group he joined more militant than the preceding and ended up in the most violent secular Palestinian terrorist group, the Abu Nidal Organization. When he ultimately was assigned a command role in the skyjacking of an EgyptAir airliner, he felt he was at last fulfilling his destiny. He was taking a bold action to help his people. He was a soldier for the revolution and all of the actions that he directed that led to the major loss of life were seen as required by his role as a soldier for the cause, a cause that ultimately would lead to the restoration of his family's lands.

ISLAMIST FUNDAMENTALIST TERRORISM

Interview with a Tanzanian Embassy Bomber

In the spring and summer of 2001, the author had the opportunity of interviewing at length one of the defendants in the al-Qaeda bombing of the U.S. embassy in Tanzania. Raised on Zanzibar off the coast of Tanzania, he was 8 when his father died and then was educated in a *madrassa*, where he was taught to never question what he was told by learned authorities. When he was the equivalent of a junior in high school his brother directed him to leave school and help him in his grocery store in Dar es Salaan. There he was miserable—alone, friendless, isolated, except for his attendance at the Friday prayer services at the mosque, where he learned from the *imam* that they were all members of *al-umma*, the community of observant Muslims, and had an obligation to help Muslims wherever they were being persecuted. He was shown videos of Muslim mass graves in Bosnia and the Serbian military, of the bodies of Muslim women and children in Chechnya and the Russian military. He became inspired and vowed to become, in his own words, "a soldier for Allah," but he was informed (I infer by a spotter from al-Qaeda) that he could not do this without obtaining training. So, using his own funds, he went to Pakistan and then on to a bin Laden training camp in Afghanistan, where he was taught weapons and explosives handling in the mornings and had four hours of ideological training each afternoon. After 7 months when he could not join the struggle in Bosnia or Chechnya, where he would be fighting against the military, although offered the opportunity to fight in Kashmir, an unconventional conflict, he declined,[1] and returned to Dar es Salaan, where he again pursued his menial existence as a grocery clerk, frustrated at his inability to pursue *jihad*. Three years later, he was called in the middle of the night and asked "Do you want to do a *jihad* job?" and without further inquiry he accepted. What had been a positive motivation to help suffering Muslims was gradually bent to his participating in this act of mass casualty terrorism.

RELIGIOUS FUNDAMENTALIST TERRORISTS IN THEIR OWN WORDS

The mosque was consistently cited as the place where most members were initially introduced to the Palestinian/Israeli conflict, including members of the secular groups. Many of the secular members report that while activism within the community was most influential in their decision to join, their first introduction to the cause was at the mosque or in another religious setting. Authority figures from the mosque were prominent in all conversations with group members and most dramatically for members of the Islamist organizations. The introduction to authority and unquestioning obedience to Allah and authority is instilled at a young age and continues to be evident in the individual members' subservience to the larger organization. This preconditioning of unquestioning acceptance of authority seems to be most evident among the members of the Islamist groups such as Hamas and Islamic Jihad:

> I came from a religious family, which used to observe all the Islamic traditions. My initial political awareness came during the prayers at the mosque. That's where I was also asked to join religious classes. In the context of these studies, the sheik used to inject some historical background in which he would tell us how we were effectively evicted from Palestine.

---

[1] When questioned as to why he would not fight in Kashmir, the subject explained that the fourth *jihad*, the *jihad* of the sword, commands observant Muslims to take up the sword against those who take up the sword against Muslims. It is thus a defensive *jihad* only. He had envisaged himself fighting soldiers in uniform, either Serbian or Russian military. Later, when confronted with photographs of the bombed embassy in Dar es-Salaan, learning of the hundred of innocent victims who lost their lives, he exclaimed "their *jihad* is not my *jihad*," explaining that nowhere in the Koran does it justify killing innocent civilians.

The sheik also used to explain to us the significance of the fact that there was an *IDF* (Israel Defence Force) military outpost in the heart of the camp. He compared it to a cancer in the human body, which was threatening its very existence.

At the age of 16 I developed an interest in religion. I was exposed to the Moslem brotherhood and I began to pray in a mosque and to study Islam. The Koran and my religious studies were the tools that shaped my political consciousness. The mosque and the religious clerics in my village provided the focal point of my social life.

Community support was important to the families of the fighters as well:

Families of terrorists who were wounded, killed or captured enjoyed a great deal of economic aid and attention. And that strengthened popular support for the attacks.

Perpetrators of armed attacks were seen as heroes, their families got a great deal of material assistance, including the construction of new homes to replace those destroyed by the Israeli authorities as punishment for terrorist acts.

The Emir blesses all actions.

Major actions become the subject of sermons in the mosque, glorifying the attack and the attackers.

Joining Hamas or Fatah increased social standing.

Recruits were treated with great respect. A youngster who belonged to Hamas or Fatah was regarded more highly than one who didn't belong to a group and got better treatment than unaffiliated kids.

Anyone who didn't enlist during that period (*intifada*) would have been ostracized.

View of armed attacks:

The more an attack hurts the enemy, the more important it is. That is the measure. The mass killings, especially the martyrdom operations, were the biggest threat to the Israeli public and so most effort was devoted to these. The extent of the damage and the number of casualties are of primary importance.

The Justification of Suicide Bombings

The Islamist terrorists in particular provided the religious basis for what the West has called suicide terrorism as the most valued technique of *jihad*, distinguishing this from suicide, which is proscribed in the Koran. One in fact became quite angry when the term was used in our question, angrily exclaiming:

This is not suicide. Suicide is selfish, it is weak, it is mentally disturbed. This is *istishad* (martyrdom or self-sacrifice in the service of Allah).

Several of the Islamist terrorist commanders interviewed called the suicide bombers holy warriors who were carrying out the highest level of *jihad*:

> A martyrdom operation is the highest level of *jihad* and highlights the depth of our faith. The bombers are holy fighters who carry out one of the more important articles of faith.[2]
>
> It is attacks when the member gives his life that earn the most respect and elevate the bombers to the highest possible level of martyrdom:
>
> I asked Halil what is was all about and he told me that he had been on the wanted list for a long time and did not want to get caught without realizing his dream of being a martyrdom operation bomber. He was completely calm and explained to the other two bombers, Yusuf and Beshar, how to detonate the bombs, exactly the way he had explained things to the bombers in the Mahane Yehuda attack. I remember that besides the tremendous respect I had for Halil, and the fact that I was jealous of him, I also felt slighted that he had not asked me to be the third martyrdom operation bomber. I understood that my role in the movement had not come to an end and the fact that I was not on the wanted list and could operate relatively freely could be very advantageous to the movement in the future. (Quote from prisoner sentenced to 26 life terms for role in several suicide-bombing campaigns)

Sense of Remorse/Moral Red Lines

> When it came to moral considerations, we believed in the justice of our cause and in our leaders....I don't recall every being troubled by moral questions.

In a *jihad*, there are no red lines.

CONTRAST BETWEEN PALESTINIAN SUICIDE BOMBERS IN ISRAEL AND SUICIDAL HIJACKERS OF 9/11

So-called psychological autopsies, that is, reconstructions of the lives of suicides, have been developed for some 93 suicide bombers of the Palestinian suicide bombers in Israel (Merari, personal communication). Although these demographic features are undergoing change, and now the age range has broadened significantly and some women have joined the ranks of suicide bombers, they were for the most part carried out by young men between the ages of 17 and 22, unmarried, uneducated, unemployed. They were unformed youth, who, when they volunteered or were recruited, were told by the recruiters that their life prospects were bleak, that they could do something significant with their lives, that they would be enrolled in the hall of martyrs, and that their parents would be proud of them and would gain

---

[2] Hassan Salame was responsible for the wave of suicide bombings in Israel in 1996, in which 46 were killed. He is now serving 46 consecutive life sentences.

financial rewards. From the moment they entered the safe house, they were never alone. Someone slept in the same room with them the night before the action to ensure that they did not backslide and physically escorted them to the pizza parlor, disco, or shopping mall to carry out their acts of suicide terrorism. Merari (personal communication) has called attention to the suicide-bomber production line, where the first step is to volunteer to become a *shahid* (martyr), then they are identified publicly as living martyrs, and finally they make the preattack video which will then be used both to memorialize their name and for recruitment purposes. These tapes, which are used for recruitment, are a crucial last step, a public declaration. He observes it is very difficult to back down after passing through these stages; the shame that would attend such a reversal would be unbearable.

What a vivid contrast with the suicidal hijackers of 9/11! Older, their age range was 28–33, with the exception of a small group of younger terrorists, brought in late for "muscle," who were probably unaware that theirs was not a conventional hijacking. Mohammad Atta, the ringleader, was 33. A number had higher education; Atta and two of his colleagues were in Master's degree programs in the technological university in Hamburg. And most came from comfortable, middle-class homes in Saudi Arabia or Egypt. Unlike the Palestinian suicide bombers, these were fully formed adults, who had subordinated their individuality to the organization, as they responded uncritically to the siren song of hatred sung by the hate-mongering destructive charismatic leader, Osama bin Laden.

Although many drawn to the path of religious fundamentalist terrorism are poor and uneducated, for some of these terrorists there are suggestive similarities to the generational dynamics of the social revolutionary terrorists. Osama bin Laden himself is the most striking example of these generational dynamics (Post, 2002). He is the 17th of 25 sons of a multibillionaire construction magnate, Muhammad bin Laden, a Yemeni émigré, whose financial empire and wealth came from a special relationship with the Saudi royal family. When Osama bin Laden railed at the corruption of the Saudi royal family and their lack of fidelity to Islam in permitting the American military to establish a base on holy Saudi land, he was striking out at the source of his family wealth, leading not only to his being expelled from Saudi Arabia but also severely damaging his family, who also turned against him.

Interestingly, and compellingly, many of the 9/11 suicidal hijackers had been living on their own in the West, in some cases for as long as 7 years, being exposed to the "buzzing, blooming, confusion of a democracy" we live in, simulating blending in, while carrying within them like a laser beam their mission to give of their lives while taking the lives of thousands. Accused of being hypocrites, they were unbearded, did not exchange Muslim greetings, were not seen in mosques, at prayer, or to be fasting.

In the al-Qaeda terrorism manual, *Declaration of Jihad against the Country's Tyrants*, which was introduced as an exhibit by the Department of Justice in the trial of the Tanzanian embassy bombers, it explains the rationale for their apparent hypocrisy. Lesson 11 explains the answer to the question "How can a Muslim spy live among enemies if he maintains his Islamic characteristics? How can he perform his duties to Allah and not want to appear Muslim?"

> Concerning the issue of clothing and appearance (the appearance of true religion), Ibn Taimia—may Allah have mercy on him—said, "If a Muslim is in a combat or godless area, he is not obligated to have a different appearance from (those around him.) The (Muslim) man may prefer or even be obligated to look like them, provided his action brings a religious benefit of preaching to them, learning their secrets and informing Muslims."
>
> Resembling the polytheist in religious appearance is a kind of "necessity permits the forbidden" even though they (forbidden acts) are basically prohibited.

FUSION OF THE INDIVIDUAL AND THE GROUP

Once recruited, there is a clear fusing of individual identity and group identity, particularly among the more radical elements of each organization. This is true both for the Islamist terrorists of Hamas and Islamic Jihad and for those of al-Qaeda. Many of the interviewees reported growing up or living in a repressed or limited socioeconomic status. Their ability to work was regulated, the ability to travel freely was severely restricted, and there was a general impression that they were denied the opportunity to advance economically. There was a common theme of having been "unjustly evicted" from their land, of being relegated to refugee status or living in refugee camps in a land that was once considered theirs. Many of the interviewees expressed an almost fatalistic view of the Palestinian/Israeli relationship and a sense of despair or bleakness about the future under Israeli rule. Few of the interviewees were able to identify personal goals that were separate from those of the organization to which they belonged. However, the appeal of al-Qaeda as well is to alienated youth, often feeling they are blocked in societies where there is no real possibility of advancement.

There is a heightened sense of the heroic associated with fallen group members and the community supports and rallies around families of the fallen or incarcerated. Most interviewees reported not only enhanced social status for the families of fallen or incarcerated members, but financial and material support from the organization and community for these families as well. "Success" within the community is defined as fighting for "the cause"— liberation and religious freedom are the values that define success, not necessarily academic or economic accomplishment. As the young men adopt this view of success, their own self-image then becomes more intimately intertwined with the success of the organization. With no other means to achieve status and "success," the organization's success becomes central to individual identity and provides a "reason for living," so that individual identity is subordinated to collective identity. Again, although this dynamic emerged clearly for the youth of Islamic Jihad and Hamas, it is also probably a strong characteristic of those attracted to the path of radical Islam elsewhere.

This fusing of the individual to the group is found across all organizations regardless of ideological affiliation. As individual identity succumbs to the organization, there is no room for individuality—individual ideas, individual identity and individual decision making—while at the same time self-perceived success becomes more and more linked to the organization. Individual self-worth is again intimately tied to the "value" or prominence of the group—therefore, each individual has a vested interest not only in ensuring the success of the organization, but also in increasing its prominence and exposure. The more prominent and more important (and often times the more violent) a group is, the greater the prestige that is then projected onto group members. This creates a cycle where a group's members have a direct need to increase the power and prestige of the group through increasingly dramatic and violent operations.

As the individuals and the group fuse, the more personal the struggle becomes for the group members. There is a symbiotic relationship created between the individual need to belong to a group, the need to ensure success of the group, and an enhanced desire to be an increasingly more active member of the group. There is thus a personalization of the struggle, with an inability to distinguish between personal goals and those of the organization—they are one and the same. In their discussion of armed action and other actions taken, the success or failure of the group's action was personal—if the group succeeded, then as an individual they succeeded; if the group failed, they failed. Pride and shame as expressed by the individual were reflections of group actions, not individual actions, feelings or experiences. There is an overarching sense of the collective that consumes the individual. This fusion with the group seems to provide the necessary justification for their actions and absolution, or loss of responsibility, to the individual—if the group says it is okay, then it is okay. If the authority figure orders an action, then the action is justified. Guilt or remorse by the individual is not tolerated because the organization does not express it. Again this is intensified among Islamist groups who feel they have a moral obligation to the cause and a religiously sanctioned justification for their actions.

Most interestingly and illustrative of this concept of individual and group fusion is the perception or characterization of "the enemy." Although there are slight differences between the secular and Islamist groups in the exact definition of the enemy, the overall experience in defining the enemy is remarkably similar. The Islamist groups are fighting for a pure Islamic state. Many interviewees cite Iran as an example of the type of state they would like to create. Although the secular groups have a type of constraint by the nature of their view of the struggle, the Islamist groups have no such restraint. There is no concern about alienating any "earthly" population because the only "audience" they are seeking to satisfy is Allah. With their direction coming in the form of religious *fatwas* (religious edicts) and sanctioned by religious clerics and other figures, the identification of the enemy is clear and simple for these Islamist groups—whether Israel or the United States—it is anyone who is opposed to their worldview.

TERRORIST PSYCHOLOGY: IMPLICATIONS
FOR COUNTER-TERRORIST STRATEGY

If these conclusions concerning the individual, group, and organizational psychology of political terrorism are valid, what are the implications for anti-terrorist policy? (It is interesting to observe how passionately arguments are waged concerning counterterrorist policies given the relative lack of reliable understanding of terrorist psychology.) This emphasizes that this is no mere academic exercise, for after all, policies designed to deter terrorists from their acts of terrorism should be based on an understanding of "what makes terrorists tick."

First, it is important to emphasize that terrorists are psychologically normal. My own comparative research on the psychology of terrorists (Post, 1990) does not reveal major psychopathology, agreeing with the finding of Crenshaw (1981) that "the outstanding common characteristic of terrorists is their normality" (p. 390). In a review of the social psychology of terrorist groups, McCauley and Segal conclude that "the best documented generalization is negative; terrorists do not show any striking psychopathology" (McCauley & Segal, 1987).

Contrary to popular belief, terrorists are not crazed fanatics. Indeed, terrorist groups expel emotionally unstable individuals; after all, they represent a security risk. It is group, organizational, and social psychology, with a particular emphasis on collective identity, rather than individual psychopathology, which is the foundation of terrorist psychology. There is no overarching explanation for the diverse spectrum of terrorism. Rather, we should be speaking of terrorisms—plural—and of terrorist psychologies. Because terrorisms differ in their structure and dynamics, counterterrorist policies should be appropriately tailored. As a general rule, the smaller and more autonomous the group, the more counterproductive is external force. When the autonomous cell comes under external threat, the external danger has the consequence of reducing internal divisiveness and uniting the group against the outside enemy. The survival of the group is paramount because of the sense of identity it provides. *Terrorists* whose only *sense of significance* comes from *being terrorists* cannot *be forced to give up terrorism,* for *to do so would be to lose their very reason for being.* On the contrary, for such individuals violent societal counter reactions reaffirm their core belief that "it's us against them and they are out to destroy us." A tiny band of insignificant individuals has been transformed into a major opponent of society, making their "fantasy war," to use Ferracuti's (1983) apt term, a reality. One can indeed make the case that left to their own devices, these inherently unstable groups will self-destruct (Post, 1987).

Similarly, for terrorist organizations for which violence is defined as the only legitimate tactic for achieving their espoused goals, outside threat and a policy of reactive retaliation cannot intimidate the organizational leadership into committing organizational suicide and ceasing to exist. For that is what ceasing committing acts of political violence would be if those acts were the sole self-definition.

For complex organizations dedicated to a cause, such as Basque separatism, where an illegal terrorist wing operates in parallel with a legal political wing as elements of a larger loosely integrated organization, the dynamics and the policy implications are again different. In such circumstances, if the overall organizational goals—in this case, Basque separatism—are threatened by societal reactions to terrorism, one can make a case that internal organizational constraints can operate to constrain the terrorist wing. However, insofar as the terrorist group is not fully under political control, this is a matter of influence and partial constraint, for as has been noted earlier ETA has its own internal dynamics and continues to thrive despite the significant degree of separatism already achieved.

For state-supported and directed terrorist groups, the terrorist group is in effect a paramilitary unit under central governmental control. In this situation, the individual, group, and organizational psychological considerations discussed thus far are not especially relevant. The target of the antiterrorist policy in this circumstance is not the group *per se* but the chief of state and the government of the sponsoring state. Because the survival of the state and national interests are the primary values, there is a rational case to be made that retaliatory policies can have a deterring effect, at least in the short term. However, even in this circumstance, to watch the children in the camps in the aftermath of bombing attacks shaking their fists in rage suggests that such tactics are contributing to rising generations of terrorists.

Just as political terrorism is the product of generational forces, so, too, it is here for generations to come. When "hatred is bred in the bone," and passed from generation to generation, it does not yield easily to peace talks. *There is no short-range solution to the problem of terrorism.* Once an individual is in the pressure cooker of the terrorist group, it is extremely difficult to influence him. In the long run, the most effective antiterrorist policy is one that inhibits potential recruits from joining in the first place, for once an individual is in the grip of the terrorist group the power of the group and organizational psychology will increasingly dominate his psychology.

Political terrorism is not only a product of psychological forces; its central strategy is psychological. For political terrorism is, at base, a particularly vicious species of psychological warfare. It is violence as communication. Up to now, the terrorists have had a virtual monopoly on the weapon of the television camera as they manipulate their target audience through the media. Countering the terrorists' highly effective media-oriented strategy through more effective dissemination of information and public education must be key elements of a proactive program.

As important as it is to inhibit potential terrorists from joining, so, too, it is important to facilitate terrorists leaving. The powerful hold of the group has been described in detail. By creating pathways out of terrorism, that grip can be reduced. Amnesty programs modeled after the highly effective program of the Italian government can usefully contribute to that goal.

Moreover, reducing support for the group—both in its immediate societal surroundings and in the nation at large—are further long-range programs to foster.

Terrorists perpetuate their organizations by shaping the perceptions of future generations of terrorists. Manipulating a reactive media, they demonstrate their power and significance and define the legitimacy of their cause. To counter them, effective education and dissemination of objective information is required.

One does not counter psychological warfare with smart bombs and missiles, although they can certainly play a useful role in a military campaign against harboring states. One counters psychological warfare[3] with psychological warfare. In the long run, the most effective ways of countering terrorism are the following.

(1) Inhibit Potential Terrorists from Joining the Group

Security alone cannot accomplish this. Alienated youth must be able to envisage a future within the system that promises redress of long-standing economic and social inequity and come to believe that political activism can lead to their finding a pathway to these goals. Otherwise, striking out violently in despair will continue to seem like the only course available. To counter the transnational *jihadi* movement will require more vigorous diplomatic intervention with autocratic Muslim and Arab nations, who are identified as apostate leaders by the Islamist terrorists. Moreover, it is critical to reform the education system. In the radical *madrassahs* of Pakistan, a virulent brand of Wahabi Islam is being taught, which identifies the goal of the West as destroying Islam and rewards the culture of martyrdom. Providing economic support to education reform, with the establishment of secular schools with moderate curriculums could assist in this effort.

(2) Produce Dissension Within the Group

The groups are virtual hothouses of tensions and rivalries. Active measures are required to magnify these tensions and pressures. When terrorists do defect from the group, information can be fed back into the group to identify other traitors within the group, exacerbating the intragroup tensions.

(3) Facilitate Exit from the Group

Once a terrorist has become a member of a group and committed terrorist acts, he is a wanted criminal, and it can seem he has "no way out." Yet, as noted earlier, a way out can be provided through amnesty programs, such as the *pentiti* program in Italy, a similar program in the Basque region, and the so-called supergrass program in Northern Ireland, where reduced sentences or amnesty are offered in return for cooperation with the authorities.

---

[3] An expansion of this argument will be found in Post (2005a).

Such programs are, in effect, "protected witness" programs, including for the Basque region plastic surgery and resettlement in Latin America. These amnesty programs can not only facilitate exit but also can produce dissension within the group as well.

(4) Reduce Support for the Group and Its Leader

This is particularly important, as important as inhibiting potential recruits from joining in the first place, indeed contributing to this goal. Thus the group or organization must be marginalized, its leader delegitimated. Osama bin Laden at the present is a romantic hero to many alienated youth in the Islamic world, and his organization al-Qaeda is a highly attractive option to consider. An effective strategic communication program will increasingly marginalize al-Qaeda as an aberrant extremist group that is contrary to mainstream Islam, and will depict bin Laden not as a heroic figure, but as a self-consumed individual whose extreme actions damage all of Islam and the future of aspiring Muslim youth.

At one time in Italy, a majority of the Italian population agreed with the stated goals if not the violent means of the Red Brigades. A vigorous public education program, framing the terrorists as murderers who were damaging the economy and hurting the entire society, rather than cultural heroes, in concert with an effective amnesty program, the *pentiti* program, was instrumental in breaking the back of the social-revolutionary movement, with a major reduction in public support for the group.

All of these goals are components of a strategic communication process that must be a central component of our antiterrorist policy. This is not a policy that will swiftly end terrorism, but it is a process that must be put in place. Just as many of the attitudes that have made the path of terrorism attractive to alienated youth have taken place over decades, it will require decades to reduce the attractiveness of terrorism for those who have been raised in a climate dominated by hopeless and despair, with hatred bred in the bone, so that extremism and violence have increasingly come to be seen as the only course.

This is not to counsel a laissez-faire approach to terrorist violence as this long-range strategy gradually effects attitudinal changes. Clearly, as a first priority, governments are required to respond to the security needs of their citizens. However, force of arms alone, without public education, political actions designed to reduce the reservoir of hatred, and a complementary strategic information operations program as outlined earlier, is doomed to failure. Force alone was insufficient to counter the nationalist-separatist terrorists of the Provisional Irish Republican Army. It was only when the strategic decision was made to involve them in the political process through their political wing Sinn Fein that progress was made in resolving the long-standing conflict, with the negotiation of the major landmark Good Friday Accords. Indeed, a single-pronged approach relying on military force and intelligence alone will be counterproductive, increasing the desire for revenge of alienated youth manipulated by hate-mongering leaders to strike out at the identified enemy responsible for their misery.

References

Crenshaw, M. (1981). The causes of terrorism. *Comparative Politics, 13,* 379–399.

Ferracuti, F. (1983). *Psychiatric aspects of Italian left wing and right wing terrorism.* Paper presented to Seventh World Congress of Psychiatry, Vienna.

McCauley, C. R., & Segal, M. E. (1987). Social psychology of terrorist groups. In C. Hendricks (Ed.), *Group processes and intergroup relations: Annual review of social and personality psychology* (Vol. 9). Beverly Hills, CA: Sage.

Post, J. (1984). Notes on a psychodynamic theory of terrorism. *Terrorism, 7*(3), 241–256.

Post, J. (1987). Rewarding fire with fire? Effects of retaliation on terrorist group dynamics. In A. Kurz (Ed.), *Contemporary trends in world terrorism.* New York: Praeger.

Post, J. (1990). Terrorist psycho-logic: Terrorist behavior as a product of psychological forces. In W. Reich (Ed.), *Origins of terrorism: Psychologies, ideologies, theologies, states of mind* (pp. 25–40). Cambridge, UK: Cambridge University Press.

Post, J. (2000). Terrorist on trial: The Context of political crime. *Journal of the Academy of Psychiatry and the Law, 28,* 171–178.

Post, J. (2002). *Killing in the name of god: Osama bin Laden and radical Islam* (Counterproliferation Papers, Future Warfare Series No. 17). Montgomery, AL: Air University.

Post, J. (2005a). Psychological operations and counter-terrorism. *Joint Force Quarterly, 37,* 105–110.

Post, J. (2005b). When hatred is bred to the bone: Psycho-cultural foundations of contemporary terrorism. *Political Psychology, 26*(4), 615–636.

Post, J., Sprinzak, E., & Denny, L. (2003). The terrorists in their own words: Interviews with 35 incarcerated Middle Eastern terrorists. *Terrorism and Political Violence, 15*(1), 171–184.

9

Creating the Illusion of Impending Death: Armed Robbers in Action

Richard T. Wright and Scott H. Decker

R *obbery is the classical example of violent crime. The goal is to deprive victims of their valuable possessions for the personal consumption of the robber. Many of these crimes are committed by young men under the influence of drugs or alcohol. Violence or threats of violence are the means by which the victims are compelled to comply with the robber's demands. In this selection, Wright and Decker examine the dynamics of the robber-victim confrontation. This selection is derived from a larger study by Wright and Decker in which they interviewed 86 active armed robbers in St. Louis. The interviews were semi-structured and conducted in a casual manner. The researchers focused on the robbers' thoughts and actions before, during, and after their crimes. In this selection, they report on the strategies used by the robbers to compel their victims' compliance.*

As such, violence is seen as instrumental to the commission of the crime. Wright and Decker's subjects reported that they created an illusion of impending death to scare victims into a state of compliance. The robbers attempted to maintain the illusion without having to actually make good on the threat. When, however, the victims did not comply as expected, the offenders usually responded with severe violence to bring victims back to compliance. The robbers reported that seldom did they want to kill their victims, although some were prepared to do so if necessary.

Unlike most sorts of street crime, successful armed robberies are never secret or ambiguous. By definition, they require offenders to confront intended victims directly. As David Luckenbill (1981, p. 25) has observed, there is a strong interactional component to armed robbery; offenders and victims must develop "a common definition of the situation" and co-orient their actions to meet the demands of the offense. This does not happen automatically. After all, why should stick-up victims willingly participate in their own fleecing?

It is important to develop a clear understanding of the strategies used by armed robbers to compel the cooperation of would-be victims. Such information could offer citizens some guidance about how best to act and react should they be confronted by a robber. It also could provide policy makers

Source: Wright, R. T., & Decker, S. H. (1997). Creating the Illusion of Impending Death: Armed Robbers in Action. *The HFG Review,* 2(1), 10–19. Copyright © Fall 1997. Reprinted with permission.

and criminal justice officials with a better appreciation of offenders' aims and intentions during robberies, thereby enabling them to make more informed crime prevention and sentencing decisions.

In an attempt to learn more about the tactics employed by offenders to commit stick-ups, we located and interviewed 86 currently active armed robbers in St. Louis, Missouri. Armed robbery is a serious problem in St. Louis. In 1994, the year our research began, the city had 6,025 stick-ups reported to the police and ranked second in the nation in robberies per capita. The armed robbers for our study were recruited through the efforts of two field-based informants—an ex-offender, and a small-time heroin dealer and street criminal. Working through chains of street referrals, the field recruiters contacted active armed robbers, convinced them to take part in our project, and assisted us in conducting interviews that lasted up to 2 hours. In the pages that follow, we report just a small portion of what the offenders said during those interviews, focusing on how they actually commit their offenses.

APPROACHING THE VICTIM

To be successful, armed robbers must take control of the offense from the start. They immediately have to impose on the interaction a definition favorable to their ends, allowing intended victims no room for negotiation. This typically is accomplished by creating an illusion of impending death.

> Robbery itself is an illusion. That's what it's about.... Here is a person that you stick a gun in his face, they've never died, they don't know how it feels, but the illusion of death causes them to do what you want them to do. (aka Robert Jones)

A large part of creating such an illusion involves catching potential victims off guard; the element of surprise denies them the opportunity to adopt an oppositional stance.

> Sometimes people be alert; they be watchin' so you got to be careful of what you do. You got to be alert.... Pretty soon [the intended victim] falls asleep, and then [h]e ain't even trippin.' He over there lookin' at some girl.... [H]e probably just take his eyes off what he's doin,' watchin' out, [which is] what he's supposed to be doin,' and just turn his head on some girls. And [the stick-up] be on. (aka Andrew)

The offenders in our sample employ two different methods to approach would-be victims without arousing their suspicion. The first method involves using stealth or speed to sneak up on unwitting prey.

> [Whoever I am going to rob. I] just come up on you. You could be going to your car. If you are facing this way, I want to be on your blind side. If you are going this way, I want to be on that side where I can get up on you [without

you noticing me] and grab you: "This is a robbery, motherfucker, don't make it no murder!" I kind of like shake you. That's my approach. (aka Richard L. Brown)

The second method involves "managing a normal appearance" (Luckenbill, 1981, p. 29). The offenders' aim is to fit into the social setting such that victims see their presence as normal and nonthreatening, thereby allowing them to get close enough for a surprise attack.

Well, if I'm walking, say you got something that I want, I might come up there [and say], "Do you have the time?" or "Can I get a light from you?" something like that. "Yeah, it's three o'clock." By then I'm up on you, getting what I want. (aka Loco)

The method chosen to approach potential victims typically is dictated more by situational factors than by the idiosyncratic preferences of individual offenders. Depending on the situation, most of the armed robbers are prepared to use either speed and stealth or the presentation of a nonthreatening self to move within striking range of their victims. The offender quoted here, for example, reported that he and his partners usually initiate their commercial stick-ups simply by charging through the front door of the establishment, ski masks pulled down and guns drawn.

When I approach the door [of a would-be commercial target] generally we got ski masks that rolls up into a skull cap; it's a skull cap right now and as we get to the door, right prior to walking in the door, we pull our masks down. Once we come in, we got these masks down [so] we got to come in pulling our weapons, might even have them out prior to going in, just concealed. As soon as we pull those masks down, we are committed [because our intention is obvious]. (aka Robert Gibson)

He added, however, that circumstances occasionally require them to enter intended targets posing as customers. Doing so helps them to avoid tipping their hand too early, which is crucial in situations where the victim is likely to be armed.

Say for instance [the target is] a tavern and the guy behind the bar ... might be the kind of guy that got a pistol. Most bartenders and most people that's cashing checks, they got pistols on them. Believe me, they got pistols....So in that particular situation, you got to ... get in the door before you go into motion because you got to know where they are at. You've got to make sure that you've got a real chance to ... get up on them and make it not worth their risk to try to reach the pistol [before you betray your intentions]. (aka Robert Gibson)

Regardless of the manner in which the offenders make their approach, the aim almost invariably is the same: to "establish co-presence" with the victim without betraying their intentions (Luckenbill, 1981, p. 29). This gives would-be victims little opportunity to recognize the danger and to take steps to repel the attack. Not only is this far safer for the offenders, it also puts them in a strong position when it comes to compelling the victim's immediate cooperation.

ANNOUNCING THE CRIME

By announcing a stick-up, armed robbers commit themselves irrevocably to the offense. Any semblance of normality has been shattered; from this point onward, the victim will act and react in the knowledge that a robbery is being committed. The offenders we interviewed saw this as the "make or break" moment. The challenge for them was "to dramatize with unarguable clarity that the situation ha[d] suddenly and irreversibly been transformed into a crime" (Katz, 1988, p. 176). In effecting this transformation, they seek to establish dominance over their intended prey, thereby placing themselves in a position to dictate the terms of the unfolding interaction.

> When I first come up on [my victims], I might scare them, but then I calm them down. It's a control thing. If you can get a person to listen to you, you can get them to do just about anything....That's the way the world is made. (aka Tony Wright)

Most of the offenders said that they typically open their armed robberies with a demand that the would-be victim stop and listen to them.

> I say [to the victim], "Look here, hey, just hold up right where you at! Don't move! Don't say nothing!" (aka James Minor)

They often couple this demand with an unambiguous declaration of their predatory intentions.

> [I tell my victims], "It's a robbery! Don't nobody move!" (aka John Lee)

That declaration, in turn, usually is backed by a warning about the dire consequences of failing to do as they instruct.

> [I say to the victim], "This is a robbery, don't make it a murder! It's a robbery, don't make it a murder!" (aka Wallie Cleaver)

All of these pronouncements are intended to "soften up" victims; to inform them that they're about to be robbed and to convince them that they are not in a position to resist. Having seized initial control of the interaction, offenders then must let victims know what is expected of them. As one armed robber reminded us: "You have to talk to victims to get them to cooperate....They don't know what to do, whether to lay down, jump over the counter, dance, or whatever." This information typically is communicated to victims in the form of short, sharp orders laced with profanity and, often, racial epithets.

[I say to victims], "Hey motherfucker, give me your shit! Move slow and take everything out of your pockets!" (aka James Love)

[I grab my victims and say], "Take it off girl! Nigger, come up off of it!" (aka Libbie Jones)

The "expressive economy" with which the offenders issue instructions can in part be accounted for by a desire to keep victims off balance by demonstrating an ominous insensitivity to their precarious emotional state (see Katz, 1988, p. 177). Clearly, the swearing and racial putdowns help to reinforce this impression.

Almost all of the offenders typically used a gun to announce their stickups. They recognized that displaying a firearm usually obviated the need to do much talking. One put it this way: "A gun kinda speaks for itself." Most of them believed that "big, ugly guns" such as 9MMs or 45s were the best weapons for inducing cooperation.

[The 9MM] got that look about it like it gonna kill you. It talk for itself. "I'm gonna kill you." Looking at a 9 pointed at you, that's what goes through your head: "He gonna kill me if I don't give him this money." (aka Prauch)

In practice, however, many of the armed robbers actually carried somewhat smaller firearms because they were more easily concealed and simpler to handle.

I like the 32 because it's like a 38, small, easy and accessible. And it will knock [the victim] down if you have to use it. (aka Bob Jones)

A few offenders maintained that very small caliber pistols (e.g., 22s, 25s) made poor robbery weapons because many potential victims were not afraid of them.

[With] 22s or 25s people gonna be like, "Man, he using this little gun. I ain't worried." A 22 is real little, they gonna be, "Man, that ain't gonna do nothing but hurt me. Give me a little sting." (aka Syco)

That said, the majority of respondents felt that even the smallest handguns were big enough to intimidate most people. As one observed: "A person's gonna fear any kind of gun you put in their face. So it don't matter [what you use]. If it's a gun, it's gonna put fear in you."

The dilemma faced by offenders in relying on a gun to induce fear is that the strategy might work too well. Katz (1988) has noted that the display of a firearm can easily be misinterpreted by victims as the precursor to an offense far more serious than robbery (e.g., rape, kidnapping, murder). Offenders are keen to avoid such misinterpretations because they can stun victims into a state of incomprehension or convince them that determined resistance represents their only chance of survival. When armed offenders warn victims—"This is a robbery, don't make it a murder!"—they are doing more than issuing a credible death threat. Paradoxically, they also are seeking to reassure the victims that submission will not put their lives in jeopardy.

TRANSFERRING THE GOODS

No doubt the most difficult aspect of pulling off an armed robbery involves managing the transfer of goods. The difficulty inheres in the fact that offenders must keep victims under strict control while, at the same time, attempting to make sure that they have gotten everything worth taking. What is more, all of this must be accomplished as quickly as possible. The longer the stick-up lasts, the more risk offenders run of being discovered by police or passersby.

The armed robbers we talked to used two different strategies to manage the transfer of goods. The first involved simply ordering victims to hand over their possessions.

> I tell [my victims], "Man, if you don't want to die, give me your money! If you want to survive, give me your money! I'm not bullshitting!" So he will either go in his back pocket and give me the wallet or the woman will give me her purse. (aka Tony Brown)

By making victims responsible for the transfer of goods, the offenders are able to devote their undivided attention to watching for signs of danger.

> I rather for [victims] to give [their valuables] to me because I have to be alert. If they reach for something, I'll have to shoot them. (aka K-Money)

There is, however, one serious drawback to giving victims responsibility for the transfer; it is difficult to know whether they really have turned over all of their valuables. Recognizing this, many of the offenders employed tough talk and a fierce demeanor to discourage victims from attempting to shortchange them.

> You say, "Is that everything?" You can kinda tell if they lyin' sometimes: "That's all I got, man, that's all!" You'll say, "You're lyin', man, you lyin'!" and just make them think that you're getting pissed because he's lying to you. So basically you got this gun [pointed] at they head, so sometimes it be like, "Okay, I got some more." (aka Damon Jones)

A few of them went so far as to rough up their victims, especially those who appeared confused or hesitant, to reinforce the message that holding something back would be a risky proposition.

> Well, if [the victim] hesitates like that, undecided, you get a little aggressive and you push 'em. Let them know you mean business. I might take [the] pistol and crack their head with it. "Come on with that money and quit bullcrapping

or else you gonna get into some real trouble!" Normally when they see you mean that kind of business they … come on out with it. (aka Burle)

But most of the offenders who allowed victims to hand over their own possessions simply accepted what was offered and made good their escape. As one explained: "You just got to be like, 'Well, it's cool right here what I got.' When you get too greedy, that's when [bad] stuff starts to happen."

The second strategy used by the armed robbers to accomplish the transfer of goods involved taking the victims' possessions from them without waiting for what was offered.

I get [the victim's money] because everybody not gonna give you all they got. They gonna find some kind of way to keep from giving it all. (aka Richard L. Brown)

A number of the offenders who preferred this strategy were reluctant to let victims empty their own pockets for fear that they were carrying a concealed weapon.

I don't let nobody give me nothing. Cause if you let somebody go in they pockets, they could pull out a gun, they could pull out anything. You make sure they are where you can see their hands at all times. (aka Cooper)

To outsiders, these offenders may appear to be greatly overestimating the risk of encountering an armed victim. Such a perspective, however, betrays a respectable, middle-class upbringing. In the desperate inner-city neighborhoods in which almost all of the armed robbers reside, and in which many of them ply their trade, weapons are a ubiquitous feature of everyday life.

As already noted, all of the crime commission strategies adopted by the offenders are intended, at least in part, to minimize the possibility of victim resistance. Generally speaking, these strategies work very well. Nevertheless, almost all of the armed robbers we talked to said that they occasionally encountered victims who steadfastly refused to comply with their demands.

[O]n the parking lot, if you grab somebody and say, "This is a robbery, don't make it a murder!" I've had it happen that [the victim just says], "Well, you got to kill me then." (aka Richard L. Brown)

Faced with a recalcitrant victim, most of the offenders responded with severe, but nonlethal, violence in the hope of convincing the person to cooperate. Often this violence involved smacking or beating the victim about the head with a pistol.

It's happened [that some of my victims initially refuse to hand over their money, but] you would be surprised how cooperative a person will be once he been smashed across the face with a 357 Magnum. (aka Tony Wright)

Occasionally, however, a robbery involved shooting the victim in the leg or some other spot unlikely to prove fatal.

[If the person refuses to do what I say] most of the time I just grab my pistol, take the clip out and just slap 'em. If I see [the victim] trying to get tough, then sometimes I just straight out have to shoot somebody, just shoot 'em. I ain't never shot nobody in the head or nothing, nowhere that I know would kill 'em, just shoot them in they leg. Just to let them know that I'm for real [and that they should] just come up off the stuff. (aka Cooper)

Although a majority of the armed robbers preferred to use nonlethal violence to subdue resistant victims, several of them admitted to having been involved in fatal encounters in the past. One of the female offenders, for instance, described how she had watched from the car while one of her male companions shot and killed an uncooperative robbery victim.

We was in the car and, I didn't get out this time, one of the dudes got out. The [victim], he wasn't gonna let nobody rob him: "Nigger, you got to kill me! You got to kill me!" And that's what happened to him. Just shot him in the head. It was like, God!, I had never seen that. When [my accomplice] shot him, it wasn't like he was rushing to get away. He shot him, walked back to the car, put the gun back up under the seat and just, you know, we watched [the victim] when he fell, blood was coming out of his mouth, he was shaking or something. (aka Ne-Ne)

Such incidents are rare; few of the offenders entered into armed robberies intending to kill or seriously injure their prey. Indeed, some admitted that they probably would abandon an intended offense rather than use deadly force to subdue an uncooperative victim.

I really ain't gonna shoot nobody. I think a lot of people are like that. I wouldn't shoot nobody myself, if they gave me too much of a problem, I might just take off. (aka Mike J.)

That said, it must be noted that armed robbers typically are acting under intense emotional pressure to generate some fast cash by any means necessary in an interactional environment shot through with uncertainty and danger. Is it any wonder that the slightest hint of victim resistance may provoke some of them to respond with potentially deadly force? As one observed: "When you're doing stuff like this, you just real edgy; you'll pull the trigger at anything, at the first thing that go wrong."

MAKING AN ESCAPE

Once offenders have accomplished the transfer of goods, it only remains for them to make their getaway. Doing that, however, is more difficult than it might appear. Up to this point, the offenders have managed to keep victims in check by creating a convincing illusion of impending death. But the maintenance of that illusion becomes increasingly more difficult as the time comes for offenders to make good their escape. How can they continue to control victims who are becoming physically more distant from them?

In broad terms, the offenders can effect a getaway in one of two ways; they can leave the scene themselves or they can stay put and force the victim to flee. Other things being equal, most of them preferred to be the ones to depart. Before doing so, however, they had to make sure that the victim would not attempt to follow them or to raise the alarm. A majority of the offenders responded to this need by using verbal threats designed to extend the illusion of impending death just long enough for them to escape unobserved.

> I done left people in gangways and alleys and I've told them, "If you come out of this alley, I'm gonna hurt you. Just give me 5 or 10 minutes to get away. If you come out of this alley in 3 or 4 minutes, I'm gonna shoot the shit out of you!" (aka Bennie Simmons)

A few offenders, however, attempted to prolong this illusion indefinitely by threatening to kill their victims if they *ever* mentioned the stick-up to anyone.

> I done actually took [the victim's] ID and told them, "If you call the police, I got your address and everything. I know where you stay at and, if you call the police, I'm gonna come back and kill you!" (aka Melvin Walker)

Some of the armed robbers were uncomfortable relying on verbal threats to dissuade their prey from pursuing them. Instead, they took steps to make it difficult or impossible for victims to leave the crime scene by tying them up or incapacitating them through injury.

> [I hit my victims before I escape so as to] give them less time to call for the police. Especially if it's somebody else's neighborhood [and] we don't know how to get out. You hit them with a bat just to slow his pace. If you hit him in the leg with a bat, he can't walk for a minute; he gonna be limping, gonna try to limp to a payphone. By then it be 15 or 20 minutes, we be hitting the highway and on our way back to the southside where our neighborhood is. (aka Antwon Wright)

Although most of the offenders wanted to be the first to leave the crime scene, a number of them preferred to order the victim to flee instead. This allowed the offenders to depart in a calm, leisurely manner, thereby reducing the chances of drawing attention to themselves.

> I try not to have to run away. A very important thing that I have learned is that when you run away, too many things can happen running away. Police could

just be cruising by and see you running down the street. I just prefer to be able to walk away, which is one of the reasons why I tend, rather than to make an exit, I tell the victim to walk and don't look back: "Walk away, and walk fast!" When they walk, I can make my exit walking. (aka Stick Going)

What is more, forcing the victim to leave first permitted the offenders to escape without worrying about being attacked from behind—a crucial consideration for those unwilling or unable to incapacitate their prey before departure.

[Afterward,] I will tell [the victim] to run. You wouldn't just get the stuff and run because he may have a gun and shoot you while you are turning around running or something like that. (aka Damon Jones)

Beyond such instrumental concerns, several of the armed robbers indicated that they forced the victim to flee for expressive reasons as well; it demonstrated their continuing ability to dominate and control the situation. The clearest example of this involved an offender who routinely taunted his victims by ordering them to leave the scene in humiliating circumstances: "I like laughing at what I do, like, I told ... one dude to take off his clothes. I just do a whole bunch of stuff. Sometimes I'll make a dude crawl away. I'll tell him to crawl all the way up the street. And I'll sit there in the alley watching him crawl and crack up laughing."

CONCLUSION

In short, the active armed robbers we interviewed typically compel the cooperation of intended victims through the creation of a convincing illusion of impending death. They create this illusion by catching would-be victims off guard, and then using tough talk, a fierce demeanor, and the display of a deadly weapon to scare them into a state of unquestioning compliance. The goal is to maintain the illusion for as long as possible without having to make good on the threat. This is easier said than done. Armed robbery is an interactive event and, for any number of reasons, victims may fail to behave in the expected fashion. When this happens, the offenders usually respond with severe, but nonlethal, violence, relying on brute force to bring victims' behavior back into line with their expectations. Very few of them want to kill their victims, although some clearly are prepared to resort to deadly force if need be.

References

Katz, J. (1988). *Seductions of crime.* New York: Basic Books.

Luckenbill, D. (1981). Generating compliance: The case of robbery. *Urban Life*, 10, 25–46.

10

Gendering Violence: Masculinity and Power in Men's Accounts of Domestic Violence

Kristin L. Anderson and Debra Umberson

*T*his chapter examines the construction of gender within men's accounts of domestic violence. The analyzed data gained through in-depth interviews conducted with 33 domestically violent heterosexual men recruited through the Family Violence Diversion Network, a nonprofit organization located in a mid-sized Southwestern city. The analysis indicated that these batterers used diverse strategies to present themselves as nonviolent, capable, and rational men. They claimed that female partners were responsible for the violence in their relationships and constructed men as victims of a biased criminal justice system. The men excused, justified, rationalized, and minimized their violence against their female partners, constructing their violence as a rational response to extreme provocation, loss of control, or an incident blown out of proportion. This study suggests that violence against female partners is a means by which batterers reproduce a binary framework of gender.

In the 1970s, feminist activists and scholars brought wife abuse to the forefront of public consciousness. Published in the academic and popular press, the words and images of survivors made one aspect of patriarchy visible: Male dominance was displayed on women's bruised and battered bodies (Dobash & Dobash, 1979; Martin, 1976). Early research contributed to feminist analyses of battery as part of a larger pattern of male domination and control of women (Pence & Paymar, 1993; Yllo, 1993). Research in the 1980s and 1990s has expanded theoretical understandings of men's violence against women through emphases on women's agency and resistance to male control (Bowker, 1983; Kirkwood, 1993); the intersection of physical, structural, and emotional forces that sustain men's control over female partners (Kirkwood, 1993; Pence & Paymar, 1993); and the different constraints faced by women and men of diverse nations, racial ethnic identities, and sexualities who experience violence at the hands of intimate partners (Eaton, 1994; Island & Letellier, 1991; Jang, Lee, & Morello-Frosch, 1998; Renzetti, 1992). This work

Source: Anderson, K. L., & Umberson, D. (2001). Gendering violence: Masculinity and power in men's accounts of domestic violence. *Gender & Society, 15*, 358–380. © 2001 Sociologists for Women in Society. Used with permission of the publisher.

demonstrates ways in which the gender order facilitates victimization of disenfranchised groups.

Comparatively less work has examined the ways in which gender influences male perpetrators' experiences of domestic violence (Yllo, 1993). However, a growing body of qualitative research critically examines batterers' descriptions of violence within their relationships. Dobash and Dobash (1998), Hearn (1998), and Ptacek (1990) focus on the excuses, justifications, and rationalizations that batterers use to account for their violence. These authors suggest that batterers' accounts of violence are texts through which they attempt to deny responsibility for violence and to present nonviolent self-identities.

Dobash and Dobash (1998) identify ways in which gender, as a system that structures the authority and responsibilities assigned to women and men within intimate relationships, supports battery. They find that men use violence to punish female partners who fail to meet their unspoken physical, sexual, or emotional needs. Lundgren (1998) examines batterers' use of gendered religious ideologies to justify their violence against female partners. Hearn (1998, p. 37) proposes that violence is a "resource for demonstrating and showing a person is a man." These studies find that masculine identities are constructed through acts of violence and through batterers' ability to control partners as a result of their violence.

This article examines the construction of gender within men's accounts of domestic violence. Guided by theoretical work that characterizes gender as performance (Butler, 1990, 1993; West & Fenstermaker, 1995), we contend that batterers attempt to construct masculine identities through the practice of violence and the discourse about violence that they provide. We examine these performances of gender as "routine, methodical, and ongoing accomplishment[s]" that create and sustain notions of natural differences between women and men (West & Fenstermaker, 1995, p. 9). Butler's concept of performativity extends this idea by suggesting that it is through performance that gendered subjectivities are constructed: "Gender proves to be performative—that is, constituting the identity it is purported to be. In this sense, gender is always a doing, though not a doing by a subject who may be said to preexist the deed" (1990, p. 25). For Butler, gender performances demonstrate the instability of masculine subjectivity; a "masculine identity" exists only as the actions of individuals who stylize their bodies and their actions in accordance with a normative binary framework of gender.

In addition, the performance of gender makes male power and privilege appear natural and normal rather than socially produced and structured. Butler (1990) argues that gender is part of a system of relations that sustains heterosexual male privilege through the denigration or erasure of alternative (feminine/gay/lesbian/bisexual) identities. West and Fenstermaker (1995) contend that cultural beliefs about underlying and essential differences between women and men, and social structures that constitute and are constituted by these beliefs, are reproduced by the accomplishment of gender. In examining the accounts offered by domestically violent men, we focus on identifying ways in which the practice of domestic violence helps men to accomplish gender. We also focus on the contradictions within these accounts to explore the instability of masculine subjectivities and challenges to the performance of gender.

FINDINGS

How do batterers talk about the violence in their relationships? They excuse, rationalize, justify, and minimize their violence against female partners. Like the batterers studied by previous researchers, the men in this study constructed their violence as a rational response to extreme provocation, a loss of control, or a minor incident that was blown out of proportion. Through such accounts, batterers deny responsibility for their violence and save face when recounting behavior that has elicited social sanctions (Dobash & Dobash, 1998; Ptacek, 1990).

However, these accounts are also about the performance of gender. That is, through their speech acts, respondents presented themselves as rational, competent, masculine actors. We examine several ways in which domestic violence is gendered in these accounts. First, according to respondents' reports, violence is gendered in its practice. Although it was in their interests to minimize and deny their violence, participants reported engaging in more serious, frequent, and injurious violence than that committed by their female partners. Second, respondents gendered violence through their depictions and interpretations of violence. They talked about women's violence in a qualitatively different fashion than they talked about their own violence, and their language reflected hegemonic notions of femininity and masculinity. Third, the research participants constructed gender by interpreting the violent conflicts in ways that suggested that their female partners were responsible for the participants' behavior. Finally, respondents gendered violence by claiming that they are victimized by a criminal justice system that constructs all men as villains and all women as victims.

Gendered Practice

Men perpetrate the majority of violence against women and against other men in the United States (Bachman & Saltzman, 1995). Although some scholars argue that women perpetrate domestic violence at rates similar to men (Straus, 1993), feminist scholars have pointed out that research findings of "sexual symmetry" in domestic violence are based on survey questions that fail to account for sex differences in physical strength and size and in motivations for violence (Dobash, Dobash, Wilson, & Daly, 1992; Straton, 1994). Moreover, recent evidence from a large national survey suggests that women experience higher rates of victimization at the hands of partners than men and that African American and Latina women experience higher rates of victimization than European American women (Bachman & Saltzman, 1995).

Although the majority of respondents described scenarios in which both they and their partners perpetrated violent acts, they reported that their violence was more frequent and severe than the violence perpetrated by their female partners. Eleven respondents (33%) described attacking a partner who did not physically resist, and only two respondents (6%) reported that they were victimized by their partners but did not themselves perpetrate violence. The 20 cases (61%) in which the participants reported "mutual" violence support feminist critiques of "sexual symmetry":

> We started pushing each other. And the thing is that I threw her on the floor. I told her that I'm going to leave. She took my car keys, and I wanted my car keys so I went and grabbed her arm, pulled it, and took the car keys away from her. She—she comes back and tries to kick me in the back. So I just pushed her back and threw her on the floor again. (Juan)

Moreover, the respondents did not describe scenarios in which they perceived themselves to be at risk from their partners' violence. The worst injury reportedly sustained was a split lip, and only five men (15%) reported sustaining any injury. Female partners reportedly sustained injuries in 14 cases (42%). Although the majority of the injuries reportedly inflicted on female partners consisted of bruises and scratches, a few women were hospitalized, and two women sustained broken ribs. These findings corroborate previous studies showing that women suffer more injuries from domestic violence than men (Langhinrichsen-Rohling, Neidig, & Thorn, 1995). Moreover, because past studies suggest that male batterers underreport their perpetration of violence (Dobash & Dobash, 1998), it is likely that respondents engaged in more violence than they described in these in-depth interviews.

Domestic violence is gendered through social and cultural practices that advantage men in violent conflicts with women. Young men often learn to view themselves as capable perpetrators of violence through rough play and contact sports, to exhibit fearlessness in the face of physical confrontations, and to accept the harm and injury associated with violence as "natural" (Dobash & Dobash, 1998; Messner, 1992). Men are further advantaged by cultural norms suggesting that women should pair with men who are larger and stronger than themselves (Goffman, 1977). Women's less pervasive and less effective use of violence reflects fewer social opportunities to learn violent techniques, a lack of encouragement for female violence within society, and women's size disadvantage in relation to male partners (Fagot, Hagan, Leinbach, & Kronsberg, 1985; McCaughey, 1998). In a culture that defines aggression as unfeminine, few women learn to use violence effectively.

Gendered Depictions and Interpretations

Participants reported that they engaged in more frequent and serious violence than their partners, but they also reported that their violence was different from that of their partners. They depicted their violence as rational, effective, and explosive, whereas women's violence was represented as hysterical, trivial, and ineffectual. Of the 22 participants who described violence perpetrated by their partners, 12 (55%) suggested that their partner's violence was ridiculous or ineffectual. These respondents minimized their partners' violence by explaining that it was of little concern to them:

> I came out of the kitchen, and then I got in her face, and I shoved her. She shoved, she tried to push me a little bit, but it didn't matter much. (Adam)

> I was seeing this girl, and then a friend of mine saw me with this girl and he went back and told my wife,-and when I got home that night, that's when she tried to hit me, to fight me. I just pushed her out of the way and left. (Shad)

This minimizing discourse also characterizes descriptions of cases in which female partners successfully made contact and injured the respondent, as in the following account:

> I was on my way to go to the restroom. And she was just cussing and swearing and she wouldn't let me pass. So, I nudged her. I didn't push her or shove her, I just kind of, you know, just made my way to the restroom. And, when I done that she hit me, and she drew blood. She hit me in the lip, and she drew blood....I go in the bathroom and I started laughing, you know. And I was still half lit that morning, you know. And I was laughing because I think it maybe shocked me more than anything that she had done this, you know. (Ed)

Although his partner "drew blood," Ed minimized her violence by describing it as amusing, uncharacteristic, and shocking.

Even in the case of extreme danger, such as when threatened with a weapon, respondents denied the possibility that their partners' violence was a threat. During a fight described by Steve, his partner locked herself in the bathroom with his gun:

> We were battering each other at that point, and that's when she was in the bathroom. This is—it's like 45 minutes into this whole argument now. She's in the bathroom, messing with my [gun]. And I had no idea. So I kicked the door in—in the bathroom, and she's sitting there trying to load this thing, trying to get this clip in, and luckily she couldn't figure it out. Why, I don't—you know, well, because she was drunk. So, luckily she didn't. The situation could have been a whole lot worse, you know, it could have been a whole lot worse than it was. I thank God that she didn't figure it out. When I think about it, you know, she was lucky to come out of it with just a cut in her head. You know, she could have blown her brains out or done something really stupid.

This account contains interesting contradictions. Steve stated that he had "no idea" that his partner had a gun, but he responded by kicking down the door to reach her. He then suggested that he was concerned about his partner's safety and that he kicked in the door to save her from doing "something really stupid" to herself. Similarly, Alejandro minimized the threat in his account of an incident in which his partner picked up a weapon:

So, she got angry and got a knife, came up at me, and I kick her. *And then what happened?* Well, I kick her about four times because she—I kick her, and I say "Just stop, stay there!" and she stand up and come again and I had to kick her again. Somebody called the police, somebody called the police. I guess we were making a lot of noise. And I couldn't go out, I couldn't leave home, because I was not dressed properly to go out. And so I couldn't go, so the only alternative I had at this moment was to defend myself from the knife. So I had to kick her.

Alejandro suggested that his partner's attack with a knife was not enough of a threat to warrant his leaving the house when he was "not dressed properly to go out."

In addition to emphasizing their partners' incompetence in the practice of violence, some respondents depicted the violence perpetrated by their partners as irrational:

She has got no control. She sees something and she don't like it, she'll go and pull my hair, scratch me, and [act] paranoid, crazy, screaming loud, make everybody look at her, and call the police, you know. Just nuts. (Andrew)

She came back and started hitting me with her purse again so I knocked the purse out of her hand, and then, she started screaming at me to get out. I went back to the room, and she came running down the hall saying she was going to throw all my stuff out and I'd just had enough so I went and grabbed her, pulled her back. And grabbed her back to the bed and threw her on the bed and sat on her—told her I wasn't going to let her up until she came to her senses...she came back up again and I just grabbed her and threw her down. After that, she promised—she finally said that she had come to her senses and everything. I went into the other room, and she went out to clean up the mess she had made in the living room, and then she just started just crying all night long, or for a while. (Phil)

Phil and Andrew described their partners' acts as irrational and hysterical. Such depictions helped respondents to justify their own violence and to present themselves as calm, cool, rational men. Phil described his own behavior of throwing his partner down as a nonviolent, controlled response to his partner's outrageous behavior. Moreover, he suggests that he used this incident to demonstrate his sense of superior rationality to his partner. Phil later reported that a doctor became "very upset" about the marks on his wife's neck two days after this incident, suggesting that he was not the rational actor represented in his account.

In eight other cases (36%), respondents did not depict their partner's violence as trivial or ineffectual. Rather, they described their partners' behavior in matter-of-fact terms:

Then she starts jumping at me or hitting me, or tell me "leave the house, I don't want you, I don't love you" and stuff like that. And I say, "don't touch me, don't touch me." And I just push her back. She keeps coming and hit me, hit me. I keep pushing back, she starts scratch me, so I push hard to stop her from hurting me. (Mario)

Other respondents depicted their partner's violence in factual terms but emphasized that they perceived their own violence as the greater danger. Ray took his partner seriously when he stated that "she was willing to fight, to defend herself," yet he also mentioned his fears that his own violence would be lethal: "The worst time is when she threw an iron at me. And I'm gonna tell you, I think that was the worst time because, in defense, in retaliation, I pulled her hair, and I thought maybe I broke her neck." Only two respondents—Alan and Jim—consistently identified as victims:

> One of the worst times was realizing that she was drunk and belligerent. I realized that I needed to take her home in her car and she was not capable of driving. And she was physically abusive the whole way home. And before I could get out of the door or get out of the way, she came at me with a knife. And stupidly, I defended myself—kicked her hand to get the knife out. And I bruised her hand enough to where she felt justified enough to call the police with stories that I was horribly abusing. (Jim)

Jim reported that his partner has hit him, stabbed him, and thrown things at him. However, he also noted that he was arrested following several of these incidents, suggesting that his accounts tell us only part of the story. Moreover, like Steve and Alejandro, he did not describe feelings of fear or apprehension about his partner's use of a knife.

Although female partners were represented as dangerous only to themselves, the participants depicted their own violence as primal, explosive, and damaging to others:

> I explode for everything. This time it was trying to help my daughter with her home-work, it was a Sunday, and she was not paying any attention, and I get angry with my daughter, and so I kick the TV...I guess broke the TV, and then I kick a bookshelf. My daughter tried to get into the middle so I pushed her away from me and I kicked another thing. So, she [his partner] called the police. I am glad she called the police because something really awful could have happened. (Alejandro)
>
> She said something, and then I just lost control. I choked her, picked her up off her feet, and lifted her up like this, and she was kind of kicking back and forth, and I really felt like I really wanted to kill her this time. (Adam)
>
> I feel that if there had been a gun in the house, I would have used it. That's one reason also why I refuse to have a gun. Because I know I have a terrible temper and I'm afraid that I will do something stupid like that. (Fred)

In contrast to their reported fearlessness when confronted by women wielding weapons, respondents constructed their own capacity for violence as something that should engender fear. These interpretations are consistent with cultural constructions of male violence as volcanic—natural, lethal, and impossible to stop until it has run its course.

Respondents' interpretations of ineffectual female violence and lethal male violence reflect actual violent practices in a culture that grants men more access to violence, but they also gender violence. By denying a threat from women's violence, participants performed masculinity and reinforced notions of gender difference. Women were constructed as incompetent in the practice of violence, and their successes were trivialized. For example, it is unlikely that Ed would have responded with laughter had his lip been split by the punch of another man (Dobash & Dobash, 1998). Moreover, respondents ignored their partners' motivations for violence and their active efforts to exert change within their relationships.

In her examination of Irigaray's writings on the representation of women within the masculine economy, Butler (1993, p. 36) writes that "the economy that claims to include the feminine as the subordinate term in a binary opposition of masculine/feminine excludes the feminine—produces the feminine as that which must be excluded for that economy to operate." The binary representation of ineffectual, hysterical female behavior and rational, lethal male violence within these accounts erases the feminine; violence perpetrated by women and female subjectivity are effaced in order that the respondents can construct masculinities.[1] These representations mask the power relations that determine what acts will qualify as "violence" and thus naturalize the notion that violence is the exclusive province of men.

Gendering Blame

The research participants also gendered violence by suggesting that their female partners were responsible for the violence within their relationships. Some respondents did this by claiming that they did not hit women with whom they were involved in the past:

> I've never hit another woman in my life besides the one that I'm with. She just has a knack for bringing out the worst in me. (Tom)
>   You know, I never hit my first wife. I'm married for five years—I never hit her. I never struck her, not once. (Mitchell)

Respondents also shifted blame onto female partners by detailing faults in their partners' behaviors and personalities. They criticized their partners' parenting styles, interaction styles, and choices. However, the most typically reported criticism was that female partners were controlling. Ten of the 33 respondents (30%) characterized their partners as controlling, demanding, or dominating:

> She's real organized and critiquing about things. She wanna—she has to get it like—she like to have her way all the time, you know. In control of things, even when she's at work in the evenings, she has to have control of everything that's going on in the house. And—but—you know, try to get, to control everything there. You know, what's going on, and me and myself. (Adam)

---

[1] We thank an anonymous *Gender & Society* reviewer for suggesting the relevance of Butler's theory to this analysis.

You know, you're here with this person, you're here for five years, and yet they turn out to be aggressive, what is aggressive, too educated, you know. It's the reason they feel like they want to control you. (Mitchell)

In a few cases, respondents claimed that they felt emasculated by what they interpreted as their partners' efforts to control them:

She's kind of—I don't want to say dominating. She's a good mother, she's a great housekeeper, she's an excellent cook. But as far as our relationship goes, the old traditional "man wears the pants in the family," it's a shared responsibility. There's no way that you could say that I wear the pants in the family. She's dominating in that sense. (Ted)

You ask the guy sitting next door to me, the guy that's down the hall. For years they all say, "Bill, man, reach down and grab your eggs. She wears the pants." Or maybe like, "Hey man, we're going to go—Oh, Bill can't go. He's got to ask his boss first." And they were right. (Bill)

These representations of female partners as dominating enabled men to position themselves as victims of masculinized female partners. The relational construction of masculinity is visible in these accounts; women who "wear the pants" disrupt the binary opposition of masculinity/femininity. Bill's account reveals that "one is one's gender to the extent that one is not the other gender" (Butler 1990, p. 22); he is unable to perform masculinity to the satisfaction of his friends when mirrored by a partner who is perceived as dominating.

Moreover, respondents appeared to feel emasculated by unspecified forces. Unlike female survivors who describe concrete practices that male partners utilize to exert control (Kirkwood, 1993; Walker, 1984), participants were vague about what they meant by control and the ways in which their partners exerted control:

I don't think she's satisfied unless she has absolute control, and she's not in a position to control anyway, um, mentally.... *When you said that, um, that she wasn't really in a position to control, what did you mean by that?* Well, she's not in a position to control, in the fact that she's not, the control that she wants, is pretty much control over me. I'm pretty much the only person that she sees every day. She wants to control every aspect of what I do, and while in the same turn, she really can't. (George)

Respondents who claimed that their partners are controlling offered nebulous explanations for these feelings, suggesting that these claims may be indicative of these men's fears about being controlled by a woman rather than the actual practices of their partners.

Finally, respondents gendered violence through their efforts to convince female partners to shoulder at least part of the blame for their violence. The following comments reflect respondents' interpretations of their partners' feelings after the argument was over:

Finally, for once in her life, I got her to accept 50/50 blame for the reason why she actually got hit. You know, used to be a time where she could say there was never a time. But, she accepts 50/50 blame for this. (Tom)

> She has a sense that she is probably 80–90 percent guilty of my anger. (Alejandro)

Contemporary constructions of gender hold women responsible for men's aggression (Gray, Palileo, & Johnson, 1993). Sexual violence is often blamed on women, who are perceived as tempting men who are powerless in the face of their primal sexual desires (Scully, 1990). Although interviewees expressed remorse for their violent behavior, they also implied that it was justified in light of their partners' controlling behavior. Moreover, their violence was rewarded by their partners' feelings of guilt, suggesting that violence is simultaneously a performance of masculinity and a means by which respondents encouraged the performance of femininity by female partners.

"The Law Is for Women": Claiming Gender Bias

Participants sometimes rationalized their violence by claiming that the legal system overreacted to a minor incident. Eight of the 33 interviewees (24%) depicted themselves as victims of gender politics or the media attention surrounding the trial of O. J. Simpson:

> I think my punishment was wrong. And it was like my attorney told me—I'm suffering because of O. J. Simpson. Mine was the crime of the year. That is, you know, it's the hot issue of the year because of O. J. Two years ago they would have gone "Don't do that again." (Bill)
>
> I'm going to jail for something I haven't even done because the woman is always the victim and the guy is always the bad guy. And O. J., I think, has made it even worse—that mentality. I know that there's a lot of bad, ignorant, violent guys out there that probably think that it's wonderful to batter their wife on a regular basis, but I think there's a lot of reverse mentality going on right now. (Jim)
>
> I don't necessarily agree with the jail system, which I know has nothing to do with you guys, but you have to sign a form saying that you'll come to counseling before you've ever been convicted of a crime. And, like I said, here I am now with this [inaudible] that I have to come to for 21 weeks in a row—for what could amount to some girl calling—hurting herself and saying her boyfriend or husband did it. (Tom)

These claims of gender bias were sometimes directly contradicted by respondents' descriptions of events following the arrival of the police. Four participants (12%) reported that the police wanted to arrest their female partner along with or instead of themselves—stories that challenged their claims of bias in the system. A few of these respondents reported that they lied to the police about the source of their injuries to prevent the arrest of their partners. Ed, the respondent who sustained a split lip from his partner's punch, claimed that he "took the fall" for his partner:

> They wanted to arrest her, because I was the one who had the little split lip. And I told them that—I said, "No, man, she's seven months pregnant." I told the officer, you know, "How can you take her to jail? She's seven months

pregnant!" And I said, "Look, I came in here—I started it, I pushed her. And she hit me." You know, I told them that I had shoved her. And after that they said, "Okay, well, we have to remove, move you out of this—out of this situation here." Something about the law. So, I said, "Well, you know. I started it." I told them I had started it, you know. And, they said, "Okay, well, we'll take you then." So I went to jail. (Ed)

When the police arrived, these respondents were in a double bind. They wanted to deny their own violence to avoid arrest, but they also wanted to deny victimization at the hands of a woman. "Protecting" their female partners from arrest allowed them a way out of this bind. By volunteering to be arrested despite their alleged innocence, they became chivalrous defenders of their partners. They were also, paradoxically, able to claim that "gender bias" led to their arrest and participation in the FVDN program. When Ed argued that the criminal justice system is biased toward women, we confronted him about this contradiction:

Ed: I am totally against, you know,—ever since I stepped foot in this program and I've only been to the orientation—[that] it speaks of gender, okay, and everything that—it seems like every statement that is made is directed toward men, toward the male party.... As I stated earlier, the law is for women. In my opinion, it—

Interviewer: Although, they would have arrested her if you hadn't intervened.

Ed: They would, that's right. That's another thing. That's right, that's right. They would have arrested her. But, you know even, even with her statement saying, look this is what, this is what happened, I'm not pressing charges. The state picked up those charges, and, they just took it upon themselves, you know, to inconvenience my life, is what they did.

Interviewer: Okay. And the other alternative would have been that she would have been going through this process instead of you.

Ed: Well, no, the other alternative, that was, that was, that would come out of this, is [that] I would have spent 30 days in jail.

Ed repeatedly dismissed the notion that the legal system would hold his partner accountable for her actions despite his own words to the contrary. His construction of men as victimized by an interfering justice system allowed him to avoid the seemingly unacceptable conclusion that either he or his partner was a victim of violence.

Another respondent, Jim, reportedly prevented his partner's arrest because he felt it to be in his best interests:

She was drunk and behind the wheel and driving erratically while backhanding me. And a cop pulled us over because he saw her hit me. And I realized that she was gonna get a DWI [Driving While Intoxicated], which would have been her second and a major expense to me, besides, you know, I think that there's a thin line between protecting somebody and possessing somebody. But I protect her, I do. I find myself sacrificing myself for her and lying for her constantly. And I told the cops that I hit her just because they saw her hit me and I figured that if I told them that I hit her, rather than her get a DWI, that we would both go to jail over an assault thing. Which is what happened. (Jim)

When batterers "protect" their partners from arrest, their oppressor becomes a powerful criminal justice system rather than a woman. Although even the loser gains status through participation in a fight with another man, a man does not gain prestige from being beaten by a woman (Dobash & Dobash, 1998). In addition, respondents who stepped in to prevent their partners from being arrested ensured that their partners remained under their control, as Jim suggested when he described "the thin line between being protected by somebody and possessing somebody." By volunteering to be arrested along with his partner, Jim ensured that she was not "taken into possession" (e.g., taken into custody) by the police.[2]

By focusing the interviews on "gender bias" in the system, respondents deflected attention from their own perpetration and victimization. Constructions of a bias gave them an explanation for their arrest that was consistent with their self-presentation as rational, strong, and nonviolent actors. Claims of "reverse mentality" also enabled participants to position themselves as victims of gender politics. Several interviewees made use of men's rights rhetoric or alluded to changes wrought by feminism to suggest that they are increasingly oppressed by a society in which women have achieved greater rights:

I really get upset when I watch TV shows as far as, like they got shows or TV station called Lifetime and there are many phrases "TV for women." And that kind of made me upset. Why is it TV for women? You know, it should be TV for everyone, not just women. You don't hear someone else at a different TV station saying, "TV for men."...As far as the law goes, changing some of the laws goes too, some of the laws that guys are pulled away from their children. I kind of felt sorry for the guys. (Kenny)

A number of recent studies have examined the increasingly angry and antifeminist discourse offered by some men who are struggling to construct masculine identities within patriarchies disrupted by feminism and movements for gay/lesbian and civil rights (Fine, Weis, Addelston, & Marusza, 1997; Messner, 1998; Savran, 1998). Some branches of the contemporary "men's movement" have articulated a defensive and antifeminist rhetoric of "men's rights" that suggests that men have become the victims of feminism (Messner, 1998; Savran, 1998). Although none of our interviewees reported participation in any of the organized men's movements, their

---

[2] We are grateful to an anonymous *Gender & Society* reviewer for the suggestion that respondents "protect" female partners from arrest to maintain control of their partners.

allusions to the discourse of victimized manhood suggest that the rhetoric of these movements has become an influential resource for the performance of gender among some men. Like the angry men's rights activists studied by Messner, some respondents positioned themselves as the victims of feminism, which they believe has co-opted the criminal justice system and the media by creating "myths" of male domination. The interviews suggest that respondents feel disempowered and that they identify women—both the women whom they batter and women who lead movements to criminalize domestic violence—as the "Other" who has "stolen their presumed privilege" (Fine et al., 1997, p. 54): "Now girls are starting to act like men, or try and be like men. Like if you hit me, I'll call the cops, or if you don't do it, I'll do this, or stuff like that" (Juan). Juan contends that by challenging men's "privilege" to hit their female partners without fear of repercussions, women have become "like men." This suggests that the construction of masculine subjectivities is tied to a position of dominance and that women have threatened the binary and hierarchical gender framework through their resistance to male violence.

DISCUSSION: SOCIAL LOCATIONS AND DISCOURSES OF VIOLENCE

Respondents' descriptions of conflicts with female partners were similar across racial ethnic and class locations. Participants of diverse socioeconomic standings and racial ethnic backgrounds minimized the violence perpetrated by their partners, claimed that the criminal justice system is biased against men, and attempted to place responsibility for their violence on female partners. However, we identified some ways in which social class influenced respondents' self-presentations.[3]

Respondents of higher socioeconomic status emphasized their careers and the material items that they provided for their families throughout the interviews:

> We built two houses together and they are nice. You know, we like to see a nice environment for our family to live in. We want to see our children receive a good education. (Ted)
>
> That woman now sits in a 2,700-square-foot house: She drives a Volvo. She has everything. A brand-new refrigerator, a brand-new washer and dryer. (Bill)

---

[3] We define high socioeconomic status respondents as those who earn at least $25,000 per year in personal income and who have completed an Associate's degree. Seven respondents fit these criteria. We define disenfranchised respondents as those who report personal earnings of less than $15,000 per year and who have not completed a two-year college program. Nine respondents fit these criteria.

Conversely, economically disenfranchised men volunteered stories about their prowess in fights with other men. These interviewees reported that they engaged in violent conflicts with other men as a means of gaining respect:

> Everybody in my neighborhood respected me a lot, you know. I used to be kind of violent. I used to like to fight and stuff like that, but I'm not like that anymore. She—I don't think she liked me because I liked to fight a lot but she liked me because people respected me because they knew that they would have to fight if they disrespected me. You know I think that's one thing that turned her on about me; I don't let people mess around. (Tony)
>
> My stepson's friend was there, and he start to push me too. So I started to say, "Hey, you know, this is my house, and you don't tell me nothing in my house." So I start fighting, you know, I was gonna fight him. (Mario)

The use of violence to achieve respect is a central theme in research on the construction of masculinities among disenfranchised men (Messerschmidt, 1993; Messner, 1992). Although men of diverse socioeconomic standings valorize fistfights between men (Campbell, 1993; Dobash & Dobash, 1998), the extent to which they participate in these confrontations varies by social context. Privileged young men are more often able to avoid participation in social situations that require physical violence against other men than are men who reside in poor neighborhoods (Messner, 1992).

We find some evidence that cultural differences influence accounts of domestic violence. Two respondents who identified themselves as immigrants from Latin America (Alejandro and Juan) reported that they experienced conflicts with female partners about the shifting meanings of gender in the United States:

> She has a different attitude than mine. She has an attitude that comes from Mexico—be a man like, you have to do it. And it's like me here, it's fifty-fifty, it's another thing, you know, it's like "I don't have to do it."...I told her the wrong things she was doing and I told her, "It's not going to be that way because we're not in Mexico, we're in the United States." (Juan)

Juan's story suggests that unstable meanings about what it means to be a woman or a man are a source of conflict within his relationship and that he and his partner draw on divergent gender ideologies to buttress their positions. Although many of the respondents expressed uncertainty about appropriate gender performances in the 1990s, those who migrated to the United States may find these "crisis tendencies of the gender order" (Connell, 1992, p. 736) to be particularly unsettling. Interestingly, Juan depicts his partner as clinging to traditional gender norms, while he embraces the notion of gender egalitarianism. However, we are hesitant to draw conclusions about this finding due to the small number of interviews that we conducted with immigrants.

Race or ethnicity, class, and gender matter in the context of the interview setting. As white, middle-class, female researchers, we were often questioning men who resided in different social worlds. Like other female researchers who have interviewed men with histories of sexual violence, we found that the interviewees were usually friendly, polite, and appeared relatively comfortable in the interview setting (Scully, 1990). Unlike Ptacek, a male researcher who interviewed batterers, we did not experience a "subtext of resistance and jockeying for power beneath the otherwise friendly manner these individuals displayed in our initial phone conversations" (1990, p. 140). However, respondents may have offered more deterministic accounts of gender and assumed more shared experiences with the interviewer had they been interviewed by men rather than women (Williams & Heikes, 1993). For example, whereas Ptacek (1990) found that 78% of the batterers that he interviewed justified their violence by complaining that their wives did not fulfill the obligations of a good wife, participants in this study rarely used language that explicitly emphasized "wifely duties."

Previous studies also suggest that when white, middle-class researchers interview working-class people or people of color, they may encounter problems with establishing rapport and interpreting the accounts of respondents (Edwards, 1990). Riessman found that white researchers feel more comfortable with the narrative styles of white and middle-class respondents and may misinterpret the central themes raised by respondents of color. These findings suggest that shared meanings may have been less easily achieved in our interviews conducted with Latino, Native American, and African American men. For example, there is some evidence that we attempted to impose a linear narrative structure on our interviews with some respondents who may have preferred an episodic style (see Riessman, 1987):

We just started arguing more in the house. And she scratched me, and I push her away. Because I got bleeding on my neck and everything, and I push her away. And she called the police and I run away so they don't catch me there. There's a lot of worse times we argued. She tried to get me with the knife one time, trying to blame me that I did it. And the next time I told her I was going to leave her, and she tried to commit suicide by drinking like a whole bunch of bottles of Tylenol pill. And I had to rush her to the hospital, you know. That's about it. *So, in this worst fight, she scratched you and you pushed her. She called the police?* A few times she kicked me and scratched me on my neck and everything, and my arms. (Andrew)

Andrew, who identifies as Latino, recounts several episodes that are salient to his understanding of the problems within his relationship. The interviewer, however, steers him toward a sequential recounting of one particular incident rather than probing for elaboration of Andrew's perceptions of these multiple events.

In contrast, racial ethnic locations can shape what interviewers and interviewees reveal. One way in which this dynamic may have influenced the interviews was suggested by Tom, who identified as African American:

I've never dated a Black woman before. Not me. That was my choice—that's a choice I made a long time ago....I tend to find that Black women, in general, don't have any get-up-and-go, don't work. I can't say—it's just down players. But I just don't see the desire to succeed in life.

Tom introduced the issue of interracial dating without prompting and went on to invoke a variety of controlling images to represent Black women (Collins, 1991). It is difficult to imagine that Tom would have shared these details if he had been interviewed by an African American woman or perhaps even a white man. Given the middle-class bias of our sample and our own social locations, future research ought to compare accounts received by differently located interviewers and a wider class and racial ethnic range of respondents.

CONCLUSIONS

Many scholars have suggested that domestic violence is a means by which men construct masculinities (Dobash & Dobash, 1998; Gondolf & Hannekin, 1987; Hearn, 1998). However, few studies have explored the specific practices that domestically violent men use to present themselves as masculine actors. The respondents in this study used diverse and contradictory strategies to gender violence and they shifted their positions as they talked about violence. Respondents sometimes positioned themselves as masculine actors by highlighting their strength, power, and rationality compared with the "irrationality" and vulnerability of female partners. At other times, when describing the criminal justice system or "controlling" female partners, they positioned themselves as vulnerable and powerless. These shifting representations evidence the relational construction of gender and the instability of masculine subjectivities (Butler, 1990).

Recently, performativity theories have been criticized for privileging agency, under theorizing structural and cultural constraints, and facilitating essentialist readings of gender behavior: "Lacking an analysis of structural and cultural context, performances of gender can all too easily be interpreted as free agents' acting out the inevitable surface manifestations of a natural inner sex difference" (Messner, 2000, p. 770). Findings from our study show that each of these criticisms is not necessarily valid.

First, although the batterers described here demonstrate agency by shifting positions, they do so by calling on cultural discourses (of unstoppable masculine aggression, of feminine weakness, and of men's rights). Their performance is shaped by cultural options.

Second, batterers' performances are also shaped by structural changes in the gender order. Some of the batterers interviewed for this study expressed anger and confusion about a world with "TV for women" and female partners who are "too educated." Their arrest signaled a world askew—a place where "the law is for women" and where men have become the victims of discrimination. Although these accounts are ironic in light of the research documenting the continuing reluctance of the legal system to treat domestic violence as a criminal act (Dobash & Dobash, 1979), they demonstrate the ways in which legal and structural reforms in the area of domestic violence influence gender performances. By focusing attention on the "bias" in the system, respondents deflected attention from their own perpetration and victimization and sustained their constructions of rational masculinity. Therefore, theories of gender performativity push us toward analyses of the cultural and structural contexts that form the settings for the acts.

Finally, when viewed through the lens of performativity, our findings challenge the notion that violence is an essential or natural expression of masculinity. Rather, they suggest that violence represents an effort to reconstruct a contested and unstable masculinity. Respondents' references to men's rights movement discourse, their claims of "reverse discrimination," and their complaints that female partners are controlling indicate a disruption in masculine subjectivities. Viewing domestic violence as a gender performance counters the essentialist readings of men's violence against women that dominate U.S. popular culture. What one performs is not necessarily what one "is."

Disturbingly, however, this study suggests that violence is (at least temporarily) an effective means by which batterers reconstruct men as masculine and women as feminine. Participants reported that they were able to control their partners through exertions of physical dominance and through their interpretive efforts to hold partners responsible for the violence in their relationships. By gendering violence, these batterers not only performed masculinity but reproduced gender as dominance. Thus, they naturalized a binary and hierarchical gender system.

References

Bachman, R., & Saltzman, L. E. (1995). *Violence against women: Estimates from the redesigned survey August 1995* (NCJ-154348 Special Report). Washington, DC: Bureau of Justice Statistics.

Bowker, L. H. (1983). *Beating wife-beating.* Lexington, MA: Lexington Books.

Butler, J. (1990). *Gender trouble: Feminism and the subversion of identity.* New York: Routledge.

Butler, J. (1993). *Bodies that matter: On the discursive limits of sex.* New York: Routledge.

Campbell, A. (1993). *Men, women, and aggression.* New York: Basic Books.

Collins, P. H. (1991). *Black feminist thought: Knowledge, consciousness, and the politics of empowerment.* New York: Routledge.

Connell, R. W. (1992). A very straight gay: Masculinity, homosexual experience, and the dynamics of gender. *American Sociological Review, 57,* 735–751.

Dobash, R. E., & Dobash, R. P. (1979). *Violence against wives: A case against the patriarchy.* New York: Free Press.

Dobash, R. E., & Dobash, R. P. (1998). Violent men and violent contexts. In R. E. Dobash & R. P. Dobash (Eds.), *Rethinking violence against women*. Thousand Oaks, CA: Sage.

Dobash, R. P., Dobash, R. E., Wilson, M., & Daly, M. (1992). The myth of sexual symmetry in marital violence. *Social Problems, 39*, 71–91.

Eaton, M. (1994). Abuse by any other name: Feminism, difference, and intralesbian violence. In M. A. Fineman & R. Mykitiuk (Eds.), *The public nature of private violence: The discovery of domestic abuse*. New York: Routledge.

Edwards, R. (1990). Connecting method and epistemology: A white woman interviewing Black women. *Women's Studies International Forum, 13*(5), 477–490.

Fagot, B., Hagan, R., Leinbach, M. B., & Kronsberg, S. (1985). Differential reactions to assertive and communicative acts of toddler boys and girls. *Child Development, 56*, 1499–1505.

Fine, M., Weis, L., Addelston, J., & Marusza, J. (1997). (In)secure times: Constructing white working-class masculinities in the late 20th century. *Gender & Society, 11*, 52–68.

Goffman, E. (1977). The arrangement between the sexes. *Theory & Society, 4*(3), 301–331.

Gondolf, E. W., & Hannekin, J. (1987). The gender warrior: Reformed batterers on abuse, treatment, and change. *Journal of Family Violence, 2*, 177–191.

Gray, N. B., Palileo, G. J., & Johnson, G. D. (1993). Explaining rape victim blame: A test of attribution theory. *Sociological Spectrum, 13*, 377–392.

Hearn, J. (1998). *The violences of men: How men talk about and how agencies respond to men's violence against women*. Thousand Oaks, CA: Sage.

Island, D., & Letellier, P. (1991). *Men who beat the men who love them: Battered gay men and domestic violence*. New York: Harrington Park.

Jang, D., Lee, D., & Morello-Frosch, R. (1998). Domestic violence in the immigrant and refugee community: Responding to the needs of immigrant women. In S. J. Ferguson (Ed.), *Shifting the center: Understanding contemporary families*. Mountain View, CA: Mayfield.

Kirkwood, C. (1993). *Leaving abusive partners: From the scars of survival to the wisdom for change*. Newbury Park, CA: Sage.

Langhinrichsen-Rohling, J., Neidig, P., & Thorn, G. (1995). Violent marriages: Gender differences in levels of current violence and past abuse. *Journal of Family Violence, 10*, 159–176.

Lundgren, E. (1998). The hand that strikes and comforts: Gender construction and the tension between body and symbol. In R. E. Dobash & R. P. Dobash (Eds.), *Rethinking violence against women*. Thousand Oaks, CA: Sage.

Martin, D. (1976). *Battered wives*. New York: Pocket Books.

McCaughey, M. (1998). The fighting spirit: Women's self-defense training and the discourse of sexed embodiment. *Gender & Society, 12*, 277–300.

Messerschmidt, J. (1993). *Masculinities and crime: A critique and reconceptualization of theory*. Lanham, MD: Rowman & Littlefield.

Messner, M. A. (1992). *Power at play: Sports and the problem of masculinity.* Boston, MA: Beacon.

Messner, M. A. (1998). The limits of the "male sex role": An analysis of the men's liberation and men's rights movements' discourse. *Gender & Society, 12,* 255–276.

Messner, M. A. (2000). Barbie girls versus sea monsters: Children constructing gender. *Gender & Society, 14,* 765–784.

Pence, E., & Paymar, M. (1993). *Education groups for men who batter: The Duluth model.* New York: Springer.

Ptacek, J. (1990). Why do men batter their wives? In K. Yllo & M. Bograd (Eds.), *Feminist perspectives on wife abuse.* Newbury Park, CA: Sage.

Renzetti, C. M. (1992). *Violent betrayal: Partner abuse in lesbian relationships.* Newbury Park, CA: Sage.

Riessman, C. K. (1987). When gender is not enough: Women interviewing women. *Gender & Society, 1,* 172–207.

Savran, D. (1998). *Taking it like a man: White masculinity, masochism, and contemporary American culture.* Princeton, NJ: Princeton University Press.

Scully, D. (1990). *Understanding sexual violence: A study of convicted rapists.* Boston, MA: Unwin Hyman.

Straton, J. C. (1994). The myth of the "battered husband syndrome." *Masculinities, 2,* 79–82.

Straus, M. A. (1993). Physical assaults by wives: A major social problem. In R. J. Gelles & D. R. Loseke (Eds.), *Current controversies on family violence.* Newbury Park, CA: Sage.

Walker, L. (1984). *The battered woman syndrome.* New York: Springer.

West, C., & Fenstermaker, S. (1995). Doing difference. *Gender & Society, 9,* 8–37.

Williams, C. L., & Heikes, E. J. (1993). The importance of researcher's gender in the in-depth interview: Evidence from two case studies of male nurses. *Gender & Society, 7,* 280–291.

Yllo, K. (1993). Through a feminist lens: Gender, power, and violence. In R. J. Gelles & D. R. Loseke (Eds.), *Current controversies on family violence.* Newbury Park, CA: Sage.

11

Retrospective Accounts of Violent Events by Gun Offenders

Mark R. Pogrebin, Paul B. Stretesky, N. Prabha Unnithan, and Gerry Venor

*T*he authors examine accounts by gun offenders to explain their violent behavior and allow them top maintain a conventional sense of self. Their data are drawn from a random sample of Colorado inmates convicted of gun-related violent crimes. Seventy-three (73) inmates from a random sample of 119 agreed to be interviewed. Respondents ranged from 20 to 67 years of age and most had been convicted of armed robbery, assault, murder, kidnapping, and attempted murder. The sample was composed of 39.1% whites, 40.6 percent African Americans, 15.6 percent Hispanics, and 4.7% Asians and Middle Easterners; 8% were female. They study revealed that inmates provide accounts in the form of justifications and excuses. Appeals to defeasibility (excuse) and denial of victim (justification) were the most common types of accounts inmates use to explain their violent behavior. The authors found that inmates who report that their victim deserved the injury rarely offer additional accounts for their violence. In contrast, inmates who claim that their violent behavior was beyond their control tended to offer additional accounts in the form of justification and excuse.

Scott and Lyman first introduced their concept of "accounts" in 1968. Since that time, researchers have expanded on the sociology of accounts to produce an impressive body of research. Interest in the study of accounts is not surprising because it allows for understanding and "insight into the human experience [in order to] arrive at...culturally embedded normative explanations" (Orbuch, 1997, p. 455). Studies of accounts are wide ranging and cover a variety of behaviors, including HIV risk-taking (Fontdevila, Bassel, & Gilbert, 2005), Medicare/Medicaid fraud (Evans & Porche, 2005), computer hacking (Turgeman-Goldschmidt, 2005), intimate partner violence (Wood, 2004), violent crime (Presser, 2004), rape (Scully & Marolla, 1984), child abandonment (Geiger & Fischer, 2003), snitching (Pershing, 2003), steroid use (Monaghan, 2002), and white-collar crime (Willott, Griffin, & Torrance, 2001). Although studies of accounts are pervasive in the sociological literature, there has been little examination of the accounts presented by

Source: Deviant Behavior, 27: 479–501, 2006 Copyright © Taylor & Francis Group.

violent gun offenders. The purpose of this research, then, is to examine the types of accounts employed by violent gun users to gain insight into their construction of reality.

The data for this study come from intensive qualitative interviews with a random sample of individuals who are incarcerated for using firearms in the commission of a violent crime. The violent encounters our study participants were involved in lasted a very short period of time, but the interviews lasted much longer and provide offenders with an opportunity to reflect on their past gun-related violent behavior. One performance norm in personally discrediting encounters is giving others the benefit of doubt by allowing them an opportunity to adopt conventional role behavior (Gross & Stone, 1964). It is within this context that our subjects provided us with accounts of their untoward acts with a gun.

THEORETICAL PERSPECTIVE

Mills (1940, p. 904) observes, "the differing reasons men give for their actions are not themselves without reasons." Mills draws a sharp distinction between "cause" and "explanation" or "account." He focuses not on the reasons for the actions of individuals but on the *reasons individuals give for their actions.* Mills views motive as "a complex of meaning, which appears to the actor himself or to the observer to be an adequate ground for his conduct" (p. 906). Yet, there is another dimension: the individual's perception of how the motive will appear to others. Mills argues that such motives express themselves in special vocabularies that must satisfactorily answer questions concerning both social and lingual conduct as well as account for past, present, or future behavior. According to Scott and Lyman (1968) accounts are socially approved vocabularies that serve as explanatory mechanisms for deviance. These linguistic devices attempt to shape others' attribution about the actor's intent or motivation, turning it away from imputations that are harmful (e.g., their personal devaluation, stigma, or imposition of negative sanctions).

It is no doubt true that, in many instances, being able to present accounts effectively will lessen the degree of one's moral responsibility. However, moral responsibility is rarely a present-or-absent attribution. Just as there are degrees of deviation from expected conduct of norms, there are probably types and degrees of accountability, as well as acceptability, to various audiences with respect to the accounts that individuals offer. "The variable is the accepted vocabulary of motives of each man's dominant group about whose opinion he cares" (Mills, 1940, p. 906).

Most people are able to draw from a repertoire of accounts in explaining their untoward acts. This is not to suggest that their reasons are either sincere or insincere. Nor does it deny the validity of their claims; they may well have committed the disapproved behavior for the very reasons that they give. However, what is important is that they require an appropriate vocabulary of motives to guide their presentation of self.

Accounts are, above all, a form of impression management that represents a mixture of fact and fantasy. Goffman, for example, argues that social behavior involves a great deal of deliberate deception as self impressions are continually created, managed, and presented to others. In short, we "put on a face to meet the faces we meet." Because accounts are often judged by others for authenticity, determining if the mixture of fact and fantasy is functional can be difficult. That is, the accounts that a social actor presents cannot be interpreted by others as deceptive and must be judged as a sufficient indicator of intentions, motivations, beliefs, and values (i.e., one's character). In short, for a social interaction to be mutually successful each social actor must assume a degree of genuineness in appearances presented by the other, as well as be able to take for granted the concomitant meanings implicit in those appearances (Goffman, 1959). As Gross and Stone (1964) point out, each participant in an interaction must present a construction of self that complements others engaged in that interaction.

An individual s commitment and performance of conventional roles are crucial for impression management. A portrayal of prosocial behavior when accounting for one's deviance may be interpreted as an attempt by the offender to reaffirm his or her commitment to conventional values and goals in order to win the acceptance of others (Tedeschi & Riordan, 1981). The demonstration of shared standards of conduct may also be seen as consistent with the wish to redeem oneself in the eyes of another in order to preserve self respect. The desire for self-validating approval becomes more important when circumstances threaten the individual's identity. In these circumstances a person will make self-presentations for purposes of securing feedback that will restore the perception of self by others (Prus, 1975). As Jones and Pittman (1982, pp. 255–256) note, "to the extent that the threatened sustains his counteractive behavior or to the extent that the counteractive behavior involves effort and costly commitments, social confirmation will have the restorative power sought."

If an offender can maintain a normal presentation of self within an abnormal situation that offender may be successful in having her or his past criminal behavior perceived by others as atypical (i.e., it is not indicative of her or his true or real self). Therefore, the offender is allowed to accept the moral responsibility of her or his violent behavior without having to accept the associated deviant identity. Thus, Goffman (1959) contends that individuals are not concerned with questions of morality about their behavior as much as they are with the amoral issue of presenting a moral self. Individuals, then, are largely concerned with moral matters, but as performers they do not have a moral concern with it.

Even where no guilt or shame is consciously felt, Goffman (1959, p. 251) argues that "one may offer accounts in the hope of lessening what could be, none the less, attributions of a deviant identity." When used convincingly accounts blur the distinction between "appearances and reality, truth and falsity, triviality and importance, accident and essence, coincidence and cause" (Garfinkel, 1956, p. 420). Thus, we believe that the offenders in our study are likely to provide us with accounts that most effectively counter their deviant identity.

FINDINGS

We present our findings in the form of detailed inmate narratives. The inmate narratives presented here offer considerable insight into the types of accounts they offer for their gun-related violence. The drawback of our approach is that lengthy narratives cannot be used to efficiently enumerate every type of inmate account. Nevertheless, the inmate narratives we chose to include in this analysis are rich in description and representative of the most common types of accounts given by inmates. Thus, the inclusion of extra accounts is not likely to provide additional insight. In short, the inmate narratives provided are accurate in that they depict the most common types of accounts and therefore represent the way most violent gun users construct reality.

We discovered that accounts of gun-related violence mainly fall into two groups—those that rely on justifications and those that rely on excuses. The most common justification used by the inmates in our sample is the denial of victim. When a subject uses the denial of victim justification she/he implies that the victim deserved the injury under the circumstances (Sykes & Matza, 1957). Excuses were also often offered as explanations of untoward acts. Specifically, many inmates presented accounts that draw on the excuse of defeasibility. Scott and Lyman (1968) point out that defeasibility is an excuse that claims an untoward act is the result of a lack of knowledge and will. Thus, an individual that uses defeasibility as an excuse is asserting that she/he is not completely free at the time of the untoward act. As demonstrated later, defeasibility was seldom used as the only account. In other words, defeasibility was often used as an excuse, but was also used together with other excuses and/or justifications.

Denial of Victim as Justification for Gun Use

The most common justification used by the gun offenders in our sample was the denial of victim. As previously stated, denial of victim implies that the victim deserved the injury. The four inmate narratives presented illustrate the diverse ways in which our subjects claim that the victim was responsible for their injury. In the first case, the offender shot his supervisor for terminating his employment. In the second case, the offender shot the victim for physically threatening him and stealing his drugs. In the third case, the offender shot the victim for failing to play by the rules and acknowledge that guns are dangerous. In the fourth case the offender shot the victim to defend himself.

Story 1

I got tired; I had been working a long time for that company. Then one day one of the tenants had not paid their rent, so they decided to put their belongings on the street. So, we went with the Sheriff and started carrying chairs, tables, that kind of stuff. There were other people that were supposed to be helping me. That would be my supervisor and another maintenance guy. I told my supervisor—his name is Robert—"Aren't you supposed to be helping me man?" He put his face in front of mine and said, "You know what, you work for me!" He said, "You do not have to tell me what I have to do, okay?" So, I got very upset because nobody yells in my face like this before. So I point my finger close to his face and started laughing, you know. He said, "That's okay I will see you crying in five minutes." After that I went to clean the swimming pool. I got a call on my radio that told me to come to the office. Robert said, "Give me your keys, your radio, and the beeper." So when this happens he said, "Good luck"— meaning that I was fired. He fired me on the spot. I was very upset. The money I was making at the apartment complex was to help my family in Colombia. The guy had to pay for what he did. I wanted to explode you know. I had a .38 caliber gun in my car. When I grabbed the weapon I knew I was ready. When I approached him [Robert] I had a sport magazine and I covered the weapon with it. I was approaching him but the other maintenance man became suspicious. He said, "Robert, watch out!" When he said that, "Boom."—I shot him. I sat down and waited for the police. It was a relief for me. You feel rested.

This particular offender had no prior criminal history. The demeaning incident that led up to the shooting of his supervisor was associated with the humiliation he experienced by his supervisor's confrontational interaction. The subject noted two important occurrences that took place prior to the shooting. First, his supervisor talked harshly to him close to his face, thereby violating his personal space that should be respected by another during face-to-face interaction. Second, the supervisor abruptly fired the interviewee from his seven-year job.

The shooter appeared to feel a deep sense of anger over his two confrontations with his supervisor. He clearly discussed his anger and desire for retaliation when he made the point that he was so angry that he felt like he was going to explode. He noted that his supervisor would have to pay for his actions. It is at this point in the account that our subjects justified his attempted murder. He also accounted for his actions by arguing that the loss of his job would adversely impact his family who still resided in Colombia. In short, from this offender's perspective, the victim was responsible for his injury.

After the shooting incident was over, the subject noted that he sat down and waited for the police. He expressed a sense of relief and claimed he felt rested. The actual retaliatory incident rapidly decreased his rage. He did what he had to do to vindicate the anger he experienced because of the victim. Nowhere in our interview did this particular participant make claims to the righteousness of his violent action, but instead laid claims and attempted to portray himself as a person who needed, at the time, to redeem his sense of self by causing pain and physical harm to the person who committed a terrible wrong against him.

Story 2

I had a gun in my pocket and I told him, you know, "Why did you jack us?" And he [victim] tried to play it off like he didn't know what I was talking about. I says, "You owe me $18,000 or your gonna give me back my dope." And he says, "Hey, you come over here running your mouth again, I'll put a fucking hole in your head." So when he threatened me like that, I turned around pulled out my gun and walked right up to him and shot him in the head. When he hit the ground I shot him 2 or 3 more times....I was selling drugs, drugs was my life, and when he went in there and jacked us for dope he was taking away from how I made my living. Word gets back on the street that me and my partner had got jacked everybody's waiting to see what we're going to do. If we didn't do nothing everybody else, everybody would come and rob us. It was like "Damn what am I gonna do?" Some of it did have to do with peer pressure, but they didn't make me do it. But, the man threatened my life and, you know, that's not good to threaten people's lives.

This subject was a gang member that was robbed of a considerable amount of drugs he was going to sell. He described his conflict of whether he should shoot the robber or not. But he accounted for his decision to get his drugs back or the money they were worth. By sharing his conflict with the interviewer, he reiterated his dilemma. The subject could either lose face as a gang member and drug dealer or do something to gain respect in the drug/gang community. In the gang environment our subject argued that he had no choice. He had to retaliate against the drug robber because the robber had threatened his livelihood and showed him a considerable amount of disrespect.

Our subject justified shooting the victim because he felt threatened. He accounted for his shooting the drug robber by arguing that "people should not threaten other people's lives." But, the shooter is also expressing his choices within a limited set of possible actions. He could lose face and have nothing left of his gang member identity or cause harm to the person who wronged him. Here, he presented a self that needed to maintain his street image. From the point of view of our subject, there appeared to be no other alternative course of action than to shoot the victim.

Those African American and Latino gang members in our study who were involved in violent gun encounters and imprisoned all expressed the importance of not losing face among their peers. The code of retaliation for both groups was sincerely believed to represent an ongoing presentation of self as tough and fearless. This image often leads to violent encounters using guns over the most incidental actions that are interpreted as disrespectful. Being disrespectful was often viewed as an act that deserved retaliation. This same presentation of self continues and is often exacerbated by gangs of all races and ethnicities within the prison.

In case after case, we observed our subjects saying that if you carry a gun you must be willing to use it. These justifications were often also related to the denial of victim in which the subject admitted the commission of the untoward act but also argued that the victim caused the offender to use a gun. In other words, the injury would not have occurred but for the victims' actions. In the following account an offender used the denial of victim justification to explain his violent actions.

Story 3

I guess there are loner criminals out there but for me there are two or three guys. I really didn't do a lot of crime by myself. We would need some money for whatever reason and then, you know, "Hey man," where can we get some money. We go rob it. We done convenience stores, liquor stores, any places we really thought had some decent money...well I get out of the military and me, my brother, a friend of mine, and a friend of his decided to do a robbery. We had an interaction with some other young people and we both stopped at a light. We got into an interaction and I pulled out my gun and shot the guy in the stomach. I was gonna fight him but I had a gun. Why fight, you know, when you have a gun? My brother looks at me and says, "Man, you're a real killer now, aren't you?" I says, "No, I'm not," but if you got a weapon you might as well use it to protect yourself. I still had a sense of trying to do the right thing. I shot a warning shot up in the air to get him (victim) away from the car. He stood there. He started talking trash and I just jammed the gun into his belly and pulled the trigger. He fell to the ground. We drove off and went and pulled a robbery. I was arrested and I am doing time for attempted murder.

In his explanation of the events that transpired during the violent altercation, our subject offered a self-perception of his integrity when he claimed he tried to do the "right thing" by firing a warning shot to let the victim know that he was serious in his demand to back down. In similar cases throughout our study, we found numerous instances when victims threatened with a gun failed to comply with the warnings given by the shooter to retreat often ended up getting shot. This usually occurred when the perpetrator actually feared physical retaliation from the victim as was the case here. As our study participant noted, why fight someone when you possess a gun? Or, when put another way, why take the chance of being overpowered physically and experiencing humiliation in front of your peers when you can avoid a physical encounter or a threatening situation by harming the aggressing victim before he harms you?

While relating his account of the events that led up to and after the violent encounter, the inmate offered two factors that tend to bolster his self image as a "bad ass" (Katz, 1988). His younger brother's admiration of him as a "genuine killer" seems to have masked his feelings of cowardice by shooting the victim instead of physically fighting him when confronting an unarmed victim. The subject presented a self that is in control of his emotions as he goes on after the shooting to commit an armed robbery. In short, he did not allow the emotional response associated with a possible homicide interfere with his original mission to rob a business for money.

Story 4

I kept the gun in the house most of the time. But this night that this happened I had it in my car with me under the seat. On my way to work I'm driving through the middle of a black neighborhood and there's these three guys out on the street corner jumping out in the middle of the street throwing rocks at cars. So this guy jumps out in the street at me throwing a rock over the hood of my car. So right away I make a U-turn right in the middle of the street and I'm going back to confront him like, "What are you doing? Why are you guys out here yelling and all that?" His partner threw something else over the top of the car. I didn't see what it was—like a rock or something. So I make another U-turn to where they were on the right side. I stopped the car and we got...got into this big argument and it escalates from there. I start to ask them why they are throwing rocks and stuff like that—jumping out into the middle of the street at cars—and they are acting all crazy and cussing at me. So, they start to approach the car and I pull out my gun. In my mind I'm figuring I'm going to scare them away. I never figured on shooting anybody. When I pulled out the gun one of them kinda backed up behind the bushes, but the other two were still standing kinda tough. The guy I ended up shooting, he was still talking to me this whole time, still cussing at me and calling me racial names and that type of stuff. I had the gun out telling him to stop, you know "I'll shoot you, if you don't stop coming toward the car." He's like, "Well, if your gonna do it, just do it. If not just drive away." I'm sitting there all confused now because I'm like "this guy thinks he's Superman or something." I couldn't figure out why he wasn't scared of the gun. I looked back at him he jumped towards the car like I don't know if he was going to come through the window or open the door, and go for the gun. But, as I look he jumps toward me and I jerked the trigger one time and it ended up hitting him in the middle of the chest. I can see him grab himself and kind of start to go down. I drove off right away.

This subject is a 16-year-old Caucasian youth who was in a confrontation with three African American teenagers. He confronted the rock throwing teenagers from the confines of his car. It is likely that he never would have driven back to the where the youth were had he not had a loaded gun in his possession that he could wield from the safety of his car.

The subject appeared to suggest that the firearm caused him to have a false sense of bravado and he implied that had he not taken his gun he would not have confronted the victim. The gun, as was true in many other cases in our study, allowed the instigator to have a self perception as a powerful person. One who can pull the weapon out during a conflict and have a more physical, threatening individual back down. This sense of power over another was exemplified in this case study. The gun gives an advantage to the more vulnerable party, and more than evens the odds that there will be no physical threat to our subject. Yet, the threat of a weapon does not always provide the desired end result. This and other cases we analyzed sometimes saw the victim pursue the gun carrier despite the threat of severe physical harm or worse. Once the victim does not adhere to the gun carrier's threats, the self perception of power on the part of the instigator immediately changes. He pointed to this feeling when he tells us that he could not understand why the threat of the pointing gun did not prevent the victim from leaving the scene afraid. At this point his account is formulated. This subject implied that if only the victim had reacted with fear when threatened with the gun, the shooting would never have occurred.

This particular inmate had no previous criminal history but seemed to be infatuated with his gun. In most circumstances in which a person is out-numbered by those who threatened them, getting away would be the logical action to take. But here the possession of a firearm directly changed this inmate's self-perception to that of a person in control, a person not to be wronged. It is clear that his feared image of a confrontational person who was wronged was not effectively communicated to his victim. Our shooter mis-cued the victim's noncompliance, even after displaying his gun. He claimed he became the threatened party and had to shoot to protect himself.

Appeals to Defeasibility as Excuse for Gun Use

Scott and Lyman (1968) stated that appeals to defeasibility are excuses that claim untoward behavior was the result of the lack of knowledge and will. In our sample, the subjects that used this excuse were essentially asserting that they were not completely free at the time they used a firearm in the commis-sion of violent act. It is interesting to note that excuses of defeasibility were always accompanied by at least one other excuse or justification. The follow-ing three accounts illustrate appeals to defeasibility. In the first case, a girl robs a convenience store to avoid losing her boyfriend. In the second case, a young girl shoots her ex-boyfriend because she has temporarily lost her mind and because he rejected her. In the third case, a young man shoots his stepfather because he was not thinking clearly and because he was encour-aged to act violently toward his stepfather by a close friend.

The first account by the girlfriend in a boyfriend–girlfriend partnership illustrates both defeasibility and scapegoating as reasons for her violence. Scapegoating is the allegation that untoward behavior is a "response to the behavior or attitude of another" (Scott & Lyman, 1968).

Story 5

The boyfriend I had at the time I don't know, we were just kind of having fun that's how I looked at it. Not that the crimes that we committed were fun or anything. We partied a lot, did drugs and stuff, but more than that we were just having fun and living it up. Then in the summer in the period of a couple months we just went on a robbery spree. . . . It all started while we were watch-ing the movie *Point Break*. He was sitting there saying, "We could do that." I was like, "Oh yeah, that is a great idea," and it just went on from there. I mean he could not stop talking about it. . . thinking about it. Then, it kinda turned to a manipulation thing. He said, "I am serious about this and I could find another partner, but I really trust you, and if I have to I will." I was in love with this guy and thinking he is not really going to do this with anybody else. We were just being dumb. I don't think we considered that it was really a violent act. We did have a gun and we pulled it on someone when we walked into the store, but it wasn't like we ran in and roared. It was weird. . . . You cannot count how many people will be in the store, who the clerk is, what they are doing, unless you study them and we really didn't. It wasn't like some big planned thing, it was really spontaneous. We didn't know if we were going to

do anything until we were there, then after go back to work [summer job] and
do it again on another day.

The pair committed three armed robberies of large discount department
stores in a short period of time. The subject's boyfriend insisted that she hide
the gun that they procured for the crimes at her parent's house. After her
boyfriend bragged to a few friends about their criminal acts, one of those
friends informed the authorities who questioned the boyfriend about the
incidents. The boyfriend told authorities where to find the gun and then
became the State's lead witness against the girl. He received a court sentence
to a drug treatment program and our interviewee received a 12-year sentence to prison.

The subject engaged in these robberies without ever thinking about the
consequences of engaging in serious crime. Of course, she implied that if
she would have thought about the consequences of her actions she would
have never engaged in the robberies. She also noted that her affection for
her boyfriend overcame her sensibilities and she argued that she had no
choice but to go along with his wishes or possibly lose him. In this particular situation, the girlfriend claims her motives were to maintain her
romantic relationship. This account might also be viewed as a justification
in the sense that it served the interests of another to which she has an
"unbreakable allegiance of affectation" had she not later argued that she
was "manipulated" by her boyfriend. She implied that she never really
thought they would commit the first robbery. However, she subsequently
engaged in multiple armed robberies prior to being apprehended by the
police. Here, Hewitt and Stokes's (1975) thematic organization of meaning applies. It is based on interactions that most often are dependent on
people's ability to interpret others' actions as types of particular identities.
When events fail to fit themes in interaction, which appears to be the case
here, identities may become problematic if the acts of others do not in reality appear sensible in light of his or her identity in the situation. Maybe her
boyfriend is not who he appeared to be.

The boyfriend's fantasy-identity as a "bad guy" was not really who he
was. For in reality he escaped any meaningful punishment but instead when
the seriousness of his criminal escapades as short lived as they were, forced
him quickly to return to a conventional status he blamed our prison subject
(also using the excuse of scapegoating) for his fantasized criminal identity.
Certainly, she miscued the veracity of his claims to want to be an outlaw
type. Instead, she became the person with the labeled identity and his excuse
was accepted (i.e., he was perceived as the one who had been led astray and
was sent to a drug rehabilitation program).

Scott and Lyman (1968) point out that a sad tale is a justification of an
untoward act in terms of a bleak past. The following account by the girlfriend who uses a firearm to shoot her boyfriend illustrates the sad tale justification combined with the excuse of defeasibility and denial of the victim.

Story 6

I was going with my boyfriend who I felt I was totally in love with and I couldn't live without and all those things. He wanted to leave me and we played this game off and on for a month. He'd leave me and then come back. The last time I was like, "I can't take this anymore. I don't want to live anymore. I am going to kill myself." I asked my mom for a gun because Randy, who had lived with us, had saw me at the 7-11, and I am afraid of him. But I want to go out so she handed me the gun and I went out. I told my mom a lie. I wanted the gun to kill myself so I told her a different story. I went out to the country to an open field and I fired the gun to make sure I could because I am scared of guns, always have been. I stopped and said to myself, "I have to know what's wrong with me first. I need to know why he doesn't love me the way he said he did." I got back in the car and I drove to an outdoor party where I knew he was at. I told him I had to talk with him and we went and talked inside. I had put the gun in my jacket pocked after I shot it in the field. We talked for like an hour and we were walking back to the car and he said something, I don't remember what, and I took the gun out and I shot him and I shot myself.

In this account our subject claimed she had no premeditated thoughts of harming her boyfriend. She began her account by referencing her mother's ex-boyfriend (who we learned about on further questioning) was sexually abusive to her while he was residing with the family. She claimed that the end of her relationship with her boyfriend was simply too much for her to take. She then went on to portray herself as a person who only meant to harm herself but presented an excuse of not really being responsible for her violent actions toward her boyfriend. The events leading up to the actual shooting of her boyfriend and herself appear vague in description and rather coincidental in nature. She clearly claimed she was not aware of her actions at the time of the shooting as she could not even remember what her boyfriend said moments before she shot him. Did his final statement (whatever it was) provoke the murder? Or, was the intention always there to dramatically take both of their lives if she was unable to reconcile her relationship with her boyfriend? The fact that her boyfriend may have said something that was hurtful in those final moments prior to the shooting seemed to us as an attempt to leave open to interviewer interpretation that he deserved to be hurt for what he said—although this justification of denial is not likely to be very effective without her sad tale and appeal to defeasibility.

This study participant's accounts for her murder are related in such a way as to justify them in terms of a sad tale and then to attempt to excuse her violent actions as if the sequence of events that occurred prior to the shooting were scripted for her to follow and she had little control over the events that followed her procuring the gun from her mother. This is an account that offers indirectly the theme of this "wasn't the real me" who committed such a terrible crime.

In a few cases, generally dealing with abusive relationships, the subjects in our study drew on justifications and excuses. In the following scenario the subject clearly invoked the defeasibility excuse, but also justified his acts by arguing that his abusive stepfather deserved to be shot. He also presented an appeal to loyalties to his mother who he asserts he saved from death.

Story 7

My stepfather would break my mom's ribs, break her jaw, break her nose. You know, he never broke anything on me....I was 18, living on my own and I went to visit my mom. She was living in an apartment, but they weren't living together at the time. She had a black eye so I called my step dad and told him, "I'm a grown man now. You hit her again and I'm coming after you." He said, "If I hit her again, I'll kill her and I'll end up killing you too." About three weeks later I saw leather indentations where she had been tied up. The morning of my 19th birthday I went out and shot him. When I decided that there was no alternative but, but to do what I did to my step dad, that's when I went and got a gun and used it. So it was like a 12 hour period of being angry and the person with me [subject's friend] was egging me on. He was having me go through every time I'd seen my step dad hit my mom and every time he hit me. Every time I started to cool down he would start in again. So he kept me pumped up ready to do this until the act occurred. I was totally disconnected from myself in the act. Once the act was complete, I saw somebody I didn't know shooting my step dad. Once the act was over, I'm back to myself, total rush, dizziness, everything was blurry, adrenaline rush, and he's still standing asking me why. I just freaked out.

Murdering his abusive stepfather was a release of pent up emotions after years of physical abuse to his mother. Yet, he accounted for the decision to shoot his abusive stepparent only after his friend kept reminding him of all the terrible abusive incidents he had experienced over the years. He used, in part, his friend's persuasiveness to help justify the shooting. True, his stepfather was a long-time abuser, and needed to be stopped. However, the subject in this case indicated that he may not have shot his abusive stepdad had it not been for his friend's constant reminders of his past beatings at the hands of his stepfather.

Our subject related the feeling that after he actually shot the victim he experienced a disconnection from his physical person and noted that he visualized someone else doing the shooting. This indicated a presentation of self as a person who would not commit such a violent act. It was as if somebody other than himself did the shooting. His account has the objective of relating the real type of person he really is, one whose self presentation consists of a nonviolent person who was overwhelmed by his circumstances. Furthermore, he justified the shooting because of his responsibility to be his mother's protector. By including his mother to help justify his fore-ground thoughts of killing his stepfather, he offered an almost heroic self image as the boy who is now a man, and therefore must confront the evil abuser. In reality it is difficult to discern if our study participant was getting even with the victim for his own years of abuse, or to rectify the years his mother experienced abuse. For this particular subject, protecting his mother heightened his image as a guardian of a weak person rather than that of an angry retaliator who was getting back for his own abusive past. The justification for his action, although wrong, is perceived as necessary.

DISCUSSION

The consequences of deviant activity are often dependent on a given "definition of the situation." When a definition of a specific situation emerges, even though its dominance may be only temporary, individuals must adjust their behavior and views to it. Alternative definitions of problematic situations routinely arise and are usually subject to negotiation. Thus, it is incumbent upon convicted offenders to have their situation defined in ways most favorable to maintaining or advancing their own interests. When "transformations of identity" are at stake, such efforts become especially consequential (Strauss, 1962). The rejection of a deviant identity has ramifications for that person's self perception of who they are. As noted earlier, the negotiation of accounts is really a negotiation of identities. Accounts serve as a management technique, or "front," that minimizes the threat to identity (Goffman, 1967). If the violent perpetrator can offer an acceptable account for his or her violent gun use, he or she increases the likelihood of restoring a cherished identity brought into question by their criminal behavior.

There is a close link between successfully conveying desired images to others and being made to incorporate them in one's own self-construction. When individuals offer accounts for their problematic actions, they are trying to ease their situation in two ways; by convincing others and by convincing themselves. An important function of accounts is to make an individual's transgressions intelligible to themselves and others. The gun users we interviewed sought to dispel the view that their deviation was a defining characteristic of who they really were. In short, they attempted to engage the centrality or primacy of a deviant role imputation. To accomplish this task they offered accounts that were mainly focused on the denial of victim and defeasibility. Their goal was to maintain or restore their own sense of personal worth notwithstanding their violent behavior. In a way, laying claim to a favorable image in spite of aberrant behavior means voiding an apparent moral reality that is apparent to the deviant.

Individuals seek a "common ground" in accounts of their deviant behavior, explaining their actions in conventional terms that are acceptable to a particular audience. It is important to point out that these accounts should not be viewed as mere rationalizations. Many offenders really believed in their accounts. Moreover, accounts do not themselves prove the cause of one's behavior. They do, however, provide contextually specific answers about the act in question and manifest a certain style of looking at the world.

Finally, it should be noted that, as retrospective interpretations, accounts often have little to do with the motives that existed at the time the criminal violence occurred. In this case, accounting for one's deviant behavior requires one to dissimulate, that is, to pretend to be what one is not or not to be what one is. Thus, it is not logically necessary that one agree with other's moral judgments in order to employ accounts. Even where no guilt or shame is consciously felt, one may offer accounts in the hope of lessening what could be, nonetheless, attributions of a deviant identity.

References

Brody, D., Acker, J., & Logan, W. (2001). *Criminal Law.* Gaithersburg, MD: Aspen.

Chase, S. E. (1995). *Ambiguous empowerment: The work narratives of women school superintendents.* Amherst: University of Massachusetts Press.

Colorado Department of Corrections. (2005). *General statistics.* Colorado Springs: Author. Retrieved September 14, 2005, from http://www.doc.state.co.us/Statistics/7General Statistics.htm

Evans, R. D., & Porche, D. A. (2005). The nature and frequency of Medicare/Medicaid fraud and neutralization techniques among speech, occupational, and physical therapists. *Deviant Behavior, 26,* 253–270.

Fontdevila, J., El-Bassel, N., & Gilbert, L. (2005). Accounting for HIV risk among men on methadone. *Sex Roles, 52*(9-10), 609–624.

Garfinkel, H. (1956). Conditions of successful degradation ceremonies. *American Journal of Sociology* 61(5): 420–424.

Geiger, B., & Fischer, M. (2003). Female repeat offenders negotiating identity. *International Journal of Offender Therapy and Comparative Criminology,* 47(5), 496–515.

Glaser, B. G., & Strauss, A. L. (1967). *The discovery of grounded theory: Strategies for qualitative research.* New York: Aldine.

Goffman, E. (1959). *The presentation of self in everyday life.* Garden City, NY: Doubleday.

Goffman, E. (1967). *Interaction ritual: Essays on face-to-face behavior.* Chicago, IL: Aldine.

Gross, E., & Stone, G. P. (1964). Embarrassment and the analysis of role requirements. *American Journal of Sociology,* 70(1), 1–15.

Hewitt, J. P., & Stokes, R. (1975). Disclaimers. *American Sociological Review,* 40(1), 1–11.

Jones, E. E., & Pittman, T. S. (1982). Toward a theory of strategic self-presentation. In J. Suls (Ed.), *Psychological perspectives on the self* (Vol. 1, pp. 231–262.). Hillsdale, NJ: Lawrence Erlbaum.

Katz, J. (1988). *Seductions of crime: Moral and sensual attractions in doing evil.* New York: Basic Books.

Mills, C. W. (1940). Situated actions and vocabularies of motive. *American Sociological Review,* 5(6), 904–913.

Monaghan, L. F. (2002). Vocabularies of motive for illicit steroid use among bodybuilders. *Social Science and Medicine,* 55(5), 695–708.

Orbuch, T. (1997). People's accounts count: The sociology of accounts. *Annual Review of Sociology, 23*, 455–478.

Pershing, J. L. (2003). To snitch or not to snitch? Applying the concept of neutralization techniques to the enforcement of occupational misconduct. *Sociological Perspectives, 46*(2), 149–178.

Presser, L. (2004). Violent offenders, moral selves: Constructing identities and accounts in the research interview. *Social Problems, 51*(1), 82–101.

Prus, R. C. (1975). Resisting designations: An extension of attribution theory into a negotiated conflict. *Sociological Inquiry, 45*(1), 3–14.

Schatzman, L., & Strauss, A. L. (1973). *Field Research: Strategies for natural sociology.* Upper Saddle River, NJ: Prentice Hall.

Scott, M. B., & Lyman, S. M. (1968). Accounts. *American Sociological Review, 33*(1), 46–61.

Scully, D., & Marolla, J. (1984). Convicted rapists' vocabulary of motive: Excuses and justifications. *Social Problems, 31*(5), 530–544.

Strauss, A. (1962). Transformations of identity. In A. M. Rose (Ed.), *Human behavior and social processes: An interactionist approach* (pp. 63–85). London: Routledge and Kegan Paul.

Sykes, G., & Matza, D. (1957). Techniques of neutralization: A theory of delinquency. *American Sociological Review, 22*(6), 664–670.

Tedeschi, J. T., & Riordan, C. A. (1981). Impression management and pro-social behavior following transgression. In J. T. Tedeschi (Ed.), *Impression management theory and social psychological research* (pp. 223–244). New York: Academic Press.

Turgeman-Goldschmidt, O. (2005). Hackers' accounts—hacking as a social entertainment. *Social Science Computer Review, 23*(1), 8–23.

Willott, S., Griffin, C., & Torrance, M. (2001). Snakes and ladders: Upper-middle class male offenders talk about economic crime. *Criminology, 39*(2), 441–466.

Wood, J. T. (2004). Monsters and victims: Male felons' accounts of intimate partner violence. *Journal of Social and Personal Relationships, 21*(5), 555–576.

SECTION IV

OCCUPATIONAL CRIME

The term *occupational crime* refers to crimes committed through opportunities created in the course of a legal occupation. In the past, the label *white-collar crime* almost always connoted crimes committed by the rich and powerful. Today, most criminologists have broadened the term to refer to crimes committed by persons in a wide range of situations. The focus today is on the nature of the crime and not on the person committing it—thus the term *occupational crime*.

Much of the research reported in this book tends to support the idea that most offenders accept responsibility for their crimes. However, the most consistent theme in the following articles, which deal with occupational crime, is that these offenders concoct elaborate justifications, excuses, and rationalizations to avoid accepting responsibility for their criminal behavior. Perhaps that is because, for most, their primary identity is noncriminal. They are health care workers, lawyers, bankers, stockbrokers, and so on. To conceive of themselves as criminals is difficult, if not impossible.

In Chapter 12, Neal Shover, Glenn Coffey, and Dick Hobbs ("Crime on the Line: Telemarketing and the Changing Nature of Professional Crime") explore the world of telemarketing fraud. Shover and his associates interviewed 47 criminal telemarketers drawn from federal prison and parolee populations. Unlike their fellow thieves, telemarketing criminals are disproportionately drawn from the middle class. They are drawn to the business of telemarketing crime because they find the work attractive and rewarding. They are also drawn to the lifestyle and the income it provides. The authors found that their subjects, like those who engage in "street crimes" pursue a hedonistic lifestyle featuring alcohol, drugs, and conspicuous consumption.

In Chapter 13, Michael Benson explains how individuals convicted of occupationally related crimes attempt to avoid the stigma of criminality by denying criminal intent.

In Chapter 14, Dean Dabney examines theft of hospital supplies by nurses in three hospitals. The author discovers that most of the nurses who admitted stealing supplies and medicines also concocted rationalizations and neutralizations regarding their behavior.

These studies are somewhat unusual in that ethnographic research of crime "in the suites" is much more difficult to accomplish than studies of crime "in the streets." Potential subjects are less likely to talk with researchers and are not as easily approached. Patricia Adler (personal communication, 1995) correctly noted that it is easier to "study down than to study up." Thus, the pool of field studies of so-called white-collar crime is small; however, the papers included here are excellent examples of what can be accomplished with a difficult population.

12

Crime on the Line: Telemarketing and the Changing Nature of Professional Crime

Neal Shover, Glenn S. Coffey, and Dick Hobbs

A lthough it has become an important part of the legitimate economy, criminals also have been quick to exploit the opportunities presented by telemarketing. Although it was nearly unheard of until recent decades, few adults today are unfamiliar with telemarketing fraud. There are countless variations on the basic scheme, but typically a consumer receives a phone call from a high-pressure salesperson who solicits funds or sells products based on untrue assertions or enticing claims. Callers offer an enormous variety of products and services, and often they use names that sound similar to bona fide charities or reputable organizations (Telemarketing Fraud and Section 568, 1993). Goods or services either are not delivered at all, or they are substantially inferior to what was promised. Telemarketing fraud touches the lives of many citizens. A 1992 poll of a national sample of Americans showed that 2% of respondents had been victimized in the preceding six months (Harris, 1992). The criminological consequences of this development are poorly charted. In this chapter, the authors examine offenders who have stepped forward to exploit one category of the new opportunities. Drawing from interviews with 47 criminal telemarketers, the authors present a picture and interpretation of them, their pursuits, and their lifestyles. As vocational predators, they share several important characteristics with the professional thieves sketched by earlier generations of investigators. Like the latter, they pursue a hedonistic lifestyle featuring illicit drugs and conspicuous consumption, and they acquire and employ an ideology of legitimation and defense that insulates them from moral rejection. Unlike professional thieves, however, telemarketing criminals disproportionately are drawn from middle-class, entrepreneurial backgrounds. They are markedly individualistic in their dealings with one another and with law enforcement. Finally, their work organizations are more permanent and conventional in outward appearance than the criminal organizations created by blue-collar offenders, which were grounded in the culture of the industrial proletariat. The findings show how the backgrounds and pursuits of vocational predators reflect the qualities and challenges of contemporary lucrative criminal opportunities. Like the markets that they seek to manipulate and plunder, the enacted environments of professional criminals embrace infinite variations, and are largely indistinguishable from the arenas that capacitate legitimate entrepreneurial pursuits.

Writing at the dawn of the 20th century, E. A. Ross (1907, p. 3) was one of the first sociologists to call attention to the fact that crime "changes its quality

205

as society develops." Ross focused specifically on growing social and economic interdependence and the variety of ways this permits both exploitation of trust and the commission of crime at a distance from victims. The transformative social and economic changes he noted only gained speed as the century progressed. In the United States and other Western nations, the middle decades of the century saw the emergence or the expansion of state policies and corporate practices with enormous criminological significance. These include a fundamental shift in the state's public welfare functions, which had the effect of expanding programs and subsidies for citizens across the income spectrum. One measure of this is the fact that by 1992, 51.7% of American families received some form of federal payments, ranging from Social Security, Medicare, and military retirement benefits to agricultural subsidies (Samuelson, 1995, p. 158).

In addition, the years following World War II witnessed a rapid growth of the domestic economy, which made available goods that either were unknown or were unattainable by most citizens just a decade earlier. Houses, automobiles, refrigerators, television sets, and a host of other commodities now were within the reach of a growing segment of the population. The disposable income available to the new owners of these commodities allowed them also to purchase the new comprehensive insurance policies offered by insurance underwriters. Increasingly, the middle-class family now was insured against not only major hazards to life, home, and business but also loss of or damage to household items (Clarke, 1990).

As the century drew to a close, there were fundamental changes also in the structure and dynamics of economic relationships and in communications technology (Adler, 1992; Lash & Urry, 1994). Most important, widespread use of telecommunications (Batty & Barr, 1994; Turkle, 1995), electronic financial transactions and consumer credit (Tickell, 1996) presage a depersonalized, cashless economy. Electronic financial transfers among banks and businesses, automatic teller machines (Hirschhorn, 1985), and home banking increasingly are used across the globe (Silverstone, 1991). In the new world of personal computers and virtual identities, individuals and organizations conduct business with remote others whose credentials and intentions cannot be easily determined.

The net result of these political and economic developments is a cornucopia of new criminal opportunities (Grabosky, Smith, & Dempsey, 2001; Taylor, 1999). Federally funded health care programs, for example, have given physicians and hospitals access to new pools of tax revenue for which oversight is so weak that it has been called a "license to steal" (Sparrow, 1996). The growth of health insurance fraud, therefore, can be seen as "emblematic of the emerging forms of . . . crime that reflect the changing economy of the late twentieth century" (Tillman, 1998, p. 197). The new criminal opportunities extend far beyond health care, however.

The changing landscape of criminal opportunities is strikingly apparent in crimes of fraud. Fraud is committed when misrepresentation or deception is used to secure unfair or unlawful gain, typically by perpetrators who create and exploit the appearance of a routine transaction. Fraud violates trust, it is nonconfrontational, and it can be carried out over long distances. In organizational complexity and reach, it ranges from itinerant vinyl siding scamsters to international banking crimes that can destabilize national economies. The number of Americans victimized by it is large and substantially exceeds the number victimized by serious street crime (Rebovich, Layne, Jiandani, & Hage, 2000; Titus, 2001). A 1991 survey of U.S. households found that compared to crimes of burglary, robbery, assault, and theft, fraud "appears to be very common" (Titus, Heinzelmann, & Boyle, 1995, p. 65). Although a number of methodological shortcomings limit confidence in the findings of previous studies of fraud victimization, there seems little doubt that it is an increasingly commonplace crime.

TELEMARKETING AND FRAUD

The rapid growth of telemarketing is one of several consequential changes in the nature of economic relationships in recent decades. In 2000, telemarketing sales accounted for $611.7 billion in revenue in the United States, an increase of 167% over comparable sales for 1995. Total annual sales from telephone marketing are expected to reach $939.5 billion by the year 2005 (Direct Marketing Association, 2001). The reasons for the growth of telemarketing are understood easily in context of the "general acceleration of everyday life, characterized by increasingly complicated personal and domestic timetables" (Taylor, 1999, p. 45). The daily schedule no longer permits either the pace or the style of shopping that were commonplace a few decades ago, and the need to coordinate personal schedules and to economize on time now drives many household activities. In the search for convenience, telemarketing sales have gained in popularity.

But although it has become an important part of the legitimate economy, criminals also have been quick to exploit the opportunities presented by telemarketing. Although it was nearly unheard of until recent decades, few adults today are unfamiliar with telemarketing fraud. There are countless variations on the basic scheme, but typically a consumer receives a phone call from a high-pressure salesperson who solicits funds or sells products based on untrue assertions or enticing claims. Callers offer an enormous variety of products and services, and often they use names that sound similar to bona fide charities or reputable organizations (*Telemarketing Fraud and Section 568*, 1993). Goods or services either are not delivered at all, or they are substantially inferior to what was promised. Telemarketing fraud touches the lives of many citizens. A 1992 poll of a national sample of Americans showed that 2% of respondents had been victimized in the preceding six months (Harris, 1992).

FINDINGS

Of all who begin employment in criminal telemarketing, some quickly discover it is not their cup of tea; they dislike it or they do not perform well. Others find the work attractive and rewarding but see it only as a means to other life and career goals. Most, therefore, pursue it only temporarily. Others, however, discover they are good at fraudulent telephone sales, and they are drawn to the income and the lifestyle it can provide. On average, the members of our interview sample were employed in these endeavors for 8.25 years. Their ages when interviewed range from 26 to 69, with a mean of 42.4 years. Their ranks include 38 white males, 3 African American males, and 6 white females. Nearly all have been married at least once, and most have children.

Organization and routine

Like its legitimate forms, criminal telemarketing is a productive enterprise that requires the coordinated efforts of two or more individuals. To work in it, therefore, is to work in an organizational setting (Francis, 1988; Schulte, 1995; Stevenson, 2000). The size of criminal telemarketing organizations can vary substantially. Some are very small, consisting of only two or three persons, but others are considerably larger (e.g., Alleged Scam on Elderly, 2000). Their permanence and mobility vary also, ranging from those that operate and remain in one locale for a year or more to others that may set up and operate for only a few weeks before moving on. These "rip and tear" operators count on the fact that up to six months' time may pass before law enforcement agencies become aware of and targets them. "Boiler rooms," operations featuring extensive telephone banks and large numbers of sales agents, have become less common in the United States in recent years, largely because of the law-enforcement interest they attract. There is reason to believe, however, that criminal telemarketers increasingly are locating them in countries with weak laws and oversight and operating across international borders (e.g., Australian Broadcasting Corporation, 2001).

Larger telemarketing operations commonly take on the characteristics and dynamics of formal organizations; they are hierarchical, with a division of labor, graduated pay, and advancement opportunities. Established by individuals with previous experience in fraudulent sales, they generally employ commissioned sales agents to call potential customers, to make the initial pitch, and to weed out the cautious and the steadfastly disinterested. We took steps to insure that our offender interview sample included persons who formerly held a variety of positions in criminal telemarketing firms. It includes 22 owners, 8 managers, and 17 sales agents.

Experienced telemarketers generally do not call individuals randomly but work instead from "lead lists" (also known as "mooch lists"). These are purchased from any of dozens of businesses that compile and sell information on consumer behavior and expressed preferences. Individuals whose names appear on lead lists typically are distinguished by past demonstrated interest or participation in promotions of one kind or another. When a person is contacted by telephone, the sales agent generally works from a script. Scripts are written materials that lay out both successful sales approaches and responses to whatever reception sales agents meet with from those they reach by phone. Promising contacts are turned over to a "closer," a more experienced and better paid sales agent. "Reloaders" are the most effective closers; much like account executives in legitimate businesses, they maintain contacts with individuals who previously sent money to the company (i.e., "purchased" from it) in hopes of persuading them to send more. As one subject told us:

> I had it so perfected that I could get these customers to buy again…. I made sure they were happy so I could sell them again. It didn't do me—I didn't want the one time, I didn't want the two-timer. I wanted to sell these people ten times.

The organization of larger telemarketing firms and the routine employees follow when handling promising calls explains why those who "buy" from them typically report contact with multiple "salespersons" (American Association of Retired Persons, 1996).

The products and services offered by criminal telemarketers span a wide gamut. In one scam, subjects identified and located unaware owners of vacant property, led them to believe that buyers for the property could be found easily, and then charged high fees to advertise it. Other schemes we encountered included collection for charities, drug education programs, and sale of "private" stocks. One subject sold inexpensive gemstones with fraudulent certificates of grossly inflated value and authenticity. The stones were sealed in display cases such that purchasers would have difficulty getting them appraised, particularly since they were told that if they broke the seal, the value of the stones would decrease and the certificate of authenticity would become invalid. "Private stocks" by definition are not listed or traded on a stock exchange, but telemarketers are able to entice investors with smooth talk and promising prospectives. Dependent on their salesmen for market reports, those who purchase soon discover that the nonexistent stocks take a nose-dive, and they lose their investments. A high proportion of the companies represented by our interview subjects promised that those who purchased products from them were odds-on winners of a prize soon to be awarded once other matters were settled. Typically, this required the customers to pay fees of one kind or another. Some of our subjects solicited money for nonexistent charities or legitimate organizations they did not represent. In the products they sell, criminal telemarketers clearly are limited only by the human imagination.

Backgrounds and careers

A substantial body of research into the lives and careers of street criminals has shown that many are products of disadvantaged and disorderly parental homes. We were interested in determining if the homes in which our subjects were reared reveal similar or functionally equivalent criminogenic characteristics. They do not. Overwhelmingly, the members of our sample describe their parents as conventional and hard working and family financial circumstances as secure if not comfortable. Their parental families were traditional in nature, with the father providing the main source of income. Nevertheless, one-half of the mothers also were employed outside the home. Although the fathers' reported occupations ranged from machinist to owner of a chain of retail stores, 32 were business owners or held managerial positions. A substantial proportion of our subjects was exposed to and acquired entrepreneurial perspectives and skills while young. Business ownership appealed to many of them:

> You're always pursuing more money, most of us are. We're raised that way, we are in this country. And that's the way I was raised. But I also wanted to do my own thing. I wanted to be in business for myself, I wanted the freedom that came with that.

Clearly, telemarketing criminals are not drawn from the demographic pools or locales that stock and replenish the ranks of street criminals. Although we questioned them at length about their early and adolescent years, their responses reveal little that distinguishes them from others of similar age and class background. Certainly, the disadvantages and pathologies commonplace in the early lives of most street criminals are in scant evidence here.

If our subjects' early years reveal few clues to their later criminality, there also are few signs that they distinguished themselves in conventional ways. Their educational careers, for example, are unremarkable; eight dropped out of high school, although most graduated. Twenty-one attended college, but on average they invested only 2 years in the quest for a degree. Five claimed a baccalaureate degree. When invited to reflect on how they differ from their siblings or peers, many reported they were aware of an interest in money from an early age. One subject told us:

> I had certain goals when I was a teenager, you know. And I had a picture of a Mercedes convertible on my bedroom mirror for years. You know, I do have a major addiction, and I don't think I'll ever lose it. And I don't think there's any classes [treatment] for it. And it's money, it's Ben Franklin.

He and others like him were aware also that there are ways of earning a good income that do not require hard work and subordination to others. Another subject said:

> You know, I was, I've never been a firm believer [that] you got to work for a company for 30 years and get a retirement. Like my dad thinks. I'm all about going out [and] making that million and doing it, doing it very easily. And there's a lot of ways to do it.

Typically, they began working for pay while young and maintained employment throughout their adolescent years.

None of our subjects said that as children they aspired to a career in telemarketing, either legitimate or criminal. Some had previous sales experience before beginning the work, but most did not. Their introduction to it was both fortuitous and fateful; while still in high school or, more common, while in college, they either responded to attractive ads in the newspaper or were recruited by friends or acquaintances who boasted about the amount of money they were making.

> [A former acquaintance] ... looked me up, found me and said "you gotta come out here.... We're gonna make a ton of money." I went out for three weeks— left my wife back home. And I got on the phones, and I was making a thousand dollars a week. I'm like, "oh, my God, Jenni, pack the stuff, we're going to Arizona." ... He was like, "man, you're, you're a pro at this shit." And I just, I don't know what it was. I was number one... I don't know, I loved it.

The influence of others is remarkably similar to what is known about the criminal careers of street criminals, particularly those who go on to pursue crime with a high degree of skill and success (Hobbs, 1995, ch. 2; Winlow, 2001, pp. 66–86).

For our subjects, many of whom were foundering on conventional paths, criminal telemarketing was a godsend; it came along at a time when they needed to show that they could make something of themselves. In the words of one of them, it was "a salvation to me as a means of income. And being able to actually accomplish something without an education." Criminal telemarketing was the reason some reported for dropping out of college:

> [It] was just something I picked up as a part time job, when I was sixteen.... When I was in college, my second year in college, [fellow students] were talking about finishing their four years of college and making $28,000 or $30,000 a year. And I was making $1,000 a week part time, you know. ... And I just couldn't see doing it. I mean, I wound up, after the end of my second year of college, I never went back. I was making too much money. It just seemed so easy.

New recruits generally start as sales agents, although most of our subjects later worked also as closers and reloaders. Employment mobility is common; individuals move from one firm to another, with some eventually taking managerial positions (Doocy, Schichor, Sechrest, & Geis, 2001).

After gaining experience, former managers told us, they were confident they knew enough about the business to strike out on their own. They did so expecting to increase their income substantially. As one put it:

> [I] n my mind I believed I was smarter than the owners of these other companies that were making millions of dollars. And I just said, "I can do this on my own."

Typically, defectors lure productive personnel from their current employer with promises of more money, and on the way out they are not above plundering the business's files and lead lists:

> I downloaded every lead in his file. I took it all. I opened up...my own office, took all those people and said "now, watch me."

Based in part on the widely shared assumption that the market is never saturated, they generally open a company based on similar products and sales approaches.

What about the criminal histories of fraudulent telemarketers? Information elicited in the interviews and a review of information contained in presentence investigation reports shows that 13 of our subjects had previous criminal records, 7 for minor offenses (e.g., petty theft and possession of marijuana) and 6 for felonies. Of the latter, three were convicted previously of telemarketing offenses. Clearly, many of our subjects are not one-time or accidental violators; they have histories of multiple arrests and convictions. Others have reported similar findings. Thirty percent of 162 sales agents employed by a California-based fraudulent telemarketing firm, for example, had records of at least one criminal offense, and another 16.4% had records of alcohol or drug offenses (Doocy et al., 2001). For members of our sample who have previous arrests, the age of onset for criminal activity is considerably higher than for street criminals. Our data do show persuasively, however, that many appear to have recurrent trouble with the law and, like street criminals, they are persistent users of alcohol and other drugs. This picture is confirmed also by information contained in their presentence reports.

Attractions and lifestyles

Overwhelmingly, our subjects told us they got into and persisted at telemarketing for "the money". How well does it pay? Only one subject reported earning less than $1,000 weekly, and most said their annual earnings were in the range of $100,000 to $250,000. Five told us their annual earnings exceeded $1 million. The fact that they can make money quickly and do so without incurring restrictive responsibilities adds to the attractiveness of the work. They find appealing both the flexible hours and the fact that it requires neither extensive training nor advanced education. Few employers impose rigid rules or strictures; generally there are neither dress codes nor uniforms. The work can be done in shorts and a tee shirt (Doocy et al., 2001).

As important as the income it yields and the casual approach to employment it permits, criminal telemarketing appeals to many who persist at it for reasons of career and identity. Despite class and parental expectations, most of our subjects had not previously settled upon promising or rewarding occupations. Asked what he "liked about telemarketing," one subject's reply was typical: "Well, obviously, it was the money." Immediately, however, he added that "It gave me a career, [and] to me it was my salvation." As with him, criminal telemarketing enables others to own their own business

despite their unimpressive educational background, their limited credentials and the absence of venture capital. As president of their own corporation, telemarketing provides both outward respectability and an income
sufficient to maintain the good life.

Other aspects of the work are attractive as well. Its interpersonal and psychological challenge, for example,

> [It] has strong appeal to many salespersons. The ability to impose one's will
> upon another person—and to achieve a measurable financial reward for doing
> so—is highlighted in many of the reports of illegal telemarketing practices. ...
> Enforcement officials told us that sellers often have mirrors in the cubicles in
> which they work. They are told to look into the mirror and see the face of a hot
> shot salesperson. Sometimes there will be a motto on the wall, such as: "Each
> No gets me closer to the Yes I want." Boiler room owners and managers...may
> put large bills on a bulletin board and say that the next sale or the highest total
> for the day will qualify for this extra reward. Often the sales people have to
> stand up when they consummate a transaction, so that the boss can note them
> and they can take pleasure in the achievement. (Doocy et al., 2001, p. 17)

Characteristically, our subjects believe they are outstanding salespersons;
they are supremely confident of their ability to sell over the telephone despite
resistance from those they contact. Doing so successfully is a high. One subject told us:

> You could be selling a $10,000 ticket, you could be selling a $49.95 ticket. And
> it's the same principle, it's the same rules. It's the same game. I like to win.
> I like to win in all the games I play, you know. And the money is a reason to be
> there, and a reason to have that job. But winning is what I want to do. I want
> to beat everybody else in the office. I want to beat that person I am talking to
> on the phone.

His remarks were echoed by others:

> [I] sold the first person I ever talked to on the phone. And it was just like that
> first shot of heroin, you know. I'm not a heroin addict. ... I've only done heroin
> a couple of times. But it was amazing. It was like, "I can't believe I just did this!"
> It was incredible. It was never about the money after that.... Yeah, it was about
> the money initially, but when I realized that I could do this everyday, it was no
> longer about the money. It was about the competition, you know. I wanted to
> be the best salesman, and I want to make the most money that day. And then
> it became just the sale. It wasn't the money. I didn't even add the figures in my
> head anymore. It was just whether or not I can turn this person around, you
> know, walk him down that mutual path of agreement, you know. That was
> exciting to me. It was power, you know; I can make people do what I wanted
> them to do. And they would do it.
>
> It was the money, but it was [also] the ability to control people, to be able to
> say over the phone, "John, go pick up your pen and write this down." And you
> write it down! You do exactly like a robot—they would do exactly what they

were told to do. And they would do it pleasingly, they would do it without hesitation, because, again, they had enough confidence and faith in you to believe that you were gonna do the right thing about it.

Another subject said simply that the work "gives you power. It gives you power." The importance of this dimension of the payoff from fraud has been commented on by others as well (e.g., Duffield & Grabosky, 2001).

Criminal telemarketers generally distinguish between working hard and "working smart." When asked, therefore, how he viewed those who work hard for modest wages, one replied, "I guess somebody's gotta do it." By contrast, work weeks of 20–30 hours are common for them, and even for owners and managers, the need for close oversight of operations decreases substantially once things are up and running. The short work week and their ample income provide considerable latitude in the use of leisure time and in consumption patterns.

The lifestyles of telemarketing participants vary by age and the aspects of the work that employees find most appealing, but ostentatious consumption is common to all. The young, and those attracted to the work and leisure it permits, live life as party (Shover, 1996). Use of cocaine and other illicit drugs is common among this segment of the criminal telemarketing workforce.

The hours were good. You'd work, sometimes, from about 9 to 2, 9 to 3, sometimes from 12 to 4. Basically, we set our own hours. It was freedom. The money was fantastic. . . . You got the best of the girls. For me, it wasn't really about the job, it was a way of life. . . . I had an alcohol problem at a young age, and to be able to support the alcohol and drug habit with the kind of money that we were making seems to go hand in hand. And then you've got the fast lifestyle, . . . up all night, sleep all day, you know. So, everything kinda' coincided with that fast lifestyle, that addictive lifestyle.

Asked how he spent the money he made, another subject responded saying:

Houses, girls, just going out to nightclubs. And a lot of blow [cocaine]. . . . Lots and lots of blow, enormous amounts. And other than that, you know, I look back, I get sick when I think about how much we spent, where the hell I put it all. I'm making all this money [but] I don't have a whole hell of a lot to show for it, you know. That lifestyle didn't allow you to save.

Heavy gambling is commonplace. One subject said that they "would go out to the casinos and blow two, three, four, five thousand dollars a night. That was nothing—to go spend five grand, you know, every weekend. And wake up broke!" Commenting on one of his employees, a subject who owned a telemarketing firm when he was arrested said that the man:

had a Porsche Speedster after he sold his Porsche 911. He had a Dodge Viper, he had a Ferrari 348, he had a Lexus LS400, he had a BMW 850i, he had a Jeep

Grand Cherokee. He liked his cars. Now, he didn't have all these at one time, but he ran through them, you know. He traded the Dodge Viper...in for the Ferrari. He always had a Porsche.

What we learned about the lifestyles and spending habits of criminal tele-marketers differs little from what is known about street criminals and other vocational predators. It also confirms what has been learned about the rela-tionship between easy, unearned income and profligacy: "The way money is acquired is a powerful determinant of how it is defined, husbanded, and spent" (Shover, 1996, p. 104).

The lifestyles of telemarketers change somewhat as they get older and take on more conventional responsibilities:

> I started to realize that, as I was getting older in the industry, it was affecting my children and my relationship with my wife. To the point that it wasn't what I wanted. I wanted more of a home-type of family, where I got home at six o'clock and have dinner and spend time with my wife and children. And with that industry, it doesn't really do that. My lifestyle? Play golf, go to the lake, you know. I had a family, but...I was also, you know, making good money. And I wanted to party and that kind of thing. So, I did that a lot. We got together and partied a lot and went here and there and went to, you know—nightlife go out to clubs occasionally, But, when you're married and have kids, it's limited. It changes. It changed a lot over those years.

For older and more experienced telemarketers, the lifestyle centers around home and family and impressing others with signs of their apparent success:

> I played some golf. [In the summer] water skiing, fishing. I'm real heavy into bass fishing, me and my dad and my brothers. Hunting. Doing things with my wife and kids. I spent a lot of time with them. Evenings, maybe just walking the golf course, or whatever. Watching the sunset.

Another subject told us that after he moved up in the telemarketing ranks: "My partner and I played, we played a lot of golf. The office was right down from the golf course. We'd go to the golf course and play two or three times a week." Save for the unrestrained hedonism of their lives when young and neophytes at criminal telemarketing, the broad outlines of their occupational careers, particularly for those who went on to form their own businesses, resemble the work careers of more conventional citizens.

Legitimation and defense

Doocy et at. (2001, p. 18) remark that the telemarketing offender they inter-viewed "conveyed the assured appearance of a most respectable entrepre-neur" and "conveyed no hint that what he was doing might not be altogether legitimate." Our subjects are no different. Notwithstanding the fact that all were convicted felons, most reject the labels *criminal and crime as* fitting descriptions of them and their activities. They instead employ a range of mitigating explanations and excuses for their offenses, although claims of ignorance figure in most (Scott & Lyman, 1968; Sykes & Matza, 1957). Some former business owners told us, for example, that they set out to maintain a legitimate operation, emulated the operations of their previous employers and assumed, therefore, that their activities violated no laws. Others said they are guilty only of expanding their business so rapidly that they could not properly oversee day-to-day operations. Some said that indulgence in alcohol and illicit drugs caused them to become neglectful of or indifferent toward their businesses. Most claimed that the allure of money caused them to "look the other way." Those who owned or managed firms are prone also to blame rogue sales agents for any fraudulent or deceptive activities. As one put it: "The owners are trying to do the right thing. They're just attracting the wrong people. It's the salesmen." Another subject likewise suggested: "I guess I let the business get too big and couldn't watch over all of the agents to prevent what they were doing." For their part, sales agents charge that their owners and managers kept them in the dark about the business and its criminal nature.

Fraud offenders typically derive moral justification for their activities from the fact that their crimes cannot succeed without acquiescence or cooperation from their victims; unlike victims of burglary and robbery, those who fall prey to fraud usually are willing, if halting or confused, participants in their own victimization (Goffman, 1952). Chief among the legitimating and defensive tenets of telemarketing criminals is belief that "the mooch is going to send his money to someone, so it might as well be me' (Sanger, 1999, p. 9). In other words, "customers" are thought to be so greedy, ignorant, or incapable that it is only a matter of time before they throw away their money on something impossible. The tendency of fraud offenders to see their victims as deserving of what befalls them was noted by Maurer (1940) more than six decades ago, and it remains true of contemporary telemarketing criminals. One of our subjects told us, "They know what they're doing. They're bargaining for something, and when they lose, they realize that they were at fault." There is neither concern nor sympathy for them. Another subject said:

> If these people can't read, so be it. Screw them, you know. It [doesn't say] everybody's gonna get the diamond and sapphire tennis bracelet. They're dumb enough not to read, dumb enough to send me the money, I really don't care, you know. I'm doing what I have to do to stay out of jail. They're doing what they have to do to fix their fix. They're promo junkies, and we're gonna find them and get them, and we're gonna keep getting them. And they're gonna keep buying. And, you know what I used to say, "they're gonna blow their money in Vegas, they're gonna spend it somewhere. I want to be the one to get it."

Telemarketing criminals selectively seize on aspects of their victims' behavior and point to these as justification or excuse for their crimes. They maintain that they were not victimizing their customers but engaging in a routine sales transaction, no different than a retail establishment selling a shirt that is marked up 1,000%. Telemarketing fraud is therefore construed by its practitioners as perfectly in tune with mainstream commercial interactions: a "subculture of business" (Ditton, 1977, p. 173).

Ensconced in their outwardly respectable and self-indulgent lifestyles, our subjects professed belief that, so far as the law was concerned, they were risking nothing more severe than a fine, an adverse civil judgment or a requirement they make restitution. They claim the entire problem more appropriately was a "civil matter" and "should not be in criminal court." As one put it: "If you have people that are not satisfied, we would be happy to give their money back."

INTERPRETATION

Our description of telemarketing crime and criminals is noteworthy for several reasons, but principally for what it reveals about the relationship between social change and the changing character of lucrative professional theft (Taylor, 1999). Defined by cultural criteria rather than legal yardsticks (see Sykes, 1978, p. 109), the concept of professional crime has become infused with contradiction and ambiguity by the evolution of this new kind of "respectable" predator.

Sociological debate over the descriptive validity of professional theft has been carried out largely as a dialogue with the tradition of Sutherland (1937), who located a behavior system of criminal specialists featuring technical skill, consensus via a shared ideology, differential association, status and, most important, informal organization grounded in a shared cultural identity. Subsequently, scholars presented alternative perspectives regarding crimes other than theft (Einstadter, 1969; Lemert, 1958). However, Shover (1973) perhaps came closest to Sutherland's original conception by locating the social organization of burglary based on highly instrumental, and constantly evolving networks of dependency as the key variable. In his view, these networks continue to evolve due to innovative strategies in policing, security and technology, and telemarketing fraudsters resemble Shover's professional burglar, in their adaptive pragmatic organization.

Telemarketers also share many core characteristics with "hustlers" (President's Commission, 1966; Shover, 1996), or "rounders" (Letkemann, 1973), offenders whose lack of commonality or consensus contradicts the notion of a cohesive tightly knit behavior system (see also Holzman, 1983; Polsky, 1964; Roebuck & Johnson, 1962). Yet Letkemann suggests that explicit commitment to criminal activity as a means of making a living is the best criterion for differentiating between professional and nonprofessional criminals, which also echoes Sutherland's classic work, and offers some support for the notion of an occupational group defined by their commitment to illegal economic activities (Becker, 1960).

Although the investigation of professional thieves and their pursuits has a long history in criminology, the canon is replete with portraits of offenders who have passed from the scene. However, for contemporary observers, "fraud masters" (Jackson, 1994) deservedly command more attention than "cut purses" (Tobias, 1967), "cannons" (Maurer, 1964) and "good burglars" (Shover, 1973). Economic and social change inevitably transform the worlds in which offenders entertain options and organize for pursuit of criminal income (Hobbs, 1997; McIntosh, 1975; Shover, 1983). The classic criminal subcultures of shared practices and beliefs as the basis of criminal community, have met the same fate as blue-collar communities based on traditional industries (Soja, 1989). The new entrepreneurial milieu is an enabling environment for a great range and variety of money making schemes (Ruggiero & South, 1997), and the perceptual templates of contemporary professional criminals feature cues that are geared to success in a sphere emptied out of anachronistic practice (Wright & Decker, 1994).

Automobile theft and "chop shop" were not found in ninetieth century society, for the obvious reason there were no automobiles to steal or sell. The shift to a postindustrial order inevitably changed selectively the human qualities and social capital requisite for successful exploitation of criminal opportunities. Traditional professional thieves hailed from locations in the class and social structure where the young generally do not acquire the human capital requisite to success in the world of well paid and respectable work. The blue-collar skills of an industrial society, however, are not equal to the challenge of exploiting contemporary, increasingly white-collar, criminal opportunities. The postindustrial service-oriented economy instead places a premium on entrepreneurial, interpersonal, communicative and organizational skills, and it is the children of the middle class who are most likely to be exposed to and acquire these.

The knowledge and skills needed to exploit criminal opportunities vocationally and successfully do not differ greatly from those required for success in the legitimate world. Like the professional thief, the new and increasingly white-collar vocational predators commit planned violations of the law for profit (Van Duyne, 1996), but they do so in the style of the middle class. They take on and publicly espouse a belief system that defends against moral condemnation from outsiders, and they are dismissive of both the world of hourly employment and the lives of those confined to it. But although the professional thieves of an earlier era publicly endorsed and were expected to adhere to norms of loyalty and integrity in dealings with one another (Cohen & Taylor, 1972; Irwin, 1970; Irwin & Cressey, 1962; Mason, 1994; Maurer, 1955/1964; McVicar, 1982; Shover, 1973; Taylor, 1984), criminal telemarketers by contrast are extremely individualistic and self-centered in their contacts with criminal justice officials and agencies. Whether this is because of their privileged backgrounds or because the nature of criminal relationships has been "transformed by the advent of a market culture," their illicit pursuits manifest qualities not only of entrepreneurial creativity but also independence and "possessive individualism" (Taylor, 1999).

Professional thieves of earlier eras found a measure of success in crime despite their humble beginnings, and much about what they made of themselves is understandable in the light of their blue-collar roots. The lives they constructed emphasized freedom to live "life as party" (Shover & Honaker, 1991) by "earning and burning money" (Katz, 1988, p. 215), to roam without restraint and to celebrate these achievements with others of similar perspective. The class origins of contemporary garden-variety white-collar criminals are more advantaged, but they live their lives in substantially similar fashion. Unlike the "foot pads" of Elizabethan England, they generally do not gravitate to a criminal netherworld or a self-contained criminal fraternity. Nor do they confine their leisure pursuits to others of similar work. The proletarian underworld was an essential network for exchanging, controlling, and disseminating information (Hobbs, 1995, pp. 21–23; McIntosh, 1971), but the telemarketing fraudster depends on networks of information that are largely indistinguishable from those that underpin the noncriminal sector.

What Benney (1936/1981, p. 263) called "the fabulous underworld of bourgeois invention" ironically has been decimated by the embourgeoisement of crime. Criminals now emerge from the economic mainstream and engage both socially and pragmatically with derivations of normative economic activity. The acquisitive entrepreneurial ethic that underpins both legal and illegal performances within the postindustrial market place, thrives upon "new technical, social, psychological and existential skills" (Bauman, 1992, p. 98), which in turn are bordered by new configurations of cultural and technological capital.

Although the old underworld was safely ensconced in the locales, occupational practices, leisure cultures and oppositional strategies of the industrial proletariat (Hobbs, 1997; Samuel, 1981), it is the bourgeois who have emerged with the education and ideological flexibility to engage with lucrative Contemporary professional crime, which is located not within a proletarian outpost of traditional transgression, but within rhetorics that legitimate and enable the entire "spectrum of legitimacy" (Albanese, 1989, p. 101).

Telemarketing fraudsters should be seen as "fluid sets of mobile marauders in the urban landscape, alert to institutional weakness in both legitimate and illegitimate spheres" (Block, 1983, p. 245). These spheres are pliant and not territorially embedded (Chaney, 1994, p. 149). Detached from an "underworld" (Haller, 1990, pp. 228–229), contemporary professional crime has mutated from an overworld in which the bourgeoisie rather than blue-collar culture is sovereign. This helps explain why telemarketing fraudsters, unlike the professional thieves of previous generations, are likely to spend their weekends on the lake, playing golf, or having friends over for a barbeque. Still, they blow their earnings on drugs, gambling, fast living, and conspicuous consumption. They earn a reasonably good return from crime, but like "box men" of yore, few spend appreciable time in jails and prisons.

REFERENCES

Abagnale, F. W. (1980). *Catch me if you can.* New York: Grosset and Dunlap.

Adler, P. S. (1992). *Technology and the future of work.* New York: Oxford University Press.

Albanese, J. (1989). *Organized crime in America.* Cincinnati, OH: Anderson.

Alleged scam on elderly by telemarketers is revealed. (2000, September 6). *Atlanta Journal-Constitution,* B3.

American Association of Retired Persons. (1996). *Telemarketing fraud and older Americans: An AARP survey.* New York: Author.

Australian Broadcasting Corporation. (2001). *Beyond the boiler room.* Retrieved September 24, 2003, from www.abc.net.au/4corners/.

Batty, M., & Barr, B. (1994). The electronic frontier: Exploring and mapping cyberspace. *Futures, 26*(7), 699–712.

Bauman, Z. (1992). *Intimidations of modernity.* London: Routledge.

Becker, H. (1960). Notes on the concept of commitment. *American Journal of Sociology, 66,* 32–40.

Benney, M. (1981). *Low company.* Sussex, UK: Caliban Books. Original work published 1936

Block, A. (1983). *East side-West side: Organizing crime in New York,* 1930–1950. Newark, NJ: Transactions.

Chaney, D. (1994). *The cultural turn.* London: Routledge.

Clarke, M. (1990). Control of insurance fraud: A comparative view. *British Journal of Criminology, 30,* 1–3.

Cohen, S., & Taylor, L. (1972). *Psychological survival.* Harmondsworth: Penguin.

Direct Marketing Association. (2001). Available from: http://www.the-dma.org

Ditton, J. (1977). *Part time crime.* London: Macmillan.

Doocy, J., Schichor, D., Sechrest, D., & Geis, G. (2001). Telemarketing fraud: Who are the tricksters and what makes them trick? *Securities Journal, 14,* 7–26.

Duffield, G., & Grabosky, P. (2001). The psychology of fraud. *Paper 199.* Griffith, Canberra: Australian Institute of Criminology.

Einstadter, W. J. (1969). The social organization of armed robbery. *Social Problems, 17,* 54–83.

Francis, D. (1988). *Contrepreneurs.* Toronto, Ontario, Canada: Macmillan.

Glaser, D. (1972). *Adult crime and social policy.* Upper Saddle River, NJ: Prentice-Hall.

Grabosky, P. N., Smith, R. G., & Dempsey, G. (2001). *Electronic theft: Unlawful acquisition in cyberspace.* New York: Cambridge University Press.

Goffman, E. (1952) On cooling the mark out: Some aspects of adaptation to failure. *Psychiatry, 15,* 451–463.

Haller, M. (1990). Illegal enterprise: A theoretical and historical interpretation. *Criminology, 28*(2), 207–235.

Harris, L. and Associates. (1992). *Telemarketing fraud.* Charlotte: University of North Carolina, Institute for Research in Social Science.

Hirschhorn, L. (1985). Information technology and the new services game. In M. Castells (Ed.), *High technology, space, and society* (pp. 172–190). Beverly Hills, CA: Sage.

Hobbs, R. (1995). *Bad business: Professional crime in contemporary Britain*. Oxford: Oxford University Press.

Hobbs, R. (1997). Professional crime: Change, continuity, and the enduring myth of the underworld. *Sociology, 31*, 57–72.

Holzman, H. (1983). The serious habitual property offender as moonlighter: An empirical study of labor force participation among robbers and burglars. *Journal of Criminal Justice Law and Criminology, 73*, 1774–1792.

Irwin, J. (1970). *The felon*. Upper Saddle River, NJ: Prentice Hall.

Irwin, J., & Cressey, D. (1962). Thieves, convicts and the inmate culture. *Social Problems, 10*, 142–155.

Jackson, J. (1994). Fraud masters: Professional credit card offenders and crime. *Criminal Justice Review, 19*, 24–55.

Katz, J. (1988). *Seductions of crime*. New York: Basic Books.

Lash, S., & Urry, J. (1994.) *Economies of signs and space*. London: Sage.

Lemert, E. (1958). The behavior of the systematic check forger. *Social Problems, 6*, 141–149.

Letkemann, P. (1973). *Crime as work*. Upper Saddle River, NJ: Prentic Hall.

Mason, E. (1994). *Inside story*. London: Pan.

Maurer, D. W. (1940). *The big con*. Indianapolis, IN: Bobbs-Merrill.

Maurer, D. W. (1964). *Whiz mob*. New Haven, CT: College and University Press. Original work published 1955

McIntosh, M. (1971). Changes in the organization of thieving. In S. Cohen (Ed.), *Images of deviance*. Harmondsworth: Penguin.

McIntosh, M. (1975). *The organization of crime*. New York: Macmillan.

McVicar, J. (1982). Violence in prisons. In P. Marsh & A. Campbell (Eds.), *Aggression and violence*. Oxford: Blackwell.

Polsky, N. (1964). The hustler. *Social Problems, 12*, 3–15.

President's Commission on Law Enforcement and Administration of Justice. (1966). Professional crime. In *Task force report* (ch. 7). Washington, DC: US Government Printing Office.

Rebovich, D., Layne, J., Jiandani, J., & Hage, S. (2000). *The national public survey on white collar crime*. Glen Allen, VA: National White Collar Crime Center.

Roebuck, J., & Johnson, R. (1962). The jack of all trades offender. *Crime & Delinquency, 8*, 172–181.

Ross, E. A. (1907). *Sin and society: An analysis of latter-day iniquity*. Boston: Houghton Mifflin.

Ruggiero, V., & South, N. (1997). The late modern city as a bazaar. *British Journal of Sociology, 48*, 54–70.

Samuel, R. (1981). *East End underworld: The life and times of Arthur Harding*. London: Routledge and Kegan Paul.

Samuelson, R. J. (1995). *The good life and its discontents*. New York: Random House.

Sanger, D. (1999). Confessions of a phone-scam artist. *Saturday Night, 114*, 86–98.

Schulte, F. (1995). *Fleeced! Telemarketing rip-offs and how to avoid them.* Essex, UK: Prometheus Books.

Scott, M. B., & Lyman, M. L. (1968). Accounts. *American Sociological Review, 33,* 46–62.

Shichor, D., Doocy, J., & Geis, G. (1996). Anger, disappointment and disgust: Reactions of victims of a telephone investment scam. In C. Sumner, M. Israel, M. O'Connell, & R. Sarre (Eds.), *International victimology* (pp. 105–111). Selected papers from the 8th international symposium. Australian Institute of Criminology, Griffith, Canberra, Australia.

Shover, N. (1973). The social organization of burglary. *Social Problems, 20,* 499–514.

Shover, N. (1983). Professional crime: Major offender. In S. H. Kadish (Ed.), *Encyclopedia of crime and justice* (pp. 1263–1271). New York: Macmillan.

Shover, N. (1996). *Great pretenders: Pursuits and careers of persistent thieves.* Boulder, CO: Westview.

Shover, N., & Honaker, D. (1991). The socially bounded decision making of persistent property offenders. *The Howard Journal, 31,* 276–293.

Silverstone, R. (1991). *Beneath the bottom line: Households and information and communication technologies in the age of the consumer.* London: Brunel University Centre for Research on Innovation, Culture, and Technology.

Soja, E. (1989). *Postmodern geographies.* London: Verso.

Sparrow, M. K. (1996). *License to steal: Why fraud plagues America's health care system.* Boulder, CO: Westview.

Stevenson, R. J. (2000). *The boiler room and other telephone sales scams.* Urbana: University of Illinois Press.

Sutherland, E. H. (1937). *The professional thief.* Chicago, IL: University of Chicago Press.

Sykes, G. (1978). *Criminology.* New York: Harcourt Brace Jovanovitch.

Sykes, G., & Matza, D. (1957). Techniques of neutralization: A theory of delinquency. *American Sociological Review, 22,* 667–670.

Taylor, I. (1999). *Crime in context: A critical criminology of market societies.* Boulder, CO: Westview.

Taylor, L. (1984). *In the underworld.* Oxford: Blackwell.

Telemarketing fraud and section 568, The Telemarketing and Consumer Fraud and Abuse Protection Act: Hearing before the Subcommittee on Consumer of the Committee on Commerce, Science, and Transportation. 103d Cong. (1993).

Tickell, A. (1996). Taking the initiative: Leeds' Financial Centre. In G. Haughton & C. Williams (Eds.), *Corporate city? Partnerships, participation in urban development in Leeds.* Aldershot, UK: Avebury.

Tillman, R. (1998). *Broken promises: Fraud by small business health insurers.* Boston: Northeastern University Press.

Titus, R. (2001). Personal fraud and its victims. In N. Shover & J. P. Wright (Eds.), *Crimes of privilege: Readings in white collar crime* (pp. 57–67). New York: Oxford University Press.

Titus, R. M., Heinzelmann, F., & Boyle, J. M. (1995). Victimization of persons by fraud. *Crime & Delinquency, 41,* 54–72.

Tobias, J. J. (1967). *Crime and industrial society in the 19th century.* London: Batsford.

Turkle, S. (1995). *Life on the screen: Identity in the age of the Internet.* New York: Simon and Schuster.

Van Duyne, P. (1996). The phantom and threat of organized crime. *Crime, Law, and Social Change, 21,* 241–277.

Winlow, S. (2001). *Badfellas.* Oxford, UK: Berg.

Wright, R., & Decker, S. (1994). *Burglars on the job: Streetlife and residential break-ins.* Boston: Northeastern University Press.

13

Denying the Guilty Mind: Accounting for Involvement in a White-Collar Crime

Michael L. Benson

*T*he author examines the excuses and justifications used by white-collar offenders to explain their involvement in criminal activities and to deny their criminality. Michael L. Benson's study is based on interviews with a sample of 30 convicted white-collar offenders. The interviews were supplemented with an examination of the files maintained by federal law enforcement authorities (prosecutors, probation officer, judges) concerned with the prosecution of white-collar offenses. The author defines white-collar offenders as " ... those convicted of economic offenses committed through the use of indirection, fraud, or collusion" (p. 586). The offenses represented in the sample included such offenses as securities and exchange fraud, antitrust violations, embezzlement, false claims, and tax evasion. All of the offenders were men.

Adjudication as a criminal is, to use Garfinkel's (1956) classic term, a degradation ceremony. The focus of this article is on how offenders attempt to defeat the success of this ceremony and deny their own criminality through the use of accounts. However, in the interest of showing in as much detail as possible all sides of the experience undergone by these offenders, it is necessary to treat first the guilt and inner anguish that is felt by many white-collar offenders even though they deny being criminals. This is best accomplished by beginning with a description of a unique feature of the prosecution of white-collar crimes.

In white-collar criminal cases, the issue is likely to be *why* something was done, rather than *who* did it (Edelhertz, 1970, p. 47). There is often relatively little disagreement as to what happened. In the words of one Assistant U.S. Attorney interviewed for the study:

> If you actually had a movie playing, neither side would dispute that a person moved in this way and handled this piece of paper, etc. What it comes down to is, did they have the criminal intent?

If the prosecution is to proceed past the investigatory stages, the prosecutor must infer from the pattern of events that conscious criminal intent

Source: Michael L. Benson, "Denying the Guilty Mind: Accounting for Involvement in a White-Collar Crime." In *Criminology*, 23 (4) (November 1985), pp. 589–599. Copyright © 1985 by the American Society of Criminology. Reprinted with permission.

was present and believe that sufficient evidence exists to convince a jury of this interpretation of the situation. As Katz (1979, pp. 445–446) has noted, making this inference can be difficult because of the way in which white-collar illegalities are integrated into ordinary occupational routines. Thus, prosecutors in conducting trials, grand jury hearings, or plea negotiations spend a great deal of effort establishing that the defendant did indeed have the necessary criminal intent. By concentrating on the offender's motives, the prosecutor attacks the very essence of the white-collar offender's public and personal image as an upstanding member of the community. The offender is portrayed as someone with a guilty mind.

Not surprisingly, therefore, the most consistent and recurrent pattern in the interviews, though not present in all of them, was denial of criminal intent, as opposed to the outright denial of any criminal behavior whatsoever. Most offenders acknowledged that their behavior probably could be construed as falling within the conduct proscribed by statute, but they uniformly denied that their actions were motivated by a guilty mind. This is not to say, however, that offenders *felt* no guilt or shame as a result of conviction. On the contrary, indictment, prosecution, and conviction provoke a variety of emotions among offenders.

The enormous reality of the offender's lived emotion (Denzin, 1984) in admitting guilt is perhaps best illustrated by one offender's description of his feelings during the hearing at which he pled guilty.

> You know [the plea's] what really hurt. I didn't even know I had feet. I felt numb. My head was just floating. There was no feeling, except a state of suspended animation. … For a brief moment, I almost hesitated. I almost said not guilty. If I had been alone, I would have fought, but my family …

The traumatic nature of this moment lies, in part, in the offender's feeling that only one aspect of his life is being considered. From the offender's point of view his crime represents only one small part of his life. It does not typify his inner self, and to judge him solely on the basis of this one event seems an atrocious injustice to the offender.

For some the memory of the event is so painful that they want to obliterate it entirely, as the two following quotations illustrate.

> I want quiet. I want to forget. I want to cut with the past.
> I've already divorced myself from the problem. I don't even want to hear the names of certain people ever again. It brings me pain.

For others, rage rather than embarrassment seemed to be the dominant emotion.

> I never really felt any embarrassment over the whole thing. I felt rage and it wasn't false or self-serving. It was really (something) to see this thing in action and recognize what the whole legal system has come to through its develop-

ment, and the abuse of the grand jury system and the abuse of the indictment system...

The role of the news media in the process of punishment and stigmatization should not be overlooked. All offenders whose cases were reported on by the news media were either embarrassed or embittered or both by the public exposure.

> The only one I am bitter at is the newspapers, as many people are. They are unfair because you can't get even. They can say things that are untrue, and let me say this to you. They wrote an article on me that was so blasphemous, that was so horrible. They painted me as an insidious, miserable creature, wringing out the last penny...

Offenders whose cases were not reported on by the news media expressed relief at having avoided that kind of embarrassment, sometimes saying that greater publicity would have been worse than any sentence they could have received.

In court, defense lawyers are fond of presenting white-collar offenders as having suffered enough by virtue of the humiliation of public adjudication as criminals. On the other hand, prosecutors present them as cavalier individuals who arrogantly ignore the law and brush off its weak efforts to stigmatize them as criminals. Neither of these stereotypes is entirely accurate. The subjective effects of conviction on white-collar offenders are varied and complex. One suspects that this is true of all offenders, not only white-collar offenders.

The emotional responses of offenders to conviction have not been the subject of extensive research. However, insofar as an individual's emotional response to adjudication may influence the deterrent or crime-reinforcing impact of punishment on him or her, further study might reveal why some offenders stop their criminal behavior while others go on to careers in crime (Casper, 1978, p. 80).

Although the offenders displayed a variety of different emotions with respect to their experiences, they were nearly unanimous in denying basic criminality. To see how white-collar offenders justify and excuse their crimes, we turn to their accounts. The small number of cases rules out the use of any elaborate classification techniques. Nonetheless, it is useful to group offenders by offense when presenting their interpretations.

Antitrust Violators

Four of the offenders had been convicted of antitrust violations, all in the same case involving the building and contracting industry. Four major themes characterized their accounts. First, antitrust offenders focused on the everyday character and historical continuity of their offenses.

> It was a way of doing business before we even got into the business. So it was like why do you brush your teeth in the morning or something. ... It was a part of the everyday. ... It was a method of survival.

The offenders argued that they were merely following established and necessary industry practices. These practices were presented as being necessary for the well-being of the industry as a whole, not to mention their own companies. Furthermore, they argued that cooperation among competitors was either allowed or actively promoted by the government in other industries and professions.

The second theme emphasized by the offenders was the characterization of their actions as blameless. They admitted talking to competitors and admitted submitting intentionally noncompetitive bids. However, they presented these practices as being done not for the purpose of rigging prices nor to make exorbitant profits. Rather, the everyday practices of the industry required them to occasionally submit bids on projects they really did not want to have. To avoid the effort and expense of preparing full-fledged bids, they would call a competitor to get a price to use. Such a situation might arise, for example, when a company already had enough work for the time being, but was asked by a valued customer to submit a bid anyway.

> All you want to do is show a bid, so that in some cases it was for as small a reason as getting your deposit back on the plans and specs. So you just simply have no interest in getting the job and just call to see if you can find someone to give you a price to use, so that you don't have to go through the expense of an entire bid preparation. Now that is looked at very unfavorably, and it is a technical violation, but it was strictly an opportunity to keep your name in front of a desired customer. Or you may find yourself in a situation where somebody is doing work for a customer, has done work for many, many years and is totally acceptable, totally fair. There is no problem. But suddenly they (the customer) get an idea that they ought to have a few tentative figures, and you're called in, and you are in a moral dilemma. There's really no reason for you to attempt to compete in that circumstance. And so there was it way to back out.

Managed in this way, an action that appears on the surface to be a straightforward and conscious violation of antitrust regulations becomes merely a harmless business practice that happens to be a "technical violation." The offender can then refer to his personal history to verify his claim that, despite technical violations, he is in reality a law-abiding person. In the words of one offender, "Having been in the business for 33 years, you don't just automatically become a criminal overnight."

Third, offenders were very critical of the motives and tactics of prosecutors. Prosecutors were accused of being motivated solely by the opportunity for personal advancement presented by winning a big case. Furthermore, they were accused of employing prosecution selectively and using tactics that allowed the most culpable offenders to go free. The Department of Justice was painted as using antitrust prosecutions for political purposes.

The fourth theme emphasized by the antitrust offenders involved a comparison between their crimes and the crimes of street criminals. Antitrust offenses differ in their mechanics from street crimes in that they are not committed in one place and at one time. Rather, they are spatially and temporally diffuse and are intermingled with legitimate behavior. In addition, the victims of antitrust offenses tend not to be identifiable individuals, as is the case with most street crimes. These characteristics are used by antitrust violators to contrast their own behavior with that of common stereotypes of criminality. Real crimes are pictured as discrete events that have beginnings and ends and involve individuals who directly and purposely victimize someone else in a particular place and a particular time.

> It certainly wasn't a premeditated type of thing in our cases as far as I can see. ... To me it's different than _____ and I sitting down and we plan, well, we're going to rob this bank tomorrow and premeditatedly go in there. ... That wasn't the case at all. ... It wasn't like sitting down and planning I'm going to rob this bank type of thing. ... It was just a common everyday way of doing business and surviving.

A consistent thread running through all of the interviews was the necessity for antitrust-like practices, given the realities of the business world. Offenders seemed to define the situation in such a manner that two sets of rules could be seen to apply. On the one hand, there are the legislatively determined rules—laws—which govern how one is to conduct one's business affairs. On the other hand, there is a higher set of rules based on the concepts of profit and survival, which are taken to define what it means to be in business in a capitalistic society. These rules do not just regulate behavior; rather, they constitute or create the behavior in question. If one is not trying to make a profit or trying to keep one's business going, then one is not really "in business." Following Searle (1969, pp. 33–41), the former type of rule can be called a regulative rule and the latter type a constitutive rule. In certain situations, one may have to violate a regulative rule in order to conform to the more basic constitutive rule of the activity in which one is engaged.

This point can best be illustrated through the use of an analogy involving competitive games. Trying to win is a constitutive rule of competitive games in the sense that if one is not trying to win, one is not really playing the game. In competitive games, situations may arise where a player deliberately breaks the rules even though he knows or expects he will be caught. In the game of basketball, for example, a player may deliberately foul an opponent to prevent him from making a sure basket. In this instance, one would understand that the fouler was trying to win by gambling that the opponent would not make the free throws. The player violates the rule against fouling in order to follow the higher rule of trying to win.

Trying to make a profit or survive in business can be thought of as a constitutive rule of capitalist economies. The laws that govern how one is allowed to make a profit are regulative rules, which can understandably be subordinated to the rules of trying to survive and profit. From the offender's point of view, he is doing what businessmen in our society are supposed to do—that is, stay in business and make a profit. Thus, an individual who violates society's laws or regulations in certain situations may actually conceive of himself as thereby acting more in accord with the central ethos of his society than if he had been a strict observer of its law. One might suggest, following Denzin (1977), that for businessmen in the building and contracting industry, an informal structure exists below the articulated legal structure, one which frequently supersedes the legal structure. The informal structure may define as moral and "legal" certain actions that the formal legal structure defines as immoral and "illegal."

Tax Violators

Six of the offenders interviewed were convicted of income tax violations. Like antitrust violators, tax violators can rely upon the complexity of the tax laws and an historical tradition in which cheating on taxes is not really criminal. Tax offenders would claim that everybody cheats somehow on their taxes and present themselves as victims of an unlucky break, because they got caught.

> Everybody cheats on their income tax, 95 percent of the people. Even if it's for ten dollars it's the same principle. I didn't cheat. I just didn't know how to report it.

The widespread belief that cheating on taxes is endemic helps to lend credence to the offender's claim to have been singled out and to be no more guilty than most people.

Tax offenders were more likely to have acted as individuals rather than as part of a group and, as a result, were more prone to account for their offenses by referring to them as either mistakes or the product of special circumstances. Violations were presented as simple errors which resulted from ignorance and poor recordkeeping. Deliberate intention to steal from the government for personal benefit was denied.

> I didn't take the money. I have no bank account to show for all this money, where all this money is at that I was supposed to have. They never found the money, ever. There is no Swiss bank account, believe me. My records were strictly one big mess. That's all it was. If only I had an accountant, this wouldn't even of happened. No way in God's creation would this ever have happened.

Other offenders would justify their actions by admitting that they were wrong while painting their motives as altruistic rather than criminal. Criminality was denied because they did not set out to deliberately cheat the government for their own personal gain. Like the antitrust offenders discussed above, one tax violator distinguished between his own crime and the crimes of real criminals.

> I'm not a criminal. That is, I'm not a criminal from the standpoint of taking a gun and doing this and that. I'm a criminal from the standpoint of making a mistake, a serious mistake. ... The thing that really got me involved in it is my feeling for the employees here, certain employees that are my right hand. In

order to save them a certain amount of taxes and things like that, I'd extend money to them in cash, and the money came from these sources that I took it from. You know, cash sales and things of that nature, but practically all of it was turned over to the employees, because of my feeling for them.

All of the tax violators pointed out that they had no intention of deliberately victimizing the government. None of them denied the legitimacy of the tax laws, nor did they claim that they cheated because the government is not representative of the people (Conklin, 1977, p. 99). Rather, as a result of ignorance or for altruistic reasons, they made decisions which turned out to be criminal when viewed from the perspective of the law. While they acknowledged the technical criminality of their actions, they tried to show that what they did was not criminally motivated.

Violations of Financial Trust

Four offenders were involved in violations of financial trust. Three were bank officers who embezzled or misapplied funds, and the fourth was a union official who embezzled from a union pension fund. Perhaps because embezzlement is one crime in this sample that can be considered *mala in se* [Editor's note: Latin for "evil in itself"], these offenders were much more forthright about their crimes. Like the other offenders, the embezzlers would not go so far as to say "I am a criminal," but they did say "What I did was wrong, was criminal, and I knew it was." Thus, the embezzlers were unusual in that they explicitly admitted responsibility for their crimes. Two of the offenders clearly fit Cressey's scheme as persons with financial problems who used their positions to convert other people's money to their own use.

Unlike tax evasion, which can be excused by reference to the complex nature of tax regulations or antitrust violations, which can be justified as for the good of the organization as a whole, embezzlement requires deliberate action on the part of the offender and is almost inevitably committed for personal reasons. The crime of embezzlement, therefore, cannot be accounted for by using the same techniques that tax violators or antitrust violators do. The act itself can only be explained by showing that one was under extraordinary circumstances which explain one's uncharacteristic behavior. Three of the offenders referred explicitly to extraordinary circumstances and presented the offense as an aberration in their life history. For example, one offender described his situation in this manner:

> As a kid, I never even—you know kids will sometimes shoplift from the dime store—I never even did that. I had never stolen a thing in my life and that was what was so unbelievable about the whole thing, but there were some psychological and personal questions that I wasn't dealing with very well. I wasn't terribly happily married. I was married to a very strong-willed woman and it just wasn't working out.

The offender in this instance goes on to explain how, in an effort to impress his wife, he lived beyond his means and fell into debt.

A structural characteristic of embezzlement also helps the offender demonstrate his essential lack of criminality. Embezzlement is integrated into ordinary occupational routines. The illegal action does not stand out clearly against the surrounding set of legal actions. Rather, there is a high degree of surface correspondence between legal and illegal behavior. To maintain this correspondence, the offender must exercise some restraint when committing his crime. The embezzler must be discrete in his stealing; he cannot take all of the money available to him without at the same time revealing the crime. Once exposed, the offender can point to this restraint on his part as evidence that he is not really a criminal. That is, he can compare what happened with what could have happened in order to show how much more serious the offense could have been if he was really a criminal at heart.

> What I could have done if I had truly had a devious criminal mind and perhaps if I had been a little smarter and I am not saying that with any degree of pride or any degree of modesty whatever, [as] it's being smarter in a bad, an evil way I could have pulled this off on a grander scale and I might still be doing it.

Even though the offender is forthright about admitting his guilt, he makes a distinction between himself and someone with a truly "devious criminal mind."

Contrary to Cressey's (1953, pp. 57–66) findings, none of the embezzlers claimed that their offenses were justified because they were underpaid or badly treated by their employers. Rather, attention was focused on the unusual circumstances surrounding the offense and its atypical character when compared to the rest of the offender's life. This strategy is for the most part determined by the mechanics and organizational format of the offense itself. Embezzlement occurs within the organization but not for the organization. It cannot be committed accidentally or out of ignorance. It can be accounted for only by showing that the actor "was not himself" at the time of the offense or was under such extraordinary circumstances that embezzlement was an understandable response to an unfortunate situation. This may explain the finding that embezzlers tend to produce accounts that are viewed as more sufficient by the justice system than those produced by other offenders (Rothman & Gandossy, 1982). The only plausible option open to a convicted embezzler trying to explain his offense is to admit responsibility while justifying the action, an approach that apparently strikes a responsive chord with judges.

Fraud and False Statements

Ten offenders were convicted of some form of fraud or false statements charge. Unlike embezzlers, tax violators, or antitrust violators, these offenders were much more likely to deny committing any crime at all. Seven of the ten claimed that they, personally, were innocent of any crime, although each admitted that fraud had occurred. Typically, they claimed to have been set up by associates and to have been wrongfully convicted by the U.S. Attorney handling the case. One might call this the scapegoat strategy. Rather than admitting technical wrong-doing and then justifying or excusing it, the offender attempts to paint himself as a victim by shifting the blame entirely to another party. Prosecutors were presented as being either ignorant or politically motivated.

The outright of any crime whatsoever is unusual compared to the other types of offenders studied here. It may result from the nature of the crime of fraud. By definition, fraud involves a conscious attempt on the part of one or more persons to mislead others. While it is theoretically possible to accidentally violate the antitrust and tax laws, or to violate them for altruistic reasons, it is difficult to imagine how one could accidentally mislead someone else for his or her own good. Furthermore, in many instances, fraud is an aggressively acquisitive crime. The offender develops a scheme to bilk other people out of money or property, and does this not because of some personal problem but because the scheme is an easy way to get rich. Stock swindles, fraudulent loan scams, and so on, are often so large and complicated that they cannot possibly be excused as foolish and desperate solutions to personal problems. Thus, those involved in large-scale frauds do not have the option open to most embezzlers of presenting themselves as persons responding defensively to difficult personal circumstances.

Furthermore, because fraud involves a deliberate attempt to mislead another, the offender who fails to remove himself from the scheme runs the risk of being shown to have a guilty mind. That is, he is shown to possess the most essential element of modern conceptions of criminality: an intent to harm another. His inner self would in this case be exposed as something other than what it has been presented as, and all of his previous actions would be subject to reinterpretation in light of this new perspective. For this reason, defrauders are most prone to denying any crime at all. The cooperative and conspiratorial nature of many fraudulent schemes makes it possible to put the blame on someone else and to present oneself as a scapegoat. Typically, this is done by claiming to have been duped by others.

Two illustrations of this strategy are presented here:

> I figured I wasn't guilty, so it wouldn't be that hard to disprove it, until, as I say, I went to court and all of a sudden they start bringing in these guys out of the woodwork implicating me that I never saw. Lot of it could be proved that I never saw.
>
> Inwardly, I personally felt that the only crime that I committed was not telling on these guys. Not that I deliberately, intentionally committed a crime against the system. My only crime was that I should have had the guts to tell on these guys, what they were doing, rather than putting up with it and then trying to gradually get out of the system without hurting them or without them thinking I was going to snitch on them.

Of the three offenders who admitted committing crimes, two acted alone and the third acted with only one other person. Their accounts were similar to others presented earlier—and tended to focus on either the harmless nature of their violations or on the unusual circumstances that drove them to commit their crimes. One claimed that his violations were only technical and that no one besides himself had been harmed.

> First of all, no money was stolen or anything of that nature. The bank didn't lose any money.... What I did was a technical violation. I made a mistake. There's no question about that, but the bank lost no money.

Another offender who directly admitted his guilt was involved in a check-kiting scheme. In a manner similar to embezzlers, he argued that his actions were motivated by exceptional circumstances.

> I was faced with the choice of all of a sudden, and I mean now, closing the doors or doing something else to keep that business open. ... I'm not going to tell you that this wouldn't have happened if I'd had time to think it over, because I think it probably would have. You're sitting there with a dying patient. You are going to try to keep him alive.

In the other fraud cases more individuals were involved, and it was possible and perhaps necessary for each offender to claim that he was not really the culprit.

Discussion: Offenses, Accounts, and Degradation Ceremonies

The investigation, prosecution, and conviction of a white-collar offender involves him in a very undesirable status passage (Glaser & Strauss, 1971). The entire process can be viewed as a long and drawn-out degradation ceremony with the prosecutor as the chief denouncer and the offender's family and friends as the chief witnesses. The offender is moved from the status of law-abiding citizen to that of convicted felon. Accounts are developed to defeat the process of identity transformation that is the object of a degradation ceremony. They represent the offender's attempt to diminish the effect of his legal transformation and to prevent its becoming a publicly validated label. It can be suggested that the accounts developed by white-collar offenders take the forms that they do for two reasons: (1) the forms are required to defeat the success of the degradation ceremony, and (2) the specific forms used are the ones available given the mechanics, history, and organizational context of the offenses.

Three general patterns in accounting strategies stand out in the data. Each can be characterized by the subject matter on which it focuses: the event (offense), the perpetrator (offender), or the denouncer (prosecutor). These are the natural subjects of accounts in that to be successful, a degradation ceremony requires each of these elements to be presented in a particular manner (Garfinkel, 1956). If an account giver can undermine the presentation of one or more of the elements, then the effect of the ceremony can be reduced.

Although there are overlaps in the accounting strategies used by the various types of offenders, and while any given offender may use more than one strategy, it appears that accounting strategies and offenses correlate.

REFERENCES

Casper, J. D. (1978). *Criminal courts: The defendant's perspective.* Washington, DC: U.S. Department of Justice.

Conklin, J. E. (1977). *Illegal but not criminal: Business crime in America.* Englewood Cliffs, NJ: Prentice Hall.

Cressey, D. (1953). *Other people's money.* New York: Free Press.

Denzin, N. K. (1977). Notes on the criminogenic hypothesis: A case study of the American liquor industry. *American Sociological Review, 42,* 905–920.

Denzin, N. K. (1984). *On understanding emotion.* San Francisco: Jossey-Bass.

Edelhertz, H. (1970). *The nature, impact, and prosecution of white collar crime.* Washington, DC: U.S. Government Printing Office.

Garfinkel, H. (1956). Conditions of successful degradation ceremonies. *American Journal of Sociology, 61,* 420–424.

Glaser, B. G., & Strauss, A. L. (1971). *Status passage.* Chicago: Aldine.

Katz, J. (1979). Legality and equality: Plea bargaining in the prosecution of white collar crimes. *Law and Society Review, 13,* 431–460.

Rothman, M., & Gandossy, R. F. (1982). Sad tales: The accounts of white collar defendants and the decision to sanction. *Pacific Sociological Review, 4,* 449–473.

Searle, J. R. (1969). *Speech acts.* Cambridge: Cambridge University Press.

14

Neutralization and Deviance in the Workplace: Theft of Supplies and Medicines by Hospital Nurses

Dean Dabney

*T*heft of drugs and hospital supplies by nurses is not an uncommon event. In one study, nurses accounted for 70% of all hospital thefts. This article focuses on the phenomenon of on-the-job deviance among nurses. Deviant behaviors such as supply theft, drug theft, drug use, and procedural shortcuts are addressed from a theoretical perspective that incorporates components of differential association, social learning, and techniques of neutralization theories. The author interviewed 25 registered nurses in critical care units in three hospitals. A snowball sample technique was used, beginning with three nurses who served as interview participants and as the core of the snowball. Each interview lasted 60–90 minutes. The data illustrate how nurses readily neutralize their deviant behaviors by using established rationalization schemes. The data suggest that the nature and limits of these rationalizations are created, perpetuated, and disseminated by the nursing work group. Moreover, evidence is presented that suggests that these rationalizations function as a priori discriminate stimuli, not simply as post hoc justifications for deviant behaviors.

The nursing profession is not without its share of employee deviance. This deviance takes many forms. Some of the most prevalent and potentially destructive examples of nursing deviance are the theft of drugs or supplies. A nationwide study of drug theft in hospitals (McCormick, Hoover, & Murphy, 1986) found that nurses were implicated in 70% of the drug losses (more than 112,000 dosage units over a 1-year period). Moreover, a large-scale survey of nurses' on-the-job substance abuse behaviors conducted by the American Nurses Association (1984) estimated that 8–10% of the nation's 1.7 million nurses are dependent on drugs or alcohol. A similar large-scale study conducted by the Michigan Nurses Association (1986) estimated that nurses are five times more likely to abuse substances than are members of the general public. The Michigan study went on to estimate that one in seven nurses will abuse substances during their careers. With these figures in mind, the research reported here attempts to provide contextuality to

Adapted from Dean Dabney, "Neutralization and Deviance in the Workplace: Theft of Supplies and Medicines by Hospital Nurses." *Deviant Behavior,* vol. 116, 1995. Pp. 312–321. Used with permission of the author and publisher.

nurses' involvements in organizational deviance, using existing criminological theory. Specifically, this analysis draws on components of differential association, social learning theory, and techniques of neutralization to explain the aforementioned forms of nursing deviance. The goal is to identify both the positive and the negative normative definitions associated with nurses' deviant behavior and to illustrate how the nursing work group supplies its members with a series of neutralizing rationalizations that are then used to modify these definitions.

THEORETICAL ORIENTATION

The learning process that leads to deviant behavior has long fascinated criminologists. Sutherland's (Sutherland, 1949; Sutherland & Cressey, 1970) differential association theory was the first to suggest that the learning process behind criminal behavior is the same as that behind noncriminal behavior. At the center of Sutherland's theory is the concept of "definitions." According to Sutherland, these definitions serve as the normative attitudes and beliefs toward behavior. When an individual has the knowledge of how to commit an act and the opportunity presents itself, that individual's behavior will hinge on his or her normative perception of the act. An excess of definitions favorable to an act increases the likelihood of its occurrence, and an excess of negative definitions decreases the likelihood of its occurrence.

Social learning theory (Akers, 1985) expands on Sutherland's (Sutherland, 1949; Sutherland & Cressey, 1970) concept of definitions. According to social learning theory, normative definitions are the result not only of association, but of imitation and differential reinforcement. More important, social learning theory asserts that definitions favorable to deviant acts can take on one of two forms: They can simply define the act as morally correct or they can redefine a morally incorrect act in a favorable light. In the latter case, a set of excuses, justifications, or rationalizations serves as vocal or internal discriminative stimuli for the deviant act. These discriminant stimuli then serve to redefine the act in one of two ways: as not really deviant or as a justifiable act.

Social learning theory incorporates the notion of neutralization from Sykes and Matza's (1957) "techniques of neutralization" theory. Sykes and Matza formulated five distinct typologies of justifications or rationalizations: *denial of responsibility, denial of injury, denial of victim, condemnation of condemner,* and the *appeal to higher loyalties.* These authors posit that each of the neutralization typologies mentioned in this article serves as a cognitive mechanism used by individuals to redefine normatively unfavorable behaviors as acceptable. The exact form of this rationalization mechanism, as well as its subsequent verbal manifestation (i.e., the excuses offered by the individual), will differ depending on which of the seven typologies is being used.

Building on the concept of normative definitions, I attempt, in this analysis to identify neutralizing definitions that manifest themselves within the nursing work group and thus facilitate various forms of organizational deviance. Interview data are used to demonstrate that the nursing work group creates and maintains its own system of work group norms. For the most part, these definitions correspond with the accepted norms of the hospital and even those of the larger society. However, in some cases, the established organizational norms of the hospital conflict with work group norms. In this case, the work group either provides the individual nurses with a set of rationalizations for violating the hospital's organizational and legal rules or institutes procedural shortcuts or innovative adaptations to circumvent existing hospital policy.

I argue that incoming nurses are aware of the formal organizational definitions against taking supplies and medicines for personal or unauthorized use. Nevertheless, observations in hospitals reveal that nurses readily engage in taking such properties. The contention here is that such behaviors are facilitated by nurses learning a series of justifications and rationalizations that portray theft as not really deviant when committed under certain conditions. Consistent with social learning theory, I argue that these rationalizations are the direct result of reinforcement from other nurses. As nurses are socialized into a particular work group, they tend to change their general normative definition to conform to that held by the work group. These norms do not compel, or require deviations from the hospital or legal regulations. Nor do they portray such deviations as something a "good" nurse should do. Rather, they simply excuse the acts as not really wrong when committed under some circumstances.

Social learning theory and techniques of neutralization theory alike have been challenged on the grounds that they do not adequately address the causal ordering issue required of etiological theories (Hamlin, 1988). In short, critics have suggested that there has been little if any conclusive evidence that demonstrates that neutralizing definitions are present before the conception of deviant behaviors. As such, theories such as techniques of neutralization (and, indirectly, social learning theory) are often labeled as little more than ex post facto explanations of deviant behavior.

In this analysis, I propose an etiological explanation of deviant behavior that borrows the issue of neutralizing normative definitions directly from social learning theory and techniques of neutralization paradigms. Thus, the causal ordering issue must be addressed. I use verbatim interview data to illustrate a number of different rationalization techniques used by the nurses, and I use retroactive neutralizations to demonstrate how individuals engage in after-the-fact rationalization that allows them to reconstruct the reality of the situation in question in such a way that it coincides with their predetermined notions of acceptable behavior. Also, evidence that nurses routinize the use of retroactive rationalizations is offered as testimony that they use these neutralization mechanisms as discriminant stimuli that serve to shape future behaviors of the same type. In short, the causal argument is as follows: Nurses are offered certain rationalizations from the nursing work group that excuse or condone certain forms of deviant behavior. In turn, the habitual use of these rationalizations increases the probability that individual nurses will internalize such redefined definitions of acceptable behavior for future reference.

I give evidence of the proactive application of the neutralization concept by presenting accounts in which nurses apply neutralizing definitions to deviant behavior committed in the past and then imply or directly assert that they will continue to engage in these behaviors in the future. Situations like this suggest that nurses have internalized the neutralizing definitions and are using them as discriminant stimuli that shape subsequent behaviors.

DEVIANCE AND NEUTRALIZATIONS IN THE WORKPLACE

Several past research efforts have approached the issue of employee deviance from a similar theoretical perspective. For example, in studying what he called "blue-collar theft" among workers at an electronics factory, Horning (1970) found evidence that employees constructed their own definitions of what did and did not constitute "real" theft within the organization. These definitions depend on the property involved. The respondents classified property into three categories: company property, personal property, and property of uncertain origin. The misappropriation of personal property or company property was seen as theft. However, a similar definition was not applied to property of uncertain origin. In this case, the workers felt justified in taking the property. The origins of these definitions were traced back to the work group. The worker was taught what was acceptable behavior and what was not. These behaviors often directly contradicted company policies, but the workers adhered to the group norms, not company policy.

Other researchers who have applied the neutralization concept to organizational deviance include Cressey (1953), Geis (1967), Benson (1985), Hollinger (1991), Tathum (1974), Sieh (1987), Dalton (1959), Gouldner (1954), Ditton (1977), and Mars (1982). Although each of these studies took on a different theoretical twist and focused on a different work setting, each illustrates how the normative definitions of the work group enable employees to redefine deviant acts that they commit while at work.

In this research, I applied the neutralization concept to a sample of nurses. Specifically, I hypothesized that certain types of hospital property, such as supplies and some forms of medicines, would be afforded uncertain ownership status. At the same time, "harder" drugs such as narcotics should clearly be defined as hospital property and should not be taken. Thus, one would expect that, in addition to offering individual nurses the motives and techniques needed to steal drugs and supplies from the hospital, the nursing work group will also offer the individual an arsenal of justifications that can be used to make these behaviors acceptable in the light of societal or administrative norms.

RESULTS

Theft of General Supplies

All of the nurses claimed to have seen other nurses stealing supplies from hospital stock, and 23 admitted to personal involvements in these activities. In fact, most of the nurses laughed when asked if they had ever seen nurses stealing supplies. When discussing the topic of supply theft, it was customary for the nurses to offer a long and diverse list of popular theft items.

All of the nurses implied that supply theft was accepted behavior among the nursing work group. This is evidenced by the fact that most nurses estimated that 100% of the nursing staff reported involvements in supply theft. Only four nurses estimated that fewer than 50% of the nursing staff were involved in supply theft.

The nurses often made statements that clearly illustrated the group acceptance of supply theft. This can be seen in the following exchange that took place between the interviewer and a 37-year-old intensive care unit nurse:

> "Do they try to hide it [supply theft] from colleagues?"
> "No, not at all."
> "So it is accepted behavior?"
> "Yes, it kind of bothers me, but..."

Despite this group acceptance of supply theft, the nurses were very cognizant of the fact that their behaviors were against the law as well as the norms established by hospital policy. For example, one 28-year-old nurse offered the following normative definition of supply theft: "Probably if you get deep down to it, it is probably morally wrong because it is not yours. But it doesn't bother me in the least. Not in the least! Isn't that awful?" Another nurse, this one a 26-year-old ICU nurse had this to say about the normative definition of supply theft:

> I steal scrubs. I have a million pairs at home. I cut them off and make shorts. I realize it is a debt but you don't think about it. You think that they won't miss it but you know they do. I mean the scrub loss is $11,000 a month. They take a beating.

Faced with a conflict between the negative societal-administrative definition and a positive work group definition, nurses chose to neutralize the negative definition and enhance the favorable work group definition through the use of work group rationalizations. The most common rationalization justified supply theft as a fringe benefit that goes along with the job. For example, a 47-year-old ICU step-down (an intermediate care unit) nurse claimed that her supply theft was "a way of supplementing one's income." In full, 88% of the nurses justified their own, and their observed, theft of general supplies in this manner. This trend is obvious in the statement made by another

28-year-old ICU nurse. When asked if she saw supply theft as a fringe benefit, she said, "Yeah, it's kind of a compensation. ... I really don't think about it. You just take it. It is no big deal."

It is interesting to note that the scope of this neutralization of supply theft was tempered by work group limitations. Not all forms of supply theft were positively defined by the work group. Only theft in moderation was rationalized. This is obvious in the quote offered by a 33-year-old ICU step-down unit nurse. She said, "If they were taking garbage bags full, people would be upset, but everyone takes something once in a while. It is a kind of fringe benefit for us."

Theft of Over-the-Counter Medicines

A similar trend emerged regarding the theft of over-the-counter medicines. Twenty-one of the nurses admitted that they had themselves stolen certain medicines, usually Tylenol, from hospital stock. Once again, the theft appeared to be quite extensive. For example, when asked to clarify her claim that someone steals Tylenol every day on her unit, a 26-year-old ICU nurse said, "Yeah, if you have a headache, you go take one [Tylenol] out of the drawer."

It was also not uncommon for nurses to say that they had engaged in over-the-counter drug theft on a regular basis. For instance, when asked how many times he had engaged in such thefts, a 48-year-old ICU nurse replied, "I don't know. I have been a nurse for 22 years and this job has given me a lot of headaches. So I guess I couldn't even give you a number." As was the case with supply theft, the theft of over-the-counter drugs was rationalized by work group definitions. This point is illustrated in the following exchange, which occurred with a 25-year-old ICU step-down nurse:

"Is drug theft looked down on by nurses?"
"Probably drugs but not stuff like Tylenol."
"Have you ever taken over-the-counter meds?"
"Oh yeah, things like Tylenol or Motrin."
"How did you get them?"
"I just walk up to the drawer and take them."
"So people see you and they don't say anything?"
"That's right."

Once again, nurses had to justify the theft of over-the-counter drugs as it was known to be against hospital regulations. These rationalizations were also usually based on the fringe benefit rationalization and were tempered by the amount taken and the frequency with which it occurred.

Theft of Nonnarcotic Medicines

A slightly different pattern arose, however, concerning the theft of medicines other than simple pain and headache remedies. In this case, nonnarcotic drugs such as Darvocet N100, a mild analgesic, or tranquilizers such as Xanax or Ativan were frequently mentioned. Although these drugs do require a doctor's prescription, they are dispensed in the same way as other non-narcotic medicines, through the unit dose system. Under this system, each patient is given his or her daily allotment of these medicines, and they are kept in each patient's room. A nurse must chart the administration of these medicines, but a key is not required to gain access to them. The majority of the nurses explained that there is often an excess of these types of medicines left on the unit. This is sometimes due to over-prescribing by physicians or because the intended patient dies or is transferred before the medication is dispensed. In the latter case, what results is a lag period between when the hospital pharmacy workers realize that the patient is no longer receiving the medicines and when they quit sending them. During this time lag, these excess medicines are stockpiled, without supervision, at the nursing station.

In all, 15 nurses described eyewitness accounts in which nurses took advantage of these stockpiled nonnarcotic drugs by taking them. For example, a 26-year-old clinical coordinator of an ICU stated, "Today one of the nurses had a sore leg so she took some Darvocet out of her patient's drawer."

The misappropriation of these stockpiled nonnarcotic drugs appeared to be accepted behavior among the nurses. For example, one 23-year-old ICU step-down nurse said, "At 6:00 anything that is left in the drawers is free game because it should have been given throughout the day."

Evidence of nurses comparing the theft of these mild analgesics to over-the-counter drugs was offered by a 25-year-old nurse working in an ICU step-down unit. When asked if she had ever seen another nurse take medicines from the hospital, she replied "Yes, stuff like Valium, Tylenol, Motrin, or even Xanax." Further questioning of this nurse showed that she made no distinction between the severity of these thefts. She brushed off the Valium and Xanax as if they were Tylenol or Motrin. Another nurse, this one a 22-year-old ICU nurse, had this to say:

"What do you think of nurses who take meds?"
"I don't think it is right to take narcs."
"Are you saying that you compare nonnarcs to taking supplies?"
"Yeah."
"Even stuff like the Ativan?"
"I don't see anything wrong with taking Ativan as long as it isn't abused."

This attitude was echoed by other nurses. For example, one 47-year-old recovery room nurse said, "I don't consider a nonscheduled drug much worse than Band-aids."

The general acceptance of nonnarcotic drug theft is underscored by the finding that, although 22 nurses reported having witnessed theft and or use of controlled substances, none reported these situations to superiors. It is relevant to note that 10 of these respondents indicated their estimates of theft incidents were likely conservative. Few of the nurses who had seen other nurses take drugs could offer what they felt were completely accurate estimates of how many different times they had seen such behavior. For instance, one female, 28-year-old step-down unit nurse explained,

> Yes, nurses do it for their own use but they only take the stuff that isn't locked up. If it isn't locked up it is fair game. I don't know how many times I have seen it happen.

This inability to estimate the prevalence of theft of these mild analgesics and tranquilizers was also illustrated by a 26-year-old clinical coordinator of an ICU. When asked how many times she had seen these drugs taken, she said, "too many times to count."

All of the nurses explained that pharmacy policy disapproved of stockpiling nonnarcotic medicines. These nurses also understood that hospital regulations did not allow them to misappropriate or ingest these drugs. Still, they rationalized doing so. These rationalizations usually resembled Horning's (1970) notion of property of uncertain ownership. He found that over time, the factory workers in his study had come to collectively redefine some forms of company property as having an uncertain ownership status and thus normatively accepted the removal of these materials for personal use. The idea was that the materials were no longer "really" the property of the company. In the present case of the stockpiled drugs, the nurses engaged in a similar process. In short, because there were no direct controls on these accumulated drugs, the work group saw them as fair game.

Theft of Narcotic Medicines

Each of the 25 nurses made a clear distinction between the theft of unit dose drugs, which are all controlled substances, and the narcotic drugs that are kept under constant lock and key. Although nurses routinely used terminology such as "no big deal" to describe the use or theft of medicines such as Darvocet N100, no such definition was afforded to the locked-down narcotics. Here, the work group norms were clearly in line with the societal and administrative definitions. When asked about narcotic drug theft, one 33-year-old ICU step-down nurse replied,

> I think it is terrible. Narcotics you mean? Yeah, I think it is terrible. They are highly addictive and it ends up being a problem. It turns into a vicious circle and something bad happens.

When asked how narcotic drug theft was viewed among nurses, a 34-year-old ICU nurse said, "I don't know of anyone who would approve of it." This trend was seen throughout the interviews. For example, a 26-year-old operating room nurse said that the theft of narcotics is viewed poorly.

> It is very bad. For instance, one day I was doing the count and came up short on the p.o. [prescribed orally] Tylenol 3's or something. I was really nervous

that someone was gonna accuse me of stealing. I looked for them for like an hour.

A negative work group definition of narcotic drug theft translated into minimal reported incidents of theft. Only one nurse admitted to stealing narcotics, and this was an isolated case that had occurred many years earlier. Furthermore, there were only four eyewitness reports of narcotics theft. Although these nurses brushed off the other forms of theft discussed earlier, they claimed that they would report nurses who stole narcotics. This once again illustrates the strong work group controls placed on employee theft among nurses. For example, one 27-year-old oncology nurse said, "it depends on what they are taking. If it is something minor then okay, but if it is something like a narc, I would report them."

A 48-year-old ICU nurse amplified this point about the theft of narcotics. He said, "I don't put up with that. If I saw it, I would have no problem busting them and turning them in."

Procedural Shortcuts

As one can see, there is a clear distinction that can be made between the work group definitions that apply to the theft of narcotics as opposed to other forms of nursing theft (i.e., other forms of medication and supplies). The nurses claim that the former is not tolerated, whereas the latter appears to be condoned if done in moderation. However, these nurses use several procedural activities that increase the opportunity for nurses to steal narcotics. These shortcut procedures in the dispensing and monitoring systems are themselves violations of the rules of governing narcotic medicines. Federal regulations, namely the Controlled Substance Act of 1970, mandate strict regulations on drugs that are categorized as narcotics. For example, all of these drugs must be kept in a secure room or cart. The keys to these facilities are to be kept in the possession of designated charge nurses. When a patient requires a narcotic, the administering nurse must have the charge nurse open the cart for him or her. Also, each dosage unit must be signed out by the administering nurse before it can be given to the patient. Finally, all narcotics in a unit must be counted by two separate nurses at the end of each 8- or 12-hour shift to verify that all of the narcotics are accounted for. If there is a discrepancy in the count, a lengthy set of administrative forms must be filled out and delivered immediately to the pharmacy. In this event, an official investigation involving security and pharmacy officials must take place.

All of these mandated procedures translate into added time and energy that the nurses must expend. Nurses view these procedures as laborious and distrusting of nurses. As a result, they have modified these procedures, using a number of shortcuts. The nurses rationalize deviant short-cutting strategies as serving to increase the quality of patient care. Work group norms accept the shortcuts, and they appeared to be routine. No nurse claimed to have a charge nurse (the nurse who monitors access to narcotics) who limited the access to narcotic keys. Instead, the keys to the narcotic cart were routinely left on or in the cart itself, a clear violation of the rules. A 26-year-old ICU nurse described this procedural shortcut as follows:

> There is a med cart that is supposed to be locked but the keys are on top. ... The only time these are locked is when JCAH [Joint Commission on the Accreditation of Healthcare Organizations] comes once a year.

Similarly, a 28-year-old ICU nurse said:

> With the narc box, it is locked but the keys are usually hanging in the lock so anyone that walks by can turn that key and open it. ... That is unless JCAH is coming. Then, we have to lock everything up and carry the keys but that is only for 1 or 2 days a year.

The nurses have also adapted a modified set of procedures that govern how drug counts are conducted. For example, they do not always adhere to the requirement that states that two nurses must conduct drug counts. Instead, one nurse often conducts the count, and a colleague simply signs the form. In these cases, it is assumed that the initial nurse conducted an accurate count. All 25 nurses described this type of modification in the interviews. A 27-year-old oncology nurse said, "Sometimes one nurse will count and the other will sign, or sometimes two do it together."

These nurses have also adapted a work group strategy for dealing with drug count discrepancies. Nurses are aware of the labor involved in filing drug discrepancy forms. They are also aware of the fact that filing these forms brings them and the work group under suspicion. As an alternative to the mandated paperwork, nurses described a more relaxed way of accounting for missing drugs that has evolved. In this accommodation, a patient who was prescribed the missing medication is simply charged with the missing dose. In all, 21 nurses either admitted to taking part in this mischarting of medicines or claimed to have seen it done by other nurses. For example, one 22-year-old ICU nurse described this mischarting as follows: "Usually you just find someone [a patient] that is using a lot and sign it out to them."

Another nurse, this one a 34-year-old ICU nurse, offered the following description of how mischarting takes place:

> Well a lot of the times, people forget [to sign out a drug] so we kind of go back and make it up as we go [laughing]. There have been times where you have been short and you say ... I am sure that they used it on this person.

These accounts of nurses' mischarting were widespread and varied in their scope and complexity. For example, a 26-year-old clinical coordinator of one of the medical ICUs described the following incident where the narcotic counts for her unit were not done for an entire weekend:

> This is a good one. I went to work yesterday morning after the weekend and they had not counted the narcs since Saturday. Here I am trying to count on

Monday. There were like five things missing for every day … I was losing it. I was so pissed off at them. There were five Phentonols, five Ativans, the morphine were missing, the Versed [a type of drug; spelling phonetic] were bad. And then they had four codes over the weekend where all four patients died so there was no way for me to track who got what. So, I just signed them out to who I thought used them.

The systematic dismissal of drug theft as the result of nurses' mischarting of drug errors was rationaized by nurses in several ways. Usually, the nurses insisted that they did not suspect drug theft among their present group of colleagues. This rationalization seemed to rest firmly on the integrity of the nursing profession. Several nurses suggested that they were certain they would know if a fellow nurse was using drugs and mischarting to acquire them. Most assumed that they were sufficiently adept to identify drug users among coworkers. For example, one 48-year-old ICU nurse said, "I think I could tell if someone was doing that [using drugs at work]."

In each case in which a nurse described the mischarting procedure, probes were used to see what the nurses thought of this behavior. None of the nurses originally thought that the missing drugs had been stolen. When I presented this possibility to the respondents, they unequivocally ruled it out.

For example, one 47-year-old female recovery room nurse had this to say when asked if mischarting might serve as a cover-up for drug theft:

I never thought of it that way. We deal in so many units that, when you are short one dosage unit, you just assume that someone forgot to chart it.

After the interview, this nurse suggested that this type of trusting attitude is customary in the nursing profession. She thought that it might be my criminological background that led me to think so suspiciously of what she called "an obviously honest mistake." In his case, an "honest mistake" serves to justify both the missing drug and the mischarting.

DISCUSSION

There are clearly two types of normative definitions functioning in the nurses' work environment: formally stated hospital policies and informal work group mores. Both of these forces serve as guides for nurses' behavior. However, these two sets of definitions are sometimes at odds with one another. For example, in the case of supply theft, over-the-counter medicine theft, or nonnarcotic drug theft, nurses are presented with two very different definitions of acceptable behavior. The administrative policies establish these behaviors as theft that is not permitted. At the same time, the work group socializes its members to tolerate and even condone such behavior as nontheft. Faced with this predicament, nurses appear more inclined to choose the latter alternative. It appears that the strength and persistence of these work group norms increase the probability that nurses will engage in these forms of behavior. This is evidenced by the fact that, for each of the above-mentioned forms of deviance (i.e., supply theft, over-the-counter drug theft, and nonnarcotic drug theft), nurses reported substantial knowledge of and involvement in these activities.

Nurses neutralize the administrative definitions and redefine the theft in a way that lessens inhibitions against the behaviors. These definitions favorable to theft take many forms. They are often determined by the nature and extent of the improprieties. The one commonality shared by all of these neutralizations is the fact that they originate from within the work group and are disseminated to the nurses through an informal socialization process. As a consequence, violations are widespread. This process is directly in line with the theoretical propositions of differential association and social learning theory.

These data illustrate situations in which administrative policies are in agreement with work group norms. The most obvious example revolves around narcotic drug theft. Here, the work group as well as the administrative policies presents unfavorable definitions of such behavior. Not only does the work group not condone narcotic drug theft, but it was also suggested that they will not tolerate it. If a nurse is thought to be stealing narcotics, he or she is not afforded the same protection that a nonnarcotics diverter would be. Similarly, the work group does not present the nurses with any viable rationalization or justification for narcotic drug theft. This situation appears to have a substantial effect on the prevalence of narcotic drug theft in this sample. Far fewer nurses offered eyewitness accounts or admitted to personal involvement in narcotic drug theft than they did with the other forms of employee theft. Violations of this type were uncommon.

The findings presented in this article lend support to the facilitating role that neutralizing definitions play in differential association and social learning theory. The accounts given by the nurses in this study portray on-the-job deviance as being closely linked to definitions favorable to the deviance. As expected theoretically, normative definitions appear to originate from various sources and are often in conflict with one another. Those definitions that receive strong work group support were more apt to prevail. When these informal work group norms allow nurses to justify theft on the job, it is likely to occur. These justifications may originally have developed following the commission of various forms of employee theft to change the normative perception of the behavior in question. However, once they become part of the work subculture, they seem to be incorporated into the occupational socialization process. Thus, new nurses appear to learn them before committing theft. This temporal ordering issue is also evidenced by the fact that nurses indicated that they will continue engaging in these various forms of employee deviance. This suggests that these normative definitions are being used as discriminant stimuli that serve to shape future behaviors.

The sources of the normative conflict between the nursing work group's and the hospital administration's definitions of proper behavior may well be traced to the overarching way in which nurses conceive of their work objective. As Hollinger and Clark (1983) observed in a study of hospital employees, nurses tend to see themselves as caregivers whose job is to help their patients at any cost. Within this self-conception, nurses are able to justify certain behaviors such as taking supplies as the patient is not harmed. Instead, it is the hospital, who they claim does not appreciate them, that incurs the loss. Similarly, when nurses condone over-the-counter or nonnarcotic drug theft, it is done under the premise that taking the drugs is done to improve the nurse's disposition. The thinking is that this allows them to better treat the patients (e.g., How can I treat a patient if I am stressed out or have a headache?). From this perspective, nurses' impairment actually enhances patient care. At the same time, taking narcotics does not fit into this paradigm as these drugs are thought to have an adverse effect on patient care. This pattern of nurses' behavior leads one to agree with Hollinger and Clark's notion that although many hospital employees enjoy their jobs from a care-giving perspective, they dislike the hospitals in which they must deliver this care. As such, the neutralizations used to justify and even condone nurses' deviance against the hospital would seem to make a great deal of sense as they are done to benefit the patients.

This research has some obvious methodological limitations. At every step of the research process, one can see problems that could affect the generalizability of these conclusions. For example, the use of such a small, nonrandom sample immediately raises questions. Moreover, one must keep in mind that these interviews involved a small number of respondents in a limited number of settings. As such, it is conceivable that these nurses' behaviors and attitudes differ substantially from those of other nurses in different settings. Similarly, the nature of the interview instrument as well as the use of content analysis raises several questions about researcher objectivity and respondent reactivity.

However, these conclusions serve as a starting point from which one may begin to explain the nature and extent of nursing deviance. One possible explanation for nursing deviance lies within a social learning perspective. By drawing on the concept of normative definitions, as is presented in social learning theory, this research attempted to shed some light on the phenomenon of nursing deviance. Of course, this is only one approach, and the reader may readily devise plausible alternatives.

References

Akers, R. L. (1985). *Deviant behavior: A social learning approach*. Belmont, CA: Wadsworth.

American Nurses Association. (1984). *ANA cabinet on nursing practice: Statement on scope for addiction nursing practice*. Kansas City, MO: Author.

Benson, M. L. (1985). Denying the guilty mind: Accounting for involvement in a white collar crime. *Criminology, 23*, 583–607.

Cressey, D. R. (1953). *Other people's money*. Glencoe, IL: Free Press.

Dalton, M. (1959). *Men who manage.* New York: Wiley.

Ditton, J. (1977). *Part-time crime: An ethnography of fiddling and pilferage.* New York: Macmillan.

Geis, G. (1967). The heavy electrical equipment antitrust cases of 1961. In M. B. Clinard & R. Quinney (Eds.), *Criminal behavior systems: A typology* (pp. 139–151). New York: Holt, Rinehart & Winston.

Gouldner, A. (1954). *Patterns of industrial bureaucracy.* New York: Free Press.

Hamlin, J. E. (1988). The misplaced role of rational choice in neutralization theory. *Criminology, 26,* 425–438.

Hollinger, R. C. (1991). Neutralizing in the workplace: An Empirical analysis of property theft and production deviance. *Deviant Behavior, 12,* 169–202.

Hollinger, R. C., & Clark, J. P. (1983). *Theft by employees.* Lexington, MA: Lexington Books.

Horning, D. (1970). Blue collar theft: Conceptions of property, attitudes toward pilfering, and work group norms in a modern industrial plant. In E. O. Smigel & H. L. Ross (Eds.), *Crimes against bureaucracy* (pp. 46–64). New York: Van Nostrand Reinhold.

Mars, G. (1982). *Cheats at work: An anthropology of workplace crime.* London: Allen & Unwin.

McCormick, W. C., Hoover, R. C., & Murphy, J. B. (1986). Drug diversion from hospitals analyzed. *Security Management, 30,* 41–48.

Michigan Nurses Association. (1986). *Fact sheet: Chemical dependency of nurses.* East Lansing, MI: Author.

Sieh, E. W. (1987). Garment workers: Perceptions of inequity and employee theft. *British Journal of Criminology, 27,* 174–190.

Sutherland, E. H. (1949). *White collar crime.* New York: Dryden.

Sutherland, E. H., & Cressey, D. R. (1970). *Criminology* (8th ed.). Philadelphia: J. B. Lippincott.

Sykes, G. M., & Matza, D. (1957). Techniques of neutralization: A theory of delinquency. *American Sociological Review, 22,* 664–670.

Tathum, R. L. (1974). Employee views of theft in retailing. *Journal of Retailing, 50,* 49–55.

SECTION V

ILLEGAL OCCUPATIONS

In the previous section, we examined crimes committed by persons in the course of their legal occupations. In this section, we consider offenders whose occupations violate formal norms. The central activities of such work are illegal, yet they share many commonalities with legal occupations. Most of those who engage in illegal occupations have regular customers, suppliers, and a formal set of roles and activities that do not substantially differ from those of people who perform legal work. Drug dealing, operating an illegal gambling operation, fencing, prostitution, and engaging in confidence games all fall under the rubric of illegal work.

In Chapter 15, "The Myth of Organization of International Drug Smugglers," Scott H. Decker and Janna Benson provide a rare look at the business of drug smuggling. Based on extensive interviews with a diverse cross section of those who engage in this offense, they study the flow of information, networks, and links, and the various "work roles" required for a successful drug smuggling operation.

In Chapter 16, "Fencing: Avenues for Redistribution of Stolen Property," Paul Cromwell and James N. Olson report on a study based on extensive interviews with 30 active, "free-world" burglars and fences. They analyzed the relationships between burglars and fences—receivers of stolen property and create a typology of fences.

In Chapter 17, the final study in this section, Romenesko and Miller, "The Second Step in Double Jeopardy: Appropriating the Labor of Female Street Hustlers," report on women who make their living from street level prostitution. They draw parallels between the patriarchal structure of the world of prostitution and that which exists in the noncriminal world. The authors report the existence of a street institution known as a pseudo-family, comprised of the pimp and the women who work for him. Within this structure, women street hustlers attempt to obtain status, but working for men in a secondary role serves to further oppress women socially and economically, making it more difficult for women to give up a life of drugs and crime. The pseudo-family is explicitly organized to exploit the female members who relinquish control of their resources for the affection and recognition of their "man" and the material goods necessary for survival.

These studies illustrate that while the activities of the participants are illegal, they tend to see themselves as "businessmen" with a product or a service for sale to the public. They have similar goals and are faced with many of the same problems and goals prevalent in legitimate enterprises.

15

The "Myth of Organization" of International Drug Smugglers

Scott H. Decker and Jana S. Benson

*U*ntil recently, most criminologists viewed international drug smuggling as a highly structured and organized operation with vertical lines of responsibility and communication. This view was based on old models of organized crime and romanticized versions of the Medellin cartels that operated in Columbia in the 1980s. The amount of money involved in international drug smuggling is enormous, and it is generally assumed that where large sums of money are present, they will be accompanied by a high level of organization. This view of group offending as highly structured is not confined to international drug smugglers. Criminologists have typically over ascribed the level of structure, organization and rationality of groups of offenders such as gangs, burglars, robbers and street level drug sellers. Often this is the case because information about organization of offending groups comes from law enforcement, which sees only a small fraction of offenders. In other cases, criminologists' interviews are restricted to "kingpins" or supposed leaders in groups, without external validation of their real role in offending.

This chapter examines the nature and extent of organization in international drug smuggling groups. Based on interviews with 34 convicted international drug smugglers, we find very little formal organization or vertical structure in drug smuggling groups. Following a description of these offenders, we discuss the literature on organization of drug smugglers and other active groups of offenders. This discussion is focuses on three major categories of organization: structure, interactions, and rationality. Having established a context for our analysis, we then use the words of convicted drug smugglers to illustrate our findings. Finally, conclusions are drawn about the sources of the "myth of organization" in international drug smuggling.

THE CURRENT STUDY

The following analysis is based on interviews conducted with 34 individuals held in U.S. federal prisons. A semistructured questionnaire was used to elicit information from individuals who were selected based on their

Source: Written especially for this volume.

extensive involvement in high level international drug smuggling. We found 135 of these individuals in federal prisons. Of the 73 individuals approached to request participation in the study 34 agreed. We compared the group who refused participation with the subjects who did take part, and found them to be similar in areas that indicate level of involvement in smuggling, specifically how serious the crime was and their role in the offense. In the end, we have a sample of 34 individuals that were heavily involved in drug smuggling. We also had access to their federal presentence reports and were able to verify their extensive involvement in drug smuggling.

Table 15.1 presents a summary of key characteristics of the smugglers we interviewed. Of the 34 subjects, the modal category for age at sentencing was 40–49. Eighty-two percent of the sample reported being between 30 and 59 years old at that time. All of the subjects were male. Although almost half of the subjects were United States citizens, Cubans and Columbians also have significant representation in the sample. Twenty-nine individuals or 85% of the sample reported being of Hispanic origin. All of the drug smugglers we interviewed operated through the Caribbean, with a majority of the drugs originating in Colombia. Smuggling activity also was described as occurring in the Bahamas, Panama, Cuba, the Dominican Republic, Mexico, Haiti, Peru, Puerto Rico, and Venezuela. The method of smuggling varied, with both private and commercial boars and airplanes being used.

All of the subjects we interviewed we arrested and charged with smuggling large quantities of cocaine. Three individuals also reported smuggling marijuana in connection with the current offense. The mean amount of cocaine the subjects were caught with was 1,136 kg, which is just less than 2500 pounds. Values ranged from 15 kg to 5,000 kg on this characteristic. The mean year of arrest was 1993, with reported values ranging from 1988 to 1997. Twenty-two members of the sample were serving a sentence of 20 years or more, with five doing life and six doing a sentence of 30 years or more. Only one subject received a sentence of less than 10 years for his involvement in the smuggling operation.

The individuals interviewed for this study were heavily involved in international drug smuggling. None of the smugglers in the sample were caught on their first act of smuggling. In fact, more than half of the subjects reported having been involved in *at least* 10 prior smuggling operations. These contentions were consistent with the results of their pre-sentence investigations. The smugglers played a variety of roles in the smuggling event for which they were caught, ranging from broker or organizer to transporter or manager. Only one of the individuals could be described as playing a minor role in drug smuggling (off loader) but this individual had an extensive history of involvement in drug smuggling.

There is also diversity in the methods of smuggling used by members of our sample, including both commercial and private vessels (boats) and private and commercial airplanes. Combinations of vessels and aircrafts were also reported. The most commonly used transportation was private vessels, with 62% of the individuals reporting experience with this method. In short, this high-level group of drug smugglers with extensive experience

Table 15.1 Characteristics of smuggler respondents

Role	Method	Region	Age Range	Weight of Drugs	Sentence Length
Recruiter	Private Vessel	Columbia/Bahamas	40–49	480 kg	30 years
Organizer	Commercial Vessel	Columbia	40–49	1,500 kg	27 years
Manager	Commercial Vessel	Columbia	40–49	630 kg	30 years
Supervisor	Vessel	Columbia	40–49	165 kg	31 years
Organizer	Commercial Vessel	Columbia	40–49	1,500 kg	8 years
Organizer	Commercial Vessel	Bahamas	40–49	3,345.5 kg	17.5 years
Leader	Private Plane/Commercial Vessel	Columbia	60–69	500 kg	30.5 years
Recruiter	Commercial Vessel	Columbia	50–59	40 kg	17.5 years
Broker	Private Vessel	Panama	30–39	59 kg	17.5 years
Leader	Private Vessel	Cuba/Dom. Republic	30–39	515 kg	17.5 years
Leader	Private Vessel	Cuba	40–49	2,350.5 kg	19.5 years
Organizer	Private Vessel	Colombia	30–39	728 kgs	27.5 years
Transporter	Private Vessel	Mexico	40–49	5,000 kg	
Captain	Private Vessel	Columbia/Haiti	30–39	150 + kg	15 years
Off-Loader	Private Plane	Columbia	40–49	500 kg	16.25 years
Organizer		Peru	50–59	500 kg	20 years
Leader	Commercial Airplane	Bahamas/Cuba	40–49	50 kg	10 years
Manager	Private Vessel	Venezuela	30–39	605.5 kg	27 years
Leader	Commercial Airplane	Bahamas	50–59	414 kg	15 years
Recruiter	Private Vessel	Colombia	50–59	15–50 kg	22 years
Leader	Commercial Airplane	Caribbean	50–59	1,450 kg	25.5 years
Manager	Private Vessel	Haiti	40–49	2,200 kg	15 years
Captain/Investor	Commercial Airplane	Bahamas	70–79	776.3 kg	27.5 years
Organizer	Private Vessel	Panama	30–39	800–1,000 kg	18.5 years
Organizer	Commercial Vessel	Bahamas	50–59	488 kg	

253

Table 15.1 Characteristics of smuggler respondents

Role	Method	Region	Age Range	Weight of Drugs	Sentence Length
Broker	Private Airplane/Private Vessel	Columbia	30–39	4,500 kg & 14,000 lb marijuana	30 years
Organizer	Private Vessel	Puerto Rico/Dom Republic	40–49	480 kg	Life
Leader	Private Airplane	Colombia	20–29	500-600 kg	Life
Leader	Commercial Airplane	Hong Kong/Puerto Rico	60–69	86 kg & 39 lb marijuana	30 years
Leader	Private Vessel	Colombia/Puerto Rico	60–69	1,000 kg & 1000 lb marijuana	Life
Manager	Private Airplane/Private Vessel	Bahamas	60–69	600 kg	30 years
Leader	Commercial Airplane	Caribbean	30–39	15-50 kg	Life
Manager	Private Vessel	Caribbean	50–59	5,543.8 kg	Life
Owner/Financier	Private Vessel	Bahamas	30–39	757 kg	20 years

in smuggling is in a position to know and understand the structure of drug smuggling organizations.

LITERATURE ON DRUG SMUGGLERS AND OTHER ACTIVE OFFENDERS

The widely held perception about groups of international drug smugglers is that they are highly structured organizations (i.e., cartels). However, some recent literature on drug smugglers and other active offenders suggests that this is not the case. We incorporate information on active groups of offenders to discount any possible criticisms that might arise about our sample only including convicted offenders. Recent ethnographic research on active offenders such as burglars, robbers, carjackers, and gang members suggest that offenders don't organize themselves very effectively. Our examination of international drug smuggling groups will concentrate on following three features of organization: structure, interactions, and rationality.

Structure

One of the most readily identifiable characteristics of a highly organized group is a hierarchical structure. Formal hierarchies have ranked levels of authority that clearly delineate super and subordinates, where those in superordinate positions are responsible for overseeing those in the lower offices (Weber, 1946). Highly organized groups have a clear chain of command which signifies the downward movement of decision making power. Such groups also have functions associated with each level in the structure. The organizational structures of these groups tend to be pyramidal or vertical in nature.

In contrast to hierarchical structures, some groups are organized in a less formal manner. Williams (1998) suggested that some drug smuggling organizations are more accurately described as networks of connected nodes that are linked across and within organizations. There is no definite vertical chain of command, as individual cells can operate independently from the larger organization due to their individual access to information and technology. This independence leaves stages of the drug smuggling process isolated from others to some degree.

Recent research on international drug smuggling suggests that many groups are organized as a series of connected nodes. Zaitch (2002) studied drug importation from Columbia to the Netherlands and found little evidence of vertical hierarchies in drug smuggling. Instead he depicted smuggling operations as flexible networks comprised of dynamic, insulated, groups that could change tactics quickly and that were relatively insulated from those earlier or later in the smuggling transaction chain.

A structure of connected nodes rather than a vertical hierarchy is supported by research on a variety of active offenders. In fact, descriptions of human trafficking and smuggling (Zhang, 2007, 2008), terrorist groups (9/11

Commission Report, 2004; Sageman, 2008), and international trafficking of stolen vehicles (Clarke & Brown, 2003) depict such groups as small networks of individuals who lack much in the way of a formal structure. In addition, research on active burglars (Cromwell, Olson, & Avery, 1994; Shover, 1996), robbers (Wright & Decker, 1997), carjackers (Jacobs, Topali, & Wright, 2003), and gang members (Decker, Katz, & Webb, 2007) also conclude that offenders do not organize themselves in an effective or formal manner.

Interviews with the 34 convicted drug smugglers provided support for the idea that drug smuggling operations are not well organized. Williams's (1998) concept of connected nodes was illustrated in the interviews of various smugglers, especially those in the role of transporter.

> (2) Transportation is one thing, okay. That office in Colombia is supposed to get the people in Miami to do the smuggling, right? And I was the head, you know, my own group. Got 20 people working for me doing the smuggling, 10 people, whatever, and it was my responsibility. They got nothing to do with that. They just pay me for me to do the job. The other offices, when you get to Miami, I did the smuggling. I brought it already in from the Bahamas, whatever. I get in contact with the people in Miami and give it to them. Then they got it through the names. ... Call those people and give it to them. Then those people got their own buyers or whatever they do.... That would be another whole operation. There would be a whole operation to sell it in. There is another office working in Colombia to deal with the money.

> (4) The original owner of the load was somebody in Colombia that I don't know. I know the guy who was, that I went to Colombia with, and he make some arrangements in there. The original owner, I don't know the owner. I never knew the original owner. Never. The owner of the merchandise gave the merchandise to a guy that I knew that I went to Colombia with. Well, the guy I went to Colombia with, he was, he was a fugitive from this country, and I was in charge of, in here, to make all of the arrangements and all of the preparations to everyone get his part, and I get mine. I didn't know the people who were going to drive the boat to Fort Lauderdale. No, I only knew one guy—two guys in this, in this enterprise, and there were about 13 or 14 people in the deal, involved there.

> (11) Well, I had a connection in New York at the airport. So, basically, [my friend] would package the drugs in '80 and he had a connection at the airport in '80 as well. Well, as far as I know, some of [the drugs] came from Colombia, but that wasn't my connection, you know. That was the person I was dealing with. My part started when it got to Haiti....I would meet with the guy and we would package everything, do whatever we do so the drugs wouldn't be able to detect by smelling it....Whenever I come back, my guys would get the drugs, and either he would arrange it with someone to get it through the airport in Haiti, or if he did come in Haiti, I would arrange it. There's a transaction that takes place between Colombia and Haiti that I don't know about. I don't know the Colombians. The only thing I know is that whatever they would give me, it would have 40 percent.

In addition to illustrating the concept of nodes, the following quote also exemplifies the independent nature of those nodes, similar to what Williams (1998) describes.

(21) The first load they asked me to bring in, I think it was—the exact amount of 383 keys....I had no idea where it was coming from. I had no idea where it was going other than I would get back, the guy would pick it up. I picked it up in the Bahamas and brought it to Jupiter [Florida]....So they recruited me and asked me to pick up the drugs and set up the operation....I had the boat reconfigured. I engineered all the little particulars like they'd call on the phone, the warehouse, and the codes for the beeper and everything.

The smugglers also explained how a load (or shipment) of cocaine would be organized in Colombia for transportation into the United States. Instead of a single company or group of individuals owning the load, as would be the case with a highly organized operation, various independent parties would contribute to the shipment that would eventually be transported:

(30) The way they do it, you have a collector, and it's—and this was interesting because I learned this myself firsthand at the time. A bunch of people will invest in the load. It's like selling shares of stock. This person will put up this amount of money. Another person will put up another amount of money, and they in effect maybe own 2 or 3 keys. Then the collector, or whoever, whatever you want to call him, puts all this together, and this joint venture goes on a plane. So a proprietary interest in this was really shared by many.

Weber (1946) described formal organizations as having a chain of command; however the current study found drug smuggling organizations to lack this structural feature. Here, a transporter retells how he did not receive commands from an authority above about how to operate his stage of the operation:

(14) I'm the transport. I'm the one that tells them this is how we're going to play the game. We're going to do it this way. We're not going to use this. We're going to do this because I'm in charge and I'm aware of surveillance. I know everything—how the Government is running things, how things are happening. So I keep constant contact with the office. All the broker does is pick up the drugs and give me the money for my services. And the broker is the one in charge of delivering the money back to Colombia for the load and the profit.

Interviews with the 34 subjects also supported Zaitch's (2002) contention that international drug smuggling groups have dynamic structures. The adaptable and dynamic nature of these organizations is described by the following individuals as they describe how drug smuggling groups adapt quickly to changes in personnel or tactics employed:

(16) When organizing a group of captains and people who could sell these drugs, they were still able to do it once I was caught. They do it with somebody else. They find somebody, they find somebody...

(5) We would constantly change the routes...through the Caribbean. You go around through the Peninsula to the west or you go to the east around the Caribbean Basin.

Interactions

Waring (2002) argued that the way groups of co-offenders are organized rarely corresponds to the structure of formal organizations. Her key focus is on behavior within offending networks, not elements of the structure, as a means to avoid a strict focus on hierarchy or structure. This approach is consistent with that championed by Burt (1992), who argues that all social structure is the product of relations between individuals. Accordingly, we will examine the nature of interactions both with and amongst drug smuggling groups to better understand their organization.

As a consequence of the vertical hierarchy of authority, highly organized groups are characterized by sustained, formal interactions between members. Interactions typically occur between specific individuals due to the vertical nature of the chain of command and the highly structured patterns of communication within such groups. In such groups, direct correspondence commonly occurs only between an individual and one other person, their immediate supervisor. Organizational communication in such groups rarely involves personal interaction. Instead, information tends to be exchanged through more formal channels, where correspondence is more easily documented (such as written messages or formal meetings).

In contrast to the concept of highly organized offenders, Best and Luckenbill (1994) suggest that deviance and deviants are generally not well organized. They created a descriptive typology of co-offending groups using the nature of association among individuals involved in offenses together. The associations between offenders were not formal, had short temporal spans, and were specific to individual offenses. We describe such associations as episodic. More recent research on the interactions between drug smugglers is consistent with these findings. In contrast to interactions based on roles or a chain of command, Zaitch (2002) found that transactions between smugglers were based on kinship, ethnicity, and language.

Our research on international drug smuggling groups supported the idea that interactions in these groups are not formal, sustained, or based on hierarchical chains of command. Consistent with Best and Luckenbill's (1994) typology of co-offending groups, the smugglers interviewed described their interactions as more episodic than sustained:

(5) I had very few people working with me. In total, about six or eight people. Some of them were part of my crew, and some of them were what we used to [call] independent contractors. If I needed him, I would hire him. If I didn't need him, he would go to somebody else.

(6) Well, I don't know anything about sale. You know what I mean? ... The load come from Haiti, but the cocaine was from Colombia. And my job, to take it from Haiti [to] the U.S. I knew the people in Haiti, but it was the first time I work with them. I knew the people in Colombia. I had not worked with them in the past. They get in touch with me because I know somebody from Haiti. I never work with him before in drugs, you know? I know him because I was there before. So he reached me here in Miami.

In a formally organized group, interactions and communication between members would be based on the hierarchy and chain of command. Interviews with the smugglers indicated that this structure was not the way their smuggling activities were organized. In fact, interactions between individuals within and between nodes tended to be based less on hierarchy and structure and more on trust and informal relationships. Consistent with Zaitch (2002), many times this trust was established through nationality or kinship.

(5) You know, they knew that I been in drug smuggling or anything. I never used a weapon in my life. I had no need for it with the people I was dealing with. They were people that would keep their word, and if I see anybody that I didn't like that would create trouble in the future, I would avoid and try not to do business with.

(18) So I called them and I told them I have an importation from Venezuela and the name of the containers, and they go and pick them up and put them in my warehouse. I don't usually bring drugs. It was my first time. I was chosen because I was trusted. They trusted me because they saw my job, my experience.

(24) So, when I was getting a pair of pants made [in South America] , some guys comes and talks to me, and he said, "Listen, how's it going? I see you're from Miami." "Yeah, I'm from Miami." He asked me if I wanted to make some money, and I said sure, that's cool. He goes "Well, next time you're in Miami, call some people and see what we can do.... And I said the hell with it, and I gave him a call. He said "Well, come on. We're at the club." I come over to a club and he just happened to be in [Miami]. I was in Miami now. I left Colombia and went back to Miami.... Three months later, after working for him, he gave me a call and told me to come to Colombia, come back to Colombia and talk to him. I get over there. I see a couple of guys. We talk and hang out, and then they start telling me what's going.

This quotation describes how trust in international drug smuggling organizations can be established simply through one's nationality. It also illustrates how interactions are less formal and involve more direct communication than in highly organized groups. This latter point was also supported by the following smuggler who describes his contact with the owners of the loads.

(6) I have to meet the people [whose drugs I am delivering]. I have to meet them. Because they give me the contract, you understand me? I mean, the owner of the boat and the merchandise, you know. The owners. All the time, owners, not representatives.

Rationality

In addition to the structure and nature of interactions, we can examine the rationality of offending groups to better understand their organization. We refer to the rationality of an organization as the degree to which the organization is structured to achieve specific goals. In other words, a rationally organized group would have a structure and operating procedures that are based on logical reasoning, not chance or other untested criteria.

Cressey (1972) used the core concept of rationality to describe the extent and nature of organization within offending groups, particularly organized crime. Role specialization and coordination are key concepts by which he describes variation in the degree of organization among offending groups. He noted that well organized groups are those that are most rationally arranged in the pursuit of efficiency and maximized profits. Therefore, according to Cressey, well organized groups will be very rational because they display high levels of specialization (division of labor based on qualifications) and coordination of activities (interdependence) in an attempt to maximize profits efficiently.

Applying the concept of rationality to offending groups, Donald and Wilson (2000) studied the organization of ram raiders, or individuals who engaged in a pattern of smash, grab, and flee at jewelry stores. They found these groups exhibited generalized roles (no specialization), had low levels of interdependence, and lacked a rational foundation for their structure. Warr (2002) examined active groups of offenders and found them to display little evidence of rational planning or calculation. Some research on gang organization also suggests that these offenders do not organize themselves rationally (Decker & Van Winkle, 1996).

Based on the interviews, it was clear that drug smuggling groups have little specialization or co-ordination of activities. The following quote shows how the lack of coordination between the nodes of the operation does not cause the entire operation to fail:

(17) I had a freighter, I knew the owner of the land strip in Guajira. Sometimes they had the loads waiting there for 2 or 3 weeks and no one would show up to pick it up. So this guy would call me to ask if I pick it up, I said yes, and the other people would call me. Sometimes they would ask me, for instance, to drop the merchandise in the Bahamas, and I would do it. But I never met those guys. The other guy, the broker, would do everything. He didn't work for anybody. He worked on commission and he trusted me.

Although these groups did not appear to be rationally organized to efficiently *maximize profits*, reports from the smugglers suggested they might be rationally organized around another goal: managing risk. In his examination of drug smuggling networks, Williams (1998) noted that while their organization is not highly formal, it does provide the group with various means of self-protection. For example, the lack a formal structure allows drug smuggling groups the ability to adapt quickly to changes in law enforcement and therefore minimize the risk of detection. The following subjects describe how smuggling operations in their groups were not based on maximizing profits, but instead on minimizing the risk of detection by law enforcement. As such, they were flexible and able to change methods, drugs, and routes.

(5) Never smuggled heroin, no. I was offered it, but [the boats] weren't ready for the loads at the time, but if we would have, probably I would have done

it, because it was a big profit of margin there. There was a big margin there. Smaller amount, and it was about three times the profit that you would get from coke.

(14) We started tightening up right after the war on drugs. Surveillance really picked up. So, I mean, the big plane was out of the question....It was getting more difficult. You know, the boats my cigarette boats were like, you know, law enforcement already knew. I mean, a 37 foot Midnight Express with four engines in the back, they knew what the boat was for. So, you know, my operation was getting obsolete already....We did [an air drop] right here in the Bahamas. It was in '89 or '90. I picked up maybe 150 keys and brought it into the Florida Keys, and after that, we waited a while and then we started changing things over here. We started air dropping right in the middle of the Gulf of Mexico. All the way from Colombia to the Gulf of Mexico....[I moved] from marijuana to cocaine, from the late '80s. Right after I moved to Georgia and I came back I'd say I came back smuggling cocaine because, you know, surveillance was heavier, and I didn't want to work bulky material. I wanted to work something that was there was plenty of money in it and something that I can get in and out and, you know, do my deliveries fast, didn't have to use a lot of people. You know, a lot more people were cooperating with the Government, and you didn't know who was who. So you wanted a small group. You wanted real trusting friends.

(29) A lot of people in smuggling are in more places than one. In other words, they not only do it in boats. They do it—now with Mexico in the business, they're doing vehicles. They're doing airplanes.

As noted earlier, trust and kinship are key concepts characteristics of the interactions between drug smugglers. The previous quote reinforces this point. Many subjects described how a structure of isolated nodes acts to protect individuals from detection when other involved in the operation are apprehended, thus suggesting the rational foundation of these group's organization is based on reducing risk.

(3) Never been stopped by law enforcement. Like I said, you know, they don't catch very much unless somebody tells them, and usually if you find out, when you interview people in prison, most of their cases or their indictments is dry. I mean, what I mean, they didn't catch the drugs. It was just a conspiracy unless somebody talked about. I'm sure you have found that out. They catch very little drugs coming through. I mean, they catch some, but very little overall. It's more dangerous after you have it here in the United States, distribution [more dangerous] than actually bringing it in.

(14) Never been arrested before this. It's been close, but no cigar. The guys who were bringing the marijuana, they were caught, but I wasn't. At the time they didn't talk. When they saw me....Well, they really didn't know me that well. I'm sure that they cooperated right away when they got caught, but they didn't know me that well. And I was you know, when you work with a lot of people, you got to you got to protect yourself. You can't, you know, you can't like, "Well, I live here. I live here. This is my last name." So [I gave them] no personal information at all.

end that international drug smuggling groups are rationally orga-
ound reducing risk *not* increasing profit. This contention is supported
one examines the persistence of their offending. Whereas a group that is
ed on maximizing profit would have high levels of persistence (continued
ctivity over periods of time), the drug smugglers we interviewed reported low
levels of persistence in their groups, in an effort to reduce risk of detection.

> (6) For a load of marijuana [I would make] 50 or $60,000. If I was single at that time, [money would last] about 3, 4 months. Party every day, you know. And that's when I look for another trip that someone needs done. [I would] get the money and party, and when the money starts to run out, I have 20 trip [offered] already. When my money starts to run out, have offers and just take one....I think I had offers from people because of both connections and I was success-ful. Because everybody knows me, you know?

> (14) Well, I knew the Government and law enforcement worked and how they set their surveillance, how they would do their interdictions, and I always I'd be a step ahead of them. My technology was always a step ahead of them. So I knew it was impossible for them to catch me....I would have taken more chances because I know I would have kept doing loads but the more you did it, that would increase your chance of being caught. You typically wait between loads, if I saw things good, it would be 2 weeks. And if [I] saw things bad, a month or two.

Although Warr (2002) proposed that groups of offenders show little evi-dence of rational planning that was not the case with the smugglers we inter-viewed. Although it is true that little planning or organization was done around the goal of maximizing profits, many subjects described their group taking advanced and deliberate measures to minimize the risk of detection. The following quote from an organizer illustrates how the groups are not searching for the most efficient means of smuggling cocaine into the United States. Instead, they consider techniques that are less likely to be subject to law enforcement detection, not produce the most profit possible.

> (1) I started meeting people, and you know, you learn. When I started doing my own stuff, I would get everybody in a room, the guys that was supposed to be involved in it, and in the planning of the project, how we're going to do it....I always figure that if all of them would come to the same conclusion that this is the best way to do it, then the police and the DEA, too, would think this was the best way to do it. So to me, the best way was to go all different [techniques].

DISCUSSION AND CONCLUSIONS

Much prior research and law enforcement descriptions over ascribe the level of organization among groups of offenders. One good example comes in the description of the organizational structure of active gang members.

Most gangs appear to be considerably less well organized than public or law enforcement conceptions of them. Similarly, descriptions of active burglars, armed robbers, and street level drug sellers depict individuals who live somewhat disorganized even chaotic lives. Very little structure is found in the offending activities of these individuals, and their behavior does not reflect a high degree of rationality. There is reason to suspect, however that high level international drug smugglers might have more formal structures, that their interactions would be more rule directed and that their behavior—as individuals and groups—would be more rational. After all, the large sums of money involved in such activities, coupled with the apparent sophistication necessary to successfully smuggle drugs and the age of the individuals involved would lead one to expect that such groups would be highly organized. Our analysis of the interviews with 34 high-level drug smugglers suggests quite a different picture.

A corporate organizational structure suggests a pyramid, with a leader on the top who passes on orders to a group of subordinates, who in turn pass on orders to their subordinates. From this perspective, organizational communication is structured by role and rank within an organization. High-level international drug smugglers describe a very different picture of their activities. Their drug smuggling groups resemble a series of loosely coupled nodes, small groups of individuals who work together largely unaware of who and what takes place at other steps in their "organization." Many of the individuals we interviewed didn't know anyone outside of their immediate group, and were recruited based on informal relationships, kinship, or ethnicity rather than the possession of a specific skill. Instead of being rationally focussed on maximizing profits, such groups are focused on the minimization of risk of detection and apprehension. We believe this is a key to understanding how their activities are organized.

It is important to have a fuller understanding of groups of offenders, whether those offenders are terrorist groups, gangs, burglars or international drug smugglers. Such an understanding is important to our ability to better understand their goals, structure, interactions and rationality. Equally important, such an understanding can more fully inform policies designed to minimize the harm caused by drug importation or gang activity or burglary. As with many offending groups, the information provided directly from offenders—in their own words—provides an important counterbalance to information gleaned from a single source of official information.

References

9/11 Commission Report. (2004). *Final report of the National Commission on Terrorist Attacks upon the United States*. New York: Norton.

Best, J., & Luckenbill, D. (1994). *Organizing deviance*. Englewood Cliffs, NJ: Prentice Hall.

Burt, R. (1992). *Structural Holes*. Cambridge, MA: Havard University Press.

Clarke, R. V., & Brown, R. (2003). International trafficking in stolen vehicles. In M. Tonry (Ed.), *Crime and justice: A review of research* (Vol. 30, pp. 197–228). Chicago: University of Chicago Press

Cressey, D. (1972). *Criminal organization: Its elementary forms.* New York: Harper & Row.

Cromwell, P., Olson, J., & D'Anne Avary. (1994). *Breaking and entering.* Thousand Oaks, CA: Sage.

Decker, S. H., Katz, C., & Webb, V. (2007). Understanding the black box of gang organization: Implications for involvement in violent crime, drug sales and violent victimization. *Crime & Delinquency, 54*(1), 153–172.

Decker, S. H., & Van Winkle, B. (1996). *Life in the Gang: families, friends, and violence.* Cambridge University Press.

Donald, I., & Wilson, A. (2000). Ram raiding: Criminals working in groups. In D. Canter & L. Alison (Eds.), *The social psychology of crime* (pp. 191–246). Burlington, VT: Ashgate.

Jacobs, B., Topali, V., & Wright, R. (2003). Carjacking, streetlife and offender motivation. *British Journal of Criminology, 43,* 673–688.

Sageman, M. (2008). *Leaderless jihad: Terror networks in the twenty-first century.* Philadelphia: University of Pennsylvania Press.

Shover, N. (1996). *Great pretenders: Pursuits and careers of persistent thieves.* Boulder, CO: Westview Press.

Waring, E. (2002). Co-offending as a network form of social organization. In E. Waring & D. Weisburd (Eds.), *Crime and social organization.* New Brunswick, NJ: Transaction.

Warr, M. (2002). *Companions in crime: The social aspects of criminal conduct.* New York: Cambridge.

Weber, M. (1946). Bureaucracy. In H. H. Gerth & C. W. Mills (Eds.), *Max Weber: Essays in sociology.* New York: Oxford University Press.

Williams, P. (1998). The nature of drug-trafficking networks. *Current History, 97,* 154–159.

Wright, R., & Decker, S. H. (1997). *Armed robbers in action: Stickups and street culture.* Boston: Northeastern University Press.

Zaitch, D. (2002). *Trafficking cocaine: Colombian drug entrepreneurs in the Netherlands.* The Hague, Netherlands: Kluwer.

Zhang, S. X. (2007). *Smuggling and trafficking in human beings: All roads lead to America.* Westport, CT: Praeger.

Zhang, S. X. (2008). *Chinese human smuggling organizations.* Stanford, CA: Stanford University Press.

16

Fencing: Avenues for Redistribution of Stolen Property

Paul Cromwell and James N. Olson

*T*his chapter is based on a study of active burglars in Texas. The authors interviewed 30 active burglars over an 18 month period. Each burglar subject was
interviewed on at least three occasions regarding their motivations to commit
*burglary, their target selection processes and the strategies they utilized to convert
their stolen good to cash. In this chapter, the authors explore the fencing of stolen
property from the perspectives of the thieves and those who purchase their goods—
the fences. They found that markets for stolen goods provide the catalyst and continuing motivation for property. Some young burglars find that they cannot sell their
stolen goods successfully and consequently soon give up stealing. However, burglars
who are able to convert their goods to cash at the first attempt may continue to repeat
this rewarding behavior. They also noted that receivers of stolen property vary widely
in the extent of their fencing activities and the level of professionalism involved.
A typology of fences is developed.*

Our study of burglary led us to consider the important role of the fence—
the market for the burglar's stolen goods. If burglary is the supply side of
stolen property, then fencing is the demand side. Without a reliable outlet
for stolen goods, burglary would have no point. Felson (1998, p. 38) states
that the significance of the fence for producing more crime cannot be overstated. Without the opportunity to sell stolen goods, the thief is limited to
stealing money only, or to very inefficient ways of selling on their own. We
sought, there-fore, to ascertain the dynamics of the thief–fence relationship;
to determine the strategies employed by receivers of stolen property; and,
how these strategies are implemented and understood by the participants
in this activity.

The role of the fence in initiating and sustaining property crime has been
recognized for centuries. F. L. Attenborough (1922), in *Laws of the Earliest
English Kings,* refers to a law from 690 A.D., which prohibited "harboring stolen cattle." However, as Steffensmeier (1986) reports, until 1691, under common law, receiving stolen goods was only a misdemeanor. He stated, "While

---

Source: Paul Cromwell and James N. Olson, *Breaking and Entering: Burglars on
Burglary.* Belmont, CA: Wadsworth Publishing Company. 2004. Used with
permission.

there was no strict law against receiving stolen property prior to the seventeenth century, it was recognized that the activity went on and that it was as bad as theft, which it may actually cause" (p. 63). Finally, in 1691 a statute (Act 3 and 4, William and Mary, c.9.s.4) made the fence an accessory after the fact and liable for severe corporal punishment or transportation. However, prosecution of the receiver was not possible unless the thief was first apprehended and convicted. In 1827, an act of Parliament made provision for an independent trial for the fence whether or not the thief was arrested (Act 7 and 8, Geo. IV c.29).

Perhaps the most notorious fence in criminal justice history was an Englishman, Jonathon Wild. McDonald (1980) described Wild as a notorious leader of a London criminal band of pickpockets, burglars, and other thieves. He set himself up as a "recoverer of stolen property," advertising in newspapers and pamphlets offering rewards for the return of stolen property with no questions asked. He bought the stolen goods and then conveyed them back to their original owners for a percent of their value. Thieves flocked to his "lost property office" with their stolen goods. Those items that were not claimed by their rightful owners, he altered so that they could not be identified and then sold them. Wild was so successful in this fencing venture that he even bought a ship to carry his plunder to Holland and other European ports. Thieves who did not cooperate with Wild were frequently turned in for the reward. It is estimated that he "captured" over 100 thieves during his 15-year career. In fact, as a well-known "thief taker" he was consulted by the Privy Council on occasion for his advice on crime control. However, becoming a public figure is something that no criminal should aspire to, for his high profile eventually brought him down. A notorious criminal who had been captured by Wild escaped from prison and publicly testified to Wild's activities. Soon other witnesses began to appear and Wild's activities resulted in his arrest and conviction. He was hanged in 1725 (McDonald, 1980).

STATE OF KNOWLEDGE ABOUT FENCES AND FENCING

Despite the fence's acknowledged contribution to crime, there has been a paucity of systematic study of this important category of offender. Due to the clandestine nature of the fence's activities, it is not surprising that so little research has been done. The professional fence has attracted the attention of some researchers, policy makers, and law enforcers (Blakey & Goldsmith, 1976; Klockars, 1974; Maguire, 1982; Steffensmeier, 1986; Walsh, 1977). Taken as a whole, although these studies provide a good overview of the activities of the professional fence, they ignore almost completely other categories of receivers. However, the nonprofessional receiver has not been overlooked completely. Hall (1952) included part-time receivers in his typology of fences. He identified the "lay receiver," who buys for personal consumption, and the "occasional receiver," who purchases for resale, but only infrequently. Stuart Henry (1978), who studied property crimes committed by ordinary people in legitimate jobs, concluded that receiving stolen property is not exclusively the province of professional criminals, but is an "everyday feature of ordinary people's lives." He states:

> The artificial distinction between "honest" and "dishonest" masks the fact that the hidden economy is the on-the-side, illegal activity of "honest" people who have legitimate jobs and who would never admit to being dishonest. (p. 12)

Henry found that many otherwise legitimate businessmen purchased stolen property when such purchases could be passed on to their customers at a profit.

Cromwell and McElrath (1994) surveyed 739 randomly selected adults in a southwestern city. Respondents were asked whether they had ever been offered stolen property for sale, whether they had bought stolen property, and whether they had friends or neighbors who had bought stolen goods. Thirty-six percent reported having been offered stolen goods. Thirteen percent had knowingly bought stolen goods and 39% reported that friends had bought stolen items. They reported that opportunity to purchase stolen goods and the motivation to buy them is related to a person's age, gender, ethnicity, and income. They stated:

> Routine activities theory predicts that buyers and sellers of stolen property must converge in time and space before an illegal transaction can occur. This convergence is facilitated when the lifestyles of buyers and sellers bring them together.... Younger persons and males were much more likely than older persons and females to be offered stolen goods for sale. These groups are also more likely to engage in "high risk" activities which might bring them into physical proximity with sellers of stolen goods. (p. 306)

A recent British study, The British Crime Survey (BCS), revealed that a large number of persons are offered stolen property by thieves. Eleven percent of respondents said that they had been offered stolen property in the previous year. A further 11% admitted that they had bought stolen goods in the past 5 years, whereas 70% thought that at least some of their friends and neighbors had purchased stolen goods for use in their home (Sutton, 1998). Further, the Youth Lifestyle Survey, also conducted in England, found that 49% of youths aged 14 to 25 years, who admitted offending in the last year, admitted that they had bought or sold stolen property in that period (Graham & Bowling, 1995).

There is little reliable and valid information regarding the extent of the fencing activities among nonprofessional receivers of stolen property, or the degree to which these amateur fences contribute to the initiation and continuing support of property crime. Some earlier studies concluded that thieves are unable to deal directly with the consuming public and must therefore operate through middlemen who have the financial resources to purchase stolen goods and the contacts to help in their redistribution (Blakey & Goldsmith, 1976, p. 1515). Indeed, this is true in large-scale theft where a thief must dispose of a truckload of television sets or a collection of fine jewelry. Most property crime, however, involves smaller quantities of stolen goods, of lesser value. Televisions, computers, CD players, car radios, most jewelry, handguns, VCRs, microwave ovens—the items that constitute the loot of the average burglar or shoplifter—may be redistributed without the assistance of a professional fence. The thief may sell many of these items directly to the ultimate consumer, to individuals who know or suspect that the items they buy are stolen property.

Some items may be traded for drugs, or sold to part-time receivers—those whose primary business activity is something other than buying and selling stolen property. Other stolen merchandise may be sold in pawn shops, flea markets, and garage sales to consumers who do not know or suspect that it was stolen.

We found that many burglars sought alternative outlets for their stolen goods. They reported selling their stolen items to ordinary citizens in bars, stores, parking lots, and even door-to-door. Others had regular customers for certain types of goods, and still others sold to otherwise legitimate businesses (bars, truck stops, etc.) who were known to be open to an opportunity to buy stolen items.

In order to understand how burglars and other thieves converted stolen property to cash, we interviewed both thieves and those who bought from them. We analyzed the thief's perspective by observations and interviews with active burglars and shoplifters, and through analysis of statements given to the police by arrested burglars and shoplifters. We obtained the receiver's outlook through interviews with professional and nonprofessional fences. We believe that amateur receivers who purchase stolen property do so primarily for personal consumption.

INTERVIEWS WITH BURGLARS

Burglar subjects were asked to describe (1) the process of locating and selecting a buyer for property they stole; (2) how items obtained in burglaries are sold or bartered; (3) the extent to which the fence determines the goods to be stolen; (4) the extent to which receivers provide aid and strategy to thieves in selecting targets; (5) the decision-making processes that determine what items are offered to which receivers; (6) the prices expected and paid for certain items; and (7) the extent, if any, to which fences specialize in one type or class of merchandise.

INTERVIEWS WITH FENCES AND OTHER RECEIVERS

During the course of this study our burglar informants introduced us to many of their regular receivers. Because we had been vouched for by burglars whom they knew and trusted, we had little trouble in obtaining their consent to be interviewed. We approached eight fences in this manner and six of them agreed to be interviewed. Four of them were interviewed extensively over several days or weeks. Interviews with two others were concluded in a session lasting an hour or two. One, a professional fence, allowed us to observe his activities from the back room of a small liquor store, which was a front for his fencing activities.

We also interviewed 19 persons who had purchased stolen property directly from a thief. These subjects were students in our classes, friends and acquaintances, or friends of friends who heard about the study and agreed to talk to us about their experiences. Some of these individuals were one-time purchasers only. Others, however, were regular customers of a thief or thieves.

These interviews—with thieves, fences, and others who knowingly bought stolen property—were subjected to qualitative analysis wherein we derived patterns and constructed typologies from the extensive descriptions.

INTERVIEWS WITH PROFESSIONAL BURGLARS AND FENCES

Professional burglars must have reliable outlets for their stolen merchandise. Most sell their goods to one or more professional fences. Dealing directly with the consumer is too irregular and an uncertain way of doing business. Other burglars, however, have limited access to the professional fence. Novice burglars, juveniles, and drug addicts often find it hard to establish regular business relationships with fences. Novices and juvenile burglars do not often steal "quality" merchandise and have not been "tested" regarding their trustworthiness. Drug addicts have a similar handicap in marketing their goods. They are considered unreliable and untrustworthy because of their drug habits. Although several addict-burglars reported that they occasionally sold their stolen merchandise to a professional fence, most had to seek less rewarding and more risky alternative channels for their goods. Many resorted regularly to direct sales to the consuming public. One young burglar, who regularly sold his stolen goods directly to consumers, said:

> I hear about somebody who want a TV or aVCR. I ask 'em how much they want to pay, and then I go get them one. If I already got some stuff, I ask around if anybody want to buy it.

A heroin-addict-burglar reported:

> I sell my stuff to [a local fence, name deleted] when I can. Sometimes he buys stuff from me. Most of the time he don't. He don't trust addicts.

Another informant told the interviewer that he had regular customers for his merchandise. He described his "self-fencing" in the following manner:

> There is this lady who buys big dresses—like bigger than size sixteen. She pays good too. Another lady will buy jewelry and stuff if I have it. I know about ten

people who buy meat. Whatever is on the price tag, they give me half price. There is even a policeman—he used to be a policeman—he buys guns if I get one.

Most of the burglars interviewed would have preferred to sell their goods to a fence. They believed the fence to be a more reliable and less risky market. However, of the 30 informants in the study, only 7 (23%) reported that they could absolutely depend on the professional fences in the community to take their goods. Others reported only occasional business dealings with professional fences. The following statement was typical:

If I get guns. Not junk—like Saturday-nite specials—stuff like Smith and Wessons—I can sell to the fences. I sold some big diamond rings and a Rolex to [local fence, name deleted] last year. They don't buy TVs and VCRs though.

Professional fences reported a strong aversion to doing business with drug addicts and juveniles. However, one fence, while expressing his contempt for drug addicts, bought stolen items from several obvious drug users while we were observing. He explained that, "So many thieves these days are addicts that you got to do a little business with them or you go broke." Another fence, more adamant in his refusal to do business with drug addicts, posted a sign over his cash register. It stated, "NO ADDICTS."

The fences reported that amateurs, drug users, "kids," and other "flakes," could not be trusted. They "snitch" and turn in their buyers when arrested. Professional thieves do not so readily "give up" their meal tickets—their market for stolen goods. Several reported that they would give up their co-offenders before their fence. One expressed his attitude as follows:

Shit! Thieves are easy to find. I can get somebody to help me do a crime any-where. Fences—they harder to replace. You turn in [local fences] and nobody gonna do no business with you after that.

INTERVIEWS WITH NONPROFESSIONAL RECEIVERS

We also interviewed 19 nonprofessional receivers. These were persons who had bought stolen items for personal consumption and/or resale, but who did not depend on fencing for all or most of their livelihood. Some had bought stolen property only once or twice. Others were regular consumers of stolen goods. One of these fence/consumers, a college professor who had been buying clothing for himself and his family from a group of burglars and shoplifters for over 20 years, described his activities as follows: "I go to [department store] and pick out what I want, and tell [thief]. He brings it around in a few days. I pay one-third of the price tag"

I know this guy. He's a pot head. He gets speakers and CD players, and all kind of stuff like that. I've bought stuff from him a lot.

A homemaker in a low-income neighborhood explained how she became a customer of a shoplifter:

> My friend said she bought meat from this drug addict. She said she could get me some meat at half price. First, I bought some steaks for half price. Now he comes by my house every payday and we. get all our meat from him. Other stuff too, sometimes.

More than one-half (n = 11) of the nonprofessional receivers we interviewed own or are employed by legitimate businesses, and occasionally buy stolen property at their place of business, primarily for resale. But, unlike the professional fence, they do not rely on buying and selling stolen property as their principal means of livelihood. To them, fencing is a part-time enterprise, secondary to, but usually associated with, their primary business activity. One of these part-time receivers justified his regular purchases from a thief, saying:

> It's not like you have anything to do with the guy stealing the stuff. He has already stole it. If I didn't buy it someone else would. I just take advantage of a good deal when I can. It's good business."

Another explained, saying:

> I don't even know for sure the stuff is hot. All I know is I can buy brand new tires for twenty bucks apiece. The last ones I got from him were Michelins. . . . I'm going to turn that down?

A dry-cleaner whose sideline was buying and selling stolen men's suits from shoplifters reported:

> I can put them in a bag and run them in with my regular cleaning. I don't make a big profit. Some weeks I don't buy anything. Mostly I sell to some friends and family. It helps out when business is slow.

ANALYSIS OF ARREST REPORTS

We analyzed 190 statements (confessions) given to police by arrested burglars in the study jurisdiction for 1 year, in which the burglars told police where and how they had disposed of the stolen property. The alleged receiver(s) of the stolen property were noted and classified as a professional fence, drug-dealer, part-time receiver, ordinary citizen, and so on, through information derived as follows: that contained in the police report; with the help of knowledgeable police detectives; with the assistance of thief "informants"; or, in some cases, through our own knowledge of the criminal community. Other information in the police report that related to the receiver (the thief's reason for choosing a particular receiver or class of receiver, the amount paid for the items, etc.) was also analyzed. The analysis revealed that only 21% of the stolen property was sold to professional fences. More than half (56.4%) was sold to nonprofessional receivers, including drug dealers. Only 12.1% was sold to pawn shops. The remaining 10.5% was reported to have been kept by the thief for personal consumption, thrown away, given away, or recovered by police before redistribution. The following statements are representative:

> We took the microwave to [address deleted] and we sold it to an elderly Mexican lady for $30.
> I traded this stuff [cartons of cigarettes] to a man named Mario on the south side for heroin.
> The place where we took the guns was a house on [street name deleted] in [town]. A man named [name deleted] lives there. He is in a motorcycle gang named the Outlaws. They buy guns.
> Then I went back to the 7-11 and sold the VCR to [a customer in the parking lot]. I sold the disc player and the VCR to [name deleted] at [name deleted] Liquor Store.
> I went in local tavern] and asked if anyone wanted to buy some cigarettes. Three or four people asked me how much. All I had was Salems and they wanted Marlboros. The bartender said he'd take 'em and sell them to some guy he knows smokes Salems.
> I sold the disc player and the VCR to [name deleted] at [name deleted] liquor store.
> About two weeks ago I met a man named [name deleted]. I met him through the wife of a friend of mine. She told me that [name deleted] might be willing to buy some stolen TVs I had from a burglary a few days before. I took the TVs over there and we plugged them in to see if they worked, and they did and he gave me $50 each for them.

WHY BUY STOLEN PROPERTY?

Buying stolen property involves many different motives. It represents a means of livelihood for some people—individuals who earn all or a significant proportion of their income from fencing. For others, as Steffensmeier (1986) suggests, "fencing they do more or less helps keep them afloat, get over the hump in their legitimate business, or gives them a little extra pocket money" (p. 118). For many others, buying (and occasionally selling) stolen property is a means of economic adaptation. Henry (1978) and Smith (1987) refer to this activity as constituting an "informal economy" or "hidden economy." Participation means more than stretching the dollar. It may, as Gaughan and Ferman (1987) suggest, be a means of economic survival. They write:

> A number of case studies have shown that low income communities rely on informal economic resources. The importance of hustling in the black ghetto,

the persistence of tight kinship networks in working-class urban communities, and the increasing visibility of street peddlers and entertainers testify to this. (p. 23)

Several informants told us that they could not survive [economically] without "hustling." One reported:

I buy my baby's clothes from this booster [shoplifter]. He sells lots of stuff—even deodorant, aspirin, and medicine. I get cigarettes from another thief. My mother gets all her meat from a booster.

A housewife/informant reported that she occasionally bought from a burglar of her acquaintance and then resold some of the various items. She stated that the income from this source allowed her to stay at home with her children rather than having to seek outside employment.

While for some, buying and/or selling stolen property was purely economic activity, we were unable to differentiate subjective motivations from economic motivations in many transactions. Psychosocial dynamics were often inextricably bound with economic motives. Some informants reported that they simply could not resist a bargain. Both thieves and receivers reported that "getting a good deal" was an important motivation for the buyer of stolen goods. Some reported buying items for which they had no immediate use, because the "price was right" or that they liked "beating the system." For still others, the occasional purchase of stolen property provided excitement in an otherwise pedestrian existence. One lawyer, for instance, asserted that he bought stolen property not just because he wanted certain items or for the money he might make reselling the items, but also for the "insider feeling" he got through these associations (also see Shover, 1971, p. 153). Another "amateur" receiver reported that she was a member of a group of office workers who bought clothing from several shoplifters who "made the rounds" in various offices and businesses in the area. The women frequently placed orders for items of clothing and paid a prearranged price for the items when the shoplifter returned with the goods. Our informant revealed that the items they purchased were often bought as gifts for friends and relatives. She described a sort of "party atmosphere" around the office on the day the shoplifter was due to arrive with the goods they had ordered days before. As described by our informant, the transaction appeared to be as much social as economic in nature.

One theme that appeared to characterize nonprofessional receivers was the tendency to neutralize or rationalize their involvement in the purchase of stolen property. Almost all of those interviewed disassociated themselves from the theft, and by extension, the victim(s). Many rationalized that "It was already stolen. If I didn't buy it, someone would." They appeared to view the purchase of stolen property as victimless crime, if crime at all. Many neutralized their purchases as "Simply getting a bargain," or that the victim was an insurance company or a big business that "expects to lose a certain amount of merchandise," and makes up for the loss by increasing prices. Many reported that they did not know for sure that the items were stolen. One informant justified her purchase of a new VCR for $50, stating:

> Okay, it's maybe too good a deal to be completely honest. I asked him if it was stolen and he said, "No," and I took his word for it. That's all I can do. I don't want to know either.

Burglars and other thieves appeared to intuitively understand the psychology of selling stolen property directly to the consumer. Most reported that the items must not be explicitly represented as stolen, yet the buyer must believe them to be illegally obtained, and therefore a "good deal." One burglar/informant occasionally purchased cheap costume jewelry from a discount store and sold it as genuine on street corners to passersby. Although he did not specifically represent the jewelry as stolen, he implied that it was. He reported that he usually made a good profit from this scam. He concluded:

> People are basically dishonest. They just don't like to admit it to themselves.

Shover's (1971) informant described the same phenomenon, stating: "It's the excitement of buying a piece of stolen goods. If you told them...that it was legitimate, they wouldn't buy it" (p. 153).

Several burglars reported that they devised elaborate stories about the source of their stolen items. They explained that buyers like a good story, even if they don't really believe it. The cover story serves to relieve the buyer's anxiety over buying stolen property. An articulate burglar, a college graduate who turned to burglary after becoming addicted to heroin, analyzed the citizen—receivers he did business with, saying:

> People need to feel good about themselves. Most folks can't accept that they are as crooked as us [burglars]. You gotta help 'em out a little. Give 'em a story about the stuff They know you're lying. Doesn't matter. They need it to keep you and them separated in their minds. You're the thief and they're the good guys.

A TYPOLOGY OF RECEIVERS

It is impossible to characterize those who buy stolen property as a homogeneous category. Rather, they are a diverse group ranging from professional criminals with ties to organized crime (Klockars, 1974; Steffensmeier, 1986) to respected citizens such as schoolteachers, business-persons and office workers who buy stolen goods for personal consumption (Henry, 1978; Cromwell & McElrath, 1994). They may be differentiated by: (1) the frequency with which they purchase stolen property; (2) the scale or volume of purchases of stolen property; (3) the purpose of purchase (for personal consumption or for resale); and (4) the level of commitment to purchasing stolen property. On the basis of these criteria, we distinguished six categories of receivers or fences:

1. Professional fences
2. Part-time fences
3. Professionals who trade their services for stolen property
4. Neighborhood hustlers
5. Drug dealers who barter drugs for stolen property
6. Amateurs

PROFESSIONAL FENCES

The professional fence is one whose principal enterprise is the purchase and redistribution of stolen property (Blakey & Goldsmith, 1976; Chappell & Walsh, 1974; Klockars, 1974; Steffensmeier, 1986). Professional receivers may trans-act for any stolen property for which there is a resale potential or may special-ize in stolen property that they can commingle with their legitimate stock or legitimate business (e.g., jewelry, dry cleaning, appliance sales, or service). The professional receiver generally makes purchases directly from the thief and almost exclusively for resale. These receivers operate proactively, establishing a reliable and persistent flow of merchandise and buying regularly and on a large scale. As a result of this commitment, the professional receiver acquires "a reputation among law breakers, law enforcers and others in the criminal community" (Klockars, 1974, p. 172). Although professional fences frequently operate "legitimate from a burglar of her acquaintance" businesses as fronts for their fencing activities, fencing is their primary occupation.

PART-TIME FENCES

The part-time fence functions in a somewhat nebulous domain between the true professional fence and other categories of receivers. The part-time fence is differentiated from the "professional" fence by frequency of purchase, volume of business, and degree of commitment to the fencing enterprise. Usually they do not buy as regularly as do professional fences, nor do they buy in volume. Further, part-time fences do not depend on fencing as their principal means of livelihood. We identified two general sub-types of part-time fences: (a) the passive receiver—who purchases stolen goods either for personal use, or for resale to an undifferentiated secondary consumer; and (b) the proactive receiver—who buys for resale only, and who may take an active role in the theft by placing orders for specific merchandise and pro-viding offenders with information about potentially lucrative targets for bur-glary in the same way as professional fences.

Passive buyers are known (by thieves) to be buyers of stolen goods. They are "passive" because they do not actively solicit thieves as suppliers, nor do they contract to buy certain items from thieves. Their commitment as receivers is only at the level of being occasionally available to buy certain items of stolen property when offered by a thief. We identified several passive buyers during the study, including a truck stop operator who bought stolen tires and tools, the manager of a video rental business who bought stolen VCRs and videotapes, and a jewelry store proprietor who bought gold jewelry and silverware. Like all part-time receivers, the passive receiver does not buy in volume, and does not depend on fencing as a principal means of livelihood. They may integrate the stolen items into their regular stock, or may personally use the stolen goods—as with the case of an automobile mechanic who buys stolen tools. Like all part-time fences, they are not considered reliable outlets by thieves. They buy only when they have funds available, and/or when they need the particular item(s) offered by the thief. They usually do not have in mind a specific customer to whom they might resell the merchandise.

Proactive receivers mimic professional fences in many respects; however, they do not rely on buying and selling stolen goods for the major part of their livelihood. Their fencing activity is an on-the-side activity, part-time crime. The proactive buyer may contract with a thief for certain items for which he or she has a market. They may actually "take orders" from customers for certain items and arrange to purchase those items from a thief or thieves. Several burglar/shoplifter informants reported that they occasionally stole certain items "on order" from both professional fences and from part-time receivers.

The part-time receiver might even have greater access than the professional fence to strategic information regarding potential victims. Because they are otherwise legitimate citizens and businesspersons, they may be trusted by their colleagues and friends with information regarding their possessions, schedules, and security precautions.

We identified three proactive part-time fences. They were each otherwise legitimate businesspersons. One owned a jewelry store and the majority of his income was from the legitimate profits of the store. However, he occasionally contracted to buy certain specific items of jewelry from a professional thief. In many cases the jeweler had originally sold the items to the victim—only to steal them back. Another proactive part-time receiver, a gunsmith, gained extensive knowledge about a customer's gun collection through his profession, and used that information to provide inside information to a thief about security arrangements and particular items to be stolen. In another case, a pawnbroker provided a thief with descriptions of a customer's jewelry and the details of the customer's vacation plans, which the customer had revealed to him during a conversation.

PROFESSIONALS WHO TRADE SERVICES
FOR STOLEN PROPERTY

These fences are persons whose legitimate occupations place them in close association and interaction with thieves, as in the case of police officers, criminal defense attorneys, or bail bond agents. These receivers may operate from a different economic motivation than other receivers in that they stand to lose financially by refusing to participate in the redistribution of stolen property. This is particularly true for bail bond agents and criminal defense attorneys, who may provide legitimate professional services to property offenders who cannot pay for these services with anything but stolen property (or the proceeds from their illegal activities). Thieves constitute a significant market for the services that these receivers provide legitimately. To refuse such trade would eliminate these "customers" and would severely curtail earnings. For some, it is but a small step from, accepting stolen property in return for professional services, to placing orders for items to be stolen. During the study, a bail bond agent showed the interviewer a matched pair of stainless steel .357 magnum revolvers that had been stolen for him "on order" by a client for whom he had posted bond. He freely acknowledged accepting stolen property occasionally in exchange for his services, justifying his actions by saying, "When they are in a bind and don't have any money, I try to help out." Another individual, a criminal defense lawyer, was completely candid about his occasional purchases of stolen property from clients, enthusiastically describing items he had received in exchange for his legal services. He described how he had agreed to represent a burglar in a criminal case, telling him that he wanted a gold Rolex in exchange for his services. He proudly displayed the $12,000 watch to the interviewer and stated, "This is a special order."

NEIGHBORHOOD HUSTLERS

The neighborhood hustler buys and sells stolen property as one of many hustles—small-time crime and confidence games—which provide a [usually] marginal living outside the conventional economic system. The neighborhood hustler may be a small-time fence, or he or she may be a middleman who brings thieves and customers together, earning a percentage of the sale for service rendered. The neighborhood hustler may also be a burglar who, on occasion, tries a hand at marketing stolen items for others. By definition, he or she is a small-time operator (Blakey & Goldsmith, 1976). Most do not have a place of business, as such. Instead, they work out of the trunk of a car, or from their home. One such entrepreneur described himself as follows: "I'm a hustler. I can get you what you want. You got something you want to sell? Tell me. I know where to go and who to see. Ain't nothing happens over here in the Flats [the area of town where he lived] that I don't know about." According to others who knew him, although he was grossly exaggerating his abilities, he was an almost stereotypical neighborhood hustler. Few experienced thieves would trust him to buy directly or to sell their merchandise for them. Several informants described him as a snitch whose hustles included "giving up" the thieves with whom he did business. He was therefore limited to buying from juveniles, drug addicts, and novice thieves who could not market their goods in a more reliable manner.

For some, hustling involves both buying stolen goods for personal consumption, and dealing in stolen merchandise. One such neighborhood hustler among our informants bought cigarettes, food, and clothing for personal use, and bought other items for resale. At the time of our interview, she had recently bought 20 rolls of roofing tar paper and 100 gallons of house paint from a thief and resold the items to a building contractor for a $75 profit. Her hustles also included some low-level street drug dealing, which occasionally involved bartering drugs for stolen goods, which she then resold.

DRUG DEALERS WHO BARTER DRUGS FOR STOLEN PROPERTY

Although not every drug dealer will barter for drugs, our interviews with thieves and fences suggest that many street level dealers consider fencing and drug sales to be logically compatible enterprises. There are two apparent economic motivations for their willingness to barter: (1) bartering increases their drug sales, opening their market to those with stolen property but without cash; and (2) they can increase their profits by marketing the stolen property at a price well above that given in trade to the addict/thief. One such fence, in discussing the advantages of the arrangement, said: "Lot of people come to me 'cause I'll take trades. Won't take no junk or TVs or shit like that. If they got guns, jewelry—then we can do business."

Several of the burglar/drug users we interviewed regularly bartered stolen property for drugs. Rather than searching for an outlet for the goods, they went directly to the drug dealer and obtained drugs in exchange. Although they reported that they did not receive the best possible price for their merchandise from the drug dealer, the speed and efficiency of the operation made the arrangement attractive. One subject said, "This is like one-stop shopping."

Wright and Decker also found that some burglars in their study sold their stolen goods to drug dealers or traded them for drugs:

Many of the tough inner-city neighborhoods of St. Louis have an informal economy that operates in part on the sale of stolen property. Local drug dealers often play a prominent role in this economy, both as buyers and sellers, because they have access to ready cash and good illicit connections to potential customers. (p. 181)

One of their informants explained: "Most of the time I want to buy drugs, so I take them stuff to the drug man. Instead of giving me money—he don't want to give out money 'cause he's making money—so he'll trade you his merchandise for your merchandise" (p. 182).

AMATEURS

With the exception of the professional thieves in the sample (n = 5) all had sold their goods directly to consumers on one or more occasions. The least experienced, the juvenile and drug-using thieves, were most likely to sell directly to the consumer on a regular basis. We distinguished two general categories of amateur receivers: (1) strangers approached in public places; and (2) persons with whom the thief has developed a relationship and who buys more or less regularly, for personal consumption.

Approaching strangers in public places is risky behavior with a relatively low success rate. It is looked upon with contempt by almost all thieves, and practiced regularly only by those with no other outlets available for their merchandise. Juveniles and drug addicts are most likely to use this technique for disposing of their merchandise. While many thieves in our study expressed their disdain for selling stolen items in this manner, the analysis of confessions given to police by burglars and other thieves revealed that much of the stolen items of these thieves was sold in this manner. Furthermore, many of the nonprofessional receivers we interviewed reported that they had previously bought stolen items from thieves who approached them in a public place. This suggests that the practice may be more widespread than was indicated in the interviews with burglars.

Wright and Decker also found that a percentage of their burglar subjects approached strangers in public places offering their stolen goods for sale. Twelve of ninety offenders in their sample said they usually sold, at least in part, to strangers. One of their subjects reported: "Man, just like if I see you on the street I walk up and say, 'Hey, you want to buy a brand new nineteen-inch color TV?' You say, 'Yeah,' and give me $75. I'll plug it up for you" (p. 189).

Our burglar informants expressed similar sentiments:

I hang at the parking lot at [local chain food store] when I got something to sell. I go up to people that looks like they might buy something. Ask them if they manna buy whatever I got.

Don't go up to no rich looking people or old people. Mostly young white dudes is interested.

Course, ya gotta be careful cause cops is mostly like that too—young, white dudes.

A second category of amateur receivers includes those who have developed relationships with one or more thieves and buy stolen property with some regularity. Most buy primarily for personal consumption. Others occasionally resell the stolen property they buy. Several reported reselling their "hot" merchandise at garage sales or through flea markets. Two of the "amateurs" resold the merchandise to friends and coworkers. One amateur fence, a public schoolteacher, began her criminal career when she was approached by a student who offered her a "really good deal" on a microwave oven. She stated that she originally bought the oven to help the student, whose family was suffering financial problems. Afterward, the student began to offer her "bargains" regularly, and she became a frequent customer. Eventually she began to offer her colleagues the opportunity to "get in on a good deal," and even posted the following note in the teachers' lounge:

NEED ATV, VCR, MICROWAVE, ETC.?????

SEE ME BEFORE YOU BUY.

½ OFF RETAIL.

Usually the teacher did not profit financially in this exchange. Instead, she garnered the goodwill and appreciation of those to whom she afforded merchandise at well below wholesale prices. Although she admitted to the interviewer that she "probably knew, deep down inside" that the items were stolen, she had never previously admitted it to herself. In explaining her motivation for purchasing goods in such an unconventional manner, she ironically described them as "a real steal."

Some individuals begin as amateur fences and become more deeply involved as a result of the irresistible gains and the virtual absence of sanctions entailed in purchasing stolen property. The overwhelming increase in profits and the thrill of "beating the system" (or at least making a good deal) tempt them into increasing their participation in the distribution of stolen property. One such amateur, turned part-time fence—a social worker—began her fencing activities when her husband purchased a household appliance from a thief he met in the course of his business as a plumber. At first, their purchases were for their own consumption. Later, they bought Christmas presents for family members. Eventually they established a thriving family business buying stolen property from thieves and selling it in garage sales and flea markets, as well as to amateur receivers cultivated by the husband through his business colleagues and customers. The informant told the interviewer that she and her husband had put their son through college with the proceeds.

SUMMARY AND DISCUSSION

The extent to which fences contribute to the incidence of property theft has been a central issue of debate. In the late 18th century, English magistrate Patrick Colquhoun (1797) called for vigorous action against fences in London, stating, "Nothing can be more just than the old observation, 'that if there were no Receivers there would be no Thieves'" (p. 298). Colquhoun's observation continues to have currency. Many believe that if fences could be put out of business, property crime rates would be dramatically reduced (Blakey & Goldsmith, 1976; Walsh, 1977). The fence is portrayed as not only providing a market for stolen goods, but also serving as an instigator and initiator of property theft.

This perspective has been criticized by other observers who argue that the "conception of the fence's role in property theft is bigger and more important than it ought to be, and that the involvement of other participants in an illegal trade is overlooked" (Steffensmeier, 1986, p. 285). Stuart Henry argues that viewing the fence as the prime mover of property theft rests on pretending that real crimes are committed by "real" criminals, not by ordinary people, and certainly not by oneself (cited in Steffensmeier, 1986, p. 286).

The extent to which ordinary people participate in the hidden economy (buying and selling stolen goods) is yet undetermined. However, our findings suggest that this part-time crime is ubiquitous (see also Henry, 1978; Cromwell and McElrath, 1994; Sutton, 1998). Unlike the professional fence, these individuals do not perceive themselves as criminal, or as part of the impetus for property crime. Yet, they provide a ready market for stolen property, particularly for the young, inexperienced, and drug-addicted thieves who lack connections with professional fences.

Markets for stolen goods provide the catalyst and continuing motivation for property. Some young burglars find that they cannot sell their stolen goods successfully and consequently soon give up stealing. However, burglars who are able to convert their goods to cash at the first attempt may continue to repeat this rewarding behavior. Mitigating the market for stolen goods might have a positive effect on halting some criminal careers before they begin (Sutton et al., 2001).

These relatively unstudied channels of redistribution of stolen property may have important implications for crime control. Research that identifies these channels and determines the extent to which stolen property is purchased directly by the consuming public or by "otherwise honest" businesspeople and citizens will assist in the development of strategies to inhibit and disrupt the distribution process.

AUTHOR'S NOTE

In the immediate years after this study was conducted, a new and widespread source for the marketing of stolen property evolved in the guise of huge international electronic auction markets such as EBay, Amazon.com, and Craiglist.com. Although these cybermarkets attempt to prevent the use of their sites as sources for sale of stolen property, the ubiquity and anonymity of the cyberworld makes them a major, albeit unwilling, player in the world of fencing.

References

Attenborough, F. L., Ed. (1922). *The Laws of the Earliest English Kings*. Cambridge: Cambridge University Press.

Blakey, R., & Goldsmith, M. (1976). Criminal redistribution of stolen property: The need for law reform. *Michigan Law Review, 74*, 1511–1626.

Chappell, R., & Walsh, M. (1974). Receiving stolen property: The need for systematic inquiry into the fencing process. *Criminology, 11*, 484–497.

Colquhoun, P. (1797). *A Treatise on the Police of the Metropolis*. London: H. Fry, Printer.

Cromwell, P., & McElrath, K. (1994). Buying stolen property: An opportunity perspective. *Journal of Research in Crime and Delinquency, 31*, 295–310.

Felson, M. (1998). *Crime and everyday life* (2nd ed.). Thousand Oaks, CA: Pine Forge.

Gaughan, J. P., & Ferman, L. A. (1987). Issues and prospects for the study of informal economics: Research strategies and policy. *Annals of the American Academy of Political and Social Science, 493*, 154–172.

Graham, J., & Bowling, B. (1995). *Young people and crime survey 1992–93*. London: Home Office.

Hall, J. (1952). *Theft, law and society*. Indianapolis, IN: Bobbs-Merrill.

Henry, S. (1978). *The hidden economy*. London: Martin Robertson.

Klockars, C. B. (1974). *The professional fence*. New York: Macmillan.

Maguire, M. (1982). *Burglary in a dwelling*. London: Heinemann.

McDonald, J. M. (1980). *Burglary and theft*. Springfield, IL: Charles C. Thomas.

Shover, N. (1971). *Burglary as an occupation*. Doctoral dissertation, University of Illinois. Ann Arbor, MA: University Microfilms.

Smith, J. D. (1987). Measuring the informal economy. *Annals of the American Academy of Political and Social Science, 493*, 83–99.

Steffensmeier, D. (1986). *The fence: In the shadow of two worlds*. Totowa, NJ: Rowman & Littlefield.

Sutton, M. (1998). Handling stolen goods and theft: a market reduction approach. Home Office Research Study, No. 178. London: Home Office.

Walsh, M. (1977). The Fence: A New Look at the World of Property Theft. Westport, CT: Greenwood Press.

Wright, R. T., & Decker, S. H. (1994). Burglary on the Job: Street Life and Residential Burglary. Boston: Northeastern University Press.

17

The Second Step in Double Jeopardy: Appropriating the Labor of Female Street Hustlers

Kim Romenesko and Eleanor M. Miller

*"T*opical" *life histories were obtained from 14 Milwaukee female street hustlers, aged 18 to 35, 11 of whom are members (or former members) of a "street" institution termed the "pseudo-family" (made up of a "man" and the women who work for him). The majority of the women interviewed were institutionalized at the time either at the Milwaukee House of Correction or at a residential drug treatment facility in Milwaukee. A putative and potential refuge to women responding to a dearth of licit employment opportunities and to the glitter and economic potential of the street, the pseudo-family actually emerges as a heteropatriarchal mechanism whose character, organization, and context serve to depress further, rather than enhance, the life chances of its female members. Once a woman is "turned out" by the "man" and enlisted in the pseudo-family, she is enmeshed in a tangled skein of conflicting emotions and motives; "wives-in-law" vie for the coveted position of "bottom woman" and for the attentions and regard of their "man," and the "man" schemes (in concert with other "men") to maintain his dominance and, above all, the profitability of the union. As female hustlers age and as their criminal records lengthen, they become marginal even to this world of last resort. Traded as chattel, often stripped entirely of property in the process of exchanging "men," and finally disowned when competition from other more naïve, more attractive, and more obedient women becomes too strong, street women find themselves doubly jeopardized by capitalistic-patriarchal structures that are pervasive in "straight" society and profound upon the street.*

This article is about Milwaukee women who make their living from street hustling. We attempt to document the operation of a patriarchal structure within the world of women's illicit work that parallels that which exists in the licit world of women's work and, ironically, further marginalizes females who hustle the streets of American cities primarily because of preexisting economic marginalization. The socioeconomic status of these women is, as a result of their experiences in this alternative labor market, even further

Source: Excerpted from The Second Step in Double Jeopardy: Appropriating the Labor of Female Street Hustlers. Kim Romeneska and Eleanor M. Miller. 1989 *Crime and Delinquency* 35: 109–135. Reprinted with permission of Sage Publications.

284 / ILLEGAL OCCUPATIONS

reduced with respect to the licit market because of the criminal involvement, frequent drug and alcohol dependency, psychological and physical abuse, and ill-health connected with the work of street hustling. A particularly tragic element of this process resides in the fact that for many, the world of the streets appears an attractive array of alternative work opportunities when compared to their experience of "straight" work. The impoverishment, dependency, and, ultimately, redundancy of women, particularly women of color, who work in "women's jobs" in the licit world of work and the impoverishment, dependency, and redundancy they experience in the illicit work world, we argue, constitute a situation of "double jeopardy."

That there are few viable opportunities for poorly educated, unskilled women like themselves in the licit job market is very clear to women who eventually become female street hustlers. That a parallel situation exists in the illicit job market, however, escapes the view of new female recruits to street hustling because that view is clouded by the appeal of feeling, many for the first time, personally desirable, agentive, and productive as women workers. Furthermore, we will attempt to demonstrate that the central mechanism by which female street hustlers are made dependent, and financially, socially, and physically insecure, the mechanism by which they, themselves, are commodified is the "pseudo-family"—a patriarchal unit made up of a "man" and the women who work for him.

Because nearly all of the literature written about street-level prostitutes (which we prefer to call female street hustlers because of the clear diversity in their everyday work that includes a broad array of street hustles), indicates that a major reason women enter street life is because of the perceived financial rewards available to them (Brown, 1979; James & Meyerding, 1976; Laner, 1974; Miller, 1986), we became interested in learning how participation in street life in general, and the pseudo-family in particular, actually affects women's financial situation and, more broadly, their life chances. It is the embeddedness of women's hustling work in the social network that is the "pseudo-family," then, that is the focus of this article.

BACKGROUND

Given the inaccessibility of lucrative legal work to most women in our society and the failure of our welfare system to maintain women and their children at a livable standard (Sidel, 1986), participation in the illegal activities of street life is a route that a certain proportion of women see as an occupational alternative. As James and Meyerding (1976, p. 178) say:

> Money-making options are still quite limited for women in this society, especially for unskilled or low-skilled women. Recognition of this basic sex inequality in the economic structure helps us see prostitution as a viable occupational choice, rather than as a symptom of the immorality or "deviance" of individual women.

One of our respondents, Elsie, described how and why she became involved in street life.

> I got married when I was eighteen. My husband, okay, when I got married, that was my biggest mistake 'cuz he never was around. I had all these little babies. When I was eighteen I had two [babies], when I was nineteen I had three. He wouldn't work, he wouldn't help support them, and there I'd sit in this little apartment with nothin'—no TV, nothin'—no milk for your babies and, you know, they gotta have milk and stuff. You know, I was so tired of runnin' to my people askin''em for, you know, favors: "Would you go buy the babies some milk?" You know, I was embarrassed doin' that. So then that's when I learned to take a check that wasn't mine and go cash it. You know that's what really drove me into it. For their sake, not to benefit myself—not at first it wasn't.

The women of this study, we argue, look to street life to obtain the status and economic stability that is largely unachievable for the children of the poor and near poor, be they male or female. The commodification of female sexuality offers them entree to the streets, often initially as prostitutes. As this analysis will show, however, street women are doubly jeopardized: Involvement in illicit street life is not a viable avenue to financial stability for women because of the institutionalized obstacles that exist in the underworld—obstacles as difficult to circumvent as those in "straight" society.

Work History

Most of the 14 female street hustlers included in this analysis worked at straight jobs at some point in their lives. (The few that did not became participants in street hustling in their early teens.) Straight work usually took place before the women's entrance into street life; however, in a few cases, women tried straight jobs in an attempt to leave street life. Although some have not given up on the idea that there is some kind of straight work that they could do as the basis of a career, most admitted that they could not go back to boring, low-paying work with inflexible hours. They believe that "the life" (short for street life, also called "the fast life") will pay off sometime in the near future. They think that things will improve, money will be saved, and they will retire from "the life" in comfort. If our analysis is correct, they are probably mistaken.

The types of straight jobs our respondents performed were low-status, low-paying, often part-time jobs that are heavily dominated by females. Examples of the types of jobs the women worked at are fast food attendant or cook, box checker at a department store, house-keeper, dietary aide, beautician, bakery shop clerk, assembly line worker for a manufacturing company, child care aide, hot dog stand attendant, cashier, waitress, hostess, receptionist, go-go dancer, and secretary.

Some women who tried to make it in straight society have been frustrated by their experience and have, essentially, given up. Brandy, a young black woman who participated in the study, had her first straight job when she was

18 years old. She performed clerical duties in Chicago but was eventually laid off. She said:

> I got laid off cuz the plant closed down and opened up in Oak Park and I didn't have a way out to Oak Park from the South Side of Chicago. After that, believe it or not, I was working at [a] hotel on Michigan Avenue in Chicago, Illinois, as a maid. After I took two tests, they gave me a promotion—I was supervisor of house-cleaning. . . . That's why it's weird for me to be goin' through the things I'm goin' through now [Brandy was incarcerated at the Milwaukee House of Correction at the time of the interview]. I'm not a bad person at all.
> How long were you supervisor of house-cleaning?
> Brandy: About two and a half years [until she was 21 years old].
> What did you do then?
> Brandy: Stayed at home and collect unemployment. . . and was lookin' for another job, but I never found one.

Other women, although they had no problem finding jobs, were not satisfied with the pay. Once women get a taste for making "fast money" on the street, it is difficult to go back. Tina describes this attraction to the street in the following comments:

> What [type of work] were you doing?
> Tina: Oh, I did a lot of things. . . . I was workin' at Marc's Bigboy as a waitress. I've been a waiter, I've been a host, I've been a private secretary, I've been a cashier. I've got a lot of job skills, also.
> You've had all these straight jobs and you've got lots of skills. What's the attraction to the streets?
> Tina: The money, the fast money. That sums it up.

Elsie, in the passage that follows, relates not only how difficult it is to live on the wages paid by many employers but also how sexism worked (and works) to keep women marginal to the job market. She is describing the first straight job that she had as a dietary aide and why she became disaffected.

> Elsie: I got the job 'cuz I really needed it. In fact, I had just turned 18 so they was payin' me $1.30 an hour. This was like in '67. Yea, '67 cuz my son was about a year old. They was payin' me $1.30 an hour. . . . See, I was stayin' at home. My mother, she was keepin' my baby. I'd get my check, I'd give her half and I'd keep half. Then, the shop was in walkin' distance, you know, from her house where we was stayin' and we'd get our lunch and stuff free cuz I was workin' in the kitchen. But still, that wasn't enough money for that hard work.
> How long did you work there?
> Elsie: I worked there nine months. . . . I would have stayed there but I was pregnant again. I was tryin' to keep it from them 'cuz back then you could only work 'til you was five or six months pregnant. And so I tried to keep it from 'em. I worked until I was nine months 'cuz, you know, I never got real big. So I was tellin' 'em I was like four months and I was really eight—so I could keep my job.

Finally, a few women reported simply being intolerant of supervised nine-to-five work and ending up getting fired from their jobs or quitting. It is interesting to note that the women who fall into this category tended to have the least skills.

What did you do then?

Rita: Worked in a hospital in the laundry department and hated it because it was hot, it was hard work, and I hated my boss.

How much did it pay?

Rita: Minimum wage.

How long did you work there?

Rita: Three months.

Why did you leave?

Rita: I've always gotten fired. But, okay, you could say that I've always gotten fired, but before they could fire me, I know when they're going to fire me, [so] I always quit. Before that "You're fired" comes out, I always quit.

What other kinds of straight jobs have you had?

Rita: Okay, my first job was in the hospital. Nurses aide was my last—I got fired there. A security guard for the telephone company.

What was the reason behind quitting most of them?

Rita: I just am not a nine-to-five person. ... Most of my jobs were during the day. I had to be there in the morning. I didn't have a car; transportation by bus, I didn't like that. So, it was like, I don't like to take buses. I like being my own boss. Work when I want to work, make good money.

For the uneducated and largely unskilled women of this study—whose experience with straight work was unfulfilling or whose jobs were unstable due to a volatile and sexist market place—participation in street life, with its promise of money, excitement, and independence, seemed the answer to their problems.

STREET LIFE

According to the women of this study, a prerequisite to working as a street hustler is that a woman must have a male sponsor, a "man," to act as a "keep-away" from other "men" who vie for a living on the street. She must turn her earnings over to this "man" in order to be considered "his woman" and to enjoy the "man's" protection. The "man," besides providing protection from other "men," gives his women material necessities and gifts and, most important, sex and love (Merry, 1980).

The following, from an interview with a respondent whom we have named "Chris," illustrates why street women need "men" to work. When asked why she worked and turned her earnings over to a "man" instead of working for herself and keeping her money, she said:

Chris: You can't really work the streets for your-self unless you got a man—not for a long length of time ... 'cause the other pimps are not going to like

> it because you don't have anybody to represent you. They'll rob you,
> they'll hit you in the head if you don't have nobody to take up for you.
> Yea, it happens. They give you a hassle. ... [The men] will say, "Hey
> baby, what's your name? Where your man at? You got a man?"

So you can't hustle on your own?

Chris: Not really, no. You can, you know, but not for long.

Women who do hustle on their own are called "outlaw" women, a term that clearly indicates that their solo activities are proscribed. Women who work as outlaws lose any protection that they had formerly been granted under the "law" of the street and are open targets for "men" who wish to harass them, take their money, or exploit them sexually.

Street life is male dominated and so structured that "men" reap the profits of women's labor. A "man" demands from his women not only money but respect as well. Showing respect for "men" means total obedience and complete dedication to them. Mary reports that in the company of "men" she had to "talk mainly to the women—try not to look at the men if possible at all—try not to have conversation with them." Rita, when asked about the rules of the street, said, "Just basic, obey. Do what he wants to do. Don't disrespect him. ... I could not disrespect him in any verbal or physical way. I never attempted to hit him back. Never." And, in the same vein, Tina said that when her "man" had others over to socialize, the women of the family were relegated to the role of servant. "We couldn't speak to them when we wasn't spoken to, and we could not foul up on their orders. And you cannot disrespect them."

Clearly, "men" are the rulers of the underworld. Hartmann's (1984, p. 177) definition of patriarchy is particularly apropos of "street-level" male domination.

> We can usefully define patriarchy as a set of social relations between men,
> which have a material base, and which, though hierarchical, establish or cre-
> ate interdependence and solidarity among men that enable them to dominate
> women. Though patriarchy is hierarchical and men of different classes, races,
> or ethnic groups have different places in the patriarchy, they also are united in
> their shared relationship of dominance over their women; they are dependent
> on each other to maintain that domination.... In the hierarchy of patriarchy,
> all men, whatever their rank in the patriarchy, are bought off by being able to
> control at least some women.

"Men," as the quotations that follow illustrate, and as Milner and Milner (1972) have written with regard to pimps, maintain a strong coalition among themselves allowing them to dominate women. As the number of women a "man" has working for him increases, the time he can spend supervising each female's activities decreases. It becomes very important that "men" be in contact with one another to assure the social and economic control of street women. With watchful "men" keeping tabs on their own and other "men's" women, women know that they must always work hard and follow the rules.

Rose gives an example, here, of one of the many ways in which "men" protect one another. Rose's sister, who is also involved in street life, was badly beaten by her "man" and decided to press charges against him. She decided to drop the charges because:

Rose: She got scared 'cuz he kept threatening her....His friends [were] callin' her and tellin' her if she didn't drop the charges they was gonna do somethin' to her. So she dropped the charges.

It is interesting to note that when working women are caught talking with "men" who are not their own, it is considered to be at the women's initiative and they are reprimanded. In other words, "men" can speak with whom they please, when they please, but women are not allowed to speak, or even look, at other "men." Ann gives another example of this element of the cohesiveness of "men":

If another pimp see you 'out of pocket' [breaking a rule] or bent over talkin' to another pimp or somethin' in their car, they will tell your man, 'Yea, she was talkin' to some dude in a Cadillac—he try and "'knock your bitch."'
hat the word they use."
What does it mean?
Ann: He tryin' to come up with her. He tryin' to have her for himself. That what they mean. That what they be sayin' all the time: "He tryin' to 'knock your bitch,' man. You better put her 'in check.— In other words, you better, how should I say it? "In check" mean, tell her what's happenin', keep her under control.
Or, if you be walkin' around on the stroll and stuff and somebody might see you sittin' down on the bench and they say, "Man, your ho [whore] is lazy! All the cars were passin' by—that girl didn't even catch none of 'em." 'Cuz they [the "men"] know you and stuff.

The mechanisms that keep women oppressed at the street level are parallel to those of the broader culture. The wage structure in the United States is such that many women cannot financially endure without men. On the street, women also need men to survive, because they are not allowed to earn money in their absence. In addition, women of the street must give all of the money they earn to their "man." A "man," in turn, uses the money to take care of his needs and the needs of his women—although, as we shall see, money is usually not distributed unconditionally but, rather, is based upon a system of rewards and punishments that are dependent upon the behavior of women.

THE PSEUDO-FAMILY

The pseudo-family is a family-like institution made up of a "man" and the women who work for him. Its female members refer to each other as "wives-in-law" and to the man for whom they work as "my man." By focusing on the pseudo-family, we try to isolate and expose a street-level mechanism for female oppression, and to explain why the "wife-in-law" is unlikely to revolt or leave her oppressive situation. Specifically, we attempt to describe how the pseudo-family, while seeming to offer love, money, and stability to the women who participate in it, is structured so that women, in fact, gain little. Our thesis, in other words, is that the security of the pseudo-family for the female street hustler is largely illusory.

The structure of the family is hierarchical and the "man" holds the top position. He collects all of the money that women earn and makes decisions about how it is spent. He is also the disciplinarian of the family: When a rule is broken, he is the person who decides upon and metes out the punishment. The "man" also has the final say about who is recruited into his family. Despite the fact that his women may oppose the idea of additional "wives-in-law," there is typically little they can do about it. If women refuse to accept their "wives-in-law" or try to make life difficult for them, they are likely to be thought "disrespectful" and, as such, will be punished. Next in the hierarchy of the pseudo-family is the position of "bottom woman." When a "man" and woman start out working only as an entrepreneurial couple who, at some later date, recruit another woman into the family to become the first woman's "wife-in-law," the most senior woman is accorded the privileged position of "bottom woman." "Bottom women" help to make sure that household is in good working order. "Bottom women" are also expected to keep tabs on their "wives-in-law" and to smooth out any differences that may occur between them.

The "man" of the family places a special trust in the woman that occupies the position of "bottom woman." It is, therefore, an enviable position and one to which "wives-in-law" aspire. To safeguard the position, then, and to control the jealousy that her "wives-in-law" may feel toward her because of her higher status, the "bottom woman" must convince her "wives-in-law"—each individually—that they, in fact, are the "man's" favorite.

Dee, a 26-year-old, self-described Puerto Rican/white woman, has been involved in street life since she was 15. She has an extensive background as "bottom woman" and described how she kept her families (of up to six "wives-in-law") together.

> Were you always bottom woman?
> Dee: Any man I had, yea. Because it was the mind, the mental thing. If you can avoid jealousy and all that and keep a family together, and me being from keepin' families together, it was an easy thing—right up my alley. [You'd have to] make them feel they were number one and you were just a peon. [It] kept them around, kept them bringin' in $400.00 and $500.00 dollars a night.
> Did you get along with your wives-in-law?
> Dee: I would force myself to get along with them....I would be protection for them so, consequently, they wouldn't really fight with me, per se, but with each other. So that I would say that I'm ... [your]...friend and her friend and be the mediator between the two. I never really had any problems unless one of them violated some type of code.

To gain the trust of the "bottom woman" and to prove that she is held in high esteem, the "man" often passes on privileged information to the "bottom woman" about her "wives-in-law." Having this information increases the "bottom woman's" feelings of power and prestige and instills confidence in her and her position, motivating the "bottom woman" to do a better job for the "man." Although the information she receives could be used to flaunt the fact that she is her "man's" favorite, the "bottom woman" must remain discreet if she is to retain her position and keep the family together.

A female street hustler can also become a "bottom woman" by working her way up through the ranks of the family. Depending upon the situation, becoming a "bottom woman" in this way can take anywhere from a week to a number of years. Generally, young white women have the best chance of promotion because they make the most money (as a result of the racism of customers and to the fact that they can work in more and "better" locations than black women without attracting attention from the police), are without lengthy criminal records when first recruited to the streets, and tend to be more obedient. At least one of our respondents said:

> Rose: ["Men"] go for young womens and for the white womens. ... They figure the young wornens will get out there and maybe catch a case occasionally until she catch on [but] she won't go to jail...and then they think that white women can work anywhere, make more money ... without catching no heat from the police.

Although there is limited advancement for women, they can never rise to a status equal to the "man." The rules of "the game" explicitly state that "men" are to dominate women, and women, as subservient creatures, are to respect and appreciate that fact (Milner & Milner, 1972). As there are opportunities for promotions within the family, and into safer and more prestigious hustles outside of the family, women cling to the false hope that "their day will come." In addition, the competition among women for these positions, and for their "man's" affection, creates such divisiveness that it is unlikely that women will conspire to fight for significant changes in the street or pseudo-family structure. Thus "men" are assured that the status quo is maintained.

Male Control

The maintenance of male dominance at the street level is dependent upon "men's" ability to control women. The control of women by "men" is made possible, first of all, by the very fact that women are not allowed involvement in the life without "men" as their sponsors. As "men" are well aware, however, women will not accept them and their rule as against the rule and control of another "man" unless given adequate enticements. These take the form of love, money, and the accompanying sense of security. Once a woman has become attached to the "man," he is then in a position to control her more effectively. Lastly, when all else fails, "men" will resort to physical violence in order to maintain control.

Getting women into positions where they can be dominated begins during the "turning out" process—the process whereby a "man" teaches a woman how to become a street hustler. The "turning out" process, as Miller (1978, p. 142) notes:

> [I]nvolves a variety of subtle techniques of social control and persuasion on the part of the pimp. ... [It] involves several steps in which the pimp initially attracts the woman through his sexual and economic appeal and later changes her mind about the propriety of prostitution and the proper relationship between men and women. ... The critical factor in the beginning of the relation-ship is the establishment of control over the relationship by the pimp.

Elsie, whom we heard from earlier, is a 38-year-old black woman. She first met her "man" when she was 28 years old; he was 35. Since about the age of 19, Elsie had been intermittently involved in forgery and other petty street crimes. She was still on the fringe of the life, however, and therefore had never worked with a "man." Elsie described for us how, and under what circumstances, she was turned out by her "man."

> Okay, I had met this guy ... I knew about stuff like that but I had never indulged in it (prostitution). I'd done, you know, check forgin' and stealin' but that's it. Me and him was talking—he was dressed up all nice and nice lookin' and he had a big nice Continental outside. So I'm lookin,' you know? So I asked him, I said, "What kind of work do you do?" He said, "I sell insurance...." He said, "You married?" I said, "No, I'm separated but livin' by myself." He said, "Well, could I call you or come by your house, could you give me your number?" I said, "Yea." So I gave him the number. He called me a couple of times and I said, "Well, come back to my house!" I was all excited—I had the house all spic and span and he came over. Right about that time I was having a few problems 'cuz I owed some back bills and stuff—my phone was gettin' ready to be cut off and stuff. I didn't have no stereo or nothin'. So he come by there that night, looked around. I still didn't really know what was happening, you know. I told him I was in financial trouble, they were gettin' ready to cut my phone off—I need a TV and stereo and stuff. He said, "Well, I'm goin' to pay your phone bill and everything for you." And he did! He paid the phone bill the next day, he brought me a stereo, he did all that. He bought me a new outfit.
>
> One of my girlfriends ... she said, "Elsie, you're too naive." She said, "You don't know what he's supposed to be?" I said, "No." She said, "I think he calls himself a pimp." I said, "He's nice, look what he did." She said, "You know, that's the way they do. He trying to set you up." I said, "Girl, go away. I know what I'm doin." I was older than she was, you know, and she's trying to tell me. And sure enough, that's what it was.
>
> How did you find out?
>
> Elsie: He told me about it, okay. When I found out, I found out on the telephone. I said, "Yea, I heard you was, you know." He said, "No, who told you that?" I said, "I just heard it 'cuz a pimp is noticed on the streets." And he used the name Peachy, that was his street name. So I said, "If that's what you is, stay away from me, 'cuz I don't even want to get involved

with nobody like that." He said, "No, it ain't like that with me and you, we can just be friends." I said, "Well, I don't even want nothin' to do with you if it's like that. I got four kids, I ain't got time for nothin' like you." He said, "Elsie, it ain't like that. If you don't wanna do nothin' like that." He said, "I admit, I do do that. I got some ladies that, you know, give me money and stuff, but you ain't gonna have to be like that." He said we could just be friends, that we could have a relationship different from that, you know.
Did you believe him?
Elsie: Yea, I did! 'Cuz I liked him! So I fell for it. And then the next thing I knew, he came by and said, "Elsie, I got somethin' set up for you."

After Elsie had serviced her first trick, her "man" came to pick her up. She said:

I got in the car and I was sittin' up, lookin' all quiet and stuff. He said, "Did you get the money?" I said, "Yea." He said, "Where is it?" I said, "I got it." He said, "Give it here." I said, "All of it?" He said, "Yea, and then if you want some I'll give it to you." That's the part that hurted. I gave it to him. [I thought], "I'll never do that no more." But then, after that, I got smart, not really smart but I got a little wiser. Okay, when I would do some-thin' like that, I would stash me some money.

Rita, a 26-year-old white woman, first met her "man" when she was 18. However, as she describes it, "I was 18 when I met my man, but I was 19 when I first put money in his hand." Rita said that for some months she had had a girlfriend/boyfriend relationship with her "man." He had a 30-year-old white woman working for him but, according to Rita:

He wanted a white girl he could turn out himself. Apparently, she [his first woman] had been turned out by somebody else. But I was his turn out completely.

Her "man," like Elsie's, made sure that there was a strong emotional attachment before any money changed hands. Rita said:

He made me fall in love with him before I put any type of money in his hand. I was working three months and still dating him and not paying him. But he knew that he was getting me.
So he was turning you out but you weren't giving him any money?
Rita: No I was not. He knew I was falling in love with him, okay? Finally, that day came where we sat in the car. We had just gone out. I was sitting in the car with him, he had brought me home from going out—we'd gone out drinking. I was sittin' in the car with him and he turns to me and says, "Well, you know, we've been going out…and you know what I'm about and my lady's get-tin' kind of mad that ain't nothin' happening and you are working. It's either, you gotta start giving me some money or I can't see you no more." And I did not want that, I fell in love with the man. So it was like, okay, here you go buddy, am I yours now?

Rita also said that her "man" would not bail her out of jail during that initial period when she was not giving him any money. She said that the reason he wouldn't bail her out was that

> He was just tryin' to show me, "Look, if you go to jail, I'm there and I'm yours and you're mine, I'll get you out. But you're alone and I can't get you out. That's going against what this is all about."

As these excerpts illustrate, the establishment of an emotional tie between the "man" and the woman is an extremely important element of the "turning out" process. Even though a woman discovers relatively early that a "man's" affection is conditional (depending on her payment, respect, and obedience to him), she believes the payoff—being "taken care of' financially, socially, and emotionally—to be worth it. When "wives-in-law" enter the picture, however, and the woman finds that she must "share" her "man" with others, jealousy and conflict arise, creating instability within the family.

GETTING DISENTANGLED FROM THE PSEUDO-FAMILY

Changes in the composition of the pseudo-family are frequent and occur for various reasons. The intervention of the criminal justice system, the inability of "men" to control adequately the jealously of their women, the heavy drug use of street women and their men, and the decreased marketability of women as they age are all factors that affect family stability.

Criminal Justice System

Because of the highly visible hustles in which street women engage, frequent contact with criminal justice authorities is inevitable. When a woman is arrested and incarcerated, a new woman is often recruited into the pseudo-family to replace the lost earnings of the incarcerated woman. When the incarcerated woman is released and returns to her family, the family must adapt to the new amalgam of personalities. Often, however, the adaptation is unsuccessful and the result is that one of the women may leave the family in search of a better situation. The woman who leaves is replaced by another, creating new stresses within the pseudo-family, and the whole process is repeated.

Also, while incarcerated, women may be recruited into new families. One of the women interviewed-a veteran of the game-chose her new "man" by telephone from the House of Correction. She was recruited by one of his women who was also serving time. Another woman reported that she was considering leaving her "man" of nine years for a new "man" whom she met and corresponded with in the House of Correction via smuggled letters. Women who are unhappy with their current family situation, then, or women who are "between" men, have opportunities while incarcerated to join new families.

Drug Use

Excessive drug use by street hustlers and their "men" also erodes family stability. "Men" have a responsibility to their women to take care of business—to pay bills and post bond, dispense clothing and pocket money, and generally behave as a responsive (if not caring) family member—and women, in return, must provide "men" with money and respect. As Joan says, a real pimp "gonna take care of her 'cuz she's takin' care of him." In other words, there are mutual obligations between "men" and women. When "men" use hard drugs excessively, they are unable to hold up their end of the bargain adequately. Similarly, women who are heavy users are unable to maintain good work habits. Both addicted "men" and women drain the financial resources of the family. In addition, "men" become dependent on their women to support their habits and thereby lose the respect of other "men" and women of the street.

> Dee: They ["men" in Milwaukee] would take and allow a woman to hold the fact that they're givin' 'em money over their heads. Where, in Chicago or New York, they would get rid of the woman—'cuz women come too easy. The women here are the pimps. And if they're payin' the man they're payin' 'em not because of some strategic level he's at, it's because they want someone to protect them. But he's shootin' so much dope nine times out of ten, that the woman runs it [the family]. She says she's not going,to work—he might get down on his hands and knees and beg her 'cuz he's such a punk he needs to go pop from the dopeman.... They're shootin' too much dope, they're doin' too much dope. Dope has become a big problem as far as the players and the females. That's taken a lot of good men who have taken the money that women have made 'em, put it in businesses, and smoked up the business. So the drugs alone has killed a lot of the men. It's a vicious circle—it all goes back to the dopeman.

Aging Out

As women age, their value as street hustlers declines and they are often discarded by "men" who favor younger, naive women who have yet to establish criminal records. As a woman becomes both increasingly cynical and less attractive (compared to her younger competitors), she is less able to assimilate into the pseudo-family. Jody, for example, said that she and her "man" permitted a "wife-in-law" of two years to remain in jail (pending $500 bail) because, "we wanted to leave the state and she was old and I had learned everything from her so she was no longer needed." When Rita, another respondent, entered a family, her "wife-in-law" left because, as Rita reported, "she knew that I was prettier than her, younger. She was 30 years old. I [was] 19 and freshly turned out."

In addition, older women are more inclined to consider their own needs rather than the needs of their man. Toni, a 29-year-old, after working as a street hustler for 11 years, seeks a secure life with a "good" man. As she says:

> You become more and more experienced and you have to do serious time and you have so much time to think about what you want. If you're going to stay

in this life, [you begin to think] about what you want out of it instead of what he wants out of it. It becomes more of a priority. Now, I want someone who does not mess around with drugs. ... Who has enough money of his own, has enough things going for himself, to where he doesn't need me. That's what I want now.

Because older women hustlers are less financially successful than younger women, and often are chary of exploitative "men," they are frequently spurned by "men."

Instability

Though women are not allowed control over their earnings, they often receive costly gifts from their "men." The process of leaving "men," however, is such that women frequently lose the material wealth that they have acquired during the relationship. Since the decision to leave a "man" is usually made in anger—after a beating, or after being left to "sit" in jail, or in a fit of jealousy—women commonly leave their families without their treasured material possessions. As Toni says, "I've had to leave without my stuff a few times. Then you gotta start all over each time. But there's been times when I've got to keep my stuff, too." In addition, women who have accomplished some occupational mobility while with a "man" must start at the bottom of the occupational hierarchy when they choose a new one.

The more frequently women change men, then, the less likely their chance of accumulating any material wealth for themselves.

SUMMARY AND CONCLUSIONS

The pseudo-family, in addition to addressing the emotional and sexual needs of its members, is explicitly organized to realize and exploit the "profitability" that inheres in its female members—that is, their sexuality. But if female street hustlers are both labor and capital "rolled into one," it is difficult to imagine how the "man" can interject himself into the lives of women who, logically, are self-sufficient—in a purely entrepreneurial sense. In fact, the women who join pseudo-families "barter" their way through their family lives, endlessly exchanging their resources as women for, variously, the affections (and recognition) of the "man" and the material goods necessary to survival. There is a twofold answer to the question, therefore, of why women relinquish control of their natural assets in the sexual market of the street. One is that they bring to the street emotional and financial vulnerabilities and so fall prey to "men" prepared to exploit them; the second is that the "sexual" street scene represents a deeply entrenched, patriarchal structure that quickly and effectively punishes independent female hustlers.

References

Brown, M. (1979). Teenage prostitution. *Adolescence, 14,* 665–680.

Hartmann, H. I. (1984). The unhappy marriage of Marxism and feminism: Towards a more progressive union. In A. M. Jaggar & P. S. Rothenberg (Eds.), *Feminist frameworks* (pp. 172–189). New York: McGraw-Hill.

James, J., & Meyerding, J. (1976). Motivations for entrance into prostitution. In L. Cites (Ed.), *The female offender* (pp. 177–205). Washington, DC: Heath.

Laner, M. R. (1974). Prostitution as an illegal vocation: A sociological overview. In C. Bryant (Ed.), *Deviant behavior: Occupational and organizational bases* (pp 406–418). Chicago: Rand McNally.

Merry, S. (1980). Manipulating anonymity: Streetwalkers, strategies for safety in the city. *Ethnos, 45,* 157–175.

Miller, E. M. (1986). *Street woman.* Philadelphia: Temple University Press.

Miller, G. (1978). *The world of deviant work.* Englewood Cliffs, NJ: Prentice Hall.

Milner, C., & Milner, R. (1972). *Black players: The secret world of black pimps.* Boston: Little, Brown.

Rubin, G. (1975). The traffic in women: Notes on the "political economy' of sex." In R. Reiter (Ed.), *Toward an anthropology of women* (pp. 157–210). New York: Monthly Review Press.

Sidel, R. (1986). *Women and children last.* New York: Penguin.

GANGS AND CRIME

The past 20 years have witnessed a renewed interest in gangs by the criminal justice system and academic researchers. Street gangs are increasing sharply in numbers and in violence. Unlike the turf-oriented gangs of the 1950s and 1960s, the gangs of today are heavily involved in a variety of criminal activities, including drug trafficking.

Chapter 18, "Gang-Related Gun Violence," is new to this edition. The authors, Paul B. Stretesky and Mark R. Pogrebin, examine how gang socialization leads to gun violence and the role that guns play as protection from the dangers of the street and in "impression management," that is, they serve to project and protect a tough reputation. These findings suggest strategies for reduction in gun violence.

In recent years, female gang activity has increased considerably. Where women once served primarily in adjunct roles, mixed gender gangs have become more common. In Chapter 19, "Gender and Victimization among Young Women in Gangs," an analysis of gender and victimization in gangs, Jody Miller found that females experience a high risk of victimization at the hands of the gang peers and from assaultive victimization from other gangs.

In Chapter 20, one of the classic studies of gang scholarship, John M. Hagedorn ("Homeboys, Dope Fiends, Legits, and New Jacks") identifies four categories of gang members based on commitment to gang life and drug dealing. He addresses a number of issues critical to understanding the phenomenon of gang life: What happens to gangs members as they age? How are drug sales and gang activity related? How might these findings be translated into effective social policy?

In each selection, the offenders—both male and female members of street gangs—provide an unfiltered glimpse into their lives and activities.

18

Gang-Related Gun Violence: Socialization, Identity, and Self

Paul B. Stretesky and Mark R. Pogrebin

*T*he purpose of this study was to examine how violent norms are transmitted in street gangs and to examine socialization as a mechanism between gang membership and violence. To explore this issue, the authors draw on in-depth interviews with 22 Colorado inmates convicted of gang-related gun violence. These data are obtained from a subset of respondents in a larger study of gun violence (see Chapter 11 in this volume). The median age of the respondents was 25, although their age at the time of the offense for which they were incarcerated was considerably younger. At the time of the interviews, the respondents had been incarcerated an average of 4.7 years. Thirteen of the subjects were African American, five were white, three were Hispanic, and one was Asian. All had been convicted of violent gun-related crimes, including murder, manslaughter, robbery, and kidnapping. All but one was male. The researchers found that gangs are important agents of socialization that help shape a gang member's sense of self and identity. In addition, inmates reported that whereas guns offered them protection, they were also important tools of impression management that helped to project and protect a tough reputation. The findings provide greater insight into the way gang socialization leads to gun-related violence, and has implications for policies aimed at reducing that violence.*

This study considers how gangs promote violence and gun use. We argue that socialization is important because it helps to shape a gang member's identity and sense of self. Moreover, guns often help gang members project their violent identities. As Kubrin (2005, p. 363) argues, "The gun becomes a symbol of power and a remedy for disputes." We examine the issue of gang socialization, self, and identity formation using data derived from face-to-face qualitative interviews with a sample of gang members who have been incarcerated in Colorado prisons for gun-related violent crimes. Our findings, although unique, emphasize what previous studies have found—that most gangs are organized by norms that support the use of violence to settle disputes, achieve group goals, recruit members, and defend identity.

Source: Journal of Contemporary Ethnography, Vol. 36 (1) 85–114. Sage Publications, 2007.

Before our analysis of gang members, we briefly review the literature on the relationship between gangs, crime, guns, and violence. In that review, we emphasize the importance of socialization and the impact of gangs on identity and self. We explain how guns help gang members shape and convey their identity. Finally, in our discussion we relate our findings to the relative efficacy of different intervention strategies that are focused on reducing gang violence.

GANGS AND VIOLENCE

Research suggests that gang members are more likely than non–gang members to engage in crime—especially violent crime (Gordon et al., 2004). According to Thornberry, Krohn, Lizotte, and Chard-Wierschem (1993, p. 75), the relationship between gang affiliation and violence "is remarkably robust, being reported in virtually all American studies of gang behavior regardless of when, where, or how the data were collected." Whereas the relationship between gangs and violence is pervasive, "little is known about the causal mechanisms that bring it about" (Thornberry et al., 1993, p. 76). Do gangs attract individuals who are predisposed to violence or do they create violent individuals? The debate in the literature about these explanations of gang violence is rather extensive.

Thornberry et al. (1993) point out that there are three perspectives that inform the debate concerning the relationship between gangs and violence. First, the selection perspective argues that gang members are individuals who are delinquent and violent before joining the gang. Thus, gang members are individuals who are likely to engage in violent and deviant behavior even if they are not gang members (Gerrard, 1964; Yablonsky, 1962). From this perspective, what makes gang members more criminal than non–gang members is that criminal individuals have self-selected or been recruited into gangs. The second perspective is known as the social facilitation perspective. This perspective argues that gang members are no different from non-gang members until they enter the gang. Therefore, the gang serves a normative function. In short, the gang is the source of delinquent behavior because new gang members are socialized into the norms and values of gang life, which provides the necessary social setting for crime and violence to flourish. The enhancement perspective is the third explanation for the relationship between gang and crime (Thornberry et al., 1993). The enhancement perspective proposes that new gang members are recruited from a pool of individuals who show propensity to engage in crime and violence, but their level of violence intensifies once they enter the gang because the gang provides a structure that encourages crime and violence (see also Decker & Van Winkle, 1996).

According to McCorkle and Miethe (2002, p. 111), the second and third explanations for gang-related crime are the most popular explanations in the literature because both perspectives rely on the assumption that social disorganization increases socialization into the gang subculture, which produces crime. Recent criminological research suggests that the enhancement perspective is the most likely explanation for the association between gang involvement and criminal behavior. For instance, Gordon et al. (2004) discovered that individuals who join gangs are, in general, more delinquent than their peers *before* they join the gang. However, Gordon et al. also found that violent behavior among individuals who join a gang significantly increases *after* they become gang members. Although the work by Gordon et al. provides some answers concerning the potential causal mechanisms of gang violence, it still leaves open the question about why gang members increase their violent behavior after they join a gang. It is for that reason that we focus our research on the concept of socialization as a mechanism that leads to gang-related gun violence.

GANG SOCIALIZATION

Research on gang socialization—the process of learning the appropriate values and norms of the gang culture to which one belongs—suggests that group processes are highly important (Miller & Brunson, 2000; Sirpal, 1997; Vigil, 1988;). In addition, Moore (1991) believes that many city gangs have become quasi-institutionalized. In these cities, gangs have played a major role in ordering individuals' lives at the same time that other important social institutions such as schools and families play less of a normative role (see also Bjerregaard & Lizotte, 1995; Blumstein, 1995; Bowker & Klein, 1983; Vigil 1988). Vigil (1988, p. 63) has found that gangs help to socialize "members to internalize and adhere to alternative norms and modes of behavior and play a significant role in helping...youth acquire a sense of importance, self-esteem, and identity." One way to attain status is to develop a reputation for being violent (Anderson, 1999). This reputation for violence, however, is likely to develop (at least to some degree) after an individual joins a gang.

The reasons individuals join gangs are diverse (Decker & Van Winkle, 1996). According to Decker & Van Winkle (1996), the most important instrumental reason for joining a gang is protection. In addition to instrumental concerns, a large portion of all gang members indicate that their gang fulfills a variety of more typical adolescent needs—especially companionship and support, which tend to be more expressive in nature. That is, the gang is a primary group. The idea that the gang is a primary group into which individuals are socialized is not new. For instance, long ago Thrasher (1927, p. 230) pointed out,

> [The gang] offers the underprivileged boy probably his best opportunity to acquire status and hence it plays an essential part in the development of his personality. In striving to realize the role he hopes to take he may assume a tough pose, commit feats of daring or vandalism, or become a criminal.

Thus, gang violence may often be viewed as expressive in nature. The value of masculinity as a form of expression plays an important role in gang social-ization (Miller & Decker, 2001). Oliver (1994) argues that gang violence is often a method of expressing one's masculinity when opportunities to pur-sue conventional roles are denied. Acts of manhood, note Decker and Van Winkle (1996, p. 186), are "important values of [a member's] world and their psyches—to be upheld even at the cost of their own or others' lives." Katz (1988) also believes violence plays an important and acceptable role in the subculture of people living in socially isolated environments and econom-ically deprived areas because violence provides a means for a member to demonstrate his toughness, and displays of violent retaliation establish socialization within the gang.

According to Short and Strodtbeck (1965; see also Howell, 1998), a good portion of all gang violence can be attributed to threats to one's status within the gang. Gang membership, then, helps to create within-group identity that defines how group members perceive people outside their formal organiza-tional structure. By way of altercasting (i.e., the use of tactics to create iden-tities and roles for others), gangs cast nonmembers into situated roles and identities that are to the gang's advantage (Weinstein & Deutschberger, 1963). Altercasting, then, is an aggressive tactic that gangs often use to justify their perception of other gangs as potentially threatening rivals, and it is used to rationalize the use of physical violence against other gangs. If the objective of a gang is to be perceived by the community, rival gangs, law enforcement officials, and others in a particular way, then their collective group and indi-vidual identities will be situated in these defining situations. Even though there is a good deal of research examining the important relationship between violence and status within the gang as it relates to socialization, lit-tle is known about the specific ways that status impacts gang violence.

Socialization into the gang is bound up in issues of identity and self. Identity, according to Stone (1962), is the perceived social location of the per-son. Image, status, and a host of other factors that affect identity are mostly created by group perceptions of who we are and how we define ourselves. "People see themselves from the standpoints of their group and appropri-ate action in relation to those groups becomes a source of pride" (Shibutani, 1961, p. 436). Berger (1963, p. 92) notes that "identities are socially bestowed, socially maintained, and socially transformed."

Moore (1978, p. 60) has suggested that "the gang represents a means to what is an expressive, rather than an instrumental, goal: the acting out of a male role of competence and of 'being in command' of things." The findings of Decker and Van Winkle (1996) and Moore suggest that although instru-mental reasons for joining a gang are important, once a member joins a gang they largely see the gang as an important primary group that is central to their lives and heavily influences their identity and personality. Because this is a primary group, the approval of gang peers is highly important. It is this expressive reason for remaining in a gang that may help to explain gang crime and violence, especially as it relates to socialization. Hughes and Short (2005) provide insight into the area of identity and gang violence. Specifically, they find that when a gang member's identity is challenged, violence is often a result—especially if the challenger is a stranger. If a gang member does not comply with gang role expectations when they are challenged, the result may be a loss of respect. It is important to project a violent reputation to command respect and deter future assaults. Walking away from conflict is risky to one's health (Anderson, 1999). Gang members must by necessity make efforts to show a continued commitment to role expectations to the group (Lindesmith & Strauss, 1968). From this perspective, it appears that character traits that are a consequence of being socialized into street gangs may result in youthful acts of violence through transformations in identity (Vigil, 1996).

Initiation rights are one important aspect of identity formation (Hewitt, 1988; Vigil, 1996). Initiation rights that new gang members are obligated to go through demonstrate commitment to the gang and attest to an individual's desire to gain official membership in the organization. Hewitt (1988) argues that these types of acts help create a "situated self," where a person's self can be defined and shaped by particular situations. Thus, notions of identity formation are highly consistent with notions of gang violence as a function of social facilitation and enhancement perspectives in that they explain why gang members may increase their levels of crime and violence once they join the gang. Moreover, research suggests that the more significant the relationship to a gang is, the more committed an individual is to a gang identity (Callero, 1985; Stryker & Serpe, 1982). In short, gangs provide a reference group for expected role behavior and shape a member's identity and sense of self (Callero, 1985). The greater the commitment a person has to a gang identity, the more frequently that person will perform in ways that enact that identity, ways that include acts of violence (Stryker & Serpe, 1982).

Guns also play an important role in many gangs and are often reported to be owned for instrumental reasons (Decker & Van Winkle, 1996). Gang members who perceive a threat from rival gangs are believed to carry guns to protect themselves and their neighborhoods (Decker & Van Winkle, 1996; Horowitz, 1983; Lizotte, Tesoriero, Thomberry, & Krohn, 1994; Wright & Rossi, 1986). Gang membership "strongly and significantly increases the likelihood of carrying a gun" (Thornberry, Krohn, Lizotte, Smith, & Tobin, 2003, p. 131). However, the reason that gang members carry guns is sill unclear. It is likely that in addition to instrumental reasons for carrying a gun, gang members carry guns for expressive reasons (Sheley & Wright, 1995). That is, guns provide gang members with a sense of power, which may be extremely important in identity formation. Guns help gang members project a tough image. Thornberry et al. (2003, p. 125) report that gang members who carry guns may feel "emboldened to initiate criminal acts that they may otherwise avoid."

Sociologists have long recognized that symbols are important indicators of identity. This is especially true of gangs (Decker & Van Winkle, 1996; Vigil, 2003). Gang members often display symbols of gang membership, and this is part of being socialized into the role of a gang member:

> Wearing gang clothes, flashing gang signs, and affecting other outward signs of gang behavior are also ways to become encapsulated in the role of gang

member, especially through the perceptions of others, who, when they see the external symbols of membership respond as if the person was a member (Decker & Van Winkle, 1996, p. 75).

Bjerregaard and Lizotte (1995, p. 42) argue that it is plausible that "juveniles are socialized into the gun culture by virtue of their gang membership and activity."

Although there is some indication that gang members are more likely to own guns than non-gang members prior to joining a gang, gang membership also clearly appears to increase the prevalence of gun ownership. Bjerregaard and Lizotte (1995) believe that future research needs to focus on why gang membership encourages gun ownership. In this vein, Sanders's (1994) research on drive-by shootings provides some insight into why gang membership may encourage gun ownership. Drawing on Goffman's (1961) notion of realized resources, Sanders argues that gangs are organizations that provide the necessary context for drive-bys. Sanders is clear when he states that guns and cars are the least important resource in producing drive-bys. However, it is also true that guns are necessary for drive-bys to occur and as such are an important part of gang culture to the extent that drive-bys help gang members "build an identity as having heart" (Sanders, 1994, p. 204). Thus, notions of character and identity provide a way to look at drive-by shootings as a product of the gang structure, where guns are important instruments in building identity. Given the importance of guns to a gang member's identity, it is interesting to note that little research exists that examines the relationship between guns and gangs in terms of identity formation.

FINDINGS

We divide our findings into four sections. First, we focus on our subjects' socialization into the gang and the impact that socialization has on their self and identity. Second, we explore the importance of gang commitment as reinforcing a gang member's self and identity. Third, we focus on masculinity as a central value among gang members. During our discussions of masculinity, gang members often referred to notions of respect and reputation. Reputation is a way that gang members can project their image of masculinity to others. Respect was often referenced when their masculine identity was challenged. Finally, we focus on the importance of guns as instruments central to the lives of our gang members in the sense that they help project and protect masculine identities.

GANG SOCIALIZATION, SELF, AND IDENTITY

Goffman (1959) argues that as individuals we are often "taken in by our own act" and therefore begin to feel like the person we are portraying.

Baumeister and Tice (1984) describe this process as one where initial behaviors are internalized so that they become part of a person's self-perception. Once initial behaviors are internalized, the individual continues to behave in ways consistent with his or her self-perception. Related to the current study, the socialization process of becoming a gang member required a change in the subject's self-perception. That is, who did our gang members become as compared with who they once were? Social interaction is highly important in the process of socialization because it helps create one's identity and sense of self, as Holstein and Gubrium (2003, p. 119 [emphasis added]) point out:

> As personal as they seem, our selves and identities are extremely social. They are hallmarks of our inner lives, *yet they take shape in relation to others: We establish who and what we are through social interaction.* In some respects, selves and identities are two sides of the same coin. Selves are the subjects we take ourselves to be; identities are the shared labels we give to these selves. We come to know ourselves in terms of the categories that are socially available to us.

Most inmates we interviewed appeared to indicate that their socialization into the gang began at a relatively young age:

> At about fifteen, I started getting affiliated with the Crips. I knew all these guys, grew up with them and they were there....I mean, it was like an influence at that age. I met this dude named Benzo from Los Angeles at that time. He was a Crip and he showed me a big wad of money. He said, "Hey man, you want some of this?" "Like yeh! Goddamn straight. You know I want some of that." He showed me how to sell crack, and so at fifteen, I went from being scared of the police and respecting them to hustling and selling crack. Now I'm affiliated with the Crips; I mean it was just unbelievable.

Another inmate tells of his orientation in becoming a member of a gang. He points out the glamour he associated with membership at a very impressionable age:

> I started gang banging when I was ten. I got into a gang when I was thirteen. I started just hanging around them, just basically idolizing them. I was basically looking for a role model for my generation and ethnic background; the main focus for us is the popularity that they got. That's who the kids looked up to. They had status, better clothes, better lifestyle.

One of our black study participants residing with his father in a predominantly white, suburban community felt estranged from the minority friends he had in his former neighborhood. He discussed his need to be among his former peers and voluntarily moved back to his old neighborhood:

> A lot of the people that lived where my father was staying were predominantly white. I mean, not to say I didn't get along with white kids but, you know, it was just two different backgrounds and things of that nature.

His racial and socioeconomic identification in the white community, where he resided with his father, offered little opportunity for him to fit in. When he returned to the city, he became involved with a gang quite rapidly:

> I started getting charged with assaults. Gang rivalry, you know, fighting, just being in a gang.

Because he was better educated and did not use street vernacular as his peers did, our participant claims he had to continually prove his racial proclivity to his peers:

> Other kids would call me "white wash" because I spoke proper English. Basically, I wanted to be somebody, so I started hanging around with gang bangers. I was planning on being the best gang member I can be or the best kind of criminal I can be or something like that.

Consistent with Goffman's (1959) observations, once our subjects became active gang members, their transformation of identity was complete. That is, consistent with the notion of social facilitation and enhancement perspectives (Thornberry et al., 1993), the self-perceptions and identity of the subjects in our study appear to have changed from what they were before joining the gang. Shibutani (1961, p. 523) explains such changes by claiming that

> a person's self-perception is caused by a psychological reorientation in which an individual visualizes his world and who he thinks he is in a different light. He retains many of his idiosyncrasies, but develops a new set of values and different criteria of judgment.

Violent behavior appeared to play an important role in this transformation of identity and self. Most gang members noted that they engaged in violent behavior more frequently once they joined the gang.

> At an early age, it was encouraged that I showed my loyalty and do a drive by ... anybody they (gangster disciples) deemed to be a rival of the gang. I was going on fourteen. At first, I was scared to and then they sent me out with one person and I seen him do it. I saw him shoot the guy....So, in the middle of a gang fight I get pulled aside and get handed a pistol and he said, "It's your turn to prove yourself." So I turned around and shot and hit one of the guys (rival gang members). After that, it just got more easier. I did more and more. I had no concern for anybody.

A further illustration of situated identity and transformation of self is related by another inmate, who expresses the person he became through the use of violence and gun possession. Retrospectively, he indicates disbelief in what he had become.

> As a gang banger, you have no remorse, so basically, they're natural-born killers. They are killers from the start. When I first shot my gun for the first time

at somebody, I felt bad. It was like, I can't believe I did this. But I looked at my friend and he didn't care at all. Most gang bangers can't have a conscience. You can't have remorse. You can't have any values. Otherwise, you are gonna end up retiring as a gang banger at a young age.

The situations an individual finds oneself in, in this case collective gang violence, together with becoming a person who is willing to use violence to maintain membership in the gang, is indicative of a transformed identity. Strauss (1962) claims that when a person's identity is transformed, they are seen by others as being different than they were before. The individual's prior identity is retrospectively reevaluated in comparison with the present definition of a gang member. Such a transformation was part of the processional change in identity that our prisoners/gang members experienced.

COMMITMENT TO THE GANG

"As a creature of ideas, man's main concern is to maintain a tentative hold on these idealized conceptions of himself, to legitimate his role identities" (McCall & Simmons, 1966, p. 71). Commitment to the gang also serves individual needs for its members. We found that gang identification and loyalty to the group was a high priority for our subjects. This loyalty to the gang was extreme. Our subjects reported that they were willing to risk being killed and were committed to taking the life of a rival gang member if the situation called for such action. That is, gang membership helped our subjects nourish their identity and at the same time provided group maintenance (Kanter, 1972). As Kanter (1972) points out, the group is an extension of the individual and the individual is an extension of the group. This notion of sacrifice for the group by proving one's gang identification is expressed by an inmate who perceives his loyalty in the following terms:

> What I might do for my friends [gang peers] you might not do. You've got people out their taking bullets for their friends and killing people. But I'm sure not one of you would be willing to go to that extreme. These are just the thinking patterns we had growing up where I did.

Another inmate tells us about his high degree of identity for his gang:

> If you're not a gang member, you're not on my level...most of my life revolves around gangs and gang violence. I don't know anything else but gang violence. I was born into it, so it's my life.

The notion of the gang as the most important primary group in a member's life was consistently expressed by our study subjects. Our subjects often stated that they were willing to kill or be killed for the gang in order to sustain their self-perception as a loyal gang member. This extreme degree of group affiliation is similar to that of armed services activities during wartime. The platoon, or in this case, the local gang, is worth dying for. In this sense, the notion of the gang as a protector was an important part of gang life. All members were expected to be committed enough to aid their peers should the need arise. The following gang member points to, the important role his gang played for him in providing physical safety as well as an assurance of understanding:

> That's how it is in the hood, selling dope, gang bangin,' everybody wants a piece of you. All the rival gang members, all the cops, everybody. The only ones on your side are the gang members you hang with.

For this particular member, his gang peers are the only people he perceives will aid him from threatening others. The world appears full of conflicting situations, and although his gang affiliation is largely responsible for all the groups that are out to harm him in some way, he nevertheless believes his fellow gang members are the only persons on whom he can depend.

Violence against rival gangs was a general subject that the majority of the inmates interviewed discussed freely. However, only a few of our study participants focused on this subject compared with the less violence-prone gang-affiliated inmates. The violent gang members perceived other gangs as ongoing enemies who constantly presented a threat to their safety. As our literature review suggests, there is some debate about whether gang members would be violent without belonging to a gang, or if formal membership in the group provided them with the opportunity to act out this way. However, we find clarity in the inmate accounts that a gang member's identity provided the context necessary to resort to violence when confronted with conflicting events, as the following inmate notes:

> I have hate toward the Crips gang members and have always had hate toward them 'cuz of what they did to my homeboys....I never look back. I do my thing. I always carry a gun no matter what. I am a gang member, man! There are a lot of gang members out to get me for what I done. I shot over forty people at least. That's what I do.

This perception of being a person who is comfortable with violence and the perception of himself as an enforcer type characterizes the above inmate's role within his gang. Turner (1978) suggests that roles consistent with an individual's self-concept are played more frequently and with a higher, degree of participation than roles that are not in keeping with that individual's self-concept. Our study subject in this situation fits Turner's explanation of role identity nicely. His hatred for rival gangs and his willingness to retaliate most likely led to his incarceration for attempted murder.

MASCULINITY, REPUTATION, AND RESPECT

For those gang members we interviewed, socialization into the gang and commitment to the gang appear to be central to the notion of masculinity.

That is, all gang members we interviewed spoke of the importance of masculinity and how it was projected (though the creation of a reputation) and protected (through demands for respect). The notion of masculinity was constantly invoked in relation to self and identity. In short, masculinity is used to communicate to others what the gang represents, and it is used to send an important signal to others who may wish to challenge a gang's collective identity. A gang member's masculine reputation precedes him or her, so to speak. On an individual level, similar attributes apply as well.

> Whatever an individual does and however he appears, he knowingly and unknowingly makes information available concerning the attributes that might be imputed to him and hence the categories in which he might be placed.... The physical milieu itself conveys implications concerning the identity of those who are in it (Goffman, 1961, p. 102).

According to Sherif and Wilson (1953), people's ego attitudes define and regulate their behavior toward various other groups and are formed in concert to the values and norms of that person's reference group. They formulate an important part of their self-identity and their sense of group identification. For our gang member study population, the attributes that the gang valued consisted of factors that projected a street image that was necessary to sustain. It was a survival strategy.

Masculinity

"Every man [in a gang] is treated as a man until proven different. We see you as a man before anything." This comment by a gang member infers that masculinity is a highly valued attribute in his gang. The idea of manhood and its personal meanings for each interviewed prisoner was a subject consistently repeated by all participants. It usually was brought up in the context of physical violence, often describing situations where one had to face danger as a result of another's threatening behavior or testing of one's willingness to use physical force when insulted by someone outside of the group.

> Even if you weren't in one [gang], you got people that are going to push the issue. We decide what we want to do; I ain't no punk, I ain't no busta. But it comes down to pride. It's foolish pride, but a man is going to be a man, and a boy knows he's going to come into his manhood by standing his ground.

Establishing a reputation coincides with becoming a man, entering the realm of violence, being a stand-up guy who is willing to prove his courage as a true gang member. This strong association between a willingness to perpetrate violence on a considered rival, or anyone for that matter, was a theme that defined a member's manhood. After eight years in the gang, the following participant was owed money for selling someone dope. After a few weeks of being put off by the debtor, he had to take some action to appease his gang peers who were pressuring him to retaliate.

312 / GANGS AND CRIME

> I joined the gang when I was eleven years old. So now that I'm in the gang for eight years, people are asking, "What are you going to do? You got to make a name for yourself." So we went over there [victim's residence] and they were all standing outside and I just shot him. Everybody was happy for me, like "Yea, you shot him, you're cool," and this and that.

A sense of bravado, when displayed, played a utilitarian role in conflicting situations where a gang member attempts to get others to comply with his demands by instilling fear instead of actually utilizing violent means. Having some prior knowledge of the threatening gang member's reputation is helpful in preventing a physical encounter, which is always risky for both parties involved. Again, the importance of firearms in this situation is critical.

> The intimidation factor with a gun is amazing. Everybody knows what a gun can do. If you have a certain type of personality, that only increases their fear of you. When it came to certain individuals who I felt were a threat, I would lift my shirt up so they would know I had one on me.

In this case, the showing of his firearm served the purpose of avoiding any altercation that could have led to injury or even worse. Carrying a gun and displaying it proved to be an intimidating, preventative factor for this gang member. The opposite behavior is noted in the following example of extreme bravado, where aggressive behavior is desired and a clear distinction (based on bravery) between drive-by shootings and face-to-face shootings is clear.

> If someone is getting shot in a drive-by and someone else gets hit, it is an accident. You know, I never do drive-bys. I walk up to them and shoot. I ain't trying to get anyone else shot to take care of business.

A final example of masculinity and bravado, as perceived by this particular study participant, illustrates his commitment to being a stand-up guy, a person who will face the consequences of gang activity. The situation he discussed had to do with his current incarceration. Here he explains how he adhered to the gang value of not being a snitch, and refused to provide information about rival gang members' involvement in two homicides to the police, which could have helped in his prosecution for murder.

> I know what I did [gang war murder], you know what I mean? I'm not gonna take the easy way out [snitch on rival gangs for two homicides]. I know what I did. I'm facing my responsibility.

An interesting note in this scenario has to do with the above inmate's continued loyalty to the values of his gang when he was outside of prison. His information on the rival gang's homicides most likely could have had the criminal charges against him reduced and subsequently he would have received a lesser prison sentence. We are taking into consideration that the inmate's cultural code is similar if not the same as the gang code, and our study participant was simply adhering to the same value system.

The image of toughness fits well under masculinity and bravado as an attribute positively perceived by gang members we interviewed. Its importance lies in projecting an image via reputation that conveys a definition of who the collective group is and what physical force they are willing to use when necessary. A clear explanation of this attribute is related by the following subject.

> Everybody wants to fight for the power, for the next man to fear him. It's all about actually killing the mother fuckers and how many mother fuckers you can kill. Drive-by shootings is old school.

The implication here is that having a collective reputation for being powerful motivates this prisoner. He notes that the tough image of shooting someone you are after instead of hiding behind the random shooting characterized by drive-bys projects an image of toughness and power.

There are others who prefer to define their toughness in terms of physical fighting without the use of any weapons—though it was often noted that it was too difficult to maintain a tough reputation under such conditions. For instance, the predicament the following gang member found himself in is one where rival gangs use guns and other lethal instruments, and as a result of this, his reputation as an effective street fighter proved to be of little value. In short, his toughness and fighting skills were obsolete in life-threatening encounters.

> Like my case, I'm a fighter. I don't like using guns. The only reason I bought a gun was because every time I got out of the car to fight, I'd have my ribs broken, the back of my head almost crushed with a baseball bat. I was tired of getting jumped. I couldn't get a fair fight. Nobody wanted to fight me because I had a bad reputation. Then I decided, why even fight? Everybody else was pulling guns. It's either get out of the car and get killed or kill them.

The fact that this prisoner had good fighting skills ironically forced him to carry a gun. The rules of gang fighting found him outnumbered and unarmed, placing him in a very vulnerable position to defend himself. The proliferation of firearms among urban street gangs is well documented by Blumstein (1995) and others. Lethal weapons, mainly firearms, have drastically changed the defining characteristics of gang warfare in the late 1980s and 1990s, when most of our study subjects were active gang members in the community.

Reputation

On a collective group level, developing and maintaining the gang's reputation of being a dangerous group to deal with, especially from other groups or individuals who posed a threat to their drug operations, was important.

The following inmate points out the necessity of communicating the gang's willingness to use violent retaliation against rivals. Guns often played an important role in the development and maintenance of reputation, though they were rarely utilized in conflicting situations:

> We had guns to fend off jackers, but we never had to use them, 'cause people knew we were straps. People knew our clique, they are not going to be stupid. We've gotten into a few arguments, but it never came to a gun battle. Even when we werne gang bangin,' we didn't use guns, we only fought off the Bloods.

In addition to a collective reputation, the group serves the identifying needs of its individual members (Kanter, 1972). Our study participants related their need to draw upon the reputation of the gang to help them develop their own reputation, which gave them a sense of fulfillment. People want to present others with cues that will enhance desired typifications of who they are. They desire to present who they are in ways that will cause those they interact with to adhere to their situated claims (Hewitt & Stokes, 1975). The following participant discusses the way gang affiliation enhanced his reputation as a dangerous individual, a person not to be tested by others.

> There are people that know me; even ones that are contemplating robbing me know of me from the gang experience. They know if you try and rob me [of drugs and money], more than likely you gonna get killed. I was gonna protect what was mine. I'll die trying.

Another study subject perceives gang membership differently. He attained a reputation through gang activity, and guns clearly played an important role in that process.

> Fear and desire to have a reputation on the streets made me do it. When I got into the streets, I saw the glamour of it. I wanted a reputation there. What better way to get a reputation than to pick up a pistol? I've shot several people.

Although each prisoner/gang member interviewed expressed a desire to be known in the community for some particular attribute, there were some gang members who simply wanted to be known, sort of achieving celebrity status.

> You basically want people to know your name. It's kind of like politicians, tike that, you wanna be known. In my generation you want somebody to say, "I know him, he used to hang around with us."

Respect

One constantly associates the subject of disrespect in gang vernacular with retaliatory violence. Interactions with rivals stemming from an affront to one's self-image often became the excuse to use a gun to redeem one's reputational identity. Strauss (1969) argues that anger and withdrawal occur when a person is confronted with a possible loss of face. For our subjects, this anger was apparent when rivals challenged their self-identity (i.e., when our subjects were disrespected).

According to the gang members we talked to, disrespect, or rejection of self-professed identity claims by others, often was the cause of violence. Violence is even more likely to be the result of disrespect when no retaliatory action may lead to a loss of face. The following inmate relates his view on this subject in general terms.

> Violence starts to escalate once you start to disrespect me. Once you start to second guess my manhood, I'll fuck you up. You start coming at me with threats, then I feel offended. Once I feel offended, I react violently. That's how I was taught to react.

The interface of their manhood being threatened seems to be directly associated with Strauss's (1962) concept of identity denial by an accusing other. This threat to one's masculinity by not recognizing another's status claims is apparently an extremely serious breach of gang etiquette.

> When someone disrespects me, they are putting my manhood in jeopardy. They are saying my words are shit, or putting my family in danger....Most of the time, I do it [use violence] to make people feel the pain or hurt that I feel. I don't know no other way to do it, as far as expressing myself any other way.

Hickman and Kuhn (1956) point out that the self anchors people in every situation they are involved in. Unlike other objects, they claim that the self is present in all interactions and serves as the basis from which we all make judgments and plans of reaction toward others that are part of a given situation. When being confronted by gang rivals who have been perceived as insulting an opposing gang member, the definition of street norms calls for an exaggerated response. That is, the disrespectful words must be countered with serious physical force to justify the disrespected individual's maintenance of self (or manhood). A prime example of feeling disrespected is discussed in terms of territory and the unwritten rules of the street by one gang member who told us of an encounter with a rival gang who disrespected him to the point that he felt he was left with no other alternative choice of action but to shoot them.

> So, as we were fighting, they started saying that this was their neighborhood and started throwing their gang signs. To me, to let somebody do that to me is disrespect. So I told them where I was from.

A little while later the gang members in question showed up in our study subject's neighborhood and shot at him as he was walking with his two small children to a convenience store to get ice cream. He continues to recite the tale:

I was just so mad and angry for somebody to disrespect me like that and shoot. We got a rule on the street. There is rules. You don't shoot at anybody if there is kids. That's one of the main rules of the street. They broke the rules. To me that was telling me that they didn't have no respect for me or my kids. So, that's how I lost it and shot them. I was so disrespected that I didn't know how to handle it.

The notion of disrespect is analogous to an attack on the self. Because many of the inmates in our sample reported that masculinity is an important attribute of the self, they believed any disrespect was a direct threat to their masculinity. For those brought up in impoverished high-crime communities, as these study population participants were, there are limited alternatives to such conflicting situations (Anderson, 1999). Retaliation to redeem one's self-identity in terms of his internalized concept of manhood precludes a violent reaction to all actions of insult. To gang members caught in those confrontational encounters, there is a very limited course of action, that of perpetrating violence toward those who would threaten their self-concept of who they believe they are.

GANGS AND GUNS

The perceived necessity by gang participants to carry handguns became a reality for our study group. They collectively expressed the danger of their life on the street, whether it was selling narcotics, committing a robbery, being a provocateur against rivals, or being the recipient of violent retaliation on the part of perceived enemies. They viewed their world fraught with potential danger, thus the need for the possession of guns. It is necessary, then, to take the person's definition of the situation into account in explaining their unlawful conduct (Hewitt, 1988). Often, the interviewed prisoners emphasized the importance of the gun as an attribute that communicated their masculinity in some situations but was protection in others. Quite often, both definitions of the situation existed simultaneously.

Our analysis of the interview data dichotomized those gun-using encounters as expressions of either power or protection, based on each participant's perceived definition of the situation.

Carrying a firearm elicits various feelings of power.

When I have a gun, I feel like I'm on top of it, like I'm Superman or something. You got to let them know.

Another participant explains that the larger the gun, the more powerful he felt:

I was fifteen at that point in time and I had a fascination with guns. It was like the more powerful impact the gun had, the more fascinated I got and the more I wanted it.

The actual use of a firearm is described in a situation that most lethally expressed the power of guns in an attempt to injure those belonging to rival gangs. In this situation, our subject points out that they were not trying to injure or kill anyone for personal reasons but rather to display a sense of willingness to commit a lethal act for purposes of dominance.

> When I was younger, we used to do drive-bys. It didn't matter who you were. We didn't go after a specific person. We went after a specific group. Whoever is standing at a particular house or wherever you may be, and you're grouped up and have the wrong color on; just because you were in a rival gang. You didn't have to do anything to us to come get you, it was a spontaneous reaction.

When not being involved in collective gang violence, individual members find themselves being involved in gun-use situations as instigators when confronting rivals on one's own.

> My cousin told me if you pull it you better use it. So you gotta boost yourself. When the time came I was just shooting.

Our findings showed that in the vast majority of gang member–related shootings, most of these violent gun-using situations involved individuals as opposed to large numbers of gangs confronting each other with firearms. Yet, we were told that in gang representation, either on an individual basis or in a small group, whether it be in a protective or retaliatory mode, gang members needed to display a power position to those confronting them to maintain their reputations, and guns were important in that respect.

The issues surrounding gun possession often have to do with interpersonal conflict as opposed to collective gang situations. The fear of being physically harmed within their residential environment, coupled with the relative ease in which a person can attain a firearm, has resulted in a proliferation of weapons in the community. Growing up in such high-crime neighborhoods and then joining a gang can shape a minority teen's perceptions of his or her social world.

> There's a lot of brutality, there is a lot of murder around us. There is a lot of violence, period. There are enemies and all. A lot of pressure, you know. If you're not going to do this, then they're going to do it to you. I'd rather get caught with a gun than without.

The perceived fear for potential harm caused this female gang member to carry a gun with her outside her home. When she expresses the violence that is prevalent in her environment, she is also telling us how random threats can often occur and sees the necessity to harm rivals before they harm her.

Individually or collectively, rival gang members constantly pose a physical threat according to the next inmate. He also discusses the need for protection and how drug sales caused him to be a target for those who would try and rob him.

I carried a gun because I knew what I was doing, especially since I was in a gang. Other gangs are gonna try and come after us. So I used it [gun] against those gangs and to make sure that my investments in the drugs was protected. I don't want nobody to take money from me.

Finally, one study subject relates the need to carry a gun all the time to protect his jewelry, which he openly displays as a symbol of his monetary success through the use of illegal means.

I basically carried a gun for protection. Just like you have a best friend. You and your best friend go everywhere. I got over ten thousand dollars of jewelry on me. People see all this jewelry and may try and beat me up. There may be two or three and just myself.

For our prisoner/gang member study population, the descriptive attributes they related all played an important role in shaping their individual gang identity. The roles they learned to play through their processional development into bona fide gang participants were accomplished by group socialization. Their acting upon those perceived valued attributes resulted in their transformed identity. Once the socializing process is complete, the novice gang member has to sustain his reputation and status personally as well as collectively with the formal group.

An individual who implicitly or explicitly signifies that he has certain social characteristics ought in fact to be what he claims he is. In consequence, when an individual projects a definition of the situation and thereby makes an implicit or explicit claim to be a person of a particular kind, he automatically exerts a moral demand upon others, obliging them to value and treat him in the manner that persons of his kind have a right to expect. (Goffman, 1959, pp. 1–5)

For Goffman, the claims (attributes) our sample of gang members desired to convey to others of just who they perceived themselves to be directly affected their sense of self.

DISCUSSION AND CONCLUSION

Gangs not only fulfill specific needs for individuals that other groups in disadvantaged neighborhoods may fail to provide, but as our interviews suggest, they are also important primary groups into which individuals become socialized. It is not surprising, then, that self-concept and identity are closely tied to gang membership. Guns are also important in this regard. We propose that for the gang members in our sample, gang-related gun violence can be understood in terms of self and identity that are created through the process of socialization and are heavily rooted in notions of masculinity. Thus, our analysis provides insight into the way gang socialization can produce violence—especially gun-related violence.

We find that related to the issue of gun violence, the possession and use of guns among gang members is relatively important because, in addition to protecting gang members, guns are tools that aid in identity formation and impression management. As many of our subject narratives suggest, guns were often connected in some way to masculine attributes. Gang members reported to us that they could often use guns to project their reputation or reclaim respect. We believe that the consequences of our findings regarding gang violence and guns are important for public policy for three reasons.

First, because our sample only consisted of those gang members who committed the most severe forms of violence (i.e., they were incarcerated for relatively long periods of time for their gun-related violence), there may be some interest in targeting individuals like the ones in our sample early in their criminal careers to "diminish the pool of chronic gang offenders" (Piehl, Kennedy, & Braga, 2000, p. 100). We believe this may be one potential method for reducing gang-related violence because the gang members in our sample often had extensive violent histories. Moreover, in studies of gang violence, researchers have generally found that a small number of offenders commit most of the crime. For instance, Kennedy, Piehl, and Braga (1996) found that less than 1% of Boston's youth were responsible for nearly 60% of the city's homicides. Thus, identifying the rather small pool of chronic gang members may be a useful approach to reducing gang violence because they are the ones engaged in most of the violence. This approach, however, is somewhat problematic because identifying chronic offenders is both difficult and controversial (Walker, 1998). Moreover, Spergel and Curry (1990), who studied the effectiveness of various gang-related intervention strategies, argue that law enforcement efforts seem to be one of the least effective methods for reducing gang-related problems.

Second, our research suggests that policies aimed at reducing gang violence should take gang socialization into account. Simply reducing gun availability through law enforcement crackdowns on violent gang members is probably not sufficient (see Piehl et al., 2000). In addition, our interviews suggest that guns are probably far more important to the daily lives and identities of gang members than most policy makers might imagine, precisely because they help project a reputation and create respect. Thus, it might be pointed out that if gang culture could be changed through the resocialization of gang members, gun-related gang violence might significantly decrease. Indeed, studies of gun initiatives such as the Boston Gun Project suggest that gang violence is reduced when gang culture is changed. As Piehl et al. (2000, p. 100) point out, one reason homicides in Boston decreased as a result of the Boston Gun Project was because that initiative focused on "establishing and/or reinforcing nonviolent norms by increasing peer support for eschewing violence, by improving young people's handling of potentially violent situations."

Overall, however, the strategy of focusing on gang socialization, however, falls most closely in line with social intervention perspectives that have not proved to be highly successful in various situations (Shelden,

Tracy, & Brown, 2001). In short, altering the values of gang members to make gang-related violence less likely may not be the most promising approach to reducing gang violence. As Klein (1995, p. 147) recently noted, "Gangs are by-products of their communities: They cannot long be controlled by attacks on symptoms alone; the community structure and capacity must also be targeted." Whether gang violence can be reduced by the resocialization of gang members appears to remain open to debate, but it is clearly one avenue of intervention that requires further attention in the research.

Third, it is not clear from our research whether simply eliminating or reducing access to guns can reduce gun-related gang violence. For example, studies like the Youth Firearms Violence Initiative conducted by the U.S. Department of Justice's Office of Community Oriented Policing Services does suggest that gun violence can be reduced by focusing, at least in part, on reducing access to guns (Dunworth, 2000). However, that study also indicates that once these projects focusing on access to guns end, gang violence increases to previous levels. Moreover, our interviews suggest that there is little reason to believe that gang members would be any less likely to look to gangs as a source of status and protection and may use other weapons—though arguably less lethal than guns—to aid in transformations of identity and preserve a sense of self. Thus, although reduction strategies may prevent gang-related violence in the short term, there is little evidence that this intervention strategy will have long-term effects because it does not adequately deal with gang culture and processes of gang socialization.

Overall, our findings suggest that gang socialization produces gang-related gun violence through changes to identity and self. Although the problems of gang-related violence appear to play out at the microlevel, the solutions to these problems do not appear to be overwhelmingly situated at this level. Instead, we believe that intervention efforts must reside at the macrolevel and impact socialization processes at the microlevel. We agree with Short (1997, p. 181) that "absent change in macro level forces associated with [gang violence], vulnerable individuals will continue to be produced" (see also Shelden et al., 2001). Thus, it may be more fruitful to focus on intervention efforts aimed at improving the economic and social environments that create gangs.

References

Anderson, E. (1999). *Code of the street: Decency, violence, and the moral life of the inner city.* New York: W. W. Norton.

Baumeister, R., & Tice, D. (1984). Role of self-presentation and choice in cognitive dissonance under forced compliance. *Journal of Personality and Social Psychology, 46,* 5–13.

Berger, P. (1963). *Invitation to sociology: A humanistic perspective.* Garden City, NY: Doubleday.

Bjerregaard, B., & Lizotte, A. (1995). Gun ownership and gang membership. *Journal of Criminal Law and Criminology, 86*, 37–58.

Blumstein, A. (1995). Violence by young people: Why the deadly nexus? *National Institute of Justice Journal, 229*, 2–9.

Bowker, L., & Klein, M. (1983). The etiology of female juvenile delinquency and gang membership: A test of psychological and social structural explanations. *Adolescence, 18*, 739–751.

Callero, P. (1985). Role identity salience. *Social Psychology Quarterly, 48*, 203–215.

Decker, S., & Van Winkle, B. (1996). *Life in the gang: Family, friends, and violence.* New York: Cambridge University Press.

Dunworth, T. (2000). *National evaluation of youth firearms violence initiative. Research in brief.* Washington, DC: U.S. Department of Justice, Office of Justice Programs, National Institute of Justice.

Gerrard, N. (1964). The core member of the gang. *British Journal of Criminology, 4*, 361–371.

Glaser, B., & Strauss, A. (1967). *The discovery of grounded theory: Strategies for qualitative research.* New York: Doubleday.

Goffman, E. (1959). *The presentation of self in everyday life.* Garden City, NY: Doubleday.

Goffman, E. (1961). *Encounters: Two studies in the sociology of interaction.* Indianapolis, IN: Bobbs-Merrill.

Gordon, R., Lahey, B., Kawai, K., Loeber, R., Stouthamer-Loeber, M., & Farrington, D. (2004). Antisocial behavior and youth gang membership: Selection and socialization. *Criminology, 42*, 55–88.

Hewitt, J. (1988). *Self and society.* Boston: Allyn & Bacon.

Hewitt, J., & Stokes, R. (1975). Disclaimers. *American Sociological Review, 40*, 1–11.

Hickman, C. A., & Kuhn, M. (1956). *Individuals, groups, and economic behavior.* New York: Dryden.

Holstein, J., & Gubrium, J. (2003). *Inner lives and social worlds.* New York: Oxford University Press.

Horowitz, R. (1983). *Honor and the American dream.* New Brunswick, NJ: Rutgers University Press.

Howell, J. (1998, August). Youth gangs: An overview. *Juvenile Justice Bulletin.* Washington, DC: U.S. Department of Justice, Office of Juvenile Justice and Delinquency Prevention.

Hughes, L., & Short, J. (2005). Disputes involving youth street gang members: Micro-social contexts. *Criminology, 43*, 43–76.

Kanter, R. (1972). *Commitment and community: Communes and utopias in sociological perspective.* Cambridge, MA: Harvard University Press.

Katz, J. (1988). *Seductions of crime: Moral and sensual attractions in doing evil.* New York: Basic Books.

Kennedy, D., Piehl, A. M., & Braga, A. (1996). *Youth gun violence in Boston: Gun markets, serious youth offenders, and a use-reduction strategy. Research in brief.* Washington,

DC: U.S. Department of Justice, Office of Justice Programs, National Institute of Justice.

Klein, M. (1995). *The American street gang.* New York: Oxford University Press.

Kubrin, C. (2005). Gangstas, thugs, and hustlas: Identity and the code of the street in rap music. *Social Problems, 52,* 360–378.

Lindesmith, A., & Strauss, A. (1968). *Social psychology.* New York: Holt, Rinehart and Winston.

Lizotte, A., Tesoriero, J., Thomberry, T., & Krohn, M. (1994). Patterns of adolescent firearms ownership and use. *Justice Quarterly, 11,* 51–74.

McCall, G., & Simmons, J. (1966). *Identities and interactions: An examination of human associations in everyday life.* New York: Free Press.

McCorkle, R., & Miethe, T. (2002). *Panic: The social construction of the street gang problem.* Upper Saddle River, NJ: Prentice Hall.

Miller, J., & Brunson, R. (2000). Gender dynamics in youth gangs: A comparison of males' and females' accounts. *Justice Quarterly, 17,* 419–448.

Miller, J., & Decker, S. (2001). Young women and gang violence: Gender, street offender, and violent victimization in gangs. *Justice Quarterly, 18,* 115–140.

Moore, J. (1978). *Homeboys: Gangs, drugs, and prison in the barrios of Los Angeles.* Philadelphia: Temple University Press.

Moore, J. (1991). *Going down to the barrio: Homeboys and homegirls in change.* Philadelphia: Temple University Press.

Oliver, W. (1994). *The violent world of black men.* New York: Lexington.

Piehl, A. M., Kennedy, D., & Braga, A. (2000). Problem solving and youth violence: An evaluation of the Boston gun project. *American Law and Economics Review, 2,* 58–106.

Sanders, W. (1994). *Gang-bangs and drive-bys: Grounded culture and juvenile gang violence.* New York: Walter de Gruyter.

Shelden, R., Tracy, S., & Brown, W. (2001). *Youth gangs in American society.* Belmont, CA: Wadsworth.

Sheley, J., & Wright, J. (1995). *In the line of fire: Youth, guns and violence in America.* New York: Aldine de Gruyter.

Sherif, M., & Wilson, M. (1953). *Group relations at the crossroads.* New York: Harper.

Shibutani, T. (1961). *Society and personality: An interactionist approach to social psychology.* Englewood Cliffs, NJ: Prentice Hall.

Short, J. (1997). *Poverty, ethnicity, and violent crime.* Boulder, CO: Westview Press.

Short, J., & Strodtbeck, F. (1965). *Group processes and gang delinquency.* Chicago: University of Chicago Press.

Sirpal, S. K. (1997). Causes of gang participation and strategies for prevention in gang members' own words. *Journal of Gang Research, 4,* 13–22.

Spergel, I., & Curry, G. D. (1990). Strategies perceived agency effectiveness in dealing with the youth gang problem. In C. R. Huff (Ed.), *Gangs in America* (pp. 288–309). Newbury Park, CA: Sage.

Stone, G. (1962). Appearance and self. In A. Rose (Ed.), *Human behavior and social processes* (pp. 86–118). Boston: Houghton Mifflin.

Strauss, A. (1962). Transformations of identity. In A. Rose (Ed.), *Human behavior and social processes: An interactional approach* (pp. 63–85). Boston: Houghton Mifflin.

Strauss, A. (1969). *Mirrors and masks: The search for identity.* New York: Macmillan.

Stryker, S., & Serpe, R. (1982). Commitment, identity salience and role behavior. In W. Ikes & E. Knowles (Eds.), *Personality, roles and social behavior* (pp. 199–218). New York: Springer-Verlag.

Thornberry, T., Krohn, M., Lizotte, A., & Chard-Wierschem, D. (1993). The role of juvenile gangs in facilitating delinquent behavior. *Journal of Research in Crime and Delinquency, 30,* 75–85.

Thornberry, T., Krohn, M., Lizotte, A., Smith, C., & Tobin, K. (2003). *Gangs and delinquency in developmental perspective.* Cambridge, UK: Cambridge University Press.

Thrasher, F. (1927). *The gang.* Chicago: University of Chicago Press.

Turner, R. (1978). The role and the person. *American Journal of Sociology, 84,* 1–23.

Vigil, J. (1988). *Barrio gangs.* Austin: University of Texas Press.

Vigil, J. (1996). Street baptism: Chicago gang initiation. *Human Organization, 55,* 149–153.

Vigil, J. (2003). Urban violence and street gangs. *Annual Review of Anthropology, 32,* 225–242.

Walker, S. (1998). *Sense and nonsense about crime and drugs.* Belmont, CA: Wadsworth.

Weinstein, E., & Deutschberger, P. (1963). Some dimensions of altercasting. *Sociometry, 26,* 454–466.

Wright, J., & Rossi, P. (1986). *Armed and considered dangerous: A survey of felons and their firearms.* New York: Aldine de Gruyter.

Yablonsky, L. (1962). *The violent gang.* New York: Macmillan.

19

Gender and Victimization Risk among Young Women in Gangs

Jody Miller

*T*his selection examines how gendered situational dynamics shape gang violence, including participation in violent offending and experiences of violent victimization. Although there are numerous studies of gangs and gang involved individuals, few have explored the concept of victimization of gang members. The author found that young women, even regular offenders, highlight the significance of gender in shaping and limiting their involvement in serious violence. Based on interviews with 20 female gang members in Columbus, Ohio Miller found that being a member increases one's risk of assaults and other physical victimization and that these risks are greater for females than for males. She suggests that the act of joining a gang often involves submission to victimization at the hands of other members of the gang and that gang activities thereafter place them at risk for further victimization.*

GIRLS, GANGS, AND CRIME

Until recently, however, little attention was paid to young women's participation in serious and violent gang-related crime. Most traditional gang research emphasized the auxiliary and peripheral nature of girls' gang involvement and often resulted in an almost exclusive emphasis on girls' sexuality and sexual activities with male gang members, downplaying their participation in delinquency (for critiques of gender bias in gender research, see Campbell, 1984, 1990; Taylor, 1993).

However, recent estimates of female gang involvement have caused researchers to pay greater attention to gang girls' activities. This evidence suggests that young women approximate anywhere from 10% to 38% of gang members (Campbell, 1984; Chesney-Lind, 1993; Esbensen, 1996; Fagan, 1990; Moore, 1991), that female gang participation may be increasing (Fagan, 1996; Spergel & Curry, 1993; Taylor, 1990), and that in some urban areas, upward of one-fifth of girls report gang affiliations (Bjerregaard & Smith, 1993;

Source: From Miller, J., "Gender and victimization: risk among young women in gangs," in *Journal of Research in Crime & Delinquency*, 35, pp. 429–453. Copyright © 1998. Reprinted with permission from Sage Publications, Inc.

Winfree, Fuller, Vigil, & Mays, 1992). As female gang members have become recognized as a group worthy of criminologists' attention, we have garnered new information regarding their involvement in delinquency in general, and violence in particular.

Few would dispute that when it comes to serious delinquency, male gang members are involved more frequently than their female counterparts. However, this evidence does suggest that young women in gangs are more involved in serious criminal activities than was previously believed and also tend to be more involved than nongang youths—male or female. As such, they likely are exposed to greater victimization risk than nongang youths as well.

In addition, given the social contexts described above, it is reasonable to assume that young women's victimization risk within gangs is also shaped by gender. Gang activities (such as fighting for status and retaliation) create a particular set of factors that increase gang members' victimization risk and repeat victimization risk. Constructions of gender identity may shape these risks in particular ways for girls. For instance, young women's adoption of masculine attributes may provide a means of participating and gaining status within gangs but may also lead to increased risk of victimization as a result of deeper immersion in delinquent activities. On the other hand, experiences of victimization may contribute to girls' denigration and thus increase their risk for repeat victimization through gendered responses and labeling—for example, when sexual victimization leads to perceptions of sexual availability or when victimization leads an individual to be viewed as weak. In addition, femaleness is an individual attribute that has the capacity to mark young women as "safe" crime victims (e.g., easy targets) or, conversely, to deem them "off limits." My goal here is to examine the gendered nature of violence within gangs, with a specific focus on how gender shapes young women's victimization risk.

METHODOLOGY

Data presented in this article come from survey and semistructured in-depth interviews with 20 female members of mixed-gender gangs in Columbus, Ohio. The interviewees ranged in age from 12 to 17; just over three-quarters were African American or multiracial (16 of 20), and the rest (4 of 20) were white.

Girls who admitted gang involvement during the survey participated in a follow-up interview to talk in more depth about their gangs and gang activities. The goal of the in-depth interview was to gain a greater understanding of the nature and meanings of gang life from the point of view of its female members.

The in-depth interviews were open-ended and all but one were audiotaped. They were structured around several groupings of questions. We began by discussing girls' entry into their gangs—when and how they became involved, and what other things were going on in their lives at the time. Then we discussed the structure of the gang—its history, size, leadership, and organization, and their place in the group. The next series of questions concerned gender within the gang; for example, how girls get involved, what activities they engage in and whether these are the same as the young men's activities, and what kind of males and females have the most influence in the gang and why. The next series of questions explored gang involvement more generally—what being in the gang means, what kinds of things they do together, and so on. Then, I asked how safe or dangerous they feel gang membership is and how they deal with risk. I concluded by asking them to speculate about why people their age join gangs, what things they like, what they dislike and have learned by being in the gang, and what they like best about themselves. This basic guideline was followed for each interview subject, although when additional topics arose in the context of the interview we often deviated from the interview guide to pursue them. Throughout the interviews, issues related to violence emerged; these issues form the core of the discussion that follows.

SETTING

The young women I interviewed described their gangs in ways that are very much in keeping with these findings. All 20 are members of Folks, Crips, or Bloods sets. All but three described gangs with fewer than 30 members, and most reported relatively narrow age ranges between members. Half were in gangs with members who were 21 or over, but almost without exception, their gangs were made up primarily of teenagers, with either one adult who was considered the OG ("Original Gangster," leader) or just a handful of young adults. The majority (14 of 20) reported that their gangs did not include members under the age of 13.

Although the gangs these young women were members of were composed of both female and male members, they varied in their gender composition, with the vast majority being predominantly male. Six girls reported that girls were one-fifth or fewer of the members of their gang; eight were in gangs in which girls were between a quarter and a third of the overall membership; four said girls were between 44% and 50% of the members; and one girl reported that her gang was two-thirds female and one-third male. Overall, girls were typically a minority within these groups numerically, with 11 girls reporting that there were 5 or fewer girls in their set.

This structure—male-dominated, integrated mixed-gender gangs—likely shapes gender dynamics in particular ways. Much past gang research has assumed that female members of gangs are in auxiliary subgroups of male gangs, but there is increasing evidence—including from the young women I spoke with—that many gangs can be characterized as integrated, mixed-gender groups.

GENDER, GANGS, AND VIOLENCE

Gangs as Protection and Risk

An irony of gang involvement is that although many members suggest one thing they get out of the gang is a sense of protection (see also Decker, 1996; Joe & Chesney-Lind, 1995; Lauderback, Hansen, & Waldorf, 1992), gang membership itself means exposure to victimization risk and even a willingness to be victimized. These contradictions are apparent when girls talk about what they get out of the gang, and what being in the gang means in terms of other members' expectations of their behavior. In general, a number of girls suggested that being a gang member is a source of protection around the neighbor-hood. Erica, a 17-year-old African American, explained, "It's like people look at us and that's exactly what they think, there's a gang, and they respect us for that. They won't bother us. . . . It's like you put that intimidation in somebody." Likewise, Lisa, a 14-year-old white girl, described being in the gang as empowering: "You just feel like, oh my God, you know, they got my back. I don't need to worry about it." Given the violence endemic in many inner-city communities, these beliefs are understandable, and to a certain extent, accurate.

In addition, some young women articulated a specifically gendered sense of protection that they felt as a result of being a member of a group that was predominantly male. Gangs operate within larger social milieus that are characterized by gender inequality and sexual exploitation. Being in a gang with young men means at least the semblance of protection from, and retaliation against, predatory men in the social environment. Heather, a 15-year-old white girl, noted. "You feel more secure when, you know, a guy's around protectin' you, you know, than you would a girl." She explained that as a gang member, because "you get protected by guys . . . not as many people mess with you." Other young women concurred and also described that male gang members could retaliate against specific acts of violence against girls in the gang. Nikkie, a 13-year-old African American girl, had a friend who was raped by a rival gang member, and she said, "It was a Crab [Crip] that raped my girl in Miller Ales, and um, they was ready to kill him." Keisha, an African American 14-year-old, explained, "if I got beat up by a guy, all I gotta do is go tell one of the niggers, you know what I'm sayin'? Or one of the guys, they'd take care of it."

At the same time, members recognized that they may be targets of rival gang members and were expected to "be down" for their gang at those times even when it meant being physically hurt. In addition, initiation rites and internal rules were structured in ways that required individuals to submit to, and be exposed to, violence. For example, young women's descriptions of the qualities they valued in members revealed the extent to which exposure to violence was an expected element of gang involvement. Potential members, they explained, should be tough, able to fight and to engage in criminal activities, and also should be loyal to the group and willing to put themselves at risk for it. Erica explained that they didn't want "punks" in her gang: "When you join something like that, you might as well expect that there's gonna be fights.... And, if you're a punk, or if you're scared of stuff like that, then don't join." Likewise, the following dialogue with Cathy, a white 16-year-old, reveals similar themes. I asked her what her gang expected out of members and she responded, "to be true to our gang and to have our backs." When I asked her to elaborate, she explained,

CATHY: Like, uh, if you say you're a Blood, you be a Blood. You wear your rag even when you're by yourself. You know, don't let anybody intimidate you and be like, 'Take that rag off.' You know, 'you better get with our set.' Or some-thing like that.

JM: Ok. Anything else that being true to the set means?

CATHY: Urn. Yeah, I mean, just, just, you know, I mean it's, you got a whole bunch of people comin', up in your face and if you're by yourself they ask you what's your claimin', you tell 'em. Don't say `nothin.'

JM: Even if it means getting beat up or something?

CATHY: Mmhmm.

One measure of these qualities came through the initiation process, which involved the individual submitting to victimization at the hands of the gang's members. Typically this entailed either taking a fixed number of "blows" to the head and/or chest or being "beaten in" by members for a given duration (e.g., 60 seconds). Heather described the initiation as an important event for determining whether someone would make a good member:

When you get beat in if you don't fight back and if you just like stop and you start cryin' or some-thin' or beggin' 'em to stop and stuff like that, then, they ain't gonna, they'll just stop and they'll say that you're not gang material because you gotta be hard, gotta be able to fight, take punches.

In addition to the initiation, and threats from rival gangs, members were expected to adhere to the gang's internal rules (which included such things as not fighting with one another, being "true" to the gang, respecting the leader, not spreading gang business outside the gang, and not dating mem-bers of rival gangs). Breaking the rules was grounds for physical punish-ment, either in the form of a spontaneous assault or a formal "violation," which involved taking a specified number of blows to the head. For example, Keisha reported that she talked back to the leader of her set and "got slapped pretty hard" for doing so. Likewise, Veronica, an African American 15-year-old, described her leader as "crazy, but we gotta listen to 'im. He's just the type that if you don't listen to 'im, he gonna blow your head off. He's just crazy."

It is clear that regardless of members' perceptions of the gang as a form of "protection," being a gang member also involves a willingness to open oneself up to the possibility of victimization. Gang victimization is governed by rules and expectations, however, and thus does not involve the random vulnerability that being out on the streets without a gang might entail in high-crime neighborhoods. Because of its structured nature, this victimization risk may be perceived as more palatable by gang members. For young women in particular, the gendered nature of the streets may make the empowerment available through gang involvement an appealing alternative to the individualized vulnerability they otherwise would face. However, as the next sections highlight, girls' victimization risks continue to be shaped by gender, even within their gangs, because these groups are structured around gender hierarchies as well.

Gender and Status, Crime and Victimization

Status hierarchies within Columbus gangs, like elsewhere, were male dominated (Bowker, Gross, & Klein, 1980; Campbell, 1990). Again, it is important to highlight that the structure of the gangs these young women belonged to—that is, male-dominated, integrated mixed-gender gangs—likely shaped the particular ways in which gender dynamics played themselves out. Autonomous female gangs, as well as gangs in which girls are in auxiliary subgroups, may be shaped by different gender relations, as well as differences in orientations toward status, and criminal involvement.

All the young women reported having established leaders in their gang, and this leadership was almost exclusively male. Although LaShawna, a 17-year-old African American, reported being the leader of her set (which had a membership that is two-thirds girls, many of whom resided in the same residential facility as her), all the other girls in mixed-gender gangs reported that their OG was male. In fact, a number of young women stated explicitly that only male gang members could be leaders. Leadership qualities, and qualities attributed to high-status members of the gangs—being tough, able to fight, and willing to "do dirt" (e.g., commit crime, engage in violence) for the gang—were perceived as characteristically masculine. Keisha noted, "The guys, they just harder." She explained, "Guys is more rougher. We have our G's back but, it ain't gonna be like the guys, they just don't give a fuck. They gonna shoot you in a minute."

For the most part, status in the gang was related to traits such as the willingness to use serious violence and commit dangerous crimes and, though not exclusively, these traits were viewed primarily as qualities more likely and more intensely located among male gang members.

Because these respected traits were characterized specifically as masculine, young women actually may have had greater flexibility in their gang involvement than young men. Young women had fewer expectations placed on them—by both their male and female peers—in regard to involvement in criminal activities such as fighting, using weapons, and committing other crimes. This tended to decrease girls' exposure to victimization risk compared to male members, because they were able to avoid activities likely to place them in danger. Girls could gain status in the gang by being particularly hard and true to the set. Heather, for example, described the most influential girl in her set as "the hardest girl, the one that don't take no crap, will stand up to anybody." Likewise, Diane, a white 15-year-old, described a highly respected female member in her set as follows:

> People look up to Janeen just 'cause she's so crazy. People just look up to her 'cause she don't care about nothin'. She don't even care about makin' money. Her, her thing is, `Oh, you're a Slob [Blood]? You're a Slob? You talkin' to me? You talkie' shit to me?' Pow, pow! And that's it. That's it.

However, young women also had a second route to status that was less available to young men. This came via their connections—as sisters, girlfriends, cousins—to influential, high-status young men. In Veronica's set, for example, the girl with the most power was the OG's "sister or his cousin, one of 'em." His girlfriend also had status, although Veronica noted that "most of us just look up to our OG." Monica, a 16-year-old African American, and Tamika, a 15-year-old African American, both had older brothers in their gangs, and both reported getting respect, recognition, and protection because of this connection. This route to status and the masculinization of high-status traits functioned to maintain gender inequality within gangs, but they also could put young women at less risk of victimization than young men. This was both because young women were perceived as less threatening and thus were less likely to be targeted by rivals, and because they were not expected to prove themselves in the ways that young men were, thus decreasing their participation in those delinquent activities likely to increase exposure to violence. Thus, gender inequality could have a protective edge for young women.

Young men's perceptions of girls as lesser members typically functioned to keep girls from being targets of serious violence at the hands of rival young men, who instead left routine confrontations with rival female gang members to the girls in their own gang. Diane said that young men in her gang "don't wanna waste their time hittin' on some little girls. They're gonna go get their little cats [females] to go get 'em." Lisa remarked, "girls don't face as much violence as [guys]. They see a girl, they say, 'we'll just smack her and send her on.' They see a guy—'cause guys are like a lot more into it than girls are, I've noticed that—and they like, 'well, we'll shoot him.'" In addition, the girls I interviewed suggested that, in comparison with young men, young women were less likely to resort to serious violence, such as that involving a weapon, when confronting rivals. Thus, when girls' routine confrontations were more likely to be female on female than male on female, girls' risk of serious victimization was lessened further.

Also, because participation in serious and violent crime was defined primarily as a masculine endeavor, young women could use gender as a means of avoiding participation in those aspects of gang life they found risky, threatening, or morally troubling. Of the young women I interviewed, about one-fifth were involved in serious gang violence: A few had been involved [in] aggravated assaults on rival gang members, and one admitted to having killed a rival gang member, but they were by far the exception. Most girls tended not to be involved in serious gang crime, and some reported that they chose to exclude themselves because they felt ambivalent about this aspect of gang life. Angie, an African American 15-year-old explained,

> I don't get involved like that, be out there goin' and just beat up people like that or go stealin', things like that. That's not me. The boys, mostly the boys do all that, the girls we just sit back and chill, you know.

Likewise, Diane noted,

> For maybe a drive-by they might wanna have a bunch of dudes. They might not put the females in that. Maybe the females might be weak inside, not strong enough to do something like that, just on the insides.... If a female wants to go forward and doin' that, and she wants to risk her whole life for doin' that, then she can. But the majority of the time, that job is given to a man.

Diane was not just alluding to the idea that young men were stronger than young women. She also inferred that young women were able to get out of committing serious crime, more so than young men, because a girl shouldn't have to "risk her whole life" for the gang. In accepting that young men were more central members of the gang, young women could more easily participate in gangs without putting themselves in jeopardy—they could engage in the more routine, everyday activities of the gang, like hanging out, listening to music, and smoking bud (marijuana). These male-dominated mixed-gender gangs thus appeared to provide young women with flexibility in their involvement in gang activities. As a result, it is likely that their risk of victimization at the hands of rivals was less than that of young men in gangs who were engaged in greater amounts of crime.

Girls' Devaluation and Victimization

In addition to girls choosing not to participate in serious gang crimes, they also faced exclusion at the hands of young men or the gang as a whole (see also Bowker et al., 1980). In particular, the two types of crime mentioned most frequently as "off-limits" for girls were drug sales and drive-by shootings. LaShawna explained, "We don't really let our females [sell drugs] unless they really wanna and they know how to do it and not to get caught and every-thing." Veronica described a drive-by that her gang participated in and said, "They wouldn't let us [females] go. But we wanted to go, but they wouldn't let us." Often, the exclusion was couched in terms of protection. When I asked Veronica why the girls couldn't go, she said, "so we won't go to jail if they was to get caught. Or if one of 'em was to get shot, they wouldn't want it to happen to us." Likewise, Sonita, a 13-year-old African American, noted, "If they gonna do somethin' bad and they think one of the females gonna get hurt they don't let 'em do it with them....Like if they involved with shooting or whatever, [girls] can't go."

Although girls' exclusion from some gang crime may be framed as protective (and may reduce their victimization risk vis-a-vis rival gangs), it also served to perpetuate the devaluation of female members as less significant to the gang—not as tough, true, or "down" for the gang as male members. When LaShawna said her gang blocked girls' involvement in serious crime, I pointed out that she was actively involved her-self. She explained, "Yeah, I do a lot of stuff 'cause I'm tough. I likes, I likes messin' with boys. I fight boys. Girls ain't nothin' to me." Similarly, Tamika said, "girls, they little peons."

Some young women found the perception of them as weak a frustrating one. Brandi, an African American 13-year-old, explained, "Sometimes I dislike that the boys, sometimes, always gotta take charge and they think sometimes, that the girls don't know how to take charge 'cause we're like girls, we're females, and like that." And Chantell, an African American 14-year-old, noted that rival gang members "think that you're more of a punk." Beliefs that girls were weaker than boys meant that young women had a harder time proving that they were serious about their commitment to the gang. Diane explained,

> A female has to show that she's tough. A guy can just, you can just look at him. But a female, she's gotta show. She's gotta go out and do some dirt. She's gotta go whip some girl's ass, shoot some-body, rob somebody or something. To show that she is tough.

In terms of gender-specific victimization risk, the devaluation of young women suggests several things. It could lead to the mistreatment and victimization of girls by members of their own gang when they didn't have specific male protection (i.e., a brother, boyfriend) in the gang or when they weren't able to stand up for themselves to male members. This was exacerbated by activities that led young women to be viewed as sexually available. In addition, because young women typically were not seen as a threat by young men, when they did pose one, they could be punished even more harshly than young men, not only for having challenged a rival gang or gang member but also for having overstepped "appropriate" gender boundaries.

Monica had status and respect in her gang, both because she had proven herself through fights and criminal activities and because her older brothers were members of her set. She contrasted her own treatment with that of other young women in the gang:

> They just be puttin' the other girls off. Like Andrea, man. Oh my God, they dog Andrea so bad. They like, 'Bitch, go to the store.' She like, 'All right, I be right back.' She will go to the store and go and get them whatever they want and come back with it. If she don't get it right, they be like, 'Why you do that bitch?' I mean, and one dude even smacked ha. And, I mean, and, I don't, I told my

brother once. I was like, `Man, it ain't even like that. If you ever see someone tryin' to disrespect me like that or hit me, if you do not hit them or at least say somethin' to them.... ' So my brothers, they kinda watch out for me.

However, Monica put the responsibility for Andrea's treatment squarely on the young woman: "I put that on her. They ain't gotta do her like that, but she don't gotta let them do her like that either." Andrea was seen as "weak" because she did not stand up to the male members in the gang; thus, her mistreatment was framed as partially deserved because she did not exhibit the valued traits of toughness and willingness to fight that would allow her to defend herself.

An additional but related problem was when the devaluation of young women within gangs was sexual in nature. Girls, but not boys, could be initiated into the gang by being "sexed in"—having sexual relations with multiple male members of the gang. Other members viewed the young women initiated in this way as sexually available and promiscuous, thus increasing their subsequent mistreatment. In addition, the stigma could extend to female members in general, creating a sexual devaluation that all girls had to contend with. The dynamics of "sexing in" as a form of gang initiation placed young women in a position that increased their risk of ongoing mistreatment at the hands of their gang peers. According to Keisha, "If you get sexed in, you have no respect. That means you gotta go ho'in' for 'em; when they say you give 'em the pussy, you gotta give it to 'em. If you don't, you gonna get your ass beat. I ain't down for that." One girl in her set was sexed in and Keisha said the girl "just do everything they tell her to do, like a dummy." Nikkie reported that two girls who were sexed into her set eventually quit hanging around with the gang because they were harassed so much. In fact, Veronica said the young men in her set purposely tricked girls into believing they were being sexed into the gang and targeted girls they did not like:

> If some girls wanted to get in, if they don't like the girl they have sex with 'em. They run trains on 'em or either have the girl suck their thang. And then they used to, the girls used to think they was in. So, then the girls used to just just come try to hang around us and all this little bull, just 'cause, 'cause they thinkin' they in.

Young women who were sexed into the gang were viewed as sexually promiscuous, weak, and not "true" members. They were subject to revictimization and mistreatment, and were viewed as deserving of abuse by other members, both male and female. Veronica continued, "They [girls who are sexed in] gotta do what-ever, whatever the boys tell 'em to do when they want 'em to do it, right then and there, in front of whoever. And, I think, that's just sick. That's nasty, that's dumb." Keisha concurred, "She brought that on herself, by bein' the fact, bein' sexed in." There was evidence, however, that girls could overcome the stigma of having been sexed in through their subsequent behavior, by challenging members that disrespect them and being willing to fight. Tamika described a girl in her set who was sexed in, and stigmatized as a result, but successfully fought to rebuild her reputation:

> Some people, at first, they call her `little ho' and all that. But then, now she startin' to get bold.... Like, like, they be like, `Ooh, look at the little ho. She flicked me and my boy.' She be like, `Man, forget y'all. Man, what? What?' She be ready to squat [fight] with 'em. I be like, `Ah, look at her!' Uh huh.... At first we looked at her like, `Ooh, man, she a ho, man.' But now we look at her like she just our kickin' it partner. You know, however she got in that's her business.

The fact that there was such an option as "sexing in" served to keep girls disempowered, because they always faced the question of how they got in and of whether they were "true" members. In addition, it contributed to a milieu in which young women's sexuality was seen as exploitable. This may help explain why young women were so harshly judgmental of those girls who were sexed in. Young women who were privy to male gang members' conversations reported that male members routinely disrespect girls in the gang by disparaging them sexually. Monica explained,

> I mean the guys, they have their little comments about 'em [girls in the gang] because, I hear more because my brothers are all up there with the guys and everything and I hear more just sittin' around, just listenin'. And they'll have their little jokes about 'Well, ha I had her,' and then and every-body else will jump in and say, 'Well, I had her, too.' And then they'll laugh about it.

In general, because gender constructions defined young women as weaker than young men, young women were often seen as lesser members of the gang. In addition to the mistreatment these perceptions entailed, young women also faced particularly harsh sanctions for crossing gender boundaries—causing harm to rival male members when they had been viewed as nonthreatening. One young woman participated in the assault of a rival female gang member, who had set up a member of the girl's gang. She explained, "The female was supposingly goin' out with one of ours, went back and told a bunch of [rivals] what was goin' on and got the [rivals] to jump my boy. And he ended up in the hospital." The story she told was unique but nonetheless significant for what it indicates about the gendered nature of gang violence and victimization. Several young men in her set saw the girl walking down the street, kidnapped her, then brought her to a member's house. The young woman I interviewed, along with several other girls in her set, viciously beat the girl, then to their surprise the young men took over the beating, ripped off the girl's clothes, brutally gang-raped her, then dumped her in a park. The interviewee noted, "I don't know what happened to her. Maybe she died. Maybe, maybe someone came and helped her. I mean, I don't know." The experience scared the young woman who told me about it. She explained,

> I don't never want anythin' like that to happen to me. And I pray to God that it doesn't. 'Cause God said that whatever you sow you're gonna reap. And

like, you know, beatin' a girl up and then sittin' there watchin' somethin' like that happen, well, Jesus that could come back on me. I mean, I felt, I really did feel sorry for her even though my boy was in the hospital and was really hurt. I mean, we coulda just shot her. You know, and it coulda been just over. We coulda just taken her life. But they went farther than that.

This young woman described the gang rape she witnessed as "the most brutal thing I've ever seen in my life." While the gang rape itself was an unusual event, it remained a specifically gendered act that could take place precisely because young women were not perceived as equals. Had the victim been an "equal," the attack would have remained a physical one. As the interviewee herself noted, "we coulda just shot her." Instead, the young men who gang-raped the girl were not just enacting revenge on a rival but on a young woman who had dared to treat a young man in this way. The issue is not the question of which is worse—to be shot and killed, or gang-raped and left for dead. Rather, this particular act sheds light on how gender may function to structure victimization risk within gangs.

DISCUSSION

Gender dynamics in mixed-gender gangs are complex and thus may have multiple and contradictory effects on young women's risk of victimization and repeat victimization. My findings suggest that participation in the delinquent lifestyles associated with gangs clearly places young women at risk for victimization. The act of joining a gang involves the initiate's submission to victimization at the hands of her gang peers. In addition, the rules governing gang members' activities place them in situations in which they are vulnerable to assaults that are specifically gang related. Many acts of violence that girls described would not have occurred had they not been in gangs.

It seems, though, that young women in gangs believed they have traded unknown risks for known ones—that victimization at the hands of friends, or at least under specified conditions, was an alternative preferable to the potential of random, unknown victimization by strangers. Moreover, the gang offered both a semblance of protection from others on the streets, especially young men, and a means of achieving retaliation when victimization did occur.

Lauritsen and Quinet (1995) suggest that both individual-specific heterogeneity (unchanging attributes of individuals that contribute to a propensity for victimization, such as physical size or temperament) and state-dependent factors (factors that can alter individuals' victimization risks over time, such as labeling or behavior changes that are a consequence of victimization) are related to youths' victimization and repeat victimization risk. My findings here suggest that, within gangs, gender can function in both capacities to shape girls' risks of victimization.

Girls' gender, as an individual attribute, can function to lessen their exposure to victimization risk by defining them as inappropriate targets of rival male gang members' assaults. The young women I interviewed repeatedly commented that young men were typically not as violent in their routine confrontations with rival young women as with rival young men. On the other hand, when young women are targets of serious assault, they may face brutality that is particularly harsh and sexual in nature because they are female—thus, particular types of assault, such as rape, are deemed more appropriate when young women are the victims.

Gender can also function as a state-dependent factor, because constructions of gender and the enactment of gender identities are fluid. On the one hand, young women can call upon gender as a means of avoiding exposure to activities they find risky, threatening, or morally troubling. Doing so does not expose them to the sanctions likely faced by male gang members who attempt to avoid participation in violence. Although these choices may insulate young women from the risk of assault at the hands of rival gang members, perceptions of female gang members—and of women in general—as weak may contribute to more routinized victimization at the hands of the male members of their gangs. Moreover, sexual exploitation in the form of "sexing in" as an initiation ritual may define young women as sexually available, contributing to a likelihood of repeat victimization unless the young woman can stand up for herself and fight to gain other members' respect.

Finally, given constructions of gender that define young women as nonthreatening, when young women do pose a threat to male gang members, the sanctions they face may be particularly harsh because they not only have caused harm to rival gang members but also have crossed appropriate gender boundaries in doing so. In sum, my findings suggest that gender may function to insulate young women from some types of physical assault and lessen their exposure to risks from rival gang members, but also to make them vulnerable to particular types of violence, including routine victimization by their male peers, sexual exploitation, and sexual assault.

REFERENCES

Bjerregaard, B., & Smith, C. (1993). Gender differences in gang participation, delinquency, and substance use. *Journal of Quantitative Criminology, 4*, 329–355.

Bowker, L. H., Gross, H. S., & Klein, M. W. (1980). Female participation in delinquent gang activities. *Adolescence, 15*, 509–519.

Campbell, A. (1984). *The girls in the gang.* New York: Basil Blackwell.

Campbell, A. (1990). Female participation in gangs. In C. R. Huff (Ed.), *Gangs in America* (pp. 163–182). Beverly Hills, CA: Sage.

Chesney-Lind, M. (1993). Girls, gangs and violence: Anatomy of a backlash. *Humanity & Society, 17*, 321–344.

Decker, S. H. (1996). Collective and normative features of gang violence. *Justice Quarterly, 13*, 243–264.

Esbensen, F.-A. (1990). Social processes of delinquency and drug use among urban gangs. In C. R. Huff (Ed.), *Gangs in America* (pp. 183–219). Newbury Park, CA: Sage.

Esbensen, F.-A. (1996). *Comments presented at the National Institute of Justice/Office of Juvenile Justice and Delinquency Prevention Cluster Meetings*, June, Dallas, TX.

Fagan, J. E. (1996). Gangs, drugs, and neighborhood change. In *Gangs in America*, 2nd ed., edited by C. R. Hulf. Thousand Oaks, CA: Sage Publications.

Huff, C. R. (1996). The criminal behavior of gang members and nongang at-risk youth. In C. R. Huff (Ed.), *Gangs in America* (pp. 75–102). Thousand Oaks, CA: Sage.

Joe, K. A., & Chesney-Lind, M. (1995). Just every mother's angel: An analysis of gender and ethnic variations in youth gang member-ship. *Gender & Society, 9*, 408–430.

Lauderback, D., Hansen, J., & Waldorf, D. (1992). "Sisters are doin' it for themselves": A black female gang in San Francisco. *The Gang Journal, 1*(1): 57–70.

Lauritsen, J. L., & Davis Quinet, K. F. (1995). Repeat victimization among adolescents and young adults. *Journal of Quantitative Criminology, 1*, 143–166.

Moore, J. (1991). *Going down to the barrio: Home-boys and homegirls in change.* Philadelphia: Temple University Press.

Spergel, I. A., & Curry, G. D. (1993). The National Youth Gang Survey: A research and development process. In A. P. Goldstein & C. R. Huff (Eds.), *The gang intervention handbook* (pp. 359–400). Champaign, IL: Research Press.

Taylor, C. (1990). *Dangerous Society.* East Lansing, MI: Michigan State University Press.

Winfree, L. T., Jr., Fuller, K., Vigil, T., & Mays, G. L. (1992). The definition and measurement of "gang status": Policy implications for juvenile justice. *Juvenile and Family Court Journal, 43*, 29–37.

20

Homeboys, Dope Fiends, Legits, and New Jacks

John M. Hagedorn

*B*ased on field research with Milwaukee gangs, gang researcher John Hagedorn delineates four categories of gang members based on their orientation to conventional values and social institutions. Focusing on core members of drug-dealing gangs, Hagedorn argues that gang members may be classified along a "continuum of conventionality," ranging from former gang members now living a legitimate life to those who regard drug dealing as a career. The study addresses several issues important to both social science and public policy. First, what happens to gang members as they age? Do most gang members graduate from gangbanging to drug sales, as popular stereotypes might suggest? Is drug dealing so lucrative that adult gang members eschew work and become committed to the drug economy? Have changes in economic conditions produced underclass gangs so detached from the labor market that the only effective policies are more police and more prisons? Second, and related to these questions, are adult gang members basically similar kinds of people, or are gangs made up of different types? Might some gang members be more conventional and others less so? What are the implications of this "continuum of conventionality" within drug-dealing gangs for public policy? The following selection includes interviews with present and former gang members Hagedorn classified as homeboys, dope fiends, legits, and new jacks. They discuss their attitudes toward drug dealing and conventional lifestyles, attitudes toward themselves, values, future plans, and life chances. Gang members were largely classified according to their level of commitment to crime as a lifestyle and particularly to drug dealing. In the conclusion, Hagedorn discusses criminal justice policy relating to gangs, drugs, and the "underclass" in society.*

A TYPOLOGY OF MALE ADULT GANG MEMBERS

We developed four ideal types on a continuum of conventional behaviors and values: (1) those few who had gone *legit*, or had matured out of the gang; (2) *homeboys,* a majority of both African American and Latino adult gang

Source: John M. Hagedorn, "Homeboys, Dope Fiends, New Jacks, and Legits." In *Criminology*, Vol. 32, No. 2, pp. 206–219. Copyright © 1994 by the American Society of Criminology. Reprinted with permission.

members, who alternately worked conventional jobs and took various roles in drug sales; (3) *dope fiends*, who were addicted to cocaine and participated in the dope business as a way to maintain access to the drug; and (4) *new jacks*, who regarded the dope game as a career.

Some gang members, we found, moved over time between categories, some had characteristics of more than one category, and others straddled the boundaries (see Hannerz, 1969, p. 57). Thus a few homeboys were in the process of becoming legit, many moved into and out of cocaine addiction, and others gave up and adopted a new jack orientation. Some new jacks returned to conventional life; others received long prison terms or became addicted to dope. Our categories are not discrete, but our typology seemed to fit the population of gang members we were researching. Our "member checks" (Lincoln & Guba, 1985, pp. 314–316) of the constructs with gang members validated these categories for male gang members.

Legits

Legits were those young men who had walked away from the gang. They were working or may have gone on to school. Legits had not been involved in the dope game at all, or not for at least five years. They did not use cocaine heavily, though some may have done so in the past. Some had moved out of the old neighborhood; others, like our project staff, stayed to help out or "give back" to the community. These are prime examples of Whyte's "college boys" or Cloward and Ohlin's Type I, oriented to economic gain and class mobility. The following quote is an example of a young African American man who "went legit" and is now working and going to college.

Q: Looking back over the past five years, what major changes took place in your life—things that happened that really made things different for you?

R#105: I had got into a relationship with my girl, that's one thing. I just knew I couldn't be out on the streets trying to hustle all the time. That's what changed me, I just got a sense of responsibility.

Today's underclass gangs appear to be fundamentally different from those in Thrasher's or Cloward and Ohlin's time, when most gang members "matured out" of the gang. Of the 236 Milwaukee male founders, only 12 (5.1%) could be categorized as having matured out: that is, they were working full time and had not sold cocaine in the past five years. When these data are disaggregated by race, the reality of the situation becomes even clearer. We could verify only two of 117 African American and one of 87 Latino male gang founders who were currently working and had not sold dope in the past five years. One-third of the white members fell into this category.

Few African American and Latino gang founders, however, were resigned to a life of crime, jail, and violence. After a period of rebellion and living the fast life, the majority of gang founders, or "homeboys," wanted to settle down and go legit, but the path proved to be very difficult.

Homeboys

"Homeboys" were the majority of all adult gang members. They were not firmly committed to the drug economy, especially after the early thrill of fast money and "easy women" wore off. They had reached an age, the mid-20s, when criminal offenses normally decline (Gottfredson & Hirschi, 1990). Most of these men were unskilled, lacked education, and had largely negative experiences in the secondary labor market. Some homeboys were committed more strongly to the streets, others to a more conventional life. Most had used cocaine, some heavily at times, but their use was largely in conjunction with selling from a house or corner with their gang "homies." Most homeboys either were married or had a "steady" lady. They also had strong feelings of loyalty to their fellow gang members.

Here, two different homeboys explain how they had changed, and how hard that change was:

Q: Looking back over the past five years, what major changes took place in your life—things that happened that really made things different for you?

R#211: The things that we went through wasn't worth it, and I had a family, you know, and kids, and I had to think about them first, and the thing with the drug game was, that money was quick, easy, and fast, and it went like that, the more money you make the more popular you was. You know, as I see it now it wasn't worth it because the time that I done in penitentiaries I lost my sanity. To me it feels like I lost a part of my kids, because, you know, I know they still care, and they know I'm daddy, but I just lost out. Somebody else won and I lost.

Q: Is she with somebody else now?

R#211: Yeah. She hung in there about four or five months after I went to jail.

Q: It must have been tough for her to be alone with all those kids.

R#211: Yeah.

Q: What kind of person are you?

R#217: Mad. I'm a mad young man. I'm a poor young man. I'm a good person to my kids and stuff, and given the opportunity to have something nice and stop working for this petty-ass money I would try to change a lot of things.... I feel I'm the type of person that given the opportunity to try to have something legit, I will take it, but I'm not going to go by the slow way, taking no four, five years working at no chicken job and trying to get up to a manager just to start making six, seven dollars. And then get fired when I come in high or drunk or something. Or miss a day or something because I got high smoking weed, drinking beer, and the next day come in and get fired; then I'm back in where I started from. So I'm just a cool person, and if I'm given the opportunity and if I can get a job making nine, ten dollars an hour, I'd let everything go; I'd just sit back and work my job and go home. That kind of money I can live with. But I'm not going to settle for no three, four dollars an hour, know what I'm saying?

Homeboys present a more confused theoretical picture than legits. Cloward and Ohlin's Type III delinquents were rebels, who had a "sense of injustice" or felt "unjust deprivation" at a failed system (1960, p. 117). Their gang delinquency is a collective solution to the failure of institutional arrangements.

They reject traditional societal norms; other, success-oriented illegitimate norms replace conventionality.

Others have questioned whether gang members' basic outlook actually rejects conventionality. Matza (1964) viewed delinquents' rationalizations of their conduct as evidence of techniques meant to "neutralize" deeply held conventional beliefs. Cohen (1955, pp. 129–137) regarded delinquency as a nonutilitarian "reaction formation" to middle-class standards, though middle-class morality lingers, repressed and unacknowledged. What appears to be gang "pathological" behavior, Cohen points out, is the result of the delinquent's striving to attain core values of "the American way of life." Short and Strodtbeck (1965), testing various gang theories, found that white and African American gang members, and lower- and middle-class youths, had similar conventional values.

Our homeboys are older versions of Cohen's and Matza's delinquents, and are even more similar to Short and Strodtbeck's study subjects. Milwaukee homeboys shared three basic characteristics: (1) They worked regularly at legitimate jobs, although they ventured into the drug economy when they believed it was necessary for survival. (2) They had very conventional aspirations; their core values centered on finding a secure place in the American way of life. (3) They had some surprisingly conventional ethical beliefs about the immorality of drug dealing. To a man, they justified their own involvement in drug sales by very Matza-like techniques of "neutralization."

Homeboys are defined by their in-and-out involvement in the legal and illegal economies. Recall that about half of our male respondents had sold drugs no more than 12 of the past 36 months. More than one-third never served any time in jail. Nearly 60%had worked legitimate jobs at least 12 months of the last 36, with a mean of 14.5 months. Homeboys' work patterns thus differed both from those of legits, who worked solely legal jobs, and new jacks, who considered dope dealing a career.

To which goal did homeboys aspire, being big-time dope dealers or holding a legitimate job? Rather than having any expectations of staying in the dope game, homeboys aspired to settling down, getting married, and living at least a watered-down version of the American dream. Like Padilla's (1992, p. 157) Diamonds, they strongly desired to "go legit." Although they may have enjoyed the fast life for a while, it soon went stale. Listen to this homeboy, the one who lost his lady when he went to jail:

Q: Five years from now, what would you want to be doing?
R#211: Five years from now? I want to have a steady job, I want to have been working that job for about five years, and just with a family somewhere.
Q: Do you think that's gonna come true?
R#211: Yeah, that's basically what I'm working on. I mean, this bullshit is over now, I'm twenty-five, I've played games long enough, it don't benefit nobody. If you fuck yourself away, all you gonna be is fucked, I see it now.

Others had more hopeful or wilder dreams, but a more sobering outlook on the future. The other homeboy, who said he wouldn't settle for three or four dollars an hour, speaks as follows:

Q: Five years from now, what would you want to be doing?
R#217: Owning my own business. And rich. A billionaire.
Q: What do you realistically expect you'll be doing in five years?
R#217: Probably working at McDonald's. That's the truth.

Homeboys' aspirations were divided between finding a steady full-time job and setting up their own business. Their strivings pertained less to being for or against "middle-class status" than to finding a practical, legitimate occupation that could support them (see Short & Strodtbeck, 1965). Many homeboys believed that using skills learned in selling drugs to set up a small business would give them a better chance at a decent life than trying to succeed as an employee.

Most important, homeboys "grew up" and were taking a realistic look at their life chances. This homeboy spoke for most:

Q: Looking back over the past five years, what major changes have taken place in your life—things that made a difference about where you are now?
R#220: I don't know, maybe maturity.... Just seeing life in a different perspective... realizing that from sixteen to twenty-three, man, just shot past. And just realizing that it did, shucks, you just realizing how quick it zoomed past me. And it really just passed me up without really having any enjoyment of a teenager. And hell, before I know it I'm going to hit thirty or forty, and I ain't going to have nothing to stand on. I don't want that shit. Because I see a lot of brothers out here now, that's forty-three, forty-four and ain't got shit. They's still standing out on the corner trying to make a hustle. Doing this, no family, no stable home and nothing. I don't want that shit.... I don't give a fuck about getting rich or nothing, but I want a comfortable life, a decent woman, a family to come home to. I mean, everybody needs somebody to care for. This ain't where it's at.

Finally, homeboys were characterized by their ethical views about selling dope. As a group, they believed dope selling was "unmoral"—wrong, but necessary for survival. Homeboys' values were conventional, but in keeping with Matza's findings, they justified their conduct by neutralizing their violation of norms. Homeboys believed that economic necessity was the overriding reason why they could not live up to their values (see Liebow, 1967, p. 214). They were the epitome of ambivalence, ardently believing that dope selling was both wrong and absolutely necessary. One longtime dealer expressed this contradiction:

Q: Do you consider it wrong or immoral to sell dope?
R#129: Um-hum, very wrong.
Q: Why?
R#129: Why, because it's killing people.
Q: Well how come you do it?
R#129: It's also a money maker.

Q: Well how do you balance those things out? I mean, here you're doing something that you think is wrong, making money. How does that make you feel when you're doing it, or don't you think about it when you're doing it?

R#129: Once you get a [dollar] bill, once you look at, I say this a lot, once you look at those dead white men [presidents' pictures on currency], you care about nothing else, you don't care about nothing else. Once you see those famous dead white men. That's it.

Q: Do you ever feel bad about selling drugs, doing something that was wrong?

R#129: How do I feel? Well a lady will come in and sell all the food stamps, all of them. When they're sold, what are the kids gonna eat? They can't eat the dope cause she's gonna go smoke that up, or do whatever with it. And then you feel like "wrong." But then, in the back of your mind, man, you just got a hundred dollars worth of food stamps for thirty dollars worth of dope, and you can sell them at the store for seven dollars on ten, so you got seventy coming. So you get seventy dollars for thirty dollars. It is not wrong to do this. It is not wrong to do this!

Homeboys also refused to sell to pregnant women or to juveniles. Contrary to Jankowski's (1991, p. 102) assertion that in gangs "there is no ethical code that regulates business ventures," Milwaukee homeboys had some strong moral feelings about how they carried out their business:

R#109: I won't sell to no little kids. And, ah, if he gonna get it, he gonna get it from someone else besides me. I won't sell to no pregnant woman. If she gonna kill her baby, I want to sleep not knowing that I had anything to do with it. Ah, for anybody else, hey, it's their life, you choose your life how you want.

Q: But how come—I want to challenge you. You know if kids are coming or a pregnant woman's coming, you know they're going to get it somewhere else, right? Someone else will make their money on it; why not you?

R#109: Cause the difference is I'll be able to sleep without a guilty conscience.

Homeboys were young adults living on the edge. On the one hand, like most Americans, they had relatively conservative views on social issues and wanted to settle down with a job, a wife, and children. On the other hand, they were afraid they would never succeed, and that long stays in prison would close doors and lock them out of a conventional life. They did not want to continue to live on the streets, but they feared that hustling might be the only way to survive.

Dope Fiends

Dope fiends are gang members who are addicted to cocaine. Thirty-eight percent of all African American founders were using cocaine at the time of our interview, as were 55% of Latinos and 53% of whites. African Americans used cocaine at lower rates than white gang members but went to jail twice as often. The main focus in a dope fiend's life is getting the drug. Asked what they regretted most about their life, dope fiends invariably said "drug use," whereas most homeboys said "dropping out of school."

344 / GANGS AND CRIME

Most Milwaukee gang dope fiends, or daily users of cocaine, smoked it as "rocks." More casual users, or reformed dope fiends, if they used cocaine at all, snorted it or sprinkled it on marijuana (called a "primo") to enhance the high. Injection was rare among African Americans but more common among Latinos. About one-quarter of those we interviewed, however, abstained totally from use of cocaine. A majority of the gang members on our rosters had used cocaine since its use escalated in Milwaukee in the late 1980s.

Of 110 gang founders who were reported to be currently using cocaine, 37% were reported to be using "heavily" (every day, in our data), 44% "moderately" (several times per week), and 19% "lightly" (sporadically). More than 70% of all founders on our rosters who were not locked up were currently using cocaine to some extent. More than one-third of our male respondents considered themselves, at some time in their lives, to be "heavy" cocaine users.

More than one-quarter of our respondents had used cocaine for seven years or more, roughly the total amount of time cocaine has dominated the illegal drug market in Milwaukee. Latinos had used cocaine slightly longer than African Americans, for a mean of 75 months compared with 65. Cocaine use followed a steady pattern in our respondents' lives; most homeboys had used cocaine as part of their day-to-day life, especially while in the dope business.

Dope fiends were quite unlike Cloward and Ohlin's "double failures," gang members who used drugs as part of a "retreatist subculture." Milwaukee dope fiends participated regularly in conventional labor markets. Of the 110 founders who were reported as currently using cocaine, slightly more were working legitimate jobs than were not working. Most dope fiends worked at some time in their homies' dope houses or were fronted an ounce or an "eightball" (3.5 grams) of cocaine to sell. Unlike Anderson's "wineheads," gang dope fiends were not predominantly "has-beens" and did not "lack the ability and motivation to hustle" (Anderson, 1978, pp. 96–97). Milwaukee cocaine users, like heroin users (Johnson et al., 1985; Moore, 1978; Preble & Casey, 1969), played an active role in the drug-selling business.

Rather than spending their income from drug dealing on family, clothes, or women, dope fiends smoked up their profits. Eventually many stole dope belonging to the boss or "dopeman" and got into trouble. At times their dope use made them so erratic that they were no longer trusted and were forced to leave the neighborhood. Often, however, the gang members who were selling took them back and fronted them cocaine to sell to put them back on their feet. Many had experienced problems in violating the cardinal rule, "Don't get high on your own supply," as in this typical story:

R#131: ... if you ain't the type that's a user, yeah, you'll make fabulous money but if you was the type that sells it and uses it and do it at the same time, you know, you get restless. Sometimes you get used to taking your own drugs.... I'll just use the profits and just do it ... and then the next day if I get something again, I'd just take the money to pay up and keep the profits.... You sell a couple of hundred and you do a hundred. That's how I was doing it.

Cocaine use was a regular part of the lives of most Milwaukee gang members engaged in the drug economy. More than half of our respondents had never attended a treatment program; more than half of those who had been in treatment went through court-ordered programs. Few of our respondents stopped use by going to a treatment program. Even heavy cocaine use was an "on-again, off-again" situation in which most gang members alternately quit by themselves and started use again (Waldorf, Reinarman, & Murphy, 1991).

Alcohol use among dope fiends and homeboys (particularly 40-ounce bottles of Olde English 800 ale) appears to be even more of a problem than cocaine use. Like homeboys, however, most dope fiends aspired to have a family, to hold a steady job, and to find some peace. The wild life of the dope game had played itself out; the main problem was how to quit using.

New Jacks

Whereas homeboys had a tentative relationship with conventional labor markets and held some strong moral beliefs, new jacks had chosen the dope game as a career. They were often loners, strong individualists like Jankowski's (1991) gang members, who cared little about group norms. Frequently they posed as the embodiment of media stereotypes. About one-quarter of our interview respondents could be described as new jacks: they had done nothing in the last 36 months except hustle or spend time in jail.

In some ways, new jacks mirror the criminal subculture described by Cloward and Ohlin. If a criminal subculture is to develop, Cloward and Ohlin argued, opportunities to learn a criminal career must be present, and close ties to conventional markets or customers must exist. This situation distinguishes the criminal from the violent and the retreatist subcultures. The emergence of the cocaine economy and a large market for illegal drugs provided precisely such an opportunity structure for this generation of gang members. New jacks are those who took advantage of the opportunities, and who, at least for the present, have committed themselves to a career in the dope game.

> Q: Do you consider it wrong or immoral to sell dope?
> R#203: I think it's right because can't no motherfucker live your life but you.
> Q: Why?
> R#203: Why? I'll put it this way... I love selling dope. I know there's other niggers out here love the money just like I do. And ain't no motherfucker gonna stop a nigger from selling dope.... I'd sell to my own mother if she had the money.

New jacks, like other gang cocaine dealers, lived up to media stereotypes of the "drug dealer" role and often were emulated by impressionable youths. Some new jacks were homeboys from Milwaukee's original neighborhood gangs, who had given up their conventional dreams; others were members of gangs that were formed solely for drug dealing (see Klein & Maxson, 1993).

A founder of one new jack gang described the scene as his gang set up shop in Milwaukee. Note the strong mimicking of media stereotypes:

> R#126: ... it was crime and drug problems before we even came into the scene. It was just controlled by somebody else. We just came on with a whole new attitude, outlook, at the whole situation. It's like, have you ever seen the movie New Jack City, about the kid in New York? You see, they was already there. We just came out with a better idea, you know what I'm saying?

New jacks rejected the homeboys' moral outlook. Many were raised by families with long traditions of hustling or a generation of gang affiliations, and had few hopes of a conventional future. They are the voice of the desperate ghetto dweller, those who live in Carl Taylor's (1990, p. 36) "third culture" made up of "underclass and urban gang members who exhibit signs of moral erosion and anarchy" or propagators of Bourgois's (1990, p. 631) "culture of terror." New jacks fit the media stereotype of all gang members, even though they represent fewer than 25% of Milwaukee's adult gang members.

DISCUSSION: GANGS, THE UNDERCLASS, AND PUBLIC POLICY

Our study was conducted in one aging postindustrial city, with a population of 600,000. How much can be generalized from our findings can be determined only by researchers in other cities, looking at our categories and determining whether they are useful. Cloward and Ohlin's opportunity theory is a workable general theoretical framework, but more case studies are needed in order to recast their theory to reflect three decades of economic and social changes. We present our typology to encourage others to observe variation within and between gangs, and to assist in the creation of new taxonomies and new theory.

Our paper raises several empirical questions for researchers: Are the behavior patterns of the founding gang members in our sample representative of adult gang members in other cities? In larger cities, are most gang members now new jacks who have long given up the hope of a conventional life, or are most still homeboys? Are there "homeboy" gangs and "new jack" gangs, following the "street gang/drug gang" notion of Klein and Maxson (1993)? If so, what distinguishes one from the other? Does gang members' orientation to conventionality vary by ethnicity or by region? How does it change over time? Can this typology help account for variation in rates of violence between gang members? Can female gang members be typed in the same way as males?

Our data also support the life course perspective of Sampson and Laub (1993, p. 255), who ask whether present criminal justice policies "are producing unintended criminogenic effects." Milwaukee gang members are like the persistent, serious offenders in the Gluecks' data (Glueck & Glueck, 1950). The key to their future lies in building social capital that comes from steady employment and a supportive relationship, without the constant threat of incarceration (Sampson & Laub, 1993, pp. 162–168). Homeboys largely had a wife or a steady lady, were unhappily enduring "the silent, subtle humiliations" of the secondary labor market (Bourgois, 1990, p. 629), and lived in dread of prison. Incarceration for drug charges undercut their efforts to find steady work and led them almost inevitably back to the drug economy.

Long and mandatory prison terms for use and intent to sell cocaine lump those who are committed to the drug economy with those who are using or are selling in order to survive. Our prisons are filled disproportionately with minority drug offenders (Blumstein, 1993) like our homeboys, who in essence are being punished for the "crime" of not accepting poverty or of being addicted to cocaine. Our data suggest that jobs, more accessible drug treatment, alternative sentences, or even decriminalization of nonviolent drug offenses would be better approaches than the iron fist of the war on drugs (see Hagedorn, 1991; Reinarman & Levine, 1990; Spergel & Curry, 1990).

Finally, our typology raises ethical questions for researchers. Wilson (1987, p. 8) called the underclass "collectively different" from the poor of the past, and many studies focus on underclass deviance. Our study found that some underclass gang members had embraced the drug economy and had forsaken conventionality, but we also found that the majority of adult gang members are still struggling to hold onto a conventional orientation to life.

Hannerz (1969, p. 36) commented more than two decades ago that dichotomizing community residents into "respectables" and "disrespectables" "seems often to emerge from social science writing about poor black people or the lower classes in general." Social science that emphasizes differences within poor communities, without noting commonalities, is one sided and often distorts and demonizes underclass life.

Our data emphasize that there is no Great Wall separating the underclass from the rest of the central-city poor and working class. Social research should not build one either. Researchers who describe violent and criminal gang actions without also addressing gang members' orientation to conventionality are doing a disservice to the public, to policy makers, and to social science.

References

Anderson, E. (1978). *A place on the corner.* Chicago: University of Chicago Press.
Blumstein, A. (1993). Making rationality relevant. *Criminology, 31,* 1–16.

Bourgois, P. (1990). In search of Horatio Alger: Culture and ideology in the crack economy. *Contemporary Drug Problems, 16*, 619–649.

Cloward, R., & Ohlin, L. (1960). *Delinquency and opportunity*. Glencoe, IL: Free Press.

Cohen, A. (1955). *Delinquent boys*. Glencoe, IL: Free Press.

Coleman, J. S. (1988). Social capital in the creation of human capital. *American Journal of Sociology, 94*, 95–120.

Glueck, S., & Glueck, E. (1950). *Unraveling juvenile delinquency*. New York: Commonwealth Fund.

Gottfredson, M., & Hirschi, T. (1990). *A general theory of crime*. Stanford, CA: Stanford University Press.

Hagedorn, J. M. (1991). Gangs, neighborhoods, and public policy. *Social Problems, 38*, 529–542.

Hannerz, U. (1969). *Soulside: Inquiries into ghetto culture and community*. New York: Columbia University Press.

Huff, C. R. (1990). *Gangs in America*. Newbury Park, CA: Sage.

Jankowski, M. S. (1991). *Islands in the street: Gangs and American urban society*. Berkeley: University of California Press.

Johnson, B. D., Goldstein, P. J., Preble, E., Schmeidler, J., Lipton, D. S., Spunt, B., at al. (1985). *Taking care of business: The economics of crime by heroin abusers*. Lexington, MA: Heath.

Klein, M. W. (1971). *Street gangs and street workers*. Englewood Cliffs, NJ: Prentice Hall.

Klein, M. W. (1992). The new street gang... or is it? *Contemporary Sociology, 21*, 80–82.

Klein, M. W., & Maxson, C. L. (1993). Gangs and cocaine trafficking. In C. Uchida & D. Mackenzie (Eds.), *Drugs and the criminal justice system* (pp. 136–148). Newbury Park, CA: Sage.

Klein, M. W., Maxson, C. L., & Cunningham, L. C. (1991). Crack, street gangs, and violence. *Criminology, 29*, 623–650.

Liebow, E. (1967). *Tally's corner*. Boston: Little, Brown.

Lincoln, Y. S., & Guba, E. G. (1985). *Naturalistic inquiry*. Beverly Hills, CA: Sage.

MacCoun, R., & Reuter, P. (1992). Are the wages of sin $30 an hour? Economic aspects of street-level drug dealing. *Crime and Delinquency, 38*, 477–491.

MacLeod, J. (1987). *Ain't no makin' it: Leveled aspirations in a low-income neighborhood*. Boulder, CO: Westview.

Matza, D. (1964). *Delinquency and drift*. New York: Wiley.

Merton, R. K. (1957). *Social theory and social structure*. New York: Free Press.

Miller, W. B. (1969). Lower class culture as a generating milieu of gang delinquency. *Journal of Social Issues, 14*, 5–19.

Moore, J. W. (1978). *Homeboys: Gangs, drugs, and prison in the barrios of Los Angeles*. Philadelphia: Temple University Press.

Moore, J. W. (1991). *Going down to the barrio: Homeboys and homegirls in change.* Philadelphia: Temple University Press.

Padilla, F. (1992). *The gang as an American enterprise.* New Brunswick, NJ: Rutgers University Press.

Preble, E., & Casey, J. H. (1969). Taking care of business: The heroin user's life on the street. *International Journal of the Addictions, 4,* 1–24.

Reinarman, C., & Levine, H. G. (1990). Crack in context: Politics and media in the making of a drug scare. *Contemporary Drug Problems, 16,* 535–577.

Rose, H. M., Edari, R. S., Quinn, L. M., & Pawasrat, J. (1992). *The labor market experience of young African American men from low-income families in Wisconsin.* Milwaukee: University of Wisconsin, Milwaukee Employment and Training Institute.

Sampson, R. J., & Laub, J. H. (1993). *Crime in the making: Pathways and turning points through life.* Cambridge, MA: Harvard University Press.

Short, J. F., & Strodtbeck, F. L. (1965). *Group process and gang delinquency.* Chicago: University of Chicago Press.

Skolnick, J. H. (1990). The social structure of street drug dealing. *American Journal of Police, 9,* 1–41.

Spergel, I. A., & Curry, G. D. (1990). Strategies and perceived agency effectiveness in dealing with the youth gang problem. In C. R. Huff (Ed.), *Gangs in America.* Beverly Hills, CA: Sage.

Strauss, A. L. (1987). *Qualitative analysis for social scientists.* Cambridge, UK: Cambridge University Press.

Sullivan, M. L. (1989). *Getting paid: Youth crime and work in the inner city.* Ithaca, NY: Cornell University Press.

Taylor, C. (1990). *Dangerous society.* East Lansing: Michigan State University Press.

Thrasher, F. (1927/1963). *The gang.* Chicago: University of Chicago Press.

Waldorf, D. (1993). *Final report of the crack sales, gangs, and violence study.* Alameda, CA: Alameda Institute for Scientific Analysis.

Waldorf, D., Reinarman, C., & Murphy, S. (1991). *Cocaine changes: The experience of using and quitting.* Philadelphia, PA: Temple University Press.

Whyte, W. F. (1943). *Street corner society.* Chicago: University of Chicago Press.

Williams, T. (1989). *The cocaine kids.* Reading, MA: Addison-Wesley.

Wilson, W. J. (1987). *The truly disadvantaged.* Chicago: University of Chicago.

SECTION VII

DRUGS AND CRIME

One of the most enduring controversies in criminology is that surrounding the relationship between drugs and crime. Although no one disputes the correlation—that drugs and crime seem to be interrelated in some manner—the issue of causation is controversial. Do drugs cause crime, or are they related in some other manner?

Recent U.S. Department of Justice data show clearly that a majority of arrestees tend to test positive for drugs. During one period, 78 percent of arrestees in Philadelphia tested positive for at least one illegal drug. Drug use for female arrestees ranged from less than 50 percent in San Antonio to over 85 percent in Manhattan.

In the first selection, "E Is for Ecstasy: A Participant Observation Study of Ecstasy Use," Wilson Palacios and Melissa Fenwick present a unique inside perspective on drug use in the club culture of south Florida. Palacios and Fenwick are particularly concerned with how and when Ecstasy is obtained and used by participants and the steps they take to avoid detection and arrest.

In the next selection, Charles E. Faupel ("The Drugs-Crime Connection among Stable Addicts") considers the role that criminal activity plays in facilitating drug use. Using ethnographic interviews with a population of stable addicts (seasoned, mature heroin users), Faupel argues that the drugs-crime connection is much more complex than the "drugs cause crime" hypothesis of popular currency. Instead, he reports that increased heroin consumption is preceded by increased criminal activity. He further debunks the myth of "crazed drug fiends" by examining the rational processes involved in maintaining a drug habit through criminal activity.

In the third chapter in this section, "Property Crime and Women Drug Dealers," Barbara Denton and Pat O'Malley examine a group of successful women drug dealers in Melbourne, Australia, and map their involvement in property crime.

21

"E" Is for Ecstasy: A Participant Observation Study of Ecstasy Use

Wilson R. Palacios and Melissa E. Fenwick

*I*n this selection, Wilson Palacios and Melissa Fenwick offer an insider's view of the Ecstasy culture in south Florida (Tampa). During a 15-month participant-observation study, they attended dozens of all-night (and sometimes several days in length) "clublike" parties, observing and asking questions of participants. Attending the nightclubs and parties where Ecstasy was freely available, the researchers were able to allay suspicion by presenting themselves as a couple interested in the music underground. In some cases they advised the others that they were researchers; in other cases, they did not, preferring to observe incognito. This chapter is a brief introduction to a continuing study—one of the first of its kind examining contemporary Ecstasy culture in America.

In *Writing on Drugs*, Sadie Plant argues that "every drug has its own character, its own unique claim to fame" (1999, p. 4). This is certainly true in the case of Ecstasy (MDMA). In 1986 Jerome Beck wrote:

> MDMA has been thrust upon the public awareness as a largely unknown drug which to some is a medical miracle and to others a social devil. ... There have been the born-again protagonists who say that once you have tried it you will see the light and will defend it against any attack, and there have been the staunch antagonists who say this is nothing but LSD revisited and it will certainly destroy our youth. (p. 305)

Beck's statements have proven to be timeless, as they accurately characterize the current media blitz surrounding the drug MDMA/Ecstasy. On July 1, 1985, at the behest of the U.S. Drug Enforcement Administration, MDMA/Ecstasy was temporarily placed in Schedule I of the Controlled Substance Act (CSA), with permanent placement achieved on November 13, 1986. Although it may seem easy to understand the DEA's objectives in banning MDMA/Ecstasy, their actions inadvertently paved the way for a large international "underground" manufacturing and distribution network worth millions of dollars, and, to a greater extent, for a larger hidden population of users.

Source: Prepared especially for this volume. Copyright © 2003 by Roxbury Publishing Company. All rights reserved. This project was supported by funds from USF Research & Creative Scholarship Grant #12-21-926RO.

Law enforcement officials and politicians have led this new charge against MDMA/Ecstasy and its users. Newspaper headlines such as "Drug's Night Club Pull Seen Hard to Curb" (*The Boston Globe*), "Raving and Behaving: The Reputation of the High-Energy, All Night Dance Parties Outpaces the Reality" (*The Buffalo News*), and "Deputies: Ecstasy Overdose Killed Teen" (*St. Petersburg Times*) have been used to usher in a new "war on drugs," which, like our previous efforts with crack cocaine, stands to dramatically increase jail and prison populations with Ecstasy users and challenge our taken-for-granted notions concerning civil liberties.

Despite the attention from the criminal justice system, Ecstasy use and abuse has received minimal attention from the social scientific community, in particular criminology. Much of what we think we know about patterns of use and abuse concerning this drug stems largely from existing self-report surveys, such as Monitoring the Future (MTF), drug surveillance systems such as Drug Abuse Warning Network (DAWN), and the Arrestee Drug Abuse Monitoring (ADAM) program. Until now, there has been little in the way of active ethnographic fieldwork in this country concerning MDMA/ Ecstasy use and its culture.

This chapter is derived from an ongoing, two-year ethnographic study concerning the use of "club drugs" (i.e., MDMA/Ecstasy, ketamine/Special K, GHB, and nitrates) and club culture in Florida. The research focuses on the emotional state of individuals who ingest MDMA/Ecstasy, the local market for such drugs, and the vernacular of this drug culture.

The drug 3, 4-methylenedioxymethamphetamine (MDMA) is commonly referred to on the street as Ecstasy (Cohen, 1998). Although other names, such as Adam, the Love Drug, Mickey, X, Raven, and M&M's, are used to refer to MDMA, the term Ecstasy is the most recognizable. In the Hillsborough and Pinellas County area, the terms *bean*(s) and *rolls* are used interchangeably to refer to Ecstasy. When asked the origin of these terms, we were told that Ecstasy pills are called *beans* because they "look like little lima beans" and *rolls* because of the way they make you feel.

Ecstasy tablets are sold on the street according to distinctive designer logos pressed on one side of the pill. For example, in the field we came across Ecstasy pills sold under such names as Mitsubishi, Smurfs, Calvin Kleins, Nikes, Anchors, Rolls Royce (RR), Starburst, Pink Hearts, Double Stack Crowns, Navigator, KnockOuts, Blue Gene, and Red Gene. Many of the Ecstasy pills we encountered in the field were of various colors, although white was the most common. Moreover, we quickly learned that the popularity of these pills was solely dependent on word-of-mouth marketing from the individual consumer level. Ecstasy represents a marketing bonanza because of its ability to induce a physiologically and psychologically euphoric state so intense without the stigma associated with drugs like crack cocaine or heroin. In addition, it is a drug that many feel they can realistically walk away from or "schedule" into their lives on an as-needed basis. The following typify this attitude for some of our participants:

It's not like doing crack or smack (heroin) ... you don't hit a pipe or needle. ... I wouldn't do that cause my friends would be like. ... Hey, crack monster ... or crack freak ... and that's not cool ... think about it ... it's a little pill which takes you for a ride and then it's over ... you don't feign (crave) for it ... you can do it every weekend or once a month or once or twice a year ... just depends on what you've got going in your life and the people around you. (Jason, a single white male, 20 years of age)

When I was in college I would roll [use Ecstasy] every weekend except for midterms and finals ... but since I've been out I haven't rolled in the last two years ... I'm not saying that I won't ... but I've just been busy with work and since I work for the system [referring to the criminal justice system] I know they drug test. ... If I will do it again I'll just plan for it ... it stays in your system from 2 to 5 days ... (Mark, a single white male, 29 years of age)

The intense physiological (amphetamine-like) rush from Ecstasy is referred to as *blowing up* or *rolling*. This experience varies across individuals. However, the overwhelming sensation of a heightened emotional and physical state was a commonly reported characteristic. The following comments typify this recurring theme:

When you're blowing up it is like you're fucking skin is going to come undone. Just imagine an orgasm but twenty or fifty times better and intense. That's the lure of X. (Jerry, a single white male, 25 years of age)

I felt like I was coming undone from the inside. You can feel every inch of your skin, even the tiny little hairs on your arms and legs ... feels that good. (Amy, single white female, 19 years of age)

Valter and Arrizabalaga (1998, p. 13) argue that "the world-wide and still increasing use and abuse of MDMA (Ecstasy) is due to its euphoriant properties and capacity to enhance communication and contact with other people." Actually, because of this last property, Ecstasy is really a member of a small class of compounds called *entactogens* or *empathogens* (which means creating contact or empathy) and therefore should not be classified as a "hallucinogenic-amphetamine" drug (see Cohen, 1998). This feeling of connecting with other people is what makes Ecstasy such a psychological draw for most people, including our participants:

I know I could go to [local nightclub] and after I eat my pill I won't care what people think of me ... I won't care if they think I'm fat, too skinny, or If I am wearing the wrong shoes ... I just don't care because it becomes about meeting people and just meeting different kinds of people. (Betty, a single white female, 25 years of age, mother of two)

It's about having a good time ... I even don't have to worry about guys trying to hook up [reference to sex] with me. ... If guys are rolling you know they are not looking at you that way ... at least not when they are rolling ... maybe later on the comedown [referring to the end of the night] but not during. (Carrie, a white Latina female, 21 years of age)

BLOWING UP

Our participants gauged the strength and purity of a pill according to the intensity of their *blowing up* or *rolling* experience. Some acute reactions experienced by our participants during the blowing up or rolling stage were bruxism (teeth grinding), trismus (jaw clenching), uncontrollable fidgeting of extremities, rapid eye movements, and a heighten sensitivity to all external stimuli (touch, lights, sounds, etc.). In order for us to tap into these varied experiences, we asked the following: "How do you know you are/were blowing up?" These are some of the responses we received:

> It usually wouldn't come on until after thirty or forty minutes but when it did you would just feel this overwhelming sensation of all your emotions being flooded [released] throughout your body. I would say after forty-five minutes into it I would feel my eyes twitch and I would have this need to just massage everything and anything around me. One night I was massaging my arms so hard without realizing it or feeling any pain that the next day I woke up and had broken my skin. I was in pain the next morning but I did not remember feeling any pain when I was doing this ... it just feel so good. (Tim, a white Latino male, 27 years of age, married)

> You can't help being or wanting to be touched. ... I've seen men touching each other without all the worry about people thinking they were gay or anything ... you know you're rolling when somebody comes up to you and begins massaging your neck, shoulders, or back ... it feels just so good that one time I had my girlfriend massage my lower back so hard that she made me pee in my pants—now that was a good bean ... you can't know what I'm talking about unless you've been there. (Stacie, a white single female 18 years of age)

> The first time I rolled I didn't feel a thing ... I was pissed because I spent some money and everyone around me was rolling their asses off and I was the only one in the group sitting there like a dump fuck ... but the second time I rolled ... that's when I can tell you that I honestly blow up.... I first noticed it because of the lights ... everything was clearer and brighter. ... I would see the bright colors from the corner of my eyes and then my feet started swaying to the music. ... I looked at my feet and it was like they weren't even mine ... I kept wanting to get up and just walk around and talk to people. ... I didn't care what people thought of ... I just wanted to be around people. (Lady X, a single white female, 23 years of age)

> I really don't like anything speedy ... my father died of a heart attack at a young age. ... I don't think I have a heart condition but I just don't want anything speeding my heart. ... I usually like the ones that are not speedy. ... I like for it [Ecstasy] to come on slow and gradually over the night. ... I want it to last ... I'm not one for dancing or stuff like that, I just want to sit there and take it all in. (Jane, a single white female, 27 years of age)

SIDE EFFECTS

Of all of the possible acute reactions—papillary dilation, headache, hypertension, nausea, tachycardia, blurred vision, hypertonicity, and tremors—that

Ecstasy induces, jaw clenching and teeth grinding (trismus and bruxism) were among the side effects most cited by our participants:

> You must always have something to chew on or you'll end up loosing your teeth. (Mary, a single white female, 21 years of age; has been using Ecstasy for 2 years)

> The only thing I hate about rolling is how your jaw feels the next morning. You just can't help chewing gum but you can chew the same piece of gum all night long and not realize it ... you can keep chewing because you need something in your mouth but you don't realize how much pain your jaw is going to be the next day. There have been times when I couldn't even open my mouth for one or two days after rolling ... it's a good thing I didn't want to eat. (Ms. S, a single Latina female, 18 years of age)

> The next day I noticed a lot of sores in my mouth ... probably from my teeth grinding down on my gums ... the inside of my mouth hurts for about 2 or 3 days after. (Joe, a single white female, 21 years of age)

A number of our participants used candy such as Gummy Bears, Starbursts, Jolly Ranchers, and BlowPops to help mitigate the unpleasantness of their jaw muscles clenching. Actually, any form of hard candy or chewing gum would do as long as it kept them from grinding their teeth and straining their jaw muscles:

> I've worn away all of my back teeth and I have four sores in my mouth from just grinding the inside of my teeth. I chipped my front teeth one night after dropping [ingesting] five beans. ... I was blowing up hard ... I felt my eyes roll towards the back of my head. I also bit my lip because I didn't realize I was biting down on it until I went to the bathroom at this club and looked in the mirror and noticed a little bit of blood from my upper lip ... no biggie but it scares the shit out of you looking in the mirror and seeing blood. (Ms. G, a single Latina female, 29 years of age)

> A Blowpop or a piece of gum never tasted so fucking good as when you are rolling ... but it helps not lose your teeth because with a good bean your teeth will chatter. (Greg, a single white male, 24 years of age)

BUYING ECSTASY

Ecstasy's street price makes it attractive and affordable. Currently, in the Tampa area the price ranges from $10 to $20 per pill, with an average cost of $15. Factors that determine the price of a pill are market availability and whether or not one is known to the dealers. Market availability is just that ... supply and demand. When a large number of pills are on the market, prices are lower. As might be expected, prices to strangers are usually higher than those to people known to the dealer. Prices at nightclubs are also more expensive than pills bought in other locations. We asked one dealer whom we had met during a rolling party whether he overcharged people at nightclubs. He offered the following view:

> If I don't know the person I will and definitely if it's in a club ... it's the price of doing business in a club. ... I have to worry about the bouncers [security personnel], off-duty undercover cops and narcs [people working for the police] ... just too much hassle. But I'm going to make my money ... people just have to pay. ... If I know you, I'll cut you a break but not by much ... I really just don't like dealing in clubs ...

Our participants preferred to buy and take Ecstasy before arriving at their destinations as a way of minimizing the risk of detection from law enforcement. The following statements are typical:

> I always buy a few days before I know I am going out. That way I don't get caught up with people saying that they can or can't get it [Ecstasy] and then having to go the club and buying something from I don't know who ... a narc or undercover, and paying something crazy like $20. (Vanessa, a 20-something Latina female)

> We would always drop [take Ecstasy] at our apartment and then go to the clubs ... we knew that we would be at the clubs like in twenty minutes so we knew that our rolls wouldn't kick in yet or they would start to kick in just as we were in line to get into the clubs ... that's how we'd do it ... we would never have anything on us ... just in case they would search you at the door. (Jimmy, a white male, 19 years of age)

ONSET OF EFFECTS

The average user begins to feel the effects from one Ecstasy pill in about 30 to 45 minutes. The time period is contingent on what and how recently people have eaten and on their unique physiology. The overall effects of Ecstasy, or an "E trip" as it is commonly known, can last from 4 to 6 hours, depending on the person's physiology, on his or her prior food intake, and most important on whether the pill has adulterants in it. In recent years the media and some ill-informed law enforcement officials have alleged that Ecstasy pills contain substances like rat poison and crushed glass, as well as other illegal drugs such as cocaine, heroin, and LSD. However, others have shown (see Beck & Rosenbaum, 1994; Cohen, 1998; Saunders & Doblin, 1996) this is to be more myth than reality.

According to DanceSafe, a harm-reduction organization, recent adulterant screening efforts have revealed the presence of such drugs as dextromethorphan, phenylpropanolamine, ephedrine, pseudoephedrine, glyceryl guaiacolate, other amphetamine-like substances (i.e., MDA, MDEA, DOM, 2-CB, and DOT), caffeine, ketamine, and only trace amounts of such substances as heroin and LSD (DanceSafe, 2001). It is believed that underground manufacturers in clandestine laboratories add many of these substances purely as a cost-saving method, although some of these ingredients do increase the risk for negative reactions, including overdose.

The fact that they could be ingesting a host of other substances in addition to MDMA did not appear to concern our subjects greatly. Our participants would take Ecstasy one of three ways: (1) orally, (2) snorting, or (3) "parachuting" or "packing." Some participants elected either one or a combination of all three methods during the evening depending on when they wanted to feel the effects of their pill. With oral ingestion, initial effects were usually felt within 30 to 40 minutes. Snorting produced effects within 10 to 15 minutes, while parachuting or packing would produce effects within 5 minutes.

"Parachuting" Ecstasy involves inserting the pill into the anus, like a suppository. Parachuters believe the pill will be absorbed faster and the effects will be felt in a shorter time. Just how parachuting is done is described in the following field note excerpt:

The time was 6:15 a.m. and we had just left an after-hours club where we had spent the last three hours with a group of people we met up with at another club earlier in the evening. In leaving this after-hours club we all got into our cars and headed for a gas station nearby. I asked David, a white male about 29 years of age, what we were looking to get at this gas station. He answered, "I need to refuel. I need to stop and get some Red Bull before we continue or I'm not going to make it." The gas station was less than ten city blocks from the after-hours club and we were there within ten minutes. All three cars pulled into the gas station, and most of the passengers got out of their cars.

In total there were five cars and ten people all together. One of the drivers, Jake, a Latino male in his early twenties, pulled his red Honda Civic to a gas pump, got out, inserted a credit card, and began to pump gas. I waited outside the car I was riding in for the rest of the group. I noticed that most were in line inside the gas station with items in their hands. Since it was early in the morning on a Sunday and no one was around, I decide to go inside just to be with the folks. In walking into the gas station I noticed that most had either Red Bull, Gatorade, or PowerAde sport drinks in their hands. Two individuals had two bottles of water, Evian, in their hands. I noticed that Fred, a white male in his late twenties was walking towards the back of the gas station.

Soon there was Henry, a white male in his early thirties, following behind him. I think Mary, a Latina female about 20 years of age, noticed I was looking at them, and, in a very low whisper, said, "They going to the bathroom to shoot." I asked, "To shoot what?" She replied, "They still have some beans left," and that's all she said. Now, I knew that shooting beans did not mean using a needle, since I have not seen anyone use this method for taking Ecstasy. So I thought she was referring to "parachuting" but I was not sure. It is a term I had heard before but I had never seen anyone actually do it. I could not help it, but curiosity got the better of me and so I headed for the bathroom, and just as I got to the door Fred looked at me and said, "Hey, professor, do you want to see something?" I replied, "What?" Henry replied, "Come see."

There we were ... in the men's bathroom, three males and I could not help think that under other circumstance this scene would represent something altogether different. However, there we were. I stood directly in front of the door and Fred, while reaching for his right pants pocket, said, "I know you've heard about "parachuting." I replied, "Yeah … but I think I know what it is." Fred's reply was, "Well, here you go …" As he said this he pulled out three beans from a small baggie … they were white in color and I knew they were known as RR or Rolls Royce because that was what the group had been taking for most of the night. As he produced the beans and threw the baggie on the floor, Henry walked over to a bathroom stall and tore off a piece of toilet paper, probably about less than one inch in length. He walks over to the faucet and just wets the piece of paper with a small amount of water. Fred then walks over and places the three beans into the center of the paper. Henry begins to fold the paper over the pills and forms a nice little wad of paper with its end twisted. He licks the twisted ends and I asked, "Why are you doing that?" His response, "To make sure that it's all nice and tight and that it doesn't come undone when it goes in." As he says this, Fred walks over to a bathroom stall, unzips his pants and lets his pants come down to his thigh area. Henry walks over to him and says, "Are you ready?" Fred's response: "Go ahead." Fred bends only halfway and Henry takes that wad of paper with the twisted ends and begins to insert it anally into Fred. There I am watching this and all I could say, "Why can't you do it yourself, Fred?" Fred stands up and as he zips up his pants he turns around and says, "I just don't like putting anything into me." Henry adds, "I do myself all the time and I do my girl this way." In almost a comic relief tone, Fred adds, "Now that's 'parachuting' professor." My only response: "No confusing that one … that's 'parachuting.'"

COMING DOWN

Toward the end of the blowing up stage of an E trip, people respond in many different ways. Some just want to engage in a free-flowing conversation about their lives and their own personal anxieties and fears. There are those that just want to sit outside to watch the sunrise and to feel the cool morning breeze brushing up against their skin. A few have some difficulty in accepting that their experience is about to end and therefore consume marijuana as a method for "kicking it back in."

> I always like to have some kind bud [high-quality marijuana] on me to smoke towards the end … takes the edge off and kicks my roll back in … it won't be as intense, but you do feel it somewhat … just relaxes me and give me a smoother roll at the end. … (Diego, a white male Latino in his early 20s)

Some also consume drugs like Valium and Xanax as a way of coping with the edginess they felt from Ecstasy:

> The morning after I take a Xane bar [referring to Xanax] then I'm OK … I can go to sleep … if I don't, my fucking mind is not going to stop talking to me … it's like you want to go to sleep because you know you're tired but your mind won't let you go … a Xane bar or some Valium would do the trick. (Keith, a white male in his early 30s)

For some of our participants, the day or days after their use of Ecstasy consisted of moderate to intense fatigue. In communicating the nature of this psychological and physical exhaustion, they used the term *ate-up*. For most, this ate-up feeling was characterized as a loss of appetite, mental exhaustion, some nausea, intense thirst, and body aches. Although it sounds remarkably similar to a hangover, many of our participants did not see such similarities:

> The only thing I hate about E is how I feel the next day ... I just can't o anything. ... I mean, I sleep all day so I waste an entire day and then I get up and just want to lay in my bed ... I can't think and if I do, I can't get the music or people out of my head. I really don't want to eat anything but I force myself to eat something ... I'm not hungry but I just force myself. (Christine, a white female in her 20s)

> I just can't do anything the next day ... all I want to is sleep ... I love to take a shower when I get home because it feels good, but then I just head for my bed ... I get no headaches or feel like throwing up, but I just don't want anything. (Mike, a white male in his early 20s)

> I really don't feel ate-up the next day ... I sleep for about six or eight hours and get up ... I eat a little something and then I just sit around, turn the TV on but I really don't watch it ... I just want to sit there and think ... my legs hurt a bit but that's from the dancing. ... If that's ate-up, then maybe yeah, but nothing like what my friends feel. (Judy, a white female in her late 20s)

> For me, the worst is about three days after I rolled. I just feel down ... can't start or really finish anything ... I just want to lay in my bed and do absolutely nothing ... I stop and think that I won't ever do that again [use Ecstasy] but then I remember I had a good time on it and well ... you know ... (Sue, a white female in her late teens)

Such after-effects are mitigated by the person's physiology, health status prior to use, frequency of use, concurrent drug use (such as with LSD, cocaine, heroin, or alcohol), and the type and amount of Ecstasy pills consumed. Therefore, the ate-up experience is never the same for any one individual.

CONCLUSION

Philippe Bourgois (1999, p. 215) argues, "A major task of participant-observers is to put themselves in the shoes of the people they study in order to see local realities through local eyes." As participant-observers we have presented a local picture of Ecstasy use among a diverse network of individuals. There is no denying that for our participants, taking Ecstasy—despite all the known risks—is pleasurable. A "local reality" is that Ecstasy is relatively affordable, does not have the same stigma associated with other illegal drugs, and is very much a part of the local youth culture (individuals between the ages of 18 and 35). Because this is an ongoing ethnographic study, there are many areas that we have not yet studied. We wanted to present a "local portrait" of Ecstasy use. We only hope that we remained true to our participants in setting out to accomplish this goal.

References

Beck, J. (1986). MDMA: The popularization and resultant implications of a recently controlled psychoactive substance. *Contemporary Drug Problems, 13*, 305–313.

Beck, J., & Rosenbaum, M. (1994). *Pursuit of ecstasy: The MDMA experience.* New York: State University of New York Press.

Bourgois, P. (1999). Theory, method, and power in drug and HIV-prevention research: A participant-observer's critique. *Substance Use & Misuse, 34*, 2155–2172.

Cohen, R. S. (1998). *The love drug: Marching to the beat of ecstasy.* New York: Haworth.

DanceSafe. (2001). Retrieved August 2001 from http://www.dancesafe.org/labtesting/

Plant, S. (1999). *Writing on drugs.* New York: Farrar, Straus and Giroux.

Saunders, N., & Doblin, R. (1996). *Ecstasy: Dance, trance and transformation.* Oakland, CA: Quick American Achieves.

Valter, K., & Arrizabalaga, P. (1998). *Designer drugs directory.* New York: Elsevier.

22

The Drugs-Crime Connection among Stable Addicts

Charles E. Faupel

*I*n this chapter, Charles E. Faupel examines in detail the lifestyles and career patterns of hard-core heroin addicts and the controversial issue of the relationship between drugs and crime. He also considers the question of whether addict criminals are skilled, rational "professional" criminals or opportunists. Faupel arrives at many of the same conclusions regarding opportunism versus rationality as have other researchers represented in this book (see Shover and Honaker; Wright and Decker). The lifestyle depicted by Faupel as representative of the addict criminal is also similar to that noted by Shover and Honaker in their study of persistent property criminals. Regarding the drugs-crime nexus, Faupel concludes that drug use does not cause crime, but may be caused by crime or at least facilitated by it. His treatment of these issues supports an understanding of the heroin addict as a much more rational being than previously believed.

Faupel notes four phases in the heroin-using career: the occasional user, the stable addict, the free-wheeling junkie, and the street junkie. In this selection he focuses on the stable addict—the mature, seasoned heroin user. He characterizes this stage in the heroin addict's life as analogous to the productive, established period in conventional careers.

In terms of research methodology this article is drawn from a long-term study of the relationship of drugs to crime. It is based on life history interviews with hard-core heroin addicts in the Wilmington, Delaware, area. Thirty heroin addicts were extensively interviewed—10 to 25 hours each in sessions lasting from two to four hours. The subjects were paid a small stipend for their time.

The subjects all had extensive criminal histories and at the time of the interviews, 24 were under correctional supervision (incarcerated, probation, parole, or work release). Women were slightly overrepresented, constituting 12 of the 30 respondents.

The sample consisted of 22 blacks and eight whites. Latinos were not represented because there is not a sizeable Latino drug-using population in the area where the study was conducted.

Source: Adapted from Charles E. Faupel, *Shooting Dope: Career Patterns of Hard-Core Heroin Users*, pp. 73–86. Copyright © 1991 by University of Florida Press. Reprinted with permission.

The complexity of the drugs-crime connection is perhaps most fully apparent during the stable-addict phase. One clear feature is the role that criminal activities play in facilitating drug use. The participants in this study strongly concurred that their level of heroin consumption was a function of their ability to afford it, which was usually enhanced by criminal activity. "The better I got at crime," remarked Stephanie, "the more money I made; the more money I made, the more drugs I used." She went on to explain, "I think that most people that get high, the reason it goes to the extent that it goes—that it becomes such a high degree of money—is because they make the money like that. I'm saying if the money wasn't available to them like that, they wouldn't be into drugs as deep as they were."

Contrary to the "drugs cause crime" hypothesis, which suggests that increases in the level of heroin consumption are necessarily followed by stepped-up criminal activity, the dynamics reported by the addicts in this study are quite the opposite: increased heroin consumption is preceded by increased criminal activity as measured by estimated criminal income. This does not necessarily imply a greater frequency of crime, for, as I shall highlight below, stable-addict status usually brings with it greater sophistication in skill and technique, often resulting in higher proceeds per criminal event.

These life history data also reveal, however, that the relationship between drug use and crime is much broader and more complex than simple causality. As I suggested earlier, increased criminal income not only enhances drug availability, but also provides the basis for an expanded life structure, an alternative daily routine. Because these criminal routines usually provide greater flexibility than do most forms of legitimate employment, they free the addict from prohibitive roles and social contacts that may be imposed by more rigid schedules. Drug-using activities are certainly facilitated under these more flexible routines. Nevertheless, criminal routines do impose certain constraints on the addict lifestyle. Moreover, they provide an important structure to one's drug-using activities. It is in this respect that Old Ray likened the routine of dealing drugs to legitimate employment: "When you're working, the world has its rhythm, its time clock. You have your eight-to-five time clock. Well, it's the same way with dealing drugs." The result is a curious paradox. Criminal activity not only enhances availability thereby providing for heavier drug consumption, but also places broad limits on the amount of heroin consumed by providing some semblance of structure and routine. There is yet another paradox in the drugs–crime relationship for the stable addict. Although it is true that crime facilitates heroin use, many of the addicts I interviewed indicated that heroin and other drugs played a utilitarian role in their commission of crime as well. Although it is commonly assumed that addicts are most likely to commit crimes when they are sick and desperate for a fix, the addicts in this study reported quite the opposite. The following comments from Joe and Belle highlight the importance of being straight (not experiencing withdrawal) when committing crimes:

> [Joe] It would be awful hard for me if I was sick to be able to hustle. A lot of times if you're sick you go in and grab stuff. And run without caution.

But if I was high it was a different story. I could take my time and get what I wanted.

[Belle] Most people say about drug addicts [that] when they're sick is when they do their most damage. But that's the lying-est thing in the world. When a dope addict is sick, he's sick. He can't raise his hand if he's a drug addict. ... They say when a dope fiend's sick he'll do anything to get money, but how the hell is he going to do it if he can't even go on the street and do it?

The prostitutes I interviewed found heroin especially functional in their criminal activities. Never knowing if their next *trick* (client) might be a freak (one who enjoys violence or sadomasochistic acts), carry a disease, or simply have unpleasant body odor, prostitutes understandably approach many of their dates with a good deal of apprehension. They reported that heroin allows them to work under otherwise difficult conditions:

[Belle] I think that a woman that tricks has to do something. If they wasn't an alcoholic, they had to be a dope fiend. 'Cause a woman in her right sense, you just can't sit up and do some of the things you do with a trick.

[Penny] If I didn't have no heroin in me, I couldn't trick, because it turns my stomach. ... I didn't feel nothin' then, I just went on and do it. ... I always was noddin' before I even get to the date. And then when I get to the date, I go to the bathroom and get off again.

[Helen] I could forget about what I was doing; I didn't give a damn about anything. I just felt good.

Heroin is not the only drug that addicts use for functional reasons in their commission of crimes. Amphetamines are also sometimes used to maintain necessary energy levels on particularly busy days. Boss, who was an armed robber among other things, reported that he would frequently use barbiturates before going out on a robbery. He found that they put him in the necessary belligerent mood to play the "tough guy" in order to pull off the robbery successfully. He also reported that he would frequently celebrate a successful robbery with heroin or cocaine or perhaps even a speedball (a heroin and cocaine combination):

They'd be like a toast. Maybe nine-thirty or ten o'clock we'd done pulled a good score off and we're sitting there and say, 'Hey man, let's go get us some good motherfucking dope.' And it would carry you until two o'clock. Nodding in the apartment, everybody feeling all right because they got away with the crime, planning what you're gonna do with your half of the money. So it'd be like the cap for you. It'd be like a toast for a job well done.

Finally, the data from these life histories suggest that both drug use and criminal behavior are interrelated elements of a broader subcultural experience that cannot be fully understood in terms of a simple causal relationship. Particularly as stable addicts, these respondents regarded both drug use and crime as important parts of a challenging lifestyle. It is true, it is true that drugs provide an important perceptual framework from which addicts interpret their behavior. Boss commented on the importance of drugs in defining the meaning that he attached to his activities:

> The money is good, but I wouldn't want the money if I couldn't have what goes along with selling the money [for heroin]. ... Like with the whores, I wouldn't want the whores if I couldn't spend the money on dope. ... It's like a working man. A working man, he wants a home and nice family. Just like in the life of crime you got to have all those essential things that go with it or it's nothing. It would be nothing if I couldn't spend that money the way [I want to].

But while heroin is an important component of the subjective experience of addicts, it is only part of a more general lifestyle, the maintenance of which motivates the addict. Also part of that lifestyle for most addicts is a nice wardrobe, fancy cars (for men), a nice crib (home), and a reputation for generosity with friends. As Boss reflected:

> See, my concern wasn't catching the habit. ... My thing was being able to make enough money to supply that habit and make enough money to keep my thing up to par—you know, my clothes, and my living standards ... to stay up to par enough so if my mother or sister or brother needed some money I could loan them some money, plus keep my habit, plus buy some shoes or something, you know, rent a car for the weekend and just hang out like the guy that didn't have the habit. And in the course of that, that called for more crime.

As important as drugs and the fast lifestyle are in motivating addict behavior, one important fact remains: crime is a way of life with stable addicts. These people take pride in their ability to hustle successfully. Criminal success is a mark of stature in the subculture, and the more lucrative or difficult the hustle, the greater the recognition one receives. "The type of criminal activity he engages in, and his success at it determine, to a large extent, the addict's status among fellow addicts and in the community at large. The appellation of *real hustling dope fiend* (a successful burglar, robber, con man, etc.) is a mark of respect and status" (Preble & Casey, 1969, p. 20; italics in original). Crime is a challenge that most stable addicts find tremendously appealing. It provides a source of excitement and a sense of accomplishment, similar to the challenge of climbing formidable mountain peaks or rafting turbulent white water. Mario compared the excitement of burglarizing a house with the anticipation experienced by a young child at Christmas time. Each package (house) has its own surprises, its own challenges. Some are located in wealthy sections of the city and have fabulous exteriors (pretty wrappings). Some of these promising houses resulted in a valuable *take* (loot), while others did not. What kept Mario going was the anticipation he experienced with each crime.

Mario's feelings reflect those of many of the addicts who took part in this study. Their perceptions defy any attempt to characterize criminal behavior as somehow being "driven" by an overwhelming need for drugs, even though heroin and other drugs constitute an important feature of a stable addict's motivational structure. For these addicts, drugs and crime are mutually reinforcing elements of a broader lifestyle, both of which play an important role in defining one's position in the criminal-addict subculture. Harry expressed it this way:

> It was never really the drug. It was the lifestyle I was trying to keep going. And the drug was a lot of that lifestyle. ... Back then [before becoming a street junkie] ... it was just that it was there and I had all this energy and no vent for it. And I had begun to vent it into getting drugs, knocking people in the head, taking their money, going into somebody's house, taking that stuff out, running into the fence, going to get the—drugs a full-time job. It was more than your basic forty hours a week. And that's what it was about, sustaining that lifestyle.

By way of summary, in contrast to the occasional-user period of addict careers where drug use and crime are independent, parallel activities, the stable-addict phase is marked by a close interdependence between these two sets of activities. This relationship is more complex than can be captured in the empiricist language of cause and effect, however. The transition to the status of stable addict is a function of increased drug availability and expanded life structure, which, in most instances, result from increased systematic criminal activities. In this respect, we might characterize the stable-addict period as one in which "crime causes drugs" or, at least, crime facilitates drug use. Having attained the status of stable addict, the user has succeeded in jockeying for position in the criminal-addict subculture. The stable addict is, at least by minimal definition, a successful participant in the subculture. Success in the subculture is defined by drug-using and criminal activity, both of which are motivating factors in the behavior of stable addicts. In this respect, the drugs-crime relationship is not so much causal as it is reciprocal, itself contributing to one's stature in the subculture.

CRIMINAL SPECIALIZATION AMONG STABLE ADDICTS

The career transition to stable addict usually entails an increasing reliance on a small number of criminal hustles or, in some cases, on a single type of crime. I pointed out [earlier] that early occasional use is a time of experimentation, not only with various types of drugs, but also with a variety of criminal roles. As in other careers, this trial period usually gives way to more focused activity as developing addicts discover what criminal skills and penchants they may have by experimenting with different criminal routines. In short, assumption of the stable-addict role usually implies the development of one or more main hustles.

Developing a main hustle implies not only the achievement of increased specialization but also of increased skill and sophistication as a criminal. Stable addicts go beyond learning the nuts and bolts of their chosen trade(s) to master the subtleties of these criminal enterprises with a finesse more characteristic of a craftsman than of a stereotyped common criminal. Old Ray may have stated it most succinctly when he remarked, "You got to have a Ph.D. in streetology." There are three broad types of skills that the successful criminal addict acquires: technical, social, and intuitive skills (Faupel 1986).

Technical Skills

This category of criminal skills entails both the knowledge of how to perform the task as well as the physical adeptness for carrying it out successfully. Shoplifters stress the importance of being able to *roll* clothing items tightly with one hand with the clothes still on the hanger. Rolling loosely will not allow as many clothes to be packed in the bag, and keeping clothes on the hanger is important because empty hangers arouse suspicion. This must all be done with one hand because the other hand is used to finger through items on the rack, thereby creating the impression that the shoplifter is a legitimate customer. A slip in any one of the maneuvers involved in the complex process may mean failure to reach a quota for the day or, even more seriously, possible detection and arrest. Moreover, shoplifters must continually keep abreast of technological innovations designed to detect theft, including cameras, one-way mirrors, and alarm devices attached inside expensive clothing items.

Prostitutes also report the importance of developing technical skills, particularly streetwalkers who regularly *beat their johns* (rob their clients) out of credit cards and cash. Belle described her strategy, for successfully stealing from her clients:

> The car was sweeter than anything else as far as getting money. Because once you get a dude's pants down, you got him where you want him. He just automatically forgets about he's got money in his pocket.... All she's thinking about is getting him in a position to get his mind off his pocket long enough for her to get in there. ... She might take his pants with her and leave him stripped for nothing—'cause I've done it.

A prostitute must also be able to determine where her trick keeps his wallet, take the wallet from his pocket, and then return it—all in a matter of minutes and without the client's being aware that this activity is taking place. These are skills not readily acquired; developing them takes time and practice, as Penny described:

> When I started off I was scared. It took a little longer. ... It might take four or five hours [on an all-night date] to get his wallet. ... [Later] it didn't take me but a minute to get it and put it back in.

The acquisition of technical skills is critical to the success of other hustles as well. The technical skills required by burglars have been extensively discussed in the literature on professional crime (Letkeman, 1973; Sutherland, 1937). These same skills were also reported by the burglar-addicts who participated in this study. An intimate knowledge of alarm systems is part of the seasoned burglar's stock-in-trade. Moreover, because most burglars prefer to enter unoccupied homes, they commonly case a residential area for days or even weeks, meticulously noting the mobility patterns of the residents. Burglars working business districts also case their working areas to determine patterns of police surveillance. Paige recalled "staying up all night watching the pattern of the police officers and seeing how regularly he made his rounds of the establishment and charting all that stuff down and trying to get a fix on when's the best time for me to rip that store off."

Stable addicts are also involved in many other types of criminal offenses. The addicts in this study reported engaging in main hustles such as armed robbery, pickpocketing, forgery, fencing stolen goods, pimping, and drug dealing at one time or another during their careers. Each of these criminal enterprises involves its own modus operandi and requires the acquisition of specialized technical skills if one is to be a reasonably successful hustler.

Social Skills

Most criminal hustles require the addict to be verbally and socially skilled as well as technically adept. These social skills involve verbally and non-verbally manipulating the setting to the criminal's advantage such that the offense can be carried out smoothly and without risk of apprehension or arrest.

Social skills, like technical skills, are quite specialized. Shoplifters who work in pairs, for example, frequently find it necessary to engage in small talk with salespersons, thereby diverting attention from the actions of their partners. Moreover, when they are detected, good boosters are often successful in talking their way out of an arrest. Gloria found that she could intimidate lower-level sales personnel from referring her to management by taking on the persona of an indignant, falsely accused customer. Some shoplifters, such as Slick, used a modus operandi that relied primarily on verbal agility. In contrast to the surreptitious strategies employed by many shoplifters, such as hiding stolen goods in garbage bags and false-bottom boxes or underneath one's own clothing, Slick opted for the bold strategy of walking out of the store with his stolen merchandise in full view of store personnel, as if he had paid for it: "I would take McCullough chain saws. . . . I would just pick up the big box, set it up on my shoulders, and even get the store security guard at the door to open the door for me. I just got bold." Then, rather than sell the chain saw to a fence for about one-third the retail value, Slick would rely on his verbal skills once again by returning the item the next day to the very store he had stolen it from (or bring it to another store in the chain) for a full refund.

Needless to say, this sort of strategy requires a unique ability to play the role of a legitimate customer. A shoplifter with highly developed social skills tends to assume this role so completely that he or she takes on the attitudes, feelings, and perspective of the customer. To use Mead's (1934) term, the shoplifter quite literally "takes the role of the other." Socially skilled shoplifters do not take the role of just any customer, however; they assume the role of an assertive customer who takes complete command of the situation. Indeed, they must do so. A legitimate customer can perhaps afford not to be assertive, but a timorous shoplifter may well forfeit his or her career by failing to command credibility as a legitimate customer.

Check forgers make use of some of the same social skills employed by shoplifters. Indeed, social agility can probably be said to constitute the principal stock-in-trade of the check forger. The entire act revolves around successfully convincing a bank employee that the signature on the check is in fact that of the individual whose name it bears, and that the forger is that individual and therefore the rightful recipient of the amount of the check. All of this involves the ability to assume the role of an assertive individual with a legitimate claim, an ability Old Ray cultivated to his advantage:

> I found the hardest teller I could find and she sent me to the manager's office. ... I went in there telling about this godsent check—a tragedy in my life. It was all acting. ... You got to story-tell. But it was my check. It became my check the minute I walked into the bank. ... Once I packed up that type attitude, I became the role. And it's easier to go to the top than the bottom. It's easier at the top to get to anybody. ... The guy at the bottom, he's gonna give you hell ... but the man at the top, he can afford to be benevolent.

Other criminal hustles require social skills of a slightly different nature. Prostitutes point out the importance of maintaining a position of dominance in the interaction between them and their tricks. Rose advised: "Always try to keep control of the conversation. Never let them see that you're soft. ... They see one time that you stutter or aren't in control, they're gonna try to take advantage of you." By maintaining such control, the prostitute is also able to direct and focus her client's attention, which allows her to engage in acts of theft. Penny was so successful at this strategy that she was frequently able to rob her clients without even having to *turn the trick* (engage in sexual acts).

Drug dealing entails social skills with still another focus. Here the primary task is to maintain a relatively stable clientele. This involves advertising one's drugs and establishing a reputation as having "righteous" dope. Harry, who was heavily involved in burglary as well as selling drugs, understood successful dealing to be little more than hype and good salesmanship:

> Conning was part of everything. The whole thing is an image. Believe it or not, it's the American way! ... So you learn how to hype. ... One of my favorite lines was "You better do only half of one of these." And that just made them get all that much more motivation to do three or four of them. And they'd do three or four and they'd come back and say, "Hey, that shit was good!" Of course, if they did three or four of them, they did get fucked up.

Inevitably, however, drug dealers are confronted with dissatisfied customers who have reason to believe that they have been ripped off with poor-quality dope. There was no consensus among the dealers I interviewed regarding how they respond to discontented clients. Some would play it tough, on the theory that to give in to a client's demands sets a bad precedent and may serve as a signal to others that here is a dealer who can easily be taken. Others saw themselves as conscientious businesspeople and would quite readily supply dissatisfied customers with more dope, urging them to spread the word that they were treated fairly. In either event, to borrow a phrase from the subculture of pick-pockets, dealers must "cool the mark out," employing all of the social skills they have at their disposal to maintain a stable clientele.

Intuitive Skills

This last category of hustling skills entails an acute sensitivity to one's environment. Sutherland (1937) describes this characteristic as *larceny sense*, a term that Dressler also employs to describe the professional criminal: "Larceny sense, it seems, is the ability to smell out good hauls, to sense the exact moment for the kill, and to know when it is wiser to desist" (1951, p. 255). Maurer (1955) applies the term "grift sense" to describe intuitive skills in his classic analysis of the professional pickpocket. But these skills are by no means limited to professional criminals. Gould et al. observe this ability among active heroin users: "Most successful dope fiends show an ability to size up people they meet in terms of trustworthiness and motivation, and have a good memory for people" (1974, pp. 45–46).

The addicts I interviewed also emphasized the importance of intuitive skills. Like technical and social skills, intuitive skills are manifested differently in various criminal contexts, but their general purpose is to help facilitate the commission of a crime or to help the criminal avoid detection and arrest.

Intuitive skills can facilitate the commission of crime by providing the addict with the ability to sense a profitable and reasonably safe opportunity. "I could see money. I could smell money," claimed Old Ray. "I could walk by a store and see if it was vulnerable. ... I could sense the whole setup." These are the skills that contribute to larceny (or grift) sense, and many of the participants in this study explicitly acknowledged their importance. Representative observations of a prostitute, a pickpocket, and a shoplifter illustrate how these skills are applied in various hustles:

> [Rose—a prostitute] Look for the nice dates. When you spot a man with the raggediest car and the oldest clothes, he's probably got the money. Because he's cheap, he don't wanna spend all of that money. It's usually the man that's got all this and that [who] ain't got a dime because he's paying out so many bills. [Rose went on to point out that she would probably have to steal his money because he is unlikely to be generous with her either.]

> [Boss—a pickpocket] As I got better, I could spot people with decent money, and you play them. Whereas in the beginning, on the amateur thing, I might play anywhere from ten to fifteen wallets. But when I got professional, I might just play one or two wallets.

> [Booter—a shoplifter] All days aren't the same for boosting.... If there's no situation where you can make some money you just don't go in and make a situation. You understand what I'm saying? The situation has to be laid out for you.

And to be really good at it, you got to be the type of person that can recognize a laid-out situation. If you get in there and try to make a situation, then you're rearranging the whole thing and it could be detrimental.

Intuitive skills are also instrumental in avoiding detection and arrest. The addict criminals in this study repeatedly stressed the importance of being able to detect and avoid undercover police officers, floorwalkers, and potential informants. This ability was regarded as absolutely crucial to their success in criminal roles:

[Harry—regarding drug dealing] I learned the ropes ... how you spot cops. He [a friend] pointed out ... those undercover detectives with the bee stingers on their cars, little teeny antennae on top; and how you could pick those cars out; and how two detectives in a car, how there were certain characteristics about them that were always the same. You could smell them a mile away. He really schooled me criminally, you know.

[Stephanie—a check forger] When she [the bank teller] sees the check, if she has to look up [or] if she has to call another teller or something like that, it ain't no good. ... If the teller has to pick up the phone, then you tell her, "That's all right, there's something I have to do."

[Penny—on shoplifting] I can tell [who the floorwalkers are]. They constantly keep walking the floor looking at me. ... They're still in that same department and ain't bought nothing.

[Fred—a drug dealer] Never take a deal that sounds too good to be true. ... This guy came by and wanted to buy fifteen bags for $10 apiece—no shorts. Now any kind of a hustler junkie coming off the street and he's got $150, he's not gonna come to you wanting fifteen bags. He's gonna come to you wanting twenty-five or thirty. You know what I'm saying? The deal was too good to be true.

These observations illustrate the diffuse qualities characteristic of intuitive skills. It was difficult even for the study respondents to articulate their precise nature. Pagie recalled: "I always had a knack for sensing the police. I don't know why. I don't know if it's an ESP thing or what, but I always could sense when the police was there." It is because of their rather imperceptible quality that I have used the term *intuitive skills* to refer to this important set of abilities. It is important to understand, however, that they are not hereditary talents. These are skills that are acquired through the same process of socialization as are technical and social skills. Together, these three sets of skills distinguish successful stable addicts from beginning occasional users.

I have attempted in this discussion to demonstrate that contrary to stereotyped depictions of addict criminality, stable addicts are skilled criminal entrepreneurs. The level of criminal sophistication required to sustain a livelihood of the magnitude reported by these hard-core addicts is acquired only after spending considerable time in the sub-culture. Such skills are simply not part of the beginning occasional user's stock-in-trade. In the process of becoming stable addicts, however, most users narrow the range of their criminal activities considerably. I certainly do not wish to represent the stable addict as a professional in the tradition of a Chic Conwell (Sutherland, 1937) or Vincent Swaggi (Klockars, 1974) nor necessarily as specialized as Preble and Casey (1969) imply in their watershed study of addict criminals. The addicts I interviewed, however, do favor a small number of crimes among the vast variety they could be committing. I am suggesting that as stable addicts, these hard-core users are sufficiently successful at their main hustles such that they seldom find it necessary to deviate from their preferred crimes. They attain a level of specialization not characteristic of amateurs nor even of their own criminal patterns during other periods of their careers. Indeed, I contend that it is only by such specialization that these addicts are able to develop the requisite skills for a successful career. There is thus a mutually reinforcing relationship between the development of a main hustle and the acquisition of technical, social, and intuitive skills that correspond to this specialization. The acquisition of these skills is, in the first place, dependent on some level of specialization; at the same time, these skills provide the very foundation for stable addicts to maintain their main hustles.

These main hustles, which constitute more or less full-time criminal roles, also have other important consequences. As I suggested earlier, they provide an alternative basis for life structure that is capable of accommodating higher levels of drug use and consumer activity generally. At the same time, however, the routine nature of the main hustle prevents one's habit from getting out of hand. The stable addict's heroin use still takes place within a rather well defined, though modified, life structure. Moreover, full-time hustler roles provide addicts with increased dependable income. Unlike the marginal criminality of occasional users, the main hustle is both a primary means of income and a source of identity and prestige in the subculture. The study respondents were quick to distinguish between a main hustle typical of stable addicts and the more amateur or impulsive *flat-footed hustling* style characteristic of less criminally routine lifestyles. Gloria emphasized her distinctive status as a booster: "I'm not a thief—I'm a booster. There's a difference between a thief and a booster. A thief ... takes anything and everything from anywhere." Booter understood his role as a pimp in entrepreneurial terms, viewing his prostitutes as an investment:

> You try not to spend too much money unless it's important. You're playing economics here. Like I got some stock.... In order for her to collect the capital, she has to be a product. You have to have something that you can sell. You don't try to give up too much, but say you are into a new girl.... You have to put some clothes on her, put some capital into that to make her look presentable.... You're expecting her to get that money back.

Thus, the stable-addict phase is characterized by a comparatively high degree of criminal specialization, complete with the technical, social, and intuitive skills that contribute to success in the criminal role. As shown by this research and in previous studies, stable addicts are successful and sophisticated criminal entrepreneurs.

References

Dressler, D. (1951). *Probation and parole*. New York: Columbia University Press.

Faupel, C. E. (1986). Heroin use, street crime and the main hustle: Implications for the validity of official crime data. *Deviant Behavior, 7*, 31–45.

Gould, L., Walker, A. L., Crane, L. E., & Lidz, C. W. (1974). *Connections: Notes from the Heroin World*. New Haven, CT: Yale University Press.

Klockars, C. (1974). *The professional fence*. New York: Free Press.

Letkeman, P. (1973). *Crime as work*. Englewood Cliffs, NJ: Prentice Hall.

Maurer, D. W. (1955). *Whiz mob: A correlation of the technical argot of pickpockets with their behavior patterns*. Gainesville, FL: American Dialect Society.

Mead, G. H. (1934). *Mind, self, and society*. Edited by C.W. Morris. Chicago: University of Chicago Press.

Preble, E., & Casey, J. H. (1969). Taking care of business: The heroin user's life on the streets. *International Journal of the Addictions, 4*(1), 1–24.

Sutherland, E. H. (1937). *The professional thief*. Chicago: University of Chicago Press.

23

Property Crime and Women Drug Dealers in Australia

Barbara Denton and Pat O'Malley

E *ngagement in property crime by drug users is often regarded as driven by the need to support a habit and/or as merely an aside to involvement in the drug "industry." This chapter examines a group of successful women drug dealers in Melbourne, Australia—most of whom are also illicit drug users—and maps their involvement in property crime. The research is based on direct observation, informal and formal discussions, and in-depth interviews carried out over more than four years with a group of 16 women drug dealers, their friends, families, and associates. Initially, the subjects were all incarcerated in a Melbourne prison; however, as they were eventually released, they continued the research relationship. The authors conclude that property crimes are tightly integrated with the women's drug businesses. Success in property offending is a characteristic of successful drug dealers, and stolen property and money plays a key role in the trade—providing a lucrative source of income, gifts, payments, and rewards. Property crime provides excitement and other valued, intangible satisfactions including status and self-esteem.*

INTRODUCTION

One of the most familiar arguments raised in the early literature focusing on drug-related crime is that illicit drug users are compelled into property offending in order to support their drug use (Anglin & Hser, 1987; Inciardi, Pottieger, & Faupel, 1982; Nurco, Shafter, Ball, & Kinlock, 1984; Sargent, 1992; Tonry & Wilson, 1990). With regard to women, this was perhaps especially thought to be the case, although the portrayal was focused far less on property offenses and far more on women's necessary resort to prostitution to support drug consumption. As Inciardi and his colleagues note "[o]ne of the most prevalent images of the female criminal generally, and more specifically of the female heroin addict, is the image of the hooker exploiting her only means of revenue for her next 'fix'" (Inciardi, Pottieger, & Faupel, 1982, pp. 244–245).

Source: Journal of Drug Issues 31(2): 465–482. 2001. Used with permission of the publisher.

These negative images of women drug users have partly been formed from research among captive populations, either in treatment or in custodial settings. In the treatment milieus, the high incidence of sex workers among drug users quite probably led to an overemphasis on this connection, with the result that other forms of criminal activity among women drug users were overlooked (Taylor, 1993, pp. 3–4). This neglect was reinforced by assumptions that women offenders do not have the resources to enter or survive as entrepreneurs in the illicit economy. Thus, for example, Covington (1985) reports that "females passively acquiesce and follow males into crime rather than launching their careers independently in female-dominated peer groups...there is no female subculture that supports and reinforces crime among women in a manner parallel to male cultures" (p. 348).

More recent research, however, affirms that many women, rather than being "driven" into crime, make pragmatic, intelligent, and rational choices about how to generate money to finance their participation in the drug economy (e.g., Fagan, 1994; Pettiway, 1987; Taylor, 1993). Such work has found that women participate in a wide variety of crimes and that prostitution plays a considerably less important role in supporting drug use than was previously thought (Hser, Anglin, & McGlothlin, 1987; Pettiway, 1987). Thus Fagan found that although women drug users in the cocaine economy who were not active in drug selling turned to prostitution to generate income, women drug user/sellers tended to become involved in property and other crimes. Fagan (1995) concluded that, "incomes from drug selling were sufficiently high to discourage or 'protect' some women from the dependence on prostitution that dominated the lives of nonsellers" (p. 179). This paper seeks to contribute to this growing line of theory and investigation.

An obvious point to be made here is that, despite the stereotypes, there is no one variety of female drug user. But perhaps more important is the implication that we should consider more closely the ways in which illicit drug use and "drug-related crime" among women are linked. Leaving aside the now generally disputed assumption that prostitution is the 'natural' or default option for women, the assumption that still recurs in much of the literature is that all drug using women's other criminal activities are drug driven. The clear implication is that such offending would not occur but for the need to pay for their drugs (and as such, is therefore simply a substitute for, or safety net against, prostitution). Thus property crime is not thought to be practiced—let alone be valued as an activity in its own right—by those women who can support the financial demands of illicit drug consumption. Perhaps most of all, this implies that women who are successful drug user/dealers would have no need to engage in property offending.

An alternative model and certainly one that has currency among studies of male drug users (e.g., Elliot, Huizinga, & Menard, 1989) is that drug use is not necessarily an all-absorbing activity among illicit drug users. Drug users and dealers are seen to be engaged in other illicit activities by choice and preference. In such cases, both drug taking and property crime could be seen to provide attractions, to be mutually supporting, intertwining and more or less continuous activities. Applying such a model to women, "drug-related crime" would not appear just as an economic safety net, nor need it be the case that dealers who engage in property crime are those 'unsuccessful' women whose businesses will not provide for all their personal drug needs. Indeed, it could be argued that failures are the last people we are likely to confront where careers in property offending are concerned. To sustain a career in property crime would appear to imply ability, skill, and resourcefulness. It might also imply the possession of social respect and of attributes to provide access to a social network that can provide markets, information, labor, specialist skills, security, and so on. The possession of such resources would suggest that the women concerned are not likely to be failures or victims in the drug market and that systematic engagement in property crime might be the sign of a social category comparatively rarely explored in the literature—that of a successful women in the drug scene. We are not, of course, proposing that all women who engage in property offenses are successful operators, whether as users or dealers. This would be to fall into a reverse and misleading stereotype. Rather the study seeks to examine some alternative connections between property crimes as revealed by close, long-term qualitative research among successful women drug dealers who are also drug users.

WOMEN USER/DEALERS AND DRUG-RELATED CRIME

Two observations supported throughout the field research form a framework for much that follows. First, the women included in the study generated money not only by the sale of drugs but also by committing a wide variety of property offenses: crimes of fraud, forgery, theft, burglary, shoplifting, and handling of stolen goods. The majority of these women were involved in the drug scene prior to entering into frequent or serious criminal activity. Most, however, had participated in some form of crime, such as shoplifting, receiving stolen goods, and credit card fraud, *prior* to entering the drug economy. No across-the-board assumptions should thus be made in their careers about crime leading to drug use or vice versa. Rather we saw more complex and variable patterns of the nexus between property and drug offending. Second—an important observation reported by virtually all participants— the women *escalated* their income-producing crimes as they became more established and successful in the drug business. Involvement in careers of property offending among these women, as emerges in detail throughout this paper, was the mark of the successful drug user/dealer, whatever role such crimes might have played in the lives of other users. But as this suggests, what also emerges is that "involvement" in property crime is a weak term if used as a single index, for it fails to distinguish between the nature of the engagement. Early in the women's careers, when most were users rather than user/dealers, such property-focused criminal activity was sporadic or otherwise limited. They largely acted in supportive roles: handling stolen merchandise, functioning as a go-between or a lookout, hiding criminals on the run, or acting as gun carriers. One such case was Kim, who worked for a street-level dealer and drug wholesaler. This dealer, early in her career, was a member of a family of criminals whose activities included armed burglary, bank hold-ups, car theft and drug dealing. Kim acted as a go-between; she would be given large amounts of money to deliver to drug and criminal associates. Another of her tasks was to visit the family's members and their associates in prison, a task for which she was deemed suitable as she had no criminal record.

Each of the women had a parallel story to tell, but as the following sections illustrate, by the time the research took place Kim and all the women in the study had become active in their own right in a wide variety of areas of crime. One of these activities, albeit the central one for all participants, was drug dealing. While some elected to act alone, most operated in leadership roles in property offenses involving "employees" and other drug users, a fact that reflected and drew upon their skills, status, and resources in the drug sector.

We suggest that just as users' forms of involvement in the drug industry may range from subordinate and vulnerable users to superordinate and capable user/dealers, so, too, their drug-related participation in property offending is likely to vary in related ways. Success in the field of the illicit drug industry is likely to be related to success in relation to property offending because of the parallel needs for accumulation of skills and resources such as those required for evading or managing criminal justice intervention, developing the experience and knowledge of leadership and business practice, and accumulating contacts and opportunities—often across a very blurred divide between drug dealing and property offending. For these reasons, this association is likely to be reflected temporally in the women's career paths. Such broad observations, which we will now explore in more detail, accord well with those emerging from Taylor's (1993) ethnographic work among women drug users and dealers in Glasgow.

SHOPLIFTING

Shoplifting has been recognized as an important means of generating revenue for both women and men in the illicit drug economy (Culliver, 1993); this appeared to be the case in Melbourne. Kim was a professional shoplifter before diversifying her activities to include drug dealing. Like most "shoppers," she established a routine and schedule to work by, usually operating late mornings and lunch times, saving the late afternoons to fence stolen goods. "I work the busy times; that way there's not that many [shop assistants] watching for you." She preferred to work alone: "I like to go on my own and do it, just me. I have no one to worry about except myself, and if it goes wrong it's just me." She wanted her independence, free from encumbrances, shying away from any responsibility that working with a partner may bring.

Certain technical skills are critical for the shoplifter, for example, the knack of rolling up clothes tightly with one hand, while the other hand sorts through items on the rack, creating the impression that the shoplifter is a genuine customer who belongs in the setting (see also Faupel, 1991). The women agreed that shoplifting had altered over the years, creating new demands for skillful work. In particular, technical innovations and security tags made the work more complex: "The game's changed so much; it's harder with the electronic and surveillance stuff they have now. You have to know what you're doing." Several women overcame this obstacle by carrying bags especially insulated to prevent electronic detection. Another demand was the market consideration. One shoplifter, Sonya, carefully planned and structured her shoplifting expeditions in relation to what her buyers, associates and friends wanted. She had a ready market for her merchandise and took orders for her customers' needs.

> I would ask them what they wanted, some would put their order in, size and all, "Sonya, can you get that coat I saw?" Mostly I'd get it back to them the same day. Better for me not to have the stuff hanging around.

At times Sonya would target up to four shopping centers a day. "I'd dress properly, tidy up and that, and I'd go to different places, wouldn't hang around the one place for long." When she returned from her "work," her customers would be waiting for her. "There was always some of them waiting for me when I got back. I'd kind of lay them [the goods] all out so they could decide what they wanted." As well as "shopping" for friends, Sonya knew a legitimate shop owner who took all the goods she obtained. She claimed that she would sell them for "two-thirds the retail price."

> I've got this Asian sheila [woman] who runs this boutique who'll take anything I get. If the others aren't around she takes it all. She's always after the stuff I get, can't get enough for her, because I get top quality gear that's hard to come by, not rubbish.

The money Sonya earned from shoplifting was channeled into her family, "lovely furniture, antiques, expensive clothes and lots of jewelry." She had a reputation for being prodigal: "I was generous with people, threw my money around." Money was also channeled into her drug business: "It was used to set me up to buy and sell the stuff." Crime, drugs, and lifestyle coexisted, a mixture of work and play. Of course, not all the women followed this model, and for some drugs were much more central. Larissa, a heroin user, relied more on shoplifting to fund her drug use. She had several outlets for her goods; her drug dealer would swap her heroin for the goods, and her friends and other associates would pay Larissa cash. But this was not the norm. Other women shoplifted intermittently depending on their specific needs.

Christmas was a special occasion, as one woman stated, "Shopping helps us get by, and gets things for the kids." Shoplifting, in short, was used by these women for a variety of purposes. The fact that they were all drug users did not mean that crime was merely a reflex of their drug needs.

In other ways, drugs did sometimes play a key role through interfering with successful property offending. One of the main risks associated with shoplifting was operating while in drug withdrawal. Kim recounted that, when she was "hanging out" badly, she deviated from her usual safe routine.

> What brings me undone is doing it when I'm sick, real sick, that's the dangerous time, I'm hanging out for that first hit, that's the only time I've been caught in all the years I've done it. Waiting for the shops to open, strung out, that's when I'm done. Once I've had a hit I'm fine. I have my hit, then I go back and do it real relaxed like.

Even so, in 15 years of shoplifting Kim received only two short sentences: "I did four months, ah, about ten years ago, and this last one where I did six months....I have never been done for drugs. That never gets a mention in court."

Coming through in the accounts provided by these women was their initiative, planning, and business acumen. Despite occasional lapses, shoplifting was not done in a random or indiscriminate way. They did not appear simply as "driven," although as Kim's case suggests, there were times when she behaved in such a fashion. As Koester and Schwartz (1993) have argued,

> Stealing requires a degree of planning and skill, and there is a delay between the time the act is committed and the time the desired end is achieved. Experienced shoplifters often take orders from customers or spend time selling their merchandise...it is possible for them (heroin users) to "work" for long periods between ingestion. (p. 194)

When considering the length of time Kim had been involved in crime, the small amount of time spent in prison indicates how well she planned her activity around the high-risk conditions. In cost-benefit terms, two short periods "inside" did not appear to her to be an excessive time to serve.

THEFT AND BURGLARY

A further observation linked with the careers of these women is that many pursue specialties in crime that were commenced before they began using drugs. Living in social contexts where crime was part of a lifestyle, it often appears a matter of chance whether in any woman's biography drug use preceded property offending or vice versa. Indeed it was often hard to sort out which came first. When Sherrie became the girlfriend of a very successful criminal, she found herself propelled into a lifestyle beyond her dreams.

Surrounding by huge amounts of money, she was able to have anything she wanted: clothes, jewelry, an up-market apartment, and expensive furniture. This abundant lifestyle brought her into contact with drugs and drug use. This pleasant but dependent arrangement came to an abrupt end when the relationship turned sour and was terminated after some years.

> I was completely under his control being with him so young, I did everything he said, but then after a while I started to think for myself and speak out and do what I wanted to do. He didn't like it, he took everything back, the jewelry, the presents, the lot, and kicked me out with nothing.

It was a shock for Sherrie to find herself out on her own and with a drug habit. "I was in a pretty bad way. I'd got used to having everything done for me and suddenly it all ended." She returned to live with her parents, who sought the services and skills of a counselor who helped her reestablish herself. But Sherrie was left yearning for her former life and companions. Having been around criminals, listening to their gossip and exploits, she concluded that crime was simple. "I thought it sounds pretty easy walking into somewhere and taking what you want...and that's how I got started. I had the contacts to get rid of any stuff I got." Other women also enjoyed being around the illicit economy, like Chris: "I found it fun listening to what the crooks got up to." Yet such social enjoyment was also linked to learning the trade and finding opportunities for gain. Knowing the right people and being one of the crowd were useful for picking up information about when, where, and what to steal. With all of the women, as with Sherrie and Chris, involvement in drug-using networks was not something divorced from property crime, in the sense that they had to be brought together by the impetus of drug needs. If there was a norm, it was that they were intertwined, with drug use supplying a social network and access to skills, opportunities, and markets, as well as one among a number of stimuli to offend.

Sonya made a point of noting the movements of prospective victims. She also familiarized herself with their location and the surrounding streets. She constantly pored over her street map before setting out on a job and developed a knowledge of alarms and surveillance systems—knowledge she had gained through her male associates. "Owen's always playing about with alarms, taking them to pieces and putting them back again, so I get to have a gig too," she explained (see also Faupel, 1991). Rita too was an experienced operator when it came to planning and carrying out a burglary. She left nothing to chance and thought carefully about every last detail. One specialty was to identify the premises of organizations that had sufficient numbers of employees to warrant the provision of staff locker room facilities. After checking out a building, Rita presented herself: well-groomed, smartly dressed, and carrying a large brief case. She walked in a business-like manner into the premises. Being challenged on the job did not faze her; she would pose as either a business associate, a prospective customer, or whatever was fitting at the time. "I'm dressed up, and I make out I'm legit and visiting someone. I say anything that comes into my head at the time. I say I'm a debt collector, anything I can think of that fits in at the time." She would make her way to the locker room and steal as many handbags as possible, quickly placing them in her own case and then exiting the building and making her getaway. Depending on the location, she would use a car, or, if the job were located in the inner city, she would have a taxi waiting.

On one occasion, while drinking coffee in a cafe, Rita told her two companions that she was going to get a cab and visit a friend in a private hospital and invited them to "[c]ome along and wait in the taxi while I drop in for a quick visit." She carried an overnight bag and had a basket of fruit and a bunch of flowers to give to her friend, and she left her companions in the taxi. In a short time she reappeared, jumped into the taxi, and said, "Let's go." As the taxi drove along, Rita produced a number of handbags and wallets from her overnight bag. She had snatched the bags while the patients were occupied in the television lounge. Swiftly and efficiently she went through the bags, putting aside any money, bankbooks, and credit cards. On leaving the taxi she dumped the bags and wallets in a nearby garbage bin and then proceeded to a bank outlet to use the bankcards. "You'd be surprised how many people have their pin number next to their card," she said. Rita explained to her companions that she did not tell them beforehand what she was up to for she wanted the scam "to look legit and natural enough."

Chris had a longtime association with criminals dating from her time as a sex worker. She had lived with two burglars, Gary and Ron, and she thought it sounded pretty simple, robbing a factory or a house. When Ron was arrested and imprisoned, she decided to try her hand at house burglary: "Ron was doing robberies and then he went to prison. Yeah, and I just thought how easy it was. So I teed up with his sister and we started doing it together. We did alright, we got TVs, videos, money, and heaps of jewelry." Being one of the crowd, mixing with criminals and their families, Chris readily found an accomplice who was willing to try her hand at house burglary. Like Chris, Ron's sister shared the view that "knocking off a house was dead easy" and working together they carried out a series of house burglaries. "We did well for a time, we got a lot of gold, all Italian gold, and then I'd give it to my drug dealer to flog." The women would randomly select a street of houses, looking in letter boxes and garages to see which of these were most likely to be unoccupied. Chris would knock on the door of a targeted house. If the occupant answered the door she would pose as a real estate agent, or a friend, who had the wrong address. If the house were unoccupied she would gain entry either by prising open the door or window with one of the small tools she carried or through an unlocked door or window. "I climb in through an unlocked door or open window. You'd be surprised how many people leave their doors open or a window. I make sure no one is home, well as much as I can." Once inside she would quickly and methodically search the premises.

> I'm looking for money, wallets, credit cards, watches, jewelry, any gold I can get, stuff that's easy to get rid of.... When I do a car I'm looking for bags and wallets. It's the credit cards I want. The money comes in handy too. Before I go,

I check outside to see if there are any witnesses and when the coast is clear I clear off.

The women belonged to networks and social contexts in which drugs and crime are linked socially and culturally. Certainly, drug consumption sets up a need for income, and in these contexts crime is seen as one way of generating it. Indeed, as the women say, it is a very "smart," "efficient," and "convenient" way of generating money. But it was not the rule that the need for drugs "drove" the women to crime (e.g., Stewart, 1987). Sometimes this was the case, but among the women in this study the need to resort to burglary to generate money specifically for drugs was usually a short-term issue, a way of dealing with a temporary shortage of funds. More often, drugs themselves are a source of income, drug dealing being one among many opportunities available. For these successful women, drug dealing, drug use, and property crime coexist within a range of related behavior under diverse circumstances.

The women who were burglars agreed that the secret of being a successful thief was to have as much "front" —nerve and audacity—as possible. "To be any good you have to have dash, and lots of it," Sherrie explained. Successful women criminals were fearless. Sherrie, Sonya, and Rita demonstrated their "have a go at anything" manner. They would enter domestic or commercial premises in the hope of finding money or "making a score." What also emerged here was that these women were attracted by what Katz (1988) refers to as the *seductions* of crime. In particular, they emphasized the thrill of committing crime. For Michelle "there's nothing like pulling off a job, it beats sex any time," and for Robyn, "the excitement of it keeps you going, trying for the next one." Thus for some women at least, property offending and drug use are integrated by another means: they relished the "rush" that went with drugs and with crime. Indeed, Sherrie thought she was more addicted to crime than to drugs.

> It's [crime] the best buzz you can get. I'm addicted to that, it beats the "slow" [heroin] every time.... For me, it's when I stand at the counter and pass over the cheque, and I'm not who I'm supposed to be. She looks at me and I look her in the face, and I'm putting one over, conning her. That's the greatest thrill at that moment. Walking out with money is nothing compared to that.

For Marcia, being a cat burglar was all risk, excitement and fun. "I get my money in certain ways, like doing cat burgles and things like that.... I dress in a dark tracksuit and wear sneakers. It's something I'm good at, getting into peoples houses." Marcia was particularly agile and athletic, and could scale fences and walls and enter premises without much effort. "That's my thing to do it in the night, I get around in the middle of the night and burgle houses." When speaking about being a cat burglar, her face lit up and a sense of pride crept into her voice. "That's my crime, and I'm good at it. I get a kick out of it." This woman obviously liked having "fun"; for her the good life was a mixture of crime and drugs.

Michelle, Marcia, and Sherrie, among others, negotiated the criminal economy as a site of pleasure by actively seeking excitement through their participation in illicit activity. On one occasion, one of Michelle's arresting police officers gave her some friendly advice. "The last pinch, one of the coppers I knew pulled me aside and told me, 'Why don't you keep yourself to just selling dope, it's this stuff [passing cheques] that keeps getting you into trouble?'" Sound advice from the police. In Michelle's lengthy criminal record, drug trafficking had never been mentioned, but the mixture of crime and drugs, putting herself on the edge, was a highly satisfying pastime. This contrasts with the views reported in Katz's (1988) study on the motivations and seductions of crime, which largely excludes women from the role of thrill seekers and in which men are presented as having "balls" and "heart," and women are viewed by their male counterparts as "pathetic" and fearful of "losing self control" (p. 243). Perhaps such views, common currency among men in the drug field, have also influenced researchers (Miller, 1991).

Although the women emphasized that success in crime was exciting and boosted their self-esteem, making money was not underestimated. "Where else can you earn five grand in half an hour's work...life on the pension gets you shit." But these women robbed, not because they were poor or because their children had insufficient food to eat (Denton, 1994). Or at least if this idea of poverty has any bearing at all, it is mostly that orthodox sources could not support the lifestyle they wanted and enjoyed. Likewise, the plea that women are driven to crime to pay for their drugs, commonly put forward to clinicians and legal bodies (D'Arcy, 1995; Fitzroy Legal Service, 1988) appeared to be only one rationale among many. A more precise reading of why women enter into supposedly male territories might begin by looking at an alternative possibility: that at least some of them, like some men, achieve success in social networks where drug use and dealing, crime, illicit commodities, stolen money, and so on, are linked together in ways that are often a source of excitement, pride, and self-esteem.

DISTRIBUTING STOLEN GOODS

It was common for the women to have a range of stolen goods for disposal, and knowing how to offload goods was an essential part of the business. The Melbourne drug dealers were constantly trading in such commodities, which were clearly a reliable and relied upon source for generating cash. Gold and jewelry would quickly be sold to a fence or traded to a drug supplier (and the drugs might then be used or resold, for cash or further stolen goods). Sonya had two regular fences who would take any goods she wanted to dispose of; one was a pawnbroker who would "do business" with her "after hours," and the other worked around the drug scene, looking for "bargains."

It also was common for the women to offload received stolen goods upon their relatives. Robyn and Chris channeled them through the networks that their respective families had built up over the years. "There's plenty in my family that would want any of this," Robyn explained as she inspected a bundle of soft furnishing and bedding that had been traded as part of a drug deal. Chris's sister, Kay, had been married to a well-established member of the illicit economy: in their time together she had built up many contacts. One of her specialities was moving stolen goods, and any goods that Chris wanted to sell were easily put through her sister's network. Kay had an established network of contacts at the local hotel through which to channel her goods. The goods sold off quickly; a rationale for direct sales was that these brought higher prices than those paid by a fence because a middleman was not in the position to pay as highly as someone who was going to use the goods themselves (see also Akerstrom, 1985). A member of Robyn's family who worked at the docks was also involved in a network that pilfered a variety of consumer goods. Robyn, at times, would purchase certain goods from this source. "My supplier puts out the word when he wants something, and I pass it on to Jeff." Pam and her family followed the horses; members of her family frequented the Totalisator Agency Board (TAB) betting outlet at their local hotel. Here was another network through which to barter and channel goods. According to Pam's sister, "down the TAB you can get anything you want, you only have to put out the word, and the same way you can get rid of things too."

There is little in this that differentiates women in the drug industry from illicit dealers in many other areas. Family networks have long been recognized as important channels for illicit goods. Many communities in the United States, Britain, and elsewhere have a long history of obtaining household goods and services from family members who inhabit the informal economy sector. In such areas, "shady economic transactions" are often tolerated, and such tolerance is relied upon by illicit traders whether or not they are in the drug trade (Johnson et al., 1985; Leonard, 1994, p. 186; Preble & Casey, 1969). In such communities and networks, the women in this study learned their crime and drug skills via men or friends or through family members. Such networks are also conduits through which to channel a variety of commodities and services to their members, of which drugs were never the sole commodity—only the most important.

BANK FRAUD

A major source of revenue generated by women was bank fraud. The women who operated bank scams operated either alone or with a single accomplice usually recruited for a specific task or operation. Rita preferred to work alone, but due to the nature of the work, she often needed to recruit a partner from her "gang" as she referred to her accomplices: "there's plenty that want to get into my rorts [illicit schemes]," she laughed. Her accomplices were attracted by the quick money that bank fraud could bring; they were frequently drug users, ex-prisoners, or people on the move from interstate. Non-drug accomplices were given a cut of the takings, and drug users were paid with drugs. In one instance, Rita and Sarah had made the rounds, trading drugs for stolen credit cards and bank books. Rita "bought a cheque book from a junkie for $200 and made $5000 out of it." It was arranged that Sarah was to be the "front" at the bank the following day: it was her job to present the forged checks, running the risk of detection if a forged check was challenged. This risk factor was instrumental in the high rate of accomplices passing through Rita's scams, and even she was cautious: "I don't do it too often. The camera's got my face a few times, so I've eased back." As there was a large network of contacts available, and invariably more than one among these who needed quick money, the illicit economy provided no shortage of "one-off" workers.

Rosie's specialty also was bank fraud; part of her skill was her knowledge of many aspects of banking and her familiarity with the checks and balances the banks put in place to guard against fraud. She had a working knowledge of the bank's computer system, and the various codes put in place to process banking accounts. Before presenting a check, Rosie, masquerading as a bank employee, would investigate the financial state of the victim's account. This involved phoning around local or interstate banks.

> I ring up the bank and say I'm from another bank, I know the bank code. The bank has a special code to say which books have been found. I rang up Queensland and found out which cheques had been cancelled, and which numbers were alright to use. I gave them the right codes and computer numbers and they gave me the information.

Having established the amount of funds in the accounts of the stolen bankbooks and credit cards, on the night before a job Rosie would set about learning the appropriate signatures. From an overnight bag, she would produce inks, pens, pencils, paper, adhesive tape, scissors, razor blades, and a "special" desk lamp. After setting up the lamp, she would examine each bankbook under a blue lamp and the previously invisible signature would be easily distinguished. "Some of them I have only to see once and I can copy them. I seem to have a flair for it, copying the signatures comes easy to me." Specific banks and times of the day would be chosen for the transactions. Bank subagencies lacking sophisticated computer systems were popular, as were large busy banks at peak periods—early Monday mornings and near to closing time on Fridays were most often chosen, as at these times bank employees were busy and preoccupied. Like Rita, Rosie often worked with an accomplice who would pass the forged check at the bank. In Rosie's words:

> I do what I'm good at, rorts. I work it all out. I put all the work in getting the stuff [credit cards, bank books]. Once I work the rort out I have to find someone to front for me. My face is never seen. I'm completely out of it. It's fool-proof. I wait outside the bank, take the money straight out of their hand and then give them their cop [share].

From prior experience Rosie had learned to be in the vicinity when her "fronts" were working. Entrusting them with large sums of money led them into temptation to abscond with the lot.

> I've been caught out by Sam and Ann who skipped out on me without giving me any money. So now I'm always waiting outside the bank and catch them when they come out. I need Ann's face in this rort to get my $15,000 back, then I'm dropping her.

Rosie's plan was to use Ann for the next job, partly to get back the money she owed. But in any case Rosie had no time to find another partner, as the job had to be done before the stolen bankbook was cancelled. She put in place a strategy which minimized the risk of being ripped off again. "As she walks out I take the money straight off her." Through the use of technical, organizational, and manipulative skills, Rosie's scams gained her various amounts of money, depending on how much cash was in the stolen bank books. When a book of company paychecks fell into her hands, she was able to put herself on the payroll, and withdrew fortnightly paychecks worth $2,000 for three months. "I did a pay cheque for $2,000. I knew this chick from Perth. I got her to pass the cheque. I gave her $500 for her trouble."

Networks in the informal economy were held together by forming and bolstering relationships that center on committing crime as well as consuming and selling drugs. All these activities overlap in variable degrees and ways. This reading of such activities raises the question of how sustainable the illicit economy would be if networks were driven by drugs alone. Or if they depended on the one dimensional drug users and dealers, especially women, that abound in some parts of the literature. In this sense, the difficulty with such simplistic typifications of women in the drug industry is not simply that they represent a misunderstanding with respect to gender. It is part of a broader failure to understand the nature of the social world of the informal economy.

SHOPPING ON THE CARD

It has been suggested that the growth of a credit-based economy in Western society has enabled more women to take part in fraudulent crimes (Biernacki, 1979), the increased opportunities for credit card fraud being noted as one major example (Steffensmeier, 1983). Although this probably applies also for men, there is no doubt that many women in the Melbourne drug economy specialized in credit card fraud. Stolen credit cards were relatively easy to obtain, through either trading or bartering with associates or directly stealing from their holder. Credit card shopping was a favorite occupation of Rita's. When she set out on a "shopping excursion," she would be immaculately dressed, with no hint of her being a heavy drug user. She would shop at large department stores, boutiques, and markets. She would make conversation with the sales assistants, asking for their advice and help. In this manner, she would build up rapport with the shop assistants creating an image of credibility and trust. When a shop assistant showed any sign of hesitation or uncertainty, Rita would cancel the sale. "I pull the plug if I think there's any danger."

Rita was calm under pressure, never looking flushed or hassled. She would shop in a carefree and casual way inventing any number of stories along the way to suit the prevailing circumstances. She also had a selection of shopkeepers to visit who were not concerned if her purchases were made with stolen credit cards. "There's plenty of them [shopkeepers] in it too, rorting the system. They don't give jack shit. It's not them that's losing out." When visiting a corrupt jeweler, Rita purchased an amount of gold that was over the credit card limit, she was instructed to come back the next day, when the daily credit limit was automatically renewed, to complete the transaction.

> I've been dealing with him [jeweler] for three years. He knows the credit cards are stolen. He told me to come in tomorrow, after six, before he closed up when things were quiet. He put through $480's worth and told me to come back tomorrow, and he'll put the rest through.

Rita had what Sutherland (1937) calls "larceny sense," similar to "business sense" when applied to a legitimate entrepreneur: an understanding whether to desist or persist with a job. Rita felt she was "very rarely wrong... you get to know if it's going to be alright."

CONCLUSIONS

We have argued in this paper that the relationship between women's involvement in drug dealing and drug use and their involvement in property crime needs to be looked at in ways that take into account both the women's own views of their activities and that recognize property offending and drug dealing as skillful accomplishments. In part, this also involves recognizing that simply because it is committed by drug dealing women, property crime is not to be seen as simply a reflex of involvement in the drug economy. Rather, drug dealing and property crime are interrelated—almost symbiotic—sources of income and satisfaction. Each of these forms of illicit "enterprise" provides opportunities, skills, knowledge, contacts, and other resources that assist with the success of the other. In this sense, they are braided together in particular lifestyles, career paths, and forms of economic activity. For the Melbourne women crime was work, and, as with the legitimate sector, such work was a source of many satisfactions other than monetary—from self-esteem and a sense of accomplishment to emotional returns including thrills and excitement. Drugs and the drug experience were central to this; they could not meaningfully be separated from—or straightforwardly given causal priority in relation to—the rest of the women's involvement and activities in the illicit economy.

None of this is meant to imply that other studies have been mistaken when they identify so many women drug users as prostitutes and/or victims, although as indicated above recent research clearly indicates that this pattern has been overstated. We stress that we are focusing on a particular and underresearched type of women drug user/dealers. Nevertheless, we wish to reassert two final points that that are of more general relevance to our understanding of women's participation in drug culture and in "drug-related" offending.

First, many women are capable operators in the illicit market, and those who deal in drugs are likely to be competent property offenders. For the successful Melbourne women, at least, property offending is thus not a sign of a failing drug selling practice. If anything, the more successful the drug business, the better connected and better skilled the women as illicit entrepreneurs and the more likely it will be they have lucrative scams in their repertory. As well, the better their drug business, the more they will have illicit goods passing through their hands, both provided in payment for drugs delivered or received and to be used as payments, gifts, or rewards to their workers. Much of this is a corollary of our observation that we need to distinguish between types of involvement in property offending, for as the women became more successful in the drug business, so too they moved from marginal to substantial participants in such crime. Consequently, to understand property offending among women drug users, we should pay attention to not just how "successful" they are in each activity, but at what points they might be in their illicit careers. Thus women in this study began as drug users, and others as partners and apprentices of men, but moved "up" into successful drug dealing and property offending.

Second, like others in illicit business, they sought to satisfy a wide range of needs and desires from their property offending: providing friends, family, and themselves with gifts; generating an effective source of income; bartering for all manner of other services, and so on. Only sometimes, and rarely solely, is property offending geared to paying for their own drug consumption. For the successful user/dealers, property crime, drug use, and drug dealing are closely bound together and are part of a pattern that changes through the course of their careers. Sometimes one leads in terms of priorities of need or opportunity, sometimes another. The changes may be related to different points in their careers, but they may also relate to changing justice environments and markets—to the variable phases in the intermittent business activity that characterizes a "drug dealership."

In all of this, this paper seeks to contribute to the developing line of theory and research that challenges more traditional views of women drug users and dealers as in some sense victims or failures. It stresses that property offending and drug dealing are closely and functionally related. As well, and most generally, the observations made in this research directly challenge assertions, such as those made by Rosenbaum (1981), that regard the careers of female drug users as involving "narrowing options," in which legitimate and thus implicitly preferred lifestyles are closed off and in which women find themselves trapped in a world of addiction. With Taylor (1993, p. 158) we would agree that "rather than a career of narrowing options, the career of these working class female drug users is one which highlights the capabilities of such women."

References

Akerstrom, M. (1985). *Crooks and squares*. New Brunswick, NJ: Transaction Books.

Anglin, M., & Hser, Y. (1987). Addicted women and crime. *Criminology, 25,* 359–397.

Biernacki, P. (1979). Junkie work, "hustles," and social status among heroin addicts. *Journal of Drug Issues, 9,* 535–549.

Covington, J. (1985). Gender differences in criminality among heroin users. *Journal of Research in Crime and Delinquency, 22,* 329–354.

Culliver, C. (1993). Women and crime: An overview. In C. Culliver (Ed.), *Female criminality: The state of the art* (pp. 119–131). New York: Garland.

D'Arcy, M. (1995). *Women in prison: Women's explanations of offending behaviour and implication for policy.* Unpublished master's thesis, School of Law and Legal Studies, La Trobe University, Melbourne.

Denton, B. (1994). *Prison, drugs and women: Voices from below* (National Drug Strategy, Research Report Series, Report No. 5). Canberra, Australia: Commonwealth Department of Health and Family Services.

Elliot, D., Huizinga, D., & Menard, S. (1989). *Multiple problem youth: Delinquency, substance use, and mental health problems.* New York: Springer-Verlag.

Fagan, J. (1994). Woman and drugs revisited: Female participation in the cocaine economy. *Journal of Drug Issues, 24,* 179–225.

Fagan, J. (1995). Women's careers in drug use and drug selling. *Current Perspectives on Aging and the Life Cycle, 4,* 155–190.

Faupel, C. (1991). *Shooting dope: Career patterns of hard-core heroin users.* Gainesville, FL: University of Florida Press.

Fitzroy Legal Service. (1988). *Women and imprisonment in Victoria.* Submission to the Social Development Committee into Community Violence, Fitzroy Legal Service, Melbourne.

Hser, Y., Anglin, M., & McGlothlin, W. (1987). Sex differences in addict careers: Initiation of use, *American Journal of Drug and Alcohol Abuse, 13,* 33–57.

Inciardi, J., Pottieger, A., & Faupel, C. (1982). Black women, heroin and crime: Some empirical notes, *Journal of Drug Issues, 12,* 241–251.

Johnson, B., Goldstein, P., Preble, E., Schmeidler, J., Lipton, D., Spunt, B., et al. (1985). *Taking care of business: The economics of crime by heroin abusers.* Lanham, MD: Lexington Books.

Katz, J. (1988). *Seductions of crime.* Chicago: Aldine.

Leonard, M. (1994). *Informal economic activity in Belfast.* London: Athenaeum Press.

Miller, E. (1991). Assessing the risk of inattention to class, race, ethnicity and gender: Comment on Lyng. *American Journal of Sociology, 96*, 1530–1545.

Nurco, D., Shafter, J., Ball, J., & Kinlock, T. (1984). Trends in the commission of crime among narcotic addicts over successive periods of addiction and nonaddiction. *American Journal of Drug and Alcohol Abuse, 10*, 481–489.

Pettiway, L. (1987). Participation in crime partnerships by female drug users. *Criminology, 25*, 741–766.

Preble, E., & Casey, J. (1969). Taking care of business: The heroin user's life on the street. *International Journal of the Addictions, 4*, 1–24.

Sargent, M. (1992). *Women, drugs and policy in Sydney, London and Amsterdam.* Dartmouth, UK: Ashgate.

Steffensmeier, D. (1983). Organization properties and sex-segregation in the underworld: Building a sociological theory of sex differences in crime. *Social Forces, 61*, 1010–1032.

Stewart, T. (1987). *The heroin users.* London: Pandora Press.

Taylor, A. (1993). *Woman Drug Users: An Ethnography of a Female Injecting Community.* Oxford, UK: Clarendon Press.

24

Researching Crack Dealers: Dilemmas and Contradictions

Bruce A. Jacobs

"Yo, Bruce", come on down the set [neighborhood]. Meet where we usually do," Luther said, and hung up the phone.[1] A trusted contact for an ongoing study of street-level crack dealers and a crack dealer himself, I had no reason to question him. "Just another interview," I thought. Notebooks and file folders in hand, I went to the bank, withdrew fifty dollars for subject payments, and drove fifteen minutes to the dope set I was coming to know so well.

Luther flagged me down as I turned the corner. The 17-year-old high school drop-out opened the door and jumped in. "Swerve over there." He pointed to a parking space behind the dilapidated three-story apartment building he called home. "Stop the car—turn it off." Nothing out of the ordinary; over the previous three months, we often would sit and talk for a while before actually going to an interview. This time, though, there was an urgency in his voice I should have detected but did not. He produced a pistol from under a baggy white T-shirt. "Gimme all your fuckin' money or I'll blow your motherfuckin' head off!"

"What the fuck's your problem?" I said, astonished that someone I trusted had suddenly turned on me. The gun was large, a six-shooter, probably a long-barrel .45. It was ugly and old looking. Most of its chrome had been scratched off. Its black handle was pockmarked from years of abuse. Why was he doing this? How did I get myself into this situation? It was the kind of thing you hear about on the evening news but don't expect to confront, even though I knew studying active offenders risked such a possibility.

I frantically pondered a course of action as Luther's tone became more and more hostile. He was sweating. "Just calm down, Luther, just calm down—everything's cool," I trembled. "Don't shoot—I'll give you what you want." "Gimme all your fuckin' money!" he repeated. "I ain't fuckin' around—I'll waste you right here!" I reached in my left-hand pocket for the fifty dollars

Source: Bruce A. Jacobs, "Researching Crack Dealers: Dilemmas and Contradictions," in Jeff Ferrell and Mark S. Hamm (Eds.), *Ethnography at the Edge: Crime, Deviance and Field Research* (Boston, Northeastern University Press, 1998). Used with permission.

and handed it over. As I did so, I cupped my right hand precariously an inch from the muzzle of his gun, which was pointing directly into my abdomen. I can survive a gunshot, I thought to myself, as long as I slow the bullet down.

He snatched the five, crisp ten-dollar bills and made a quick search of the vehicle's storage areas to see if I was holding out. "OK," he said, satisfied there were no more funds. "Now turn your head around." I gazed at him inquisitively. "Turn your motherfuckin' head around!" For all I knew, he was going to shoot and run; his right hand was poised on the door handle, his left on the trigger. "Just take your money, man, I'm not gonna do anything." "Turn the fuck around!" he snapped. "OK," I implored, "I won't look, just lemme put my hand over my eyes." I left small openings between my fingers to see what he was really going to do. If he were truly going to fire, which he appeared to be intent on doing—the gun was being raised from the down-low position in which it had been during the entire encounter to right below head level—I would smack the gun upward, jump out of the car, and run a half block to the relative safety of a commercial street.

As I pondered escape routes, he jammed the gun into his pants as quickly as he had drawn it, flung open the door, and disappeared behind the tenements. I hit the ignition and drove slowly and methodically from the scene, grateful to have escaped injury, but awestruck by his brazen violation of trust. All I could do was look back and wonder why.

If this were the end of the story, things would have normalized, I would have learned a lesson about field research, and I would have gone about my business. But Luther was not through. Over the next six weeks, he called my apartment five to ten times a day, five days a week, harassing, taunting, irritating, baiting me. Perhaps twice over that six-week period, I actually picked up the phone—only to find out it was him and hang up. Luther would call right back and let the phone ring incessantly, knowing I was there and letting the answering machine do the dirty work. On several occasions, it became so bad that I had to disconnect the line and leave the apartment for several hours.

I'd arrive home to see the answering machine lit up with messages. "I can smell the mousse in your hair—huh, huh, huh," his sinister laugh echoing through the apartment. "I know you're there, pick it up." More often than not, I would hear annoying dial tones. One message, however, caught my undivided attention: "897 Longacre—huh, huh, huh," he laughed as I heard him flipping through the phone book pages and identifying my address. "We'll [he and his homeboys] be over tomorrow." I didn't sleep well that night or for the next six weeks.

What was I to do—report the robbery, and go to court and testify to stop what had become tele-stalking? Some researchers contend that when crimes against fieldworkers occur, staff are to "report them to the police to indicate that such violations will have consequences."[2] I did not feel I had this option. Calling the authorities, no matter how much I wanted to, not only would have endangered future research with Luther's set and those connected to it, but would also have risked retaliation—because Luther's homies knew where I lived and worked.

So I called the phone company and got caller ID, call return, and call block. These devices succeeded in providing his phone number and residence name, which I used to trace his actual address, but I could still do nothing to stop him. Changing my number was the last thing I wanted to do, because those who smell fear often attack. As other researchers have noted, concern about "violence may cause ethnographers to appear afraid or react inappropriately to common street situations and dangers. ... Fearful behavior is easily inferred by violent persons" and may often lead to violence itself.[3] Thus, Berk and Adams stress the importance of maintaining one's cool when threatened: "The investigator will be constantly watched and tested by the very people he is studying. This is especially true [with] delinquents who ... value poise in the face of danger."[4] Danger, it must be remembered, is "inherent" in fieldwork with active offenders, "if for no other reason than there is always the possibility of dangerous cultural misunderstandings arising between researchers and subjects."[5] This is especially true of research among active street-corner crack sellers, who routinely use violence or threats of violence to gain complicity.[6]

After enduring six weeks of this postrobbery harassment, and with no end in sight, I had to do something. I called the police and told them the story. An officer came out and listened to messages I had saved. As he listened, the telephone rang, and Luther's number displayed on the caller ID. "Do you want me to talk to him?" the officer asked sternly. "No," I replied, feeling more confident with a cop three feet away. "Lemme see if I can work things out." I picked up the phone and started talking.

> "What do you want?"
> "Why do you keep hangin' up on me? All I want is to talk."
> "What do you expect me to do, *like* you? [sardonically, on the verge of losing it]. You fuckin' robbed me and I trusted you and now you call me and leave these fuckin' messages and you want me to *talk* to you? [incredulous]"
> "I only did that 'cause you fucked me over. I only ganked [robbed] you 'cause you *fucked me.*"
> "What are you talking about?"

He proceeded to explain that without him, none of the 40 interviews I obtained would have been possible. True, Luther was the first field contact to believe that I was a researcher, not a cop. He was my first respondent, and he was responsible for starting a snowball of referrals on his word that I was "cool."[7] But after he could no longer provide referrals, I moved on, using his contacts to find new ones and eliminating him from the chain. My newfound independence was inexplicable to him and a slap in the face. He wanted vengeance; the robbery and taunting were exactly that.[8]

ETHNOGRAPHY AND SOCIAL DISTANCE?

Such are the risks ethnographers take when studying dangerous, unstable offenders. Although "robbery, burglary, and theft from field staff are uncommon, [they] do occur. In fact, many crack distributors are frequent and proficient robbers, burglars, and thieves."[9] Not so ironically, someone I had trusted and considered a "protector"[10] had become someone to be protected from. Such flip-flops are entirely possible in the world of active offenders, who themselves often admit an inability to control or understand their behavior.

All of this merely underscores the changeable, unpredictable nature of fieldwork relations, especially with active offenders. Johnson notes that "[i]t is incumbent on the investigator to assess the influences of these changes."[11] The important point is for researchers to put themselves in a position where they can do this. Unfortunately, the very nature of criminological fieldwork may work against this.

Much of the problem revolves around the dilemma between social distance and immersion in fieldwork, and the difficulty researchers have in resolving it. The notion of "social distance" is thought to be in some ways foreign to the ethnographic enterprise. Wolff, for example, contends that successful fieldwork inevitably requires surrender—psychological, social, and otherwise—to the setting, culture, and respondents one is studying. It requires "total involvement, suspension of received notions, pertinence of everything, identification, and risk of being hurt."[12] Ethnographers are advised to immerse themselves in the native scene,[13] to become a member of what they are studying.[14] They are told to become an actual physical and moral part of the setting.[15] As Berk and Adams put it, "The greater the social distance between the participant observer and the subjects, the greater the difficulty in establishing and maintaining rapport."[16]

Building rapport with active offenders typically becomes more difficult, though, as the "deviantness" of the population one studies increases.[17] With any offender population, trying to become "one of them" too quickly can be downright harmful. Some contend that the most egregious error a fieldworker can make is to assume that the fieldworker can gain the immediate favor of his or her hosts by telling them that he or she wants to " 'become one of them' or by implying, by word or act, that the fact that they tolerate his [or her] presence means that he [or she] is one of them."[18] Similarly, Polsky warns that "you damned well better not pretend to be 'one of them,' because they will test this claim out and one of two things will happen. Either the researcher will get drawn into participating in actions one would otherwise not engage in, or the researcher could be exposed as a result of not doing so, the latter having perhaps even greater negative repercussions."[19] The more attached the researcher gets too early in the process, the more vulnerable she or he may be to exploitation. The researcher is still a researcher, no matter how close the researcher thinks she or he is getting. Subjects know this and may also know there will be few if any serious repercussions if they try to pull something, especially at the beginning of research when the fieldworker tends to be the most desperate for acceptance. Problems are only compounded by the fact that researchers tend to be far more streetwise by the end of fieldwork than they are at the beginning. Perhaps the least important time to be streetwise is at the end; both the number and seriousness of threats tend to decline with time. Where threats are often highest—at the beginning, when the researcher may be labeled a narc, a spy, or simply a suspicious character—the researcher may also be least capable of handling them. This only makes the threats that do materialize more threatening.

Researchers who are victimized at this early stage may often be barred from reporting it; doing so threatens to breach promises of confidentiality and anonymity made to subjects. The practical matter of being labeled a narc who "sold someone out" is a separate issue and potentially more problematic: snitching violates a sacred norm of street etiquette, even if the person being snitched on is in the wrong. At best, snitching will terminate future chains of respondents. At worst, it will label the researcher a "rat" and subject him or her to street justice. Both outcomes are of course undesirable and will likely bring an end to one's research.

Being immersed while remaining to some degree objective is the key. Some researchers stress the importance of using "interactional devices and strategies that allow the fieldworker to stay on the edges of unfolding social scenes rather than being drawn into their midst as a central actor."[20] Others recommend engaging in a paradoxical and "peculiar combination of engrossment and distance."[21] Like the Simmelian stranger, researchers are told to be familiar yet not too familiar, involved yet not too involved, all the while making the balance seem natural.[22] Some modicum of social distance is thus critical to the ethnographic enterprise—"as a corrective to bias and overrapport brought on by too strong an identification with those studied."[23]

In some sense, then, social distance between the researcher and the active offenders she or he studies can be beneficial. As Wright and Decker observe, "[T]he secrecy inherent in criminal work means that offenders have few opportunities to discuss their activities with anyone besides associates, a matter which many find frustrating."[24] By definition, criminal respondents will often have "certain knowledge and skills that the researcher does not have."[25] This asymmetry may empower them to open up or to open up sooner than they otherwise would. Offenders may enjoy speaking about their criminal experiences with someone who is "straight." Perhaps it is a satisfaction gained from teaching someone supposedly smarter than they are, at least in terms of academic degrees. The fact that respondents may see something in the research that benefits them, or an opportunity to correct faulty impressions of what it is they actually do,[26] only facilitates these dynamics.

All of it may come down to dramaturgy. Yet, the very nature of criminological fieldwork dictates that the researcher either can't or won't "act" in certain ways at certain times. Acting inappropriately can compromise the research itself, the fieldworker's ability to remain in the setting, or the ability to remain there safely. The moral and practical conundrum between social distance, immersion, and "participant" observation in criminological fieldwork may, in many ways, be unresolvable.

My failure to manage the distance, immersion dialectic with Luther appeared to have more to do with a practical shortfall in managing informant relations—a myopia if you will—than with going native. Clearly, I had lost objectivity in the process of "handling" Luther. Whether this was a function of over immersion is open to question, but it undoubtedly played some role. Whether it was avoidable is also open to question, particularly when one considers the practical and methodological paradoxes involved in fieldwork with active offenders. Although myopic (mis)management led to my exploitation by Luther, without putting myself in such a position, I would never have been able to collect the data I did. In many ways, the "shortfall" was necessary and, at some level, advantageous.

The bottom line is that no matter how deft the fieldworker is at managing relations, he or she ultimately never gains total control. Criminological fieldworkers exist in a dependent relationship with their subjects.[27] This makes one wonder who is indeed the "subject" and what he or she can be "subject to" at any given moment. Some contend that the hierarchical relationship between interviewer and subject in social research is "morally indefensible"[28] and should be thrown out. Perhaps the hierarchy may be jettisoned as a matter of course, by the very nature of the fieldworker-active offender relationship. Luther's actions toward me stand as an exemplary case.[29]

Studying Active Offenders

Studying active drug dealers is problematic precisely because their activity is criminal. Active offenders are generally "hard to locate because they find it necessary to lead clandestine lives. Once located, they are reluctant, for similar reasons, to give accurate and truthful information about themselves."[30] "Outsiders" are often perceived as narcs seeking to obtain damaging evidence for juridical purposes.[31] Indeed, the most common suspicion that subjects have about fieldworkers is that they are spies of some sort. As Sluka notes, "It is difficult to find an [ethnographer] who has done fieldwork who has not encountered this suspicion."[32]

Collecting data from drug dealers, particularly from active ones, is likely to be difficult and dangerous unless one can construct friendships within a dealing community.[33] Because of this difficulty, some researchers target institutional settings.[34] Such settings afford the chance of obtaining data without the risk of physical harm associated with "street" interviews.[35] Unfortunately, collecting valid and reliable data in such settings may not be entirely possible, as criminologists have "long suspected that offenders do not behave naturally" in them.[36] Sutherland and Cressey argue that "[t]hose who have had intimate contacts with criminals 'in the open' know that criminals are not 'natural' in police stations, courts, and prisons and that they must be studied in their everyday life outside of institutions if they are to be understood."[37] Polsky is more emphatic, commenting that "we can no longer afford the convenient fiction that in studying criminals in their natural habitat, we ... discover nothing really important that [cannot] be discovered from criminals behind bars. What is true for studying the gorilla of zoology is likely to be even truer for studying the gorilla of criminology."[38] There are fundamental qualitative differences between the two types of offenders. Institutionalized drug dealers, for example, may represent those not sophisticated or skilled enough to prevent apprehension, or those who simply do not care about getting caught and who sell to anyone with money. Studies of incarcerated offenders are thus open to the charge of being based on "unsuccessful criminals, on the supposition that successful criminals are not apprehended or are at least able to avoid incarceration." This weakness is "the most central bogeyman in the criminologist's demonology."[39]

Knowing this, I entered the field and began frequenting a district near a major university that is both prestigious and expensive, yet which borders a dilapidated neighborhood with a concentrated African American population and heavy crack sales. A lively commercial district, with restaurants, quaint cafes, bars, theaters, and stores, splits the two. The area is known for racial and ethnic diversity, making it relatively easy for most anyone to blend in. Over a nine-month period, I frequented the area and made myself familiar to the regular crowd of hangers-out in the dividing commercial district. Some of these individuals were marginally homeless and spent entire days in the district smoking, drinking, playing music, and begging. Although not crack dealers themselves, they knew who the dealers were and where they worked. After gaining their trust, I was shown the dealers' congregation spots and quickly took to the area.

At first, I would simply walk by, not explicitly acknowledging that anything was going on. Sometimes I would be escorted by one of the "vagabonds," but most of the time I went alone. My objective was simply to let dealers see me. Over the days and weeks, I walked or drove through slowly to gain recognition, trying to capitalize on what Goffman has called second seeings: "[U]nder some circumstances if he and they see each other seeing each other, they can use this fact as an excuse for an acquaintanceship greeting upon next seeing…"[40] Unfortunately, this did not go as easily as Goffman suggests, as dealers openly yelled "SCAT!"—a term for the police undercover unit—at me.[41] Jump-starting participation was clearly the toughest part of the research because dealers suspected I was the police. Ironically, it was the police who gave me my biggest credibility boost.

Police and Credibility

Ferrell notes that "a researcher's strict conformity to legal codes can be reconceptualized as less a sign of professional success than a possible portent of methodological failure … a willingness to break the law," by contrast, "[opens] a variety of methodological possibilities."[42]

Hanging with offenders on street corners, driving them around in my car, and visiting their homes must have been a curious sight. My appearance is somewhat akin to that of a college student. Shorts, T-shirts, cross-trainers, and ball caps with rounded brims, "just like SCAT wear 'em" (as one respondent put it), make up my typical attire. Further, I am white, clean-cut, and affect a middle-class appearance, traits the relatively poor, African American respondents associated with the police. These traits appeared to make them even more leery that I was SCAT, or that I worked for SCAT in some capacity.

To offenders who hadn't gotten to know me well, or to those waiting to pass judgment, I was on a deep-cover assignment designed to unearth their secrets and put them in jail. To cops on the beat, I was just another college boy driving down to crackville with a user in tow to buy for me. Such relations are commonplace in the street-level drug scene and have generalized subcultural currency: users serve as go-betweens and funnel unfamiliar customers to dealers for a finder's fee, usually in drugs and without the customer's consent, but generally with his or her tacit permission. When cops see a relatively nicely dressed, clean-shaven white boy driving a late-model car (with out-of-state plates, I might add) and a black street person in the passenger seat, they lick their chops.

Several police stops of me in a one-month period lent some credibility to this proposition. I had not obtained, as Wright and Decker had, a "prior agreement with the police"[43] whereby the police knew what I was doing and pledged not to interfere. I chose not to; the last thing I wanted was to let police know what I was doing. As Polsky explains, "Most of the danger for the fieldworker comes not from the cannibals and headhunters but from the colonial officials. The criminologist studying uncaught criminals in the open finds sooner or later that law enforcers try to put him on the spot—because, unless he is a complete fool, he uncovers information that law enforcers would like to know ... "[44] Because my grant was not a federal one, I could not protect the identity of my respondents with a certificate of confidentiality (which theoretically bars police from obtaining data as it pertains to one's subjects). My work was undercover in a sense and eminently discreditable. However, contrary to admonitions by some to avoid contact with the police while doing research with dangerous populations,[45] my run-ins with police turned out to be the most essential tool for establishing my credibility.

My first run-in came two weeks after making initial contact with offenders. I was driving Luther through a crack-filled neighborhood—a neighborhood which also happened to have the highest murder rate in a city which itself had the fourth-highest murder rate in the nation.[46] We were approaching a group of ten mid-teen youths and were about to stop when a St. Louis city patrol car pulled behind. Should I stop, as I planned on doing, and get out and talk with these youths (some of whom Luther marginally knew), or would that place them in imminent danger of arrest? Or should I continue on as if nothing was really going on, even though I had been driving stop and go, under ten miles an hour, prior to and during the now slow-speed pursuit? I opted for the latter, accelerating slowly in a vain attempt to reassert a "normal appearance."[47]

Sirens went on. I pulled over and reassured Luther there was nothing to worry about since neither of us had contraband (I hoped). As officers approached, I thought about what to tell them. Should I say I was a university professor doing field research on crack dealers (a part I clearly didn't look), lie, or say nothing at all? "Whatcha doin' down here?" one of the officers snapped. "Exit the vehicle, intertwine your fingers behind your heads, and kneel with your ankles crossed," he commanded. The searing June sidewalk was not conducive to clear thinking, but I rattled something off: "We used to work together at _____. I waited tables, he bussed, and we been friends since. I'm a sociology major up at _____ and he said he'd show me around the neighborhood sometime. Here I am." "Yeah right," the cop snapped again while searching for the crack he thought we already had purchased. Three other police cars arrived, as the cop baited Luther and me as to how we really knew each other, what each other's real names were (which neither of us knew at the time), and what we were doing here. Dissatisfied with my answers, a sergeant took over, lecturing me on the evils of crack and how it would destroy a life others in this very neighborhood wished they had. I found no fault with the argument, listened attentively, and said nothing. After a final strip search in the late afternoon sun revealed nothing, they said I was lucky, vowed to take me in if I ever showed my face again, and let us go.

On a second occasion, Luther and his homie Frisco were in my car when we pulled up to a local liquor store. The two became nervous upon seeing two suits in a "tec" (detective) car parked at the phone booth. I told Luther and Frisco to wait, and I went into the store. As I exited, the two men approached and showed their badges. "What you doin' with these guys—do you know 'em?" "Yes," I said, deciding to tell them who I really was and what I was doing. "Mind if we search your car?" one asked. "No problem," I replied. "Go right ahead." As one searched my car (for crack, guns, or whatever else he thought he'd find), his partner cuffed both Luther and Frisco and ran warrants. As I soon learned, both detectives knew the two as repeat violent offenders with long rap sheets. They took Frisco in on an outstanding warrant and let Luther go with me. "I respect what you're doing," the searching officer said as he finished and approached, "but you don't know who you're dealing with. These guys are no good." I told him thanks and promptly left with Luther, feeling remorseful about Frisco being taken in only because he was with me.

On a third occasion, I was sitting on my car making small talk with four or five dealers when a patrol car rolled by. The officers inside gave a stern look and told us to break it up. "All right," I said, not going anywhere. We continued to talk for a few minutes when the officers, clearly agitated, rolled by again and demanded in no uncertain terms, "Break it up and we mean now." I hopped in my car, drove four or five blocks, made a left, and heard sirens. "Here we go again." This time, I was not nearly as nervous as I had been on the other occasions, ready to dispense my professor line, show my consent forms and faculty ID, and see their shocked reaction. "Get out of the car and put your hands on the trunk," the driver predictably ordered as I began my explanation. They searched me anyway, perhaps thinking it was just another mendacious story, but I kept conversing in a relaxed, erudite tone. Cops are known to have perceptual shorthands to render quick and accurate typifications of those with whom they're interacting,[48] and I could tell my conversational style was creating a good impression. I told them that I was doing interviews, that I was paying respondents for their time, and that the research was part of a university grant designed to better understand the everyday lives of urban youth. This was, of course, specious. The study's true purpose was to identify how crack dealers avoid arrest, something I dared not admit, for obvious reasons. "You can do what you want," one of them said, satisfied after a thorough search revealed no contraband, "but if I were you, I'd be real careful. You don't want to mess around with these punks." His words rang all too true several weeks later when Luther pointed the gun at my abdomen.

I did not realize it at the time, but my treatment by police was absolutely essential to my research. Police provided the "vital test"[49] I desperately needed to pass if my study were to be successful. The differential enforcement practices of these police officers (and many others around the country)—in which young, minority males are singled out as "symbolic assailants" and "suspicious characters" deserving of attention[50]—benefitted *me* immensely. Police detained *me* because I was with "them." Driving alone in these same areas at the same time, though suspicious, would not likely have attracted nearly as much attention. I was "guilty by association" and "deserving" of the scrutiny young black males in many urban locales receive consistently. For my research, at least, this differential enforcement was anything but negative.

As Douglas notes, it is often necessary for researchers to convince offenders they are studying that the researchers do not represent the authorities.[51] Sluka adds that subjects "are going to define whose side they think you are on. They will act towards you on the basis of this definition, regardless of your professions."[52] Words may be futile in convincing offenders who or what one really is. Ultimately, "actions speak louder than words. ... [T]he researcher will have to demonstrate by ... actions that he is on the side of the deviants, or at least, not on the side of the officials."[53] The police had treated me like just another user, and had done so with offenders present. This treatment provided the "actions" for me, the picture that spoke a thousand words.

Offenders' accounts of my treatment spread rapidly through the grapevine, solidifying my credibility for the remainder of the project and setting up the snowball sampling procedure I would use to recruit additional respondents. Without the actions of *police* I may not have been accepted by *offenders* as readily as I was or, perhaps, never accepted at all. A skillful researcher can use the police—indirectly and without their knowledge or, as in my case, without even the researcher's own intent—to demonstrate to offenders that the researcher is indeed legitimate and not an undercover police officer. Often thought to be a critical barrier to entry, the police may be the key to access. Of course, undercover officers themselves can manipulate this very dynamic to gain credibility with those they target—something savvy law enforcement administrators may exploit by setting up fake arrests in plain view. Such tactics may make a researcher's identity even more precarious; in my case, though, this did not occur.

Why police never attempted to confiscate my notes during these pull-overs I'll never know. Perhaps it was because the notes appeared to be chicken scratch and were indecipherable by anyone but me. Perhaps it was because my notes didn't reveal anything the cops did not already know, or at least thought they knew. Regardless, the law is clearly against ethnographers, who can be held in contempt and sent to jail for protecting sources and withholding information.[54] As Carey points out, "There is no privileged relationship between the ... researcher and his subject similar to that enjoyed by the lawyer and client or psychiatrist and patient."[55] This, of course, says nothing about issues of guilty knowledge or guilty observation.[56] Being aware of dealing operations and watching transactions take place makes one an accessory to their commission, a felony whether one participates or not. Fieldworkers are co-conspirators by definition, no matter their motive or intent. As Polsky concludes, "If one is effectively to study adult criminals in their natural settings, he must make the moral decision that in some ways he will break the law himself."[57]

Researching Active Crack Sellers: In Perspective

By definition, criminological, fieldworkers regularly intrude into the lives of individuals engaged in felonies—felonies for which these individuals can receive hard time. The more illegal the behavior, the more offenders as research subjects have to lose if found out. Obviously, this makes it tougher—and more risky—for researchers to gain access.

Street-level crack selling is thus a paradox of sorts: there is perhaps no other behavior so openly visible and so negatively sanctioned by law as crack selling. It must be this way for sellers to be available to their customers. This is particularly true in a declining drug market such as St. Louis[58] where demand is finite and dwindling, while the number of sellers has remained constant or increased. To compete in such conditions, sellers will often stand out longer and in more difficult conditions than they previously would, in greater numbers, and in greater numbers together. Individual sellers also may rush to customers to steal sales from competitors, drawing even more attention. This situation creates ideal conditions for police—or researchers—to identify open-air sellers and infiltrate them.

Access notwithstanding, the importance of a strong indigenous tie to the research setting at the beginning of field relations—as a way of vouching for the researcher—cannot be overstated. Access and safe access are two wholly different notions. In my case, this tie was Luther—or at least so I thought. More generally, it is an indigenous offender or ex-offender turned fieldworker who acts as gatekeeper and protector. Yet, in a twist of sorts, field research with active offenders often requires strong ties in order to generate weak ones—that is, to initiate the methodological snowball. Micro-structurally and methodologically, this is unique; multiple weak ties rather than one or two strong ones are thought to be indispensable for social-network creation.[59] Indeed, one or two strong ties may actually cut off an actor from an entire social network.

In field research, developing strong ties with the wrong person or persons can, at a minimum, bias the sample or, worse, generate no sample at all.[60] Researchers may gain entry, but it may be with the wrong person. As my encounter with Luther attests, the outcome can be far more threatening than obtaining a biased sample or no sample. Perhaps the larger point here is that, no matter how strong or safe one's ties, danger is inherent in fieldwork with active offenders. Nowhere is this more true than among street-corner crack sellers. Although many dangers can be addressed through planning and preparation, more often than not, danger management hinges on a creative process of "trial and blunder"[61] and results from a combination of skill and luck.[62] As Sluka notes, "[G]ood luck can sometimes help overcome a lack of skill, and well-developed skills can go far to help overcome the effects of bad luck. But sometimes no amount of skill will save one from a gross portion of bad luck."[63] Inevitably, criminological fieldwork is unpredictable and less subject to rational planning than we want it to be. How researchers handle this problem ultimately is a personal choice.

Researching active offenders requires one to balance conflicting agendas. Such agendas emanate from specific audiences—whether police or criminals—each with their own biases toward the ethnographic enterprise. Simply taking sides or currying favor with one audience over the other is not the issue, though this may be done at some point. Research strategies must be weighed carefully because their consequences are inevitably dialectical: police can get you "in" with offenders, but offenders can get you "in trouble" with police. Personal security is dependent on offender acceptance, yet security can be compromised by dependency. Police can be researchers' last bastion of hope against volatile offenders, but reliance on authorities may undermine the very purpose for being in the field. Caught among these contradictions stands the researcher, a true one-person "island in the street."[64] In this lonely position, the researcher must decide when to shade the truth and when to be forthright, when to offer and when to omit, when to induce and when to lie back. Such judgments are subjective and context specific, as any ethnographer will tell you. They must be made with the audience in mind, whether that audience is legal or illegal, academic or social. Each choice affects the kinds of data obtained and revealed. And how far an ethnographer is willing to go to get such data intertwines with the results that ethnographer hopes ultimately to obtain—as my encounter with Luther attests.

Notes

1. All names are pseudonyms to protect identities.
2. Terry Williams, Eloise Dunlap, Bruce D. Johnson, and Ansley Hamid, "Personal Safety in Dangerous Places," *Journal of Contemporary Ethnography,* 21 (1992): 365.
3. Williams et al., "Personal Safety," 350.
4. Richard A. Berk and Joseph M. Adams, "Establishing Rapport with Deviant Groups," *Social Problems* 18 (1970): 110.

5. Jeffrey A. Sluka, "Participant Observation in Violent Social Contexts," *Human Organization* 49 (1990): 114.

6. Williams et al., "Personal Safety," 347.

7. Patrick Biernacki and Dan Waldorf, "Snowball Sampling," *Sociological Methods and Research* 10 (1981): 141–163.

8. See Harold Garfinkel, "Conditions of Successful Degradation Ceremonies," *American Journal of Sociology* 61 (1956): 420–424.

9. Williams et al., "Personal Safety," 364.

10. Williams et al., "Personal Safety," 350.

11. John M. Johnson, "Trust and Personal Involvements in Fieldwork," in *Contemporary Field Research*, ed. Robert M. Emerson (Prospect Heights, IL: Waveland, 1983), 205.

12. Kurt H. Wolff, "Surrender and Community Study: The Study of Loma," in *Reflections on Community Studies*, ed. Arthur J. Vidich, Joseph Bensman, and Maurice R. Stein (New York: Wiley, 1964), 237.

13. Robert H. Lowies, *The History of Ethnological Theory* (New York: Farrar and Rinehart, 1937), 232.

14. Hortense Powdermaker, *Stranger and Friend: The Way of an Anthropologist* (New York: Norton, 1966), 19.

15. E. E. Evans-Pritchard, *Social Anthropology and Other Essays* (New York: Free Press, 1964), 77–79.

16. Berk and Adams, "Establishing Rapport," 103.

17. Berk and Adams, "Establishing Rapport."

18. Rosalie H. Wax, "The Ambiguities of Fieldwork," in *Contemporary Field Research*, ed. Robert M. Emerson (Prospect Heights, IL: Waveland, 1983), 179.

19. Ned Polsky, *Hustlers, Beats, and Others* (Chicago: Aldine, 1967), 124.

20. Robert M. Emerson, ed., *Contemporary Field Research* (Prospect Heights, IL: Waveland, 1983), 179.

21. Ivan Karp and Martha B. Kendall, "Reflexivity in Field Work," in *Explaining Human Behavior: Consciousness, Human Action, and Social Structure*, ed. Paul F. Secord (Beverly Hills, CA: Sage, 1982), 261.

22. Georg Simmel, "The Stranger," in *Georg Simmel*, ed. Donald Levine (Chicago: University of Chicago Press, 1908), 143–149.

23. Emerson, *Contemporary Field Research*, 179.

24. Richard T. Wright and Scott H. Decker, *Burglars on the Job: Streetlife and Residential Break-ins* (Boston: Northeastern University Press, 1994), 26.

25. Berk and Adams, "Establishing Rapport," 107.

26. See Polsky, *Hustlers*.

27. Peter K. Manning, "Observing the Police: Deviance, Respectables, and the Law," in *Research on Deviance*, ed. Jack D. Douglas (New York: Random House, 1972), 213–268.

28. Annie Oakley, "Interviewing Women: A Contradiction in Terms," in *Doing Feminist Research*, ed. Helen Roberts (London: Routledge and Kegan Paul, 1981), 41.

29. Luther's stalking came to an end only because police picked him up on two unrelated counts of armed robbery and armed criminal action. He is now serving 10 years in a Missouri state penitentiary. With the help of colleagues, I moved. My phone number is now unlisted and unpublished, something I recommend to other ethnographers researching active offenders.

30. John Irwin, "Participant Observation of Criminals," in *Research on Deviance*, ed. Jack D. Douglas (New York: Random House, 1972), 117.

31. See Erich Goode, *The Marijuana Smokers* (New York: Basic, 1970).

32. Sluka, "Participant Observation," 115.

33. See Patricia Adler, *Wheeling and Dealing: An Enthography of an Upper-Level Drug Delain and Smuggling Community* (New York: Columbia University Press, 1985).

34. Diana Scully, *Understanding Sexual Violence* (Boston: Unwin Inman, 1990).

35. Michael Agar, *Ripping and Running: A Formal Ethnography of Urban Heroin Addicts* (New York: Seminar Press, 1973).

36. Wright and Decker, *Burglars*, 5.

37. Edwin Sutherland and Donald Cressey, *Criminology*, 8th ed. (Philadelphia: Lipppincott, 1970), 68.

38. Polsky, *Hustlers*, 123.

39. George McCall, *Observing the Law* (New York: Free Press, 1978), 27.

40. Erving Goffman, *Relations in Public: Micro Studies of the Public Order* (New York: Basic Books, 1971), 323.

41. SCAT is an acronym for "street corner apprehension team." This 15-man undercover team is charged with curbing street-level drug sales by apprehending dealers immediately after sales to one of their "buy" officers. Hiding nearby in unmarked cars, personnel "swoop" down on offenders in an attempt to catch them with marked money just given them by buy officers. This money either has traceable dye or serial numbers previously recorded that link dealers to undercover transactions. SCAT units were highly feared because they were reportedly merciless in their arrest procedures (i.e., they conducted strip searches).

42. Jeff Ferrell and Mark S. Hamm, *Ethnography at the Edge: Crime, Deviance and Field Research* (Boston: Northeastern University Press, 1998).

43. Wright and Decker, *Burglars*, 28.

44. Polsky, *Hustlers*, 147.

45. See Sluka, "Participant Observation."

46. Federal Bureau of Investigation, *Crime in the United States* (Washington, DC: Government Printing Office, 1995).

47. See Erving Goffman, *Stigma: Notes on the Management of Spoiled Identity* (Englewood Cliffs, NJ: Prentice Hall, 1963).

48. See John Van Maanen, "The Asshole," in *Policing: A View from the Streets*, ed. Peter K. Manning and John Van Maanen (Santa Monica: Goodyear, 1978), 221–238.

49. Erving Goffman, *Frame Analysis: An Essay on the Organization of Experience* (Cambridge, MA: Harvard University Press, 1974).

50. See Jerome Skolnick, "A Sketch of the Policeman's 'Working Personality,'" in *Criminal Justice: Law and Politics*, ed. George F. Cole (North Scituate, MA: Duxbury Press, 1980).

51. Jack D. Douglas, "Observing Deviance," in *Research on Deviance*, ed. Jack D. Douglas (New York: Random House, 1972), 3–34.

52. Sluka, "Participant Observation," 123.

53. Douglas, "Observing Deviance," 12.

54. Irving Soloway and James Walters, "Workin' the Corner: The Ethics and Legality of Fieldwork among Active Heroin Addicts," in *Street Ethnography*, ed. Robert S. Weppner (Beverly Hills, CA: Sage, 1977), 175–176.

55. James T. Carey, "Problems of Access and Risk in Observing Drug Scenes," in *Research on Deviance*, ed. Jack D. Douglas (New York: Random House, 1972), 77.

56. See Adler, *Wheeling*, 24.

57. Polsky, *Hustler*, 133–134.

58. Andrew Gollub, Farrukh Hakeem, and Bruce D. Johnson, "Monitoring the Decline in the Crack Epidemic with Data from the Drug Use Forecasting Program," unpublished manuscript (1996).

59. Mark Granovetter, "The Strength of Weak Ties," *American Journal of Sociology* 78 (1973): 1360–1380.

60. Douglas's research on nudist beach goers, for example, was jeopardized because of his early bond with a marginal and generally disliked participant (something Douglas did not know until later)—a participant with whom he was able to bond precisely because of that person's marginality; see Douglas, "Observing Deviance."

61. See Karp and Kendall, "Reflexivity."

62. Robert F. Ellen, *Ethnographic Research: A Guide to General Conduct* (London: Academic Press, 1984), 97.

63. Sluka, "Participant Observation," 124.

64. Marin Sanchez-Jankowski, *Islands in the Street: Gangs in American Urban Society* (Berkeley: University of California Press, 1991).

QUITTING CRIME

Do criminals continue their careers over a lifetime? Do they desist at some point or begin to engage in less serious offenses? What motivates causes these changes in criminal activity? Desistance has been a controversial topic in criminology. Research has generally shown a decline in criminal activity as offenders age. In this final selection, "Aging Criminals," Neal Shover's research reveals that as offenders get older, two factors have significant impact on their lives: (1) development of conventional social bonds and (2) strengthened resolve to abandon crime entirely of to restrict their criminal activities. Other factors related to desistance identified by Shover include greater a greater interest in the rewards of a noncriminal lifestyle and a more rational decision making process. The risk-gain calculus employed by criminals tends to shift as they age and mature exhibiting a greater concern with the possibility of apprehension and punishment.

25

Aging Criminals: Changes in the Criminal Calculus

Neal Shover

*I*n this selection, Neal Shover compares the decision-making processes of juvenile and young adult offenders to those of older criminals to discover the changes in the criminal calculus—the perception of risk and gain associated with a criminal opportunity—as offenders age. "Clearly," he argues, "something about advancing age produces reduced participation in ordinary crime, even by those with extensive criminal records." Shover concludes that aging offenders undergo a number of changes, including development of new commitments and increasing fear of incarceration. This causes them to alter their calculus—to evaluate the risks and benefits of crime differently.

Shover's research methodology involved identifying, locating, and interviewing a group of men aged 40 and over who were involved in ordinary property crime earlier in their careers. Shover and his assistants interviewed 50 subjects whose dominant criminal pattern consisted of ordinary property offenses such as grand larceny, burglary, robbery, and auto theft. All had been convicted of such offenses at least once. The research subjects were identified through the files of the U.S. Probation Offices in Baltimore and Washington, DC (22), and U.S. Probation Offices in other cities (5), through introduction by an ex-convict employed to work on the project (13), and by referral from an ex-convict who had been part of an earlier study (4). Six additional subjects were interviewed in federal prisons. Interviews, which were tape recorded and later transcribed, lasted from 30 minutes to three hours, averaging two hours.

CALCULUS AND OFFENSES OF YOUTH

For many juveniles, involvement in delinquency contains a rich variety of motives and subjective meanings. Juveniles "slide into" their initial delinquent acts for a variety of nonrational, often situationally based reasons (Matza, 1964). Although there is little new in this, it is interesting that the

Source: Adapted from Neal Shover, *Aging Criminals*, Sage Publications, pp. 105–126. Copyright by Neal Shover. Reprinted with permission.

interview subjects recalled their earliest crimes this way. A 45-year-old man said,

> I was, like years ago, I was a peeping Tom—when I was a kid, you know. ... I enjoyed this, you know. ... But, anyway, then I got married young, and I had two children. And I had bills, you know. I was a kid and I had a man's responsibility. ... Now, what's the best way to make money? With something you know. I had been peeping in windows when I was a kid. So, I knew, you know, like where the windows would open, where the—you understand what I mean? And then [I] broadened my sense. After awhile I started mixing business with pleasure, you know. I would peep and then later come back and, you know, take this or that.

Another man told of his adolescent fascination with automobiles. As a youth, he often roamed through parking lots, admiring the steering wheels of cars. From there it was a short, tentative step to breaking into the cars and stealing their contents.

A great deal of delinquency begins simply as risk-taking behavior and it is only later, with the benefit of accumulated incidents, that it takes on the character and meaning of "crime" (Short and Strodtbeck, 1965). Braley (1976, pp. 11–12) writes,

> I began to steal seriously as a member of a small gang of boys. We backed into it, simply enough, by collecting milk and soda bottles to turn in for the deposits, but, after we had exhausted the vacant lots, empty fields, and town dumps, we began to sneak into garages ... and, having dared garages and survived, we next began to loot back porches, and, finally, breathlessly, we entered someone's kitchen. ... Clearly, this was an exercise of real power over the remote adult world and I found it exciting. I liked it. ... [A]nd it is only now, some forty years later, that I begin to see how stealing cast me in my first successful role.

Many of the crimes committed by youth are impulsive and poorly planned:

> Q: Did you do a lot of stickups [when you were young]?
> A: Oh yeah, you know. ... [We] stole and shit like that, you know. I didn't give it no thought, no plan, don't know how much money's in it. You know what I mean? Just go in there and say, "we're gonna do it, we're gonna do it." ... That was it.

The spontaneous pursuit of fun and excitement provides the impetus for some delinquency:

> [When I was a kid] I wasn't a sports enthusiast. I played sports very rarely, but it just wasn't exciting enough. ... None of [the "normal" adolescent activities] were exciting to me. ... It's just that we, there was a feeling of participating in something that was daring and dangerous.

To some extent, these collective definitions of misconduct based on expressive vocabularies of motive explain why participants do not always see their activities as criminal. Instead of resulting from a rational decision-making process, they simply "happen," and participants do not appreciate sufficiently the seriousness. A former gang member writes,

> It's funny, but we didn't see ourselves as delinquents or young criminal types. Most of what we were into was fighting other gangs. ... Sure, we got into other kinds of scrapes sometimes, like vandalism and petty larceny from a street vendor or a store. Most of the time we thought of that kind of stuff as "just playing around"—never as crime. (Rettig et al., 1977, p. 28)

For other youths, participation in delinquency results from the interactional dynamics of peer groups. Some boys experience a situational need to maintain personal status and face with their peers (Short and Strodtbeck, 1965; Jansyn, 1966). Theft or other acts of delinquency may function to buttress or solidify one's informal ranking within a small group. Youths may occasionally use them as a dramatic, incontrovertible demand for a higher as compared with a lower rank:

> Everybody would look up to me, you know, when I was young. ... And seem like every time they wanted something, they'd come to me and say, "Jack, well, come on and do this," or "help me do this," you know. Fuck it, you know. I had an image I had to live up to, you know. I'd say, "fuck it, man, come on."

Precisely because many of the criminal incidents of youth are responses to group dynamics or moods, they occasionally "break out" in situationally propitious circumstances. An interview subject related an incident of armed robbery that occurred when he was young. His account illustrates some of the foregoing observations about the impetuous nature of juvenile crime:

> [One day] we were just walking up First Street and [one of my companions] said as we were approaching Rhode Island Avenue, "let's go in here and rob this drug store," because [another companion] had a gun. We said, "okay, let's go in here and rob the drug store." Went in there, the soda fountain was filled up ... robbed everybody on the stools. Went back in the post office, stole money orders and stamps and stuff, took the cash box. And we turned our backs on everybody in the store, going out! We didn't know whether the proprietor had a gun or what, but it just so happened that he didn't. But, that's just the atmosphere in which, you know, that took place.

Overall, the interview subjects said that as juveniles and young adults they pursued crime with considerable intensity:

> [W]hen you're young, or when—the people that I've known who are young, it was nothing to go out and break into two or three places a week just *looking* for money.

Similarly, a retired English thief writes that "when you're young you tend to have a go at anything" (Quick, 1967, p. 142).

Although juvenile crime is impetuous and fun, it is also monetarily rewarding. Indeed, to juveniles from economically deprived backgrounds it may appear more rewarding than any legitimate employment available to them. The sums of money garnered from crime may seem princely indeed. Crime opens up for them new worlds of consumption and leisure activities. The 49 imprisoned armed robbers studied by Petersilia et al. reported that often their youthful crimes were motivated by a desire for and pursuit of "high times" (1978, p. 76).

It seems apparent that many youth become involved in property offenses without having developed an autonomous and rationalized set of criminal motives. Petersilia et al. discovered a similar pattern in their research on imprisoned armed robbers. Their subjects reported using little or no sophistication in planning the offenses they committed in their youth (1978, pp. 60–65). At the same time, they found that the juvenile offenses committed by men in their sample included "expressive elements" far more than was true of the offenses they committed later (1978, p. 76). (Expressive reasons for committing offenses include such things as hostility, revenge, thrills, or peer influence.)

Juveniles and young adults often have little awareness or appreciation of the legal and personal repercussions of their criminality. This is true especially of their perceptions of time spent in institutions such as training schools and prisons:

> I've seen the time in my life, man, where it might seem foolish, 'cause it seems foolish to me now. When I was in the street, hustling, I'd say, "if I get knocked off and don't get but a nickel"—five years—I said, "hell with it," you know. The only thing would be in my mind, if I got busted could I hang around, try to have my lawyer try to get me some kind of plea or something so I wouldn't get but a nickel. 'Cause I knew I could knock five years out.

A 47-year-old man echoed these remarks, saying that when he was young,

> I don't know, man, I just didn't give a fuck, you know. I was young, simple, man. I didn't care, you know. Shit, doing time, you know, I didn't know what doing time was all about. Doing time to me was nothing, you know.

The net result of these youthful meanings and motives is that the potential repercussions of crime to some extent are blunted. Juveniles neither possess nor bring to bear a precise, consistent metric for assessing the potential consequences of delinquent episodes. They fail to "see" or to calculate seriously their potential losses if apprehended. For many youth, crime is a risk-taking activity in which the risks are only dimly appreciated or calculated.

CALCULUS AND OFFENSES OF YOUNG ADULTS

This poorly developed youthful calculus is transformed both by the approach of adulthood and by the experience of arrest and adult felony confinement.

Young adults develop the ability to see, to appreciate, and to calculate more precisely some of the potential penalties that flow from criminal involvement. Consequently, by late adolescence to their early 20s men begin to develop a keener awareness of the potential costs of criminal behavior. Gradually supplanting the nonrational motives and calculus of youthful offenders is a more clearly articulated understanding of the price they will pay if convicted of crime. In this sense, aging and its associated experiences are accompanied by an increasing rationalization of ordinary property crime.

Their growing rationalization of crime seems to be a turning point for many ordinary property offenders. As Zimring (1981, p. 880) has noted,

> At some point in adolescence or early adult development, most of those who have committed offenses in groups either cease to be offenders or continue to violate the law, but for different reasons and in different configurations. Either of these paths is a significant change from prior behavior.

A substantial majority of the uncommitted apparently drop out of crime at this point.

Paradoxically, others—this includes many unsuccessful and most successful offenders—respond to their developing rationalization of crime with a strengthened belief that they can continue committing crime and make it a lucrative enterprise. This is because they convert their developing rationalization of crime into an increased confidence that they can avoid arrest.

For those who continue at crime, theft increasingly springs from a more autonomous set of motives and meanings. The salience of "expressive elements" gradually declines in the process of criminal decision making. Offenders also develop an awareness of the importance of making crime a rational process. They learn the importance of assessing and committing crimes on the basis of an increasingly narrow and precise metric of potential benefits and costs. In this sense as well, their crimes became more calculating and rational. Money increasingly assumes more importance as a criminal objective. After serving a term in the National Training School, one subject and his friends began robbing gamblers and bootleggers. I asked him,

> Q: Did the desire for excitement play any part in those crimes?
> A: No, I think the desire for excitement had left. It was, we recognized that it was a dangerous mission then, because we knew that gamblers and bootleggers carried guns and things like that. And it was for, you know, just for the money.

Another man made the same point succinctly, saying that "whatever started me in crime is one thing. But at some point I know that I'm in crime for the money. There's no emotional reason for me being into crime." Finally, an ex-thief has written,

> When I first began stealing I had but a dim realization of its wrong. I accepted it as the thing to do because it was done by the people I was with; besides,

it was adventurous and thrilling. Later it became an everyday, cold-blooded business, and while I went about it methodically ... I was fully aware of the gravity of my offenses. (Black, 1926, p. 254)

Interestingly, during their young adult years the 49 California armed robbers expressed a new confidence in their ability to avoid arrest for their crimes (Petersilia et al., 1978, pp. 69–70). They reported a marked increase in the sophistication of their criminal planning (although the researchers indicate the men never achieved tactical brilliance) (1978, p. 60). Pursuit of "high times" declined in importance as a motive for crime (1978, p. 78) and the need to meet ordinary financial exigencies became more important (1978, p. 76). Concern about arrest declined substantially (1978, p. 70).

Young men, however, tend to exaggerate their ability to rationalize their crimes and to commit them successfully:

Whenever I began to steal it was always with the rationale I wouldn't make the mistakes I had made before. ... It didn't occur to me there were literally thousands of ways I could get caught. I was sustained by the confidence nothing truly awful could happen to me. (Braly, 1976, p. 65)

Often they confidently assume there are a finite, manageable number of ways that any particular criminal act can fail (Shover, 1971). Consequently, they analyze past offenses for information they believe will lead to ever more perfect criminal techniques and success. Parker's interview (Parker and Allerton, 1962, p. 149) with an English thief reveals this reasoning process:

Q: When you're arrested, what are your reactions at that moment?
A: I think the first thing's annoyance—with myself. How could I be so stupid as to get nicked? What's gone wrong, what have I forgotten, where have I made the mistake?

In most cases, young adult offenders' newly acquired faith in their ability to rationalize theft and thereby make it safer proves to be self-defeating. Few of them are equipped by temperament, intelligence, or social connections to follow through on their plans and dreams. Consequently, subsequent offenses usually only repeat the pattern established in their youthful criminal forays.

CALCULUS AND OFFENSES OF AGING ADULTS

As men age, fail at crime, and experience ... [other] contingencies, their rationalization of the criminal calculus changes apace. Now they enter a third and final stage of their criminal careers. Increasingly, they realize that the expected monetary returns from criminal involvement are paltry, both in relative and in absolute terms.

Simultaneously, their estimation of the likelihood of being arrested increases, as do the objective probabilities of arrest. (Petersilia et al., 1978, pp. 36–39).

Because of the nature and length of their previous criminal record, they generally assume that they will be sentenced to prison again if convicted of another felony. There is evidence to support this assumption (Petersilia et al., 1978, p. 39). Also, older men assume that any prison sentence they receive, given the length of their previous criminal record, will be long. Finally, those who experience an interpersonal contingency are increasingly reluctant to risk losing their new-found social ties. For all these reasons, aging men begin to include factors that previously were absent from their calculus of potential criminal acts. A 46-year-old former addict said,

If I go out there and commit a crime now, I got to think about this: Hey, man, I ain't *got* to get away. See what I'm saying? I have—man, it would be just my luck that I would get busted. Now I done fucked up everything I done tried to work hard for, man, you know, to get my little family together.

Perhaps it is not surprising that they increasingly begin to see that their potential losses, if imprisoned again, will be immense.

In sum, as offenders age, their expectations of the potential outcome of criminal acts change. Their perception of the odds narrows. Now the perceived risks of criminal behavior loom larger. Note that the Rand Corporation's research on 49 armed robbers found that fear of arrest increases during this age period (Petersilia et al., 1978, p. 70). Little wonder then that a 56-year-old man said,

I realized that, even though in crime, even though you might get away, let's say 99 times, the one time eliminates your future. You don't have no future. Regardless of what you have gained, you lost all of that. A rabbit can escape 99 times and it only takes one shot to kill him. So, I was a rabbit. ... I want to enjoy life. But I know I can't do it successfully by committing crimes.

This does not mean that men cease *thinking* about crime altogether. Rather, they develop a more complex set of reasons for avoiding it in most situations. However, in more advantageous circumstances, some believe they still are capable of resorting to crime:

Now, I'm not going to tell you that if you put $100,000 on that table and I saw an opportunity, that I felt that I could get away with it, that I wouldn't try to move it. But there's no way, even now, there's no way that I would endanger my freedom for a measley four, five, ten thousand dollars. I make that much a year now, you know. And I see the time that I wasted—well, I figure I wasted four or five years when I was younger.
Q: What do you mean, you "wasted" it?
A: In and out of jail.

Those men who continue to pursue a criminal career change their approach to crime. Most decide to avoid some of the crimes more characteristic of their youth. They shift to offenses that are less confrontative and, therefore, less *visible*. Armed robbery is the prototypical highly visible and highly confrontative offense. Shoplifting or selling marijuana represents the other extreme. An imprisoned man said,

> When I go out, I'm goin' for the "soft" stuff. I'm going to book the numbers, you know … but *hard* crime … I gave that up a long while ago.

Thus, there is evidence that ordinary property offenders, once their fear of arrest and confinement increases, shift to other types of criminal activities. In doing so, they believe that they simultaneously reduce the chances of arrest and, even if arrested, increase the chances of receiving less severe penalties:

> You know, it's funny but there's only a few things that a man goes to the penitentiary for: burglary or robbery or something like that. But how many ways of making money are there that you don't have to revert to robbery or burglary? Thousands. I mean [where you're] between being legit and being crooked. You're skating on thin ice and if that ice breaks it's not going to break bad. You might get your foot wet, you might get a fine or something. What they're [police, prosecutors, courts] really concerned with are these violent cases, man, these people who are causing these headlines and stuff. … If I am going to be a thief I might as well be the one who is skating on that thin ice. And a person who is skating on thin ice is less likely to go to the penitentiary. … 'Cause if you get arrested boosting, shoplifting, it is generally a fine. If worse comes to worst, you're going to have to have to do a year in the county jail—in some places, nine months.
>
> I caught one number—that ten years, all them robberies—and then, you know, everything I did then was more like a finesse thing. … I'm not gonna stick no pistol in nobody's face, man, you know. I'm not gonna strong arm nobody, you know. I'm not gonna go in nobody's house. You understand what I'm sayin'? I'm not gonna do that.
>
> Q: You figure as long as you don't do those things you won't go to the penitentiary?
> A: Hey, you better believe it. You better believe it.

Along with this reduction in the visibility of their offenses, men try to reduce the *frequency* of their crimes. One subject, who still engages occasionally in nonviolent felonies, told me how he had changed:

> I done got a little *softer*, you know. I done got, hey man, to the point, you know, where, like I say, I don't steal, I don't hustle, you know. But I don't pass the opportunity if I can get some free money. I'm not gonna pass. … I don't hustle, you know. I don't make it a everyday thing. I don't go out *lookin'* for things, you know.

Another man said,

> When you're younger, you can ... steal to pay the rent, you know. Hell, you can go out and steal seven days a week. And sooner [or later] ... you learn that—to me, it's exposure time, you know. You don't want to get "exposed" too much.

Petersilia et al. (1978, p. 27) found the same pattern. The average monthly offense rates reported by their subjects decreased from 3.28 when they were juveniles to 0.64 in their adult years. After changing their approach to crime, some men do continue to commit crime for several years, but eventually they desist from crime. Only a handful of ordinary property offenders continue their criminal behavior into old age.

NEGATIVE CASES

Three aspects of the experiences of successful offenders distinguish them from the other types of offenders. First, the former usually develop an autonomous, rationalized calculus of crime at an earlier age, albeit in the same general fashion discussed here. By their late teens, some successful offenders are engaging in carefully planned crimes primarily for the expected monetary gains. Even some successful thieves, however, never entirely slough off all nonmonetary meanings of and motivations for crime:

> I know a guy who's relatively well connected, if you know what I mean, with the Outfit. [Nevertheless, he would] [g]o on any score! Now he needed money like I need a double hernia. But [he] just loved—don't care if there's any money there or not. "Let's go." [It was] [t]he thrill. I never got any thrills like that myself. ... The only thrill I got [was] counting the money.

Second, the crimes of successful offenders generally are substantially more rewarding than the crimes committed by other types of offenders. Third, they are more successful than other types of offenders in avoiding incarceration; they spend fewer years in prison. For these reasons, failure at crime does not produce in successful offenders the same impetus to modify their criminal calculus as it does in their unsuccessful peers.

Despite these differences, however, some successful offenders also experience one or more of the contingencies described [earlier]. ... In such circumstances, they respond in ways similar to unsuccessful offenders (Hohimer, 1975).

Unlike unsuccessful offenders, however, they sometimes make adjustments in their criminal activities without discontinuing them entirely. They can do so, in part, because their theft activities provide them late career opportunities not available to unsuccessful offenders. For example, because some of them establish extensive social contacts through their work, they can change the nature of their criminal involvement. They are able to shift to other roles in the social organization of theft. Now they eschew the role of *front-line participant* in favor of the role of *background operator* (Mack and Kerner, 1975; Shover, 1983a). Still others manage to save enough money from their working years to retire with a degree of material comfort. One man suggested these two strategies account for most late-life patterns of successful offenders like himself. As he put it, "[T]hey're either sitting in the rocking chair or out finding something soft for somebody else to pick up."

Nevertheless, a substantial percentage of successful offenders apparently continues "going to the well" despite advancing age. An English thief, who already had served several prison sentences, has written,

> I content myself with the dream—the one that all criminals have—that one day I'll get the really big tickle. ... That's all I can do now, take my time and wait for the chance to come. I've no intention of going straight, I'm just being more careful, that's all—and I'm getting cagey, I won't take unnecessary risks. It used to be I wanted a fifty-fifty chance, now I want it better than that, somewhere like seventy-five to twenty-five. But sooner or later it'll come, the job will be there, I'll do it, get the big tickle, and then I'll retire. ... This is it, this is the dream, the great rock candy mountain that beckons us all. (Parker and Allerton, 1962, p. 189)

This man subsequently was reimprisoned several times (T. Parker, personal communication, July 10, 1981).

Among the unsuccessful offenders, there are two distinctly different categories of negative cases. Some men simply do not experience the orientational and interpersonal changes described [earlier], and so they fail to modify significantly their calculus of ordinary property crime. In assessing their past criminal behavior these men use almost identical verbalizations: "They [police and the courts] could never get even." They use this description to support their contention that they have avoided arrest and prosecution for so many crimes that, even if they were caught in the future, the ledger books still would show an advantage for them. A man who shoplifts almost daily as a means of support had this to say:

Q: Have you ever thought that you were a good thief, or a good hustler?
A: Yeah, I am...
Q: What makes you think you're a good hustler?
A: 'Cause I *produce*.
Q: Yeah, but you've done a lot of time, too, haven't you?
A: Yeah, but considering, you know, in comparison, I ain't did that much. I think, if they gave me 199 years they couldn't get even. ... They couldn't get even.

References

Black, Jack. (1926). *You Can't Win*. New York: A. L. Burt.
Braley, M. (1976). *False starts*. New York: Penguin.

Hohimer, F. (1975). *The home invaders*. Chicago: Chicago Review Books.

Jansyn, L. R., Jr. (1966, October). Solidarity and delinquency in a street corner group. *American Sociological Review, 31*, 600–614.

Mack, J., & Kerner, H.-J. (1975). *The crime industry*. Lexington, MA: D. C. Heath.

Matza, D. (1964). *Delinquency and drift*. New York: John Wiley.

Parker, T., & Allerton, R. (1962). *The courage of his conviction*. London: Hutchinson.

Petersilia, J., Greenwood, P. W., & Lavin, M. (1978). *Criminal careers of habitual felons*. Washington, DC: National Institute of Justice.

Rettig, M., Torres, J., & Garrett, G. R. (1977). *Manny: A Criminal Addict's Story*. Boston: Houghton Mifflin.

Quick, H. (1967). *Villain*. London: Jonathon Cape.

Short, J. F., & Strodtbeck, F. L. (1965). *Group Processes and Gang Delinquency*. Chicago: University of Chicago Press.

Shover, N. (1971). *Burglary as an Occupation*. Unpublished doctoral dissertation, University of Illinois, Urbana.

Zimring, F. (1981, Fall). Kids, groups, and crime: Some implications of a well-known secret. *Journal of Criminal Law and Criminology, 72*, 867–885.